Computer-Based Instruction:
Design and Development

Computer-Based Instruction: Design and Development

Andrew S. Gibbons
Utah State University

Peter G. Fairweather
T. J. Watson Research Center
IBM

Educational Technology Publications
Englewood Cliffs, New Jersey 07632

Library of Congress Cataloging-in-Publication Data

Gibbons, Andrew S.
    Computer-based instruction : design and development / Andrew S.
    Gibbons, Peter G. Fairweather.
        p. cm.
    Includes bibliographical references and index.
    ISBN 0–87778–300–4 (hardcover).—ISBN 0–87778–301–2 (softcover)
    1. Conputer-assisted instruction.   2. Instructional systems-
-Design.   I. Fairweather, Peter G.   II. Title.
LB1028.5.G487   1998
371.33'4—dc21   97–34702
                                                             CIP

Printed in the United States of America.

Library of Congress Catalog Card Number:
97–34702.

International Standard Book Numbers:
0–87778–300–4 (hardcover).
0–87778–301–2 (softcover).

First Printing: January, 1998.

Dedication

We dedicate this book, with love, to our families.

ACKNOWLEDGMENTS

The kind help of many people supported the preparation of this book.

We give special thanks to a review panel whose members received an early version of the manuscript and commented extensively on it. Two editions of the manuscript have been produced since their review, largely based on their concerns and generous sharing of time to give us detailed feedback. The reviewers were: Valorie Beer, Netscape Communications, Inc.; Richard Boutwell, Newport News Shipbuilding Company; Olin Campbell, Vanderbilt University; Dexter Fletcher, Institute for Defense Analysis; Michael Karim, University of North Dakota; Greg Kearsley, George Washington University; and M. David Merrill, Utah State University.

Key sections of the manuscript, particularly those relating to the Authorware and Quest authoring systems, were reviewed by Craig Rushton and Ron Johnson of Allen Communication, Inc. and by Michael Allen of Allen Interactions. We appreciate their willingness to take the time on our behalf to perform a review. If there are still inaccuracies in the book concerning their products, we must accept that they are our own inadvertent misinterpretations of their feedback.

The manuscript was reviewed by faculty colleagues Kimberly Lawless and Steve Soulier, both of Utah State University, to whom we are most grateful. In addition, reviews by business contacts John Fox of Pacific Bell and Derron Bishop of United Education Centers, Inc. were most helpful.

We thank Marsha Gibbons for entering editorial changes and performing a reading of the manuscript during the final stages of its production. Stephen Gibbons of the American Stores Company also read the manuscript and took delight in pointing out opportunities for improvement.

We also thank numerous instructional technology students at Utah State University and many other CBI professionals in corporate training settings throughout the world who, over a ten year period, have used various portions of this book as a learning tool. They, as much as anybody, contributed to the book's evolution from a set of guidelines to a full-fledged, balanced, and, we hope, usable discussion of key principles and methods. Special thanks go also to the former Gail Yamizake, then of the U.S. Air Force.

Despite these numerous reviews, there are doubtless errors and mistakes. As authors we accept that responsibility and sincerely thank all those who have been of service to our preparations.

Andrew S. Gibbons
Logan, Utah

Peter G. Fairweather
Yorktown Heights, New York

PREFACE AND OVERVIEW

Who is our reader?

This is a book of practical concepts and development techniques intended for developers of instruction to be delivered using a computer. Our audience is the average CBI developer. This may be an educator in the schools looking for increased instructional leverage or reach, a training developer in industry trying to increase productivity while reducing cost, or a college academic in any field who wants to use the power of the computer to make the invisible and subtle concepts of a discipline accessible to beginning students.

This is a practical book. It teaches sound instructional design principles, but it recognizes that not all CBI designers have the time or patience for scholarly discussions. We have tried to make our descriptions simple, interesting, and concrete. Suggested readings at each chapter end help the reader who has a continuing curiosity to bridge into academic studies. Self-directed learning projects, also at chapter end, begin the reader on his or her own journey into the world of practical yet effective CBI design. A CBI designer does need not be a trained instructional psychologist, but we are foolish if we ignore principles with known influence on learning, and we hope that our readers will desire to continue their education in this most fascinating and dynamic technology.

Unlike most instructional media, most CBI today is being developed by the audience we have described—non-programmers and non-instructional designers. It is imperative that these workers have support to develop the best possible products, because they will do much to set the vision and the expectations for future CBI products. They must not only have effective instructional principles to work with but also must understand the implications of their design decisions for production and delivery costs. The lessons to be learned must be learned quickly, because many of those entering the world of CBI are doing so with limited time and resources and yet work within an atmosphere of high expectations for quality and effectiveness.

The ongoing test of the CBI technology

Despite its widespread use and growing popularity, CBI as a technology is still on trial. Technologies like television, aviation, and refrigeration have become so ingrained into our living patterns that losing them would cause personal hardship for us individually and severe economic distress in general. This is not true of the technology of computer-based instruction.

Every promised new technology meets two important tests—one to see if it is effective, and one to see if it is affordable. If a technology can't pass both tests, it either dies or finds a specialized niche to fill.

The test of the CBI technology will be difficult for several reasons. Easy-to-use development tools seem to make it so easy to build a CBI product that anybody *ought* to be able to do it. Anybody *can* build a pretty screen using a sophisticated graphics program, but the fact is that *not just anybody* can build effective computerized instruction, any more than just anybody can stand in front of a class and be converted automatically into an excellent teacher. There are principles of learning and instruction, and they apply just as certainly to computer-based instruction as they do to classroom or any other form of instruction. We have written this book placing heavy emphasis on the principles of instruction and on the conceptual structures of CBI, realizing that you can learn to build attractive screen displays and to use specific development tools from other sources.

The convergence of CBI technologies

CBI is actually a combination of several hard and soft technologies. The main hard technologies—computers and programming—already stand with such other indispensable technologies as automobiles, refrigeration, and human language.

The main soft technology—the technology of instruction by computer—is not at the same mature stage of development. We are still using computers instructionally at very low levels of sophistication. We have much to learn about the basics of using this technology, and that learning will come from informed developers in the field as much as it will from academic research. Therefore, we hope that the readers of our book will eventually become contributors to the field in significant ways. Hence, our emphasis is on principles.

There is an exciting revolution going on right now in the field of CBI. On the one hand, there are CBI designers who follow traditional lines of thinking to create CBI products which look much like older and familiar forms of instruction. On the other hand, there are designers who realize that the power of the computer to instruct is not found in the traditional forms and that the computer represents the first completely new instructional medium since the book. These designers are discovering the great variety of instructional approaches which the computer has made available that were impossible before—in many cases even to live teachers.

How do you write a book about CBI design in this atmosphere of change and discovery? CBI designers must have tools and concepts that they can begin to use immediately to produce effective results. At the same time, a book that teaches just today's tools and techniques will be obsolete the day it is published. We have tried to provide a bridge between the accepted, proven practices of today and the wonderful possibilities which will soon become the new standard. We hope to give new CBI developers tools for disciplined but innovative thought as they encounter and solve new CBI problems and advance the state of the art.

CBI still faces a period of testing to see whether effective, general, and universally usable principles for computer-based instruction can be discovered and whether efficient tools can be developed that allow designers to create powerful new experiences at affordable prices. It is to help this come to pass that we have written this book.

Here is an outline of the book chapters:

SECTION I: WHAT IS CBI?

A survey of the CBI experience in all its forms for those who have never been CBI students themselves. This section will help you stretch your conception of CBI.

Chapter 1—The Big Difference

A contrast between CBI and traditional instructional forms. This chapter points out the five features of the computer as an instructional tool that allow it to create instructional experiences possible with no other medium.

Chapter 2—CBI On the Surface

A description of the major forms of CBI products from the user's point of view, on the surface. This chapter describes the kind of experience created by each form of CBI and relates the different forms to each other in real-world applications.

SECTION II: BENEATH THE SURFACE

A look inside of CBI products to view the inner logical structures that make them work the way they do. Two major forms of logical structure are identified which strongly influence the power of CBI, the types of CBI created, and the costs of creation.

Chapter 3—The Evolution of CBI Authoring Tools

A short discussion of how CBI authoring tools have developed over time. We discuss the basic instructional logic-building element and the implications it holds for CBI developers—now and in the very interesting future.

Chapter 4—Frames

A description of a useful building block of CBI, the frame. A study of the basic family of frame varieties, how frames behave, and how a designer can use frames.

Chapter 5—Frame Patterns

A description of how individual frames fit together into larger patterns capable of making familiar surface CBI events take place. A discussion of the limitations of frame-based authoring systems.

Chapter 6—Objects

The persistent run-time object is described as an emerging technology that will revolutionize the way we think about and build instruction.

SECTION III: PRINCIPLES OF INSTRUCTIONAL STRATEGY

Principles derived from knowledge of the learning process to guide the design of instructional messages and interactions. The beginning of a book-long exploration into strategies and their origins.

Chapter 7—Learning: The Student

A non-technical discussion of learning processes and their implications for CBI developers.

Chapter 8—Instructional Strategy I: Foundations

An examination of where instructional strategies come from and a derivation of several general strategy principles from examples.

Chapter 9—Instructional Strategy II: Applications

A closer look at the goals and elements that make up an instructional strategy for direct tutorial instruction.

Chapter 10—Memory Instructional Strategy

A description of different varieties of memory performance and a set of principles for supporting learners as they attempt to store and later recall memory content.

Chapter 11—Procedure-Using Instructional Strategy

A description of the nature and variety of procedures and a guide for applying the structured approach to instructional strategy to the instruction of procedures.

Chapter 12—Process-Using Instructional Strategy

A description of process-using behavior. A discussion of the importance of processes and their usefulness as a form of knowledge. Guidelines for designing instruction for processes.

Chapter 13—Concept-Using Instructional Strategy

A description of the notion of *concept*. A catalog of the ways in which concept classes vary. A set of guidelines for instructing concepts.

Chapter 14—Principle-Using Instructional Strategy

A description of principle-using behavior. A description of the special preparations required for principle-using instruction.

Chapter 15—Instructional Strategy III: Fragmentation and Integration

Principles and techniques for instructional strategy design at levels above the individual objective. Introduction of the work model and instructional event structural elements as tools for building macro-strategies. Introduction of the ideas of scope and challenge as elements of a strategy.

Chapter 16—Instructional Simulations

A description of the simulation as an instructional tool and how it is employed within the larger context of instruction. A description of the types of instructional simulation. Principles for merging instructional features into simulations. A description of six types of instructional features for simulations.

Chapter 17—Simulation Logic Patterns

A non-technical description of the inner workings of the environment and model simulations. Approaches to simulation development which save time and effort through the use of drivers and object programming.

SECTION IV: PRINCIPLES OF INSTRUCTIONAL DELIVERY

Specific practices to improve the instructional power of the message, the interactions, and the CBI display.

Chapter 18—Message Management

Methods for capturing a complete and accurate instructional message and then expressing it with economy and clarity.

Chapter 19—Display Management

Methods for arranging a *display*, which consists of all of the channels of communication to the student, in order to communicate the maximum information and interaction with the minimum time and energy.

Chapter 20—CBI Barnum: How to Use Showmanship Without Becoming a Clown

Ideas about appropriate and inappropriate uses of the special effects capabilities of the CBI medium to attract student attention and try to generate motivation.

SECTION V: HOW TO DESIGN CBI

Design processes for tutorials and simulations, including key structural elements, the order of design, and principles to guide the design process. Examples of two different approaches to the design of CBI products: tutorials and simulations.

Chapter 21—Creating Tutorials

An easy and logical step-by-step method for designing and documenting CBI tutorial instruction.

Chapter 22—Creating Simulations

A guide to the design of CBI products which do not present a structured message to the student. An alternative approach to design which integrates the several levels of structure in a CBI simulation.

Chapter 23—CBI and Distance Learning

The application of CBI design principles when instruction occurs at a distance. A re-examination of the four areas of CBI design: strategy design, message management, display management, and special effects usage.

SECTION VI: TRENDS

Our look into the crystal ball.

Chapter 24—Looking Ahead

A necessary look into the future of CBI in the spirit of preparing designers not only to create today's products using today's tools and design concepts, but to prepare the designer for the inevitable shifts in both which will make tomorrow even more interesting.

CONTENTS

Computer-Based Instruction:
Design and Development

SECTION I

WHAT IS CBI?
A survey of the CBI experience in all its forms for
those who have never been CBI students themselves.
This section will help you stretch your conception of CBI.

1

THE BIG DIFFERENCE

Chapter Objectives:

1. *Recognize that good instruction is media independent; good and bad instruction can be created in any medium.*

2. *Recognize that the most sound motivation to learn comes from the satisfying experience of learning.*

3. *Identify the five features of the computer which give it strength as an instructional delivery medium.*

4. *Recognize that the computer can provide kinds of instruction not possible with other forms of instructional media.*

5. *Recognize that the design of CBI instruction consists of more than simply transferring instruction from other forms of instructional media.*

An experience in motivation

A group of Army trainees sits at computer terminals in a small classroom converted into a computer-based instruction lab. These students are taking part in the initial testing of a computer-based system for teaching guided missile maintenance. At some terminals only one student works; at others, there are groups of students. Most have passed through a set of introductory lessons and have entered a series of simulated troubleshooting exercises in which actual maintenance skills are being tested.

The students concentrate intently on their screens, even though it is the second full day of instruction on the system. The sergeant assigned to monitor the evaluation recalls that the Space Shuttle is scheduled to land today. Feeling that this will be something of interest to the students, and hoping to reward them for their diligence in studying by giving them a break, he steps over to the wall-mounted television set behind the students and switches it on.

His timing is right. The Shuttle is on its final approach. "Look at this," he says to the group, "the Space Shuttle is about to land!" The students appear not to notice him. After a few moments, he repeats the invitation more urgently. Still there is no result. Finally, exasperated by the lack of interest, and perhaps puzzled at this unusual behavior, the sergeant suggests in strong terms that there is a kind of patriotic responsibility to watch this historic landing. In response, the students turn around momentarily barely enough to see the screen. They watch until the Shuttle touches the ground and then return their attention immediately back to their terminals.

Surprising? Several observers thought so as this small group of Army students showed totally unexpected levels of motivation toward very technical instruction. Yet, subsequent experience has shown on many occasions that this was only one example demonstrating the tremendous motivational forces that can be released by excellent, interactive, computer-based instruction. Technicians, professionals, children, and learners of all ability levels become deeply engrossed in good instruction delivered by computer.

In a completely different area of instruction, Fred O'Neal, a colleague, describes a large group of medical doctors in Germany attending an international medical convention. They struggle at two o'clock in the morning, arguing vehemently over the diagnosis of a fictitious, computerized patient's rare combination of symptoms. This level of motivation has become commonplace when excellent CBI is involved.

5

But computer-based instruction is not the only medium that can produce this effect. All of us can remember intense moments of complete engrossment in instruction of many different forms—a book, a lecture, a film—experiences where the enjoyment of comprehending and discovering itself produced the desire for more learning. These experiences are too rare. They are moments of highly productive learning, and they leave lasting impressions on our minds.

The quest of this book is two-fold: first, to identify the properties of good instruction and to capture them as principles that can be used in design; and second, to identify how to incorporate these principles specifically within computer-based instruction. Identifying these principles will cause us to engage in a few somewhat abstract discussions at the beginning of the book, but by the end of the book, these discussions will have brought us to specific techniques for designing effective computer-based instruction of many forms.

The computer as an instructional medium

A good place to begin will be to investigate the features of computers which give them strength for delivering instruction. What are the characteristics of the computer that make it capable of producing instructional moments? What sets CBI apart from other instructional media? We will find that it is not just one characteristic but a complex of characteristics. Taken together, and applied with sound instructional technique, they can make computer-based instruction an engrossing and powerful experience. Let's review five qualities: the computer's dynamic display, the ability to accept student input, the computer's speed, its ability to select, and its flawless memory.

Difference #1: Dynamic display

The computer display is the most flexible and dynamic of all instructional display surfaces. It can depict events which are cosmic in their scope and those which are microscopic. Even imaginary events and objects can be shown. As the student watches, objects can evolve and change into new forms with audio or text messages annotating each change. The student can be given the power to experiment and observe as the results of decisions appear in realistic form.

The computer display for instructional purposes consists of more than a monitor screen. A CBI display consists of all of the sounds, sights, and sensations that the computer is capable of producing. Many elements add to the power of the computer's display.

Speed and timing: The speed of the computer's display, operating on powerful graphic, video, and audio programs, accounts for much of the computer display's dynamism. The display can show events taking place in fast motion, slow motion, or frozen motion. And the speed can be placed under the student's control. Perhaps the first time through, a student will choose to see process steps slowly, with full commenting and explanation. Later, the student may choose to see the speed of the steps increase by degrees, to get a more complete *feel* for how the process steps flow together.

Moreover, the computer can place graphics events or combinations of graphics, text, audio, and video on the screen at just the right moment. Research indicates that timing is an important dimension of the instructional message. (Chapter 19 on Display Management deals with this dimension.)

Selective change: The computer display can change any portion of itself at any time. During the simulation of a boiler room control panel, an instructional designer can cause only those parts of the display to change which are affected by a student input. When the main steam valve is closed and pressure begins to build in a boiler, the pressure needle alone can be made to move, the pressurized lines can be shown to build pressure, and all other parts of the display can remain unchanged.

Selective changing of the screen is very useful in tutorials also. The developer who knows how to arrange lesson content into logical categories dedicates areas of a screen to the categories: one to main ideas, one to examples, and another to explanations or notes. These areas become symbolic to the student, who learns to use location as a cue to the type of information being given. Research shows that information uptake by the student is more efficient under these conditions.

Graphics: Today's graphics programs make complex, full-color, high-resolution graphics and video effects easier to create on the computer than using traditional tools and methods. Graphics can be quite detailed, and the use of windowing effects can provide the illusion of zooming-in to areas of a graphic for a closer look at the details. The old monochrome and four-color standards have been replaced by computer graphic systems capable of sixteen, 256, or over a million different colors on the screen at one time. The computer's graphic capability invites us to place a greater portion of the instructional message in non-verbal form. Instead of describing the steps and mechanical interactions within an internal combustion engine verbally, a graphic display can show each step in animation, pausing to point out each cause-effect relationship.

Video: Recently the storage capacity of the personal computer and the speed of data handling have become equal to the task of supporting low-cost computer video—both motion and still. The inclusion of video into computer-based instruction opens new worlds of realism, makes possible the visualization of things difficult to illustrate graphically, and creates an immense instant resource of existing video which can be considered for re-use within computerized instruction through a process called *repurposing*. Most CBI systems which allow the use of video in the display also make possible the overwriting of the video with graphics simultaneously. This is a critically important feature which allows video materials to be enhanced, modified, or emphasized for instructional purposes at the time of instruction and used for multiple instructional purposes.

Video can be stored for the computer in many forms. The videodisc, the CD-ROM, and digitized video files can act as sources of video display content. These display sources make possible video motion as well as stills. Good systems allow these sequences to be stopped, slowed, and stepped forward or backward one frame at a time—under student control. These display tools also excel in some cases where computer graphics cannot produce sequences of animated motion with sufficient levels of realism or where they cannot do it within required timing limits.

Audio: Under computer control, media devices such as an audio board, videotape, CD-ROM, or videodisc may be used to supply music, voice, and sound effects. Computers can be equipped with voice-generation or digitized audio capabilities which allow immediate random access to spoken messages. Moreover, as the technology of voice recognition continues to mature, computers will be increasingly equipped with voice recognition programs. When controlled by the computer, this capability will permit students to carry out verbal dialogues with the computer for instructional purposes, such as for teaching languages, management skills, customer skills, sales techniques, or any skill in which the use of the voice is an important ingredient.

The multiple *channels* of communication described above make up the computer's display. Combined together, these display capabilities enable students to interview and treat patients; simulate operation and/or maintenance of electronic and computer equipment; pilot oil tankers, tanks, and aircraft; or tour the geosphere, the human body, dangerous areas of a nuclear plant, the solar system, or the inside of an atom. Students can even be given the media and the controls to tour history, meet famous persons, converse with them, view historical events, and enjoy historical locations the way they used to exist in a kind of mediated time machine. All of these things are well within the realm of possibility with current CBI display capabilities.

External devices: Recently, the visible portion of the computer display has been extended beyond the screen—even beyond the virtual reality headset. Innovative developers have used real objects connected to the computer as part of the display. Chemistry tools—sensors, electrical probes, measuring devices—can be connected to the computer. Experiments can be run by the student using such systems, with the computer aiding, coaching, directing, evaluating, providing feedback, and even warning of danger. Beyond virtual reality, there is reality itself.

This extension of the display to outside the computer's box is a trend which will continue and accelerate. One form of CBI is called *embedded* instruction. In this type of CBI, instead of a CBI system trying to mimic real equipment, it becomes a part of real equipment. A CBI capability is embedded in the real equipment, making the equipment capable of administering its own instruction and support for users. During periods of non-use, the equipment's embedded instructional capability provides tutorials, practice, feedback, and testing for students who are unable to detect that they are not using real equipment in a real application.

The computer-based instruction system has, indeed, the most flexible and dynamic of all instructional display surfaces. If you can imagine it, the computer, either alone or coupled with other media devices, can probably do it.

Difference #2: Ability to accept student input

The common but erroneous stereotype of computer-based instruction envisions a student in front of a computer's terminal screen, normally in some sort of cave-like, walled carrel, typing at a keyboard. We have just discovered that the CBI display goes far beyond the terminal screen. Let us look now at ways for accepting input from the student that go far beyond the keyboard. The computer's display surface is the most flexible of instructional display surfaces, and the instructional computer provides the most flexible and powerful of input surfaces for communicating with the computer. Most of these input channels do not involve the keyboard.

Students at the computer use several input channels to express choices, enter answers, control exploration, and perform motor tasks. Input mechanisms vary widely in the amount of information they can carry to the computer, and so different input devices are suited to different purposes.

Screen location devices: One whole family of input devices allows the student to select or point to a location on a computer screen. This location may be tied to a choice or an opportunity which has been presented on the screen, so by selecting a screen location the student can answer a question, express a decision, change the settings on the computer's controls, or order instruction on a particular topic. The location is the key that the computer uses to decode the student's intentions.

Touch screens are one kind of location device used to simplify student input. No special training is required to use a touch screen; the student simply touches one of the choices shown on the screen. In the process of pointing at the display feature, the finger either breaks a light beam or generates an electrical signal, and the computer can read the position of the touch. The touch pad is a variant of the touch screen. The principle of operation is the same: The student touches a location which corresponds to a choice. The touch pad, however, is not located on a computer screen; it is normally placed on the desktop in a horizontal position. The touch pad surface may be overlaid with a drawing, a chart, or a control matrix. By touching the drawing, the student is at the same time touching the underlying pad, and the location of the touch is correlated with a choice or control action, just as it is with the touch screen.

Light pens operate on the same physical principle, though by a different electronic mechanism. A light pen, either connected by wire to the computer terminal or powered by a battery, is pressed onto the screen surface instead of a finger. The computer reads a light signal from the pen and computes the location of the touch.

Possibilities with tools like light pens are only limited by imagination and programming skill. The clever use of the light pen by developer David Hon allowed students to "weld" metal using a light pen which was built, with plastic, into the shape of a welding torch. The light pen/welding torch was held near the surface of a computer screen displaying two pieces of metal. The student's task was to use the light pen as a welding torch to join them together. To do this, the student placed the light pen near the screen and drew it across the seam between the metal sheets, with the tip of the pen just the right distance from the screen, just as an expert welder would. The computer was able to sense (through tricky programming) whether the light pen/welding torch was being held too close or too far from the screen, and it gave visual feedback to the student in the form of an actual welding "bead" (the glow and color of hot metal), which was supplied by a videodisc image. The result was a display that mimicked the look of a real weld taking place. The programming and videodisc design skills for this product were considerable. It is not a project that the average designer would attempt, but this product illustrates how a change in perspective can take an otherwise simple and underrated tool and use it for a variety of instructional purposes.

The term "mouse" has become a household word. Whereas most computer input used to come from a keyboard, much of it is now accomplished using a mouse. Few computers are sold these days without a mouse. In CBI, a mouse is used in the same fashion as a touch screen or a light pen to choose screen locations. The mouse does have one added dimension of control which touch screens and light pens lack: the mouse buttons. A mouse may have one, two, or three buttons for the user to press to effect control or express choice. If a designer assigns consistent functions to these buttons, the student is given a more powerful channel for expressing options. However, if the button definitions shift and change frequently, or if they are used in illogical ways, the student can become confused, and the power of the buttons is lost.

A close cousin to the mouse is called the trackball. In effect, a trackball is a mouse turned upside down. A trackball presents a sphere to the user which is cupped within a housing and can be rotated in any direction. When the user of a trackball moves the ball, sensors in the housing read the direction in which the ball is turned and send that information to the computer. A trackball also has one or more buttons which can be pressed to mark locations or to express choices. These buttons have the same effect as the mouse buttons.

The joystick is another variant of the location input device which operates, in principle, like a mouse or a trackball. The joystick's control is exerted by positioning a vertical handle-grip rather than by moving a mouse or a sphere. Most joysticks have one or more buttons for selecting a location, just as the mouse and trackball. Joysticks are constructed for rapid precise actions like those required to play video games, and their use in instructional systems has been relatively limited.

These location input devices—the touch screen, the touch pad, the light pen, the mouse, the trackball, and the joystick—have a variety of uses in computer-based instruction for an imaginative developer. These include making menu selections from a textual or graphic menus, drawing graphic objects, outlining areas of the screen to be enlarged and examined in detail, tracing paths through complex pathways such as arteries or electronic circuits, and operating switches and valves. With these devices, students can move things around, build structures, draw, activate processes, lasso screen areas, and adjust values. Frequently these devices are used in harmony with standard interface conventions to reduce the amount of attention required to express choice or control. These conventions make use of familiar elements from the student's surroundings such as information and menu boxes, desktops, file cabinets, index cards, and notebook pages. One of the main advantages of this class of input devices is that they can normally be used rapidly and with little distraction from the student's main thinking task. There is no need to hunt for keys or to encode verbal responses.

However, many kinds of subject matter require a verbal response. This brings up the need for verbally-oriented channels of student input: the keyboard and voice control.

Keyboard: Years of CBI experience have produced very capable and flexible computer routines for the analysis of short text messages from the keyboard. Given a string of text from a student, the more sophisticated CBI answer processors can look within that string for exact matches, key word matches, and synonym matches. It can throw away certain irrelevant parts of the input, such as "noise" words, and it can accept and recognize words in any order, but only if the developer has specified it. It can also judge for the presence or absence of capitalization, punctuation, and blank spaces, and it can recognize a word that has been misspelled, despite the misspelling. For partially correct answers, it can award points based on the portion that was correct.

Voice input: The computer technology for accepting voice input in natural language has improved rapidly in recent years. Some computer manufacturers are beginning to equip their products with built-in voice control systems, and this must be interpreted to show their confidence that this technology will continue its rapid advance. There are many computer instructional applications where no-hands control is important. In many instructional areas, the skills to be learned are verbal skills, such as language learning. In other areas, such as interpersonal communication training, voice input is important to increase the natural feel for the student making a response.

The development of the computer's ability accept and respond to voice input, a skill which humans take for granted, has required the development of two complicated computer technologies: voice recognition and natural language parsing. These are both difficult tasks which require fast, powerful computers and complicated programs, so the length of a verbal input is an important limiting factor at present, especially in CBI. The longer the input, the more potential there is for misunderstanding of the student's content or intention, and the more work is required to set up the evaluation of the response.

External sensors and mechanisms: Several varieties of sensor external to the computer and not normally classed with the computer as input devices have important instructional uses.

Real equipment of almost any type can be connected to a computer, and the controls (and indicators) of the real equipment can be used to effect action (and then show the results). Aircraft simulators are simply a very sophisticated form of computer-based instruction in which realistic equipment sets have been substituted for displays. One very interesting development in the more modern aircraft is the increased use of computer-like displays in the actual aircraft controls and indicators, in place of the traditional knobs and gauges. In this sense, CBI and real equipment are converging, which not only improves the systems themselves, but makes CBI easier to develop.

Connecting real equipment to computers for CBI purposes goes far beyond the common terminal-based stereotype of CBI. Many designers readily see the difference between fully terminal-based and fully equipment-based varieties of CBI. Increasingly in the future, it will be important for them to see the instructional value of CBI systems which lie between these two extremes: systems in which some elements of interaction are provided through the CBI display and some are provided through realistic equipment.

Olympic athletes use specialized sensors connected to computers to record the motion of their bodies during training. These sensors are a type of computer input device, and their use constitutes a form of computer-based instruction. The computer can capture the athlete's performance as data, and the computer can analyze it for patterns in the data which indicate either excellent performance or deficient performance. This data can be used to recreate or replay the athlete's performance for review and feedback and also to judge the performance and to prescribe modifications which will lead to improvement.

Another way to look at the use of such sensors is as controls within a CBI experience. One inventive approach to the instruction of cardio-pulmonary resuscitation created by David Hon uses a mechanical dummy attached to the computer. Within the dummy are pressure sensors which can detect whether the life-saving procedures are being applied with sufficient force and accuracy. A display screen and a system of sounds is used to provide feedback for the student as she or he operates on the dummy. Thousands have learned CPR using what they may not have recognized as computer-based instruction and a non-keyboard input channel device.

The current growing interest in *virtual reality* provides another demonstration of the use of sensors as inputs from a student. Humans wearing helmets and gloves for control operation during virtual reality exercises are becoming common. The technology is now readily available that enables control to be exerted using eye movement, and even brain waves.

It is not hard to imagine the instructional uses of sensor-equipped psychomotor instruction on CBI. Beginning ballet students may learn more precise control and learn it earlier through the use of such systems. Paraplegic students of all ages can be given the ability to converse with the rich educational world of the computer through the use of head movements or any other available motion capability they possess. These uses of the computer rely on servo-mechanistic and electronic sensors as input devices.

Another channel for accepting input from a student is the stylus. The stylus is a type of pen which can be recognized by the computer but which does not work by light. The stylus has recently begun to appear with specially-designed computer screens for the purpose of allowing the user to write words directly on the computer screen. This alternative use of the pen promises to open new areas to computer-based instruction. Writing and art instruction come to mind readily as areas where physical control and precision are being learned. We can also see this tool helping physically challenged students regain or attain improved control over motor functions of many kinds.

Timing of input: The computer can not only time its output to the student, it can check the timing of the student's input as well. The most frequent use of this ability is in timed drills. After a given number of seconds, a lesson or test can time-out if no response has been received from the student. Within that time limit, students may have very little time—just time enough to touch the correct answer on the screen or to type one letter or number. This timing ability is also important in sophisticated applications like simulations. During instruction for pipeline technicians or brain surgeons, a simulation may require that a particular action be taken before a critical pressure or volume of fluid is reached. By checking the timing of responses, the computer can determine when to inform the student that acid from the pipeline is now eating a hole in his home town or that the patient is experiencing convulsions.

Difference #3: Fast processing of the input

The computer can do what it does because it is so fast. The good news for CBI is that the trend toward faster and more powerful computers is accelerating. The speed of today's computers is actually becoming a problem for designers who discover that the computer can process a student input and accomplish its response in less time than it takes to look up from the keyboard to the screen. Students are actually being denied the ability to see the changes to the display based on their actions, and it may be that special timing buffers will become an important element of CBI software to allow responses to be brought back from computer speed to human speed. Computing for instructional purposes puts an unusually heavy processing load on a computer. At one time speed was a major problem for even the simplest forms of instruction, but most CBI systems today do not have major timing problems unless full-screen bitmapped images are being displayed. The computer in an instructional setting is so fast at getting its part done that it spends most of its time waiting for the student to do something.

Difference #4: Ability to select between courses of action

As once-beleaguered former school teachers, both of the authors have regularly faced classes of 30 to 35 students. During instruction, we found that some students moved along well without much coaching. Others had the ability to understand and perform but required individual attention for other reasons. Had we been able to work one-on-one with those students, they would have moved along well also, but attention was demanded by the entire class, and we had to attend to the group first. The amount of time we had to respond to individuals, even under the best time management practices, was severely limited.

In contrast, though students can work at the computer in groups, they can also work individually, and this means that the computer only has to face one student at a time. Because of this, and because of its great speed, the computer can interpret every student input from several points of view and supply what it interprets to be the most needful thing at a given moment—missing information, additional practice, coaching, feedback of a special type, or even reassurance.

The limits to the treatment a student can receive are the limits in the expertise and skill of the instructional designer and the designer's tools. For instance, the computer can analyze complex textual input from the student during composition instruction and identify common writing practices which require special attention. It can then pick out suitable instruction and practice material and present it to the student and monitor the results until the signs of the problem are gone. It can periodically check the student's future productions for recurrence of the problem. Most importantly, it can do all of this, if desired, in the context of instruction on a completely unrelated topic. That is, while instruction is being given on punctuation, the computer can be searching the student's work for dangling participles.

This ability of the computer to process student input rapidly on an individual basis and respond in a tailored fashion to student needs is probably its single most powerful capability as an instructional device. This capability increases the amount of practice one student can squeeze into a unit of instructional time, and it improves the precision of the feedback a student can receive. This makes computerized instruction vastly more productive than the thirty-to-one ratio that the classroom setting imposes for certain learning tasks.

Computer users have long been aware of the "Garbage In, Garbage Out" principle. It is a reminder that computers can only process according to the instructions the designer or programmer gives them. If the computer is given good recipes for instruction and good materials to use, it will produce good instructional experiences. If, on the other hand, the computer is given poor material and poor instructional rules, then no amount of computer involvement will turn out good instruction. This is one of the reasons that this book tries to emphasizes good instructional principles. We must never accept the position that the instructional computer, no matter how pretty or amusing its display capabilities, can be used as a cosmetic to cover up the blemishes of poor instructional practice.

Difference #5: Memory

If it only had high speed and the power to make decisions, the computer would be restricted to judgments involving only the most recent student responses during instruction. But with the added power of memory, the computer can remember past things about the student to use in future decisions. That is, it can keep a constantly changing profile of the student's progress and performance and use it to plot the future path of instruction. What kinds of things can the computer remember that are instructionally useful? Here are a few ideas:

First, the computer can remember responses and scores. As an exercise progresses, students are continually answering questions and exerting choice and control. As responses are given by the student, the computer can store them away after taking the proper immediate action. Later, it can retrieve them for further analysis. This may occur while the student is still in the exercise, or later, after the student has left. From this stored data, the computer can derive a wealth of helpful information, including error patterns and areas of misunderstanding. The mass of scores accumulated for one student can be summarized into grades if desired, or pass/fail decisions.

Second, the data accumulated for several students can be examined for areas of weakness in the instruction itself. For instance, if a specific test item (either a verbal question or a simulation problem) is deficient, it will become apparent as the data for all students is examined, since most students, achiever and non-achiever alike, will have trouble with it. If a concept is poorly taught, that will also be reflected in generally low scores on one or more assessments. This process of response pattern analysis is important to the operation of any instructional system, computerized or not. Having the computer to keep the data and analyze it automatically is a great time-saver and allows the teacher to deal with errors that were otherwise inaccessible or undetectable.

Third, the computer can remember course structure and mastery data. As students work through a computer-based course, as in any well-developed course, they are mastering certain instructional objectives that are a part of a well-organized and clearly defined network of objectives. Courses based on this system of organization allow student progress to be charted clearly and unmistakably. The computer can record items of progress for a student automatically and present a full report of where the student has been and where to go next. On the basis of this report, the student or the computer can be given the choice of what to do next. This use of the computer's memory is called CMI, or Computer-Managed Instruction. The ultimate expression of this management function is found in systems which are capable of moment-by-moment adjustment of the nature or content of the instruction to student needs and performance. Of course, CMI today falls far below this ideal.

Fourth, the computer can remember personal student information, such as knowledge levels attained or learning style preferred. Because the computer can notice and store data about a student's performance, it can adapt the instructional presentation to his or her needs and preferences. The search has been going on for years to find a practical way to chart student knowledge and then use it to adapt instruction to the individual student. One missing fact or concept can prevent the assimilation of other facts and principles. Using special techniques for representing knowledge, the computer programs of the future will keep knowledge data for the individual student and be able to react when the student is missing something critical. Once again, current practice is far from the ideal.

Fifth, researchers continue to seek for the elemental set of learning variables that make up a person's learning style. If these can be charted, then instructional strategies can be designed which supply the optimal amounts and types of information, interaction, feedback, and helps to suit the needs of a style. Given that students differ in learning styles, the computer's memory will be capable of storing a learner's set of needs and preferences and then administering the right mixture of instructional elements and practice. In the early days of CBI, this was an important part of the vision for computerized instruction, but it was a distant and elusive goal. However, the advancing speed and size of the computer's memory brings this goal closer to realization, given the expected progress in research.

Where does it lead?

We have considered five characteristics of the computer that make it the most flexible and powerful instructional device ever invented. The intent of this chapter was to broaden some perspectives and change some limiting stereotypes. Let us now take a few moments to consider several current trends that lead toward the future. These may help us to see what the totality of these simple capabilities of the computer might add up to as they are brought to work together more completely and harmoniously.

Consider microworlds and learning environments: For years, students have been learning thinking and problem solving skills by actually solving problems within what is called a microworld. A microworld is a defined setting created on a computer within which a learner may encounter and solve problems of a specific type. If problems are carefully selected, they can lead the student through lower-level learning through gentle steps toward increasingly challenging problems, and can do so without increasing levels of error and anxiety.

New programming tools make it simple to create entire worlds to explore, through which the student can literally wander as an observer, an inquirer, an investigator, or a participant in some larger learning event. Environments like this are appearing in increasing numbers, and the varieties of learning experience they make possible are increasing rapidly.

Consider more robust learning support: For the most part, past CBI design practices have perceived instruction mainly as an informing activity. New design concepts and programming tools are changing this perspective. They allow us to look at CBI instruction as a supported inquiry by the learner: an inquiry in which the learner assumes a greater responsibility for personal learning but does so with the help of an observant support system capable of monitoring learning, coaching, advising, judging, providing feedback, and assisting in the selection of beneficial learning paths.

Consider learning through "cognitive" apprenticeship: Not only are individual instructional activities changing in nature, but the concept of the larger context of instruction is changing as well. CBI is benefiting from new applications of the age-old apprenticeship method, in which a student learns by carrying out progressively challenging real-world tasks set by a perceptive master performer. This new perspective is turning a previously fragmented view of instruction into one which describes for the student an integrative approach for building complex skills out of less complex ones.

Consider agents that remember the student: The computer has been in the past a dispenser of instruction, and the student has approached it alone. Future CBI systems will provide an agent which will meet the student who has logged on and will accompany the student through instruction and through instructional choices, remembering the student's preferences and plans, and helping the student to chart a productive instructional course.

Consider adaptive instruction: Older tool metaphors have encouraged designers to create instruction in one flavor. However, the original conception of computer-based instruction conceived the computer as a provider of instruction adapted to the individual learner. Our ability to adapt instruction is improving, and our tools are rapidly introducing new design capabilities which will make adaptive instruction a reality in the future.

Consider shared instruction for groups and networks: Groups of students appear to benefit from CBI, just as individuals can. Recent experiences in computer-based instruction have included groups of students at distant locations and have engaged them in cooperative learning experiences beyond the walls of the classroom. This will become increasingly common in the future as the electronic highway becomes more accessible to schools and industries both.

Some of these new perspectives are laboratory concepts at present, but all of these trends are emerging rapidly into common CBI design practice. They are changing and will continue to change the nature of computer-based instruction and our own perceptions of what can be done. This places the CBI designer in an exciting atmosphere of productive change. But it also requires the designer to approach CBI as a new type of instructional medium in its own right.

Conclusion: Not just another medium

CBI is not just another instructional medium. It represents a major leap in the capacity of instructional delivery systems. The magnitude of this leap has been compared in power with the introduction of the textbook during the middle ages into a previously memory-based instructional system, one in which knowledge was passed from master to student by oral repetition and memorization. The introduction of the textbook created fears and suspicions. There were those who predicted that it would lead to the decline of human memory because students would be able to forget things which were written down.

The rise of CBI as an instructional tool has created similar fears. Predictions that students would be turned to robots have by now been put to rest by demonstrations that the computer is capable of teaching inquiry and problem-solving skills and powerful knowledge structures in a way hitherto difficult and restricted to the lucky few. Instead of creating a monster, CBI promises to create more thoughtful and inquiring students capable of taking a greater measure of responsibility for informing, instructing, and educating themselves over a lifetime and at their own rate of progress.

Attempts to equate CBI with other instructional media have failed. CBI is a unique instructional delivery medium with its own unique demands on the thinking of designers and developers. Instruction does not translate directly between the CBI medium and other media. To illustrate, a business friend of ours decided to convert some programmed instruction to computerized form. Thinking there would be a direct conversion, he entered the material in a form that directly corresponded to the original material and changed nothing. He called us in to review it with him. We acted as students and did not do well. Before many minutes had passed, we were confused and disoriented by the instruction.

Our friend was disturbed to find that the product which had worked so well in one medium was not working at all in the new one. We were unable to correctly answer many of the questions the computer asked us, so it refused to let us pass certain spots in the instruction. We did not understand where we were much of the time because many of the roadsigns we were used to in the original medium were gone. This led to frustration on our part and confusion. We also found the instructional style which had been interesting in the original medium to be ill-suited to the new medium: Whereas the original medium allowed the user some flexibility in moving about forwards and backwards in the material, the computer focused the attention of the learner on only one spot in the instruction and prevented any wandering at all. All of these mismatches between the instructional method and the instructional medium added up to a negative experience for us all, both the designer and the learners.

It became apparent during that review—as it has to so many others who have tried to use the instructional computer under the instructional metaphors of other media—that the computer brings with it special strengths that enable new forms of instruction; capabilities and requirements possessed by no other medium. These demand that instruction be designed to those strengths. In order for designers to create excellent CBI, they must catch a vision of CBI's unique capabilities, and that requires them to be open to new ideas of instruction, new images in their own thinking about what could be and what ought to be. Most CBI designers experience a breakthrough where they recognize that the instructional techniques by which they were educated can be expanded and modified in beneficial ways through the capabilities of the computer. This is not a barrier of education, but one of imagination, and anyone can pass through it and begin to conceive instruction for the computer. As you read, keep this idea paramount in your mind, and stretch your imagination to encompass the instructional computer.

Self-directed activities

- Make a checklist or a profiling list that allows you to differentiate good instruction from bad instruction. Make a secondary list containing characteristics which apply only to computer-based instruction.

- Begin a list of learning moments which you experienced as a student that were particularly enjoyable or memorable (after they were over, at least). Try to identify the elements which made these experiences memorable. Do the same for learning moments which were not enjoyable (after they were over) or which were counterproductive. Analyze the elements of those negative experiences.

- Collect the names of several standard instructional media varieties. Assess the instructional strengths and weaknesses of each medium as a provider of instructional experience. Suggest for each one ways in which the basic medium can be altered or augmented to be more interactive. Suggest ways each medium might be used in conjunction with the computer for instructional purposes. Determine which media had their weaknesses removed by combining with the computer.

- List the techniques and activities of the live instructor which the computer finds it hard or impossible to carry out. Form and express an opinion on the extent to which computers can and should replace the live instructor. Decide whether the computer can replace the live instructor.

- Describe as many ways as you can think of for uniting the live instructor with computer-based instruction. Describe how this impacts the activities, techniques, or teaching style of the instructor. Describe how the role of the instructor is changed. Describe the types of computer-based instruction which work well in coordination with an instructor and which ones don't. Identify qualities of the instructor that suit it for use by an instructor and those which make it more difficult for an instructor to use.

- Inventory the computers used for instructional purposes at your own place of work or schooling. Identify for each one the display and input options which it supports. Identify the potential value of those options which are not supported to the average learner, to learners with handicaps, and to learners who wish to learn and explore on their own. What additions or changes would you recommend be made to the computers you surveyed? Which input and control systems are more attractive because of the specific nature of the content instructed at your location?

- Select a piece of instruction currently delivered through a non-computer, non-instructor medium. Describe the changes which would be necessary to convert the instruction for computer delivery. Describe improvements you feel would result from the conversion. Describe ways in which you feel the instruction would suffer. Describe ways in which the goals of the instruction might change due to the conversion.

Further reading

Alessi, S., and Trollip, S. (1991). *Computer-based instruction: Methods and development (2nd ed.)*. Englewood Cliffs, NJ: Prentice-Hall.

Atkinson, R., and Wilson, H. (1969). *Computer-assisted instruction: A book of readings*. New York: Academic Press.

Bailey, G. D. (Ed.). (1993). *Computer-based integrated learning systems*. Englewood Cliffs, NJ: Educational Technology Publications.

Bork, A. (1987). *Learning with personal computers.* New York: Harper & Row.

Clark, R. (1989). *Developing technical training: A structured approach for the development of classroom and computer-based instructional materials.* Reading, MA: Addison-Wesley.

Fletcher, J., Hawley, D., and Piele, P. (1990). Costs, effects, and utility of microcomputer-assisted instruction in the classroom. *American Educational Research Journal, 27,* 783–806.

Fletcher-Flinn, C., and Gravatt, B. (1995). The efficacy of computer-assisted instruction: A meta-analysis. *Journal of Educational Computing Research, 12*(3), 219–41.

Lee, W., and Mamone, R., with Roadman, K. (1995). *Computer based training handbook.* Englewood Cliffs, NJ: Educational Technology Publications.

Lewis, R. (1993). *Special education technology: Classroom applications.* Pacific Grove, CA: Brooks/Cole Publishing.

Papert, S. (1980). *Mindstorms: Children, computers, and powerful ideas.* New York: Basic Books.

Papert, S. (1993). *The children's machine: Rethinking school in the age of the computer.* New York: Basic Books.

Steinberg, E. (1992). *Teaching computers to teach (2nd ed.).* Hillsdale, NJ: Lawrence Erlbaum Associates.

U. S. Congress, Office of Technology Assessment. (1995). *Teachers and technology: Making the connection.* OTA-EHR-616. Washington, DC: U. S. Government Printing Office.

2

CBI ON THE SURFACE

Chapter Objectives:

1. *Recognize the major forms of CBI product and how they relate to each other in formal instructional settings and in the workplace.*

2. *For each major form of CBI instruction, describe the kind of experience it provides to a student, the varieties it exhibits, its practical applications, and its cost and benefit factors.*

3. *Recognize the value of computer-managed instruction and its importance to increased CBI use in the future.*

4. *Place several key trends in CBI in perspective relative to their place in the growing CBI movement.*

Many forms of CBI

Up to this point we have discussed CBI as if it were just one kind of product, but there are many forms of CBI, and each one has its own uses and benefits. This chapter examines the forms of CBI applied to a variety of instruction and job support functions in order to paint a clearer picture of the CBI experience. For many of us, this will fill an experience gap, because the majority of those who design and develop CBI materials today did not use CBI products as learners during their own training. It is a situation analogous to the early days of the automobile and aircraft industries, when designers had only modest experience with the types of products they were designing, cars and aircraft.

To begin with, let's consider where CBI fits within the larger context of instruction that goes on around us every day at school, in industrial and commercial training, and in the workplace. There are four major forms of CBI activity in these areas: (1) tutorial instruction, (2) simulation and modeling, (3) learning coaching and job aiding, and (4) certification testing. Figure 1 places each of these four activities against the background of the school, the training place, and the workplace to show how they relate to each other throughout the instructional lifetime that spans both formal schooling and training in the workplace.

As the figure shows, tutorial instruction is frequently used during formal training for initial instruction on basic topics. It is also used in the workplace for direct instruction on advanced issues and for refresher instruction. Tutorial instruction often provides the foundation of basic understanding and knowledge and leads toward the advanced forms of practice provided by simulations.

Simulations and their realistic responses to the student provide the tool by which students can integrate skills and knowledge into a mature performance capability. Simulations also prepare students more fully to enter the real working world by giving them experience in realistic performance situations. Moreover, simulations can provide the bridge of certification testing that verifies when a student is ready to enter the professional world.

Learning Coaches and Job Aids (also referred to as Performance Support Systems, or PSS) are introduced for use early in formal learning, and they follow the student into the work place. They are actually slightly different forms of the same instructional tool. The Learning Coach is used during formal instruction to coach the student through complex processes and procedures for the first few times, assisting, commenting, supplying steps, supporting decisions, providing references, and helping students check their performance. As the student becomes

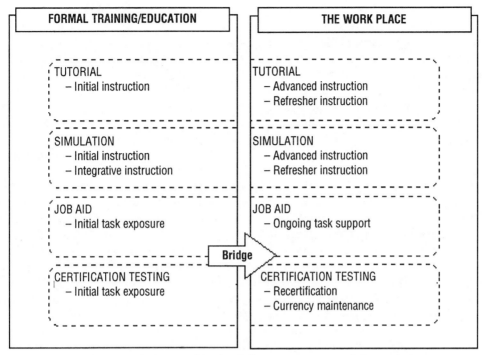

Figure 1. How CBI spans the school, the training area, and the workplace.

experienced, the student can continue to receive support at work from a job aid. A job aid (PSS) in the workplace can consist of:

- Reference support for memory:

   "What was the payment schedule for new homes?"

- Process support for steps and sequences:

   "Once the policy has been approved, who has to see it next?"

- Decision support for complex or crucial decisions:

   "What is the decision rule for determining eligibility?"

- Access to examples of completed work:

   "How do we set up the schedule for single-level structures?"

The learning coach or job aid is the only computer-based instructional tool that is never left behind by the student. It follows the student into the workplace.

Each of the forms of CBI serves its purpose, and each one has its own range of variations, strengths, limitations, costs, and benefits. Let's begin to survey this variety starting with tutorial instruction.

Tutorial instruction

Most people have a composite mental picture of computer-based instruction, and frequently it looks like a tutorial. A tutorial is a lesson which explains a principle, teaches facts, or instructs a procedure. Some tutorials combine together facts, procedures, and principles to be instructed within one lesson, and some teach them separately. Within a tutorial, there are traditionally two elements—a presentation portion, and a practice portion. Though these may be inter-mixed in various patterns and textures within the tutorial, they are almost always considered important. The presentation portion of a tutorial conveys in a message some body of infor-mation the student will need in order to perform a particular activity. The practice portions of the tutorial ask the student to perform target behavior(s) in ways that are visible and can be evaluated. In most cases, if a tutorial is shortened, it is the practice portion that suffers. How-ever, as you will see in a later chapter, the quality of the practice provided by a tutorial is one of the most important measures for judging its overall quality.

Most tutorials proceed along the lines of a deliberate, pre-planned instructional strategy. That strategy may be centered around the delivery of the message or around giving the student an opportunity to practice. The better tutorials emphasize practice. As a student moves through a tutorial, there are usually several paths, defined by the instructional designer and set by com-puter program code, which the student must follow. Some designers provide multiple, branch-ing paths through a tutorial, trying to make it seem less limited, but the student is still restricted to those paths. Pathing, whether navigated by the student or by the computer, is one of the iden-tifying features of a tutorial, and a sequenced message is a natural outgrowth of that path.

A well-developed tutorial contains certain essential primitive elements which make it ca-pable of doing its job. These elements include various classes of instructional messages (graphic as well as verbal), demonstrations, opportunities to explore, and requirements to in-teract with the computer. Some tutorials are designed so that the control over the sequence of lesson elements is almost totally in the hands of the lesson developer. This is called *system control*. At the other end of the spectrum, some tutorials simply provide a menu of instruc-tional elements along with a set of controls which the student can use for browsing through the available instructional messages and interactions. This is a technique called *learner con-trol*. Most tutorials fit somewhere between these two extremes, in what is called *mixed-ini-tiative* control.

The major strategic elements of a tutorial are its presentations and the practice it affords. There are several styles of presentation and several ways to provide appropriate practice. De-signers may carry out these functions using the computer alone or a mixture of computer and traditional media. They have a great range of options for designing tutorials using very basic patterns in different arrangements. Chapters 10 through 14 discuss the elements of tutorial in-structional strategy in detail, and Chapter 9 shows how the intermixing of strategic elements creates a great variety of interesting instructional patterns from a few basic strategic elements.

We can speak in general terms of three media plans for tutorials. These represent the most common forms that you will encounter, and you may want to begin to identify the tutorials you encounter by the pattern they use.

Form #1: On-line presentation only: This type of tutorial omits on-line practice and concen-trates on excellence of presentation. Tutorials of this sort rely on several techniques to increase their effectiveness, ranging from detailed message analysis and careful arrangement of message elements to special graphics and multimedia effects which hope to communicate efficiently.

In some highly-technical subject-matters, the high resolution and plasticity of the com-puter display make it a desirable medium for presenting visual displays of complex phenom-ena—atomic reactions, equipment panels, or interpersonal body language messages—but other factors, such as existing laboratory facilities, equipment simulators, or the importance and availability of person-to-person interaction, may make it less costly or more effective to practice off-line.

Another version of the presentation-only type of tutorial exists at the borderline between instructing and simply informing, and this is a special area of concern for CBI. CBI which presents information without asking for a response from the student at some point is easier and in many cases less expensive to build. It can also be made very attractive with the assistance of appealing design, color, motion video sequences, audio, sound effects, and animations. But it is not instruction without practice. One of the crucial tests that CBI will face in the decade to come will be the ability to separate instruction from mere presentation.

Why is this an important issue? Because it is a temptation for instructors to feel they have accomplished their task of *instructing* when they have simply *informed*. Instruction and learning—two sides of the same coin—are a cooperative activity. They have been called a *negotiation of two wills*—the student's will and the instructor's will—working cooperatively toward a goal. The instructor hopes to know when the student has learned, and the student seeks confirmation that adequate levels of learning have occurred so that the new knowledge can be applied when the need arises and the instructor is no longer present.

In order to confirm that learning has occurred, both instructor and student need the experience of practice. It not only confirms when learning has occurred, but it provides the occasion for remedying errors in learning and filling in the knowledge and performance gaps that are discovered.

Tools for the easy creation of interesting and impressive presentations are proliferating in business and education. The new multimedia capabilities of the computer are making presentations ever more interesting and engaging. However, if education leaders and corporate decision-makers confuse a beautiful or flashy presentation with effective instruction, then they will gravely underestimate the costs and preparations necessary for using the computer (or any medium) as an instructional tool, and the instructional computer will be trivialized. The presentation-only tutorial form must be carefully used by CBI designers; they must never accept the no-practice alternative as a real instructional solution.

Form #2: On-line practice only: Many practice-only tutorials have been created because of the great power of the computer to provide realistic and responsive practice environments. From the earliest days of CBI, tutorial practice consisted of drill-and-practice routines, but also of true-false and multiple choice question banks, question trees (interactive dialogues), problems to be solved, situational quizzes, and simple case studies organized into pathed structures for student practice. Practice-only CBI assumes that students have obtained knowledge from other sources which they need a chance to apply.

Form #3: On-line presentation and practice: The computer is made responsible in many cases for both presentation and practice. The presentation and practice elements of the instructional strategy in such tutorials are often intermixed, and the varieties of experience possible within tutorials of this type are almost endless. Moreover, the mixing can take place at several levels. When a practice is followed by instruction, followed by another practice, the pattern is pretest-instruction-posttest. When intermixing occurs at the level of the individual message, a student-computer dialogue can be set up in which the computer tests (diagnoses) what the student knows at a detailed level and then delivers information which the student is asked immediately to use in some way to ensure learning. This is called the Socratic dialogue, and creating a dialogue mechanism that allows the student to converse with a knowledge base (a network, a set of propositions, a set of rules, etc.) was one of the first experiments attempted by designers of intelligent tutoring systems and is a quest which endures in the work of many CBI laboratories today.

Improving tutorials

Tutorials are a robust form of instruction which will probably continue to be a staple of computer-based instruction. Tutorials have particular strengths, especially when they are properly designed, and among them is that they can be effective and yet relatively inexpensive. They are currently the workhorse of CBI. However, they are an often misused form of CBI, and in the future, designers must concentrate on improving the effectiveness of tutorials. There are some specific things they can do to accomplish this.

Improvement #1: Increased focus: The focus of a tutorial refers to the range of topics it tries to cover. Tutorials which are more focused tend to be more effective and easier to use. Focused tutorials leave out information and activities which are extraneous to the purpose of the tutorial.

Improvement #2: Increased use of prescribed instructional strategy: Technologies improve as the precision and leverage of their tools improves. CBI improves instructional technology by employing powerful instructional strategies for presentation and interaction which are optimized for specific classes of skill and knowledge. The application of many of these strategies has been hampered in the past due to the inability of most instructional media to execute all of the required moves for a complete strategy. The interactive power of the computer is leading to increased application of appropriate instructional strategies and the discovery of new dimensions of strategy. Chapters 8–16 deal with strategy.

Improvement #3: Increased emphasis on completeness: Because our media systems in the past could not fully implement instructional strategies, designers became inured to the fact, accepting instructional shortcuts because there was no alternative. The habit of omitting practice is one example of a shortcut which has been generally accepted. Non-computerized forms of instruction chronically under-practice; many fail to provide any practice at all. CBI designers must require their products to provide adequate, relevant practice.

Tutorial costs

Before leaving the subject of tutorials, some attention should be given to tutorial costs and benefits. The cost of CBI tutorials has been historically low relative to other forms of CBI. This is one of the factors which has contributed to their high level of use. As authoring tools have been created, they have favored the development of tutorial logic and tutorial-type message delivery. The internal logical structure of tutorials tends to be quite repetitive, and a few simple logical structures can be used to build very good tutorials. Tutorial costs are declining due to improvements in authoring tools which permit the use of logic templating and graphics library storage. (Although the creation of more sophisticated graphic and video display materials are also pushing costs higher.)

The major benefit of the tutorial form is its self-containedness. Most tutorials can accomplish their instructional function with a minimum of instructor involvement. This makes them ideal for distance learning and for learning unattended by an instructor. Moreover, tutorials can administer tests, giving the training organization some assurance of instructional effectiveness. Tutorials might be called the staple of CBI. They can be called upon to rapidly make up for instructor personnel shortages. Many organizations experiencing instructor shortages or temporary surges in student load have found a lifesaver in tutorials.

Simulation

Simulation is so powerful as an instructional tool that it is generally considered by most to be an instructional form in its own right, separate from other forms of CBI. This has placed an undesirable distance between it and other CBI forms in the minds of most designers. In reality, simulation is closely connected with all of the other forms of CBI.

Simulation is not technically a form of instruction; it is a type of computer program. In order to be used for instruction, a simulation has to be integrated within a larger instructional plan, and in many cases it has to be complemented with additional instructional features which are not part of the simulated model itself. As an instructional tool, simulations are currently used primarily for two functions: to provide demonstrations, and as an interactive base for practice exercises. However, it is one of the goals of this book to show that the full instructional power of simulations has been much overlooked.

Tutorials have both demonstration and practice elements. Could a simulation be used within the boundaries of a tutorial to support those functions? The answer is yes. Can a simulation be used independently of tutorials as an instructional tool? Again, yes. But it is always important to keep a clear perspective on the purpose for which a simulation is being used in order to see how it fits into the larger instructional plan. A simulation is normally used as one instructional element in conjunction with other instructional tools in pursuit of one or more specific instructional goals. Let's consider three basic plans for using instructional simulations.

Plan #1. An embedded simulation may be used to carry out one or more parts of a tutorial instructional strategy leading to the attainment of an instructional goal. Instruction for processes, like photosynthesis, procedures, like the operation of a copier machine, and concepts, like Neutron Star, can benefit from the inclusion of a simulation model. Models need not be complicated to be effective. A model of a copier machine inserted within the context of a tutorial allows students to try various setting combinations to see the result. This may constitute a useful practice and testing environment (depending on the instructional goal). If a designer wanted to construct practice which allowed not only correct responses and their consequences to be visible but incorrect ones and their consequences as well, and if the designer did not want to use a simulation, the amount of authoring system branching logic necessary to create the exercise environment just described would be considerable. In fact, most designers would create a small model of the copier within their tutorial (this can be done with most authoring systems with effort). This simulation would provide the basis not only for interactive practice but for demonstrations and perhaps the presentation as well.

Plan #2. A simulation may be used as a stand-alone instructional tool used to support one or more parts of an instructional strategy independent of the tutorial setting. Instructional objectives are not all of the same size. Some focus on the instruction of one procedure or one relatively simple process. Others focus on groups or families of procedures held together with a glue of decision-making and judgment. These are higher-order objectives closer to real-world performance, but often they are the ones which are sacrificed when training decisions are made and budgets are weighed, because as important as they are, they are also the most difficult to instruct and to design and the most costly to build.

Instruction for the larger-sized instructional goal still follows the basic outline of presentation, demonstration, and practice that is used for smaller, tutorial objectives, but most often the provisions for demonstrations and practice are so significant, and the presentation portion of the instruction is so slight that the single-package tutorial form is abandoned, and students encounter what seem to be independent instructional events—a presentation event and a simulation-based practice event—rather than a single tutorial. The instructional functions performed are the same, even if the total interactive experience is more complicated. Free-standing simulations, ones which exist as separate computer programs and are not embedded within a tutorial, are sometimes used to create demonstrations and practice exercises for this type of instruction.

Plan #3. A simulation may be constructed as a base upon whose surface many instructional goals may be pursued. More frequently, when a free-standing (non-tutorial embedded) simulation is created, it is designed to support the attainment of not just one instructional objective but many. Functionalities of the simulation used for one objective or group of objectives overlap with those used for others. Such simulations are therefore designed to possess as many common functions as possible.

In the past, such simulations have been created as replicas of real world systems and not as instructional simulations, because they were created without the inclusion of instructional functions. They did not act as if they were a part of an instructional system and could not provide coaching, feedback, or other instructional help.

This condition should be expected to change in the future. The concept of an instructional simulation sharing control of and working in coordination with an instructional strategy is becoming increasingly important as more and more designers show that such simulations can be built at relatively low cost. Not only are the strategic concepts necessary becoming more popular and widely-used, but the higher-level complexes of performance which use such simulations are receiving increased attention from instructional designers who have mastered the tutorial form and are ready to move on to something more challenging.

Types of simulation

There are many forms of simulation routinely used for instructional purposes. So many are the variations of instructional simulations that one cannot point out a single instructional simulation that represents the whole range of possibilities: there is simply too much variation. It is possible, however, to point out three general classes of instructional simulation which are common. A simulation can create three things: a model of a system, a model of an environment, or a model of expert behavior. A simulation can also contain all of these at the same time, so the four classes of simulation are: (1) model simulations, (2) environment simulations, (3) expert simulations, and (4) hybrid simulations, which include models, environments, and experts.

Within the worlds created from these types, a student can interview and diagnose patients, track patient progress following treatment, fly passenger jets, adjust telephone switch configurations, locate switch defects, run a business and either succeed or succumb, converse with foreign nationals in their own language, save heart attack victims, repair guided missiles, and perform countless other real-world activities, all without leaving the computer. CBI can create a miniature world which replicates some portion of the real world of an electrical power control center, an electronic circuit, or an oil tanker's navigation system. It can also create non-equipment related micro-worlds such as economic systems of businesses or nations, weather systems, or human physical systems. When a student interacts with a micro-world, the simulation computes the result and displays it to the student. Then it makes ready to accept the student's next input. A simulation may be as complicated or as simple as the designer decides. It may simulate an entire system, a portion of it, or only selected parts of it. Moreover, a simulation may be either highly realistic or highly contrived, depending on the objectives and imagination of the designer.

Simulation costs

The cost of simulation has been traditionally somewhere between moderate and high. This is largely due to the authoring tools of the past which did not favor simulation construction. Today tools have emerged which make simulation costs much more agreeable. Moreover, accumulating experience in the construction of simulations is widening the pool of CBI designers who have the conceptual and procedural tools as well as the programming tools to build them.

The complexity and the attendant cost of simulations spans a wide range, from large aircraft simulators to simulations which can be executed on the personal computer using PC software. The most complicated forms of simulation—aircraft, networked military exercises, and control room simulators—often require several dedicated computers to run, years to design and build, and large teams of designers, programmers, and engineers to create. From there the costs range downward, depending on the scope of the simulation, the reusable elements available, and the tools chosen by the designer. We have ourselves produced families of simulation problems based in a common simulation environment whose cost per problem was less than the cost of the average tutorial. When cost is the issue, a great deal depends on the logical structure and programming tool chosen by the designer for building the simulation. Two designers choosing different logical approaches and/or different tools will develop the identical simulation for widely differing costs.

CBI developers must be careful not to over-commit. Before agreeing to the creation of a specific simulation, there must be a careful assessment of feasibility and, in some cases, a willingness to scale down expectations. A designer can design a simulation beyond a CBI system's capabilities and his or her own skills or the capabilities of the programming tool, so design decisions must be informed either by experience or by many small proof-of-concept experiments which precede major commitments.

The extra cost and effort of simulation can be offset by the return on investment from a good product. A well-designed simulation can achieve impressive instructional gains, at the same time paying for itself through saved training costs. It is not universally true, however, that simulations will save instructional time and money, so a designer should perform careful cost-benefit studies to ensure that a return is possible. Failing a return, the designer must be able to make a case based on the improved quality of instruction resulting from the simulation. Many organizations are willing to pay somewhat more for CBI products like simulations if the training result is better than is being achieved by traditional approaches.

The future prospects for simulation development costs are also very good. New techniques and tools are emerging within the skills of the average instructional designer which improve the quality of instructional simulations that can be built. This helps to remove the economic factor from the designers' decision whether to use simulation. The cost of simulations will continue to fall. This difference will change the face of the curriculum as we know it today, bringing dramatic changes to the look and feel of computer-based instruction.

The simulation is only the second of the four major varieties of CBI application. The third is the *learning coach* and the *job aid*.

Learning coach and job aid

If a good picture is worth a thousand words, then a good job aid can be worth a thousand minutes of instruction. Designers sometimes decide too quickly that instruction is the best solution to their performance problem. In many cases a job aid or some combination of instructing and job-aiding can save development time and instruction time, and still improve performance.

The job aid is designed for use at the workplace: (1) as a substitute for training, and (2) to support the worker in difficult tasks that require heavy information processing or memory loads. Job Aids can help workers perform their functions faster and with higher levels of accuracy. Like simulations, they can pay for themselves in many cases.

A job aid consists of some form of media (manual, workbook, reference sheet, slide set, videotape, computer program, etc.) which provides memory, prompting, or decision support for a job performer. Job aids are referred to most frequently as *performance support systems*. When they are computerized, they are called *electronic* performance support systems. The idea of the job aid—even the computer-based job aid—has been around for a long time. The principles for building them are not difficult. Intelligent job aids which employ expert systems can actually participate in job execution by making some or all of the decisions for or with the performer.

Electronic job aids become necessary when our modern technological systems increase in complexity beyond the point of the average human's capacity or when the speed and accuracy demands exceed normal human ranges under the given set of work conditions.

Airline pilots use printed checklists to avoid working totally from memory. The number of systems on the passenger jet, the huge number of checklist occasions, and the number of steps in each checklist places a too large of a demand on the human memory. Pilots use checklists even in emergencies—a time when it is most important to do the right thing and when stress can overload the attention and memory of the pilot. You may also feel comfortable to know that the maintenance worker who last serviced the generator on your aircraft's #2 engine used one or more job aids while performing the work. Incidentally, if you are one of those who dislikes flying because you think it may be unsafe, you might be surprised to hear that you are many times safer in a regulated passenger aircraft than in a car on the freeway. Check the numbers out for yourself using the figures supplied by an almanac. To some degree, this safety is a result of the use of flight and maintenance checklists.

Let's consider the options regarding the use of a job aid. A procedure which you want people to perform may contain twenty steps, seven of them involving major decisions which require the activation of seven controls and the scanning of ten indicators. There are different ways you can teach this procedure to a novice performer:

1. Provide instruction for the whole procedure with no job aid: This plan calls for training a student in the procedure, allowing the procedure to be practiced thoroughly. Following instruction, the student is expected to perform the procedure completely from memory. If at some point the student's memory fades, it has to be retrained. This type of instructional plan is necessary when the subject of training includes critical, dangerous, highly-timed, or costly procedures during which it is impossible or impractical to use a job aid. Surprisingly, there is less of this type of situation than you might think.

2. Provide instruction before use of the procedure and a job aid at the time of performance: In this instructional plan, the job aid serves as insurance that the instruction will be remembered and that the procedure will be performed correctly. The cost of this redundancy (training and then aiding) is slightly higher, but in ultra-critical or difficult procedures it may be justified. As we have already noted, airline pilots are trained in this way. When safety is at stake and the costs of error are high, this is the approach of choice.

3. Provide instruction for only those portions of the procedure that require it and provide a job aid for the remainder; train students to use the job aid: This instructional plan is often the best economically and also in terms of performance. It avoids costly instruction where possible and maximizes the use of the job aid to support non-trained tasks. Instruction provides knowledge and practice in the difficult parts of the job, and the job aid assists the student's memory during performance.

4. Provide a job aid only; omit training: A surprisingly large number of tasks do not really require instruction. This includes: (1) procedures in which there no new and unfamiliar steps, (2) procedures where mistakes are not costly, (3) procedures which are not dangerous, and (4) procedures in which timing is not an important element. This includes a large number of every-day work tasks.

For solving performance problems there are two other reasonable alternatives in addition to those listed above. These alternatives are somewhat more radical. Given appropriate resources and a strong enough need, they can be the best solution, so we mention them here:

5. Re-engineer the work environment so that neither instruction nor job aid is required or so that reliance on them is reduced: Re-engineering may include anything from redesigning or re-arranging controls and indications to redesigning the way that the task itself is performed. This approach is common in the design of equipment which must be used frequently by a variety of people. Certain copying machines, for instance, lay out and label their controls in such a way that almost anyone who can read can operate them. If you cannot afford to train everybody how to use the copy machine, you change the machine.

6. **Devise an intelligent job aid:** An intelligent job aid is one which is itself involved in the performance of the procedure along with the user. Such a tool is made aware of results of each step and participates in choosing or executing subsequent steps. It is not a trivial or inexpensive task to create a job aid of this type, but in certain critical and very complex tasks, or when reduction of task time can result in savings, it is a good way to proceed. It is also a means of making the job aid into a learning coach at the same time. Students can learn the task initially using the learning coach, which is like a live coach in most respects, and then have the intelligent job aid monitoring their performance even on the job.

Job aid functions

At least three main functions are performed by job aids in support of the worker: (1) reference, (2) procedural support, and (3) decision-making support. These functions are normally blended together within a specific job aid to meet the needs of the job they support. For convenience, they are described below as if they were different types.

Reference job aids: A reference job aid is one which supplies task-related data to the performer. We once consulted with a government agency responsible for procuring complex computers for very tailored applications, one-of-a-kind computers for special purposes. The building of custom computers is common but complex, and the process of designing and producing them is of necessity an extremely detailed and lengthy one. So long was the entire process that many workers assigned to monitor the development of a custom computer in this particular agency never saw one product all the way through to its completion.

The custom computer development process involved numerous stages from expression of the concept through final testing and acceptance of the product. Each stage had a prescribed set of events, documents, meetings, reviews, approvals, and forms. Each meeting had a prescribed agenda. Each document had prescribed contents. The documentation describing this process and its standards stood taller than the tallest person responsible for using it. Learning this process and committing it to memory was out of the question for any person. Instruction was not the solution. There were some technical knowledges and skills required for the process, but special personnel were hired for those tasks.

The challenge to the instructional designer in this case was to develop tools which would provide access to the mountains of information, protocols, regulations, agendas, and forms to supply the manager of the process with the essential backbone of the process. To prepare for a Critical Design Review (a meeting), a team member needed a job aid to furnish details on the memoranda and documents which were necessary preparations for the meeting, the list of persons and organizations who were to attend, the role of each attendee, the process of handling approvals and disagreements before, during, and after the meeting, and many other details. Moreover, each entry in the job aid had to relate directly back to the original pile of regulatory documents, in case team members should need to refer there for further clarification.

One of our co-workers developed a prototype computerized job aid for this job. Her prototype took the form of a tree structure of menus which led at the lowest levels to summary pages of information. The pages were designed in a way that provided a readily useful summary sheet of information on one meeting, one document, one agenda, or one procedure. Pages were designed not only to provide information but to serve as worksheets for the user while preparing an agenda, writing letters, scheduling the meeting, and all of the other normal tasks.

Having found a page of interest, the user was permitted to print the page by pressing a designated key, producing a ready-made worksheet. Provision was made for browsing through this job aid using easy-to-learn controls. Keeping the controls simple was essential to ensure that the job aid was a help rather than an additional encumbrance to the user. This was an excellent example of a reference job aid.

Procedural job aids: The second type of job aid, the procedural job aid, supports the user by providing step-by-step direction, data, and illustrations to the user relative to tasks to be performed. One manufacturer, whose manufacturing processes involved stationary production machinery, found that repairs to the machines were faster when a computerized job aid walked repair personnel step-by-step through fault diagnostics, repairs, and post-repair testing. Videodisc images selected and controlled by the computer were shown at each step to confirm part identities, show signs of part wear for comparison, and show the steps in part repair for broken parts. Repair personnel using such a system can require less instruction if the job aid is complete and clear.

Procedural job aids are common in our society. Remember that bike you assembled last birthday? Remember the last store-bought cake mix you used? There were job aids with both of those products in the instructions that came with the product. You may have become aware as you assembled the bike, however, that most procedural job aids are inadequate. Remember that the brakes fell off the bike and that the cake was a bit doughy. It is not at all easy to prepare a good procedural job aid. That is because normally experts rather than novices prepare them, and they prepare them out of their expertise, rather than seeing through fresh eyes the information and support needs of the novice.

For a procedural job aid to really work, there is much more information and data required than most developers (and even users) realize. It is failure to provide these sometimes elusive pieces of information or to provide them in a readable form that caused us to put bolt "L" in the wrong place or to select the wrong item as bolt "L."

Decision-making job aid: The third type of job aid is the decision-making job aid. We found a need for this type of tool in a large insurance company which used a complex process for rating business insurance policies in order to determine the premium to be paid. The rating process involved a great deal of decision-making that resulted in a categorization of the insured business: "Is this a type A building or a type B?" "Is this type C construction or type D?" "Is this a type E location or a type F?" And so forth.

Raters found that what they needed in order to perform their jobs faster and more accurately was not better training but a system of job aiding that would support them during the making of the literally hundreds of decisions that were required; a system that would make decision criteria clear, consistent, and readily-obtainable; a system that would supply look-up data rapidly and through easy commands; a system that could be used to record intermediate decisions; and a system that would produce documentation automatically. What was needed was a decision-making job aid.

Job aid costs

The cost of creating job aids is relatively low. However, in light of what has just been said, a job aid must be constructed with some caution and much testing to ensure that it is both complete and usable. The strength of a job aid is that it almost always speeds the execution of a task and reduces the likelihood of error if it is used conscientiously. Its weakness is that it forms a dependency and becomes itself one of the performer's tools for doing the job. If the job aid is lost or disabled in some way, it can affect or prevent performance. The well-designed computer-based job aid is probably the most overlooked opportunity in the tool box of instruction. Developers should use this valuable tool more frequently, experimenting where necessary to learn the working attributes of job aids and the principles for constructing them.

Learning coaches

Job aids are built for use on the job. During the period of formal training or education there is an analogous tool which supports learning called the learning coach. Learning coaches might be called a *hands-on* form of tutorial, because they lead a student through a learning experience by performing some task with the student as she or he learns. Although they are involved in learning in a hands-on way, learning coaches can include support for learning of any kind, from the simplest memory learning to the most complex reasoning: the target behavior need not be a manual task, and the instruction need only be called up on student demand or in the event of failure to perform.

A learning coach often instructs a person how to perform actions in a realistic work setting. The activities of the learner are almost always performed on one or more elements of the work setting, not on the computer itself. A student may be asked to dissect a frog to learn anatomy, build a structure of balsa wood to learn engineering principles, examine a flower closely to learn about pollen, conduct a chemical experiment to learn about oxidation and reduction, or assemble an engine to learn its parts and their functions.

If the learner's hands are going to be busy or dirty while using a learning coach, the designer can make the computer responsive to vocal commands through the use of a microphone and a voice recognition system (of the sort which can be dropped into the computer or inserted through software). The student can be given a small set of commands with which to command access to information, displays, action guides, tool depictions, demonstrations, reference material, procedural descriptions, explanatory material, instructional elements, and any other learning supports provided within the coach.

We have already described the intelligent job aid. In the same manner, a learning coach can be made intelligent as well. This requires that the designer create a model of an expert performer capable of performing the steps and decisions required by the performance being learned. As the student acts (following the directions of the coach), the coach asks for confirmation that the action has been performed and asks what the learner saw as a visible result. The expert model can then deduce what is happening in the same way a live instructor can and be able to correct mistakes, describe and perhaps explain internal system states, and otherwise participate as a sensing, intelligent member of the learning partnership.

Learning coaches are an interactive and highly interesting form of CBI instruction whose experience is very much like having a live instructor work directly with a student. A learning coach can teach guitar playing, lead a mechanic through the repair of an engine for the first time, and teach the subtleties of structure of a DNA molecule. The cost of a simple learning coach is approximately the cost of a simple tutorial. The cost of an intelligent learning coach is somewhat more but need not be prohibitively high.

The fourth and final major variety of CBI is the use of the computer in certification testing systems.

Certification testing

The use of CBI in certification testing is important because it, like the job aid, is an opportunity to improve performance and safety and save money at the same time. Certification testing is carried out frequently in schools, business, and the military. In college we pass summary exams in the process of earning a degree, and following technical training in industry, there is frequently a test to certify that a worker is ready to function competently on the job.

The importance of certification testing is only being increased by the presence of complex network software tools in the workplace. Workers with special training are required to administer these systems and keep them running for an entire office. These are specially-trained and certified office personnel who must be measured at a level of skill sufficient to keep the business-critical network system operating reliably, an economic necessity in the modern workplace. Not only is certification testing performed for network installers, operators, and maintainers, but for those who operate the application software that runs on it as well, such as word processors, spreadsheets, and data bases. Companies that manufacture application products are becoming aware of the importance of certification testing to the success and continuation of their product.

Tests for certification take many forms. An advanced degree-seeking student at a university must pass extensive written and oral examinations which evaluate at great depth readiness to enter the professional world. Lawyers must satisfy professional bar organizations that they know the details and application of the law by passing a written exam. Certified public accountants pass similar exams; that is why they are called *certified* public accountants. An aircraft assembler who has been trained in applying adhesive to certain surfaces of a high performance aircraft wing must pass at least a written examination and in some cases a performance test on that technique. Workers who will operate with or around explosives must be certified safe, as must a host of workers who work in the presence of other dangerous substances. A brain surgeon has not only passed a host of written and oral exams but has been certified by professional colleagues through observation as being competent to practice. All or part of the certification testing for these and other skills can be, and in some cases are, conducted using a computer.

Certification tests are of two types: diagnostic and non-diagnostic. A non-diagnostic test samples only the behavior or knowledge of interest to the test. A diagnostic test contains sub-tests which are of interest only if the main test is failed. When it is failed, performance on the sub-test is used to isolate the specific area of knowledge or skill that is deficient so that remediation can take place. Diagnostic tests of this type are of interest in fields where training of job candidates has been costly and time-consuming and where the failure of students has a larger impact on lives and organizations. Diagnostic tests allow remediation and retesting to fill minor learning gaps.

Assuming that the tests themselves are adequate and have been proven reliable and valid, the issues which most often surround certification tests are security and cost of administration. Test security issues often cause organizations which must administer large numbers of tests to prepare several alternate versions of their tests in order to foil cribbing and answer swapping. In addition, during the administration of tests, organizations are often obliged to post test monitors in the testing area to discourage and detect cheating. These measures are costly. Finally, even those tests which have low security risk involved are frequently administered at locations throughout the nation or even across the world, creating additional expense. The computer is a natural solution to these problems. It makes cheating difficult, can be used a distant locations, can create tests which are different for every user, and can lower the cost of test administration. In addition, it can make the scheduling of tests more flexible, since testing can be administered to small numbers of persons at one time and since the testing is monitored by the computer.

Computerized testing takes advantage of the computer's ability to remember large numbers of details. Once a student has taken a test, the computer can remember not only the score obtained but the identity and order of the individual items that made up the original test. Moreover, it can ensure that on re-tests, the same items will not be used. This ability of the computer to remember, coupled with its ability to select randomly from a pool of items, enables it to construct tests, printed or terminal-delivered, which are unique for each student in the composition and ordering of items. Moreover, when testing is completed, it permits automatic tallying and storage of test results, followed by complete item analysis reports by student and by test item.

One option for testing which is being considered increasingly by organizations which do a large volume of testing or whose tests are prohibitively long is called *adaptive* testing. This type of test, which is somewhat more expensive to prepare, can lead to appreciable savings in examination time while at the same time measuring the student's level of attainment with equal or greater accuracy than before.

An adaptive test is made up from a pool of items, each of which is scaled precisely in terms of difficulty through a rigorous calibration process. When the test is administered, a student is given items starting at the center of the difficulty scale. As the student answers each item, the answer is judged immediately. If the student response is correct, a more difficult item is selected. If the response is incorrect, a less difficult item than the first one is chosen. This judging and selecting process continues throughout the test. As long as the student answers are correct, the test continues to produce harder questions, up to the point where an error occurs. When an answer is incorrect, an easier item is selected. Rapidly the test homes in on the capability level of the student and does it with as few items as possible. These tests are shorter than standard tests and yet are quite accurate if the calibration of items has been done properly. Such a test is natural for computer delivery and would be quite difficult, if not impossible, to deliver any other way.

Even when the factors of test security and cost have been dealt with, there is an additional area in which the computer greatly benefits certification testing programs. This is with the issues of validity and reliability. The validity of a test is a measure of how well it tests what it purports to test, and the reliability is, just as it sounds, a measure of how well the test score actually represents the student's real and consistent level of ability. There are difficult theoretical arguments involved in validity and reliability issues, which is why the vast majority of instructors who build tests never deal with these issues, so it is safe to say that all tests do not test exactly what they say they are testing nor what they intend to test. The results can be: (1) that capable talent that is wasted because it was not measured fairly, and (2) that deficient performers obtain certification by squeaking through or fooling the testing process. This can happen for a number of reasons.

Of most interest to us here is the fact that many tests currently used for certification lack the proper form to adequately test what they suppose they are testing. It is common, for instance, to test a person's readiness to handle hazardous materials situations by asking twenty to thirty true-false or multiple-choice questions. People's verbal knowledge and their actual practices often differ. A more valid test of performance ability and habits will include an actual performance of key processes or steps, supplemented by verbal testing.

A more reliable test will include the requirement to perform key actions and decisions repeatedly on multiple occasions and under a variety of circumstances while being observed and evaluated. The problem is that testing in these ways is prohibitively expensive. The computer is an obvious candidate if such tests are to be improved. We have already described how the computer can create a realistic, simulated worlds in which real-world responses and reactions can be practiced. In preparation for landing on the moon, astronauts were placed in a simulated moon world and given an opportunity to rehearse and test their moves multiple times to certify that they were ready to perform them during a real mission. Airline pilots demonstrate their readiness to pilot an aircraft, not in the aircraft, but in a simulator. This is done because the simulator can actually provide a better, more complete test than the aircraft can. In a simulator, where there is no risk to life or property, an examiner can schedule not only normal procedures for testing but can program emergencies to occur unexpectedly, testing the pilot's ability to respond promptly and accurately. So it is that airline pilots for many years have been allowed to pass their certification tests in high-fidelity flight simulators instead of aircraft. The excellent safety record of the airlines shows that this decision to base the test in a computer was a sound one.

In many applications in the schools, industry, and the military, there are opportunities to improve the level and quality of certification testing through the use of computer-simulated environments. Tests may include full simulation of complete performances, or they may include the presentation of multiple problem scenarios, each of which presents a different challenge to the student and each of which must be reacted to appropriately. Instructional designers can save their organizations money and time and at the same time improve the validity of certification testing programs through test computerization, and they should be alert for opportunities to do so.

Computer-as-tool

Though it is not a formal instructional event type, it is important to consider the use of the computer as a reactive learning tool during instruction. Designers often think of the computer as an active delivery agent for instruction. However, the computer is frequently used as a patient adjunct for instruction to provide reference access, media support, data recording, and communications. In these roles, the computer plays a part in the overall strategy of instruction, but it is not for the delivery of a presentation, control of the learning, nor for guided practice. Instead, the computer serves as a tool which the learner uses to take charge of the learning process. The possibilities for using the computer in this manner are enormous. Consider the following:

Reference: Increasing numbers of today's elementary school students go to the computer rather than the book shelf when they want to look up something in the encyclopedia. Major encyclopedia publishers have created their products in the form of CD-ROMs. In some cases, articles on the CD encyclopedias are illustrated with graphics, sound bites, photographs, or motion video sequences, creating greater immediacy. In most cases, students can call up note-taking utilities as they read and can make personal notes or copy quotations for later use.

To supplement the material found in the on-line encyclopedia, a student can change CDs and access a visual data base. Numerous products of this type have been produced which are simply catalogued visuals, normally dealing with a central theme. Visual data bases have been produced for almost all basic school subjects, including science and mathematics, social studies, language learning, cultural studies, geography, and history. These resources can be used within their own thematic areas or as adjuncts for reading, report writing, mathematics, and language studies. The presence of the computer in the classroom as a tool is what makes these resources desirable and usable.

Data Recording: With emphasis in science and mathematics instruction turning toward application of knowledge rather than its accumulation, the use of the computer as a data recording device in the classroom is increasing. Several varieties of laboratory support systems have been developed and marketed by computer and software firms in order to meet this growing market. Digital signal converters make it possible for laboratory computers to support experimentation in biology, chemistry, physics, and general science. Schools in some states are beginning to receive computer programs which allow the classroom to become a weather reporting station, entering weather data taken through standard procedures into a data base which can be sent to the weather archive. This has the effect of multiplying the number of weather recording stations within a state enormously—so much, according to one television weathercaster, that now he would be able to see the front "moving across the valley."

Computing: Once you have collected all of that data, don't forget that it has to be processed to find a result or conclusion of some kind. Basic number-crunching computing capabilities are an important part of the computer-as-tool in the classroom. This includes the ability of students to use statistical packages to perform analysis on their data as well as the ability to write programs to perform their own data analysis and display.

Communications: When you have collected and analyzed the experimental data, the computer-as-tool allows you to communicate the data and the results to other schools everywhere. Computers provide an important link through satellite and fiber optic communication systems between schools. Networks of school classrooms have begun to form and have carried out significant experiments jointly as a network. Electronic mail and teleconferencing by computer are also options open at reasonable cost to classrooms wanting to communicate with other classrooms. The computer makes these available to every student.

Media Support: The results are in, the experiment is a success, and now it is time to report the results. The computer-as-tool becomes involved in this process also. For little cost, student groups working on a report can have access to sophisticated graphics packages, spreadsheets, word processors, and data bases. Though it may seem that these are tools beyond the reach and use of the average student, that impression seems to be mistaken, especially with the development of simplified versions of these tools just for school use. For example, the "I Hate Algebra™" spreadsheet makes using one easy—even for an adult. And don't forget the presentation software that makes your presentation look like a million bucks while teaching the concept of outlining at the same time.

The virtual classroom: These developments and similar developments in the construction of instructional products that are intended to open the learning process to groups have led to what John Bransford calls the "virtual classroom." Just as the computer can be made to seem as if it had unlimited memory through special techniques, and just as the computer's graphic display can be made to seem as if it was a small window into a large graphic, classrooms can be made to feel as if they had no dividing walls and no barriers to communication with each other.

Both teachers and students can benefit from this electronic leveling of the walls if it is done intelligently and with a plan. Teachers who have for years felt hesitant to approach subjects because they thought they were inadequately prepared—or who felt their currency in an area slipping away—can now call upon a network of other school teachers, experts, and consultants from higher academic sources as co-teachers in the virtual classroom. Students who may have had only a local perspective and who may feel isolated in small schools or in small towns can now join with students in classrooms of any size and in any location and share the learning process. This is made possible by the computer-as-tool.

These are interesting and productive uses of the computer for educational purposes. They represent a major cutting-edge area of the use of computers in education. The focus of this book, since it is on the use of the computer for instruction or practice purposes, does not include further discussion of applications of these types, but there are several excellent books covering these uses.

Computer-managed instruction

How do the various types of instruction, job support systems, and testing systems described above work together? That question is one of the primary issues of computer-based instruction which still awaits an innovative and practical answer. Clearly, if students are to obtain all or some of their instruction from a computerized base, then there must be some tool for managing their progress.

The need for a computerized tool to do this arises from the immense body of data on each student that can result when a computer becomes involved in instruction. The computer's data capturing capability can supply more information about the student when instruction is finished. Better testing systems also produce more data on the student than traditional systems. This data could be thrown away, but it would be an immense waste, akin to taking the patient's temperature in the hospital and then deciding not to write it down.

When the computer enters instruction, its increased capabilities for data gathering, handling, and decision-making make it a natural choice as a tool which can be used to increase the adaptability of instruction to the individual. Classroom teachers are often overwhelmed by the mass of data available to them on student performance levels. They are unable to find time to record it all, and the subsequent decision-making task using that data presents still more challenges as teachers try to meet the differing needs of students.

Today, computer management systems in classrooms nationwide and worldwide record data that no human teacher could possibly manage to record, and assist the teacher in making decisions about progress levels, remediation, and future instruction for each student individually. Alarms in these systems identify students who are progressing at slow rates so that they can obtain extra attention. Students who are excelling can be identified and given opportunities for additional learning experiences—either on-line or off-line.

The original vision of the computer as an instructional device placed the computer first and foremost at the center of the management process. Early researchers envisioned instruction that was adjusted on a moment-to-moment basis by a learning management program lying at the heart of the instructional system. This management process was expected to monitor student responses on a constant basis, changing the characteristics of instruction according to its interpretation of data on student characteristics, performance trends, and task demands.

It was not originally realized then how great a task this would be to accomplish. Scientists and technologists have labored for nearly twenty-five years and have yet to realize that original dream except in the laboratory. In the meantime, it has become apparent through research that the dream is possible and that computers can manage instruction adapted to the needs of the individual student. Today, a variety of approaches to computer management are in use, some from commercial firms and some created by designers of individual instructional products. They must evolve to support newer visions of instruction and testing. Computer-based management systems are discussed in more detail later in this book.

Keeping perspective

Many varieties of CBI experience have been described in this chapter. Progress in the field of CBI has been difficult, and many technical problems have required solutions to reach this point. The work of researchers and technologists from many related fields has converged to form the industry and technology of CBI as it exists today. It is important to envision this field as a constantly-changing scene into which promising new trends flow, and out of which some less useful ideas fall from time to time.

This final section of the chapter will name and briefly describe current trend words in CBI to give you a broader perspective of the current flow of ideas in this vigorously changing field. Some of the terms introduced below will be relics within a short time; others will continue and develop into central ideas for the advancement of computer-based instructional technology.

Perspective: Hypermedia: Hypermedia is a computer-based experience which allows a student to follow threads of interest through a large base of information. Links between key elements of the information base allow a student to move through articles, picture files, and audio and video resources in a completely user-controlled sequence. Links join words in documents with pictures, words with other words, or any resource with any other resource. Links are the paths which a student travels in a self-chosen journey through the body of knowledge.

Hypermedia systems are not, strictly speaking, instructional systems. They do not express or embody instructional goals, and they do not take the initiative in interacting with the student. Their structure may suggest paths to the student to explore, but there is no directiveness to hypermedia. Some recent hypermedia products have begun to feature embedded models with which a student may have an undirected but interactive experience. The student may operate controls which are placed on the model and watch model responses. Recently, simulation designers have experimented with ways to make models capable of expressing themselves either spontaneously or in response to inquiries. This is an example of simulation models being embedded within a hypermedia environment.

Perspective: Integrated Learning Systems: It is one thing to create one or two tutorials or simulations for use in educational (school) settings and quite another to create complete courses. Several large CBI companies have concentrated on the design, production, and marketing of complete courses for educational use. Each course normally corresponds to the length of the semester or the school year. This means that these courses are roughly one hundred to two hundred contact hours long. Creating such courses is a major logistical, financial, and design accomplishment, and these companies have each invested literally tens of millions of dollars in their products.

Of course, these companies have not stopped with the production of just one course product; each one markets several courses. The largest concentration of courses is in the basic skills area of elementary education (reading, arithmetic, spelling, language arts); however, there is also an interesting variety of courses at the middle school and high school levels which include science, algebra, geometry, and computer science.

As one course is produced, it becomes clear to a designer that a major instructional management problem is created. Students taking course instruction will produce data and scores which must be tallied, summarized, reported, and archived for later use. This implies a management system, which these companies have found is as important, or more so, than the instructional products themselves. When a group of courses is implemented under the control of a management system that controls the administration of the course events and maintains the base of instructional data which results from instruction, the resulting total system is called an Integrated Learning System (ILS).

Integrated Learning Systems have the benefit of providing a consistent instructional product which moves students through an entire course of study. They do so by supplying instructional events in a sequence which builds one learned concept upon the other over a prolonged period of learning. Several benefits accrue to the learner: The style of the instruction and the control mechanisms for operating it are consistent across the product, progress is monitored by the management system, and performance trends can become apparent, leading when necessary to remedial attention. Finally, the degree of coverage of knowledge and skills within the area of study is known, since curricula designed by ILS firms are published and can be correlated with local curriculum standards.

Perspective: Games: The issue of games is controversial, both inside and outside of the community of instructional designers. Outside are the parents, in many cases concerned with the proportion of time spent by their children playing popular video games. Talking with this group about instructional games often brings up a painful subject. Many parents think games have no place in education and question their value.

Within the instructional design field, designers themselves are split over the issue of games. Some appreciate the motivational force of competition and the ease with which games stimulate the interest of students—sometimes in learning. However, others do not trust the type of motivation provided by games and correctly note that not every learning pursuit can be turned into a highly motivating game, which produces the dilemma of how to integrate adrenaline-producing games within the larger fabric of the curriculum without making other parts of the curriculum look boring in comparison.

Introducing games into a curriculum is a difficult engineering task. The game must be designed in such a way that it does not diminish the effectiveness of the surrounding instruction. This can be done by reducing the importance of the competitive element, by devising multi-dimensional scoring schemes, and by selecting games which are demonstrated to have effectiveness as learning as well as motivational tools. The popularity of games in any society cannot be denied, and designers cannot simply ignore the fact that humans find enjoyment in them, but as designers import the game concept into learning systems, they must be careful to ensure that learning retains its position as the central goal and that the game works harmoniously, increasing the value of the entire instructional suite.

Perspective: Microworlds: The term *microworld* is used to refer to the capability of a computer simulation to create a miniature replica of some portion of the real world—some environment or model—with which the student can interact. Within a microworld, the student can give commands, express plans, and take action and then watch the result. A major emphasis of the later parts of this book is to establish the use of microworlds, not only as a CBI technique, but as a critical structure in curriculum design. Since many chapters are devoted to that emphasis, we will not worry the issue here other than to stress its importance.

Perspective: Intelligent tutoring systems: Very early in the history of CBI, the conceptual development of the field spilt into two main schools of thought. One group moved toward the development of the frame-based concept of CBI which is predominant today in commercial authoring systems. Instruction created by this group tended to consist of pre-composed messages delivered in sequence as the student moved along paths within the lesson logic.

The other group from this split moved toward instruction which used messages composed at the time of instruction. Messages were composed from primitive elements under the control of artificial intelligence programs. Among the major research questions explored by this group included: (1) what kinds of primitives to build messages from, (2) how to store knowledge in a knowledge base and use it later to construct messages, and (3) what rules of instruction to use to build useful, effective messages and interactions from these primitives. This field of study has been called Intelligent Tutoring Systems (ITS).

A great variety of systems has been produced by ITS researchers. Many of the systems produced have been for laboratory use only and would not be practical in actual instructional settings because they lack range of application or flexibility. Some instruct well, and some do not. Interestingly, many of them have not been extensively tested for their instructional power and were intended strictly to demonstrate the feasibility of a particular programming or knowledge base approach. Some systems from the ITS community, however, have demonstrated the ability to instruct effectively and have been tested extensively in real training settings.

The range of ITS system concepts and structures is quite broad. Some systems concentrate on the learning of propositional knowledge or facts, while others teach principles. Some systems use semantic networks for storage of knowledge, and others build simulations from which students can learn. Some have extensive and well-developed instructional plans and rules, while others are quite simple in their organization and operation. The history of ITS is a very worthwhile study, especially since many of the ITS concepts are emerging from the laboratory and finding application in real CBI instructional products.

Perspective: Multimedia: The term *multimedia* has a long and interesting history within the field of instructional technology, and only recently has the term been introduced into general use by the public at large. In earlier days, multimedia referred to any use of instructional media in synchronized combination with each other. In the 1960s, for instance, multimedia referred to sound/slide presentations which employed banks of projectors and a synchronized audio track capable of changing slides in a timed sequence. Special fades were also used to dim one slide slowly as the next appeared gradually. The recent rapid increase in personal computer power, coupled with high-powered hardware (sometimes) and software (always) have made possible combinations of several media forms under computer control to produce sound, video, motion, vivid color, and interactivity all at once. Today this is what is called multimedia, and it can be exciting to experience.

Expectations have been raised that the new multimedia represents a major improvement in the instructional capability of the computer. This is partly true and partly false.

The new capabilities for video and audio are extremely useful and open up instructional message channels that were inaccessible to the CBI designer not long ago. How much instructional benefit is added by multimedia? Your answer to that question will depend on where you think instructional benefit comes from and how it is measured. The motion and sound of a multimedia presentation can stimulate an immediate interest in almost anyone, but the motivational boost provided by glittery techniques wears off over time, and when that happens, there must remain in the instructional experience something of substance which the student perceives as having true instructional value and power in the longer view. Multimedia is important, but it must be joined by good instructional technique.

Having taken a somewhat conservative position on the subject of multimedia, now let us take a realistic one and relate the experience of an instructional designer with another CBI innovation which was at that time new: the color display. Back in the days of monochrome (single color) computer terminals, this designer had created hundreds of hours of instruction and was facing the decision of whether to colorize it. The constant improvement in technologies had made that possible and the attractiveness of color seemed to be winning the interest of clients. It was a non-trivial decision whether to colorize, because it would be costly, and there were many hours of instructional material to convert. The developer delayed, feeling that no direct instructional benefit would result from colorization of already proven and effective CBI. The bulk of educational research seemed to support this conclusion.

Before long, the developer discovered that his decision was trying to stop the clock. Color displays had, in fact, become the accepted standard among his competitors, so eventually the developer did make the conversion, but only after losing some key marketing opportunities to competitors who had already colorized.

How do *you* evaluate multimedia? You must decide which of its features improves your instruction, but remember also that you cannot stop the clock, and multimedia today is the *de facto* standard which CBI designers must meet.

Perspective: Networks: Computer networks may not seem to be related to CBI, but they are very important to it and that importance is increasing rapidly because of other new technological developments. Administering CBI to a large audience of students requires not only the ability to instruct, but to maintain the records that result from instruction: scores, completion records, and student profiles. If students receive instruction at individual terminals which have no connection with other computers, then the scores achieved by the student reside only in the isolated terminal. They cannot be effectively archived, and they cannot be used in future instructional decisions unless they are carried manually on a floppy disk to a central records computer.

However, if a network exists between instructional computers, score collecting is a simple transfer, along with several other functions. Computer-managed instruction (CMI) programs are frequently large and demand much of a computer's attention. Placing the management software on a central computer frees the student terminal for instructional computing. Then, during future instructional sessions which may be carried out on a different student terminal, the student's scores are available to influence instructional decisions over the network.

The conception of computers is changing rapidly these days. We are becoming as a society much more connected through networks. The "information highway" we hear about is nothing more than a massive system of interconnected computer networks. Interestingly, though it is being made to seem new, this highway has existed for decades. Will the connection of outside networks to homes, schools, and businesses make a difference? It has already begun to do so. In schools, educational networks that link the schools are creating communication pathways which allow classes in one state or nation to communicate regularly with classes in another. The messages sent over the networks range from personal communications with electronic pen pals to class projects which link scores of schools together to collect weather data.

In the future, we will see increased presence of networks all around us. They may become increasingly commercialized and costly, or they may stay in the hands of the people, where their costs will continue to be borne by governments. Whichever way the trend goes, the increasing presence of networks will greatly influence instructional computing. Students may find before too long that they need carry no books home because textbooks and reference materials will be available on the computer, and homework over the networks is a concept which is possible now.

Perspective: Virtual reality: There is a lot of excitement when a new display technology emerges, and virtual reality is one with great promise. When virtual reality matures into a standard instructional medium, it will be by combining its visual realism and the ability to totally immerse the student in a visual world with many of the other features of an instructional simulation. Those features are described in Chapters 15 and following.

Virtual reality is exciting because it allows a student to be present inside something or at something. As this medium matures, we will find ourselves as spectators at historical events (e.g., the signing of the Constitution or the driving of the Golden Spike), inside famous places (e.g., the Parthenon, or the structural members of a skyscraper under construction), inside otherwise inaccessible places (e.g., the atrium of the heart, or the heart of an atom), and outside of things as well (e.g., climbing Mount Everest, climbing the Space Shuttle's skin). With virtual reality, we are able to tour any space and examine any object closely and without danger.

However, the virtual reality display technology—just like multimedia, which we have already discussed—is only remarkable for the world of CBI if it finds appropriate application within a larger instructional plan or strategy. Many elements must work together to produce an instructional product, and the display technology is only one of them. Therefore, we might imagine students within the virtual reality experience speaking to the objects they encounter and asking questions of them, interacting with objects and watching them respond just as real ones would, and listening as objects explain how they operate and why.

To place things in perspective, it is worthwhile to see virtual reality not as a totally new technology for instruction as much as an extension of display technology into the realm of the 3-dimensional. Display technology can take us now into the heart of an atom, into an aorta, and to a famous event. This happens all the time in well-illustrated books, in videos, and on 2-dimensional CBI displays. What is missing is the ability to surround students with these things and allow students to be *at* and *in* them. And for this to happen, the costs of creating reality environments must come down, and experience must accumulate telling us where and how this new display medium is effective.

Conclusion

This survey of CBI varieties is intended to give you a broader view of CBI. It presented a surface view of each of those varieties to stimulate your thinking and broaden your mental picture of what CBI feels and looks like. In addition, it was intended to prepare you for the discussion which follows in the next chapter of what goes on under the surface of a CBI product.

It would be unfortunate if this chapter caused you to think that the world of CBI was complete and unchanging. Exactly the opposite is true. Our conceptions of what the computer can do instructionally are yet in their infancy. Our ideas must remain fluid and ready to change as the technology continues to develop at a rapid pace. This chapter has described things as they are today, using today's technologies for hardware and software. But the CBI medium is very young and will undoubtedly be put to new uses in ways we have yet to imagine.

Self-directed activities

- Start your own collection of computer-based instructional products. As you select new items, stress variety. Only add new products which demonstrate some new approach or feature not possessed by products already in your collection. Record the date that you acquired each product. If you can, find out the date the product was first released and record that.

- In your product collection, when an older product is replaced by a newer product version, calculate the lifetime the older version. (Decide on your own whether you think there is a good enough reason to purchase the upgrade.) Calculate the cost of the product if you were to buy each new version issued. Calculate the benefit of each new version by comparing features between the new and old versions. Begin to notice the average life of usability of a commercial CBI product. Note the characteristics or features of the products most often responsible for the change: content, instructional strategy, or hardware/software considerations.

- Pick the form of CBI that you think will become most common in the future. Describe why you feel this form will proliferate more rapidly than others. Name specific factors which favor proliferation.

- Try to obtain estimates for the costs of creating each of the major forms of CBI from several different local sources or from sources working under conditions which most closely resemble your own. Pick sources with some experience. What are the most difficult issues and questions that surface as you gather this data? What are the factors that make it difficult to compare costs and benefits across CBI forms?

- Contact businesses that develop CBI products (both off-the-shelf and custom) of several varieties (e.g., tutorials, simulations, job aids, etc.). Find out costs not only for initial design and development but for lifetime product update and maintenance. Find out also, if possible, the marketing costs associated with different products. Which of the costs is largest: initial development, maintenance, or marketing?

- Assume the role of a commercial CBI developer. Make a list of the benefits you feel your customers will realize from using your products as opposed to the traditional products they are using. Make a list of the features you think people will look for that will make them want to buy your products instead of a competitor's.

Further reading

Acovelli, M., and Gamble, M. (1997). A coaching agent for learners using multimedia simulations. *Educational Technology, 37*(2), 44–48.

Baker, F. B. (1978). *Computer-managed instruction: Theory and practice.* Englewood Cliffs, NJ: Educational Technology Publications.

Baker, F. B. (1981). Computer-managed instruction: A context for computer-based instruction. In H. F. O'Neil, Jr. (Ed.), *Computer-based instruction: A state of the art assessment.* New York: Academic Press.

Bunderson, C. V., Inouye, D. K., and Olsen, J. B. (1989). The four generations of educational measurement. In R. L. Linn (Ed.), *Educational measurement (3rd ed.).* New York: Macmillan Publishing Company.

Gery, G. (1991). *Electronic performance support systems: How and why to remake the workplace through the strategic application of technology.* Boston: Weingarten Publications.

Lajoie, S. P., and Derry, S. J. (Eds.). (1993). *Computers as cognitive tools.* Hillsdale, NJ: Lawrence Erlbaum Associates.

Nitko, A. J. (1989). Designing tests that are integrated with instruction. In R. L. Linn (Ed.), *Educational measurement (3rd ed.).* New York: Macmillan Publishing Company.

Sloane, H. N. (1989). *Evaluating educational software: A guide for teachers.* Englewood Cliffs, NJ: Prentice-Hall.

Stevens, G. H., and Stevens, E. F. (1995). *Designing electronic performance support tools: Improving workplace performance with hypertext, hypermedia, and multimedia.* Englewood Cliffs, NJ: Educational Technology Publications.

SECTION II

BENEATH THE SURFACE

A look inside of CBI products to view the inner logical structures that make them work the way they do. Two major forms of logical structure or flow are identified, which strongly influence the power of CBI, the types of CBI created, and the costs of creation.

3

THE EVOLUTION OF
CBI AUTHORING TOOLS

Chapter Objectives:

1. *Define three factors of authoring system use which influence the amount and quality of instruction the system is capable of producing.*

2. *Describe the products of authoring systems in terms of objects. Identify the attributes they possess and how variations in attribute values influence the student's experience.*

3. *Describe how differences in the answers to the three questions of authoring systems cause the great variety of authoring systems available today.*

4. *Identify three major generations of authoring tool and describe how each produces objects.*

5. *Discriminate between non-persistent objects, author-time objects, run-time objects, persistent run-time objects, and post-instruction persistent objects.*

6. *Create your own list of useful instructional objects.*

7. *Define two types of instructional flow control made possible by authoring tools. Describe how each type may be a strength or a weakness during instruction.*

What are the atoms in the chemistry of CBI?

National Geographic magazine published some fascinating photographs during the renovation of the Statue of Liberty for the Statue's Centennial. The pictured showed an extensive inner framework constructed of metal rods to hold the surface of the statue rigidly in place. This framework, invisible to the observer from the outside, supports the multitude of heavy copper plates which cover and form the surface of the statue. The framework keeps this surface from buckling and sagging. It makes the statue possible, for without the framework, the weight of the immense copper plates would immediately reduce the statue to a pile of scrap metal.

Those pictures provide a metaphor which sums up the theme of this chapter. Just as there is a framework inside that relates the inner structure of the statue with its outer appearance, there is a structure of logical elements within a CBI product which cannot be seen but which makes possible the visible surface of the product. In both the statue and a CBI product, there is more to the product than can be seen on the surface, and what appears on the surface is different from the structure that lies buried inside. A designer—of statues or of CBI—must understand not only the surface, but the inner workings that make the surface possible.

The structure deep inside a CBI product depends almost entirely on the production tool that the developer uses. Different kinds of tool create different inner logical structures. In this chapter, we will try to discover whether there is any common ground on which all authoring tools meet so that we can discuss the inner structure of CBI products in a generic way. In other words, is there a set of *universal* structures—a common CBI *language*—underlying the CBI surface that is common to all authoring tools?

This is an important question and one whose answer will be of great use to you as a CBI designer. Many designers find it hard to come to grips with different authoring tools and their function because they have no answer to this question. We hope to show you, in this and in several other chapters (see Chapters 4, 5, 6, and 17), that the answer to this question is the key to understanding today's authoring tools. Even more important, just as authoring tools have evolved over time to reach their present capability, we hope to help you understand the continuing evolution which is taking place in authoring tools and therefore in the underlying structures used to build CBI products. Before long, this evolution process will have changed the way we think about and create computer-based instruction. Soon it will be as hard to understand the output of today's authoring tools as it is now to understand the output of the authoring tools that were used a decade ago.

The trade-offs of authoring tools

Before we begin to discuss the inner workings of authoring tools, we need to introduce some measurement standards for evaluating their progress from generation to generation, since the tools we use now are not the first generation of tools and certainly won't be the last. How do we assess the relative value and usability of authoring tools?

First, realize that the main purpose of CBI authoring tools is to make programming easier. If this were not true, all CBI products would be created using standard programming languages. (In the same way, programming languages are created to make programming easier. If this were not so, all programmers would do their work in machine language, which is extremely difficult for humans to read, but easy for computers.) Basically, a CBI authoring tool is a compromise that allows CBI authors and computers to understand one another. The trick is to pick a tool: (1) that allows you to express your powerful ideas in a computer program without compromising them, and (2) that allows you to create, read, and maintain the program as easily and efficiently as possible.

Figure 1 shows three factors balanced against each other in any authoring tool. They create a three dimensional (x,y,z) space in which you can locate your particular favorite tool. These factors are: Productivity, power, and ease of use.

Productivity is the amount of work that can be accomplished using the tool per unit of time. An authoring tool is more productive if it increases the amount of instruction that can be generated per hour, day, or week.

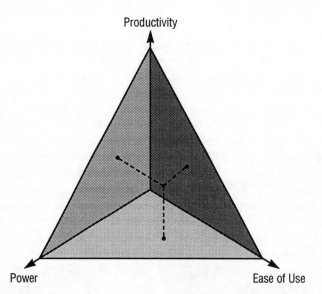

Figure 1. The balance of productivity, power, and ease of use in authoring systems.

Power is the ability of an authoring tool to do things. A tool has more power than another if it allows the author to accomplish more or if it allows the author to approach and solve a particular problem in more ways. Power is the ability to use more of the power of the computer: to use sizzly new screen techniques, to accomplish more flexible logic and branching, to deliver more *intelligent* instruction, or to design more sophisticated interfaces and interactions.

Ease of use, as it sounds, is the ability of the author to use the tool with less specialized knowledge and skill or with less complex decision-making at the time of use.

Any authoring tool (or for that matter, any program development tool or programming language) can be evaluated against these three factors. A tool may be easy to use but reduce the options of the designer, making the tool lower in power. Another tool may provide great power to the designer for specialized effects, but in doing so become harder to use. Another tool may increase productivity but do so by either restricting power or by demanding specialized skills from the designer, making it harder to use.

Some tools try to maximize one of the three factors in hopes of attracting users who value that factor. Thus there are authoring tools which stress ease of use or speed of use, while making fewer claims about power. Others promote their tool's power and do not try to appeal to the unskilled user. Others try to reach an optimal balance of the three factors, maximizing them all as far as possible. The three-dimensional scheme in Figure 1 will be useful as you evaluate the authoring tools described later in this chapter.

Inside the computer

Now to return to the original question: What are the basic structures common to all authoring tools? We are trying to identify the *internal language* of authoring systems. To answer the question, imagine yourself inside a computer, observing the internal goings-on during a session of computer-based instruction.

What can you see? What changes from moment to moment as instruction occurs? You may see streams of electrical pulses fly past you on their way to a display screen. Other signals jostle their way toward the computer's memory. Others sit, just waiting in RAM. It's hard to make any sense of what's happening at this level of detail. All you can see is bits, bytes, and electrical pulses. You may realize that groups of these pulses probably represent numbers to the computer, but if all you can see at this level is numbers, you don't understand what's going on. Maybe you are looking at things too closely. Adjust your focus to a higher level.

At the higher level you do not see bits and pulses any more; you see what might be called objects. We are not talking about *object-oriented* objects, merely things which we will for the moment call objects. The objects you see at this level are of many types. Some are screen objects—for instance, a line. The line object that you see (that appears on the screen) exists inside the computer as a collection of several numbers that describe it. These numbers are the values of its attributes. The line's color is represented by one number, its thickness by another, and its beginning and ending points by four more numbers. You realize that if you change the values of any of the numbers (the values of the attributes of the line), you will change some aspect of the object. The object that you see at this level is defined in terms of the numbers that you saw flashing about at the lower level. The objects that you see are defined in terms of the *values of their attributes*.

There are other objects which you can see at this level. Some are objects in memory. One may be a string of characters representing the student's last answer, or an identification number, or a score. For these objects, the value of their attribute is the string of numbers that they contain. Still other objects are neither graphics nor strings; they may be individual numeric values connected with an instructional strategy that is being used—say, the number of questions in the current quiz.

You can discover at this level of watching that: (1) large numbers of very small objects are required to make CBI happen at the lowest level, (2) there are still higher levels of organization, and what you see at the current level are the details of that higher level. So, let's move up to the next level and see what we can see there.

As you watch things at this higher level, you see what you saw at the lower level: objects. But the objects you see at this level are made up of the objects you saw at the lower level. The ones at this level are therefore larger and are involved in the performance of higher-level functions. For instance, at this level, the line that you saw defined by several numbers at the lower level is only one part of a larger graphic object. If you looked at still higher levels, you would see that this graphic object was only a part of the entire screen display. The student's last answer and the numeric strategy value you saw at the lower level would both appear now as a part of a larger strategy object: one quiz question. This question, like everything else is made up of smaller objects: text string objects that ask the quiz question when displayed on the screen, objects ready to contain the student's answer, objects that contain various feedback messages ready to be used once the answer is judged. This quiz question object is in turn a part of an even larger strategy object found at higher levels—the quiz or the test—and they in turn are part of an entire instructional strategy—all made up of smaller objects.

The common language of authoring tools

The objects or entities we have been discussing make up the primitive language of all CBI authoring tools in some way or another. It is the interaction of objects that makes things happen: Screens appear and change, values kept in the heart of the computer trigger strategy actions, and the student moves through the instruction experiencing a sequence of events made possible by the coordinated action of many objects. *All authoring tools allow you to build objects.* For instance, every authoring tool lets you build a line; every authoring tool allows you to adjust the number of items in a quiz. They just do these things in different ways. That is why objects as we have talked about them so far are the primitives of CBI.

Since all authoring systems create objects, they all can answer the same set of basic questions about themselves:

1. What are the objects created by this authoring system and how big are they? Some systems deal only with graphic primitives such as lines and pixels and with data primitives such as integers, strings, and real numbers. Others deal with *larger* elements such as menus and buttons. Still others deal with tests and practice sequences as their smallest object.

2. What attributes can change over the life of an object, and when can they change? Some authoring systems permit an attribute such as the color of a circle to change only at authoring time, but not while the instruction is running. This restricts the choices of the author and the range of effects that can be created at the time of instruction.

3. What are the attributes for a particular type of object? How many attributes of a circle can the author influence? How many attributes of a quiz? How many attributes of an instructional strategy? Must the author be restricted to those provided by the authoring tool, or can the attributes be extended by the author (that is, can the circle be given a new attribute such as line thickness if it was not provided in the authoring original tool)? Can the extension of attributes take place during instruction, or must it be done at authoring time? It is natural for a circle to have the attribute of *color*, but what if the circle could be given the attribute *touching something* or *touched by something*? Could that attribute not be useful?

The answers that an authoring system gives to these three questions determines to a great extent the *power* factor of the authoring system as depicted in Figure 1. Other questions about the authoring interface determine the system's *productivity* and *ease of use*.

Objects in early languages

Using an authoring tool—a language or an authoring system—an author creates objects. These in turn make instruction. In the early days of CBI, authoring tools were simply computer languages, such as the TUTOR authoring language used on the PLATO[1] CBI system, or Coursewriter[2], or DAL[3]. These languages had but one type of authorable object: the procedure. Two samples of such procedures from the TUTOR language are shown in Figure 2. TUTOR called its procedures by the name of "unit." One of the procedures, named *drawc*, draws a circle. The author specifies data to specify the mode of drawing (write), the center point of the circle (50,50), and its radius (75). Using these attribute values, the authoring language causes its routines to draw the circle—to create the circle object. The second procedure named *erasec*, erases the circle. It does so by setting the mode to erase and drawing a circle—creating a second circle object—using the same computer subroutine.

Some important characteristics of objects are shown in this simple example. First, there is an object which the author *authors*. *Unit* is the authorable object in this example. Another authoring tool may call its authorable objects by different names. Whatever the case, authorable objects themselves are never seen by the student. At the time of instruction the authorable object creates an *instructional object* (in this case, a circle), which is what the student actually experiences.

```
unit    drawc
*       this unit draws a circle
mode    write
circle  50,50,75

unit    erasec
*       this unit undraws the same circle
mode    erase
circle  50,50,75
```

Figure 2. Procedural objects from an early version of TUTOR.

Persistence

For the vast majority of authoring tools in use today, once an object (say, a circle) is created at the time of instruction, the circle is forgotten so far as the computer is concerned. Once it is drawn, the computer keeps no record of the existence of the circle. Therefore, nothing further can be done to the circle or with the circle unless the author remembers where the circle is and performs the function manually, using another authorable object. This is the reason for the second unit in Figure 2 (the unit *erasec* that erases the circle). Any additional manipulations of the circle, like changing its color, size, line thickness, or fill color would similarly have to be done using additional objects, created by the procedures in other units.

An object which is created and then forgotten by the computer in this way loses any persistent identity. It simply ceases to exist and has no life, as far as the program is concerned, past the moment of its creation. Even though it might be something that can be seen on the screen, its appearance is simply a trace of a procedure that, once executed, ceases to be. There is no record of the object (the circle), its attributes (centerpoint, radius, draw mode), or their values (50, 50, 75, and write) to be found in the computer's active memory.

So what? What difference does it make whether something called the circle exists or not? This is a subtle question, but it has been a major stumbling block in the development of better authoring systems for over twenty years. You will see how as this story continues to unfold.

Let's return to the circle. Actually, what we have said about the circle you could say about any structure of a CBI program you wish: a complex graphic, or the logic structure of a quiz. We can ask the following about objects and their persistence (in the computer's memory):

Question: If an object has no persistence, how does one find out one of its attributes later?

Answer: One can't.

Example: The program draws a circle in blue color at one point, but later it needs to inquire after its color in order to make a decision about the circle. How does it find the color except by storing it somewhere in memory?

Implication: The author must program the storage of attribute values for any non-persistent object used. Later, when the value of the attribute is needed, the author must program its retrieval. This is a lot of detailed and error-prone work. Authoring tools ought to make the process easier than this!

Question: If an object has no persistence, how does a program change its attributes?

Answer: The programmer must do it manually.

Example: The program needs to change the color of the circle (for some good reason, we assume). How is this done except by re-invoking the circle-drawing routine?

Implication: The author has to program the re-drawing of the circle if the object is non-persistent. It is not possible to simply change its attribute. Of course, if the circle has moved since it was drawn.... uh-oh!

Question: If an object has no persistence, how does one debug it?

Answer: One can't.

Example: The program tries to color the circle by mixing two other colors, but something goes wrong. How does the author look at the circle to find out what color it actually turned out to have?

Implication: The author cannot directly debug the attributes of a non-persistent object. This increases the amount of work for the programmer while programming.

These three questions appear to make persistent objects very valuable. We used simple objects like circles in the examples, but during the creation of a real CBI product, the objects involved are more complex and difficult to deal with if they are non-persistent.

To give you an example of the value of persistent objects, consider a problem which is common in the experience of many CBI designers. It is the problem of the moving display object. It is important on many occasions during CBI instruction to show a gradual change in some element of a graphic display. Normally the change consists of a movement, such as the movement of a needle across the face of a dial or gauge. Educators instructing children in time concepts recognize this as the problem of making a moving clock hand. Trainers in the technical area recognize this as the fuel gauge or altimeter problem.

Creating displays with gradually moving objects of this sort using authoring tools without persistent objects can be a nightmare. Not only must the moving needle graphic be placed on multiple displays in all of its various positions, but in order to erase old versions of the needle, special erasing displays must be created which remove the old needle position and restore the background which was removed with it. It is true that some authoring tools permit programs to be written which animate needles in this way, but this introduces the need for specialized programming skills.

In contrast, if an authoring tool has persistent objects at instruction time, it can create one version of a needle object and send to it messages which tell it its current position. The object, capable of managing its own screen representation, then undraws itself from its old position and redraws itself in the new position automatically. This represents a quantum leap in authoring capability, and designers who have been through something like the needle experience will immediately recognize the value of this development. Persistence is a topic that will re-surface later in the chapter because it so clearly influences all three of the authoring tool factors shown in Figure 1.

Author-time objects

As useful as the early authoring languages were, in about 1980, CBI developers started looking for an alternative to the error-prone and expensive drudgery of coding procedures like those in Figure 2. This search began despite the growth within the languages of powerful instruction-oriented features such as question-asking and quiz-organizing procedures and despite the discovery that language subroutines commonly used by designers could be created once and reused as often as desired. A major part of the problem seemed to be that instructional designers did not want to work at arm's length from the tools used to create CBI. They wanted to be able to try out and test ideas easily, but they did not want to have to become programmers to do so.

The way out of this difficulty appeared in the form of several what are called *frame-based* authoring systems. The name frame-based came from the attempt of these authoring systems to create pre-fabricated *frames* of instructional macro-procedure which carried out pre-packaged instructional functions: display-presenting, menu-presenting, question-asking, response-accepting, answer-judging, score assignment, feedback-delivery, and many others. To use these macro-procedures, which were nothing more than high-level objects used by the author to create run-time objects (the ones you saw when you were inside the computer), the author only had to add a few *attribute values* to tell the frame how to act. Then at the time of instruction, these frames executed, creating objects for the student to experience.

The majority of today's authoring tools for CBI use this approach to authoring. For instance, two of the more sophisticated and powerful of today's systems, Authorware[4], and Quest[5], use macro-procedure building blocks out of which instructional sequences are built. Authorware uses eleven of these basic building blocks. They are listed in Table 1. Quest 5.0 for Windows uses five classes of them—a total of 27 basic building blocks. These are listed in Table 2. You will find it worthwhile to compare these lists to get a sense of the types of objects offered to the author. There are many similarities, and even the differences can be used to understand how authoring systems use objects.

More recently, useful super-groups of these basic building blocks are being provided with the products, allowing for reuse of even larger bundles of pre-structured logic. These super-groups are called *models* in Authorware and *Fast Tracks* in Quest. Most other frame-based authoring tools either supply templated logic of this sort or allow the designer to construct and store them for later use. As you will see in later chapters of this book, the ability to define generalized logic patterns is an important theme in CBI today and one of the keys to attaining lower costs in CBI development.

Many useful instructional objects can be built from the basic author objects provided by frame-based authoring systems (referring now to the basic objects, not the super-group templates). For instance, a menu in Authorware can be thought of as the combination of a presentation object (one which specializes in placing visual material on the display screen) with a decision object (one which specializes in accepting a response from the user and then branching to a destination frame correlated with the user's choice).

Some very sophisticated special-purpose objects have been built as authorable objects. One frame-based authoring system popular in the eighties contained a graphing object that permitted authors to have students interact with a graph and express their responses in terms of points and plots on the graphing surface. This was especially useful for designers teaching mathematics and could not be easily built from other existing objects in the authoring system. This same system also contained a specialized test construction frame capable of creating complex pooled, randomized, and sampled testing logic at instruction time with the only authoring requirement being to enter a few parameter values and to specify the question frames to be used in the test.

Table 1. The authorable objects of Authorware.

Object Name	Object Function
Display	Displays information in the form of text, graphic, imported bitmap, or other authorized format.
Animation	Moves a displayed object from one point to another along a defined path, transforming it as specified by the designer.
Erase	Removes a displayed object, possibly with special effects.
Wait	Pauses execution until a condition is met (e.g., time elapsed, keypress, mouse click).
Decision	Permits execution to either branch based on a certain set of conditions or iterate until a certain condition has been met.
Interaction	Gets input (mouse click, characters, etc.) from the user.
Calculation	Permits the evaluation of one or more expressions to either get, set or transform some variable data or to change the state of the system.
Map	Permits the author to insert any set of objects into the flow of objects; much like a subroutine made up of author objects.
Movie	Permits the author to insert a digital movie into the flow.
Sound	Permits the author to insert an audio message into the flow.
Video	Permits the author to reference an external video source such as a videodisc.

Table 2. The authorable objects of Quest 5.0 for Windows.

Object (Tab) Group	Object Name	Function
Graphics	Rectangle	Displays a rectangle
	Ellipse	Displays an ellipse or circle
	Line	Displays a line
	Text	Displays text
	Fill	Fill a graphic object with color
	Graphic	Displays a bitmap graphic
Animation	Bounce	Bounces a displayed object within an area
	Path	Moves a displayed object along a defined path
	Drag	Permits user to drag an object in a specific area
	File	Displays information as an animation file
	Cycle	Cycles display objects
	Dissolve	Dissolves display objects
Audio/Video	Audio	Plays an audio file
	CD Audio	Plays audio from a CD
	Video	References external video source (videodisc)
	Video file	Plays a digital video file
Controls	Button	Places a button on the display
	Text box	Accepts and judges a response from the user
	Timer	Inserts a clock onto the display
	Scroll bar	Adds scroll bars to the display
	Smart spot	Adds an irregularly shaped user selection area
	Windows help	Adds Windows(help file to a product
Interact	Watch for	Persistently watches for user input or time delay
	Wait for	Delays object until user input or time delay
	Branch	Branches to a frame along path or path color
	Service	Permits change of object attributes at run-time
	Coach	Permits the author to declare variables, use standard C, Quest, and Windows functions to manipulate objects at run-time and extend tool functionality

These kinds of author-time objects greatly increase author productivity and avoid program coding by bundling up the kinds of things authors want to do and packaging them as authorable objects. This is a great strength.

But author-time objects also have a weakness. It is that the instructional objects they create during instruction do not persist any better than the objects created by the programmed run-time procedure objects of the early authoring languages. And if an object doesn't persist past its creation point, there are no attributes whose values can be manipulated to create instruction-time or computed effects. If you draw a rectangle on the screen during instruction, changing its color requires that the rectangle continue to exist in the computer's memory past the point when it is drawn.

Both Authorware and Quest retain knowledge of some objects—that is, they have some persistent objects. Both retain display objects in memory, making it easy to remove or reposition objects without engaging in the details of screen management. Quest also retains in memory non-display objects, making it easy to interact with all program objects. In Quest, the memory for display objects also makes it possible to change the characteristics of display objects at the time of instruction.

Do we really need it?

Some designers do not see the need for persistent run-time objects whose attributes can be changed while instruction is underway. The consequence of this view is that the designer is forced to anticipate and specify *in advance and in detail* all of the possible states that the display and instructional logic can exhibit. Some designers don't try to develop complicated instructional interactions because their thinking has been channeled and confined by the non-persistent object tools that they have had to work with. But as interest in simulation as an instructional tool increases, it becomes apparent that the systems to be simulated have extremely large numbers of states, which make it impractical to simulate them by anticipating all possible eventualities and creating them in advance within frames.

If the simulation deals with a traffic light having three bulbs, in order to simulate it, you must include in your pre-planned objects three sequences—a red-off-off; an off-yellow-off; and an off-off-green—to represent the three states of the signal. This is easy enough for a simple three-state system, but if the system is an electronic circuit with many thousands of state combinations, having to anticipate them and represent them all as separate objects can easily overwhelm a development project.

Here the wisdom of the move of authoring tools like Authorware and Quest toward persistent objects becomes apparent. That movement must not only continue, but will accelerate as new tools are created which take advantage of the benefits of persistent objects.

Run-time objects

In reality, the degree to which an authoring tool permits the creation, destruction, and manipulation of objects during courseware execution will probably come to be the measure of its power in the future more than any other feature. The persistence of objects at the time of instruction allows authors to develop the most complex and the most responsive courseware. Whether or not this increase in power will come at the expense of ease of use and productivity is a tale yet to be told. The fact is that increasingly sophisticated types of CBI products are now being created and will produce new user expectations, making products like them the rule, rather than the exception they have been in the past. The building of this type of instructional product favors and in some cases demands authoring systems that supply persistent run-time instructional objects. A first generation of object-oriented authoring tools are on the market or are rapidly approaching it: ToolBook[6], Visual Basic[7], Delphi[8], Quest 5.0 for Windows, SK8[9], mTropolis[10], and others yet in the developmental process are changing the types of instruction we design and create.

What kinds of objects?

Having been introduced to the power of instructional objects which persist and can be manipulated at run-time, you might now think that an authoring system should simply permit you to identify all of the objects and attributes that you wish to interact at run-time and enable you to change them. However, such a system would quickly bring you face to face with intolerable complexity. For this reason, the creators of object-oriented authoring tools will probably exercise some selectivity in the objects that they make available to the author and the attributes which authors are able to change. The set of offered objects and their manner of authoring will, in fact, become the major competitive decision these tools make.

The goal of authoring system developers will be to select the smallest useful set of objects and give them the most flexible and useful set of attributes. Interface design will determine how easy it is to create and arrange objects within the object community. From basic objects, the instructional designer will also build combination objects which perform a wide range of instructional functions. By keeping the set of primitive objects small and universal, the skills required of the tool user can hopefully be kept simple and easy to learn.

Persistence beyond run-time?

Naturally, if we have considered authoring tools that offer non-persistent objects, and ones that offer objects which are persistent at author-time and run-time, shouldn't we ask whether there is any value in objects that persist *beyond* run-time? To date, no authoring system has taken advantage of this means of preserving data from session to session: data on the outcome of instruction, student profiles, or progress records. However, general-use programming systems have already realized the power of this concept. It is the basis of all object-oriented data bases, and we predict that as such data bases find relationships with CBI authoring tools, we will see a breakdown of the barriers between those systems and the ones used to manage student learning. In the future, the computer-managed instruction (CMI) system will be an object-oriented data base, which by definition means that the objects created during instruction will persist and *live* as long as the student or the system they describe is active.

Instructional flow—linear flow

We have talked up to this point about CBI objects whose attribute values can change, but we have said little about the nature of the interaction between objects. In short, as individual objects "do their thing," what controls the flow of instruction?

Early CBI programming systems worked just like all programming systems of their time, which executed commands in a linear, statement-by-statement fashion. The order in which statements were placed into a monolithic program was for the most part the order in which they were executed. Jumps in the order of execution could be planned in advance and built in by the author through the use of branch and branch return statements. The flow of instruction, controlled by the execution of the program, was essentially linear.

The arrival of author-time objects (frames) on the scene around 1980 did nothing to change this essentially linear pattern of instruction. Whether in the form of individual statements or grouped statements called *frames*, the programs tended to flow from beginning to end, with inserted eddies of conditional or iterative (loop) logic providing only minor relief. One of the implications of this is to force all instructional decisions onto a single processing path, whether the decisions are selecting the next display or computing the student's readiness for the introduction of a particular new task demand.

Authorware owes much of its attractiveness and ease of use to this linearity. The main activity of the author creating instruction is to first populate a *flow line* with *icons* (objects, frames of bundled logic) and then specify the *attribute* settings for each icon, using the family of dialogue boxes related to the icon type. The order of icon (or object) execution during instruction is defined by the flow line, top to bottom, with the possibility of jumps and conditional branches between major sections of otherwise linear flow. Virtually all frame-based authoring systems share this characteristic with respect to the order of instructional flow. The IconAuthor[11] authoring system allows the user to diagram the flow of instructional logic using standard flowcharting symbols and conventions in place of writing program statements.

In the Quest authoring system, the author creates the flow within a product by executing what is termed "title design." The author creates independent frames, groups of frames called *modules*, external program calls to other applications, and then specifies the default flow patterns between them by constructing flow lines and connectors. The author then populates the individual frames with objects to create graphic displays and instructional sequences. Within the frame there is a flow pattern, just as between frames. Conditional execution and jumps are possible as a relief from the otherwise linear order of object execution.

One advantage of linear flow within an authoring system is that the product created this way is easy to maintain. A frame of instruction in need of maintenance can be located and modified relatively easily—or even removed and the logical flow closed up where it used to be. The high costs of courseware maintenance make this a hard feature to ignore.

The reason that the flow of control can be so easily and clearly diagrammed in a frame-based authoring system is that the objects which are connected into sequences do not persist beyond the point where they are used. This makes things run faster at instruction time, because the computer has fewer things to remember and track. But heavy emphasis on forward-moving sequence also makes it impossible for students to move about on paths not planned and explicitly programmed in advance by the author—for instance, to move backward in the presentation, to review a just-seen movie segment. Moving backwards at any point is possible only if the author has *anticipated* the need at every point and has placed into the flow sequence the controls and logic which enable the student to move backward from that point.

Instructional flow—network flow

An alternative form of inter-object flow provided by newly-emerging authoring tools involves a type of *network* flow in which there is not a central controlling thread of processing. Instead, the objects form a sort of society and communicate through messages sent between themselves when some internal or external event triggers the need for communication.

The implication of this type of flow control is that its sequence can be hard to predict. From any given point in instruction, a student can be given the freedom to go a large number of directions, perform a broad spectrum of actions, and request any of several paths (actually, non-paths, which is the whole point) for the program to take. Of course, for this type of flow to be used, the objects which communicate with each other must all persist at run-time, ready to receive or send messages at any time. Because Quest authoring system objects persist at run-time, there is some deviation from the flow defined by the author between frames and modules. Objects do communicate through services, events, and functions. Several navigation options are available, and the author is not completely tied to paths specified in the title design.

Luckily, the metaphor of message-passing between objects is easier for humans to master than the algorithmic and variable-heavy metaphor of the sequenced-statement program, so the added complexity of multi-level objects is still easier to deal with. For instance, many people think of objects as if they were a community of people talking to each other in order to bring about various outcomes. This conversational metaphor is very close to our daily experience, and it applies well to objects.

Multi-threading

The real benefit of the conversation of persistent objects will become apparent in later chapters. For now, we are introducing the concept of objects and outlining in broad terms their impact on CBI. Consider, however, one last point about object conversations. If it is possible for a single conversation to take place among one set of objects, then we might ask if it is possible for two different conversations to be underway among different groups of objects within the same computer at the same time. The answer is that with some object-oriented authoring tools and development systems, it is.

Not only can separate conversations take place, but through cross communication between themselves, the separate object communities can act upon each other. For instance, if there exists in the computer's memory a complex object which represents some natural system under study—perhaps the processes within a leaf—and if there is another object in the computer's memory at the same time which is capable of carrying out instructional functions with respect to leaf system models, then the instructional object can act upon the system object and produce appropriate instructional messages and interactions. This is one form of *model-centered instruction*, a term defined more completely in later chapters. Instructional functions can be created separately from simulation models, tutorials, and even reference works.

The catch is that the simultaneous processing of two communities of objects normally must be made possible at the operating system level. Some operating systems do support this capability, which is called *multi-threading*. However, demand has not pushed all commercial operating system vendors to provide this capability, or to make it easily accessible. Luckily, there are ways provided in some object-oriented development systems to convince even non-multi-threaded systems to manage inter-community conversations, so the concepts we are describing have reality using many object-oriented tools today. The Quest authoring system offers multi-threading capability with the concurrent module in Quest 5.0.

Later chapters will show that the untangling of the logic of the display and interactions from the logic of the instructional process makes it possible to construct more interactive and realistic practice environments. It allows the construction of these models, at the same time permitting a parallel computing process to monitor the student's responses to instruction, make instructional decisions, and adjust the flow of the instructional experience independently.

Conclusion

Perhaps this chapter has brought you to a place that you did not expect. It has described in a disjointed way the history and evolution of CBI authoring systems, doing so in a way that highlighted the innermost issues of authoring systems and their features of greatest interest to the future of CBI.

This has not been a status quo chapter, because the status quo is changing, and as a CBI developer, you can expect the change to accelerate. What we have tried to do was prepare you as a CBI designer to live in two worlds: the world of CBI authoring systems that exists today and is capable of producing genuinely quality instruction, and the world of object-oriented authoring systems that will grow rapidly and bring with it new instructional forms, new development thinking, and new power for the designer to use.

We feel that it is important for you to see how these two worlds relate to each other. In fact, the evolution that is taking place is not so much a complete disruption of all that has gone on in the past as it is an extension of it with improvements—improvements which are made possible by the great increase in personal computer power, new programming techniques, and new conceptions of computer programming. We hope you feel comfortable living in both worlds. To make it more likely that you will, we have filled the three chapters which follow with more detailed understandings of both the present authoring systems and the newer object-oriented systems and how they relate to instructional plans.

Self-directed activities

- Begin to assemble and maintain a list of CBI authoring tools. Obtain the name and contact information for the company which maintains and sells each tool.

- For each of the authoring tools on the list your created in the previous activity, have your name placed on its mailing list and begin to assemble a file of literature on each tool. Also, find as many articles as you can describing the tools, their features, their economies, and the strengths and weaknesses and capacities of each tool.

- Create a master feature list for the authoring tools you have discovered. Use the list to compare authoring tools. If possible, obtain an examination or demonstration copy of the authoring tool and verify for yourself how the feature is implemented through the interface. Compare the ease-of-use of the tools you analyze. Share your list and your comparisons with other CBI developers.

- Describe the types of objects created by the tools of most interest to you. Describe the actions the author must carry out to create each kind of object.

- Group authoring tools according to all of the information you have learned about them. Identify which tools you would use for a simple project as opposed to a complex one. Which one would you use for a project with an impatient client? Which would you use if there was a high volume of material to be produced? Which would you use if you knew there would be much revision and maintenance of the product over time? Which would you use for a project where development cost was the most important issue?

- Learn more about the history of individual authoring tools: their date of origin, the original purpose for which they were developed, their migration from computer to computer, their patterns of ownership, their patterns of marketing and distribution, their patterns of use, and the major landmark events in their growth and history.

- Examine the shape of the learning curve for each of the authoring tools of interest to you. Determine how easy it is to begin using a given authoring tool. Determine how easy it is to arrive at the first plateau of user confidence and capability. Identify how many levels of mastery—how many plateaus—are associated with each tool and how difficult and time-consuming it is to arrive at each one. Identify special skills associated with each level. Assess the pool of users qualified at each level of use which might be available to your project if you selected a given authoring tool.

- Contrast the training and support offered by the vendor of each tool. Look for supplied tutorials, example sets, coaching systems, provision of copyable models, documentation sets, classes offered, workshops, training sessions, user conferences, user support groups, special interest groups at conferences, user support hotlines, newsletters or periodical publications, and other similar products and services. Determine the costs associated with each of these.

Further reading

Bunderson, C. V. (1981). Courseware. In H. F. O'Neil, Jr. (Ed.), *Computer-based instruction: A state-of-the-art assessment.* New York: Academic Press.

Gibbons, A. S., Fairweather, P. G., and O'Neal, A. F. (1993, May). The future of computer-managed instruction. *Educational Technology, 33*(5), 7–11.

Larkin, J. H., and Chabay, R. W. (1992). *Computer-assisted instruction and intelligent tutoring systems: Shared goals and complementary approaches.* Hillsdale, NJ: Lawrence Erlbaum Associates.

Milheim, W. D. (Ed.). (1994). *Authoring-systems software for computer-based training.* Englewood Cliffs, NJ: Educational Technology Publications.

Spector, J. M. *et al.* (1993). *Automating instructional design.* Englewood Cliffs, NJ: Educational Technology Publications.

Endnotes

1   The PLATO™ system was originally developed at the University of Illinois (Urbana) and further developed and disseminated by the Control Data Corporation. The name is currently a trademark of TRO.

2   The Coursewriter™ series of authoring languages were developed and distributed by IBM.

3   DAL™, for Digital Authoring Language, was developed by Digital Equipment Corporation for its VAX™ series of computers.

4   Authorware™ is a trademark of Macromedia Incorporated.

5   Quest 5.0 for Windows™ is an object-oriented authoring system registered by Allen Communications, a Times-Mirror Corporation.

6   ToolBook™ is an object-oriented software construction set registered by Asymetrix Corporation.

7   Visual Basic™ is an object-oriented programming system registered by the Microsoft Corporation.

8   Delphi™ is an object-oriented programming system registered by the Borland Corporation.

9   SK8™ is an object-oriented software development system registered by Apple Computer, Inc.

10   mTropolis™ is an object-oriented programming system registered by mFactory.

11   IconAuthor™ is an authoring system marketed by the Asymetrix.

4

FRAMES

Chapter Objectives:

1. *Describe how the frame object provides templated logic for repetitive instructional functions.*

2. *Identify the four generic types of authoring frame.*

3. *Trace the logical operation of the four generic frame types, showing how changes to individual frame property values control or modify frame behavior.*

4. *Given a set of frame property values for one of the four generic frame types, describe how the frame will behave.*

The frame object

In the previous chapter, we described the importance of objects in the creation of CBI programs. Basically, authors create objects—graphic ones and logical ones—and the sequenced execution of those objects is what makes instruction happen. At the beginning of the discussion on objects, we asked you to envision what it looks like inside the computer during instruction. Some of the objects you saw there at lower levels were quite small: individual lines, numerical values, strings of text, and so forth.

Just as a house is an assemblage of very small objects (nails, short boards, metal plates, etc.), CBI is also an assemblage of very small objects (lines, circles, fills, strings, branches, etc.) which are sequenced in various ways to produce different sensory and interaction effects for students to experience. But if you want to study the structure of houses, you don't concentrate your study on nails; instead you pay attention to larger structural units of which nails are a part. Nails are important, but the structures nails make possible are *more* important to the overall appearance and serviceability of the final product. Housing contractors have discovered that in order to build houses within the economic range of the average home buyer, they have to think of buildings in terms of pre-assembled units of objects (like the rafter units that hold up the roof, for instance) rather than as individual nails and boards. Houses can be built board-by-board, but only at higher cost.

The same principles of construction apply to CBI. If CBI authors are forced by their tools to pay attention to each detailed element of structure that they put into their product, then productivity falls dramatically, and instead of thinking about design issues, the author is forced to think about nuts-and-bolts programming issues. This was a reality that early CBI developers faced very soon after the invention of CBI technology, and it continues to be a major concern for designers today. It is the primary reason that CBI authoring tools are created. How do you increase the rate of authoring productivity while at the same time maintaining or improving the quality of the product?

The solution that has been produced by the current generation of authoring tools is generally referred to as the *frame*. A frame is an author object. That means that the author uses it to enter data which will be used later to create dynamic experiences (instruction-time objects) for the student. A frame represents a grouping of smaller objects which are assembled into a kind of pre-fabricated unit. As an author creates a frame, he or she simply supplies attribute values for the smaller objects which are grouped together within the frame. This process is called *authoring*. Most current authoring systems use the frame as their basic unit of structure. Each authoring tool implements the frame concept in a way they think provides their user with the best blend of power, ease of use, and productivity (see Figure 1, Chapter 3). The most used and most productive frame-based authoring tools of this generation not only offer the author the productivity gains of frames, but also provide the author with a user interface that makes the process of frame construction easier, accessible to more people, and less costly to use. As you also learned in Chapter 3, sometimes this ease and accessibility come at some cost in power and flexibility, but this is a type of optimization dilemma every technology faces, and CBI is no different.

In this chapter we explore the implications and inner workings of four generic frame types as a basic structural unit of CBI authoring. We do this in some detail because it will give you a notion of the tools within the average authoring system from which you can build the surface and instructional features of CBI.

We also have deliberately chosen to describe frames, the building blocks out of which instructional strategies are crafted, before describing the principles of strategy themselves. This is so that as you read about strategy you will have *thought tools* for considering different ways that strategic plans could be carried out by one of the present generation of authoring tools.

It is important that you recognize that we are not saying that your strategic designs should be pre-determined or confined by the frame types available to you or that you should think of frame types before you think of instructional principles. However, we do want you to be aware of the main path that is easily walked using most authoring tools. Once you understand frames, you will know what the average authoring system can do for you easily and without extra cost. Then you can begin to plan extensions of frame functions using the supplemental programming tools which are built in to nearly all of the current authoring systems. You can also begin to consider the alternatives to frame structures.

Basic frame components

Frame, as it is used here, refers to an authoring object which allows the author to define either or both: (1) an expressive *display* element (something which can be seen, heard, or felt), and (2) a pattern of unseen computer branching *logic*. The expressive element of a frame once consisted exclusively of a graphic or textual screen display, but the advent of multimedia is changing that definition to include any combination of graphics, text, animations, audio, video stills and motion, and other sensory experiences for the student which the computer can administer. In this book, the term *display* is used to refer to this broader meaning, which encompasses messages to *all* of the senses.

The logic of CBI is made up mainly of a small number of functions which are carried out rapidly and repeatedly. These functions consist of actions like accepting input from the student, branching to a menu location, judging input, responding to input, and so forth. Since these are the things authors want to happen during instruction, authoring tools must make them easily available to authors, and different systems do this in different ways. Some authoring tools, such as the Quest Multimedia Authoring System (Version 5.0) allow you to control the order in which frame events occur. Quest allows you to *build* a frame by assembling into it the basic functions you want, in the order in which you want them to occur during instruction. Other authoring systems like, Authorware and IconAuthor, use specialized, pre-packaged function icons. By assembling these icons into a desired sequence on a flow line or a flow chart, you control the sequence of function execution during instruction.

Other "frames"

Since the term "frame" has had extensive use in the field of artificial intelligence (AI), it is important to stress here that we are not talking about AI frames. An AI frame is a generalized structure of knowledge. There is a *frame* for the concept "car," for instance. That frame consists of the normally expected qualities and descriptors of a car, like color, size of engine, type of transmission, and make. There can also be a *frame* for an experience, like a visit to a restaurant. This frame consists of a structure of details that gives a description of a particular visit to a restaurant: who went, which restaurant, what was ordered, how the bill was paid, and so forth. In a later chapter, we will appeal to this notion of *frame* as we talk about ways to capture and control instructional message content, but in the present chapter, we will restrict our interest to the meaning of *frame* which refers to a construction created by an authoring tool.

The term "frame" was also originally used in programmed instruction to refer to one isolated element of an instructional program. Each *frame* element in programmed instruction had a specific function that was meaningful in the context of behavioral psychology, but the principles upon which programmed instruction was built have not been supported by time and research. At one time there were those who felt that CBI was nothing more than programmed instruction on a computer. No knowledgeable CBI developer makes that claim today, and the meaning of *frame* used here has no real relation to the meaning it was given in the days of programmed instruction.

Generic frame types

Let's begin to look at the four types of frame. *These will be generic frame types; they will not correspond exactly to the frame organization of any specific authoring system.* But you will find that this idealized set of frames makes possible the description of several basic frame patterns in Chapter 5 which begin to have important instructional implications and uses. *Moreover, you will see that these generic frame types can be constructed using any mature and full-featured authoring system in use today.* Therefore, frames are a kind of lowest common denominator for CBI as it is currently practiced, a kind of common design language which all authoring systems speak. We look at the frame types as a kind of "Rosetta Stone" for CBI designers. We will try to interpret each generic frame type in terms of its implementation within two popular authoring systems: Authorware and Quest 5.0.

The frame types we will describe are differentiated from each other by their logic patterns. For simplicity, we will assume that three of the four frame types have a display component bundled with the frame. Once we have described each frame type, we will provide examples to show how each frame can create a great variety of surface effects during instruction.

The four basic frame types we will study are: the *presentation* frame, the *menu* frame, the *question* frame, and the *calculation* frame.

The presentation frame

The presentation frame is the simplest frame type. A generic logic for the presentation frame is diagrammed in Figure 1, showing the sequence of functions normally associated with a presentation frame:

- Execute the display, if one is specified.

- Accept a branching signal, if one is specified.

- Execute the time-out, if one is specified.

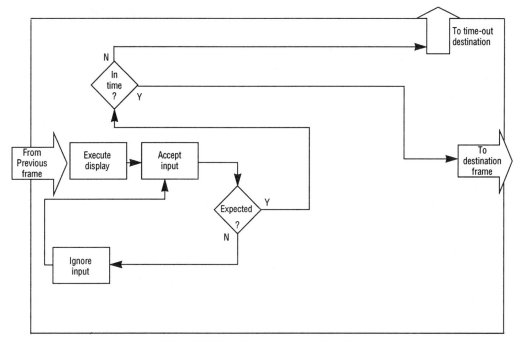

Figure 1. Generic presentation frame logic.

Let's examine these functions.

Execute display: The display function of the presentation frame appears in Figure 1 as the logic element labeled *execute display*.

When the display of a presentation frame is executed, it is executed as a sequence of synchronized events. In the days when *display* meant only a computer screen filled with text and graphic content, the sequence that was executed was called a "display list." Essentially, the display list was a list of the graphic and text objects to be placed on the screen in the order they were to appear.

Today, in the days of multimedia, there is something comparable to the display list, but instead of controlling the appearance of graphic objects, it controls the coordinated appearance of all of the multimedia resources assigned to the display. Because some resources such as video, audio, and animations are *played* rather than just displayed, timing and synchronization of message channels is now a much more important element of display management. To achieve maximum effect with the message, an author will often desire to synchronize the occurrence of display elements, and sometimes this becomes quite tricky. In effect, with multimedia, the author becomes a stage manager or a director, calling together the various effects of the display in a coordinated sequence. One popular program especially adept at coordinating multimedia resources in this way is, in fact, called (Macromedia) Director.

The average authoring system has some difficulty with exotic timing and sequencing requirements. Some media forms hog the computer's output channels while they are playing and make it impossible for certain other media to be active simultaneously. Moreover, some authoring systems have good tools for specifying the relative timing of display events, while others leave authors to their own inventiveness at using a few simple (and sometimes blunt) tools.

Whereas early authoring tools possessed (and most still do have) built-in graphic drawing tools, the rapid growth of powerful graphic application packages has surpassed the capabilities of these built-in tools, and many designers prefer to use imported graphics. This means that an authoring tool must be capable of displaying a variety of graphic file formats. The designer must specify what portion of the existing display (if any) to erase as a new display is executed: all, part, or none. If the screen is not erased, or if only part is erased, then material placed on the screen by previous frames remains visible, and the display content of the currently executing frame is added to it. Overlaying or *building* displays in this manner is a very useful technique for creating the feeling of display continuity—a principle discussed in more detail in Chapter 18.

Managing the display portion of a frame can be simple, but if certain effects or timing sequences are chosen it can become complicated. Designers prescribing fancy effects should be prepared to encounter a few timing and synchronization challenges. Inventiveness can sometimes overcome the failings of an authoring tool. For instance, it is sometimes possible to link multiple timed presentation frames together into an automatic sequence which achieves a desired timing effect that would be difficult or impossible within the boundaries of a single presentation frame.

With regard to frame-related displays in general, we would offer an important caution. It is easy to imagine display effects more complicated than your authoring tool can deliver. We strongly advise designers to allow their display designs to be guided by what is needed to implement a sound instructional strategy and to avoid glitz for the sake of glitz. It is not only costly and time-consuming, but displays that are too busy can actually detract from learning.

Accept input and time-out: Once the display has been executed, the generic presentation frame determines what branching instructions are in force and carries them out (the *accept input* box in Figure 1 and all of the boxes above and to the right of it). Conditions for branching may be: branch automatically after X seconds (or immediately), wait for a student signal to branch, or branch on student signal only if it is given within a specified time. If the designer wants a timed branch, he or she must specify the amount of time to elapse before the branch. If a time-out value is not set, it means that the designer wants the frame to terminate execution upon some signal from the student, placing the pace of the message under student control. For this to happen, the designer must tell the frame the expected input, which may be "press any key," or "press a specific key." For all of these branching possibilities, a destination must be specified—the name or number of the next frame to be executed—and the destinations may be different for the input and time-out branches.

Early CBI products used the "Press Enter to Continue" method of screen advancement so much that it was making CBI look like a book. Pressing Enter became the equivalent of turning a page in the book. In fact, the technique is still referred to as *page turning*, and it is never intended as a compliment. If you use page turning (and there are some times when it is difficult not to), do not to let it run on for too many frames. The timed advance also has its abuses. Since not all students read at the same pace, fast readers will be bored and slow readers will not be able to keep up with a timed presentation. Moreover, some students will miss information or will want to go back to review, and a timed presentation makes this difficult.

One possible time setting for a presentation frame is the time-out value of "instant," which means that the presentation frame will execute its display and then branch immediately to another frame. This is a good technique for adding content to the display just before or during a complex interaction. Later in this chapter, you will see some variations in the surface features of instruction made possible by the presentation frame and its variations in settings.

Attribute summary: According to this description of the generic presentation frame, all of the varied textures of the presentation frame are brought about by giving values to just a few frame attributes. They are:

- Erase? (yes/no)

- Area or objects to erase

- Graphic file name (or display event list, in order of execution)

- Time-out? (yes/no)

- Time-out value? (in seconds or computer clicks)

- Time-out destination (frame name)

- Advance signal expected from student? (yes/no)

- Advance signal(s) identity? (keys, click areas)

- Destination frame for time-out? (frame name)

- Destination frame for signaled branch? (frame name)

By giving specific values to the frame attributes (properties of the frame object), the designer specifies the behavior of the frame. This is an example of giving values to an object, as described in Chapter 3.

Presentation frame logic, which is the same for all presentation frames, is a kind of subroutine, or as a programmer would refer to it, a function. By passing different values to the function and then telling it to execute, the reusable logic of the frame is made to appear to act differently on the surface. This notion of the parameterization of logical structures underlies and is the core mechanism for the bulk of our standard authoring tools today. In menu-based systems and icon-based systems both, the menus are simply a convenient method for allowing the designer to enter the variable values into a data file. The entered values are used at run time to make the basic frame logic act in a certain way. In authoring languages, the subroutines of logic which are used are built by a programmer and are normally not supplied with the language, but there is little alternative to building subroutines if the designer wishes to keep the costs of programming reasonable. From this point on in this chapter, watch how the remainder of the frame types use this generic logic principle. The list of functions performed by each frame type will differ, but the basic frame mechanism will be the same from frame type to frame type.

Application to popular authoring tools

To provide a contact with reality, let's correlate the presentation frame we have described with the basic elements of two currently popular authoring systems: Authorware and Quest 5.0. We will do this for each of the frame types discussed in this chapter, so a little background on each authoring tool is also in order.

Authorware: Authorware builds instruction by arranging *icons*, which represent repeatable logical functions, on a "flow line," which represents the sequential flow of the logic. Table 1 in Chapter 3 lists the Authorware icons and their functions.

The Display icon of Authorware corresponds to the *execute display* component of the generic presentation frame described here. The Display icon's time-out setting is always *instant* (that is, branch immediately), and the destination for the branch is normally to the next icon on the graphical flow line upon which all Authorware icons are placed during logic construction. In order to effect a timed or action-based branch after a Display icon, an additional icon must be placed in the flow line below the Display icon (since motion along the flow line is downward). Usually the Wait icon is used for this. For a control-initiated branch, either the Wait or the Interaction icon may be used. For erasing, an Erase icon is provided. Using this icon, you may erase complete objects from the display quite readily without erasing their surrounding area at the same time. This is a benefit provided by a persistent-object graphics system.

Quest 5.0: In Quest 5.0, the author designs each frame during frame edit and connects frames to each other logically during title design. Designing a frame involves populating it with objects which are selected from a list of available objects. These are objects in the same way we described objects in Chapter 3: Each one is a pattern of computer logic which carries out a specific set of functions, according to directions supplied by the author in the form of numerical, binary, or textual data. In Quest, each object within a frame acts as an independent object with which the author can communicate at runtime through pre-built events, services, and functions. The objects which can be included within a frame and their functions are listed in Chapter 3, Table 2.

An author selects the order in which Quest objects are added to a frame. The order in which they are added is the order in which they will be executed during instruction. (Though the author can change object attributes at runtime to adjust the order of presentation.) An author can also hide objects (make them invisible) and show them at the desired moment during the instructional sequence. The ordering of objects within a frame accomplishes basically the same sequencing function as does the flow line in Authorware. An author may add to one frame a large number of features—stuffing an entire lesson if desired within the confines of a single frame. It should be clear from this description that an author may select and sequence frame objects which act together exactly like the generic presentation frame described here.

Defaulting and globalization

Before moving to a discussion of the Menu frame type, it is worthwhile to digress here to mention two techniques used to reduce the number of separate data points a designer must enter into a frame: defaulting and globalization.

Defaulting: Even though a designer wants different frames to look and act differently, there are certain settings of the frame which the designer wants to remain the same from frame to frame. Much time is saved by having the authoring tool automatically set all of those unchanging objects of a frame to a standard *default* value. The branch timing values may be set to "wait for signal" within an authoring system. This means that all frames automatically have that value pre-set within them when the frame is created. Exceptions to the default can be made at each frame, but if no change is specified, the default value will be used. By using defaulting, an authoring tool makes it possible to author *by exception*. That is, the only values that must be entered are those which differ from standard default values, and this is a great time saver.

Globalization: Another method for reducing the amount of data to be entered during authoring is globalization. This consists of specifying a default value only once for the whole instructional event, rather than at the level of each frame. For instance, a designer may decide to specify an instructional event termination key: the key which when pressed, terminates the instructional event. Each frame must be aware of this key because the student may choose to end the instructional event at any moment. Most authoring systems provide an event-level default for termination. If a designer wished to change this default to some other key, doing it at the level of each frame would be enormously time consuming and costly. By placing this default value, which operates within each frame, at the global level for setting and changing, a real economy is achieved.

Now let's move on to a discussion of the menu frame type.

The menu frame

The menu frame is quite simple. The logic of the menu frame is illustrated in Figure 2 below. The functions of the menu frame are:

- Execute the display, if one is attached.

- Accept a menu choice from the student.

- Handle unexpected input.

- Branch to the frame attached to the selected menu item.

- Execute a time-out, if one is specified.

The menu frame is somewhat like a question frame, since both ask the student to enter a response. The difference between the menu frame and the question frame is that a menu frame simply branches the student to the menu item selected and does not judge the input, whereas the question frame does judge it. The menu frame creates no score, and it is not particularly interested in what the student has selected. Many of the functions of the menu frame are the same as those of the presentation frame, with the exception that the menu frame must branch contingent upon the student's choice, while the presentation frame has only one main destination.

Execute display: The menu frame display acts identically with the presentation frame's display in all respects. This is likewise true of the question frame which we will discuss later. What was said of presentation frame displays is true also of menu and question frame displays. This is true with one exception: the menu and question frame displays must in addition display (1) input confirmation, and (2) input response.

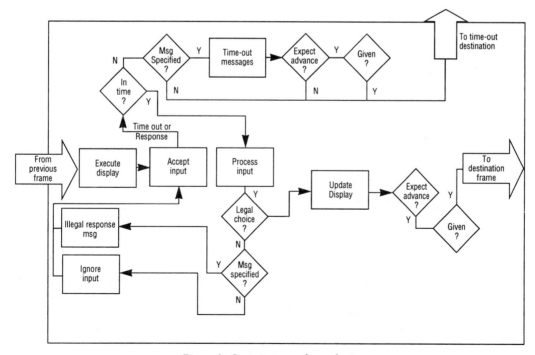

Figure 2. Generic menu frame logic.

Input confirmation. Input confirmation means that when a response is made the frame acknowledges with some visible sign that the response has been noticed. The most familiar example of an input confirmation in a mouse-operated program is that the selection of a pushbutton with the mouse is followed by the visual depression of the button. This type of confirmation is a positive sign to the student that the mouse selection has taken effect.

Input response. Input response means that the program has made a decision concerning what to do next and is in the process of doing it. An input response normally asks the student to wait ("One moment please" or "Processing your request"). If a delay of longer than two seconds is expected, the input response may tell the student what the computer is trying to do ("Preparing the Workplace simulation problem..."). The most familiar example of this kind of input response is the hourglass cursor in Windows and the clock cursor in the Apple Finder that lets you know the computer has not wandered off to oblivion when it takes a long time to respond. In fact, in order to comfort the user, both these cursor messages have motion components which confirm that the computer is not halted: The hourglass sometimes moves its sand, and the clock moves its hands.

Other than the features of input confirmation and input response which are used on menu and question frames for student comfort and assurance, the display portion of every frame type described in this chapter works the same. For the purposes of this book, we combine the display and the frame logic within the generic frames because the content of a display and the logic of a frame must in most cases interact with each other.

Accept input: The menu frame is more administrative than instructional. It is a means of turning choice and control over to the student without making a judgment about the choices. Menus may be used to give students access to a number of options:

- Content options
    - Choice of next instructional event
    - Choice of next problem
    - Choice of next topic

- Control/strategy options (locus of control)
    - Choice of instructional strategy
    - Choice between full and mixed-initiative control
    - Choice of strategy element (e.g., practice)

- Treatment/messaging options
    - Choice of representational form
    - Choice of technical language level
    - Choice of explanation level

- Optional support services
    - Access to glossary, menu, and other services

Menu choices may be expressed by the student in a number of ways: through key presses (sometimes followed by Enter, sometimes not), screen touches, or mouse clicks. Chapter 18 gives suggestions for placing menus and questions into CBI. In addition to branching after input, a menu frame can also branch after timing out. This implies that the author must specify a time-out period and a destination frame. It also suggests that a designer might provide a message to the student when a time-out branch is occurring, followed by either an automatic branch to the time-out destination or a pause for the student to confirm the action (see Figure 2). This might be considered by a designer for the opening menu of a course which was constructed as an idling loop of several menus, each of which timed out to the next in line and eventually back to the first.

Not all menus are simple in their operation. In some cases, a designer may wish to present a menu from which the student makes more than one selection at a time before proceeding to multiple sequenced destinations. To use this type of menu, the student must be able to turn selections on and off and then indicate that the selection process is finished by selecting at a separate response point, such as a "Done" button. Authoring systems do not provide this type of menu, so they must be constructed using more primitive frame types, in conjunction with system variables (which are described under the section on the calculation frame type). It is an interesting and challenging assignment to diagram the logic of this type of super-frame (or frame pattern, see Chapter 5).

Process input: When a student responds to a menu and does so earlier than the time-out (if there is one), then the frame must process the response and execute the appropriate branch to the next frame. Occasionally through accident, curiosity, or mischief, a student will respond in a way that is unexpected. The designer has the option of responding to the unexpected input with a message or simply ignoring it.

Update display and branch: Once a student has selected from the menu, the menu frame's job is to branch to a pre-planned destination frame. Therefore, every menu item must have the name of a destination frame associated with it. Before the branch to the new frame is executed, the designer may allow the student to finalize preparations before moving to the destination. Following that, the branch is executed.

Attribute summary: According to this account, the variations in the menu frame are caused by setting the following attributes (attributes identical with the presentation frame's attributes are *italicized*):

- *Erase? (yes/no)*
- *Graphic content?*
- *Time-out? (yes/no)*
- *Time-out value? (in seconds or computer clicks)*
- Time-out message? (yes/no)
- Time-out message content (message)
- Time-out advance signal expected? (yes/no)
- Time-out advance signal? (normally a list of key presses)
- *Time-out destination? (frame name)*
- Selection mode? (mouse, key press, touch, matched string)
- Input termination? (yes/no)
- Input terminator? (name of a key or keys)
- Selection names? (list of option names for internal use)
- Destinations? (list of corresponding destination frames)
- *Advance signal after selection? (yes/no)*

- Advance signal value? (name of key or keys)

- Message unexpected input? (yes/no)

- Message content? (message for unexpected)

- Message on selection? (yes/no)

- Message content on selection (message)

It should be apparent from this list and from the logic diagrammed in Figure 2 that much of a frame's logic is tied up in handling exceptions (time-outs, unexpected input, advance messages, etc.) and not in doing the main work of the frame. This is not unusual in computer-based instruction in general. One of the burdens imposed on the designer of instructional technology—forms of instruction which may be used in the absence of a human teacher—is that of anticipating and providing for the contingencies that arise during instruction due to student error or choice. The built-in logic of the frame is a great help with handling the large logical overhead due to anticipating all possible situations and providing a constructive administrative response to them.

Application to popular authoring tools
Let's correlate the logic of the generic menu frame with the structural elements of Authorware and Quest 5.0.

Authorware: Authorware's icons can reproduce the behavior of a menu frame in more than one way. The most sensible way is to use the Interaction icon, which allows branching contingent upon student selections automatically. The display of the Menu frame may be executed using a Display icon. Many of the response checking, messaging, and time-out functions are contained within the logic of the Interaction icon and can be set easily through the icon's menu structure. For those functions not supplied by the Interaction icon, additional icons placed in the flow line out of each of the branches can be used.

Quest 5.0: The generic menu frame may be built in Quest 5.0 in the same way its objects were able to construct the presentation frame. In the case of the menu frame, the display-related objects are used to build the display, and the performance object can be used to compute the branching. Some additional logic is required to provide time-out and messaging functions, but that is added as objects in the same fashion, and the resulting frame logic can look identical to the generic menu frame logic or be even more sophisticated. Both Quest and Authorware allow the designer to save frame logic creations for later re-use.

The question frame
The question frame has the most complicated logic of the generic frame types. It has the most built-in functions and must handle more instructional and administrative decisions and contingencies than any other type of frame. The logic of the generic question frame is illustrated in Figure 3 below. A question frame allows the student to make a response: true-false, multiple choice, or textual. Upon receiving the response, the frame performs several functions:

- Execute the display, if one is attached.

- Accept answer input from the student.

- Handle unexpected input.

- Judge the input.

- Give feedback based on the judgment.

- Adjust scores based on the judgment.

- Execute a time-out, if one is specified.

- Manage re-tries.

- Branch to an answer-contingent destination.

Let's describe each of these functions from Figure 3 separately. As you sort out the logic of Figure 3, you may find it helpful to look for those areas of the frame responsible for the following functions: response judging, feedback, scoring, timing, entry checking, and max re-tries checking.

The first thing apparent from Figure 3 is that some functions are carried over from the relatively uncomplicated presentation and menu frame types into the question frame type. These functions have been left in the same location as in Figures 1 and 2 to make it easier to read the logic diagrams.

The time-out function at the top of the diagram is already familiar for this reason, as are the accept input, and handle unexpected input functions. The unique functions of the question frame are those for response judging, providing feedback, keeping scores, and counting re-tries following incorrect answers.

Execute display: The display function for the question frame does not differ materially from the function described for the displays for the other frame types. However, the relationship between the display and the frame logic in a question frame is much more active than in the others, which is described next.

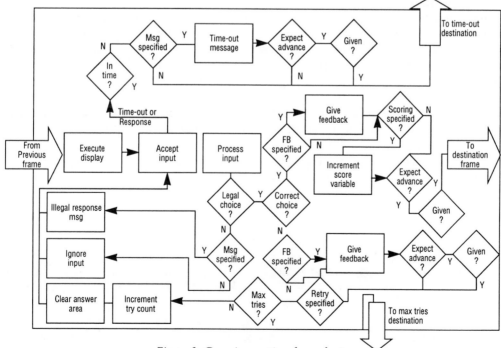

Figure 3. Generic question frame logic.

Accept input: The answer supplied to a question frame may take several forms. True-false and multiple-choice answers consist of a single symbol for the computer to process. Free-response or constructed-answer questions come in the form of extended verbal strings which must be analyzed by complex judging routines.

Whereas the presentation frame had little relationship between the display and the frame logic and the menu frame also had a relatively simple relationship, the question frame uses the display to a great extent. It must provide space on the display surface (screen, sound, etc.) to acknowledge acceptance of the input that it receives. It must also echo that input to the display surface for the student to observe, review, and possibly edit before submitting it for judging. Moreover, the answer must be left accessible to the student until a judgment has been made. If the judgment is adverse, the display must be cleared of previous answers and frame-generated messages before it can accept a new answer.

The display must in some cases provide the functions of a minor text editor and must participate heavily in the logical activities of the question frame for constructed response questions. The screen in effect becomes the construction area for the answer, and what is typed by the student does not become a real answer until the student approves it and sends it to be processed. Not only is there a close relationship between the frame logic and the display, but sometimes much display space is required for answers to be entered and manipulated. This closer relationship between display and frame logic in the question frame is important for a designer to understand, because display management becomes a design problem for complicated interactions and must be factored in early in the display design process.

Handle unexpected input: The chance of receiving an unanticipated answer is greater in a question frame than in a menu frame. An unanticipated answer may result from leaning on the keyboard accidentally or typing in a totally mistaken answer for which the designer has made no provisions. The handling of unexpected input for the objective forms of answer (true-false, multiple-choice) is done much as in the menu frame. The handling of unexpected input for textual answers is described below.

Judge the input: When objective answers are judged, a simple comparison takes place that matches the answer given with the few right and wrong answer possibilities, and there are not normally many of them. When a textual answer is judged, however, the process becomes one of the most difficult challenges that exist for authoring tools. The number of possible judgments increases geometrically with the length of the text and the number of dimensions of the answer the designer wants judged.

The process of judging textual answers is analogous to the process for judging objective answers; that is, successive matches are made against test strings until one is found that matches. The complexity of the process comes from the large number of possibilities that must be checked for (punctuation, capitalization, synonyms, word order, spaces, spelling tolerance, etc.) and the enormous number of potential matches this generates.

If no match is found, then a safety net is normally provided by the last match. It is normally designed to match anything, even meaningless garbage. This *matches anything* approach is normally the method for handling unanticipated responses. The designer attaches a message to this match which says something like, "I didn't understand that answer. Please try again." That is another way of saying, "I don't have any anticipated matches for your response. Try again."

If you were programming a CBI product without an authoring system, or even using an authoring language, the amount of code that would be required to handle textual answer judging would be immense and complex. You would only want to create it once. Answer judging using the specialized routines of the question frame logic is a great work saver. It takes a lot of data entry to create one judging sequence, even with an authoring system, but it is far better to do that work than to program from scratch.

Give feedback: When a symbol or a text string has been judged, the computer only knows whether it was acceptable or unacceptable; it does not know the specific ways in which it was good or bad. This is known only to the designer who creates the matching sequence. Therefore, in order to provide useful feedback that is related to the specific error made by a student, the designer must attach a feedback message to each matchable answer. This is part of the variable data that the designer must supply, and often this is the largest part of that body of data.

Adjust scores: Some parts of the built-in logic of the question frame are not visible to the user. Most authoring systems include a set of system variables which are automatically updated during instruction without the designer asking for it to happen. Each authoring system has its own set of variables, but there are certain common variables that systems tend to keep track of. One of these is a running score variable that keeps a tally of the number of points accumulated by a student during a test or practice exercise.

Authoring systems vary widely in the power they give the designer to compile and display scores. Some systems allow a numeric point value or weight to be attached to each matchable answer. Others simply increment their system variables and assume that each question will be of equal weight in scoring. All of the mature systems allow the designer to use something like the calculation frame (described in the next section) to change the value of system variables or to keep a separate set of user-defined variables for scoring purposes. Frequently it is also left to the calculation frame to report the score to the student. This means that a question frame sometimes implies the use of additional frame types to complete the desired interaction with the student.

Time-out: The time-out function for a question frame is identical to the time-out function for the menu frame. There is an additional use of the function, however. In addition to timing-out students who have waited too long to respond to the system, the time-out in a question frame can be used to create realistic timing pressures during the production of an answer. This is a useful capability when the performance being learned has a timing criterion. If the student does not respond to a menu in time, there is no penalty, but if the student does not respond to a question in time, it may influence the need for feedback, scoring, and the selection of the next question.

Manage re-tries: The opportunity to retry a question once it has been missed is a unique feature of a question frame. A designer can specify the number of attempts a student will be given on each question in most authoring systems. In order to make the retry possible, the designer must specify a number and may be allowed to specify the number of reduced points awarded if the answer is correct on a retry. No system allows a modified version of the question to be presented on a retry, so that requires a separate question frame.

Branch to an answer-contingent destination: After all of the other frame responses to the student's answer have been made, the question frame terminates its execution by branching to another frame. A branching destination is sometimes attached to each matchable answer of a question frame. If the designer was successful in achieving all of the feedback and correction functions necessary using the capabilities of a single question frame, then the branching destination for all answers can be to the same next frame.

The more common case, however, is that the designer does not find the question frame to provide enough options inside of itself to perform all of the remedial or extra instructional functions that are needed, so the destination attached to each matchable answer often takes the student to other frames outside of the question frame which deal with the messages and consequences of that particular answer in isolation.

Attribute summary: Just as in previous frame types, the behavior of the question frame is controlled by the setting of key attributes which enable and disable frame functions and give values to them where appropriate. The attributes for the question frame are shown below. Those which are shared with the menu frame type are *italicized*.

- *Erase? (yes/no)*
- *Graphic content?*
- Location of input echo area (coordinates)
- *Time-out? (yes/no)*
- *Time-out value? (in seconds or computer clicks)*
- Scoring consequence for time-out violation? (yes/no)
- *Time-out message? (yes/no)*
- *Time-out message content (message)*
- *Time-out advance signal expected? (yes/no)*
- *Time-out advance signal? (normally a list of key presses)*
- *Time-out destination (frame name)*
- Answer input mode? (symbol, text string)
- *Input termination? (yes/no)*
- *Input terminator? (name of a key or keys)*
- Answers to match for? (list of symbols or strings)
- Processing preferences?
- Word orderings (maintain/ignore)
- Spelling tolerance (often a percentage)
- Check for synonyms (list of synonyms)
- Punctuation (check/ignore)
- Feedback message? (one for each matched string)
- Scoring value? (for each matched string)
- Re-try possible? (yes/no)
- Maximum re-try value? (an integer)
- Maximum re-try message? (a message)
- Maximum re-try destination? (frame name)
- *Destination? (destination on match)*
- *Advance signal after feedback? (yes/no)*
- *Advance signal value? (name of key or keys)*
- *Message unexpected input? (yes/no)*
- *Message content? (a message)*

The complexity of the question frame's logic is suggested by the number of attribute values which must be specified in order to define one frame. Though question frames are laborious to define in most authoring systems, and a bit tricky, even for an experienced designer, the programming alternative is more difficult and much more expensive.

Application to popular authoring tools

Let's coordinate the question frame with the structural elements of Authorware and Quest 5.0.

Authorware: Several icons working together are required to create the generic question frame described here. That is both good news and bad news. It is bad news, because it means that authors must construct larger units of logic and keep track of the internal branching and behavior of their own constructions. It is good news because authors are not restricted to the confines of the logic for the generic question frame and are free to build more flexible patterns of frames which interact with the student in precisely the manner the designer wants.

This is an important point to note: The generic frame types described here are used for explanatory purposes only. Notice that neither of the major authoring systems being used as examples has these frame types (except for the calculation icon in Authorware). When a generic frame type is used, it in some way confines the designer, because any assemblage of basic frame functions is likely to be inadequate for some designers under certain design conditions. It will always be the case that a designer wants to do something that the generic frame does not do well or do at all. In such cases, a crisis occurs for the designer, and the frustration generated can be great if the designer has already invested much time on the assumption that an authoring tool would perform the design.

As an alternative to putting the designer in this kind of bind, the authoring tools described here have provided a flexible set of primitives and allow the designer to specify the ways in which they will be combined to produce the behavior of the finished product. This is a good example of the trade-off between productivity, power, and ease of use described in Chapter 3. Power of an authoring tool comes partly from the ability to create interesting and useful instructional effects. If a tool denies the designer an effect, it is less powerful. Ease of use and productivity, however, argues that the designer should not have to think and act like a programmer, keeping logic designs and instructional designs in mind at the same time. The decision of these two authoring systems in providing specific primitive logic elements for the construction of products can now be clearly seen in terms of this balancing of power, ease of use, and productivity.

Now back to Authorware and the generic question frame. The interaction icon is the base icon for creating questions in Authorware. Its function is to accept responses from the student, process, and branch. The display function is possible within the interaction icon, but frequently a designer will choose to create the base display for a question using the display icon or by using a residue of display created by any combination of previously-executed icons.

Time-out and retry are handled within the interaction icon, however, provisions for feedback and unexpected response handling are handled outside by attaching additional icons to the branching output of the interaction icon. Branches are contingent upon the answer matched by the interaction icon.

Quest 5.0: The flexibility of the Quest frame is that it allows the designer to create complex logic within the boundaries of one frame without being confined by the pre-set logical patterns of a generic frame type. This means that in Quest, the question frame described here may be accomplished either by constructing the exact replica of the question frame described here or by creating an architecture of separate frames designed for specialized parts of the question frame function (such as feedback).

The decision for which approach to use depends on the complexity of the designer's intentions. If, for instance, only simple feedback messages are intended following a correct or incorrect answer, those messages can be easily managed within the confines of a single Quest frame. However, if as a result of an error, the designer wishes to move the student through an involved diagnostic process, the choice remains whether to include the diagnostic routine within the frame or place it outside. If the routine is to be used repeatedly, then the natural choice would be to place it outside. If, however, it is only used once, then the designer can choose either approach.

The calculation frame

The generic calculation frame allows variable values computed during instruction to influence the course of that instruction. If a designer decides to keep track of a certain type of error, then when the number of errors made by a given student during instruction reaches a certain critical value, the calculation frame can be used to branch the student into a path of instruction which supplies extra attention, slower pace, or other specialized instructional treatment tailored to the student. This type of branching is called *conditional* branching because whether or not the branch occurs depends on certain conditions being met: a certain score on a quiz, a certain number of errors, or the value of some index or variable. Conditional branches allow the designer to take certain actions under certain conditions but not under others. This version of the calculation frame is just a simple branching mechanism; it checks a variable to see its value, and based on the value, it makes its branches.

There is a second version of the calculation frame used in some existing authoring systems. It allows the designer to incorporate into the standard logic of the authoring system a body of specially-written code produced by the designer or a programmer. This code permits the designer to extend the capabilities of the authoring system, incorporating features and patterns of behavior that might otherwise be unattainable using only the logical building blocks supplied with the system. Virtually every mature authoring system allows the designer to supplement the system's code in this way.

What does this extra code accomplish, and why is it needed? Most often extra code in a calculation frame is used for the purpose of dealing with the values of variables that are kept and updated during instruction. Every authoring system allows the designer to keep track of the value of certain variables, and most systems allow the designer to influence the value of the variables or use those values in computations prior to decision-making and branching. Normally the variables in an authoring system are of two types: (1) system variables, which are created and updated automatically during instruction, and (2) user-defined variables, which the designer may specify, but which the designer must also keep updated through special program code.

Not all of the variables provided by an authoring system are related directly to student performance or instruction. For instance, the creation of a simulation normally requires the designer to create a small family of variables, each one related to the state of some part of the simulated system. A boiler simulation may require variables for water temperature, steam pressure, and so forth. The calculation frame allows the designer to both observe and change the values of both system and user-defined variables.

There is a price for this extra capability: The designer must either learn to write the programming code of the target authoring system or hire the services of a programmer to do it. Calculation frames allow the designer to use program code for any function that can be performed with the programming language. Not only do most authoring systems supply their own unique programming language, but most also allow the designer to write independent programs outside of the authoring system and then run those programs from within the system during instruction. The outside program may be as simple as a routine to check some value in the operating system or as complicated as a complete simulation model whose computations are handled outside the authoring system but displayed using the built-in graphics and branching capabilities provided within the authoring system.

Among the actions possible using a calculation frame is to calculate the number of the destination frame to branch to. This uses both of the capabilities of the calculation frame: the conditional branching, and the ability to execute designer code. Computed branches are possible because most authoring systems assign each frame or logical primitive that is created a serial number as well as a textual name.

Computed branches have been extremely useful in the past, especially for simulation developers. It is hard to imagine how without seeing examples, so consider this one from a much earlier time when authoring tools were very primitive.

A CBI aircraft simulation found it necessary to display altitude values on the screen that matched the computed altitude values that were being constantly computed by a simple aircraft model. If the aircraft was descending, the model would compute a new altitude every few seconds, and the display had to show the altimeter needle in the new position. The challenge was to keep the needle in calibration with the computed altitude, which could either go up or down, depending on student input.

Needle motion on the display was accomplished by placing altimeter needle graphics on a family of presentation frames, each with a specific frame number (this had to be planned very carefully in order to work right). The graphic showing the needle at 100 feet was placed on frame number 100. The graphic for 200 feet was placed on frame 200, and so forth. Then a calculation frame was used to control the branching to the presentation frames, looking first at the current computed altitude and then making a conditional branch to that frame number.

This worked very effectively, and it made it unnecessary to prescribe the sequence of altitudes. It made the simulation completely responsive to the student in this dimension. Luckily, the authoring system used for this project was one that allowed frame numbers to be non-sequential and assigned by the designer. Otherwise this approach would not have worked. We would also emphasize that this was a technique used years ago in the infancy of authoring systems. Today some authoring systems have new capabilities that make this approach unnecessary. As you will see in Chapter 6, even these new capabilities are about to be challenged by a newer generation of authoring tools that will make this approach obsolete and handle such things as indicator displays automatically.

Application to popular authoring tools

Let's coordinate the calculation frame with the structural elements of Authorware and Quest 5.0.

Authorware: Authorware supplies two icon types which together account for the features of the calculation frame: the decision icon and the calculation icon.

The decision icon can examine the value of a variable (which is chosen by the designer) and branch depending on the value of that variable. The value must be greater than one, and there must be branches for all of the possible values of the variable. This is a very useful icon. The calculation icon allows the designer to observe a variable value, set it, make a calculation using it, or take conditional action based on its value. Together, these two icons are capable of providing both conditional branching and variable management.

In addition to these capabilities, additional conditional branching is provided by the perpetual feature of Authorware. A *perpetual* is an icon which continues to exist in the memory of computer even after it has finished executing. It is a type of persistent object at run-time. Because it remains an active object, it can continue to monitor the keypresses and other actions of the student even after other icons have started to execute, monitoring the input for a particular action and resuming execution as an icon when it sees the action it is looking for. Using this feature, a designer can create branches at any time to glossaries, lesson menus, and other auxiliary functions quite easily. The perpetual is a valuable feature for subroutining, a frame pattern that is described in the next chapter.

Quest 5.0: Quest contains several tools the author can use for calculation frame features: C Coach, Watch/Wait-for objects, concurrent modules, and C code.

The C Coach tool permits the author to create and initialize local variables which can be updated later, during instruction. The update is accomplished by placing C code in the object list of the frame. Since this object list is the major factor in the order of frame execution, it executes the C code in its proper order, as if it were an object. Across frames, global variables can be declared for an entire instructional product.

Watch/Wait-for objects within a frame constantly watch for some event to occur. The event may be a specific key press, a message from another frame, a Windows message, the expiration of a time limit, a specific menu selection, or an object event, such as the movement of the mouse over the surface of a button or other object. When the watched-for event occurs, the Watch/Wait-for object can cause an appropriate contingent action to be executed, for instance, causing a video play to be halted. Watch/Wait-for objects are an example of a perpetual object, since they continue to exist and to execute once they have been created by the computer.

Concurrent modules in Quest permit the author to cause two objects to be in execution at the same time. This allows the author to not only execute a simulation model but to *observe* the execution from another module running at the same time, watching for specific events to occur which act as the trigger for other instructional actions such as coaching or feedback. Objects in a concurrent module can provide data gathering, navigation, continual audio or video play, tracking of event records, and the manipulation of variables.

As mentioned above, C Coach permits the author to add standard C code to a frame's object list. Quest supports communication between Windows and Quest frames as well.

Caveat

This completes the final round of comparison between the generic frame types and two popular authoring systems. We stress that this is not intended as a review or comparison of the authoring systems but rather an attempt to illustrate the concept of generic frame types and how they can be created by two widely-used, mature authoring tools. Both Authorware and Quest 5.0 are much more powerful than the previous sections suggest. They are both highly developed authoring tools, and they both possess capabilities not even hinted at in this chapter. This chapter is specifically focused for the reader who is trying to become familiar with frame-based authoring system principles and structure, and so its coverage is basic. For an exhaustive review of these authoring systems, we recommend the books and articles referenced at the end of this chapter and the technical manuals for the authoring systems themselves.

Examples

The discussion to this point has identified the features of four generic frame types. This section will provide examples of how these underlying frame types are used in a variety of settings and for a variety of purposes and how that is accomplished by adjusting the values that are given to the frame object attributes.

Presentation frame examples

The set of examples below shows how a presentation frame object can be suited to different purposes by giving its variables different values. Tables 1 through 3 describe three commonly-used configurations of the presentation frame.

Table 1. Presentation frame example #1.

Description: Typical page-turning presentation frame.	
Prior frames in sequence: Very likely a frame just like this one: one of a string of page-turning presentation frames.	
Attribute Settings:	
Erase?	Yes
Area to erase?	Whole screen
Display event list?	Any combination of graphic, audio, or video
Time-out?	No
Time-out value?	N/A
Advance expected?	Yes
Advance identity?	ENTER key
Time-out destination?	N/A
Advance destination?	The next presentation frame in the page-turning sequence.
Logical sequence:	
The display is executed, whatever it contains; no timer is set; the keyboard is monitored for any press of the Enter key.	
Surface appearance:	
The screen clears of its former contents before displaying a completely new screen full of graphics, text, and video. The new screen probably has a different layout and framing than the old screen. (If this were not so, then only part of the old screen would have been replaced.) At the lower right corner of the screen, a symbol or displayed text indicates that the student may press Enter. Nothing happens until the key is pressed.	
Points of interest:	
This is page-turning. The logic of the frame punctuates the surface of the instruction. Page-turning is unavoidable in some instances. Wherever possible, it should be avoided, because it is annoying to the student to have to re-orient to the layout and framing of the computer screen each time a new element of message is presented.	

Table 2. Presentation frame example #2.

Description: A timed fall-through display-building sequence. The student will be given a special "freeze" key which can pause the build-up at any moment to give the student a chance to study the display before going ahead. The content of this building sequence may be anything from the steps in folding an origami figure to the steps in photosynthesis to the steps in the construction of one of the pyramids from the inside out.

Prior frames in sequence: A frame much like this one, which adds its own element to the build-up of the display.

Attribute Settings:	
Erase?	No
Area to erase?	N/A
Display event list?	One element of a graphic. This element was originally a part of a larger graphic unit, such as a complete diagram of the inside of the heart. This element has been separated from the other elements with which it was originally created so that it can be added incrementally as part of a sequence of frames that will build up the entire graphic of the heart interior.
Time-out?	Yes
Time-out value?	Three to five seconds. (There is no absolute right value to select for this purpose. Timing depends on the speed with which the audience will be able to recognize the addition and the complexity of the addition and the entire graphic.)
Advance expected?	Yes
Advance identity?	Any key which you wish to use as a "freeze" key; perhaps the space bar.
Time-out destination?	To the next presentation frame in this building sequence.
Advance destination?	To a pause frame whose function it is to wait until the student signals readiness to proceed with the build-up sequence.

Logical sequence:

No erase occurs; the display is executed, placing only a portion of a graphic on the screen, on top of other graphic objects which have already been deposited there; the timer is set, and a counter begins to monitor the passing of time; the keyboard is monitored for any press of the "freeze" key; when it is pressed, it branches to the advance destination; when it is not pressed before the time-out elapses, the branch is to the time-out destination.

Surface appearance:

This type of frame can have literally thousands of looks. The instructor has in this case decided to present a complex graphic in a way that doesn't seem complex. The first parts of the graphic appear in earlier steps of the unfolding graphic sequence. Each one adds slightly to what was already there, either adding detail or adding a new part to the graphic.

Points of interest:

Building the graphic step-by-step with the opportunity for the student to pause and examine the new additions gives the separate elements of a complicated graphic a kind of unity at a lower psychological cost to the student and may be a means of enhancing student interest and understanding.

Table 3: Presentation frame example #3.

Description: Use of a presentation frame to supply a display during a video-based simulation. Assume that the setting for this presentation frame is within a simulation on interpersonal skills. The student has made a choice of action and is about to see the result of the action, which is a particular video sequence which shows the other person's reaction to the student's choice. Remember that which presentation frame to use may be either a destination branch from a question frame or a computed branch from a calculation frame. What matters is not how the student got here but what the presentation frame does as its part of the simulation.	
Prior frames in sequence: The screen may have a general framing which is used for the simulation, or there may be areas of the screen already designated for special purposes, one of them being the presentation of the video this presentation frame will present. The use of screen real-estate is the subject of Chapter 18.	

Attribute Settings:	
Erase?	No. (Prior presentation frames used for this same purpose leave no video residue on the screen, so the area devoted to video plays is now empty.)
Area to erase?	N/A
Display event list?	Play one video sequence. This seems too simple, doesn't it. Actually, it *is* simple. This is because video playing these days has been made easy by special routines for video play which take care of all of the functions the designer used to have to do by hand. These functions include putting up video play controls to give the student control over the playing of the video as well as the program routines to actually control the video in response to the student's commands. The video capabilities of authoring systems aren't what they used to be, and *vive la difference*.
Time-out?	No. The student will control the movement from the frame by dismissing the video once the student has seen all that he or she wants of it.
Time-out value?	N/A
Advance expected?	Yes
Advance identity?	Whatever the designer has decided to use for advances after video plays. This may be as automatic as using the "stop" control to dismiss the video or may involve pressing a key or clicking a window closed. Designer's choice.
Time-out destination?	N/A
Advance destination?	The advance destination may be any of several possibilities, depending on how the student got to the presentation frame in the first place. If the branch was a hard-coded destination branch, the branch away from the presentation frame is likely to also be a hard-coded destination branch to either a menu or another question frame (to make another response). If, however, the branch to the presentation frame was a computed branch, then the branch from the presentation frame is likely to be a return branch that takes it back to where it came from in the first place. Major authoring systems all have this return branch option, and it is a standard feature of the subroutining pattern of frames described in Chapter 5.

(Continued)

Table 3: Presentation frame example #3 (continued).

Logical sequence:
The logical sequence for this frame is simple: Do not erase; play the video sequence and wait for the special video controls that are a part of the video play routine to be used by the student. Wait for the appointed signal that the play is finished; branch to either the advance destination frame or back to the original point of control.

Surface appearance:
The student observes the video's appearance, plays it and replays it as much as desired, and then dismisses it using the appropriate control.

Points of interest:
The presentation frame in this case does not punctuate the surface. Because there are areas of the screen in which things like video plays are expected to happen, the video in this presentation frame just seems to appear there and then vanish when dismissed. Instead of seeming like a page-turning (which in actuality this could be), the presentation frame fits in naturally as part of a larger instructional message environment which has many informational windows and conventions for delivering instruction. It is this larger frame of instruction that the student notices, not the presentation frame itself. Note the great contrast between this feel and the feel created by obvious page-turning.

Menu frame examples

The examples in tables 4 through 8 show you the variety of ways the menu frame appears in instructional events. Notice that the list of values to be specified gets a lot longer for the menu frame. It will be even longer than this for the question frame. Notice also that many of the values like "Erase?" are carried over from the presentation frame as practical necessities.

Table 4. Menu frame example #1.

Description: A menu frame used for content selection.	
Prior frames in sequence: The prior frames to this one do not matter. The Menu frame here serves as a kind of break point from whatever went on before it.	
Attribute Settings:	
Erase?	Yes
Area to erase?	Whole screen erase is often used, but some menus are placed on top of an area of the screen cleared specially for the purpose or within a window opened just for the menu to be placed in. In this case, we will assume that the designer has cleared a section of the screen only and that the menu will appear there. (Note: It is possible also to leave a menu on the screen at all times during instruction. The designer must simply designate an area of the screen to be used for the menu purpose and defend that area against anything else overwriting or clearing the area.)
Display event list?	Display menu items and instruction prompt in cleared area.
Time-out?	No
Time-out value?	N/A
Time-out message?	N/A

(Continued)

Table 4. Menu frame example #1 (continued).

Message content?	N/A
Time-out advance?	N/A
T-O advance signal?	N/A
Time-out destination?	N/A
Selection mode?	Mouse click
Input termination?	None after mouse click
Input terminator?	N/A
Selection names?	Photosynthesis Demonstration
	ADP-ATP Cycle Demonstration
	Plant Metabolism Demonstration
Destinations?	Names of the frames which correspond to the three choices listed above
Advance signal after select?	No
Advance signal identity?	N/A
Message unexpected input?	No
Unexpected input message content?	N/A
Message on item selection?	No
Message content on item selection?	N/A

Logical sequence:
The display is executed after a partial screen erase; no timer is set; the frame waits until a mouse click is detected in one of its selection areas; illegal clicks are ignored; on detecting a legal click, the frame branches immediately to the destination frame associated with the clicked item.

Surface appearance:
The area of the screen devoted to menus erases whatever was occupying its space, and a list of menu items appears with a direction prompt and areas for mouse selection. Immediately after a mouse click in one of the selection areas, the screen changes to accommodate the display of the selected content.

Points of interest:
A very straightforward menu. Notice that it was a textual list menu. It could as easily have been a graphic item menu and may not have looked like a menu at all, such as in the next example.

Table 5. Menu frame example #2.

Description: A menu frame used a part of a zoom-in, zoom-out exploration structure. For this example, assume that the subject-matter is a large, multi-layered graphic model of a natural ecosystem you wish the student to understand at several levels. You provide an initial view of the whole system and then give the student the ability to zoom in on parts of the system. At each level of zoom, the student finds there is another layer of detail accessible by zooming in yet closer.

Prior frames in sequence: The frames in this complete zoom-in structure will be arranged like tree branches, tree roots, or a pyramid of menu frames. The present frame is just one element of that whole structure, arranged somewhere within the pyramid. The Menu Tree frame pattern is described in more detail in Chapter 5.

Attribute Settings:	
Erase?	Yes
Area to erase?	Whole screen in this case, but an alternative is described below.
Display event list?	Display the graphic of the location which has been zoomed to (full screen).
Time-out?	No
Time-out value?	N/A
Time-out message?	N/A
Message content?	N/A
Time-out advance?	N/A
T-O advance signal?	N/A
Time-out destination?	N/A
Selection mode?	Mouse click on graphic display
Input termination?	No
Input terminator?	N/A
Selection names?	At each menu frame, the content of the displayed graphic determines the number, location, and identity of the selection areas. This is a graphical menu and does not present its options as a list of textual items. Instead, the student is in effect moving through a virtual conceptual space by selecting an element off the displayed graphic to examine up close and in more detail.
Destinations?	The destination for each selectable area is another menu frame just like this one, with its own unique display and its own areas to zoom in to.
Advance signal after select?	No
Advance signal identity?	N/A
Message unexpected input?	Ignore unexpected input
Unexpected input message content?	N/A
Message on item selection?	N/A
Message content on item selection?	N/A

(Continued)

Table 5. Menu frame example #2 (continued).

Logical sequence:
The display for this frame is executed; no timer is set; the frame waits for a legal mouse click to be detected; illegal clicks are ignored; on detection of a legal click, the frame branches immediately to the destination frame associated with the selected area.

Surface appearance:
It appears to the student that he or she is zooming around a conceptual system, examining details as desired by zooming in to any visible part of the system which will respond to a mouse click. This is an exploration. It could be the exploration of a cave, an archaeological dig, the interior of a famous landmark, or an entire country. Though the description here has the screen erase completely as a new zoom-in is executed, alternatively, locations zoomed to could be presented without total screen erasure. Each new location could instead be placed within a pop-up window which was superimposed on the face of the already-visible display, and not fully covering it. In this way, zooming in to a location would not totally eradicate the traces of the location which was zoomed from, keeping it visible around the fringes of the display. This type of screen handling would provide additional orientation cues for the student, making it less likely he or she would become lost in a maze of locations.

Points of interest:
This menu frame does not feel like a menu. Its underlying structure is identical with the first example, which was plainly a list-form content menu. This menu is also a content menu, allowing the student to obtain specific categorized information on demand, but it is a graphic menu and uses a much different visual and interactive metaphor. This is a good example of how similar underlying structures can provide widely varying surface experiences for the student.

Table 6. Menu frame example #3.

Description: A multiple-selection menu. This menu will allow the student to select more than one item from the menu before moving to the items themselves, which will occur in the order the items were chosen.
Prior frames in sequence: The prior frames in this sequence do not matter, because the menu frame here serves as a break point from what has gone on before.

Attribute Settings:	
Erase?	In this case, yes. However, Example #1 in Table 4 shows that this is not essential.
Area to erase?	Whole screen
Display event list?	In this case, the subject of the instruction is jungle animals, and the designer wishes to have a video image of the biome in which the animals live visible behind the menu items, which will be textual in nature. Therefore, the display event list includes: — Display video backdrop for biome — Superimpose select areas as graphic — Superimpose text items on areas — Place "Done" button on menu
Time-out?	No
Time-out value?	N/A
Time-out message?	N/A

(Continued)

Table 6. Menu frame example #3 (continued).

Message content?	N/A
Time-out advance?	N/A
T-O advance signal?	N/A
Time-out destination?	N/A
Selection mode?	Mouse click
Input termination?	Yes. The "Done" button at the bottom of the menu screen is the student's signal that selecting is finished.
Input terminator?	"Done" button click.
Selection names?	A list of the names of the animals living within this biome.
Destinations?	A corresponding list of frame names that begin the presentations for each of the animals on the menu.
Advance signal after select?	N/A
Advance signal identity?	N/A
Message unexpected input?	No
Unexpected input message content?	N/A
Message on item selection?	N/A
Message content on item selection?	N/A

Logical sequence:

The display is executed; no timer is set; the frame waits for a legal mouse selection to be detected; illegal clicks are ignored; on detection of a legal click, the frame records or sends to a calculation frame the identity of the destination frame related to the selection. The calculation frame stores these destinations in order, and after the selection is complete, as indicated by a click on the "Done" button, the calculation frame is given control and executes the branches as a sequence of subroutine calls (with return to the calculation frame) until all have been executed.

Surface appearance:

The video backdrop appears (if you have a fast machine; otherwise, it slowly appears). The menu selection areas appear over the face of the video image, and the text appears on top of the selection areas at the same time. When the student selects one of the areas, the screen acknowledges it and marks the selection as having been made. An second selection of the same item de-selects it. When selections are complete and the student clicks the "Done" button, the presentation related to the first selection begins, followed in order by the rest.

Points of interest:

The use of the video background is a fairly typical treatment of menus in multimedia presentations. The impulse is normally to supply as much visual richness and incidental material as possible. There is no reason to present an opaque background to menus when you can show something of interest instead which may have incidental learning or interest value. The multiple selection feature is used here. Most authoring systems do not contain this capability as a simple connection of a few frame elements. Instead, this pattern is most often accomplished as a construction of several frames which use user-defined variables to record choices. Notice that the time-out feature has not been used yet in any of the examples, nor has the illegal entry feature. These are specialized features which are used infrequently but which are needed badly when they are needed. You will see a use of the time-out feature for a menu in a later example.

Table 7. Menu frame example #4.

Description: Use of a menu to allow the student to tailor the instructional strategy.	
Prior frames in sequence: This frame would normally be executed in one of two contexts: (1) near the beginning of an instructional presentation as an offered option to the student, or (2) at the student's bidding through the use of a *lesson options* feature which allows the student to change instructional parameters at will.	
Attribute Settings:	
Erase?	Not necessary. In this case, a window simply appears over the top of the existing instructional display. The window will disappear when the student's setting of values is completed.
Area to erase?	N/A
Display event list?	Display window containing strategy-tailoring options.
Time-out?	No
Time-out value?	N/A
Time-out message?	No
Message content?	N/A
Time-out advance?	N/A
T-O advance signal?	N/A
Time-out destination?	N/A
Selection mode?	Mouse click. Touch and keyboard are not used in these examples because of their relatively lower rate of use in current systems. Keyboard, which was once the only means of entry, has been eliminated as much as possible by most designers (unless it is specifically required by the skill being learned) because it introduces a new mode of control which is more prone to errors and which is not a skill universally held by students. Some students have real difficulty typing and find that it slows them down considerably. Touch screens are costly compared to the mouse, have specialized technology which is comparatively fragile, and add complexity to an already complex instructional station, therefore, their use is not as widespread as mouse control.
Input termination?	No
Input terminator?	N/A
Selection names?	The names of the controls the designer wishes to make available to students. This may include controls over the pace of presentation, the type of explanations given, the degree of interactivity, the level of the presentation (technical, etc.), the completeness of the instruction (give demonstrations?), the type of practice given, or the extent or difficulty of practice. There are many other strategic variables that can be given over to student control. This list is only suggestive. For more detail, see Chapters 8 and 9 which discuss instructional strategy.

(Continued)

Table 7. Menu frame example #4 (continued).

Destinations?	The destination frames from this menu frame will not be directly to instructional presentations or interactions, but will be to a calculation frame. This frame will record the student's choices as variable settings within the system. When instruction is presented, the logic of the instruction will contain embedded calculation frames which read the settings of the variables the student has made and select subsequent frames based on their values, tailoring the message to the student's request. This is not an often-used technique because frame-based authoring systems make it hard to implement, and because the cost of this type of logical structure is higher than the usual cost and more complicated to design for and produce. The original concept of CBI included instruction adaptable to the individual student (either at the student's request or by computation of the student's needs). This is an example of a vision of instruction which is not yet practical because of the state of the tools we use. This is an area where we need to consider tool improvements.
Advance signal after select?	Yes. This is a multiple-selection menu like Example #3 (Table 6), and the menu will not disappear until some termination signal is given by the user to signal that choosing is finished.
Advance identity?	Probably a "Done" or an "OK" button at the bottom of the menu.
Message unexpected input?	No
Unexpected input message content?	N/A
Message on item selection?	No
Message content on item selection?	N/A

Logical sequence:

The logical sequence of this frame is identical to that of Example #3 (Table 6). The only differences between these two frames is surface.

Surface appearance:

The menu presented in this example is a textual menu, rather than the more graphic menu used in Example #3 (Table 6).

Points of interest:

The important point here made is that menus are not just a means of branching to other frames for immediate execution. Menu choices can be stacked for later execution (Example #3, Table 6) or be used during instruction to change variable values which then influence the future execution of the instruction.

Table 8. Menu frame example #5.

Description: A menu frame acting as part of a timed cycling menu system, such as one that might be used at a demonstration, in a consumer kiosk, or at an exhibition. This kind of menu is often used because it can contain more menu items than can be fit onto one screen. It is also used as a means of offering to a diverse audience a multi-sectioned menu with specialized sub-menus of interest to different parts of the audience.

Prior frames in sequence: The prior frames to this one do not matter. The cycle of menu frames of which this menu frame is one serves as a kind of centralized point to which all menu selections return. Most likely, this menu frame cycle is the first thing in the program. Each menu frame in the cycle times out to the next menu frame in the cycle and so forth back to the first one in the cycle until a selection is made. When the selection is executed, the branch returns the user to the menu cycle for further selections. The program runs in this cyclic path forever, until it is terminated.

Attribute Settings:	
Erase?	Yes
Area to erase?	Whole screen
Display event list?	Display Menu, Part 1.
Time-out?	Yes
Time-out value?	8 seconds (designer's choice)
Time-out message?	None. Simply branch to the next menu frame in the cycle.
Message content?	N/A
Time-out advance?	None
T-O advance signal?	N/A
Time-out destination?	Menu, Part 2
Selection mode?	Mouse click
Input termination?	None after mouse click
Input terminator?	N/A
Selection names?	The names of the selections for this part of the menu.
Destinations?	The destinations related to each of the selections.
Advance signal after select?	No
Advance signal identity?	N/A
Message unexpected input?	No
Unexpected input message content?	N/A
Message on item selection?	N/A
Message content on item selection?	N/A

Logical sequence:

The menu display, consisting of a background and the menu items (which may be either textual or graphic), is executed after a complete screen erase; the timer is set to 8 seconds and begins to click off the seconds; the frame waits until a mouse click is detected in one of its selection areas; illegal clicks are ignored; on detecting a legal click, the frame branches immediately to the destination frame associated with the clicked item; if the time-out goal is reached before there is a legal selection, the branch to the next menu frame in the cycle is executed. It is identical to this frame except that it has a different display, different menu items to select, and a different set of destinations.

(Continued)

Table 8. Menu frame example #5 (continued).

Surface appearance:
The screen erases and the new menu appears. No indication of timing is evident, but if there is no selection made within 8 seconds, the screen erases and presents a new menu (the next one in the cycle). Immediately after a mouse click on one of the legal selection areas, the screen changes to begin display of the selected content.
Points of interest:
A very straightforward menu. Notice that it was a textual list menu. It could as easily have been a graphic item menu and may not have looked like a menu at all, such as in the next example.

Question frame examples

The examples in Tables 9 and 10 show the variety of ways the question frame appears in instructional events. The list of values to be specified for a question frame is the longest of all of the frames. That is because the question frame carries out more functions.

Table 9. Question frame example #1.

Description: A standard textual question frame, like any you might encounter during a quiz or a verbal interaction embedded within a tutorial.	
Prior frames in sequence: The prior frames in the sequence are not important in this case, since this frame is assumed to be an isolated and independent question as might be drawn at random from a pool of question frames during a quiz. An example of the use setting for this frame can be found in the Selected Question frame pattern described in Chapter 5.	
Attribute Settings:	
Erase?	Yes
Area to erase?	Whole screen
Display event list?	Display the text of the question (in this case a constructed response or textual answer question).
Time-out?	Designer's choice. In this example there is no time-out.
Time-out value?	N/A
Time-out message?	No
Message content?	N/A
Time-out advance?	N/A
T-O advance signal?	N/A
Time-out destination	N/A
Answer input mode?	Textual
Input termination?	Yes
Input terminator?	"Done" button on the question screen which is used after the student has edited the answer to some desired state. (Note: If the Enter key is used as the input terminator, then that restricts the use of the Enter key while the student is editing the response. It is better to avoid using the Enter key, unless the answer is not to be edited.

(Continued)

Table 9. Question frame example #1 (continued).

Processing type	Text matching—keyword.
Observe word order?	No. Use keyword matching only. This means that the frame will look only for certain keywords in the student's answer. The words may appear in any order and be acceptable, but all keywords must appear in the answer at least once. You can see that this is a difficult answer processing form to control and that it is difficult to judge with exactness the content of a student's answer when you are restricted to using statistical and loosely coupled techniques to do so.
Spelling tolerance?	No tolerance—exact match required.
Use synonym list?	No synonyms, although this is a designer's choice and depends on the nature of the judgment. If this were instruction on exact terminology, then synonyms might not be appropriate. Elsewhere, it probably is, but once again, you see the added designer effort required to specify each acceptable synonym for this particular question.
Name of synonym list?	N/A
Observe punctuation?	No. Punctuation is not important in this answer. Though it might be for a question on grammar or punctuation.
Provide feedback?	Yes
Feedback per answer?	A list would have to be supplied here of the anticipated answers and the feedback message attached to each. It can become tedious work, but using a frame to create this effect is far better than programming each question by hand.
Scoring per answer?	A list would have to be supplied here of the anticipated answers and the scoring value to be added or subtracted for each answer.
Retry possible?	Yes
Max retry value?	3
Max retry message?	"Sorry. You did not answer correctly in three tries. Please contact the instructor."
Max retry destination?	The "contact instructor" frame, a special frame that will not unlock the presentation until an instructor enters a code. This ensures that the instructor will be called and notice the student's need.
Answer destinations?	A list of acceptable answers must be provided, with a destination branch for each. The branches may be all to the same destination frame, but if feedback is not provided within the confines of this frame, the destinations will most likely be to a frame outside which can give a more extensive feedback and interaction for the specific answer.

(Continued)

Table 9. Question frame example #1 (continued).

Advance signal after feedback?	Yes. This allows the student to read the feedback carefully before moving ahead—either to retry the answer or to an outside destination frame, whichever the designer has specified.
Advance signal value?	Mouse click on "Done" button.
Message unexpected input?	Yes. In this case, unexpected input means any answer that does not match any of the recognized answers listed and given to the frame for judging. In the case of an unexpected answer, you want to be able to say something to the student to the effect that they need to try the answer again.
Unexpected input message content?	"I don't recognize that answer. Please enter your answer again."
Message on selection?	No. There are no selections in this frame, since the answer is textual.
Message content on selection?	N/A

Logical sequence:

The display clears and the new display containing the question is placed on the screen; no timer is set; the input area is placed on the screen, ready to receive the student's answer; the student enters an answer, including editing it, and selects the "Done" button; the answer processor compares the words in the student's answer with a list of keywords supplied to the frame by the designer; it does not judge the order of the keywords nor look for synonyms nor punctuation, but it looks only for the presence of all keywords in the answer with exactly correct spelling; the judging routine returns the identity of the answer matched; the frame provides the feedback message matched with the answer and if it is an incorrect answer, offers the student another attempt to answer; the student's score is adjusted according to the answer matched; if the answer is correct, the correct feedback message is given and the frame waits for an advance signal to move to the associated destination frame; if the correct answer is not given after the maximum retry count is reached, the last feedback message is given, followed by a "call instructor" message.

Surface appearance:

The appearance of this frame is much like a computerized version of the constructed-response test questions we are all used to encountering in paper form. The display appears, showing the student the question and an answer box is placed on the screen with a cursor in it, ready to accept an answer. As answers are attempted and the student submits them using the "Done" button, messages appear in designated areas of the screen which give feedback and direct further attempts toward a correct answer. When the correct answer is given, a feedback message is presented, and the display changes to the next quiz item.

Points of interest:

It is a complicated process just to get one verbal question onto the display and accept an answer, judge it, and give feedback before branching. Even after all of the detail described here has been given, there are a few omissions which have been made intentionally to simplify the example. Yet without the information detailed here, how can the computer know how to act in response to the student under all conditions?

Table 10. Question frame example #2.

Description: A question frame used as part of a simulation (that is, to process a non-verbal answer to a non-verbal question).	
Prior frame(s) in sequence: Prior to the appearance of this frame, a simulation has been in process for some time. The student has been given a problem to solve within a simulated environment. The environment in this case is not a free-play environment but simulates a path of behavior which, if the student is responding correctly, will carry the problem to successful completion. (See Chapter 16 for a description of both path and free-play, or model, simulations). The current frame is one of the steps along that path. Its job is to accept one action from the student (and it knows what action to expect at this point), and then either advance the student along the path by displaying accurate consequences to the student, or to halt the simulation momentarily to inform the student of an error and suggest appropriate actions to take to resume movement along the correct-response path.	

Attribute Settings:	
Erase?	No. The display that has been built-up by this point represents the result of all of the student's correct answers to this point. In effect, it has created the set of conditions and indications to which the student is now to respond. The student's *question* at this point is to read the indications, decide what the correct action is at this point, and take that action by mouse clicking some control or response area that is visible on the screen. Previous correct answers have created the *question* at this point—the context for a performance rather than a verbal answer. To erase the screen at this point would be like erasing the question.
Area to erase?	N/A
Display event list?	No new additions to the display. The question is in the residue already on the screen.
Time-out?	Time out should be set only if the appropriate action at this point is a timed action. In this example, no timing is set.
Time-out value?	N/A
Time-out message?	N/A
Message content?	N/A
Time-out advance?	N/A
T-O advance signal?	N/A
Time-out destination	N/A
Answer input mode?	Mouse click on selection area. Areas of the screen have been designated which represent actions the student can take at this point. A selection area positioned over a switch or over a facial expression (indicating the correct way to address a customer in the simulation) represent answers the student can give. One will turn a switch on, and the other will cause the customer to hear a particular message.
Input termination?	None
Input terminator?	N/A

(Continued)

Table 10. Question frame example #2 (continued).

Processing type?	Selection area. This type of processing is the easiest. It is identical to the processing of a multiple-choice or true-false question. Mechanically, it is like processing a menu choice.
Observe word order?	N/A
Spelling tolerance?	N/A
Use synonym list?	No
Name of synonym list?	N/A
Observe punctuation?	No
Provide feedback?	No feedback. The response to the student in both correct and incorrect answer situations will be handled by frames outside this question frame.
Feedback per answer?	N/A
Scoring per answer?	Scoring can be handled either within the frame (one point for each correct response) or in a manner more global (such as keeping track of the steps correctly taken using a calculation frame). In this case, scoring will not be handled within the frame: designer's choice.
Retry possible?	No
Max retry value?	N/A
Max retry message?	N/A
Max retry destination?	N/A
Answer destinations?	A list must be supplied for each selection area designating the destination frame for each. Normally, in this type of simulation, the correct answer will go to one frame, and all of the incorrect answers will go to another. The correct answer destination is normally a presentation frame which does no more than add to or modify the display to show the results of the student's correct answer (graphically or in video). The incorrect response destinations, on the other hand, are normally verbal messages which tell the student an error has been made, informing what the correct response is at this point, and then branching (after a signal from the student) back to the original question frame to try the correct answer this time. In some cases, the designer may wish to tailor the feedback message linked to each correct response separately. This allows you to say such clever things to the student as, "You have just blown up the factory by waiting too long to make adjustments to the steam pressure. Try again."
Advance signal after feedback?	Normally, you would say "Yes" here. This gives the student a chance to read the message and gives you the ability to clean the message off the screen when the feedback advance signal is given.
Advance signal value?	Usually a "Done" button.
Message unexpected input?	No

(Continued)

Table 10. Question frame example #2 (continued).

Unexpected input message content?	N/A
Message on selection?	No
Message content on selection?	N/A
Logical sequence:	
No display changes are made; the frame begins to look for a mouse click in one of the designated selection areas; no timer is set; when a legal mouse click is detected, the branching routine branches to the destination frame linked with the selection area.	
Surface appearance:	
The student does not perceive that the question frame has begun to operate. All he or she sees is a display slightly modified following the last correct response to reflect the new state of the simulation. Now the student must perceive that another action is appropriate and take that action. When it happens, the student either sees the correct-action result (without any verbiage), or sees an error message directing the correct action. Following a confirmation of the message by the student, the screen returns to looking as it did at the beginning of the question, ready for a new response from the student.	
Points of interest:	
This relatively simple construction can be used to create interesting and highly interactive simulation problems and scenarios which are very powerful in the early stages of training, the period where students normally benefit from a higher degree of structure.	

Calculation frame examples

No examples of calculation frames are provided here. In Chapter 5, which discusses frame patterns, several pattern types will be shown which involve calculation frames, and you will see that calculation frames seldom act alone but are always part of larger frame patterns. You will see them there as the main moving force behind the more powerful and flexible frame patterns.

Conclusion

The frame examples provided in this chapter demonstrate the great variety of textures in screen and interaction events that can be created using just a small number of underlying frame types (or logic structures) with their controlling attribute values and surface features configured differently. Another reason we have given a large number of examples is to supply plenty of material for the study of the inner workings of the frame. Understanding this basic building block is important for those who want to use frame-based authoring tools. One thing that should be most evident from these examples is the effect of both the surface and the underlying logical context of the frame on how it will appear and act.

However, it is not what the frame types can do that should dictate a designer's choices; it is what the designer desires to do that should determine what type of frame and what type of tool will be used. The tool (in this case, available frame types) should not be allowed to constrain the designer in what can or cannot be done. Tools must be used which can execute the designer's plans, and if tools can't be found that do what the designer wants, then new tools must be created.

Self-directed activities

- Design the *super frame* capable of carrying out any instructionally-relevant action. Is it possible? If so, what are its shortcomings?

- Select one of the basic frame types (presentation, menu, or question) and invent as many different surface appearances of it as you can.

- Design a complex surface action that you have seen in an existing CBI product or that you think might be an interesting new technique. Try to achieve the effect using the presentation, menu, and question frame types. Once you have done that, try to achieve the same effect using calculation frames. In what ways does the use of calculation frames simplify things? In what ways does it complicate things?

- Analyze the logic of an existing CBI product in terms of frames, whether the product was created using frames or not. What features of the product can be accounted for by creative uses of the basic frame types and which cannot?

Further reading

Authorware reference manual. (1993). San Fransisco, CA: Macromedia, Inc.

Milheim, W. D. (Ed.). (1994). *Authoring-systems software for computer-based training.* Englewood Cliffs, NJ: Educational Technology Publications.

Quest 5.0 for Windows reference manual. (1995). Salt Lake City, UT: Allen Communication, Inc.

5

FRAME PATTERNS

Chapter Objectives:

1. *Given a surface effect desired as part of a CBI product, suggest how one or more of the eleven basic patterns described in this chapter can be used to produce the effect or how patterns can be combined to achieve it.*

2. *Describe how a pattern can be modified or extended to create a new pattern which meets a given surface requirement.*

3. *Identify structures which are possible with frame-based authoring tools and limitations which can be overcome through the use of persistent run-time objects.*

4. *Describe how frame patterns might be useful as notions of CBI evolve and new forms of logic and surface effect become more important.*

Introduction

Before beginning, let's place things in perspective. In Chapter 3 we described the common element of CBI authoring tools—the object. In Chapter 4 we described a basic object for authors—the frame—used by the current generation of authoring tools to simplify the work of authoring and increase productivity. In this chapter we want to show how combinations of frames work together to create larger instructional objects which have real applications during instruction.

Certain patterns of frame arrangement tend to be repeated frequently in CBI products. These patterns become, as it were, the basic building blocks of an instructional product when a frame-based authoring system is being used. This chapter examines several of the most common conglomerate frame patterns to see how they can give a product its unique surface appearance and interaction texture. This will further illustrate the point that a relatively small number of basic structures clothed in different surface features accounts for the rich variety of CBI products. In fact, the patterns we will describe in this chapter account for the logical structures used in the vast majority of CBI products being developed using frame-based authoring tools.

We will give a number of examples of how each pattern of frames can be used instructionally. Particularly, we will try to point you ahead toward the use of patterns in the service of instructional strategy, which is the subject of Chapters 10 through 14. These strategies will form the basis of a tutorial design created in Chapter 21.

As you become familiar with the details of different authoring systems, you will see that in many cases, the creators of these systems have anticipated the desire to use the patterns of frame logic described in this chapter. The toolmakers realize the tremendous productivity increase that these patterns make possible and so provide methods within their tools for constructing and then filling these patterns. You should be especially alert in this respect for new developments in "models" if you are an Authorware user, "FastTracks" if you are a Quest 5.0 user, or "templates" or "scripts" if you use another authoring system.

The frame types which are used to build the patterns in this chapter were named and described in detail in Chapter 4. They are: the presentation frame, the menu frame, the question frame, and the calculation frame. Let's look at the patterns these frames make.

Linear pattern

Description: The linear pattern in Figure 1 is a simple sequence of presentation frames which branch one to another in an invariant, linear order. Advancement from frame to frame may be under student control (press a key, touch the screen, etc.) or under system control through automatic time-out. Each new frame may totally refresh the display, or simply make only additions or changes to it.

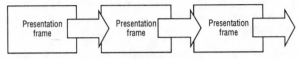

Figure 1. The linear pattern.

Common uses: Many occasions are right for the use of a linear sequence. For example, during the introductory section of an instructional event a linear sequence can be used to present several items of information about the instructional event itself: its objective, its length, its difficulty, reference works or accompanying printed materials to be used with the instruction, and so forth. During introductory parts of instruction, there are sometimes several things which just must be said to orient the student, and a linear sequence is one way (but not the only way) to take care of these preliminaries.

Sometimes for the presentation of a complex graphic step-by-step, a timed linear pattern is used. One new element of the graphic is added, followed by a pause of some length, followed by the next addition. One use of this pattern is to demonstrate complex cycles of activity, such as mitosis, a chemical reaction, or the internal workings of a complex machine. A more flexible version of this pattern allows the time-out period for all frames to be varied by the student. Rate control is a convenient way to offer the student some means of influencing the presentation, a contributing factor to how he or she will accept the CBI, if not to how effectively he or she learns from it.

Common abuses: Most instructional events, even the most interactive ones, have within them one or more lengthy stretches of message which must be presented, and even the most inventive developer is sometimes hard pressed to avoid the linear pattern in presenting them. This brings up the potential for *page-turning*. Page-turning may not so much be a characteristic of an interaction as it is an attitude in the mind of student. Page-turning occurs when the student says, "This computer isn't doing anything but turning pages." If the student never says this, then page-turning isn't really occurring, even if the designer has created a long linear sequence of frames.

Long sequences of reading and advancing the display followed by more reading and advancing is bothersome to students, however, when they are aware that is taking place. They do not accept very much of that treatment from books, and from a computer they tolerate even less. Sometimes there is no graceful way to avoid the presentation of a sizable linear sequence. In such cases, the only option seems to be page-turning—either obvious or in disguise—but in CBI, the presence of a high proportion of page-turning is a signal of weak instructional strategy. Some developers mistakenly assume that if they put the information on the screen for the student to read, the student will actually read it, but during page turning sequences especially, students sometimes skip the reading.

The key to avoiding page-turning is to recognize that it is in the student's attitude. There are many times when a linear pattern is the best one to use, but in those cases, proper use of the display can make it seem on the surface very different from a linear sequence. Our chapter on Display Management (Chapter 19) describes in some detail the things that can be done with the display along these lines. To summarize now what you will read there in more detail: Use the structure of the message and structure of the display to create an "information center" appearance and feel to the screen. Also, divide the message into its natural parts and consider using the menu-and-limb pattern described later.

Inserted question linear

Description: The inserted question linear pattern consists of a linear pattern into which one or more question frames has been inserted. Whether the feedback pattern following the questions uses the built-in feedback capacities of the frame itself or uses outside frames, the same basic pattern emerges that is shown in Figure 2.

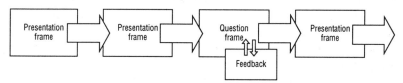

Figure 2. The inserted question linear pattern.

Common uses: Occasionally you will need to break up a linear pattern which has grown too long and where the display tactics of Chapter 19 can't save you from page-turning. However, we hope that this is not one of the major uses you will have for this pattern.

A more defensible reason for using this pattern is as a means of highlighting information—causing the student to use information which has just been given in some way. Using information increases the chance that it will be learned. The inserted question can be either verbal,

> *"What is the fluid inside the cell membrane called?"*

or graphic,

> *"To show that you know where the mitochondria are, click on one of them."*

The question may even consist of a challenge to perform one or more steps in a sequence being learned:

> *"Turn the power on now."*

Testing for knowledge or understanding or skill in this way during instruction can provide the designer with information on student learning speed and can reveal areas of instruction which are weak.

In some cases the inserted question may be used to ask for information which the student has not yet learned. For instance, in a discovery learning strategy, you may ask a question intended to start the student thinking, to shift responsibility for inquiry to the student, or to increase motivation through curiosity:

> *"If ice is just frozen water, then why does it float to the top of the water in a glass?"*

Asking a question before information is presented can increase the chances that the information will be attended to and remembered.

Inserted questions are also a useful way to tap and preserve student thinking at a specific moment. Consider several possibilities. A designer may insert questions in order to test student opinions toward the lesson or the subject matter. This is a clearly useful evaluative function. For completely different purposes, the student may be asked to summarize information that has been presented as a means of producing a benchmark or snapshot of the student's understanding at a given moment. Later, after a good deal more information has been encountered, this snapshot can be re-presented to the student for comparison with a more recent snapshot.

This technique is especially useful in instruction where the student is asked to deal with a value question, to try to see both sides of an argument, or to become aware of the influence of persuasive arguments on him or herself. Consider its use also in exercises to develop observation skills. The student may be shown a scene to be observed and remembered. After each of several repeated observations of the same scene followed by questioning regarding what was seen, the student might be expected to develop improved skills of observation.

Outside the tutorial world, the inserted question pattern finds use in job-aiding. A procedural job aid may use a linear sequence to present the steps in the procedure. One of the steps may require access to data which is not required by all users (for instance, if it has already been learned by the user). This data can be accessible to the user through a question inserted into the job aid's otherwise linear pattern. Why not use a menu frame? Because the designer wants to know how rapidly users are coming to have memorized the information that is accessed, and the question frame normally keeps an automatic tally of answers. A menu frame would have to be accompanied by one or more decision frames to do so.

Common abuses: One common abuse of the inserted question is to assume that it satisfies the needs of the student for interaction simply because it is easy for the designer to construct. For too many designers, the concept of interaction means, "Ask a question every so often." This is hardly sound design thinking.

Another common abuse of the inserted question concerns the use of feedback following the question. When students answer a question correctly, the next branch is normally in the forward direction, so that the student can continue the instruction. Following an incorrect answer, however, several varieties of feedback pattern are possible:

1. Branch ahead, regardless of the wrong answer (in cases where the right answer is not critical or where the student's error will become evident after progress).

2. Branch ahead after feedback which contains the correct answer.

3. Branch back to the question following corrective feedback (in order to re-try the question).

4. Branch to an alternate question (for diagnostics or remediation).

What to do following a missed question in CBI has always been problematic. In the most extreme attempts to be responsive to the student, some developers spend many times the effort designing clever feedback messages for various student responses than they spend on the main message itself. Sometimes too-clever feedback leads to the somewhat perverse outcome where the students deliberately make mistakes just to experience interesting feedback. One of the authors made this mistake in the design of some early arithmetic materials and was shocked to find students who clearly knew how to do the arithmetic gleefully showing their friends the elaborate displays that the computer produced when a problem was done improperly.

In trying to avoid this problem, some developers unwittingly place students into a kind of trap following a wrong answer. Instead of trying to anticipate and remediate student errors, they try to brute-force the student into a correct response. They branch the student back to the original question after telling the student, "Wrong. Try again." With no feedback giving a clue to the correct answer, and with no way to go backward from the question to review the instruction and find the correct answer, the student is trapped in the question. There have been instructional design books which advocate this as a defensible tactic during instruction, but it has been our experience and the experience of many students we have watched that this technique produces angry, frustrated students.

Linear question

Description: The linear question pattern shown in Figure 3 consists of an unbroken sequence of question frames. As with the inserted question pattern just described, there are some options for connecting feedback following questions, however, as you will see, the linear question pattern can have uses which do not call for feedback.

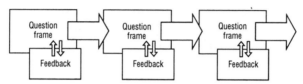

Figure 3. The linear question pattern.

Common uses: The most obvious use of the linear question pattern is in the construction of quizzes or tests in which the designer wants an invariant item order. In one variant of this type of quiz, a set of test questions is ordered so that earlier questions will not give away answers to later questions. However, in the complement of this variant, questions are asked in a particular order which are intended to draw the student toward a specific realization, conclusion, or observation. In this variant, the questions take part in a structured discovery process. This approach is particularly useful in early stages of instruction for complex decision-making such as would be found in a business case study. It represents a major step upward in sophistication from our standard concept of a quiz, which normally consists of a series of loosely related questions not pointing toward any single performance goal.

One example of instruction using the linear question pattern for decision-making instruction was created by one of the authors for instruction in basic troubleshooting skills for electronics technicians. The training was really trying to accomplish two instructional goals: (1) training how to troubleshoot a specific set of electronic circuits, and (2) training in the process of troubleshooting itself.

A set of exercises was created which walked students step-by-step through the solution of individual troubleshooting problems. In each problem of the set, regardless of how different the problem itself was from the others, the same set of decisions had to be made in a set order. A linear question pattern was used to make this happen. Each question in a sequence followed a set format: First, it provided information on the results of the last decision, then it provided options for the next decision that needed to be made. Feedback for correct decisions consisted of one new bit of information—the result of a test, a reading, or new data—and most often it was the information they would have obtained if they had made the correct decision. For incorrect decisions, the correct path was pointed out, and the student was returned to the original question to select again.

The results of this simple application were surprising. The exercises alone were sufficient to teach the troubleshooting skill as measured by a performance test, but not quite to the high level desired. However, using the exercises as an initial instruction vehicle prior to a more complete free-play simulation did create the desired level of skill. Surprisingly, the simulation without the linear question exercises was also incapable of bringing students to the desired level of skill. When students were given the simulation without prior experience with the linear question exercises, their performance fell. They found the simulation much more difficult to deal with because their problem-solving processes lacked the needed structure. The use of the linear question pattern in this case provided us with a type of limited simulation. We gave it the name *path* simulation, which referred to the single correct path that students had to follow to accomplish a solution. The path simulation turned out to be a good vehicle for inculcating a pattern into the students' approach to problems. Certainly this use of the linear question pattern contrasts strongly with the standard quiz applications which use the same pattern.

Tests using the linear question pattern of frames are not common. They most frequently use the selected question pattern described in a later section. However, if an instructor wanted to construct a problem-solving test or exercise which unfolded the problem one step at a time, giving the student a chance to respond to each phase of the problem as it developed, the linear question pattern would be very appropriate. This would create tests and exercises somewhat like case studies. Other forms more frequently used for tests which randomize or sample problems from a pool would not work for this type of application, since sequencing of items is a key ingredient to the unfolding process.

When the linear question pattern is used for quizzes, the developer must decide how to use feedback after correct and incorrect answers. In making that decision, there must be a way for students to avoid entrapment in a negative feedback cycle.

Common abuses: The most common abuse of the linear question pattern is its trivialization. When students are quizzed or have interaction with instruction, they judge the value of the interaction. If it contributes to learning, students increase their confidence toward the instruction. On the other hand, if they perceive that the interactions are a waste of time or are trivial, the estimate of the instruction lowers.

Developers sometimes misjudge the value of a given interaction and ask questions for which the student feels no need. To avoid trivializing interactions, developers should be careful to see that the linear question pattern is used in significant ways—not as a textbook question-answering drill.

Another common abuse of the linear question pattern is the improper use of feedback. Occasionally, a designer creating questions for a quiz feels that students should be made to sweat for the right answer. A common approach to this is to adjust the feedback messages so that they are cryptic, difficult to understand, and provide little assistance. The reasoning is that doing this will cause the students to think things through for themselves.

Though this approach is stimulating to the well-motivated and well-prepared student, it often uses up the limited pool of motivation that less-well-prepared students have, because they perceive that they are fighting rather than using the instruction. Moreover, it becomes apparent to students in this situation that they are being manipulated, which creates suspicions and a distancing from the instruction that detracts severely from the learning. This instructional technique is akin to teaching swimming by throwing a child into the water; it produces a swimmer, but the swimmer does not want to go back into the water often.

A more reasonable solution is for the developer to provide feedback which is adequate to correct misunderstandings, but also to re-structure the questions themselves so that they represent a more realistic and relevant exercise for the student. In addition, the original instructional message itself might come under scrutiny in hopes of finding better, clearer expression. The doctrine that students must suffer to learn is an anachronism which should be quickly replaced with a commitment to the fair and relevant exercise of skills being learned.

Selected question

Description: The selected question pattern shown in Figure 4 goes one step beyond the linear question pattern and allows questions to be selected from a pool of questions in different orders. The rules of selection determine the type of surface activity that results.

Common uses: The two main uses of the selected question pattern are: (1) to administer tests and quizzes in which the question order must vary, and (2) to carry out drill and practice exercises.

The selected question pattern is common, but so much effort is required to create sampling systems of the type needed that some authoring systems have developed a meta-frame or executive frame type called the test construction frame. The Wise authoring system, now out of general use, is an example of this. The frame asks for the identities of the (individual) question frames which are to be pooled and then asks several questions about the form and function of the test. There are so many varieties of test—each of them valid and important for certain applications—that many attributes must be specified in order to construct each one. A sample—but not a complete list—of the types of data that must be supplied to provide controls for a test includes:

1. Number of items in the test.

2. Method of sampling.

3. Replacement of missed items.

4. Criterion for ending the test (score, number of items, time).

5. Pass/Fail criteria.

6. Reporting of results.

7. Existence of question sub-pools.

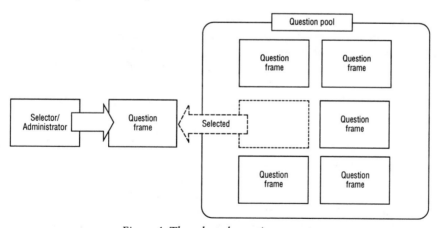

Figure 4. The selected question pattern.

And the list goes on.

When the sampling method is set to "random" and when the type of test is set to "practice" as opposed to "mastery," then the selected question pattern becomes a practice exercise. Questions are sampled from the pool in random order with replacement of missed ones. Normally, even correctly-answered questions are replaced back into the pool until a criterion for correct successive responses is reached for each one. When the criterion for a question is reached, it is removed from the pool, and the drill continues until the pool is exhausted.

An especially interesting problem arises when you consider what happens to the feedback for each question in a question selection pattern. During practice, feedback for questions is desirable, because it is part of the learning process. During a test, however, especially one in which the questions are sampled in any order, feedback for one question may give away the answer to another, which is unacceptable. The most logical solution (assuming that the designer realizes the instructional value of feedback and wants to take advantage of it following the test) is to present the feedback in a batch at the end of the test. Questions answered correctly can be given *knowledge of results* feedback ("That was the correct answer."). Questions answered incorrectly may be given more robust and useful feedback.

The bind that is created by this solution clearly exposes to view a problem that is encountered in the frame-based authoring world. The feedback for a question must be bundled with the question, or else each question placed into the pool must be placed there complete with all of the connected frames which provide its feedback. This is impractical.

Moreover, if the feedback is placed into the pool with the questions, then it will occur directly after the student enters an answer to the question—not at the end of the test. And there is no mechanism for splitting the question from its feedback that maintains the ties between question and feedback so that they can share the data on the student's answer when it comes time to present the feedback.

This problem is representative of a type of difficulty which is found in other areas of frame-based design as well. The manner of bundling logic and storing data within frames causes what we call the problem of compartmentalization of communicating processes. This high-sounding phrase means that the frame logic is sometimes not broken into chunks in a way that you, the designer, want to use them, but in order for the instructional event to work the way you want it, two smaller functional chunks of logic—in this case the question and the feedback for the question—must act at separate times but must also share data. That is, the outcome of the question must be known in order for the feedback to be given. These two processes—questions and feedback, when compartmentalized, find it difficult to communicate, and the designer who wants them to do so must create several variables to store the needed data that would otherwise be forgotten by the computer after the questions were answered.

Without a complex set of decision frames to manage the great amount of data-handling that would be required to make batch feedback work, this problem cannot be solved by a frame-based authoring system without major adjustments to the test construction frame type. We bring up this issue at this point without proposing a solution. Because run-time persistent objects (like a question, for instance) can still exist at feedback time, and since objects can store and recall their own data (in this case, the answer given by the student and the correct answer), the data needed to provide either delayed or immediate feedback is readily available. This is an advantage possible with object-oriented authoring.

In order to make a final point about the selected question pattern, we want to make a guess about what you might be thinking. We guess that the assumption you have been making during this section of the chapter is that questions pooled are verbal in nature and that they are most likely to be multiple choice questions. If that has been your mind set, then you join the great mass of designers who have (as we all have at times) fallen into the verbalism trap. We just assume that instructional presentations are a verbal activity (we *tell* the student) and we also just assume that the test will be some sort of reverse verbalization to the instructor in an easily-checked question form. This is the legacy of the verbally-based education we all have had.

As designers of computer-based instructional systems, when we stay in the verbal mode for presentations, practice, and tests, we are robbing this dynamic instructional medium of most of its power. May we brainstorm for a moment on some *non-verbal forms of the selected question test?*

Consider first that the computer is an excellent tool for asking graphic questions and for drawing non-verbal responses from the student through mouse actions, touches, or cursor movements. Now think of the almost unlimited number of graphical non-verbal questions you can present to the student in this environment. Present the student with a picture (say, for instance that every question in the pool has precisely the same graphic to respond to) then ask the student to select (point to, click, etc.) specific parts of the graphic, to click of pairs of things that are associated in some way, or to drag one part of the graphic over to another part of the graphic with which it is associated. Perhaps your test items will ask the student to drag the states of the USA from an area where they appear one at a time into their proper position on a steadily-growing map of the nation. These are only a few quick suggestions for breaking the verbal mode of thinking which it is so easy for designers to fall into. Be on constant guard, and invent your own varieties of the non-graphic selected question test or exercise.

Common abuses: The construction of tests is a specialized area of study called *psychometrics* (literally, *mind measure*). The abuses of the selected question pattern most frequently occur in the creation of questions and question pools. When questions do not match instructional objectives or when questions are poorly constructed, there is no amount of computer logic that can correct the problem. Because test item analysis and validation is expensive and somewhat mysterious, instructional developers sometimes skip them, relying on their intuitions as to what makes a "good" question. This makes such tests of questionable worth.

What is the implication? Do we recommend that in order to develop sound tests you must become a psychometrician? That isn't practical. However, sometimes being aware of a problem stimulates us to watch for opportunities for improvements as they are possible. This is what we recommend. Many excellent books and papers have been written containing guidance for teachers on how to create test items of all kinds. The principles which apply to teacher-constructed tests apply as well to tests which you will place in the computer. Over time, we recommend that you become acquainted with this guidance and that you exercise the best quality control you can over your own tests. Moreover, we recommend that you become aware of the steps and decision points in the instructional systems development process which are intended to add validity to your tests by basing them on well-constructed instructional objectives and maintaining faithfulness to the behavior expressed in the objective as you plan the test behavior. These recommendations, if followed, will improve the quality of most tests—verbal or non-verbal.

Question tree

Description: The question tree or question hierarchy pattern consists of a series of question frames which branch to other frames in a cascading pattern as shown in Figure 5.

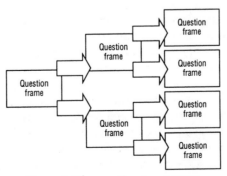

Figure 5. The question tree pattern.

Common uses: The question tree pattern is useful any time a conversational type of interaction is needed. For example, a student may practice foreign language skills in a conversational setting by seeing or hearing a communication, accompanied by three or four possible responses. Each response may lead to a different outcome and a different question frame.

As you learned in the last section, a question frame need not look like a question is being asked. In the case of a question tree pattern, each frame may present a communication to the student in the form of an audio or video sequence in which an actor speaks something in the foreign language. The answer options to the student may be presented either in foreign language or the student's native language and can even require non-verbal responses. A student answer causes a branch to another question frame—with its own language message and its own options.

As far back as the late 1970s, videodisc instruction pioneers were constructing interactions of this sort, in which the foreign language communications were supplied by way of videodisc sequences spoken and acted by foreign actors in real foreign settings. In effect, students conversed with foreign nationals in their own language and in their own country. Students dealt with doctors, taxi drivers, storekeepers, and a host of other real people in real situations.

The reason for using the question frame for this application rather than the menu frame is that the question frame can keep score. Assuming that all the responses offered the student may be appropriate, some can be made more appropriate than others, earning a differential score.

Common abuses: The problem created by the question tree pattern is the immense number of frames and branches which are produced within only four or five rounds of interaction. For instance, one question may branch to three destinations. If each destination produces in turn three more branches and the pattern is continued, then by the fifth interaction a total of 121 frames will be required to handle all of the branching. By the tenth interaction the number of frames will total 29,524.

Unmodified, this pattern produces unreasonable development burdens. Some variations of this pattern, however, are quite reasonable. First, a developer can limit the length of the chain and the number of options available on each question. A chain of five questions with two options per question results in a very do-able 31 frames.

A second possibility is to create dialogue with breaks or resets so that some question choices branch to a common destination, regardless of the response given. This can be done easily by managing the choice of options. A little planning makes this possible with no loss in the realism of the dialogue.

Menu-and-limb

Description: The menu-and-limb pattern shown in Figure 6 consists of a single menu frame connected to two or more frame patterns appended to menu choices. The patterns attached may be any of the patterns described in this chapter. After executing the pattern of any limb, the control may be returned to the menu to allow the student to select another limb. A choice of limb may also move the student away from the menu, never to return.

Common uses: The menu frame in this pattern is used to turn some degree of control—some type of choice—over to the student without consequences. A question frame used in this pattern would score responses, and each choice would be judged right or wrong. By using the menu frame, the developer avoids that and is able to use this pattern to give an unjudged choice to the student. Although the diagram shows that the sequences linked with the menu are linear sequences, literally any pattern can be used there. With a return path to the menu, this pattern is a means of showing the student parallel sequences of information. The choice presented by the menu might be:

1. A content choice:

   "Click on the part of the cell that you want to learn about next."

2. A management choice:

   "Select one: (a) Pre-Test (b) Instruction (c) Review (d) Post-Test"

3. An instructional strategy choice:

   "Select one: (a) Main Idea (b) Examples (c) Practice Items (d) Simplified Discussion"

4. An instructional quality choice:

   "Select the level of presentation in this instructional event: (a) technical/mathematical (b) conceptual/graphical."

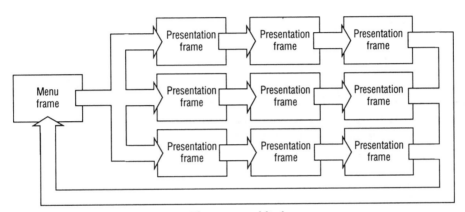

Figure 6. The menu and limb pattern.

This pattern might become an invitation for a student to explore the features of a new product one at a time or to query the several elements of a complex conceptual structure.

Common abuses: The most common abuses of this pattern are: (1) its overuse and (2) failure to provide for maintaining the orientation of the student who has made a choice.

In the CBT medium, some of the orienting features available in a book are missing, and it is much easier to get lost. After one menu branch in computer space, it is relatively easy for students to remember where they have been and where they are going. After two successive branches, it is somewhat harder. After three or more such branches, students begin to feel they are in a maze, both ahead and behind, and some very negative emotional reactions can occur. This disorientation occurs much more easily and quickly on the computer than in almost any other medium, but if you can recall experiences you have had with audio tapes where you could not find a particular song or with videotapes where you could not find a particular motion sequence, then the feelings of being closed off or hemmed in can be readily identified. This problem, which is unique to certain forms of technological media, is discussed in Chapter 19 on Display Management, along with methods for averting it.

Menu tree

Description: The menu tree pattern consists of a series of menu frames arranged hierarchically. The branch from each selection of one menu frame leads into another menu frame as shown in Figure 7.

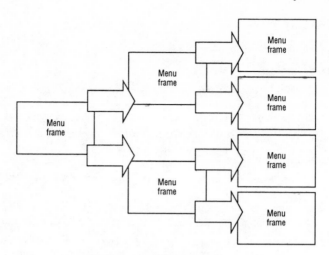

Figure 7. The menu tree pattern.

Common uses: The most frequent use of the menu tree pattern is to create a zoom experience. This allows a student to browse through a large body of packaged information freely or to zoom around some physical or conceptual structure. During simulations, it is often desirable to give the student free travel privileges to all of the locations in a complex suite of equipment. An electronics simulation designed by one of the authors allowed students to zoom from high-level views of equipment (in which all parts could be seen at once) down to individual controls and indicators in order to read and set them. During simulation problems, students were allowed to zoom behind the equipment panels to locations where measurements could be taken.

Another simulation created by the authors allowed a student to solve a complex planning problem, obtaining information and resources for the solution from several physical locations at an airport. This simulation led to others like it and to the development of the concept of a *location simulation* which is discussed in Chapter 16. A similar environmental simulation might take the student through the halls of a school, the work benches of a laboratory, or the cloak rooms of the Capitol where laws are being made.

Using the zoom capability is like taking a self-guided tour of something, and there are few things in a zoom simulation that deny access. During a zoom, it is possible to offer the student the opportunity to question individual components about themselves. A school teacher might consider providing students the chance to zoom through the inner workings of a flower, a digestive tract, or an atomic reactor, asking each thing they see what it is and what it does.

The self-guided tour can take the student through any physical system, including an atom, an oil refinery, an electronic circuit, the galaxies of the universe, or an electrical power grid on the East Coast. The student can also be allowed to tour a conceptual model: a nonphysical system such as a period of history, or the structure of a written composition such as a novel or a poem. During tours, a student may be allowed to disassemble objects, ask questions about objects or to objects, leave messages, take notes, or even be quizzed about what is being observed.

Common abuses: A hazard for this pattern is the same as for the all menu-type patterns—disorientation. However, this problem is easily prevented by following the principles outlined in Chapter 19 on Display Management. Furthermore, developers can put short circuit paths in courseware, allowing the user to back out one step at a time in order to exit from the instruction or begin another chain of exploration. Menu trees must be augmented with ways of going easily to frequently-sought limbs, and to specialized support services such as glossaries, helps, or note taking utilities. These moves must be relatively simple and intuitive so that students don't have to become experts in operating the controls of the CBI product. This, by the way, is a problem which is difficult to manage with current frame-based authoring tools, but it is relatively simple to manage with tools that create persistent run-time objects (see Chapter 6 for more detail).

Computed branch

Description: The computed branch pattern as shown in Figure 8 consists of at least one decision frame which computes a branch destination. There is no return to the decision point once the computation has been made and the branch has been executed. A return creates another type of pattern described later as the event-driven loop pattern.

The identity of the destination frame in the computed branch pattern may be computed by comparison with a range of values (X=1, X=2, X=3, etc.), or it may be computed by formula ("if boilertemp=500 then go to frame 55"). This pattern operates in essentially the same way as the basic decision frame described in Chapter 4. It is included here to provide a further opportunity to describe ways in which such frames are used.

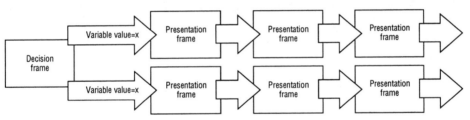

Figure 8. The computed branch pattern.

Common uses: It is sometimes hard to see the need for the computed branch until you begin to use it, but then it becomes almost indispensable. The more non-sequenced your design thinking becomes, the more important this pattern becomes. It can be used to compute either the graphic or logic frame which will be executed following an action by the student. This makes it ideal for simulations. It may be used to change the graphical position of a knob or to cause a hypothetical patient to change his or her complaint—say, after the passage of a certain period of time without a correct solution by the doctor. In chemistry lab experiments, when an explosion occurs after the addition of a substance to the beaker, it is almost always some form of decision frame logic that calculates the need for the blast.

Within tutorials this pattern can be used to choose a treatment style best suited to a particular student's scores. Differences in treatment may include simplified versus technical explanation modes, low versus high density verbal messages, depth versus surface content coverage, or any of several other variations.

Common abuses: The computed branch, though powerful, can create maintenance and modification nightmares. It is too easy for a computation to be done improperly such that the courseware will transfer control to a sequence that doesn't exist. Tilt!

To guard against this problem, each computed branch should have a mechanism that delivers the flow of the courseware to a reasonable location where an appropriate error message or continuation of instruction (whichever) can be given if the computation yields a location that is not in the correct range.

Subroutining

Description: The subroutining pattern shown in Figure 9 consists of a decision frame capable of adding or subtracting a series or pattern of frames from a lesson at the time of instruction, based on the results of a computation. After the subroutine of frames to which the pattern branched is completed, execution returns to the main line of instruction.

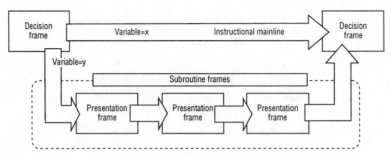

Figure 9. The subroutining pattern.

Common uses: One important use of the subroutining pattern is to automatically supplement the presentation in some way to better meet the needs of the student. During the learning of a mathematical operation, a student may be given extra practice on simple items if the scores on previous practice sections has been low. This can be accomplished through the addition of a subroutine of extra problems. Also, if a particular pattern of errors has been detected, the mixture of practice items can be skewed in favor of remediating the error pattern by subroutining in the same fashion.

For students whose knowledge of mathematics is weak, a presentation on statistics may automatically add certain simplified explanation frames which graphically or through concrete examples elaborate on a concept which has just been explained mathematically. Since not all students need this treatment, it can be subroutined for only those who do. The presentation of review material just prior to the introduction of new concepts which build on that material may be necessary for only a few students out of a total population. For those, a subroutining pattern can provide the review. If you are familiar with the history of computer-based instruction, you can see that the subroutine pattern is one of the key ways a designer can apply one of the original intentions of the CBI pioneers—individualization of instruction to each student's needs. This is a greatly underused pattern for these purposes, and we recommend that designers begin to think along these lines to a greater extent, now that authoring system technology makes individualized designs easier to accomplish.

In a simulation, random events which influence the course of a problem may also be inserted through subroutining. This can include unexpected hazards or windfalls.

Common abuses: There has not been much evidence of abuse of this pattern except for its under-use.

Simulation cycle

Description: The simulation cycle pattern shown in Figure 10 consists of a series of decision frames connected in such a way that they form a ring that leads back to its own beginning to begin executing again. This creates a continuous cycle of computing based on inputs from the student or on changing values in a simulated model. The simulation cycle is the same basic pro-

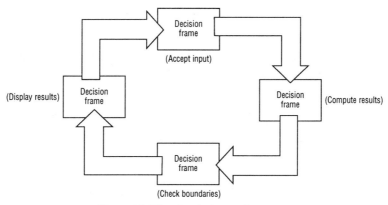

Figure 10. The simulation cycle pattern.

gram pattern that lives at the heart of large aircraft simulations, but this basic pattern has its humble applications as well and can be very useful to a CBI designer.

The exact identity and function assignments of the decision frames included within simulation cycles vary somewhat from application to application, but most cycles contain at least the following basic functions:

1. Display current indications.

2. Accept student input.

3. Compute results of input.

4. Check for legal boundaries and problem completion..

Completion checking is the computer's means of determining when it is time to exit the cycle. It is necessary because the computer continues to cycle around the ring of decision frames. Another similar pattern, the event-driven loop which is described next, only cycles when an event occurs, and then it only cycles once or a few times.

Common uses: The most common use of the simulation cycle is, of course, in building simulations. A discussion of this pattern and its application to the various forms of simulation is contained in Chapter 17, so it is not elaborated here.

Common abuses: See Chapter 17.

Event-driven loop

Description: The event-driven loop pictured in Figure 11 is used for simulation. As its name suggests, it is a simulation loop, but it does not cycle continually as does the simulation cycle pattern just described. Instead, its loop contains a decision frame which waits and watches waits for events to occur that say it is time to complete another (one usually) cycle around its loop. When a triggering event occurs, the loop reacts, usually by executing one or more of the patterns of frames described in this chapter. Following the response, control is most frequently returned back to the idler (or latch) decision frame of the simulation loop, which begins again to watch for another event to handle.

Common uses: Interesting simulations can be organized around an event-driven loop. Triggering events can be:

1. External events, such as mouse clicks, keyboard character presses, or the arrival of data from an external source.

2. Time-based periodic events, such as a timer that continually counts off a specified number of "ticks" and then sends an event to the loop.

3. Time-based but non-periodic events, such as an alarm that warns a student pilot that too much time has elapsed since de-icing procedures were last performed.

4. Internal events, where an event is generated by one of the frames set off by the loop's own reaction.

The frames in the simulation loop that detect events watch a list of variables and compare their values with a set of predefined conditions or values to which the simulation should react. For instance, when the temperature of the simulated greenhouse reaches 77 degrees, the flower-blooming subroutines are invoked by the simulation loop.

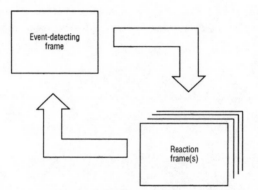

Figure 11. The event-driven loop pattern.

Event-driven loops help keep the arch-enemy, complexity, at bay. They reduce the variety of possibilities to which your program must react down to comparatively easy-to-manage stream of single events. For example, if you are trying to simulate your car radio, the idler frame will only bestir itself when a radio button is pushed. When that happens, you will invoke subroutines which change the tuner setting, stop the audio associated with the old station, move the graphical dial indicator, and start the audio associated with the new station. But in between there is little else to do. A broad variety of (perhaps most) educational and training simulations can be handled with this type of pattern, which is termed a discrete simulation (as opposed to a *continuous* simulation).

Common abuses: Event-driven loops can require certain levels of support from your authoring software, operating system, and hardware, depending on the simulation's requirements.

What happens, for example, if your CBI system is off reacting to another event when an important event takes place? Should the new event be handled when it occurs or should the one presently being processed be finished first? What happens if two events occur while the system is off reacting to something else? Does it store them or does it just forget one of them? (And if so, which one?)

Two issues, in particular, must be dealt with when event-driven loops are used: (1) event priority, and (2) the density and frequency of events.

Priority. CBI authors sometimes make the mistake of trying to treat all events as they occur as if they were of equal importance or priority. When this is done, for instance, when the driver education simulator is off making the dashboard clock hand move and the student slams on the brakes, the system can't drop what it's doing and handle the braking, to return to the clock when things have quieted down. That is, it can't do this unless the designer has built into the loop the ability to recognize when new events have occurred and the ability to place one subroutine on hold while others are activated. This priority problem is not a problem with most educational simulations and is only a real problem for technical simulations in which the timing of the response to events is critical.

Density and frequency of events. Some CBI authoring software systems can't handle events if they occur too close together or more often than a certain rate. This is not hard to understand if you keep in mind that most computers can do only one thing at a time. As the number of events to be checked increases, loops can slow down to unacceptable rates. Once again, here the solution may include building priority mechanisms to support handling events of different importance.

If, for example, any of 10,000 events can occur at any point (not unreasonable in a simulation of a complex piece of equipment but very unreasonable for most educational simulations), then each time around the loop, the system must check against an average of 5,000 events before it matches. Let's say that events crowd into the system at a fairly sluggish rate of five per second. This means that the system must perform 25,000 checks per second—not only that, but it must react to whatever events have happened as well!

A question worth asking, then, is what kind of support your authoring software gives to these kinds of demanding search tasks. If there isn't any, and if you plan to design technical simulations, you can outrun even the most powerful computer's resources. Authoring systems that can be extended with programming offer one kind of escape route: You can develop search management strategies yourself, or arrange for it to be done. Many of the present generation of frame-based authoring systems can be extended by programming. The coming generation of systems will most likely have much more sophisticated capabilities of this sort.

Thinking constructively—frame-based thinking

Why this long discussion of frames and frame patterns? The answer is that it enhances the productivity of the CBT designer to think in terms of structures, and these structures are one set which can be used. Chapters 8 through 14 present ways for thinking structurally about instructional strategies, which can incorporate the patterns described here to implement those strategies.

It should be evident by now that when a frame-based authoring system is being used, instructional events and tutorial instructional strategies can be constructed in a picture puzzle fashion by linking together patterns of frames as they are needed. This is a useful mental image for the CBT designer to possess, because using common patterns to solve recurring structural problems can save the designer from re-inventing the wheel every time a new instructional event is designed. Moreover, new and creative designs can be built by modifying or extending the basic patterns described in this chapter.

Essentially, we have described a certain number of wheel types to stimulate your thinking, and we now invite you to use them, modify them, or invent your own as needed. We stress the importance of using these patterns creatively rather than slavishly. These patterns do not exhaust all of the possibilities, and you must not think that they constitute a kind of final word that must be followed like a formula.

Does using patterns mean that all of your products will look and act alike? Not at all. As we have discussed frame and pattern types, we have tried to emphasize how the visible surface of frames can be changed a million ways to obscure and yet use the same logical structure underneath. An enormous variety of surface effects is possible using only a small number of underlying structures. An inventive mind working on just the basic elements described here can work a long time before exhausting all the possibilities.

Thinking constructively—object thinking

In a previous chapter (Chapter 3) and in a later chapter (Chapter 6) we describe what we feel will be a major innovation in the way we think about and design CBI that will be brought about by the rapidly changing nature of authoring tools that are becoming available. Does that peek into the future invalidate what we have said in this chapter and Chapter 4 about frames and frame patterns? To be perfectly clear, the answer is "yes" and "no."

The answer is "yes" because the new tools will ask us to think in new and different ways about what constitutes instruction. We will invent new forms, new looks, new modes of interaction, new conventions, and new styles. Everything will be up for review—all of our entrenched ideas about what CBI is—because these new tools will open up to the average designer more powerful techniques which have been the province of relatively few up until now. As this review of CBI happens, some of the traditional ways of instructing by computer—particularly the ones which mimic other forms of instruction like the lecture or the videotape—will probably be de-emphasized and fall into less frequent use, while other forms of instruction—some of which we are not used to now and whose concepts have not yet been fully developed—will become of much greater importance. As this happens, some of the patterns of communication and interaction represented in the frame patterns of this chapter will have less value, and some of them will become unpopular.

At the same time, some of the patterns described here will persist because they still represent a useful way of interacting with the student and a useful way of thinking about instructional structures. Therefore, the answer is also, "No." You won't have to give up the important structural things you have learned in this chapter. And since frame-based authoring tools themselves are evolving, you won't have to give them up either.

In order to prepare you for tomorrow as well as today, the next chapter introduces the kind of structural thinking that is important when you design and develop CBI using authoring systems with persistent run-time objects.

Self-directed activities

- Select a frame pattern from this chapter and use it to generate as many different surface appearances and behaviors as you can.

- Analyze an existing CBI product in terms of frame patterns, whether or not the product was created using frames.

- Identify one or more new patterns not described in this chapter.

- Consider how you would use a single frame pattern to execute a complete lesson by reusing the logic frames over and over again, supplying only new content and/or data each time the pattern executed. What are the implications of this "live template" approach to using frame patterns in terms of production effort? In terms of cost? In terms of instructional effectiveness?

- Examine the user interfaces of several authoring systems, comparing them in their ability to create patterns of frames and then fill them with content and data. Suggest improvements to the interfaces which would improve the speed of entry.

- Compare the same authoring systems that you studied in the previous activity on their ability to support the "live templating" described earlier.

Further reading

Dempsey, J. V., and Sales, G. C. (1993). *Interactive instruction and feedback.* Englewood Cliffs, NJ: Educational Technology Publications.

Jonassen, D. H. (Ed.). (1988). *Instructional designs for microcomputer courseware.* Hillsdale, NJ: Lawrence Erlbaum Associates.

6

OBJECTS

Chapter Objectives:

1. *Identify the benefits of object-oriented development from both the software and the instructional perspective.*

2. *Describe how objects can be used to create frames.*

3. *Describe how objects can used to create qualitative and quantitative simulation models.*

4. *Describe how objects can be used to create basic instructional functions related to a simulation.*

5. *Define the difference between an intelligent instructional system and object-based instruction without intelligence.*

The impact of frames

It would be hard to overestimate the positive impact that frame-based authoring systems have had (and continue to have) on the use and acceptance of CBI. There is little doubt that without these valuable tools, the industry would be at a fraction of its present size, evidence of CBI use would be hard to find, and we would not have the useful educational and training products that we now have, most of which supply evidence that CBI is an effective instructional medium.

Yet technology advances in stages, and in retrospect we always wonder how we could have lived with things as they were in the old days, doing things the old way. Someday in the not too distant future, these will be "the old days," and frame-based authoring will be "the old way." We must look ahead to "the new way" now, because in the field of CBI, a new way is rapidly emerging, and CBI designers need to prepare for the new tools and approaches that will become the standard.

Every technology has its strengths and its weaknesses. Previous chapters in this book have shown the strengths of frame-based authoring and have not attempted to cover up its weaknesses. The main shortcoming of frame-based authoring is that frame-basing itself requires that we express instructional plans (a set of conceptual structures) and instructional messages (a set of content structures) in terms of frames (a set of logical structures). Because the product must always be expressed in the logical structures, this conflict almost always focuses the designer on the authoring tool and its capabilities rather than on the instructional task and what is needed to accomplish it.

Frames make certain kinds of CBI product relatively easy to build, particularly linear and branched-linear tutorials. Other types of product—such as simulations, expert-guided instruction, learning coaches, and performance testing systems—are harder to build, so it is not surprising to see a proliferation of the former products and slower growth in the latter. CBI designers hope for improvements in tools, but many are uncertain where the next quantum leap in the three factors of authoring tools—productivity, power, and ease of use—ought to come. The purpose of this chapter is to describe new tools for CBI development which may make the answer to this question, "all three."

Many computer publications today testify to the promise of object-oriented programming technology, extolling its virtues in language normally reserved for advertisements of over-the-counter diet preparations. Some CBI designers bet heavily that object orientation of authoring tools represents the next step forward they are looking for. Others doubt, and yet others are waiting to see. Scraping away the gloss and excitement produced by new hope, we find that object technology will have some impact on the programming of CBI, but far more on methods of teaching and learning than the literature would lead us to suspect. Let's examine the two benefit areas of software production and instructional power. But first, let us provide a brief review of object-oriented programming terms and principles. Readers already familiar with object-orientation can skip the next section without missing anything.

Principles of object-orientation

What are the basic terms and principles of object-orientation? How does it differ from traditional programming? The following survey of key terms and processes explains how.

Program structure and execution: Object-oriented programs differ from the traditional sequential programs in structure and order of execution. A traditional sequential program consists of commands listed in the order they will be executed. The order of execution of an entire program is essentially first-to-last. When the program executes the last command in the list, the program is terminated.

In contrast, an object-oriented program does not execute in the same type of sequential order. It defines a small community of objects and creates them within the computer's memory. Program execution proceeds as these objects send messages to one another. When no more objects have messages to send to other objects, the program is terminated. Program execution is very much like a chain reaction. Since each object is a separate entity, and since it is hard to predict which object will receive a message at any given moment, the order of execution for an object-oriented program is almost impossible to predict.

Objects, properties, and values: Objects created by an object-oriented program differ from each other and, like objects in the real world, have properties (or attributes). A circle object, for instance, has properties for line color, line thickness, fill color, center point, radius, and so on. In order for one instance of a circle to exist in an object-oriented program, specific values must be given to its properties.

This may not sound new. It may seem to resemble the principles of object creation and value-setting we have been talking about since Chapter 3—during the discussion of the frame-based variety of authoring system—so what's the difference? While creating frame-based CBI objects, the author supplies values to a sequential program. The objects exist in the designer's mind, but don't really exist in the program. Creating object-oriented objects means creating real program objects, because that is the only kind of program the system can create. When you give values to object properties, you are giving values to program objects, and when the object-oriented program executes, it is through the interaction of independent objects, not through the execution of a sequence of commands in the traditional sense.

Data encapsulation: Whereas in a traditional program the data for the whole program is kept in a common data area, objects in an object-oriented product keep their own data, and except for certain shared global variables, data is not shared between objects. This is called data encapsulation. Data is encapsulated inside the object, and each object remembers, maintains, and handles its own data.

Methods and messages: An object-oriented program executes as objects it has created send messages to each other. It is much like a conversation between the objects. Each object normally has several program subroutines called methods attached to it. When an object receives a message from another object, these methods are what recognize and respond to the message. Each method of an object is usually attuned to hearing and processing only one particular message.

As an object receives a message (as one of its methods recognizes a message it can process) it may send its own message as a result. The method processing the incoming message may itself send one or more outgoing messages to other objects. The methods possessed by an object determine what messages it can receive and send. If a message is sent for which an object has no corresponding method, the object will ignore the message and do nothing.

Classes: Each object in an object-oriented program does not have to be created from scratch. Instead, objects can be created as instances of classes. These classes come with the programming language or authoring system and are built in. They constitute a kind of library of objects which the designer can borrow temporarily as a pattern for the creation of new object instances. There is normally a ready-made class of objects called *circle* in an object-oriented programming system, and it is possible to create an instance of a circle using the class object *circle* as a pattern. The instance (that is, the new object) is formed by copying the structure of the class object and then giving specific values to its properties (radius, centerpoint, line color, etc.).

Why is it done this way? So that the programmer doesn't have to write a complete list of new methods each time a circle object is created. Instead of writing all of the program code necessary for the methods and data handling for each new object created, a designer can simply copy the code that is common to all objects of that type from the class object and then give specific values to the instance object which makes the object unique. The original class object is not changed, but the instance is given data that defines it. This saves tremendous amounts of programming time.

Inheritance: Object classes in the object library are related to each other. The object class Circle, for instance, is a sub-class of the object class Oval, because all of the properties of an oval are also properties of a circle. In effect, a circle is a specialized oval—or a sub-class of oval. In the same way, the object class square is a sub-class of the object class rectangle.

In these examples, oval and rectangle are parent classes and circle and square are respectively *child* classes. So what? The parent class objects have methods and data storage just as do the child class objects. However, the child has all that the parent has plus some extra. Therefore, when you create a circle, you are creating an oval with a few extra characteristics, and you get all of the oval's methods and data structures as well for no extra effort. This is called inheritance.

The object revolution: Programming perspective

With these basic terms in mind, we can discuss the benefits to CBI programmers from object-orientation.

Inheritance and development by exception: Inheritance works to the benefit of CBI programmers. First, by creating object instances from object classes, the designer saves huge amounts of time, because new objects—complete with methods and internal data structures—can be created rapidly. Also, since object classes inherit methods and data structures from parent classes, each object automatically has all of the parent's capabilities as well.

Inheritance gives rise to *development by exception*. This means that designers can take the object classes supplied by their programming tool and modify them slightly (make exceptions to them) and so create new object classes which can be stored in the class library and used in the same manner. This makes it possible to create reusable objects.

Reusability: The holy grail of computer programming is to put software engineering on the same footing as computer engineering, where computers are assembled from standard, off-the-shelf components. Our brief review of the CBI authoring systems suggests the same theme: Those things done over and over again in instructional computing were made objects of the authoring system, accessible to all users.

The objects that result from object-oriented programming are, in fact, reusable. Once you make a dial or a pushbutton object, it can be copied and used anywhere. This is made possible by the almost complete independence of objects. Each object contains all of its own data (except globals), so it is not tied to a central data area, and it also contains its own methods, so it knows how to behave. The benefit to CBI from reusability is that designers need create certain basic objects only once in order to be able to reuse them in the future. Reusable objects can range from menus to graphical chemical molecules.

Persistence: In Chapter 3, while laying the foundation for understanding objects, we described persistence as an important characteristic of objects that was for the most part missing from frame-based authoring systems (with the exception of Authorware's graphic and perpetual objects) and some quest objects also.

Persistence is the continued existence of run-time objects in the computer's memory after their creation. We have described how most authoring tools draw objects on the screen but then forget them after doing so, making modification of the objects, erasure, movement, and general screen management sometimes very complicated. We have also described the utility of Authorware's object approach to graphics as a useful and welcome exception.

Object-oriented programming by definition creates objects which persist as long as the program is running. Only if an object exists in the computer's memory can it receive and then send messages. In an object-oriented program, not only can a circle draw itself on the display, but it can erase itself, move itself, change its color, or grow by changing its own radius. This is a powerful tool for display management, and for non-graphic objects, there is a comparable increase in power with a comparable reduction in programming effort which is achieved because of object-orientation.

The object revolution: Instructional design perspective

Though there are considerable benefits to the CBI programmer from object-orientation, there are even greater instructional powers afforded to designers that before were beyond reach. It is in the creation of newer forms of instruction and simplifying the process of instructional design that objects will have their greatest impact.

Designable objects: A compelling benefit of objects is that almost any kind of logical structure could be created with objects.

Frames. Frame structures could be created using objects, each frame type being equipped with component objects and handlers that would allow it to carry out the standard frame functions. An author would supply certain variable values to the frame which consists of structured objects, just as in a traditional authoring system. Frame objects would be linked to each other by specifying to a frame-object the message it is to send to activate the next frame-object when it is through executing itself.

Beyond frames. Structures much more flexible, versatile, and useful than frames could also be built using objects. Moreover, these more useful structures could be built with relative ease and speed. It is possible that the shift from frames will direct the designer's thoughts to these logical structures so strongly that the result will be a revolution in the way designers think about their instructional products, how they are built, and how they operate.

Instructional metaphor: Whereas in the past designers have tended to create message-centered instructional forms in which the crafting and delivery of a more or less sequential message was the essential pursuit, designers can now capitalize on the ability to design interactive models of reality for the student to interact with and learn from. The sequenced verbal message will become an embedded appendage to this new form of instructional experience. Chapter 16 describes at length a shift toward what we call model-centered instruction.

The principle of model-centered instruction is simple: Students learn from direct experience with the world's systems or faithful representations of them. In addition to experiencing models first-hand, students may also learn from a set of instructional features which accompany the model and provide the auxiliary information, guidance, and structure that helps the student learn from the direct encounter.

Instructional applications of model-centering

The notion of model-centering instruction is not so much new as it is underused in comparison with the more message-structured approaches to CBI. Up until now, the imaginations of instructional designers have not been given free rein because their tools did not allow them to depart from the message-centered, frame-based metaphor. That condition is rapidly changing, and designers are using a variety of new instructional forms and features made possible by object-oriented development tools.

Centering instruction on a model—a model of an environment, of a system, or of expert behavior—suggests several ways that models may be brought back into the instructional setting, appropriately supplemented and supported by independent instructional features. Models can supplement, complement, and perform functions live teachers find difficult—performing them more completely and rapidly. In addition, models can supply living, interactive books, making the library an interesting place to go. Best of all, models extend the teacher's reach as have earlier technological successes like the blackboard and the book.

Models and instructor-led classroom instruction: The best uses of CBI, and especially model-centered CBI, lie in extending rather than replacing the teacher. Teachers have found the blackboard—a brave and startling innovation in its own time—unyieldingly static as a surface on which to display dynamic ideas and representations. A projected model placed under complete instructor control for both normal and abnormal operation modes places the most dynamic and repeatable blackboard displays under the control of the least technological teacher.

Consider the instructor who is able to demonstrate the correct functioning of the central nervous system in small increments of new information which build toward the dynamic modeling of the entire system in full operation. Consider the ability to fault that same system and display instantly in full motion and color the impact on system function and external indications. Consider this same modeling capability demonstrating for high school biology students the dance of the molecules as DNA replicates both normally and in various mutation modes, or the operation of a new computer network or data entry system. A teacher can use models of any of these to improve his or her dialogue with the student's understanding.

Models and individual or small-group work: The term "individualized," due to our lack of adequate technology to truly individualize, has become synonymous with "isolated." Instead of individualizing instruction, we have evolved a system of mediating set, non-responsive messages which students witness by themselves, alone, and often do not even interact with. Models not only invite participation, they demand it because they do not operate or change without being controlled.

Models have several applications in small group and individual work:

Learning coach. A learning coach is, among other things, a process guide that participates in the process with the learner. A student conducting a chemistry experiment might have with him or her to the laboratory a computer which moved with the student through the experiment, as a living lab book, explaining outcomes in terms of a model of the experiment which it had within itself. By carrying out a dialogue with the student, it could compute the expected result and be ready to discuss it with the student, recommending steps to re-trace in the event of errors. This computer need not be a large presence sitting with its keyboard on the counter top. Instead, it might be ruggedized and placed in a relatively small package plugged into the laboratory wall, communicated with through a microphone-headset unit worn by the student.

Another form of learning coach might be useful to the owner of a new car. A program delivered with the car could supply a guided tour, show systems in operation, and allow the owner to ask questions of the system as it operated. Speak to me, my Porsche!

Intelligent tutor. The functions of the intelligent tutor are much like the functions of the non-intelligent tutor at the bottom of the imagination scale, but many of what are called instructional tutors do not conform to our mental image of the standard tutorial. Complex systems have been modeled, from electronics to boiler systems to DNA molecules, which allow the student to perform manipulations under either guided or unguided conditions, observing the response of the system and instructing at the same time.

Plaything. Though it was not originally intended to be a toy, the LOGO system was intended to be interesting and fun, but it is fun which instructs. There are many products begging to be built which involve interactions with the student which are almost as enjoyable as they are instructive. Instructive playthings will become an important product for both home and school use and hopefully can compete with the glitter of the current staple, the less-nourishing combat video game.

Guided exploration. Guided exploration activities, in which the student is given a tour through the human body or through the interior of the sun, are easily possible through model-centering. Certainly we are able to simulate such tours by providing animations on videotape, but what if during the tour you have a question? What if you want to see something repeatedly without having to rewind (and perhaps get lost)? What if you want to stop and look at details before proceeding? What if you want to act on the system you are touring to see a result?

Tool. Simulations—models of systems—have been a tool of modern technology for decades. We have described how our economy and new technologies could not advance without simulations. Students must learn to use these tools of our society. We must therefore present students with serious simulations and ask them to derive new knowledge from observing the influences of changes to input configurations.

Base for project. Students alone or in groups do projects as a normal part of learning not only school content but social interactions. Models should become a part of these projects. If students are asked to report on the water cycle and the effects of ground pollution on streams and rivers, can't we ask them to draw from the library the model of the water cycle for their grade level and then run tests using it to determine the information for their report? Could not a student-commented version of the model itself become a central feature of the report presentation?

Base for problem solving. Students can learn problem solving best by solving problems. Models can create simulated worlds within which problems can be presented, along with action controls for use in solving, taking action, and observing results. Following problems, students can be given feedback on the course of their activities, learning more effective strategies for problem-solving as well as specific content knowledge.

Models as a resource. Models and libraries have been connected in the paragraphs above. It is hard to understand why books should not become computer-based collections of, among other things, interactive models and interfaces to them. Students learning about weather and its effects should have models of the atmosphere and local weather zones, perhaps ones near their own home, to help them understand. The idea of model-centered instruction alone could redefine the concept of the library.

Later chapters of this book, particularly Chapter 15, enlarge upon the concept of model-centered instruction and describe many of its features in detail. For now the discussion must center on one question. How do object-oriented programming and authoring tools support the transition of CBI into a new and more powerful teaching metaphor?

Applying objects to model-centered instruction

The two main functions of model-centered instruction—executing simulations and providing instructional services—can be accomplished by object-oriented programming and authoring tools in a way not possible using strictly frame-based tools. In this section we begin to describe different structural approaches to doing this and discuss the types and arrangements of objects which are required.

We do not presume that this chapter will equip you with skills and knowledge to accomplish the things we describe, but we feel that much of what we describe in this chapter and in Chapters 15 and later will be within the grasp of the average CBI designer using available tools. Additional study will equip the intrepid and adventuresome designer with skills for more difficult challenges and provide targets for the future.

Intelligent instructional systems

One form of model-centered instruction is termed *intelligent instruction* or *intelligent tutoring*. "Intelligent," when applied to instructional systems, means that the system generates its instructional acts from knowledge about how to teach and about what to teach rather than from pre-formed messages and logic. This means that the system has the ability to make decisions about instruction rather than simply executing decisions which have already been made. In order to form instruction on-the-fly at the time of instruction requires that the instructional program have encoded within it certain functions and knowledge:

Knowledge of how to teach: This normally equates to having internal to the system an expert teacher function which has been equipped with the best rules for constructing messages and interactions from raw knowledge and resources. This is often referred to as the *teacher model*.

Knowledge of what to teach: This refers to a base of knowledge to be taught, but its form and nature is a matter of much discussion among CBI designers and AI practitioners. In the model-centered approach to structuring instructional products, the knowledge is understood to come from the model itself, describing itself, its operation, and its status. That is, as the simulation executes, it generates dynamic knowledge about itself, in addition to the static knowledge of itself which it also possesses.

Knowledge of the person being taught: In order to say or do the right instructional thing, an intelligent system must know who it is saying and doing things for. Knowledge of the student of two types is necessary: (1) knowledge of the student's characteristics, styles, learning patterns, and (2) knowledge of what the student knows at any given moment. The student's knowledge is sometimes tracked in terms of what is known compared to what could be known from the knowledge base. This is often referred to as the *student model*.

An intelligent instructional system may be intelligent in one area (for instance, next problem selection) and not intelligent in another (for instance, feedback). Remember that intelligence refers to the system's ability to make instructional decisions as opposed to carrying out pre-made decisions. In those areas where an instructional system is making decisions on the spot, it is intelligent. In others, it is not. Moreover, it is possible for a wide variety of intelligence-producing mechanisms to be employed—some of them very smart, and others not as smart. This leads to a wide expanse of possible intelligent instructional system configurations.

These ideas make the concept of an intelligent instructional product less frightening and suggests more adaptive instructional products. If object tools are used to construct them, there is also hope of their reusability.

The things that appear complex today will soon become commonplace, and rather than being an area of specialty as intelligent systems are now within the CBI community, they soon will be common knowledge, and familiarity will have risen to the point where intelligent features will be the rule and easy to implement with the improved tools which will be available.

Building instructional objects

Since we have spent time in earlier chapters showing how useful frame structures work and are joined together into combinations that make instruction possible, we should do the same for objects. How do objects combine for instructional purposes? We would like to explore three cases: building frames out of objects, building interactive models for students, and building instructional features as objects.

Case #1. Using objects to build traditional frame-like structures: Different approaches to design using objects abound. Entire books are written for programmers, showing them how to build efficient and reusable object structures. We will try to tie together ideas from previous chapters and demonstrate how objects can be organized to carry out the familiar higher-order functions of frames.

We will design a menu frame capable of displaying a menu of choices, accepting a choice from the student, and branching control to the appropriate next *frame* object, based on the choice. In Chapter 4, we diagrammed this type of frame (see Figure 2, Chapter 4).

Our most important structural choice will concern whether to build a single object with many function-specific methods (attached handler routines) or several separate objects contained within a larger container object, each one performing a prescribed portion of the frame's functions. While making this decision, we may recall that object reusability is an important benefit of object-orientation. Therefore, we may decide to create the many-object frame and count on being able to reuse the individual function-objects to build yet other frame types. Taking this approach means that creating new frame types will consist of: (1) selecting existing function-objects to be included into the new frame type, (2) creating additional function-objects as needed for the unique specialized functions of the new frame, and (3) uniting the selected and the newly-made objects under the control of the container object.

This approach to frame design will have the following benefits:

- Not only the function-objects, but the container object as well will be reusable for the construction of other frame types with minor modifications.

- The authoring of the frame (that is, giving the frame the specific data that will enable it to function correctly) will consist of supplying data to only one object, the container object, which will send that data to the individual function-objects at the appropriate runtime moment.

- The ordering of functions carried out by the frame will be very flexible, following the sequence given as data by the author to the container object.

This style of frame construction—the assembly of functions within a larger frame—should remind you of the mechanism used by the Quest authoring system. All versions of that system have used this basic approach of populating a container with functions. In effect, we have shown how reusable objects could be used to achieve this result.

As function-objects for our menu frame we might create an object that executes a display, another which begins a timer for the time-out function, another that displays a response area and accepts input, and so forth. In order to obtain more control and flexibility in the display, we may place individual display function-objects within their own display object container inside the larger frame container. One object might have the assigned function of placing bitmaps on the screen, another may move bitmaps across the screen along a designated path to create an animation effect, and another object may remove a bitmap from the screen. The display container could be designed to choreograph the action and timing of these display function-objects, and the effect would be to create a display management system with some of the capabilities of a tool like Macromedia Director.

The point we hope we have made is not that these sophisticated authoring tools can be built by the average designer using off-the-shelf tools, but that objects can be used to build a variety of frame-like structures.

Case #2. Using objects to construct models with which students can observe and interact: Object-oriented tools were originally made for the purpose of creating models of things, so it is no surprise that they are very good at it. Object orientation as we know it had its roots in the work of Alan Kay, an American computer scientist, who was assigned as a graduate student to analyze a programming language called Simula (its name suggests its function), written by two Norwegian computer scientists. The lessons he learned from Simula and from other experiences came together in an object-oriented programming language Kay designed, called SmallTalk.™ SmallTalk is now a very popular and powerful object-oriented programming tool.

To construct a model for students to experience and interact with means constructing one of three types of models: a model of an environment, a model of a system, or a model of expert behavior. These types of models and their hybrid varieties are described at length in Chapter 16. For illustrative purposes, we will construct a hybrid model of a portion of the electrical system of a house, showing the types of objects which are created and the manner in which they communicate.

The model we create will simulate the operation of two light switches and two lamps in two locations of the house—the entryway inside the front door and the front porch. This will entail not only representing the switches and the lamps but as well the environmental locations: Entryway and Front Porch.

We begin by itemizing the elements of the simulation which must be created: an Entryway, a Front Porch (environmental locations), a front porch lamp, an entryway lamp, a front porch lamp switch, and an entryway lamp switch. Since these real-world objects have to be related to each other spatially, we will place the switch for both the front porch lamp and the entryway lamp in the entryway. There will be no switch at the front porch location.

Having identified these real-world objects, we can create a program object to represent each one. Each program object will have properties and behaviors which mimic those of the real objects. Properties will store current values of the object. For instance, the front porch lamp will have the property *illuminated,* and that property will have one of two values at all times: either *on* or *off.* The front porch lamp switch will also have properties, among them *setting* with possible values of *on* and *off.* It will have the behavior (expressed in a method attached to the object) of telling the lamp what position it is in every time the switch position changes. Whenever the switch position is changed, the switch will send a message to the lamp telling it the value of the new position (on or off). From this, the lamp will be able to determine if it needs to take any action to change its own values. Attached to the lamp will be a method which contains the rule: "When the switch value changes to ON, then set the value of ILLUMINATED to YES." There will also be a rule in the lamp's method to change the lamp's ILLUMINATED to NO when the switch moves to the OFF position.

Note that because the switch for the front porch lamp is in the entryway, the lamp on the front porch will not be apparent until the student moves from the entryway location to the front porch location where the front porch lamp is visible. Chapter 17 describes the simulation logic patterns that are involved in displaying locations and the model values related to each one.

A third model with potential instructional value is a model of expert behavior. Such a model could easily be constructed and capable of interacting with the two other models: capable of moving from location to location, making decisions on how to reach a particular commanded goal, and showing its own reasoning process and actions as it does so. This model is a model of behavior that is to be learned.

This simple illustration shows that the design of a simulation model is easier because the model itself is often expressed in terms of the components which make up the real system being simulated. This is not always true, but it is so in the large majority of cases. When an object model is designed, the designer does not need to translate the design for the simulation into a language that the computer understands, because with object-oriented tools, the language of the computer is objects and the messages which they can send to each other. The language for program design parallels the designer's language of thought.

Case #3. Using objects to create instructional features: The hardest and yet most interesting challenge is to create instructional features using objects. Instructional features exist at a level of abstraction above the specific content or skill being taught, and that is one of the things which make it difficult for designers to think of them. The other contributing factor to this difficulty is the broad variety of opinions as to what constitutes good instruction. Each designer, it seems, has his or her own private set of beliefs about what is good instructional technique, and mixed in with the research results and proven principles is a lot of folklore, personal experience, and personal bias.

We will define a simple instructional feature and show how that feature can be made to work using programmed objects. We will leave the creation of more objects to you and to your own insights on instruction.

We will design a feedback feature which is capable of spotting erroneous patterns of performance and signaling them to the student when one is detected. Our feedback provider will be silent for most of the time while the student operates the simulation, but every action of the student upon the simulation and every response of the simulation to those actions will be sent in a message to the feedback object, which will then compare the latest action with patterns of previous actions, looking for patterns of events which signal an error. When an error pattern of events is detected (and the feedback object may have many, supplied to it through any of several different program mechanisms), the feedback object presents to the student a message (either pre-composed or composed at the time the error is detected) signaling the concern. The decision-making capability of this feedback object depends on the insight of the designer, and it may range from very stiff and mechanical built-in decisions to very intelligent and adaptive decisions based on details of the performance pattern.

This is a simple feedback messaging instructional feature. What happens once the error has been signaled to the student depends on the designer's principles and theories of feedback, and subsequent activities may include entering into a diagnostic dialogue with the student, supplying some form of instructional message, asking the student to correct his or her own error, or any of several other forms of messaging and interaction. These types of interactive and extended feedback may require additional objects to carry them out.

There is no doubt that an object used to provide complex forms of feedback for a complex modeled system and a complex problem to be solved will be a complicated thing to create. That is the bad news. The good news is that it is possible to define an object capable of providing feedback and then modifying or evolving the object into a more general and more reusable object. It is not an easy task, and there are technical problems to be solved, but over time, not just one, but multiple solutions to this and the other instructional problems will evolve, and as they become public knowledge, we will see that the problem was not as complicated as we thought, and that the construction and modification of instructional feature objects has become easy and common.

In Chapters 15 and 16, we describe the importance of models in CBI in greater detail, and in Chapter 17, we describe the basic structures used to create both environment and system models.

Object-oriented authoring tools

We have referred in several places in this chapter to programming and authoring tools that either are or will become commercially available for designers to use for object-oriented design. Some of them, such as SmallTalk and C++, are object-oriented programming languages which require much expertise to use. Others, however, have simplified the user interface considerably, placing object-orientation within the grasp of the designer who is willing to expend enough effort to learn their basic elements. In selecting a tool, the designer should keep in mind that object-orientation is not an all-or-none quality. The principles and features of object-orientation can be applied to a tool in degrees, and some tools are fully-featured object systems, while others are traditional imperative (sequential) programming tools to which have been added some (but not all) of the features of object-orientation.

We will mention a representative sample of the more user-friendly object-oriented tools suitable for CBI design and development.

Programming systems: Of the object-oriented programming systems available for use by instructional designers, several stand out as desirable options, depending on the willingness of designers to learn a new language. These tools offer great power to the designer and so are very tantalizing. They will see increasing use in the future by instructional designers and their programmers.

Visual Basic and Delphi. Microsoft's Visual Basic and Borland's Delphi products are a blend of the Basic and Pascal programming languages respectively, structured programming techniques, and some object-oriented features (for instance, method-like subroutines and encapsulated data). They have a flat set of object classes and therefore no inheritance other than from the immediate class. However, they are a powerful and efficient programming option and can accomplish advanced instructional applications while relieving the designer of much of the normal programming load.

ToolBook. The Asymetrix ToolBook product is object-oriented to a high degree. It does not have the sequential programming capability that Visual Basic and Delphi do. It allows users to create objects from a small number of classes and attach to them *handlers,* which are the methods described earlier in this chapter. The operation of ToolBook is more fully within the metaphor of object-orientedness described in this chapter. ToolBook has also proven to be an economical tool, and Asymetrix has issued a specialized CBT version which provides reusable, frame-like object structures from which the designer can assemble traditional forms of instruction. ToolBook is especially well-suited for the creation of simulation models and allowing instructional features to be added to them.

mTropolis. The mTropolis programming system provides an easy-to-use system for defining objects and adding to them handlers which give them unique behavior. The product tries to simplify its representation of object interactions with diagrams, which have something of a learning curve, but do make programming easier once they are mastered. A variety of pre-programmed handler behaviors are supplied to the developer on a palette which can be dragged and dropped onto objects under construction. Extension of handlers beyond the basic set provided is possible in several programming languages.

SK8. SK8 is the internal code name for an object-oriented programming environment by Apple Computer. SK8 is a fully object-oriented and very powerful programming environment which uses a friendly, natural-language-like scripting language for the creation of its methods.

Authoring systems. Some authoring systems designed specifically for the production of CBI have properties of object-orientation.

Authorware. Many of the object-oriented features of the Authorware Pro product from MacroMedia were described in Chapter 4. These presently include the object-oriented graphics features and the perpetual feature which allows multiple objects to persist at run-time.

Quest 5.0 for Windows. Quest, traditionally a frame-based authoring system, is transitioning toward object-orientation. Quest 5.0 for Windows is an object-oriented authoring system which retains its compatibility with frame-based structures, but also opens an object-oriented capability to designers who have the desire to use it.

Conclusion

This chapter has attempted to peek over the horizon to see what awaits the CBI designer in terms of metaphors and tools for future design and development. The new developments are close on the horizon. Some have already become visible, and others will follow in their train. It is important for the CBI designer to become conversant with the two schools of thought in CBI design and tools—the traditional and the model-centered—in order to be functional in the near term, but also to be able to adapt as the tide of products and tools changes.

Self-directed activities

- Analyze an instructional product that you know was developed using frame-based tools. Design the same product using object structures instead.

- Reverse the previous activity and analyze a product you know was developed using an object-oriented tool. Design the same product using frame structures.

- Design each of the frame types described in Chapter 4 using object structures.

- Design a unique instructional interaction pattern of your own and show how object structures would be used to create it.

- Design the operation of an instructional feature that gives coaching or hinting messages upon student demand. Design the feature using objects.

- Begin to collect names and information for object-oriented programming systems and authoring systems. Collect information that can be used to compare features and capabilities of the systems as well as information on limitations or weaknesses of each system.

Further reading

Booch, G. (1994). *Object-oriented design and analysis with applications (2nd ed.).* Redwood City, CA: Benjamin/Cummings Publishing.

Coad, P. (1992). Object-oriented patterns. *Communications of the ACM, 35(9),* 152–159.

Coad, P., and Yourdon, E. (1991). *Object-oriented analysis (2nd ed.).* Englewood Cliffs, NJ: Yourdon Press, Prentice-Hall.

Coad, P., and Yourdon, E. (1991). *Object-oriented design.* Englewood Cliffs, NJ: Yourdon Press, Prentice-Hall.

Coad, P., and Nicola, J. (1993). *Object-oriented programming.* Englewood Cliffs, NJ: Yourdon Press, Prentice-Hall.

Gamma, E., Helm, R., Johnson, R., and Vlissides, J. (1995). *Design patterns: Elements of reusable object-oriented software.* Reading, MA: Addison-Wesley Publishing Company.

Polson, M., and Richardson, J. (Eds.). (1988). *The foundations of intelligent tutoring systems.* Hillsdale, NJ: Lawrence Erlbaum Associates.

Psotka, J., Massey, L., and Mutter, S. (Eds.).(1988). *Intelligent tutoring systems: Lessons learned.* Hillsdale, NJ: Lawrence Erlbaum Associates.

Shasha, D., and Lazere, C. (1995). *Out of their minds: The lives and discoveries of 15 great computer scientists.* New York: Copernicus.

Shlaer, S., and Mellor, S. (1992). *Object lifecycles: Modeling the world in states.* Englewood Cliffs, NJ: Yourdon Press, Prentice-Hall.

Towne, D. (1995). *Learning and instruction in simulation environments.* Englewood Cliffs, NJ: Educational Technology Publications.

Wenger, E. (1987). *Artificial intelligence and tutoring systems: Computational and cognitive approaches to the communication of knowledge.* Los Altos, CA: Morgan Kaufmann Publishers.

SECTION III

PRINCIPLES OF INSTRUCTIONAL STRATEGY

Principles derived from knowledge of the learning process to guide the design of instructional messages and interactions. The beginning of an exploration into strategies and their origins.

7

LEARNING: THE STUDENT

Chapter Objectives:

1. *Recognize the influence of the student's energy state on the course of learning.*

2. *Identify the stages of instructional message processing which constitute the student's "information highway."*

3. *Describe the effect of interruptions in the processing flow on message interpretation and learning.*

4. *Identify the processes by which students draw knowledge from instructional messages and connect message patterns with what is already known.*

5. *Define the influence of the student's strategic control on learning.*

6. *Relate the four factors of excellent CBI to the processes of message and experience processing during learning.*

The legs of the stool

Excellence in computerized instruction is a chemistry that occurs only when two requirements are met: (1) it must be good instruction, and (2) it must be designed properly for the computer as a medium.

When you evaluate CBI products, you can measure them in terms of four main factors which function as if they were the legs of a stool. If one of the factors is faulty, the instruction works, but like the stool with one leg missing, it is difficult to use. With two of the factors faulty, then like a two-legged stool, the instruction is hard to use and unpredictable. With three of the factors are missing, only the most persistent students will find the product useful. On the other hand, if all four factors are present, then you can expect good results when the product is used with the population of students for whom it was designed, and you can consider it excellent—instruction which will be motivating and highly productive.

The four factors of excellent CBI—the four legs of the stool—are the topic of this chapter. As guiding principles, they have been shaped and improved during the creation, revision, and testing of hundreds of hours of CBI. Understanding the choice of these factors requires some understanding of how students learn, so before naming the factors, we digress long enough to talk about learning processes. That is because instruction is intended to support the needs of the learning process, and only by understanding the process can you supply it with the appropriate raw materials—experiences and information.

A new look at the student

The four factors of excellence in CBI products are based on the premises that:

1. Human learning requires information processing.

2. Information processing consumes massive amounts of student energy.

3. Humans have limited energy and information processing capacities.

We are so used to thinking about the human mental capacity as being boundless, and we are so transfixed by the mind's power and scope that we often fail to take some of its limitations into account. But just as seemingly unlimited supplies of fossil fuel tempted us as a society to waste the earth's energy resources, the seeming unlimited supply of mental processing power of students can tempt a designer into instructional practices that waste the student's learning resources. We can be extravagant in the way we use the limited pool of energy and the limited channels of communication that students have for learning.

Let's take a moment to review just how finite and relatively narrow are some of the passages within the human information processing mechanism. Let's catalog some of the *finite dimensions* of the human mind:

- *Our brain has only 10 to 15 billion nerve cells. We stress only because that number, though it seems large, is far less than the number of bacteria growing in your mouth at this moment; ten billion, which seems like so much to us, is a pittance on nature's scale.*

- *Our brain can record 86 million bits of information each day. This is again, a pittance, especially when you consider the massive consolidation of those bits into chunks which takes place during the learning process. The fact is that when we view a scene we actually encode only a small portion of the information within it, and that, most often, not accurately.*

- *Each second, 100,000 different chemical reactions are occurring in your brain, and they burn up huge quantities of your body's energy.*

- *It takes about 1/500 of a second for the brain to recognize an object after the light from the object enters your eyes. That's fast, but this recognition is only the first of hundreds of steps that the brain must execute in order to make that object have meaning or to be employed in any useful way. Consider the fact that at this moment about 10 billion bits of information are streaming across the bridge between the right and left halves of your brain as you read—a path that is essential to your understanding and acting.*

- *Brain nerve impulses travel at about 250 miles per hour. That is much slower than the speed of light and the speed of electricity. It is slower than the speed of the space shuttle, and is only about half the normal cruising speed of the average passenger jet.*

As awesome as the human brain is, it is finite and limited, and it burns up energy at prodigious rates. Your brain's metabolism, if converted to the equivalent electrical energy, would consume the equivalent of a 20-watt light bulb. Your brain uses up 40% of your body's total energy. That's why the brain is so easily damaged by a lack of oxygen.

Think of that energy consumption! Nearly half of your body's energy is consumed by less than 5% of the body's bulk! Something impressive has to be going on there. We live in a society which requires more mental than physical exertion, yet we still come home after a day of hard mental activity as tired as if we had been hauling bricks.

Energy production and consumption

We learn in elementary school that humans oxidize the chemicals contained in food using the oxygen we breathe. This liberates energy, which the body can capture and allocate to various physical and mental body functions. Energy production is a constant process in humans that requires a steady stream of raw materials. Since we use energy constantly, the energy supply runs out quickly, requiring production of still more. Our energy store is finite, and when our energy runs out, so does our ability to think and act.

Each of us has come to understand through personal experience that there are limits to the amount of energy that we can produce and consume each day. Part of the wonder of our energy system is its ability to manage our pool of energy and mobilize it in support of those activities which we or our body's built-in mechanisms decide have the greatest benefit to us. One of those activities is learning.

In order to learn by study, we as humans must desire to learn. We must participate in learning by directing our attention and by directing our own processing of incoming information. Just as instructing is an act resulting from the designer's intention, learning is an occurrence resulting from the learner's intention.

But in the real world of real life, learning is only one mental process which must compete with many other mental and physical processes which draw on the body's energy. The constant demands for attention, processing, and action experienced by the average human all reduce the likelihood that time and energy will be spent on intentional, focused learning. This is a fact of great relevance to the instructional designer.

Energy management

As part of becoming competent individuals, we become competent managers of our own energy resources. We learn early in life to allocate available energy carefully, so as not to run out before our intentions for action are fulfilled. We are frequently forced into trade-off choices: "If I chop all of this wood now, I won't be in very good shape for the baseball game this afternoon," or "If I mow the lawn now, I won't feel like studying for the test later."

One parent described her son as a small child, before he had learned how to self-manage energy. On numerous occasions, after playing hard outside all day, he would come to dinner very hungry, but as he had failed to save any energy, she would look over at him in his high chair only to find his face buried in his food, sound asleep. Over time, this child mastered energy management, as we all do; few of us sleep in our food any more. We have learned to forecast our planned activities and to save energy for those activities. We actually arrange our activities so that they do not interfere with one another. "I'm going to eat a small lunch today so I will not be drowsy during the meeting this afternoon," is actually the expression of an energy management plan.

Those who have become proficient learners have discovered that learning is one of the activities for which we reserve energy. The saving of energy is not what makes learning occur, but without it, we do not have the energy to spare for learning. Research indicates that each mental process takes a finite, even measurable, amount of time. We may assume also that each one also consumes a finite and measurable amount of energy. Therefore, each decision of the instructional developer represents a tax on the limited pool of energy which the learner has allocated for learning use.

The practices of the instructional designer must be informed by the principles of energy management which are constantly active within students:

1. Designers must require the expenditure of energy for activities and interactions which support the student in carrying out learning.

2. Designers must avoid placing unnecessary roadblocks in the path of the student in the form of meaningless mental processing.

In order to maximize learning benefit for the student, the computer-based instruction designer must organize an instructional experience which complements student needs and either influences or responds to student expectations and goals moment by moment. The designer must refuse to be indiscriminate, haphazard, or careless in the design of instructional events, whether they employ fixed or adaptive logic, and regardless of what primitive elements are combined to form the instructional message and interaction.

This means that the designer is committed to assisting the learner in:

- Directing attention

- Extracting the central message of displays

- Interpreting patterns within the message

- Forming goals

- Structuring memory

- Organizing information processing habits

- Building recall associations

- Constructing action plans and patterns

- Acting

- Automating performance

- Evaluating performance.

Furthermore, it means that the designer does not trifle with or become irrelevant to the student's organization of these activities unless the intent is to teach something to the student directly about the activities themselves. By making this commitment, the designer takes the best advantage of the student's process of energy management by allowing that energy which has been allocated to the process of learning to be spent as profitably as possible. This is the main justification for all of instructional design.

The intelligent instructional designer can carefully control the factors of instruction which influence the amount of energy that the learner must exert in order to learn. This means that the developer will maximize the energy used in encountering new ideas and gaining new skills and minimize the energy used up in wrestling with the faults and quirks of the delivery medium and the instructional message.

Instruction that is clumsy is relatively unproductive and requires more energy to be used by the learner than is necessary. As anyone who has been a classroom teacher will tell you, when a student's energy is used up, the instruction is effectively over, whether the teacher is finished or not. Only the foolish teacher will waste learning energy, and the best way to control the energy drain during instruction is to carefully manage the information processing burden placed on the student.

The human information highway

We hear a considerable amount about the "information highway." Consider the highway for information created during instruction by the *continuous stream* of incoming data through a student's senses. Highway engineers become nervous when they see the highway they designed becoming crowded, because they realize that under those conditions, the potential for a traffic jam increases rapidly. If somebody slows down or crashes, it can cause a chain reaction that will quickly turn their superhighway into a parking lot. The human information highway is always crowded and moving at top speed. It is very vulnerable to information "accidents."

What can the instructional designer do to keep a student's information highway from becoming a parking lot during the instructional experience? Are there things that designers do innocently which cause pile-ups to happen? Clearly, the answer to this question is "Yes." Preventing mental traffic jams is one of the central issues of this book—keeping information flowing freely and rapidly to supply the voracious appetite of learning.

Let's travel the human information highway for ourselves. In the process, we will pass some intersections where intelligent work by the designer can spell the difference between full speed ahead and gridlock. First, a road map. Figure 1 diagrams our version of the information processing functions of a learner.

The functions shown in Figure 1 are mental functions or processes rather than things or locations in the brain. The function labeled "decoder" does not really exist as a localized thing or place in the brain. It is a set of functions carried out by several parts of the brain in interaction with each other. The more we learn about mental functions, the more we find they are distributed in complex patterns throughout the brain. Vision was once thought to be concentrated within one area of the brain. It is now believed to be the product of nearly twenty interacting centers of visual processing. We assume that the learning functions are no differently distributed.

Decoding the incoming message

The information highway shown in Figure 1 begins with the entry of sensory data into a sense receptor: an eye, an ear, the nose, the tongue, the touch sense, the sense of balance. Incoming sense data must be decoded into terms that the brain can understand. This is done by a set of functions which in Figure 1 are labeled as the decoder.

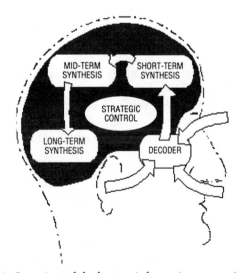

Figure 1. One view of the human information processing system.

The decoder performs several actions. It:

- Scans the experiential surface (the incoming data to all of the senses).

- Coordinates the data from multiple sensory channels.

- Identifies familiar elements of the incoming data through pattern-matching.

- Temporarily stores the identities of detected familiar elements.

- Identifies unfamiliar elements in the incoming data.

- Makes specialized analysis of unfamiliar (undecodable) elements in an attempt to decode them.

- Attempts to store the details of still-unfamiliar elements when decoding attempts fail.

- Detects the pattern of organization (e.g., temporal, spatial, kinetic) between elements.

- Sends detected patterns to temporary storage.

This list of functions accomplishes a kind of decoding or analysis of the incoming message into constituent parts which can be processed by the brain. This decoding or decomposition process has an analog in the disassembly line of our digestive system, which breaks food into constituent chemicals which can be used by the body for nourishment. Just as the absorption of the food value is impossible without this "decoding" of the food into usable form, the absorption of an instructional message through the senses is impossible without the decoding of the incoming sense data. According to Richard Restak's *The Modular Brain*, in the visual sense, there appear to be separate processing areas responsible for "seeing" motion, "seeing" color, and "seeing" facial patterns. These are some of the stations on the disassembly line for incoming visual information.

In a small percentage of newborn infants, the decomposition function of the digestive system does not operate properly because the body fails to supply the correct mixture of enzymes and juices that are required to break down food material. These children must temporarily use special formulas which contain the chemicals for body nourishment in pre-digested form, until their own body can supply them. Without this, the infants waste away for lack of energy and can eventually die. In a like manner, a student with no processes in place for digesting or decoding incoming sense data or one whose processes are somehow faulty finds it more difficult to extract meaning from experience and thereby learn.

Once the function identified as decoding has analyzed the incoming sensory data into its constituents (and remember that this is a complex function involving many areas of the brain and consisting of many steps or stages), the decomposed raw elements of the incoming message are kept within temporary memory, waiting for further processing to make use of them. Figure 1 identifies a sequence of waystations which are labeled "Short-Term," "Mid-Term," and "Long-Term" Synthesis. It is here that the processing takes place, by which the student constructs an understanding of the message and uses it to either build structures of new knowledge or modify existing structures.

Synthesizing the elements

These waystations are the mind's mechanism for building larger and more useful structures from the raw elements of the decoded incoming message. Whereas the decoding process sifts through a blizzard of incoming sensory data, looking for recognizable patterns, these synthetic building processes begin with the patterns which have been found and connect them into larger patterns of meaning. Figure 2 illustrates the type of process that is carried out during this synthesis. The process involves:

- The accumulation of decoded message elements in memory.

- Pattern matching against the student's existing knowledge, which allows individual elements to be related to each other through chunking.

- Retention of un-matched elements in memory for advancement to the next round of pattern matching.

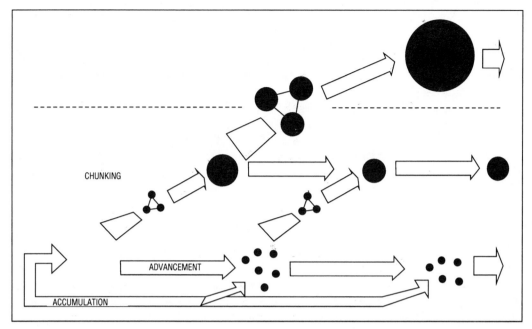

Figure 2. The processes of accumulation, chunking, and advancement in message processing.

The continuous application of these three actions—accumulation, chunking, and advancement—allows the mind to relate the structure of the incoming message with the knowledge structures it already possesses.

Accumulation

Accumulation is the process of marshaling together all of the message elements which have been recognized by the decoding process and stored in temporary memory. Keeping just one set of elements in this highly volatile memory requires a certain amount of attention and constant review and rehearsal. It is a task much like juggling, but the task is made even more difficult by the constant addition of new elements to be juggled, which happens because the information highway continues to process the stream of incoming sense data.

Though it is easiest to think of learning as a context in which the student receives only one instructional message at a time and digests it in a leisurely way, that is never the way things really happen. An instructional message flows to the student in a steady stream of varying length and density. With computerized instruction, that stream can be punctuated by pauses, but when the message is flowing, it still comes in a stream that requires some degree of mental juggling by the student.

The decoded elements of the incoming message find their way into temporary memory. But temporary memory—sometimes called by psychologists, *short-term memory*—does not have a very large capacity, and furthermore it does not have a very long time span of remembering. A famous study of memory capacity by Miller determined that the memory span for numbers for the average human was between 5 and 9 digits at one time. Beyond that, forgetting erased not only the excess digits, but the already-learned ones as well. This is an experiment you can try on yourself.

Because of this upper limit on short-term memory, the number of elements stored there must be reduced as quickly as possible to make way for the constantly-arriving stream of new elements which have been recognized by the decoder. The mind has two ways of emptying its temporary memory: (1) the automatic method: forgetting, and (2) the learning method: reducing the memory load through chunking.

When the temporary memory runs out of room, it simply refuses to store any more elements. This event normally causes some confusion and breaks your concentration, so when overloading takes place, you don't just forget the extra elements that don't fit; you also forget much of what was already being held safely in temporary memory. This means that overloading not only reduces learning capacity but has cataclysmic effects that interrupt the chain of learning in a more general way. It has the same effect that an overturned truck has on a highway: It causes a traffic blockage and makes a parking lot out of your information highway. This realization should cause you as a designer to look for ways to avoid overloading the student's short-term memory.

Chunking

The alternative to forgetting the content of temporary memory is *chunking*. Chunking happens when a synthesis function (short-, mid-, or long-term, see Figure 1) is successful in spotting a familiar pattern among the elements which are being juggled within temporary memory. When such a pattern is found, the independent elements begin to be recognized as one single pattern and are no longer handled by memory as separate entities.

This is a mental activity we all use. If you are given the phone number "224-3456," you can remember seven individual digits—seven separate items of temporary memory—even though that is near to the limit of the average person's short-term memory. On the other hand, you may notice a pattern in the numbers which allows you to remember fewer actual digits. There is a sequence of digits in this telephone number, and you can remember its beginning digit, "3," the number of digits following, and the direction of the sequence (ascending). This reduces the memory load for the second half of the phone number from four things to three things.

If there is only one telephone prefix in your town—"224"—then you are probably so familiar with it that it represents a familiar pattern within your existing knowledge and can be remembered as if it were one digit.

Even if there is more than one prefix in town (e.g., 224, 225, and 226), then all that you have to remember is the "4," the "5," or the "6." However, if you live in New York City, where there are huge numbers of prefixes, then you will probably have to remember the prefix as three separate digits.

Chunking reduces the load on temporary memory by reducing the number of things to be remembered. Figure 2 shows that chunking is capable of reducing memory at every stage of processing. The decoder creates chunks from the raw message, then it can create chunks from those chunks by combining them together. Once the low-level elements of the decoded message have been through one chunking, the higher-order elements that result can themselves become a part of a larger remembered pattern. This can lead to the formation of chunks of memory of considerable size, a desirable state of affairs. This is how we build useful mental structures that eventually correspond with what we already know and allow us to understand and learn from the instructional message.

These processes of accumulation and chunking (through pattern-matching) go on in the short-term synthesis, the mid-term synthesis, and the long-term synthesis (see Figure 1). The only difference between these stages is the size of the chunks that are being remembered, matched against existing knowledge, and chunked into larger chunks.

You may ask whether these processes should be shown separately in the illustration if they all represent the same basic function. You may also ask whether there are really only three levels of synthesis. The answer to both questions is that the figure is representative and conceptual, not specific. It depicts the types of processes which allow us to receive and decode the steady stream of experience contained in an instructional message.

As a designer, you will be the creator of many messages which must travel the information highways in the minds of your students, and if you can begin to think of the message-handling processes as a continuous activity rather than as a still-life painting, you will avoid many instances of mental gridlock for your students.

Learning

The process of chunking, in which we match the incoming message with what we already know, depends upon the students' ability to recognize patterns which are already in their knowledge. But if learning depends upon the ability to recognize knowledge patterns already held in the mind, how can the student learn anything new, since no patterns exist in the mind to match the new?

The answer lies in the ability of the mind to match partial patterns. When we are unable to readily recognize the content of an incoming message, we have the capacity to apply inferential processes in order to find near-matches in what we already know. Once we find partial matches, we can use them to create new knowledge patterns. This is learning.

When we use this process of partial pattern matching, it is deliberate, intentional, and goal-driven. It is the direct result of: (1) a realization on the part of the learner that the patterns within existing knowledge are not adequate to match the incoming message, (2) a determination by the learner to resolve the discrepancy, (3) a search for partial patterns within the learner's existing knowledge which have some chance of being valid, and (4) the selection and remodeling of an existing pattern to create a new pattern or to bring about a re-organization of the old pattern.

This process involves the student's realization that learning needs to take place. It requires the student's active participation in the process of learning. An important stage of the instructional process is to create the anomalous state within the student—one in which it becomes apparent to the student that he or she needs to learn something not already known. Without reaching this anomalous state, students interpret new messages just in terms of what is already known. They match the incoming message with existing patterns of knowledge, and new learning does not occur.

Advancement

What does happen to elements of the decoded message which are never matched and so never become included within a chunk? They are handled through advancement and forgetting. Advancement is the third of the three functions carried out during the synthesis of chunks. As Figure 2 shows, the accumulation of new elements from the decoder continues on after chunking has begun to remove things from short-term memory. Elements that are not matched may either be retained in the temporary memory pool—in hopes of finding a match later—or they may be forgotten when they become so unrelated to the other elements in temporary memory that the strain of remembering them becomes great.

The process of retaining unmatched chunks in memory in hopes of finding future matches is a common, perhaps universal, experience. When you read a long sentence, you begin to accumulate decoded message elements in temporary memory in hopes of tying them together with a known pattern of existing knowledge. A well-constructed sentence allows you to detect a pattern early in the sentence, in some cases even before you have read half of the sentence.

Then that central structure can serve as the organizing theme around which the addition of detailed information can take place. Having the pattern facilitates your reading of the remainder of the sentence, and the message seems to flow in more rapidly, with less effort.

A poorly-constructed sentence, on the other hand, frequently tricks you by retaining clues to the central idea until near the end of the sentence, when you have all of the detailed elements of the message crowded into your short-term store. Some sentences are so convoluted, and their pattern is hidden so far toward the end of the sentence, that the capacity of short-term memory is exceeded by the sentence before a pattern can be found to chunk the elements and remove them from temporary memory. These are the sentences which you cannot understand just from one reading; instead, they must be decoded element by element. This requires reading the sentence several times slowly, analyzing the elements of the message and then relating them together to known patterns of knowledge in a deliberate, step-by-step process, which is the exact, visible analog of the otherwise invisible processes we have been describing. This type of sentence is found in a certain class of textbooks and is the enemy of learning. There are techniques for expressing all forms of instructional message—textual, graphical, auditory, and tactile—that will help you, as a designer, to prevent such convoluted communications from finding their way into your products. These techniques are a main concern of this book.

Strategic control

Figure 1 (see page 133) includes a function called strategic control, which is not connected directly with any of the other functions. Strategic control is critically important during learning. Strategic control consists of all of those functions which are necessary to help learning occur. These include the administrative and environmental functions that maintain the background processes, the stage of the mind, upon which learning takes place:

- Setting and revision of learning goals.
- Selection and prioritization of learning tasks.
- Monitoring of progress toward learning goals.
- Management of volatile memory.
- Monitoring and judgment of personal performance when activity is required during learning.
- Formation of opinions and judgments about the source of learning.
- Credibility filtering of the instructional message and the derived knowledge.

Strategic control is the function that allows us to think about and direct our learning processes. The scientific term for it is *metacognition*. Metacognition allows us to monitor and judge for ourselves how well our learning is progressing and how well our performance measures up when we are asked to respond. Since learning consists of more than just memorizing information and sequences of action, some parts of the instructional message, such as feedback, are targeted toward this Strategic Control function. Feedback affirms to the student the quality of a performance during practice. This information not only corrects knowledge errors, but it can be used in forming self-judgments of performance quality. That is, it is the kind of information that allows us to act independently of the instructional source once instruction is completed.

Implications

This description of learning processes is simplified and has tried to remain as non-technical as possible. It describes learning mechanism in terms which suggest things the designer can do to influence learning positively and avoid detracting from learning. As we move along the information processing highway, it becomes clear that the quality and organization of the instructional message does influence its use and usability by the student. The remaining chapters of this book attempt to convey principles that enhance the processing of instructional messages of all types by students and the conversion of knowledge into competent performance.

It is interesting to observe students as they encounter excellent instruction in any medium and to speculate on what mechanism is behind the increase in motivation which almost always follows.

We believe that increases or decreases in a student's motivational state are observable signs of the student's own internal allocation to or withdrawal of energy from learning. When students discover instruction which really instructs, motivation soars. We believe that this is evidence of a student's commitment of energy reserves to learning which might otherwise be saved for other activities.

Students are good judges of excellence in instruction. They know when they are learning, and one of the principles which we accept as a given is that learning is an inherently pleasing experience to humans. If a student begins with even a minimal interest, excellent instruction will compound that interest.

There is a great deal that a developer can do to increase the impact and efficiency of instructional communication, especially using the computer. Therefore, more learning can be accomplished in a given instructional time if the developer has arranged things to make that happen. The four factors of excellent CBI which form the subject matter of the remaining sections of this book are areas in which developers can improve the efficiency and effectiveness of their instructional materials.

Factor #1: Use of appropriate instructional strategy

Strategy is a set of communications and interactions which the developer makes possible to take place between the student and an instructional source. A proper strategy makes available information which is directly relevant to what is being learned. Good strategy also includes interaction between student and instructional source of a type which leads to a desired kind and level of performance. Selection of appropriate instructional strategies is the first leg of the four-legged stool and is discussed in Chapters 8 through 16.

Factor #2: Disciplined message management

Message management involves, first, capturing the content needed for a complete and accurate instructional message and, second, forming that content into a properly-paced, clear, and properly-expressed communication which uses all the relevant senses. Message management is the second leg of the stool and is discussed in Chapter 18.

Factor #3: Creative display management

Used without careful planning, the CBI display, whether visual, auditory, or tactile, can detract from an otherwise good instructional message and make interaction clumsy. On the other hand, used with disciplined creativity, the display can become an attractive and efficient window for the student to use while looking into the content—and at the same time a highly interactive interface between the student and the power of the computer. Display management is the third leg of the instructional stool and is discussed in Chapter 19.

Factor #4: Appropriate use of CBI Barnum showmanship

Occasional seasoning of an instructional message with the appropriate kind and amount of fun or special interest pays dividends, but too much, too little, or the wrong kind of fun quickly becomes either a distraction or a bore. There are techniques for injecting excitement and delight into instruction which complement and aid the learning process. CBI Barnum is the fourth and most difficult leg of the stool. It is discussed in Chapter 20.

Conclusion

These factors of CBI can, by their presence or absence, strengthen or weaken a CBI product. Each factor can be measured and controlled. It is the goal of the remaining chapters in this book to show you the principles behind each factor and how to control them to the student's benefit.

In this chapter, we have identified some of the main information processing issues related to instruction and learning. We have barely scratched the surface. A great deal is known about the learning process that we do not have time or space to treat here. We strongly urge CBI designers to make a deeper study of the learning process, for it is only by understanding the process that they can go beyond the recipes of others and create innovative and effective instructional designs of their own.

Self-directed activities

- Collect the names of as many learning theories and learning theorists as you can. From articles and books, begin to collect key elements of each theory. Make a one-page summary of each theory/theorist, giving key principles of learning.

- Explore the difference between learning theory and instructional theory. Make a table in which to begin recording their contrasts and their similarities. Keep this table and add to it throughout your design career.

- Using the one-page theory summaries created during the two previous activities, list the instructional implications for each major theoretical principle of both the learning theories and the instructional theories you collect.

Further reading

Anderson, J. R. (1993). *Rules of the mind.* Hillsdale, NJ: Lawrence Erlbaum Associates.

Bruer, J. T. (1995). *Schools for thought: A science of learning in the classroom.* Cambridge, MA: MIT Press.

Driscoll, M. (1994). *Psychology of learning for instruction.* Boston: Allyn & Bacon.

Gagné, E. (1985). *The cognitive psychology of school learning.* Boston: Little, Brown.

Gredler, M. E. (1992). *Learning and instruction: Theory into practice (2nd ed.).* New York: Macmillan Publishing.

Hofstadter, D. (1995). *Fluid concepts and creative analogies: Computer models of the fundamental mechanisms of thought.* New York: Basic Books.

Mayer, R. E. (1992). *Thinking, problem solving, and cognition (2nd ed.).* New York: W. H. Freeman and Company.

Miller, G. A. (1956). Human memory and the storage of information. *IRE Transactions of information theory, 2–3,* 129–137.

Norman, D. A. (1976). *Memory and attention: An introduction to human information processing (2nd ed.).* New York: John Wiley and Sons.

Posner, M. I. (1993). *Foundations of cognitive science.* Cambridge, MA: MIT Press.

Restak, R. M. (1984). *The brain.* New York: Bantam Doubleday Dell.

Restak, R. M. (1994). *The modular brain.* New York: Charles Scribner's Sons.

Schank, R. (1984). *The cognitive computer.* Reading, MA: Addison-Wesley.

Schank, R. (1990). *Tell me a story: A new look at real and artificial memory.* New York: Charles Scribner's Sons.

Shuell, T. J. (1992). Designing instructional computing systems for meaningful learning. In M. Jones and P. H. Winne (Eds.), *Adaptive learning environments: Foundations and frontiers.* Berlin: Springer-Verlag.

8

INSTRUCTIONAL STRATEGY I: FOUNDATIONS

Chapter Objectives:

1. *Identify the main reasons for which we instruct students.*

2. *Recognize the difference between learning and instruction.*

3. *Identify the key characteristics of an instructional act.*

4. *Describe the strategic processes used by a live instructor which have implications for technology-based instructional strategy design.*

5. *Define the two main historical approaches to the design of instructional strategy for CBI.*

6. *Differentiate micro-strategy from macro-strategy.*

7. *Describe how categorization of instructional goals facilitates the design of instructional strategies.*

8. *Name the two main varieties of goal taxonomy and give examples of each.*

9. *Describe how strategy designs arise from common best practices, practical considerations, and theory.*

Why instruct?

Not all learning is a result of instruction. In fact, most of what we know as individuals is probably learned without instruction. Some current educational philosophies place less emphasis on instruction, and alternatives to instruction are recommended. If learning can take place without instruction, then why do we instruct? We instruct for several reasons:

- Because it increases the amount of learning which is possible in a given period of time.

- Because without it, students may rest in false assurance that they know something which they in fact know incompletely or incorrectly.

- Because it allows us to suggest proportion to the student and point out learning which is more important, more powerful, more generative, and more useful than what the student might discover on his or her own.

- Because students often run out of energy for learning before they have learned all they should or need to, and because often we can reduce the energy required to learn.

- In order to give the student a better assurance of the completeness of what he or she has learned, thus to be better prepared for later learning, which otherwise might be impeded by lack of knowledge or skill.

- In order to help the student make connections between already-learned knowledge and new knowledge, or between distant bodies of already-learned knowledge which the student might not connect on his or her own.

- In order to integrate new performance abilities with old ones through practice.

142

- In order to help the student reach levels of performance which are robust under varying conditions and performance criteria.

- So that students can learn how to learn and how to evaluate their own performance, which frees them increasingly from the need for instruction.

- In hopes that the experience of learning might be pleasant and desirable for all students, not just for the self-directed and capable few who find learning their natural bent.

- In order to certify to others that the student has achieved specific skills and knowledge within a given subject area.

We should not expect all of a student's formal learning to come from instruction any more than we should expect all of it to come from non-instructed learning. Over the course of a student's career as a student, the skills of learning themselves can be taught to help the student become a self-directed, lifetime learner. However, we must plan so that the experience of learning by being instructed is rewarding enough for the student to desire more.

What is instruction?

Instruction is a harmonious activity in which the two wills and the two sets of intention cooperate temporarily in a mutual venture from which the student (and the teacher) can benefit. Instruction needs a definition so that it will not be confused with activities which appear similar but are carried out for different reasons. A definition of instruction will help us distinguish between:

> . . . an informative presentation to the Board of Directors and the presentation of a business problem scenario to a student problem solver

> . . . an interesting afternoon of research in the library from a directed research project executed in the library

> . . . an interesting chance encounter with a tricky word puzzle from a series of planned encounters devised to help students learn to solve specific varieties of word puzzle

Instruction has the following characteristics:

Instruction is a purposeful activity: Instruction doesn't just happen; it is planned. Of course, learning can be incidental: it can occur even when it is not intended. Instruction, however, requires a deliberate act on someone's part. A teacher must intend to instruct. The student must also intend to learn. The purposes to instruct and to learn are always present during instruction.

Instruction involves an instructor: A student can learn through self-directed exploration, experimentation, inference, deduction, and generalization. When this happens, learning takes place, but not instruction. Instruction is an interaction between two people or between a person and technology. The student relies upon the instructor to supply some degree of support for learning, which includes some combination of goals and means. The activities of an instructor can be internalized, and a learner can become capable of deliberate *self*-instruction. One of the key goals of the instructor should be to provide enough awareness of the instructional processes to students that they can become *self*-instructors.

Instruction is goal-directed: Instruction always has a goal, even though some instructors are content to leave the goal fuzzy and ill-defined. The purpose of instructing is to assist the student in reaching a conceptual or performance goal. The existence of the goal is the only reason for instructing. Either the teacher sets the goal and the student agrees to be instructed, or the student sets the goal and enlists some degree of assistance from the teacher in reaching it.

Instruction involves a judged response from the learner: One or more responses must be drawn forth from the student during instruction. The purpose of the response is to measure the effect of the instruction—to gauge the type and degree of learning which has occurred compared to what was intended. Without a response, it is not possible to tell whether instruction has produced a result, and attainment of the goal is uncertain. A student response may be judged either by the student, a teacher, or by a third party, but interaction alone is inadequate to tell either the student or the instructor whether instruction has had an effect and if so, what kind. The judged response is an important element of instruction.

Many instruction look-alikes differ from instruction only in this quality of requiring a judged response from the learner. People can learn from just presentations, but if *artful telling* alone qualifies as instruction, then every television show, movie, news broadcast, radio talk show, billboard, magazine article, advertisement, cereal box and lecture—every presentation-centered informational event of our culture, including "no smoking" and "no parking" signs—must be included within the class of things called instruction. Where this book is concerned, if no judged response is drawn from the user, then instruction will not have occurred, just information presentation.

The function of strategy

An instructional strategy is: (1) a planned path of, or (2) a permitted but non-predetermined sequence of interchanges between a student and an instructional source intended to support learning. The order of interactions may be fixed in advance or may be determined as instruction progresses. The key element is that strategy proceeds according to an underlying plan or principle. Strategy is the plan by which the teacher teaches or by which the learner chooses experiences and thereby learns within an organized field of provided instructional elements. Live teachers plan strategy in advance or make strategy decisions at the time of instruction as they observe student responses; sometimes they do both. Technology-based instruction sometimes has a fixed strategy, but CBI is capable of very dynamic strategies.

The live teacher makes strategic moves in order to achieve specific goals, which change from moment to moment. Though the overall learning goal does not change, the teacher's strategic goals change momentarily as the teacher acts, observes the student response, and interprets the meaning of the response. The teacher's interpretation tries to identify the student's changing momentary need. The teacher adjusts the strategic goal of instruction to one which best meets the student's need at any given moment. This is how live instruction proceeds.

The designer of automated instruction uses technological devices to supply some of the functions of a teacher so that one-on-one instruction can take place. While implementing technology-based instructional strategy, however, the designer is at arms length from the learner, because the designer will not be present in person to perform any teaching actions or make decisions. Therefore, he or she will either (1) set a fixed strategy in place, or (2) create some means by which the instructional system can interpret student responses, determine need, and shift the momentary strategic goal appropriately. In this way, the technologist can create an automated instructional delivery capable of some of the acts of a live teacher. The key to doing this lies in the ability to identify, moment by moment, the best performance and strategic goals to set.

Execution of instructional strategy

Execution of an instructional strategy consists of carrying out four functions in a continuous cycle: (1) goal selection, (2) means selection, (3) means execution, and (4) assessment.

Means execution is the execution of instructional actions. Instructional actions are the things that teachers do and designers design. They are the events of instruction. Each instructional act is carried out to satisfy an existing goal. Instructional acts include: providing information, emphasizing or highlighting aspects of the information, posing a problem, or calling for a judgeable response from the student. These actions sound quite plain and uninteresting, but because they can occur in so many varieties, they are in fact interesting and highly varied. Discovering creative, diverse, and effective ways for these basic activities to be carried out is one of the designer's most interesting challenges.

Means selection includes selecting instructional actions: pairing instructional ends with instructional means. The strategic goals of instruction change moment by moment in the same way that the goals of a busy executive change moment by moment. Each time an instructional goal changes or is modified, means for supporting the new goal must be selected. In addition, a new means must be selected when it is determined that an already-selected means is not supporting student learning effectively.

Goal selection includes both deciding when to select a new instructional goal and performing the selection. A goal may be selected: (1) when a previous goal has been satisfied, (2) when a current goal appears to be unreachable under the current strategy plan, or (3) when a student reaches a breakthrough and is ready to advance to a more challenging version of the current goal.

Assessment is the determination of the effects of instruction. It requires that the student do something which can be observed and judged. Assessment should be directly related to the selected goals of instruction; otherwise there is no reason to assess and no way to determine what to assess.

At any moment in time during instruction, a teacher, live or technological, is engaging in either means execution, means selection, goal selection, or assessment.

A historical note on strategy and CBI

As designers first began to explore the ways in which computer technology could be used instructionally, it became apparent that live teachers make decisions moment by moment during instruction, which influence or re-direct the course the instructional strategy takes. Early CBI pioneers felt that in order to be effective instructionally, computers had to make decisions in this same way. Just as live teachers judge student responses before deciding what to say next, they believed that a computer ought to take into account the student's most immediate previous response and history of responses before making its next strategy decision. They also believed that strategy should be computed following each response and be adapted to the momentary needs and performance of the student.

This early conception of computer-based instruction was not very easy to implement. Those early pioneers were hampered by the newness of the computer technology. The computers were much less powerful than the ones we are used to today, and the programming tools and concepts they worked with were quite primitive compared to the ones we are used to using. The result was an inability to create any appreciable amount of adaptive instruction.

From that point about thirty years ago, the history of CBI headed down two separate paths which are only now just beginning to rejoin. Down one path, the group we refer to today as the intelligent tutoring system (ITS) group continued to hope that fine-grained instructional strategy decisions (means execution, means selection, goal adjustment, and assessment) could be made at the time of instruction by a computer. These researchers began to invent sophisticated new programming tools and techniques. They believed that computers would, over time, become more powerful and faster. The conceptions of instructional strategy they invented relied upon knowing how the student was responding moment by moment, and in some cases, could recognize what the student knew or didn't know.

Those who took the second path of CBI resigned themselves temporarily to a simplified concept of instructional strategy. This group felt that strategic decisions could be made during product development and could be encoded within the CBI program in advance. This group constitutes the vast majority of CBI practitioners today. Authoring tools and techniques today are built with pre-planned strategy in mind, and though varying degrees of flexibility have been afforded in these tools, it is still extremely difficult to build instruction with them which can adapt the details of the instructional strategy to the individual student.

The point of this historical account is to alert you that the conceptions of CBI instructional strategy are undergoing a change. ITS developers are now achieving some degree of success. Many of their products are impressive instructionally and have features that CBI designers in general would like to incorporate into their own products. Moreover, the power of the average computer has increased enormously, and tools which used to require specialized computers can now be used on personal computers and are much easier to use because of improved interfaces.

As we continue our discussion of instructional strategy, keep in mind that the level of the discussion has been chosen for two purposes: first, to equip you with the understanding you need today to create effective and excellent CBI using current tools and techniques, and second, to equip you with an understanding of instructional strategy which will not be made obsolete as these two currents continue to merge and as strategy thinking continues to evolve.

A more modern development

Having described this rejoining of two long-estranged currents in strategic thinking, it is important also to describe a third current which is merging with the other two. It arises from a basic change in thinking about what instruction is and what kinds of strategy and interaction promote the most effective learning. To summarize this third current briefly, we can say that much of instructional practice in the past has assumed that:

- Teaching and learning were processes for transferring knowledge from one brain to another.

- The best form of teaching was telling information to the student, then having the student practice what he or she had been told.

- A direct, head-on approach to instruction, where the teacher controlled and the student complied, was the best arrangement between teacher and learner.

These propositions have come under serious scrutiny recently, and if they have not been discarded, then at least they are being modified. Designers today tend to look for ways to reverse this formula. They look for ways to:

- Allow students to construct knowledge themselves from raw elements and experiences during the solving of a problem.

- Bring students into more active involvement with the learning process, requiring them to participate heavily in inquiry, planning, searching, practicing, and problem-solving.

- Make students take greater initiative during the learning process and participate in selecting and forming their own learning goals and strategies.

You will see evidence of both currents of strategic thinking in this book. Personally, the newer current influences us the most heavily. We hope to show how the two long-separate currents of strategy actually have elements in common and can enrich each other if the best practices of both are combined. Both approaches emphasize the importance of goal-directedness, intentionality, and judgment of performance in instruction. This may remind some readers only of instruction of the more traditional style. However, the new hardware and software technologies make possible new strategic technologies which support learning along guided paths, but which do so by involving the learner and the learner's agency more actively in the learning process. The earlier chapters in this book emphasize a highly-structured approach to strategy, along with techniques for making that approach produce wonderfully varied and interesting instruction which does not appear structured. Later chapters emphasize simulations and arrangements of simulation problems designed not only to support the student during the learning of performance, but also to instruct the student in more subtle and less direct ways, with the student retaining much of the instructional initiative.

This is our view of instructional strategy. We feel the best course is to borrow the best principles from both the older and the newer strategic traditions, providing structure, but inviting the student into the learning process as a more active agent. We hope you recognize this philosophy behind the prescriptions and principles we provide in this and the following chapters.

Macro-strategy and micro-strategy

As a professional group, instructional designers are constantly improving their understanding of instructional strategy. Nowhere is the evolutionary nature of instructional strategy more apparent than in the distinction between macro-strategy and micro-strategy, as defined by Charles Reigeluth. This distinction relies upon a structure with which all of us have long familiarity—the lesson.

Macro-strategy is the term commonly used to describe the application of instructional strategy *above* the lesson level: strategic decision-making *between* lessons. Macro-strategy determines the order in which lessons and tests are or can be encountered and defines the paths which a student may take through a course. In contrast, the term *micro-strategy* refers to strategy *inside* of the lesson. It is concerned with the ordering of message elements, the structure of messages, and modes of practice and interaction. The twin concepts of macro- and micro-strategy rely on the concept of *lesson*, because the lesson boundary is the watershed between the two.

But what *is* a lesson? It is the division of instruction and instructional time into more or less useful blocks. In the literature of instructional design you will not find anywhere a precise and consistent definition for the term "lesson," yet it is one of the most frequently-used terms for referring to instructional structures. Companion and equally meaningless terms include "course," "module," "unit," "segment," and "section"—all container terms with equally fuzzy meaning. A "course" may last two hours, two weeks, two months, or two years, and may contain any amount of instruction, covering any body of knowledge and/or skills.

This an important point for instructional strategy because it demonstrates that designers frequently rely on practical rather than theoretical boundaries in their definitions of strategy. The previous section explained how strategy conceptions have been generally simplified in order to accommodate the inability to implement more sophisticated strategies with present technologies. The acceptance of the lesson as the boundary between two types of strategy is one example of that simplification.

As you will discover later in this and the following chapter, strategy is concerned with the sequencing of instructional experiences at multiple levels, and the same rules which drive strategy at low levels of instruction are related to those that govern instruction at higher levels. From this point on through Chapter 14, discussions of strategy will refer to micro-strategy unless otherwise specified. Then in Chapter 15, we will introduce ideas which break down the more traditional distinction of "lesson" and require us to think in terms of more interesting macro-strategies.

Good-bye "lesson"

One thing that we will do at this point is abandon the term *lesson* in favor of a term which will come to have much more clearly defined meaning later in the book. We use the term *instructional* event to denote the instructional encounter, whether it lasts for ten minutes or ten hours, as long as that encounter centers around the same prescribed set of instructional goals. In a later discussion of instructional structures in Chapter 16, we will give a specific meaning to this term in relation to a technology called Work Model Synthesis. Until then, if you want to think of the terms *lesson* and *instructional event* as being synonymous, then do so, but be ready later to give up some of your old notions about lessons and take on some new conceptions of how instructional experiences are packaged. We believe instruction at all levels to be made up entirely of instructional events of different size and scope.

Designing the right instructional strategy

How does an instructional designer design a strategy? It seems that there is such a variety of raw ideas from which to select. How is a designer to know the *right* thing to do?

Let's first deal with the word *right* in the phrase *right strategy*. Instructional design is a goal-driven technology, and as in any technology, there are many ways to accomplish a goal. That means that there is not just one right way to do anything: not just one right way to instruct, not just one right strategy. Technological choices—and that includes the selection of instructional strategy—are not judged by whether they are "right" or "wrong," but by whether they are *effective* and *efficient*. That is, do the designer's solutions work? And are they affordable in terms of the time, money, and energy they require? Properly chosen instructional strategies: (1) reduce the effort of, (2) increase the probability of, or (3) improve the quality of learning.

Categories of instructional goals

Since instruction is purposed for and guided by instructional goals, the only place to begin the design of an instructional strategy is with the instructional goal. Most instructional technologists today believe that instructional goals can be grouped or categorized in some way; few believe that each instructional goal is unique. The reasoning is that even though human behavior is wondrously varied and complex, there are patterns of performance which recur again and again. By identifying and naming those patterns of performance, designers feel they can simplify and standardize (within reasonable limits) the strategies for teaching them to students.

It is a generally accepted principle of instructional design that for each category of instructional goal, there is a corresponding strategic formula for instruction which defines, in general terms, an efficient and effective path for that type of instruction to follow. This, as it turns out, is a fairly robust principle; it works well in most cases. If this is so, then the key to making instructional strategy choices is to identify the category of the instructional goal and then to adapt its corresponding general strategy prescription to your specific content. This is the system used by many designers for strategy design, though the categories of goal that designers use and the strategy prescriptions which they apply can vary quite a bit.

Several systems for categorizing instructional goals, called *taxonomies,* have been proposed, and it is from these taxonomies that designers select or fashion their own preferred set of goal types. In general, category systems fit into two groups: atomistic systems and integrated systems.

Atomistic systems: Atomistic systems break instructional goals into very small compartments of behavior believed to have some relationship to the basic elements of performance which people actually use in their everyday thinking and acting. One early and popular version of this type of category system was proposed by Robert Gagné, whose classes were derived to a great extent from learning theory and research in experimental psychology. Early versions of Gagné's category system differed greatly from later ones, as Gagné's own understanding and the understandings of psychologists in general evolved over the years. This type of evolution is the rule among atomistic taxonomies, rather than the exception, because taxonomies are proven by being applied to new problems, and as new problems are encountered which can't be solved by the old categories, new taxonomies have to be proposed. Thus, taxonomies have proliferated and continue to evolve as experience accumulates.

Gagné's early taxonomies included the categories: classical conditioned responses, operant conditioning, motor chains, verbal associations, multiple discriminations, concepts, principle-using, and problem solving. In later years, Gagné's research identified clear distinctions in the way verbal and non-verbal content were learned. This prompted Gagné to extend his taxonomy to two levels of definition, as shown in Figure 1.

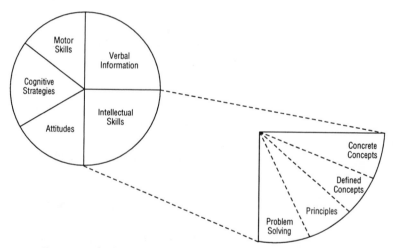

Figure 1. The later, 2-layer Gagné taxonomy of learning types.

At the upper level, Gagné divided the universe of human behavior into five categories: verbal information, motor skills, attitudes, intellectual skills, and cognitive strategies. Within one of these divisions, Gagné created a second level of definition by placing many of the earlier learning categories (concrete concepts, defined concepts, principles, and problem solving) into one of the five divisions: intellectual skills. Gagné's naming of the cognitive strategies category was a significant recognition that there are higher (or *metacognitive*) levels of execution and control within human thinking, and that the higher levels can and ought to be instructed as well as the lower levels.

David Merrill has also proposed multiple versions of instructional goal taxonomies. One of his early schemes contained categories for fact learning, concepts, rules, and problem solving. Later, additions were made, including procedure-using and principle-using. Merrill's research moved him in the direction of considering behavior separately from the content that it acted upon. This led to a two-dimensional taxonomic diagram which showed how recall and performance behavior both applied to many types of content: facts, concept definitions, principle wordings and formulas, and procedural lists, as shown in Figure 2. The changeability of the category schemes of Gagné and Merrill (as only two examples) should suggest to you that the issue of learning or behavior categories is still under vigorous study and debate. More recently, Merrill has defined a family of transaction types between the learner and a learning source, which represent prototypical strategy patterns capable of tremendous variations because of the particular parameterized method of implementing them.

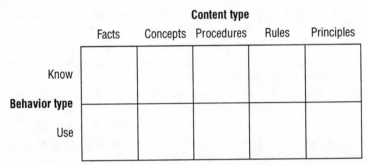

Figure 2. An earlier Merrill taxonomy defined in two dimensions.

Integrated systems: Integrated systems for categorizing instructional goals focus above the level of the single behavior atom or information processing act. They prefer to define larger complexes or *integrated* combinations of everyday human behavior.

One of the earliest of these systems was Benjamin Bloom's taxonomy (see Table 1). Bloom's work was stimulated by the need to classify test item types, but he and his colleagues discovered that their test item categories corresponded with general classes of common human behavior, independent of the specific content of the behavior (history, literature, physics, etc.).

Bloom divided the universe of human behavior into three main categories or *domains:* the cognitive, the affective, and the psychomotor. (Compare these with Gagné's five upper-level divisions.) Subdivisions of behavior within each of Bloom's three domains guided the forming of instructional goals.

The cognitive domain was Bloom's domain for what today might be called skill and conceptual knowledge learning. He and his co-workers divided this domain into numerous subcategories shown in Table 1. It is clear that there is some correspondence between Bloom's taxonomy and the atomistic taxonomies, especially at the memory level. However, at the upper levels of Bloom's scheme, the behaviors become elongated, multi-stepped, and complex. They represent, if anything, integrations of the atomistic elements found in Gagné's and Merrill's taxonomies into larger, but still unified, collections of behavior.

A second example of the integrated approach to instructional goal taxonomies began with the attempt in the 1950's to inspect the inner mechanisms of the human mind at work. At that time a shift in psychological theories was taking place—from behaviorism to cognitive psychology—which created great interest in the detailed mechanisms of human thought and behavior. One of the directions this new interest led was toward the classification of frequently-repeated patterns of information processing behavior.

Which taxonomy?

The ultimate quest of the instructional designer with relation to goal taxonomies is to find the one that leads to the best strategy prescriptions—that is, the one whose prescriptions are

Table 1. Bloom's objective categories within the cognitive domain.

1.00 Knowledge
    1.10 Knowledge of specifics
        1.11 Knowledge of terminology
        1.12 Knowledge of specific facts

    1.20 Knowledge of ways and means of dealing with specifics
        1.21 Knowledge of conventions
        1.22 Knowledge of trends and sequences
        1.23 Knowledge of classifications and categories
        1.24 Knowledge of criteria
        1.25 Knowledge of methodology

    1.30 Knowledge of the universals and abstractions in a field
        1.31 Knowledge of principles and generalizations
        1.32 Knowledge of theories and structures

2.00 Comprehension
    2.10 Translation
    2.20 Interpretation
    2.30 Extrapolation

3.00 Application

4.00 Analysis
    4.10 Analysis of elements
    4.20 Analysis of relationships
    4.30 Analysis of organizational principles

5.00 Synthesis
    5.10 Production of a unique communication
    5.20 Production of a plan or proposed set of operations
    5.30 Derivation of a set of abstract relations

6.00 Evaluation
    6.10 Judgments in terms of internal evidence
    6.20 Judgments in terms of external criteria

the most effective and the most efficient for the entire range of instructional goals. This presumes that a classification system can be complete across the entire range of human behaviors, from the most atomistic to the most complexly integrated of behaviors. This is a proposition which has never been tested. In fact, the existing taxonomies are clearly incomplete when compared to each other. Nevertheless, they are still very useful.

Recently, taxonomic systems like those we have described have come under some criticism because they tend to fragment the designer's thinking and concentrate instructional strategy on low-level instructional goals only, leaving open the question of how individual skills and knowledges are integrated into larger and more comprehensive conglomerates of skill and knowledge. However, goal taxonomic systems have proven to be so useful to instructional designers that they are not prepared to give up their use until something can be supplied which works better than they do. One approach is to recognize that learning is often a process which begins with fragments and then expands toward larger, more integrated levels of behavior. For this reason, we describe instructional strategy for what would normally be considered *fragmented* performance types in this chapter and Chapter 9, but we also describe techniques for integrating instructional goals and strategies through the use of problems, problem environments, and simulations in Chapters 15 and later.

The benefit that has been realized from goal taxonomies is that thinking about instructional strategies has become more consistent and more orderly. Progress appears to be occurring throughout the profession of designers in the application of consistent instructional patterns. That is both a blessing and a curse: a blessing because it is generally improving the quality of instruction throughout CBI, and a curse because many designers take this useful simplification of the world and treat it as a doctrine, causing a kind of narrow orthodoxy to develop that is capable of smothering new thinking about approaches to strategy.

The shortcoming of the taxonomies is that they are incomplete, mostly unvalidated, and yet in their early stages of development (the older ones are only forty years old). For instructional designers to affix their techniques to such an incomplete specification of human behavior and performance is like the attempts of the early astronomers to determine the place of the earth in the universe with their poor telescopes and tools, which led many decision-makers to form hasty and, as time showed, incorrect impressions of who, what, and where we are.

For the purposes of this book, we will use as the basis for describing instructional strategy an eclectic and loosely-held set of categories gathered from various taxonomic systems, which has proven useful for the majority of the design needs of the authors. It relies heavily on the atomistic taxonomies of Merrill and Gagné and includes within its preferred classes: factual learning (of several types), concept-using, procedure-using, principle-using, and process-using behavior.

In addition to them, it recognizes a general class of *integrated* behaviors. Integrated behaviors are everyday performances performed in real-world settings. They are made up of flexible and sometimes lengthy sequences of atomistic behaviors which involve decision-making as well as the performance of procedures, interpretation of processes, and the recall of facts. Decision-making is an especially important part of integrated behavior and often constitutes the most important new learning at the integrated level.

General principles of instructional strategy

The specific atomistic strategies prescribed for our selected goal types are the subject of Chapters 10 through 14, and in Chapter 15, we begin to describe the principles for instructional strategy at the integrated level, which normally involves simulation environments. In this chapter and Chapter 9, our purpose is to identify general principles of instructional strategy. We lay a foundation of general strategy principles by examining examples of common strategies and by inducing principles from them. From each example, we try to draw some new understanding of what a strategy is and what one is made of.

Example #1: Procedure instruction

Let's begin with the instructor script in Table 2, which teaches the relatively simple procedure for starting the diesel engine of a passenger car or pickup truck. This is a useful procedure for illustration purposes because the diesel's starting procedure is slightly different from that of the gasoline engine, but the basic content will be familiar to most readers.

The instructor script in Table 2 is in the form of the outline a hypothetical driving school might give to one of its instructors in an attempt to impose quality control and standardize its instruction. It is an outline of a strategy to be used by the instructors as they instruct. The script begins, as most scripts do, with instructional amenities—an introduction, an objective,

Table 2. The driving instructor's lesson plan.

AAAJAX DRIVING ACADEMY
INSTRUCTOR OUTLINE
DIESEL STARTING PROCEDURE

Introduction

Set the student at ease with friendly conversation before introducing the purpose of the lesson. The purpose is:

To learn to start the passenger diesel without damaging it.

Tell the student that you expect the lesson to take about ten minutes and that the student will be asked to perform three correct engine startings before leaving the lesson.

Presentation

Present in your own words the following message. Be sure not to omit any of the information. As much as you can, describe the steps one at a time.

Starting a diesel engine correctly is important because it can save you a lot of repair bills over the life of your engine. A diesel engine is started differently from a gasoline engine. The procedure you will learn to-day applies to engines when the outside air temperature is above twenty degrees below zero, Fahrenheit.

The steps used to start a diesel engine are:

STEP 1: *Place the vehicle in park gear. The engine will not start with the transmission engaged in any other gear. If the vehicle has a manual transmission, then place it in neutral. In either case, put the emergency brake ON.*

STEP 2: *Insert the key into the ignition and turn the key to the first detent, which is labeled "ACC" on the ignition plate and stands for "Accessory Power." As you turn the key, two indicator lights on the dashboard will illuminate, and a loud buzzing will begin. These indicate that the engine is not ready to start.*

STEP 3: *Wait until the lights go out and the buzzing stops. If this does not happen within ten seconds, then turn the key off and try again. If by three tries the problem still exists, contact a mechanic.*

STEP 4: *After the lights have gone out and the buzzer is silent, turn the key momentarily to the "START" position and release it the moment that the engine starts. Starting is indicated by a rising sound.*

This means that the speed of the engine is increasing on its own. If the engine does not start within five seconds of the start of cranking, release the key. Before trying to crank the engine again, allow the starter motor to cool for fifteen seconds. If the engine does not start after cranking six successive times, follow the procedure for ENGINE NON-START (Instructor Outline #25–3).

WARNING: *Failure to wait fifteen seconds may result in overheating of the starter, and the starter may be damaged to the point where it cannot start the vehicle. Expensive repairs will result.*

STEP 5: *Allow the engine to run for fifteen seconds before engaging the transmission. This allows the en-gine oil to reach the upper part of the engine and reduces engine wear.*

Demonstration

At this point, repeat the steps in the procedure aloud while demonstrating them to the student one more time. Be sure that you speak each step before you actually perform it and that the student sees the detail of what you are doing. Perform steps slowly, and do not rush the demonstration. Keep the steps separate as much as possible. Repeat the demonstration until the student is satisfied.

(Continued)

Table 2. The driving instructor's lesson plan (continued).

Student Practice

Practice is conducted in two stages. In Exercise A, the student is asked to perform the procedure one step at a time as you name the step. In Exercise B, the student is asked to perform the procedure without any help.

Be sure that the students are able to perform Exercise A comfortably and confidently before moving on to Exercise B.

EXERCISE A: Tell the student that you are going to name the steps in the starting procedure one at a time. Tell the student to perform each step as you name it. Watch the student as each step is performed to ensure that it is being performed correctly.

EXERCISE B: Tell the student that you want him or her to start the engine without any assistance from you. Watch carefully to see that each step is performed completely and that no steps are omitted.

---

and some information about the instructional event itself. Following these, the writer begins the presentation which forms the core of the script. It is a description of the procedure itself.

The script at this point begins to present information in a certain deliberate order. In the instructor script, the scriptwriter controls that order, but during instruction, the instructor will control it, based on observations of the student and the strategy ordering of the instructor. The essential point is that the instructor: (1) convey all of the core information, and (2) that it be conveyed in a manner (order of ideas, expression, and style) which communicates to the student.

The prose in the script is divided into sentences, and there are no labels pointing out the individual elements of the designer's strategy, but we can find some of the elements with a little searching. For instance, the script is divided into blocks, each pertaining to one step of the procedure. Within each step, a regular pattern of information is provided: the step action, indications seen or heard during the step, cautions related to the step, and so forth. This pattern of information is repeated more or less regularly for each step, though not necessarily in a set order. For some of the steps, certain categories of information are left out. For instance, not every step has a caution associated with it. This plan of information management is, in fact, an important part of the strategy. Chapter 18, Message Management, describes how you can determine and manage the content of the instructional message during development.

Having detected the patterns of information in the procedure, we can see some of the author's strategy plan, but only part. The strategy proceeds from a presentation to a demonstration, for which the designer gives specific instructions. Directions for administering practice are also explicit: They define two levels of practice.

From this simple example we can make a few observations about instructional strategy:

Observation #1: The instruction is roughly divided into three phases: the presentation of information, the demonstration, and the practice.

Observation #2: The author caused certain information to be conveyed. The information contained in the instruction was not random and was focused on the goal: starting the engine.

Observation #3: The chunks in the script message consisted of repeated, logically-categorized information types (e.g., step actions, step cautions, step indications, etc.).

Observation #4: Chunks of information did not correspond to sentence boundaries. This means that the informational building blocks of the strategy were not merely linguistic units or sentences, but rather definable categories of information, all having a particular logical relation to the topic.

Some of the strategy (categories of information, stages of instruction) was found in the script; some of it (judgment of practice, momentary student assessment, goal- setting on behalf of the student) was assumed to be a part of the instructor's personal expertise and judgment.

During the instructional encounter, the student in this case is free to ask clarifying questions or guide the instructor to repeat some portion of the strategy. These are some of the cues that the instructor uses to adjust instructional goals moment by moment.

Example #2: Memory instruction

Let's study a second example of an instructional strategy. In this one, the student is asked to learn a list of ten associated memory pairs. Find the script in Table 3. This is the script for a slide-sound presentation. In this example, we can analyze the script, just as we did in the previous example, to find the structures and sequences used by the author. There are three main script structures: an introduction, a presentation section, and a practice section (with two parts).

The introduction to this script is much the same as that of the first example. The presentation section, however, is radically different. For each item in the list of ten, only two categories of information are presented: (1) the name of the class, and (2) the associated class description.

In addition, the script specifies a graphic to be presented which hopes to associate the two in a memorable way. These graphics are a critical part of the writer's strategy for making the association between class number and class contents. Such memory tools are common in memory instruction and are called *mnemonics* (say this word slowly if you wear dentures). They are definitely a part of the strategy, but they are not necessarily verbal in nature. Several varieties of mnemonic are described in Chapter 10.

Not everything that makes an instructional strategy work is expressed verbally. This is a critically important point whose value increases as you move toward the integrative levels of performance. Instruction is much more than a verbal process and much more than the simple conveyance of information. This example allows us to make three more observations about instructional strategy:

Observation #5: Different strategies are used to achieve different instructional goals. The strategies for these two types of learning are organized differently. The strategy for memory instruction is structured differently from that of procedural instruction. Different information is presented, there is no need for a demonstration, and the practice takes on a different form.

Observation #6: The items sequenced and manipulated by the designer are not limited to raw verbal content. They include a variety of representation forms (in this case graphical) as well as additional non-content messages intended to aid the student in processing, storing, and later retrieving information during performance. This example includes the use of a mnemonic (memory-supplementing information), and quizzing (a performance).

Observation #7: Sometimes more than one form of practice is desirable or necessary as a part of the strategy. You may have noticed this exemplified in the driving school script as well. The adjustment of practice types and difficulty levels is done to ensure: (1) the opportunity to exercise all of the varieties of behavior that the student will be asked to perform in real-world situations, and (2) sometimes, advancing difficulty levels which begin within the student's performance capability and gradually move beyond that level in stages which the student can sustain a successful performance.

Observation #8: Proper strategy hopes to decrease instructional time and improve performance. Although you could not tell it by reading, the instruction that was created from this script during an actual development project reduced instructional time by 80% and increased recall of the information by 40%. Moreover, the strength of recall by students months after instruction is quite high. Students can learn the information without a mnemonic, but that way of learning is harder, takes longer, is less pleasant, and is more liable to be forgotten. In short, there are good reasons for sometimes using structured strategies directed at specific classes of learning or performance.

Table 3. The slide-sound script.

TEN CLASSES OF SUPPLY SCRIPT
Slide: 1 Slide content: Title—"The Ten Classes of Supply" (Pause 3)
Slide: 2 Audio: "Supply is divided into ten classes. In this lesson you will learn the name and content of each class." Slide content: Pie chart divided into ten sections. (Pause 4)
   **Slide: 3** Audio: Class One contains food items. (Pause 10)
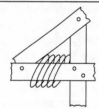 **Slide: 4** Audio: Class Two contains footwear of all kinds. (Pause 10)
 **Slide: 5** Audio: Class Three contains petroleum, oil, and lubricants. (Pause 10)
Slide: 6 Audio: Class Four contains construction supplies. This includes timbers and wire. (Pause 10)
Slide: 7 Audio: Class five contains clothing items. (Pause 10)
 **Slide: 8** Audio: Class Six contains sundries. (Pause 10)
Slide: 9 Audio: Class Seven contains repair parts. (Pause 10)

(Continued)

Table 3. The slide-sound script (continued).

	**Slide: 10** Audio: Class Eight contains medical supplies. (Pause 10)
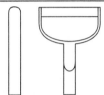	**Slide: 11** Audio: Class Nine contains precision tools, like micrometers. (Pause 10)
	Slide: 12 Audio: Class Ten contains agricultural supplies. (Pause 10)

Slide: 13 Audio: Now see how many of the classes you can identify. Write your answers on a sheet of scratch paper. Slide content: Title—"Quiz #1" (Pause 5)
Slide: 14 Audio: "What is in class Five?" Slide content: Title—"5" (Pause 6)
Slide: 15 Audio: None Slide content: Repeat slide #7.
[The next several slides (from #16 to #33) repeat this pattern of asking one of the category contents and then revealing the answer in the following slide.]
Slide: 34 Audio: None Slide content: Now name the supply class for each item that follows.
Slide: 35 Audio: "Which class contains shoes?" Slide content: Title—"Shoes" (Pause 6)
Slide: 36 Audio: None Slide content: Repeat slide #4.
[The slides (from #37 to #54) repeat this pattern of asking one of the category numbers and then revealing the answer in the following slide. Following the last quiz item, the instruction terminates.]

In this case, all of the strategy (categories of information, stages of instruction, representations, response occasions, judgment, and goal structure) was found in the script. None of it was assumed to reside within the instructor's actions, because an instructor will not necessarily be present during this instruction.

Example #3: Instruction for a concept

Let's consider a third sample of instruction. It is found in Table 4. This is neither a script nor an instructor's outline. It is a poster which a teacher will use while teaching the concept periodic sentence. The goal of this instruction is the ability to discriminate between examples and non-examples of *periodic sentences*. Classification behavior is essential in our day-to-day functioning as humans, and it is sometimes referred to as discrimination or categorization behavior.

Table 4. The concept poster.

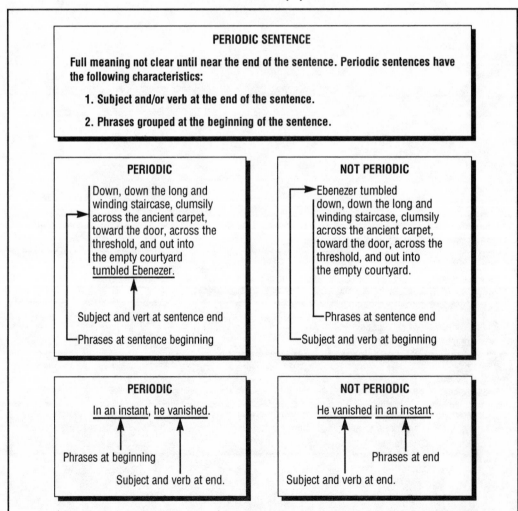

The incomplete instruction in Table 4 contains only a part of the presentation portion of an instructional strategy—no more—and the presentation section of this script differs again radically from the two previous examples. In this example, the categories of information supplied are particularly suited to teaching classification or concept-using behavior.

The categories of information supplied include: (1) a class definition, (2) a set of examples, (3) a set of non-examples, (4) emphasis notes for each example and non-example. And they are presented in an orderless way. The poster is not a sequenced message. It can be scanned by a student in any sequence. Moreover, when a teacher uses it, the teacher's message may point out the parts of the message in any order.

The technique of this strategy (David Merrill's concept strategy) is to provide for the student a clear contrast between class members (examples) and non-members (non-examples). An important but invisible feature of this strategy is that the examples were carefully selected and placed in pairs in order to provide the maximum information to the student. The creator of this poster realized that one example only gives one example's worth of information, whereas properly matched and sequenced example/non-example pairs provide considerably more than two examples' worth of useful information to the student. The rules for ordering examples are discussed at length in Chapter 13.

Even without knowing the details of those rules, we can still make more observations about strategy in general.

Observation #9: Careful selection and relationship of information categories and their counterbalancing against each other greatly multiply the amount of information available to the student from the instruction without multiplying the size of the instructional message. A student doesn't have to be told everything explicitly if the instructor sets up the information field properly.

Observation #10: Though it may seem that careful sequencing of the instructional message is essential to use of a strategy, it is seldom so. An expert teacher, given the core elements of an instructional message for one objective, can arrange them in a multitude of orders, weaving them into a coherent message sequence which seems to unfold step by step. But there are several orders of the core message elements which could have been used by the same teacher. This is an idea we will examine in more detail later in this chapter.

Observation #11: Part of the strategy includes emphasizing parts of the message and drawing the attention of the student to specific features and implications of the information presented. These highlighted features must be assumed to be directly related to the student's processing of the information and its transformation into usable knowledge or skill. In this we see another non-verbal element of instructional strategy.

The three strategies we have examined conform to guidelines which are accepted by numerous instructional designers. Where are these strategy rules found? How are they discovered? Who makes them up?

Where does strategy come from?

How are the guidelines for effective instructional strategy determined? In the field of instructional technology, our normal impulse is to seek answers from instructional research, but it might surprise you to realize that probably more of our thinking on instructional strategy comes from sources outside formal research. Indeed, formal research is frequently influenced by traditional practice.

There may be many reasons for this, including the relative newness of emphasis on structured strategy and the vast reservoir of traditional instructional practices from which designers can more easily borrow. The reliance on experience and "best practice" of the past has been one of the largest contributors to current instructional strategy practice. It is also one of the forces that opposes new approaches to instructional strategy.

There are many contributions to instructional strategy from practical concerns. For instance, strategies must be implemented within the administrative units of time ("periods") by which we structure the instructional day, and they must be implemented for students whose limited energy stores give them finite staying power in an instructional setting.

The sources of instructional strategy, then, include: (1) common practice, (2) practical considerations, and (3) practices recommended by theory. Let's discuss these sources one at a time.

Strategy and common practice

Instruction has been going on for many centuries; instructional technology as a field has existed only for about thirty to forty years. Teaching has been going on for millennia; the formal study of teaching has occurred on and off during that time, but if that amount of study were collected, pressed down, and measured, it would amount to a few hundred years at most. The common practices of instruction have had a great deal of time to mature, while our attempts to formalize the instructional process and place it under deliberate beneficial control have not. It is no surprise that in the absence of guidance from instructional technologists, teachers have gone ahead and invented their own techniques.

All of us were taught by teachers using those techniques, so we should be careful not to be too harsh in our condemnation of the barbaric practices of the past. Few, if any, of us were educated by computers, so as a group of technologists we have yet to see whether the promise of computer-based instruction can be fulfilled. If anything, that should teach us humility.

The teachers of the past learned from the practices of their own teachers. They sifted out the worst practices and kept the best ones with which to educate us. They have learned to perform the dual juggling act of structuring their message to us so that it communicates with our existing knowledge, while at the same time finding ways to make the experience interesting, involving, appropriately challenging, and varied. Some of our teachers succeeded exceptionally well, and that is perhaps why many of us are even reading a book on this topic.

What did the teachers of the past learn to do? Many things. They learned to form complex ideas and principles into expressions and experiences. They learned that by using analogies and metaphors, they could cause those ideas to communicate with our existing knowledge more efficiently. They learned the power of the example and of demonstration, all of which are respected instructional techniques, even if the budgets of our teaching institutions do not allow us to give all of the examples and demonstrations that are needed. They learned that practice is the most beneficial part of the instructional process, and they frequently engaged us in such practice as their tools and means allowed. They noticed the beneficial effects of feedback following a performance and have in many instances advanced the technique of feedback to a high art, a feat we have yet to even discuss within the field of instructional technology. They realized also the great benefits of coached practice, and have elevated coaching to an art as well. Because of this, we have musicians, singers, speakers, dramatists, athletes, debaters, inventors, technologists, engineers, scholars, and problem-solvers.

They realized the relationship between desire and learning, and learned how to inspire our minds with goals for learning and mental images of what we could attain. They then devised sequences of instruction which brought us by careful stages through a series of experiences that opened our imaginations and our visions to broader understandings of the world, ourselves, and each other. They did all this, being patient until we finally realized that we did not know what we thought we knew and were able to face our own need to learn. Our teachers have achieved an educational system unparalleled in history, and the instructional strategy techniques they have used on us, though flawed in many instances and not always pleasant, have been sufficient to educate us.

What did our teachers fail to do? Why are we trying to improve on their practices? In what ways can the pursuit of instructional technology studies in general and the pursuit of instructional strategy refinements in specific improve instruction? Actually, in this respect, we have the advantage of a new technology—the computer. With that technology, we can address one student at a time, which is a privilege that our teachers only had in a limited number of cases, usually after the school day was over.

Because we can address one student at a time (or small groups of students), we have the opportunity to make instruction which is tailored to the needs of individual students. In fact, the time and cost pressures on our educational institutions may make this a responsibility that we cannot ignore in the future. True individualization was one of the visions that drove technologists to consider the computer as an instructional device in the first place. It is a dream which we have not yet begun to realize on any scale, except in laboratories and a relatively few isolated instances of general practice.

We have learned how to give students individual computer experiences from which they can learn, but in order to truly individualize instruction for them—a thing that we have not yet accomplished—we must know a great deal more detail than we know now about all of the techniques of instruction which our own teachers used. What we need in order to improve over the teaching practices of the past is to refine the techniques themselves—saving only the most beneficial—and then to apply techniques tailored to the individual, the small group, and the large group. Chapter 1 describes the unique features of the computer as an instructional device that make this goal possible.

As technologists, we must now learn the underlying formula for giving an effective demonstration, when to give a demonstration, and what must be included or excluded from a demonstration. We must learn whether to provide one demonstration or multiple demonstrations, and whether to create layered demonstrations which increase in detail and explanatory power each time they are given. We must learn which types of learning require demonstrations and what varieties of demonstration exist which have a differential effect on learning. We must learn what those effects are and learn to tailor the demonstration for a specific content, and for a specific student.

As we learn to do these things, it is possible that we will find that the computer has capabilities which allow us to use a few techniques our teachers did not think of because they were beyond their capacities to implement. As technologists, we may find that having these capacities in the computer, we can now contemplate techniques that our own teachers could not, but for the great majority of our studies, we as technologists can expect to be refiners of existing techniques more than inventors of new ones—and scientists more than seers. Our own teachers were pretty good, after all.

Strategy and practical considerations

In Chapter 7, we described some of the dimensions of the human brain—its speed and some of its capacities—that dictated certain conventions for instructional communication. Other parts of the human body place restrictions on the instructional experience as well. The ability to sit still for only a short period is a factor which, more than almost any other consideration, has defined the length of the average instructional session and has introduced the concept of the "break" during sessions which need to be longer.

What are the *other* practical considerations which influence instructional strategy? We have tried to compile at least a partial list:

Cost: Cost is a major factor in determining what designers design. The production of instructional representations (graphics, video, audio, animations, etc.) for the computer is still expensive. The representation of ideas for communication is part of instructional strategy. It would not be impossible to design an extremely effective graphical or video sequence which used computer-generated graphics to illustrate cell function, DNA replication, or the interaction of atoms during chemical bonding. This representation would have extreme detail and fidelity, a zooming-flying perspective point, colorful and textural differentiation of objects, animated interactions of objects, and the whole thing would be amenable to student control. The cost of such a representation could be somewhere between colossal and astronomical. The average chemistry, biology, and physics courses can use literally hundreds of such representations to illustrate everything from the time-space continuum to the response of the forest floor and sub-soil over time to burning. Teachers would give a lot for such responsive visualizations, but they do not have enough to give, or else these tools would have been created and made widely available long ago.

Making representations on the screen interactive and responsive in real-time is a dream still reserved mainly for video games (and, unfortunately, they choose to picture mainly monsters and mass-killers). Education will have interactive and responsive real-time graphics much later than they appear in games and on television if the trends of the past continue. New tools for object-oriented graphics development will be a major step toward greatly improved representations, as will the continued emphasis on tools and techniques for digitized graphics creation and storage. Until such tools become generally available, ideas like virtual reality and high-end visual representations will remain costly.

Organizational schedules: Instruction is delivered by organizations which have schedules of operation. Instructional functions have to fit within these organizational schedules. If the organization is a school, instruction must, with few exceptions, fit into 45 to 50 minute time slots. When the administrative time associated with some classes is taken into account, another ten to fifteen minutes is subtracted, leaving about half an hour for real instruction.

Certainly there are schools which have longer periods, open class schedules (particularly in the elementary grades), and other arrangements to lengthen the instructional period. Whether the figures used here are completely accurate or representative is not the point. What is important for the moment is to realize that whatever the organizational schedule, an instructional strategy must be in some way molded, sized, or influenced by that schedule. Developers of commercial products for both education and training are especially aware of this time constraint.

Learner energy: Learners, whether in schools or in industry, have schedules and responsibilities of their own in addition to their learning responsibilities. As they pursue their daily schedules, their attention and their energies must be apportioned to cover all of their affairs, and instruction is only one of them. Learner energy levels are a factor which influences instructional strategy, and therefore, energy levels must be taken into account when designing strategies.

For example, when airline pilots are trained in emergency techniques, a session in the simulator is used for the practice portion of instruction on some set of tasks that are being learned. Students engaging in these simulator sessions are subjected to an intense experience. A forty five minute session can leave a student wet with perspiration and rubber-legged for the rest of the day. This is the extreme end of a continuum of energy-using in instruction. The design and use of instructional strategies must take the student's energy levels into account. What if, for instance, the simulator session were made ten hours long?

Learner motivation: It was once thought that young children had short attention spans, but some parents noticed that their children become completely absorbed during play with some tasks which occupied time far beyond the supposed attention span. This showed that attention span is relative to the to personal interests of a child, just as it is in an adult. Though there may be age group averages, they are only averages, and actual attention spent depends on interest.

But even a video game or a television set can hold the interest only for a limited time, and instruction is the same. If students draw energy for learning from their total pool of energy, then there is no guarantee of how much they will choose to draw out, and therefore, continued learner motivation is a variable of instruction. Designers cannot tell in advance how much attention students will give to instruction. Therefore, the strategy must be designed within the average limits of learner motivation.

Prior learning and knowledge about how to learn: Students arrive for instruction with widely varying past experience. Some realize that they are the best managers of the learning process and take an active role in directing their own education. Other students do not realize their own powers and abilities and are convinced that the best way to learn is to be taught. Much less is required to instruct the first type of student than is required for the second. For the first, providing raw materials in an instructional form and a few directions or suggestions suffices. For the latter type of learner, much more direction may be needed, as well as small-step transitions between carefully-planned instructional experiences and more explanation during messaging.

Delivery platform: The technological term that describes the computer used for instructional delivery is *platform*. Platform considerations are extremely important to computer-based instruction because there have been rapid advancements in computer power and capability. This means that there are all kinds of computers which might be used for instruction: some of them large and powerful, having many peripheral devices, and some small, underpowered, graphically limited, and with no peripherals. One of the greatest impediments to what we can do instructionally with computers in the public schools is not the design nor the development of innovative instructional forms; it is the existing installed base of under-sized and under-featured computers that have found their way into the schools and now remain there, limiting the possibilities.

Administrator preferences: Though it is frightening to contemplate, much of the instruction purchased by organizations, both for schools and businesses, is approved by administrators who will not administer the instruction themselves and who have had only brief experiences with an entire curriculum. These decision makers come to the decision process with preconceived notions of what constitutes good instruction, and most of them have never used the instructional computer themselves as students. Strategies which do not conform to their preconceptions of what is "good" face an uphill battle, so these preconceptions influence the design of instructional strategies—often limiting them.

Teacher/instructor preferences: To some extent, instructors viewing computer-based instruction share the difficulties of the administrator. When instructors—school teachers or commercial trainers—inspect a CBI product, they also filter what they see through their own expectations and try to envision the learning process of students they have taught in the past and estimate how this new tool will perform with that image of the learner. They also try to imagine how this tool will fit within their own current techniques and patterns for teaching. Sometimes they are prisoners of limited vision or lack of experience in this respect.

It is a difficult assessment for them to make, and one problem inherent in the judgment that must be made is that it can be unduly influenced by the surface appeal of a CBI product, while issues of real instructional substance go unnoticed. Instructional strategies are influenced by the vision of teachers as well as administrators, and designers must be aware of techniques for communicating the need for effective strategy as well as for a pleasing and interesting appearance in CBI products. More importantly, they need to produce convincing evaluation data that discriminates good strategy features from ones having little effect.

These considerations cause us to design instructional strategies which can be administered within certain time limits or which can be segmented into such lengths. They limit to some extent the "look and feel" variations which will be tolerated. They limit the budget for producing graphics and video and also limit the power and capability of the delivery platform. They are clearly factors which influence instructional strategy.

Strategy and theory

Chapter 7 described the student during instruction and suggested several ways that instructors can inadvertently slow learning. There are equally many ways designers can facilitate learning. Many strategy guidelines can be derived from the designer's goals with respect to the student's information processing and the formation of mental structures. Given the outline of information processing stages in the previous chapter, a designer might form any of the following goals:

- To assist the intake and decoding of instructional messages by the student.

- To enliven or awaken existing knowledge structures which are related to the targeted learning.

- To assist the student in extracting elements from the incoming message which can be chunked and then matched with the student's existing knowledge.

- To influence within the student a feeling that there is knowledge which is desirable and learnable but which the student does not possess.

- To engender confidence in the student that the present instructional source can assist in that learning.

- To assist the student in making matches with existing knowledge patterns.

- To assist the student in extending knowledge through partial matches and the creation of new structures of knowledge.

- To assist the student in detecting larger and larger chunks of meaning from the elements of the instructional message.

- To assist the student in reaching long-term assimilation of new structures.

- To assist the student in converting knowledge structures into performance-ready structures.

- To assist the student in becoming a self-prompting and self-monitoring (self-evaluating) performer who is therefore independent of the learning source.

It is important to keep the perspective that instructional strategy does not *cause* learning. Learning is under student control and is subject to the learner's intentions. Instructional strategy does no more than arrange to deliver information and interactions to the student in hopes that it will complement the student's own learning needs and desires.

Strategy can supply information and highlight patterns in that information, but strategy consists of much more than just informing the learner. It consists of engaging the learner in a cooperative effort whose goal is learning. In order to do this, strategy must do its part by supplying different types of messages at different times in order to support different and constantly changing momentary goals. At some points during instruction, the strategy's goal is to disquiet the student, convincing him or her that learning is needed. At other times, strategy must be ready with many categories of information to either supply on the student's demand or to anticipate the student's need. Most importantly, at other times the strategy must challenge the student to use knowledge to accomplish an acceptable *performance* and must know what to say to the student to remedy failures in that performance.

Conclusion

In this chapter, we have tried to establish a foundation for thinking about instructional strategy by describing its origins and purposes. We have tried, through examples, to examine some higher-level principles of strategy and remove some of the mystique from what is a very practical subject. In the next chapter, we become more specific and describe structural ways for conceiving and designing instructional strategies.

Self-directed activities

- Write two definitions: one for "learning theory" and one for "instructional theory." Contrast these two types of theory, describing what each one is used for and what each one is *not* used for.

- Compile a list of activities during which people learn. Divide the list into two parts: activities where instruction is taking place as well as learning, and activities where instruction (as defined in this chapter) is not taking place. Be able to defend your categorization of each item.

- Examine your own tools and habits for self-instruction. Evaluate how effective they are and what you can do to increase: (1) their number, and (2) the effectiveness with which you use them. Watch for self-instruction techniques used by others and revealed in things they say and do while learning.

- Analyze as many CBI products as you can to determine which ones use the student's most recent response to determine the future path of instruction. Also, identify products which use some record of the student's response history to make strategic decisions after instruction. Identify products which keep a record of what the student knows and doesn't know. Learn how the inner logical mechanisms of these products work, if that is possible.

- Select two instructional products. Contrast the two in terms of the macro-strategy and the micro-strategy they employ. What is the central design structure used in each product? Is it the "lesson"? The "activity"? The "problem"?

- Analyze the script or transcript of an instructional session. Try to identify the structural elements of the strategy used. Identify patterns which the designer or instructor has used for strategically managing the instructional message and the interaction.

- Contrast two instructional transcripts for their use of deliberate instructional strategy. Identify the structural elements of the strategy and the rules the instructor was apparently using to control the use of those elements.

- Examine your own use of instructional strategy during design for both computer-based and non-computer-based instruction. Trace the origins of each decision you make to find the principle on which it rests. Is the principle: (1) practical, (2) theory- or research-based, or (3) based in tradition?

Further reading

Bloom, B. S. (1956). *Taxonomy of educational objectives, Handbook I: Cognitive domain.* New York: Longman.

Gagné, R. M. (1985). *The conditions of learning (4th ed.).* Fort Worth: Holt, Rinehart, and Winston.

Jonassen, D. H. (Ed.). (1988). *Instructional designs for microcomputer courseware.* Hillsdale, NJ: Lawrence Erlbaum Associates.

Joyce, B., Weil, M., and Showers, B. (1992). *Models of teaching (4th ed.).* Boston: Allyn and Bacon.

Kearsley, G. (1982). *Costs, benefits, and productivity in training systems.* Reading, MA: Addison-Wesley Publishing Company.

Merrill, M. D. (1994). *Instructional design theory.* Englewood Cliffs, NJ: Educational Technology Publications.

Merrill, M. D., Li, Z., and Jones, M. K. (1991). Instructional transaction theory: An introduction. *Educational Technology, 31*(6), 7–12.

Moore, D. M., and Dwyer, F. M. (Eds.). (1994). *Visual literacy: A spectrum of visual learning.* Englewood Cliffs, NJ: Educational Technology Publications.

Reigeluth, C. M. (Ed.). (1983). *Instructional design theories and models: An overview of their current status.* Hillsdale, NJ: Lawrence Erlbaum Associates.

Reigeluth, C. M. (Ed.). (1987). *Instructional theories in action: Lessons illustrating selected theories and models.* Hillsdale, NJ: Lawrence Erlbaum Associates.

van Merriënboer, J. J. G. (1997). *Training complex cognitive skills.* Englewood Cliffs, NJ: Educational Technology Publications.

9

INSTRUCTIONAL STRATEGY II: APPLICATIONS

Chapter Objectives:

1. *State three principles of instructional goals which influence the design of instructional strategies.*

2. *Diagram the dynamic interplay of performance and strategic goals which takes place during instruction.*

3. *Describe the five levels of design for strategic goals and strategy plans for direct instruction by tutorial.*

4. *Describe the problems currently encountered by designers trying to achieve adaptive instruction.*

5. *Explain how similar strategic structures can give rise to very dissimilar surface features of instruction.*

Instructional goals and strategy

The instructional goal is the focal point of all instructional strategy plans. But what is the state of the art in our current use of instructional objectives—those expressions of our instructional goals?

- Trainers and school educators routinely write instructional objectives *after* the instructional products "based" on them have been produced, in order to satisfy regulations.

- Designers of simulations and other advanced forms of instruction find the current technology of instructional goals insufficient and too trivial to guide them in product design or to help them integrate their products into curricula.

- Parents and business operators are discouraged to find that high scores on tests have no direct relationship to real performance capability in students and employees, despite the fact that their education and training are said to be "objective-based."

- Students in school and industry find the major portion of their instruction consisting of verbal presentations, followed by verbal paper-and-pencil tests.

Many instructional designers have grown so impatient with the confusion, lack of definition, and unresolved issues surrounding instructional objectives that they have either defined their own definitions and procedures for using objectives or have begun to work *around* instructional objectives—an area that is fundamental to their craft. Instead of relying upon objectives as an important design tool, some designers have found them to be a costly and confusing inconvenience.

This is symptomatic of a serious dis-ease which exists between designers and the doctrine of instructional goals. No serious designer can do *without* them, but many designers do not know what to do *with* them either. In the minds of too many designers, instructional designs have become *uncoupled* from explicit instructional objectives written in advance of the instruction. In too many cases, instructional objectives are an afterthought and a formality that post-date the design of instructional strategies and tests. Moreover, the current use of instructional goals—which are almost always stated as designer or instructor intentions—tends to deprive the student of active participation in the instruction/learning process and instead promotes instruction which is designer-centered and message-centered. Most often, objectives are written containing verbal rather than hands-on or realistic behavior.

All of these problems with objectives are most unfortunate, because future advances and improvements in the implementation of instructional strategy will depend on our understanding of the dynamics and interplay of student and designer goals during instruction. Instructional designers must devise more useful and detailed conceptions of student and instructor goals and the manner in which they interact during instruction.

Contributions from artificial intelligence

In contrast to the state of affairs in education and training, work in artificial intelligence and tutoring systems has given the notion of instructional goal more meaning and specificity in order to make it a useful tool for generating instruction. Many intelligent tutoring systems (ITS) incorporate engines for generating and then satisfying sequences of transient instructional goals—in a sense, dynamic instructional objectives—which change from moment to moment, governing instruction. This can in some systems result in different performance goals being selected for different students and different strategic approaches to satisfying those goals. We feel that if progress is to be made in the formation of objectives and their application during instruction, it will be along these lines. Instructional goals must become much more closely linked with instructional acts. If it is not practical to emulate the ITS example right now with respect to instructional goals, then perhaps it can become a vision to draw us, for it will cause our discussions of instructional goals to become more substantive, more searching, and at the same time both more theoretically and more utility-oriented.

A useful philosophy of instructional goals based on the example of AI systems can be summarized under three principles:

Principle #1. At least four sets of instructional goals are active during instruction: An instructor/designer has two sets of goals during instruction, and so does the student. If all of these goals work together harmoniously, learning is improved and speeded; if these goals do not harmonize, difficulty in instructing and learning occur, and frustration is the result. The goals during instruction are enumerated below.

1. *The instructor/designer performance goals.* These are what we normally refer to as "instructional goals" or "instructional objectives." They express the type and level of performance the instructor/designer hopes the student will attain as a result of instruction. The instructor traditionally imposes these goals. That may or may not be the best way, which we will discuss later, but that is how it tends to be done.

2. *The instructor/designer strategic goals.* These are goals that express what specific actions the teacher/designer will take to support the student's learning processes and attainment of the current performance goal. These goals express the instructor's *strategic plan.* They correspond directly to the instructor's performance goals, but they are more numerous. While one performance goal persists as the instructional target, a sequence of related strategic goals may be selected, applied, assessed, and discarded, until one is found to which the student responds. There may be many strategic goals formed by the instructor before the student finally attains the desired performance. Strategic goals are adjusted dynamically, depending on the results being obtained from instruction. When the instructor runs out of

strategic goals, he or she runs out of approaches and doesn't know what to do next, though the performance goal still exists.

(Note: It is important not to confuse the instructor's strategic *goals* with the instructor's strategic *means*. Just as there may be more than one strategic goal for a single performance goal, there may be more than one specific strategic means—message sequence, interaction sequence, or message representation—for one strategic goal. If speaking words doesn't work, then maybe drawing a picture will. If one type of practice doesn't help, then what about another?)

3. *The student's performance/learning goals.* These goals express what the student intends to learn or what the student understands as the learning target. A student always forms or accepts a performance goal upon entering into an instructional relationship with another person. The student's goal may originate in one of two ways: (1) it may be suggested to the student, or (2) the student may form his or her own goal as an outgrowth of self-directed learning desires and then enlist instructional assistance in reaching it. Most frequently, when an instructor fails to provide a learning goal, the student will reverse engineer the goal from the instruction (and tests) provided. This is called "psyching out" the instructor, and it is a survival strategy in high school and college for many students.

If an instructor suggests the goal, there is no guarantee that the student will understand what is intended. Frequently, a mismatch between student and instructor goals occurs. This is evidenced by a number of common instructional mishaps, all of them filled with frustration:

- The student studies the wrong things for the test.

- The instructor spends ten minutes eloquently answering a question that the student didn't really ask, and the student still wants to know the answer to the original question but is afraid of being misunderstood again.

- A student has to turn in a research paper three times, making revisions each time, uncertain of what is wanted, until the instructor sees what he or she wanted to see in it and accepts the paper.

4. *The student's strategic goals.* These goals express what the student intends to do in order to achieve his or her learning goal. Student strategic goals include either self-directed activities in which a teacher is cooperatively engaged or the student's acceptance and active use of a teacher's proposed or implied strategic plan. Under different conditions, either of these alternatives may be desirable.

Performance goals represent a target for focusing instruction. Strategic goals consist of strategic plans by which the target may be reached. Performance and strategic goals are what the designer constructs as the basis for making design decisions. Performance and strategic goals help students to focus attention and energy and manage learning processes during instructional experiences, helping the student obtain as much benefit as possible from them.

A student's strategic goals are expressed in terms of actions he or she knows how to use for self-directed learning. At any stage of education for any learner, this set of goals may be sound, or it may be faulty or incomplete. *Therefore, one of the purposes of instruction and instructional strategy is to help the student achieve a better set of learning skills with which to form better, more productive strategic goals.*

Principle #2. Goals exist at several levels: Instructional designers tend to think of instructional goals in a monolithic sense. A single large goal is often expected to give rise to several minutes or even hours of instruction. However, it is common for live instructors—deliberately during pre-planning or without realizing it at the moment of instruction—to break a large instructional (performance) goal into several sub-goals.

A goal may be broken into sub-goals in two ways: (1) by reduction or fragmentation into smaller self-contained behaviors, or (2) by reduction to a series of partial-performance plateaus which build in graduated steps toward complete performance. For instance, the goal of bowling a strike may be fragmented into the sub-goals: (1) grasp the ball correctly, (2) assume the starting position, (3) make the approach, (4) make the delivery, (5) complete the follow-through.

Likewise, the same goal of bowling a strike can be broken into successive plateau sub-goals: (1) get the bowling ball to the far end of the alley, (2) keep the ball from falling into the gutter, (3) knock down at least half of the pins, (4) roll a spare each time, (5) put the ball in the strike pocket each time.

The function of either form of sub-goal is to provide choice points at which either in-structor or student can: (1) select goals, (2) select means, (3) execute means, and (4) assess the result. We presented these steps in Chapter 8 as the basic activities of instruction, and they ap-ply to both *instructor* and *student* actions during instruction.

As performance goals break into smaller sub-goals, the strategic goals which correspond to them undergo a parallel decomposition. The manner of this happening will be described later in this chapter.

Principle #3. All goals are dynamic during instruction: As instruction progresses, perfor-mance goals change from moment to moment, as do the strategic goals selected to lead to their attainment. The goals and subgoals described in Principles #1 and #2 above are taken up and achieved in some order. Moment by moment, performance goals are being selected, taught, as-sessed, and either re-selected or traded for a new goal. Just as the performance goals (of both student and instructor) change dynamically in this way, the related strategic goals (of both stu-dent and instructor) also change.

Nowhere is this more evident than following an error during instruction. The forward progress of instruction halts momentarily, as it were, and the instructor carries out corrective activities in which a new momentary instructional goal is selected: a sub-goal of the one which directed instruction only moments before. When the sub-goal is satisfied, it is discarded, and instruction continues, restoring the former performance goal as the focus of instruction. Sev-eral situations during instruction illustrate this happening:

- The association pair which is retained longer in the drill and practice pool because it has been missed more times than the others and appears to need additional practice.

- The concept discrimination dimension for which additional example-non-example pairs are shown to the student who has trouble making the discrimination of that dimension.

- The process step for which the student is unable to make correct predictions and which is singled out for additional instruction and practice.

- The short passage of decision-making steps in a larger integrated performance which causes the student to falter and which accordingly receives additional prac-tice opportunities with coaching.

As performance goals change moment by moment, strategic goals correspondingly adjust moment by moment in order to support their attainment. This creates a dynamism in the instruction which has been possible in the past only for human instructors, but which can be accomplished with the computer if instructional strategy is designed in such a way as to allow it to happen. Chapter 1 emphasizes the qualities of the computer which suit it for delivery of this type of instruction. It is in the dynamic adjustment of instructional strategy that these qualities all come together to create an adaptive computer-based instructional experience.

Levels of design: Dissecting a strategy

Having talked about goals in the abstract, we now want to illustrate these principles by looking within a generic instructional strategy and observing how its structure is related to the four kinds of goals we have identified:

- The designer's performance goal
- The student's performance/learning goal
- The designer's strategic goals
- The student's strategic goals

A generic instructional objective for procedure-using instruction is:

> *"The student will be capable of performing procedure X under a specified range of conditions, to a specified competence criterion."*

Figures 1 through 5 and the sections that follow below describe a useful technique for breaking down or decomposing the designer's goals in a way that leads to strategy designs. This breakdown creates a strategy design at five levels:

- *The Didactic Activity level*—The level at which the designer specifies major types of didactic activity that will occur during the instruction: presentations, practice opportunities of different varieties, tests, pre-tests, demonstrations, and so forth.

- *The Content Structure level*—The level at which the designer impresses the structure of the content onto the existing structure from the previous level, creating additional strategic structures.

- *The Message Element level*—The level at which the designer defines the structural elements of instructional messages and interactions and adds these new structures to the evolving design.

- *The Representation Element level*—The level at which the designer makes decisions regarding the specific verbal, graphic, and other representations and media channel assignments that will be used to convey the message and provide the interaction.

- *The Implementation Logic level*—The level at which the designer merges all of the structures formed by the previous four steps with the logic structures provided by an authoring tool or a programming language being used, giving computerized expression to the entire strategy plan.

We will now provide an extended example of the design decisions that are made in succession at each of these levels of strategy planning for procedural instruction. *We will try to show how making design decisions at each of these levels is the essence and order of design for direct tutorial instruction.* The process begins with the instructional goal and leaves the designer with a strategy plan. The final sections of this chapter will show the many different ways this strategy plan can be used to create variety without abandoning underlying structure.

The didactic activity level

At the Didactic Activity level of design, the designer makes decisions regarding the main strategic structures—the major types of instructional activity that will be carried out within the instructional product being designed. The structures included in the design will be determined by several constraining factors: the goal of instruction, the resources available for both development and delivery of instruction, the needs of the students, and the context of instruction in which the product will be used.

At this point, though the instructional objective specifies that the student will be able to "perform Procedure X" following instruction, remember that there will be four sets of goals operative at the time of instruction, and they will influence what the designer should design.

First, to ensure that the performance goals are aligned between student and instructor, the designer will create as part of the instructional strategy a block of messages and interactions for instructional goal setting. The goal will be selected, formed, reviewed, discussed, acknowledged, negotiated, and/or understood by both instructor and student during this block of activity.

Major didactic activities normally include either a *presentation* activity or a *practice* activity or both. These are placed into the strategy structure at the didactic activity level. As you will see later in this chapter, there are many ways in which these blocks may be rearranged. Figure 1 shows the addition of these blocks to the strategy.

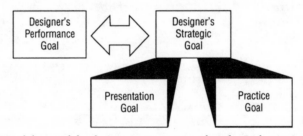

Figure 1. Breakdown of the designer's strategic goal at the Didactic Activity level.

As the major didactic activity blocks are added during this level of design, the single controlling instructional goal is either deliberately or tacitly being divided to form sub-goals. By creating presentation and practice blocks, the designer has automatically created the following practice goals:

Designer's practice performance goal:

Student will perform procedure X acceptably

Designer's practice strategic goal:

I will provide occasions to perform procedure X with appropriate coaching and feedback until criterion performance is reached.

As well, the designer has created the following presentation goals:

Designer's presentation performance goal:

The student will encode the propositional knowledge necessary for procedure X performance.

Designer's presentation strategic goal:

I will supply access to core information essential to procedure X performance along with supports that will help the student encode the information: (1) in long-term storage, and (2) in a form that is readily usable when it is needed for performance.

At the time of instruction, these sub-goals must come to be understood and shared by the student in some way if the instruction is to proceed effectively. The student must form corresponding performance and strategic goals which either match the instructor's or include the instructor's. Otherwise, the instructional communication will be ineffective.

In response to the instructor's goals for practice, the student might form the following performance and strategic goals:

Student practice performance goal:

I will learn to perform Procedure X to the standards expected.

Student practice strategic goal:

I will use appropriate attentional, memory, and conceptual knowledge-forming techniques during the practice and will make an active attempt to synthesize knowledge into larger, usable wholes; I will hold myself accountable for performance capability and will rehearse the procedure until I am confident I have learned it adequately.

In response to the instructor's goals for the presentation, the student might form the following performance and strategic goals:

Student presentation performance goal:

I will encode the conceptual knowledge related to Procedure X in a form that can be used during practice attempts to guide decision-making and action.

Student presentation strategic goal:

I will analyze the incoming message of the presentation, looking for specific items which fill the slots of my procedure-using knowledge template, including the slots for: step name, step action, step indications, step criteria, step warnings, and so forth; I will be responsible for placing these items in memory in a way that retrieval is facilitated and reliable.

Of course, if the role assignment negotiated between instructor and learner made the student responsible for learning, then this goal's wording would change.

The designer may add as many or as few blocks as are needed at this Didactic Activity level of design. Other candidates for blocks of strategy include: one or more varieties of demonstration, alternate forms of practice, alternate forms of presentation, and so forth.

The content structure level

At the second level of design, the designer determines how to apply the structure of the content to the didactic activity blocks just created.

In a procedure, the content is segmented into steps. This has implications for the structure of the strategy. Each step in the procedure must be taught and must be practiced, and appropriate structures must be created for doing that.

For instruction of behavior other than procedure-using, the content does not divide naturally into steps. Each type of content divides along structured lines appropriate to its own type.

For instance, process content decomposes into cause-effect relationships and transmission pairs (see Chapter 12); concept content breaks down in terms of classification rules and exemplars of specific attribute combinations (see Chapter 13); and memory content fragments in terms of either single associations or complexes (schemata) of association (see Chapter 10).

Figure 2a shows the Practice block of the strategy divided according to the steps in the procedure—with one block created for each step. Figure 2b shows the same thing for the Presentation block of the strategy. (For more detail on procedure-using instructional strategies, see Chapter 11, and for an extended example of procedure-using design, see Chapter 21). The instructional goals which were divided by creation of the didactic activities in the previous step are now divided again.

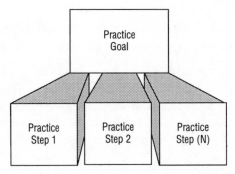

Figure 2a. Imposition of the content structures on the practice block of the strategy.

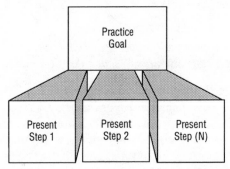

Figure 2b. Imposition of the content structure on the presentation block of the strategy.

The message element level

Instructional activities consist of some combination of:

* Information elements

* Interaction elements

During the Message Element level of design, the designer will determine the information elements to be provided and the types of interaction to be used within each of the strategic blocks which have been created so far.

Certain types of message element are essential to and support learning of each type of behavior. Every behavior type has its corresponding family of message elements. For learning a body of facts, it is essential that the student be informed of the facts. For learning a process made up of cause-effect relationships, it is essential that the learner be told or discover the exact nature of the relationships. For concept instruction, the student must either be told or discover the concept definition.

The same principle is true for interactions: Some kinds of interaction contribute to the learning of a procedure, while other kinds of interaction don't. Recall how different the message contents and practice activities were for the three instructional strategies we examined in Chapter 8.

This level of design is preoccupied with the types of information and interaction that must be supplied within each strategy block to support the student's learning of: (1) the propositional knowledge, and (2) the performance knowledge for each step of the procedure.

For strategy purposes, information is measured in terms of *categories* of information: *types* of message. Categories of information are place holders where real message content will be inserted during instruction. For procedure instruction, the essential core of information consists of step names, step beginning cues, step actions, step indications, step terminating cues, and step cautions or warnings. At this level of design, the designer does not create the *exact content* of the message elements nor decide its media-channelization. What is determined here is simply the set of *categories* of message that will be included during instruction.

Practice does not consist of informing; it consists of providing the student an opportunity to act and observe the outcome. Therefore, the message elements for practice name types of interaction with the student. These include: providing the setting within which to respond, providing the occasion for a response, providing interactive controls through which to act, providing a dynamic response to student actions, providing a judgment of student action, providing feedback to the student (both natural and artificial), and providing guidance for error correction.

Just like the presentation message place holders, these interaction place holders will be filled with specific message content in later steps of design. For now, they only represent empty slots in a strategic plan to be filled at some point.

Just as at all the previous levels of design, message element blocks created during this level of design represent both performance and strategic goals for both student and instructor. Each represents the strategic goal or intention of the designer to present a specific item of information or conduct a specific phase of interaction for the student's benefit. Message elements have the performance goals: "Encode the propositional knowledge for step (N)" and "Perform step (N)." Figure 3 shows the breakdown of the content blocks of the strategy into Message Element blocks.

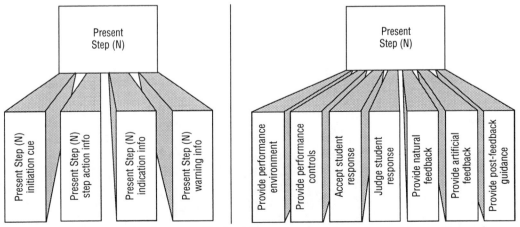

Figure 3. Division of each content block of the strategy by information and interaction needs.

The representation element level

In order to present the message, the designer must plan how each Message Element defined in the previous level of design will be represented to the student. Frequently, one information element or one interaction element will require more than one method of representation. Presenting the indications which attend the performance of a specific step in the procedure may require both graphic/video representation and text or audio. At this point, the designer plans the use of the available media channels for: (1) the representation of the message content for each information block, and (2) the interactive mechanisms for each interaction block.

This includes a plan for single versus multiple channelization and for synchronization of message parts sent through different channels. For instance, a designer may plan that the representation of step indications for each step will be presented using a particular pattern of verbal content, visual content, and auditory content, using a particular pattern of timing between them. The designer must form a representation plan for each strategic Message Element block created at the previous design level.

Figures 4a and 4b show that the strategic goals for presentation and practice message elements are subdivided at this level of design into goals for the representation of each message element block. There is a one-to-one correspondence between Message Elements and Representation Elements for practice. This is because the message and the representation are very closely related during a performance; to a great extent the representation is the message for practice. In those situations, the artifice of designed textual messages is proportionally less.

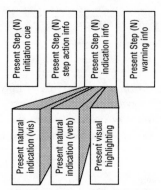

Figure 4a. Division of presentation message element blocks of the strategy into representation blocks.

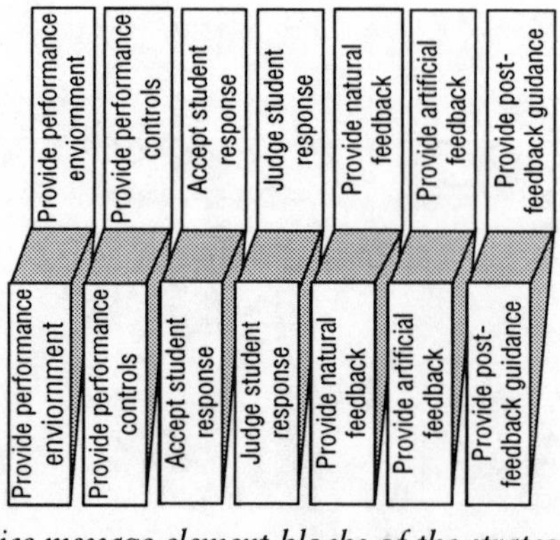

Figure 4b. Division of practice message element blocks of the strategy into representation blocks.

The implementation logic level

Finally, once representations are designed, their conveyance to the student must be planned in structures corresponding to computer program logic elements. Each Representation Element must have designed for it a plan for Implementation Logic that will cause the required displays to be shown, and the interactions to occur.

Figures 5a and 5b show that at this level of design, the elements produced begin to resemble basic instructional acts and also resemble some of the basic frame patterns described in Chapter 5.

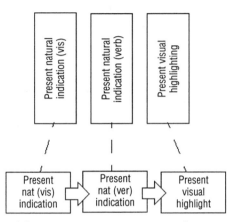

Figure 5a. Mapping of the presentation representation elements onto logical elements.

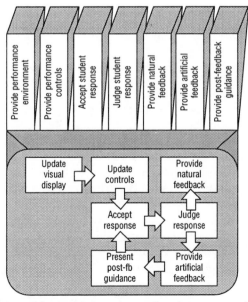

Figure 5b. Mapping of the practice representation elements onto logical elements.

Multiple strategic goals

The above analysis has taken what appeared on the surface to be a simple procedure-using performance goal and derived from it a pyramid of matched performance and strategic goals. At the top of the pyramid, the blocks represent major didactic activities, and after applying content, messaging, and representational structure to these blocks, the result is a detailed plan for an instructional strategy, including even the computer logic structures necessary to carry out the plan. Most importantly, every block in the pyramid embodies four instruction-related goals, so there is a direct, traceable relationship between the original goal and the structures created to support its attainment.

Does this correspond to how teachers really teach? We think it does. We think that teachers can and do address goals at a high level of decomposition as a natural part of interacting with students instructionally. It is the thing that enables live teachers to adjust their strategy moment by moment, and it is this type of mechanism which will enable technological "teachers" to do the same.

Figures 1 through 5 have shown provisions for only one strategic plan. What does an instructor do if that one plan does not work? Repeat it again? Speak louder? Provide more practice problems? This is a dilemma which has always plagued both technology-based and live instruction. We suggest that the designer consider either: (1) providing alternative strategic plans (more than one set of strategic goals), or (2) providing the basic instructional elements under the control of rules which can form alternative approaches to instructional in a way that can adapt to the student's need.

Why so many goals?

We have built our discussion of instructional goals on the premises that:

1. Both students and instructors have two sets of goals each which are active at the time of instruction.

2. These goals decompose into sub-goals dynamically during instruction.

3. One of the main functions of goals during tutorial instruction is to allow the student and the instruction (or the instructor) to negotiate a sequence of experiences and information which will support the student's learning processes.

In effect, we have taken a subject (instructional goals) which used to be simple and have made it more complicated. Why have we done this, and what do we expect to gain from it?

We feel this different view of instructional goals and their interplay during instruction not only prepares you to understand the manner in which many of the CBI systems of the future will operate, but we believe it represents what actually occurs during instruction. If you watch great teachers at work and watch students learning from them, you will witness the subtle negotiation of goals, expressed in the form of questions, remarks, pauses, and even body language.

A second reason we favor this view of goals is that it makes clear those initiatives which occur during instruction, and therefore makes it easy to design instruction in which initiative is shared or negotiated between student and instructor. These sets of goals and levels of goals constitute, as it were, a menu from which the student and the instructor can design an experience.

We feel this view of goals is also useful because it has diagnostic value: It can help us understand the source of certain common instructional problems. Consider the four sets of student and instructor goals as a matrix, as shown in Figure 6.

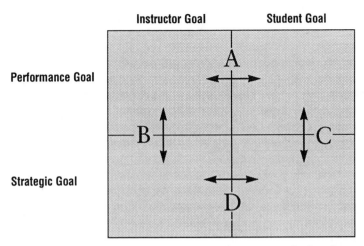

Figure 6. Instructional problems arising from mismatched goals.

To this point, we have emphasized the importance of harmony between these goals. However, a specific, goal-related instructional malady occurs whenever there is disharmony in any direction between these goals.

Take, for instance, the situation where the instructor's performance goal does not match the student's (Arrow A). The result is a goal crisis which leaves the student unable to comprehend the performance expectations and judgments of the instructor. When the instructor's performance goal does not match the instructor's choice of strategic goal (Arrow B), there is a strategy mismatch, and though the student may understand the performance goal and be ready to learn, the experiences and information supplied will not seem to be supporting that specific learning, so the student will learn what is presented, adapting as much as possible to the circumstance. When the student's performance goal does not match the student's strategic goal (Arrow C), the student is working against himself or herself and will attempt to apply inappropriate strategies to the learning task, making it harder than necessary, frustrating, and perhaps impossible. Finally, when there is a mismatch between the instructor's strategic goal and the student's strategic goal (Arrow D), the information and experience supplied by the instructor are difficult for the student to process and use for learning purposes.

All of these goal mismatches can be observed daily in classrooms and training rooms everywhere. They result in difficult or ineffective instruction. Understanding these potential problems by understanding the goal dynamic which exists during instruction can help designers, instructors, and students. It gives instructors some idea of how to improve communication during goal negotiation to avoid mismatches. It gives the student an analytic tool for determining what is going wrong when the instructional experience becomes overly difficult or confusing. With their understanding, students can not only diagnose the problem, but also have a ready vocabulary for asking for the remedy.

To summarize, we feel this more complete view of instructional goals as tools rather than as static entities leads directly to application during design and during instruction. The goals at all five levels help the designer to focus on instructional strategy which is relevant to the learning task, and discipline that strategy in support of the student's needs, rather than the instructor's habits and preferences.

Goals and the student

Let us now try to place the designer's goals into perspective with the student's goals and discuss how considering student goals leads to designs for increased sharing of initiative and control during instruction.

The designer's strategic goals consist mainly of providing information and interaction opportunities to the student in hopes of supporting the student's own learning and strategic goals. Though the designer may select goals and design strategies, the designer cannot make the student learn. The designer can only provide relevant information and interactions—raw materials with which the student can construct knowledge and performance capability.

The student's strategic goals depend on his or her perceived role as a student. Students aren't born as students; they learn to be students by being taught, and every instructional encounter teaches not only content knowledge, but also knowledge on "how to be a student," "what is a student," and "what kind of a student are you?"

Student strategic goals are based on the student's understanding of what kind of effort and activity it takes to learn, what self-initiated activities improve learning, what level of initiative it takes to be a self-directed learner, what resources are available, and how to learn from different types of resources. The student's strategic goals also depend on the invitation from the instructor to the student to participate. Such invitations are frequently non-verbal, but experienced students have normally learned when to speak up and when to remain silent. If the student perceives that the instructor prefers to do most of the work, then the student's strategic goals include doing what is possible to engage in learning without disturbing what the instructor is doing. If the student realizes that the instructor intends to turn some portion of responsibility and initiative for learning over to the student, then a much different set of strategies is selected.

The communication and balancing of instructor and student strategic goals is a negotiation which occurs each time instruction takes place.

The student watches the instructor and either directly or silently negotiates a set of strategic goals. Ideally, students see learning as an opportunity, desire it, want it to be a satisfactory experience, and adjust their strategic plans according to the signals they are given or can pick up from the instructor.

Students interpret technology-delivered instruction with the same keenness. They try to judge the role that the technology will place them in just as carefully as they would try to judge the role a live instructor would give them. One of the tasks of the CBI designer is to define the student role, create designs compatible with that role definition, and then help students recognize and accept their role as active, responsible learners. It helps if students are given encouragement and opportunity for forming their own performance and/or strategic goals. In many cases, students may need direct coaching or indirect experience in order to learn the techniques of learning, but this is one of the most important goals of instruction, so the designer must design for it.

Structured strategy: Pro and con

The strategy design approach we have just presented is called *structured* strategy. It is a suitable method for defining instructional strategies for direct content- and message-centered instruction. As you will see in Chapter 15, other types of instruction call for an indirect approach to instruction which this method of design does not support. Methods for designing those types of instruction are presented in later chapters.

There are many different reactions to the structured approach, voicing concerns about implications for the designer as well as the student. Let's deal with the most common of those concerns in hopes of at the same time clearing away some misconceptions about the structured strategy method.

Level of detail: Clearly the structured approach to instructional strategy generates more detail than other approaches to designing. However, it is useful detail. It helps you describe what you are designing, gives you a rational basis for decision-making at each level of design, and helps you to be systematic and thorough. Many designers find that it speeds up the design process, as they become familiar with the decision process involved.

Instructional designers have been hampered in the past by inadequate vocabulary for discussing instructional strategy. The approach we describe here also supplies some new terms for that discussion. The structured approach identifies design decisions for a complete strategy—decisions which otherwise might be overlooked and discovered later under unhappy circumstances.

Completeness: Is the structured approach all that is need for complete instructional strategy planning? We believe not. There is much more to instructional strategy than we have discussed here. That is because excellent strategies for instruction ultimately call upon all that we know about how people learn, and that is a very comprehensive body of knowledge.

What we have presented is actually a way for structuring the development of strategies. We have told you that you should determine your Message Elements at a certain stage of design, but *which Elements you select (or invent) depends on your own understanding of what will be effective.* We have told you that you should design interactions which are appropriate to the instructional goal, but the interactions you select (or invent) depend on your understanding of the way in which practice influences learning, and that is a subject which has undergone intensive study for many decades. The effectiveness of your instruction will not be guaranteed by using the design approach we have advocated, but the use of the structured strategy technology will leave more time and energy for you to spend on the important issues which at present have no structural approach and no simple set of alternatives to choose from. These decisions are the point where you weave the teaching-learning principles to which you adhere into the fabric of the instructional product.

How can the designer keep track of all the details that are created by the structural approach? In the long run, the structural approach will actually reduce the complexity of the designer's task and the level of detail which must be recorded and dealt with. Here's why.

In the early days of CBI, some designers felt that creative approaches to design were paramount to an enjoyable CBI experience for students. Every lesson created by those designers was an entirely new creative effort. Lessons, by design, were not allowed to look alike nor share the same style. The philosophy was that this variety would stimulate interest and keep instruction from being boring.

This striving for difference in every product may have been a reaction to the many look-alike drill-and-practice forms that were created early in the history of CBI. However, students reacted to the resulting avalanche of creative variety by getting *lost* in the lessons that were created—but not *lost* in a positive sense. Since every lesson was a whole new experience, and since each one unfolded in its own unique way, students had no familiar orienting landmarks to tell them where they were, where they were going, and how far it was to get there. They were, in a sense captured by and at the mercy of the lesson, and each lesson became an endless maze of creative branches.

The structured approach to strategy brings order and regularity to CBI, not only for the designer but for the student as well. The designer is able to design strategic patterns once which, with modification, can be reused in many places. These repeatedly-used patterns are commonly called strategy *templates*. By using strategy templates, designers save not only large amounts of design time but similar amounts of development time as well.

The student benefit is that even though the surface appearance of the message may differ radically from tutorial to tutorial (you will see how by the end of this chapter), familiar surface features at key points throughout the experience provide the students with familiar landmarks telling them where they are, where they can go, and how far it is. This issue of maintaining student sense of place and control is a key issue in CBI, and it is treated at length in Chapter 19 on Display Management.

Sameness of instruction: Does structured strategy create instruction which is all the same? Are we creating ticky-tacky boxes of look-alike tutorials using this approach? Our own experience says no. Though underlying structures are often nearly the same in the structured approach, surface appearance of instruction diverges as different content is applied to the structure. What results is an amount of variety that eliminates boredom but also provides sufficient regularity for the student to anticipate the instruction. This regularity has a tremendous influence on the ability of the student to take control of and become active in the learning process. It allows the student to anticipate the structure of the instruction and take initiative in setting and reaching personal strategic goals. Therefore, this regularity of underlying strategic structure allows the student to become a more involved, active, self-directed learner, and we consider that to be a very important outcome.

Reductionism: Isn't this reductionistic approach directly counter to the trends in instruction today? Breaking things down into smaller and smaller units has been a practice within instructional technology for the past forty years. Though Robert Gagné has been credited with the reductionistic approach to instructional goal definition, the trend toward analysis of elements began long before. Gagné's approach had wide appeal, and Gagné's background as an experimental psychologist gave it the seal of theoretical respectability.

The reductionistic approach to instructional design—the approach in which wholes of behavior are broken into small elements of behavior so that they can be given individual instructional attention—has been criticized recently for *fragmenting* instruction and failing to teach behavior at higher, more integrated levels. Interestingly enough, Gagné expressed this criticism himself, indicating the possibility that his original ideas may have been misinterpreted. There is a tendency among instructional designers to perform an analysis of tasks and then to base instruction on the fragmented tasks, never revisiting the tasks at an integrated level, which would allow the learning of higher, more real-world-like patterns of performance.

Are we suggesting here a process that will only lead to continuation of that type of fragmentation? We believe not. The structured approach to strategy does imply that designers will break strategy elements down to their lowest level and then design instructional treatment for each of the low-level elements thus obtained. It brings designers face-to-face with the decisions which must be made during design, and gives them a checklist for determining when a design meets the criteria of completeness and wholeness. However, properly used in conjunction with integrative forms of instruction described later in this book (see Chapter 15), this approach will improve the integration of design elements and allow designers to create integrated suites of instruction.

We think that the analytical method of the structured approach is a strength rather than a weakness. The elements of strategy which we have identified here and in later chapters (see Chapters 10 through 14 for detailed discussions of instructional strategies) are in the natural makeup of *every* procedure strategy—systematically derived or not. Can you think of a way to teach a procedure which does not in some way convey to the student (either verbally or nonverbally) what the procedure steps are, or in what order they occur? Can a procedure be taught without somehow conveying or making available to students information on the indications used to begin and end actions?

The structured strategy approach defines by analysis all of the underlying elements of instruction which would be identified by designers wrestling with the same design problem. But it leads the designer to design items which tend to be omitted due to the lack of a systematic approach.

Practicality: How practical is this approach for designers who are under heavy time pressures and must produce instruction in large volumes? Experience shows that it is very practical. In fact, most large-scale commercial developers of CBI could not stay in business if they did not apply some version of templated strategy techniques in the design, development, and production of their products.

Developing CBI is simply too costly to build customized products one at a time. Many years ago, formulas were reached which allowed the mass production of cars with acceptable optioning to meet the needs of almost all drivers. This same approach, over time, has become the standard for the production of computer-based instructional products as well, and if good strategy templates are used as the basis for those products, the result is high quality and effective instruction.

The practicality issue in relation to structured strategy has deeper implications for the technology of CBI than most designers realize. We believe that CBI is a technology trying to pass a test of both excellence (effectiveness) and economics (cost of development, cost of delivery). The CBI developer mindset in the past has favored the creation of small, isolated CBI programs rather than families or contexted groups of linked products. The reasons are mainly economic: CBI still costs too much.

We administer courses in our schools which run for months at a time, but we have few CBI products whose span of use is longer than ten hours. If CBI is to become a mainstream, essential technology, used at the level required of such a technology, then we must find ways to produce consistent products of extensive size at low cost. Yet these must be quality, interesting products which deliver instruction possible from no other medium. The structured approach to strategy design is *one tool* for reducing the cost of CBI through standardization of internal structures with benefit for both designers and students.

The generality of structured strategy

In Chapter 8 we maintained that some modern instructional techniques are in part the result of imitation and refinement of the best instructional techniques from the past. If the principles described so far in this chapter are general, then they ought to be evident in instruction that was created in the past as well as instruction designed today. If instruction from the past can be described in terms of the present system, then this system provides a kind of Rosetta Stone which makes sense of different approaches to strategy.

We believe this to be the case. If you analyze existing instruction from any medium, you can identify the elements of structured strategy described here embedded within its message. It is sometimes confusing to perform this kind of analysis because of: (1) the many surface forms which can be assigned to underlying strategic elements, making them look dissimilar when they are in fact serving the same function, (2) the intermixing of multiple strategies within one instructional event, which is a common occurrence, (3) the variations in order with which strategic elements may be included in a script, (4) the unintentional omission of important strategic elements from some scripts, and (5) the addition in many cases of strategic elements which are irrelevant to the instructional goal.

What makes it possible for instructional scripts which look quite different on the surface to share the same internal strategic structure? There are two answers:

- Multiple surface forms
- The shuffling of strategic elements

Multiple surface forms

There are several different ways to convey a single message. You can convey it graphically, textually, in audio, through animation, or through iconic symbols. You can use literal communication, analogy, metaphor, or suggestion. Five different designers presenting the definition of a concept will do it in five different ways. The presentations will vary on the surface, even though the essential content of the message is the same. The concept definition doesn't change, but the surface methods used to present it may change. There are several ways to carry out each strategic intention, but so long as certain essential elements are included, the strategic effect is the same, regardless of what the surface looks like. It is one of the important challenges of the designer to create varied surface forms to fulfill standard, underlying instructional intentions.

Shuffling of intentions

We have so far said nothing about the instructional ordering of the blocks of instructional intention (goals) that were derived by analysis in Figures 1 through 5. In addition to identifying the goals of instruction, a strategy plan must determine an order for setting and satisfying them, and this plan must be determined either before instruction begins or at the time of instruction.

The ordering of goals is one of the major design opportunities and one of the most interesting design challenges that a designer faces. Ordering is one of the primary sources of differences in the surface appearance of instructional products which are based on the same underlying strategy plan.

Think of the goal blocks at the Content level of a particular instructional strategy as if they were cards in an instructional deck. Remember that at this level you have designed the major didactic functions to be carried out and have impressed the content structures on them. In our example, this left us with instructional goals like, "Present step 1," and "Practice step 3."

Shuffle the cards in this deck of goals mentally and turn the top card. Whatever strategy goal appears, think of how you would design the instruction for that goal if it were the first goal that had to be satisfied in an instructional presentation. Then turn the next card in the deck and answer the same question, until all of the cards have been turned.

It takes a strong imagination to make something of some of the orderings that will occur this way, so let's imagine something simpler. Think of the same deck of strategy cards and consider whether the following different orderings of those cards make sense and could be used in a reasonable instructional strategy.

For instance, does the following order make sense for a three-step procedure?

> Step 1 presentation
>
> Step 2 presentation
>
> Step 3 presentation
>
> Step 1 demonstration
>
> Step 2 demonstration
>
> Step 3 demonstration
>
> Step 1 practice
>
> Step 2 practice
>
> Step 3 practice

This is a somewhat disjointed ordering, but it is reasonable and could instruct adequately. Now shuffle some of the cards into a new order:

> Step 1 presentation
>
> Step 1 demonstration
>
> Step 2 presentation

Step 2 demonstration

Step 3 presentation

Step 3 demonstration

Step 1 practice

Step 2 practice

Step 3 practice

Can you envision what this instruction would look like? Does this order of goals make sense? It simply folds the demonstration in temporally with the presentation. It makes better sense than the first shuffling, because it moves the demonstration closer to the presentation of step information. Now change the ordering once more to get:

Step 1 presentation

Step 1 demonstration

Step 1 practice

Step 2 presentation

Step 2 demonstration

Step 2 practice

Step 3 presentation

Step 3 demonstration

Step 3 practice

This ordering is even more attractive. You present a step, give a demonstration of it, and then ask for the student to perform the step. This could be the best sequence of the three.

All three shufflings of the intents (Content design level goal blocks) make sense, and there are many others which make sense as well. Some of these place the demonstration first, return for the presentation, and then execute the practice. Another reasonable shuffling of the goals places all of the practice first. This creates a pre-test. This same ordering of the intents can also be used in a kind of after the fact instructional strategy where feedback after each missed step can consist of a presentation of the step. Could a student learn the entire procedure from only the practice cards (with feedback) ordered in this manner? If many students are expected to have a high degree of familiarity with the procedure on entering instruction, it would be appropriate, or if the instruction was for review for already-trained students preparing for a recertification test.

In the days of programmed instruction, Thomas Gilbert recommended that the last step of a procedure could be the first thing presented, demonstrated, and practiced. Then, he recommended, the next to the last step of the procedure should receive the same treatment. The sequence in this recommended ordering of the strategy elements proceeded backwards, step by step, until the first step was presented, demonstrated, and practiced. By that point, the student was performing the entire procedure.

This technique, which he called *mathetics,* was suggested as a strategy for teaching a small child to tie a shoe. The parent ties the bow all except for pulling the "rabbit ears" tight into a knot; that's the last step. Then the parent ties the bow all except the last two steps, and so forth. It works, and it represents just one more reasonable way to shuffle the goal-cards of strategy.

This section has attempted to illustrate the notion of intent (goal) shuffling and to show how one set of structured strategy goal blocks could produce multiple, very different but useful instructional surfaces. As you analyze existing instruction, this idea will help you to recognize the designer's pattern for the ordering of instruction. As you will discover, orderings sometimes appear to be deliberate but often appear to be inadvertent, and that is the clue that tells you that some designers carefully plan their strategies while others devote less attention to them. In some instruction you will find key cards missing—a clue to the confusion or concern of students.

Adaptive instruction

The idea that an instructional strategy could be adjusted—adapted—moment by moment based on student performance during interactions was part of the original dream of the CBI pioneers. The idea that some level of control could be made available to student choice came later and is referred to as *learner control.*

The pioneers probably had little concept of the complexity and number of the decisions that would have to be made in order to provide robust and responsive instruction that is adaptive to the individual student. Today, we are still struggling to create adaptive instructional systems, and though there are some extremely interesting and positive examples beginning to appear in public education and training, it is still not common for the average designer to design or create adaptive systems.

In order to achieve adaptive instructional systems, we must think of our intentions (goals) in greater detail and with greater precision. We also must come to see instructional strategy as a multi-level rather than a single-level structure. And when this vision of strategy matures, the computer will be the only instructional medium besides the human teacher capable of implementing it.

Interaction, feedback, and strategy

Interaction: The choice and handling of interactions by the designer is probably the most important part of an instructional design. Recent learning theory suggests that people learn in two ways: they learn *about* and they learn *how to.* That is, they can learn knowledge in a propositional (or semantic) form and then they can convert that knowledge to a second action-ready form which makes performance possible.

It has become the common practice of our education and training systems to teach the propositional knowledge but to fail to support its conversion into performance capability. That is left for the student to accomplish. . . . somehow. The result is people who can *verbalize* about things but feel unprepared and somewhat anxious when asked to do things. The main contributor to this habit of mainly propositional or verbal learning is the selection of verbal practice behaviors by teachers and instructional designers, creating the multiple-choice-matching-essay-true-false monster.

In the chapters which follow this one, several varieties of instructional strategy are described in some detail, and each one has its own pattern of interaction with the student. In each case, you can assume that the behavior asked of the student should be as realistic—as real-world-like—as possibly attainable. Though sometimes the actual observable response in these strategies (for example for concept-using) may look like a true-false monster or a verbal-response monster, the performances called for by the strategy are real-world because of the mental processing they ask the student to perform, which is the form of behavior they would engage in under real-world conditions.

Concept-using strategy requires what looks like a true-false response from the student, but only because that is the form the behavior takes in the real world. Moreover, notice that the response of the student is given to carefully-structured, unencountered practice items that ensure that the performance is concept-using and not memory behavior. Notice also that the procedure-using strategy calls for students to perform the procedure, not to just verbalize about it.

In later chapters, this book gives emphasis to simulations as an instructional tool simply because a simulation is capable of engaging a student in actual performance, whereas other forms of instruction tend to lead to verbalized behavior. Verbal behavior should be called for if verbal behavior is what you want the students to learn, but if your goal is performance, you should ask students to perform and then provide a computer-based environment in which they *can* perform.

In the past, some designers have felt that interaction of any kind by itself was meritorious. Interaction has been promoted as a way to keep students "engaged" in learning and "attentive." This is a restricted and potentially self-defeating view of the value of interaction. There is little evidence to support the idea that interaction for interaction's sake is beneficial. On the other hand, there is an abundance of evidence—from both common practice and research—that particular types of interaction are beneficial for particular types of learning.

Not only is it important for a designer to select the right form of interaction for the instructional goal, but in many types of instruction—for instance, procedure learning—there must be sufficient variation in the interaction conditions and performance criteria to ensure that the student will become proficient across the desired range of performance ability. Providing adequate practice opportunity for students in many cases requires development of extra practice items, problems, or scenarios. However, the cost of this additional development must be balanced against the benefits from confident, prepared performance of students more fully experienced through adequate practice. Moreover, the additional cost in training development may be balanced against the savings from on-the-job training programs which may be canceled or reduced because students are better prepared upon entering the work world. You may also add to that balancing sum the reduction in on-the-job errors, which are a real but normally unaccounted training cost.

Feedback: The feedback which follows an interaction is almost equal in importance to the opportunity for interaction. Feedback is more than a means of reporting to the student the correctness or error of a response. It provides information used by a student to: (1) correct erroneous knowledge, and (2) learn to self-monitor and evaluate his or her own performance, thus gaining confidence. This second purpose of feedback is almost more important than the first as a means of establishing the student as an independent, self-judging performer.

But feedback is a badly neglected area of instructional design principles for instruction beyond the memory level. We have few guidelines from research, and what research has been done has been for very limited and somewhat unrealistic forms of memory instruction. There is little there to guide the active designer who wishes to design feedback systems for performance above the memory level. Most of the guidelines actually used by designers for providing feedback are derived from common practice and common sense.

A designer can learn some useful principles of feedback from the techniques of excellent sports coaching. Some interesting principles are also being learned by tutorial systems from artificial intelligence, but not enough research in this important area has accumulated to provide firm feedback guidelines to designers. Despite the lack of clear guidelines for feedback design, the importance of the subject requires that we notice the issue. We recommend that you, as a CBI designer, be inquisitive and watchful in the future, as usable guidelines emerge in this area of design practice. In place of firm guidance, we would like to share our own observations on feedback, gained from practical experience and common sense.

Feedback may respond to a single student action or to a lengthy sequence of student actions. The common practice of focusing on fragmented performances has led to feedback which responds to single student choices. In an integrated instructional world, feedback will probably respond to single student responses early during instruction, but as integration of fragments of performance into conglomerates takes place and monitoring of performance is expected to shift from the instructor to the student, feedback will respond to longer and more varied performances and will have to do so with greater insight. For instance, feedback should be able to comment differently on mistakes in problem solving due to inadequate knowledge of specific content and inadequate problem solving process. If feedback does not lengthen in span as the student progresses toward real-world performance levels, then the student's ability to self-evaluate and self-correct is crippled. Therefore, the student must be weaned, as it were, from immediate, prescriptive feedback as instruction proceeds.

Feedback messages can contain several different kinds of information and can be delivered in many different ways. They can be direct and blunt, announcing to the student the corrective information, or they may be delivered as hints from which the student is expected to figure out the correct answer with the least help possible. Replays of performance can be an effective feedback technique, and the performer replayed can be the student, a peer, or an expert. When replay is provided, it helps to have it accompanied by controls to allow the student to view it repeatedly and with pauses at key points. When a replay is used, it may be accompanied by commentary, or the student may be asked to provide the comments and judgments. One of the keys for this commentary is that it should make the expert performer's invisible thinking visible to the student so that the student can use it as a model for revising his or her own patterns of reasoning.

The subject of instructional feedback is gravely in need of attention by researchers and designers in the future, because we are about to witness increasingly sophisticated instructional designs, and we must be able to incorporate adequate feedback systems within them.

Conclusion

In summary, we recommend the following general strategy-building principles to designers of directed-instruction, objective-based tutorials:

1. **An instructional strategy should be designed only after examining its instructional goal.** Instruction is intended to help the student attain a specified performance goal. This goal is expressed in an instructional objective. Strategy design begins with that objective and proceeds in support of its attainment.

2. **An instructional strategy should be designed as a multi-level structure.** CBI causes us to turn away from the "hour of instruction" as a unit of measurement. This chapter has described techniques for focusing strategy decisions at several levels.

3. **An instructional strategy should make accessible to the student a core of information directly related to the type of learning and performance expected.** As we saw in the examples of Chapter 8, different strategies make use of different information categories.

4. **An instructional strategy should exclude information and interactions unrelated to the instructional goal.** One function of objectives is to allow the student to focus attention and assume a greater role in the learning process. The strategy should not detract from that focus by including the irrelevant.

5. **The behavior required during practice should match the behavior expressed in the instructional goal.** From reading the instructional goal, a student should be able to tell what the practice will look like. Many developers misunderstand this function of objectives and feel that once objectives are written and approved, the instruction and practice may take any form, regardless of its relation to the objective. This can be very confusing if the student has focused on the objective and prepared to perform one action, only to find that something else is asked

for. Ignoring this principle leads to a game of intention-hide-and-seek between the teacher and the student, especially at test times.

6. The behavior practiced should be the same behavior that is later tested. Some teachers feel guilt if they allow students to practice and test the same type of behavior; they feel they have been guilty of "teaching to the test," so they go out of their way to reserve some unexpected and unpracticed performance requirement for tests. Some even boast about it. However, if we specify objectives that contain real-world-like performances, and if the student can attain those performance levels, then we can conclude that we have prepared the students for the real world and not just for a test.

7. The behavior expressed in an objective should be as real-world as possible and should get away from the memory level whenever possible. A great deal of our instruction teaches people *about* things rather than *how to do* things. This is not because we expect students to do nothing in the real world. It is more due to the limitations of traditional instructional media and their inability to interact with students in life-like or world-like ways.

With the recent increase in our ability to create complete practice "worlds," developers can reduce the distance between training and the real world to the point where it is difficult to tell where one ends and the other begins.

In many cases, memory-level performance must be taught. However, failing to move beyond memory-level instruction places an unfair burden on the student.

8. Instruction should order objectives in such a way that each new objective adds a new skill or knowledge to that which has already been learned in a rational, building sequence. As developers, we must ensure that prerequisites are learned by students before the more complex forms of behavior based on prerequisites are required. The developer must also regulate the size of the steps the student is required to take from performance to performance as he or she advances through instruction. Courses can expect too much or too little advancement between performance levels as instruction progresses. Ideally, the designer should provide for those levels to be suited to the individual student. Realistically, the design should provide for steps attainable comfortably by the largest possible number of students. More of this issue will be discussed in Chapter 15, on simulations. Designers should aim for a reasonable *staircase* progression of student skills from basic to complex and integrated behavior.

Self-directed activities

- Analyze a recorded passage of classroom instruction from any class. For each utterance or action, try to determine the performance or strategic goal that motivated it. Express the instructional interchange in terms of the moment-by-moment change in instructional goals. Chart not only the instructor's goals in this way, but the student's.

- Select two examples of procedural instruction, instruction to teach a concept, instruction on a process, or instruction on a principle (see Chapters 10–14). Compare the selected examples in terms of their use of the structured approach as it is described in this chapter.

- Analyze an instructional product in terms of the decisions which had to be made at the five levels of strategy design described in this chapter: didactic level, content level, message element level, representation level, and implementation logic level.

- Collect as many writings as you can in which an instructional design expert describes the preferred principles of instructional strategy. Compare these principles and begin to build your own notebook of design guidelines and rules.

Further reading

Butler, D. L., and Winne, P. H. (1995). Feedback and self-regulated learning. *Review of Educational Research, 65*(3), 245–282.

Gayeski, D. M. (1995). *Designing communication and learning environments.* Englewood Cliffs, NJ: Educational Technology Publications.

Jonassen, D. (Ed.). (1988). *Instructional designs for microcomputer courseware.* Hillsdale, NJ: Lawrence Erlbaum Associates.

Leshin, C., Pollock, J., and Reigeluth, C. (1992). *Instructional design strategies and tactics.* Englewood Cliffs, NJ: Educational Technology Publications.

Merrill, M. D. (1994). *Instructional design theory.* Englewood Cliffs, NJ: Educational Technology Publications.

Mory, E. H. (1996). Feedback research. In D. H. Jonassen (Ed.), *Handbook of research for educational communications and technology.* New York: Macmillan.

10

MEMORY INSTRUCTIONAL STRATEGY

Chapter Objectives:

1. *Name four varieties of memory behavior.*
2. *Name two types of memory performance.*
3. *Describe the function of mnemonics in (a) simple associative memory, and (b) network memory.*
4. *Given a memory objective, design an appropriate practice strategy for it.*
5. *Explain the value of models of information in the design of memory instruction.*
6. *Describe the special challenges associated with network memory recall.*
7. *Name the types of mnemonic especially suited for network memory instruction.*

Varieties of memory behavior

A memory instructional objective supports the student's effort to store a fact or group of facts for later recognition or recall. A memory instructional strategy is the developer's technique for helping that process occur efficiently, effectively, and pleasantly.

Studying the human memory has occupied an army of research psychologists for decades. Among other things, we have learned that the memory is very complex but subject to influence by proper training. Likening human memory to computer memory appears to be a great misconception. If humans remembered things in the same way computers do, none of us would ever forget a fact nor hesitate to recall it exactly and rapidly.

Memory behavior comes in several varieties:

- Fact recognition—The ability to recognize that something has been seen, heard, or felt before.

- Associated fact recall—The ability to recall one half of an associated fact pair, given the other one.

- Ordered fact recall—The ability to recall an ordered sequence of facts in their proper order.

- Networked fact recall—The ability to recall multiple associations for one object and to follow linked paths of recall.

There is no distinction between memory objectives based on the size, composition, or sensory modality of the fact being recalled. Therefore, associated fact recall can cover recall of the names of art works, historical dates, technical terms, definitions, memorized verbal statements like poems, tunes, perfume scents, or any other associated sensation. The thing to be remembered need not be verbal or even verbalizable. Much if not most of what we remember is non-verbal.

The instructional techniques for one variety of memory instruction will be very similar to those used for other varieties. Therefore, when we speak of memory instructional strategy in this chapter, we will be speaking of a general strategy applicable to all varieties with minor modifications.

Memory behavior is at the foundation of all higher-order behaviors. It is required as a component in each of them. For instance, it is hard to predict the effects of changes in the Hotwell temperature when you can't remember what a Hotwell is, what it does, and how it relates to other components.

It is perhaps best to look at the teaching of factual material as a necessary but potentially dangerous activity—necessary because it is indispensable, but dangerous because it can seduce developers into creating courses which do not go above the memory level. A very popular approach to memory instruction today stresses the importance of learning facts and propositions *in the context of performance*, eliminating the need for direct memory instruction and helping the student to understand how memorized knowledge will be used in the real world.

Strategy for memory instruction

A generic strategy for memory instruction normally includes: (1) presentation of the content to be memorized, either in raw form or in some embedded context, (2) sometimes, provision of additional memory aiding content, and (3) practice at performing recall. These three stages are described in this chapter.

Memory instruction can be approached in two main ways. The first can be termed *rote* memorization. This method involves presentation of the facts, followed by recitation practice until the repetition of the facts from memory becomes second nature. We all have several lists of such facts which we have learned rotely, including:

- "Sunday, Monday, Tuesday..."
- "Stop, drop, and roll..."
- "January, February, March..."
- "One, two, three..."
- "A noun names a person, place, or thing."
- "Washington, Jefferson, Adams..."
- "Stomach, liver, humerus, aorta..."
- "Two times two is four..."

Lists like these are the basis for most of the defining verbal knowledge we possess. Other facts committed to rote memory include faces, tunes, and types of pain (sharp versus dull versus ache, etc.). These imply that memory is more than just a verbal phenomenon.

A second approach to memory can be emphasis on aided or *reconstructive* recall. It usually involves the teaching of the facts to be remembered plus certain additional facts calculated to improve recall. These additional facts are termed *mnemonics* (mne-MON-ics). Mnemonics can be either very obvious or very subtle. Either way, it is likely that most of us use some form of mnemonic or reconstructive device for the majority of our recall processes.

Mnemonics in memory instruction

Mnemonics are simply easy-to-remember facts which help you pick out from among the literally millions of things stored in your memory exactly the right one on demand. Mnemonics remind you where information is stored when you need to recall it. Mnemonics provide either a seed which allows you to reconstruct information when it is needed or a partial hint which helps you to recall the complete information.

Mnemonics come in a variety of types. Some of them are quite familiar to you. Others, perhaps the more powerful and subtle ones, are not. Within this chapter we will discuss both types. Among the more common types of mnemonic are the following:

Initial letter mnemonic: This mnemonic takes the first letter of each item in a list of things to be remembered and forms them into a word or sentence.

EXAMPLE: *The name ROY G. BIV is familiar to students, who sometimes use it to re-call the order of colors in the visible light spectrum—Red, Orange, Yellow, Green, Blue, Indigo, Violet. Remembering the name stimulates recall of both the colors and their proper order.*

Event sequence mnemonic: This mnemonic takes advantage of some already-learned se-quence that the student knows. It attaches one item of new learning to each item in the already-known sequence.

EXAMPLE: *The arrangement of furniture around their living room wall is a sequence most students know by heart. By taking a sequential tour of each piece of fur-niture and imagining one memory item associated with each piece, a student can remember long lists.*

In a more practical application of this principle, once students had learned the physical lay-out of a control panel, the procedure for checking values on the panel during a start-up pro-cedure might be linked to some imaginary pattern superimposed on the face of the panel, as if it were a line which had been drawn there. Some pilots use this principle to remember the or-der of checklist items.

This type of mnemonic takes advantage of the fact that memory for episodes, sequences of action, is one of our strongest forms of memory. We can recall stories and sequences of events very well. Perhaps the last time you lost your car keys you re-lived your actions leading up to the point where you discovered you had lost them. By rehearsing the episode, you were recalling a long list of places where you might have lost the keys.

Shape mnemonic: This mnemonic uses the shapes of objects to make them memorable.

EXAMPLE: *Instruction in letter recognition for early reading students may turn an um-brella upside-down to associate the shape of the letter "U" with an already familiar shape.*

EXAMPLE: *Morse code can be taught with a series of shapes assisting the recall process. For instance, the dot-dash-dot sequence which represents the letter "R" can be fit into the shape of a rabbit's face— each dot representing an eye, and the dash representing the nose.*

Distortion or emphasis mnemonic: This mnemonic isolates one feature of an item to be re-membered and distorts it in a way that makes it memorable.

EXAMPLE: *The memory lesson presented in Chapter 8 formed the squeezing from a toothpaste tube into a "6" to link sundry items with Class Six.*

High frequency association mnemonic: Some specialty areas have facts which are commonly and well-known within the specialty. New facts can be attached to those already-learned facts.

> EXAMPLE: *In the memory lesson in Chapter 8, the student population was expected to be familiar with the fact that shoes come in pairs. It was natural to use shoes shown in a pair to symbolize Class Two.*

Generative mechanism mnemonic: This mnemonic supplies the student with a rule which can be used to reconstruct the items of information to be recalled. Frequently we use this type to recall a phone number or an address.

> EXAMPLE: *A beginning computer student can be taught to remember rotely the binary number sequence, "1, 2, 4, 8, 16,...." As an alternative, the same student could be taught to generate the sequence when it is needed, by starting with "1" and multiplying repeatedly by "2."*

Each type of mnemonic above provides the student with a handle for drawing facts, once learned, out of memory. It attaches something that is to be learned to something that has already been learned or to something that can be reconstructed.

This list of mnemonic types is not complete. We have not touched on graphic methods which can be used to promote recall. The sample memory strategy in Chapter 8 used graphic mnemonics to promote recall. The list of mnemonics presented here and the few more which are presented later in the chapter are intended to stimulate your thinking. How can you use mnemonics? What if you encountered a situation where none of the types you knew of worked? Could you invent a new type that worked? The real list of mnemonic types is only as limited a your imagination. It is a challenge to designers to recognize new opportunities for mnemonics and create them where they can be used profitably.

In doing this, it would be well for designers to keep some basic principles in mind to regulate their use of mnemonics:

1. Keep mnemonics **simple** so that the learning of the mnemonic does not become harder than the learning of the target information.

2. Do not use a mnemonic if it will **slow down or interfere** with the normal speed of performance. One colleague describes a mnemonic used to teach note reading to music students which prevented them from playing faster than a certain speed—the top speed at which students could apply the mnemonic.

3. Don't use so **many** mnemonics that the student begins to forget them. Initial letter mnemonics are good tools, but they become their own kind of memory problem when students have been given so many of them that they can't remember what each one stands for.

4. Use mnemonics which are as **meaningful** as possible so that they will spring readily to mind. Avoid stretching to make a mnemonic fit content, and avoid the lo-o-o-ng reach linking of two or three inference steps just to make a mnemonic work. (That should remind you of this.... Which should remind you of that.... Which....)

Introduction of mnemonics can be an important stage of memory instruction. However, mnemonics do not replace practice.

Memory drill and practice

If you have ever used flash cards to drill yourself, then you are already acquainted with the basics of memory drill-and-practice. Drill and practice is an essential part of memory instruction whenever a particular criterion of performance is required of the student. Practice may not always take the exact form of your early experience with flash cards, but the principles involved in computer-based drill and practice are essentially the same. Figure 1 illustrates the general sequence of events in a memory drill. Imagine two friends quizzing each other on the names of state capitols as you read the diagram.

Depending on the type of information being learned, drill and practice can vary in any of several important ways. Consider the following:

Length of the drilled list: How many memorized items should be drilled at once? Obviously there is an upper limit where the list is so long that items are seldom repeated and a lower limit where the list is so short that there is not adequate time between repeats. The size of the list of facts to be drilled depends on the type of facts involved, whether a mnemonic has been provided or not, and the experience level and motivation of the student.

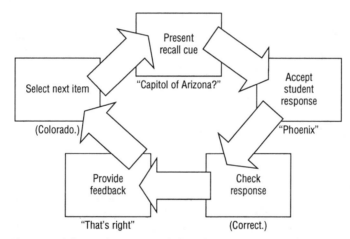

Figure 1. The general form of a memory drill-and-practice is a repetitive cycle of asking, responding, checking, feeding back, and selecting the next item to be asked.

Method of presentation: What stimulus shall be presented to the student? Is it verbal? Is it visual? Is it aural? The answer depends on the intended use of the knowledge and how the real world will ask the student to recall it. Whatever the real world will ask of the student, that is what you should ask also.

Method of selection: Shall items be presented for recall in a set sequence, or shall they be drawn randomly from a pool of items? Once an item is drawn and missed, shall it be replaced in the pool to be drawn at random again? Shall it be replaced if it is answered correctly? These answers depend on the nature of the list and upon the criterion which has been set.

If the objective requires sequenced recall, then sequence must be part of the drill. Otherwise, the items may be sampled randomly. Normally, missed items are returned to the pool, and in drills where the criterion is more than one correct answer or more than one in a row, each item must be returned to the pool until its criterion has been reached. You may choose to leave items, once mastered, in the pool just for review purposes, and new pools of items may contain something like 10% repeat items from previously mastered pools for the same reason.

Scoring and reporting: Should the student see the score as the drill progresses? This is a judgment call. Some groups of students will demand to know the score. Students whom you are trying to get to take responsibility for their own learning will almost certainly want to see the score as they go. For others, the score may be a great motivator. Scoring turns out to be de-motivating only if the original instruction was poor or if the rules or dimensions of the drill have been made impossibly hard.

Some characteristics of drill and practice do not remain unchanged over the entirety of the experience. The criterion may be made to change, the amount and type of prompting may change, and the amount and type of feedback may change.

Criterion: How perfect is recall expected to be? and how long-lasting? You may set a criterion of 100% or less, depending on the importance of the information being learned. You may also require that there be perfect recall three times in a row, or two, or only once. You may require that level of recall on three successive days, or on just one.

The setting of the ultimate criterion—the criterion for certification—depends on the criticality of the student's ready knowledge of the information. Multiplication tables, for instance, must be learned perfectly on all days, all of the time. State capitols may not require the same criterion. A high school student does not require prefect recall of the parts of the brain, but a brain surgeon does.

The level of the criterion may change over time, in a pattern that encourages student progress. In early practice sessions on the state capitols, some students may be defeated if they encounter too many errors. As practice progresses over time and in multiple occurrences, the criterion should advance.

Prompting: What about giving hints? Just as the criterion factor can be scaled from being at generous levels in the early stages of practice to being less generous and more demanding in later stages, you should also fade the amount of prompting available to the student as performance increases. Prompting which continues too long can discourage self-reliance and weaken the student.

Timing of responses: Shall there be a time limit on the student's answer? Once again the decision depends on what the real world will expect of the student. If there will be a timing requirement in the real world, then in the final stages of practice, there should be a timing requirement. In the early stages there may be no timing imposed until the student demonstrates a certain level of recall ability. Then there may be a generous time limit introduced which gradually is reduced until the real world criterion is reached.

This principle of sliding criterion, timing, and prompting actually applies to the practice of all forms of behavior where the real world conditions and criteria are too difficult for students to reach in one jump. The challenge facing the designer is to decide how to implement these sliding scales.

Feedback type: What do you tell the student who is right? Who is wrong? Students who are right may simply need to know that they are right. Wrong answers on the other hand, should be an occasion for the student to be reminded of at least the correct answer. If you have supplied any mnemonic, a wrong answer may be a good occasion to restate it. The content of feedback may change over time also, from rich and full to less complete as student proficiency and response speed increase.

The drill and practice principles above apply to drills for any type of memory content, even though the implied emphasis was on memory for discrete facts. Some of the memory content we learn is in the form of easily-identifiable facts, lists of facts, or sequences of facts. Most of it, however, is not. The great bulk of our memory learning assumes the form of a vast network of connected facts. Since it is such an important part of memory instruction, let's discuss the implications of networked memory learning separately.

Networked memory content

We swim constantly in a sea of facts. As we see things, hear things, decide things, and do things, our mind is bombarded with a steady stream of experiences which we are capable of turning into factual knowledge. From that stream, we select those items perceived to be of value and makes an effort to store them for later use.

As life progresses and experience accumulates, we form a set of mental structures which we use to process this constant inflow. These structures help us identify memorable elements of knowledge, sort them, and retain ones we perceive have value by attaching them to existing knowledge structures.

The nature of these structures (often called *schemata* or *mental models*) is a topic of great interest to learning psychologists. We know much less about them than we need to, but we do know that they make the storage, handling, and later recall of the facts possible.

Even though we don't know the exact form of facts when they are stored in memory, we do know that they tend to consist of related complexes in complex patterns, one factual item being linked to many others. It is appropriate to refer to what gets stored as a *network* of facts.

During an average day, we receive, store, and retrieve facts from our own personal networks pertaining to cats, dogs, traffic laws, TV schedules, family genealogy, automobile engines, clothing styles, historical events, child behavior, economic trends, and the origins of the universe.

The networked information we hold in memory is complexly organized, because every fact in it is theoretically relatable to every other one. One object in memory can have a lot of different things "known" about it. That is, one object can be associated with a lot of other objects and qualities.

Most of us have an object in memory called *baseball*. In addition, we can relate many fats about the baseball's qualities (hard, round). We can talk about functional relations between baseballs and other objects (bats hit baseballs, baseballs break windows, etc.). Baseballs are only one object out of hundreds of thousands, perhaps millions, that each of us holds within our memory network.

As designers of memory instruction, we deliberately plan ways to help students enter new things into their memory network so that these things will enter easily, stay long, and be easy to recall when needed. There are a few things we can say about networked memory content which make it easier for us to deal with it as designers:

Proposition #1. One object in a memory network may have many, many associations: Associations are what make up the network. Think of your current automobile and of all of the associations you have for it:

> Car...
>
> > ...is red
> >
> > ...is fast
> >
> > ...has wheels
> >
> > ...has a dent in the fender
> >
> > ...runs well
> >
> > ...cost a bundle
> >
> > ...is still under warranty
> >
> > ...starts easily

This list does not begin to scratch the surface of what you know about your car, or for that matter, any one of its parts. For instance:

Radio knob...

> ...is soft and rubbery

> ...turns easily

> ...changes stations too fast

> ...pulls off easily

> ...doesn't get cold in the winter

Most of us know of literally hundreds of car (or computer) parts. We also have a network of associations that ties each one into our knowledge.

Proposition #2. Relations are grouped within a network: A network has many dimensions and is not just a flat structure. We won't even try to illustrate a network; we will leave that to your imagination. When you pull one fact out of memory, you are likely to pull other, associated facts out with it. When Jane thinks of Tom, she is likely to think about Tom's appearance and way of acting. She is less likely to think about quarks, unless she and Tom are both nuclear physicists. This example is trivial, but another one will show that there is some practical importance to the fact that associations are grouped.

If the object of interest is car, we can see that there are levels on which we organize our information about it. This means that when we are dealing with an object at one level, we are more likely to bring up the associations we have for it at that level and less likely to bring up associations at a different level. As we think about the car as a totality, we are more likely to recall its shape and condition and less likely to bring up associations concerning the shape and threading of its lug nuts (which hold the wheels on and are located underneath the hubcaps).

The organization of our memory, which is mostly learned and does not occur spontaneously, allows us to deal with the complexity of our world in an orderly fashion. It allows us to form notions of whole and part, which are themselves associations.

This organization allows us to hold in our network at the same time the notions of body, skeleton, skull, and occipital condyle, as well as universe, galaxy, solar system, planet, continent, country, state, city, street, house, living room, sofa, cushion, and grape juice stain.

Instructionally, it is important for us to know this because as we instruct in memory networks, we are responsible for helping students create these levels and very often cross the levels multiple times in order to explain one idea. To assist this learning process, we must be aware of it. An example from an article in the June, 1985 *Science Digest* will illustrate this:

> *No matter what size, a floppy disk is a circular wafer of Mylar, an especially durable and stretch-resistant variety of polyester.... The wafer is coated with an adhesive (for which each disk company has its own recipe) filled with particles of ferrous oxide, a chemical compound of iron and oxygen. As the adhesive dries on the disk, an electromagnet turns the particles into tiny bar magnets about a millionth of an inch long and a tenth as wide. They line up perpendicular to the disk's radius and retain their direction after drying.* (Page 12)

Even this straightforward description of a physical object contains three different levels of organization—the level of the Mylar disk, the level of the compound on the disk, and the level of the constituents of the compound. Most process descriptions of this type are multi-level, and it is very difficult to find one which is not. This means that we understand—and remember—things in terms of a multi-level networking of the information.

Proposition #3. Memory networks are so subtle and complex in reality that we cannot predict with precision in advance exactly what a student will learn from a given piece of instruction: As we learn networked memory content, we are seldom learning just what the developer or writer intended us to learn. Readers form questions, and curious, probing minds are constantly picking up incidental facts, integrating them with other facts, inferring, deducing, and creating their own new knowledge. This is a side-effect that we want to promote—the use of networked information and principles by the learner to extend what is known. It is one of the skills of a self-guided learner. Amid all this self-directed learning activity, however, the developer must still ensure that the organization and presentation of the target message is sufficient to promote also the learning which is intended.

Proposition #4. Developers can identify those associations within the memory network that are intended to be learned so that a strategy can be designed to teach it thoroughly, practice it thoroughly, and test it thoroughly: Even though we can't predict in advance what side effects our instruction will have, we can arrange things so that the main learning intended will have a high likelihood of taking place. The first step is to identify the objects to be instructed and the important associations relating them. Once identified, these things can be managed systematically by the strategy, and the instruction can present them with the proper focus and emphasis. By failing to identify associations to be taught deliberately, the instructor is leaving that decision to chance. The best method we know for capturing a network is in what we call a model of information.

Models of information

When a network of facts is the body of content to be learned, it is sometimes described as a *model* or a *system* of information. A model in this case consists of a set of facts and relations between them which are to be learned.

For the developer's purposes, it is useful to represent a model of information in some form so that it can be dealt with systematically in the instruction. In doing this, the developer is identifying what belongs to the model and what does not. One way of representing a model is to create a table of information and some form of graphic representation. Figure 2 is the diagram portion of the model of information *living cell*, and Table 1 contains tabulated information for this model.

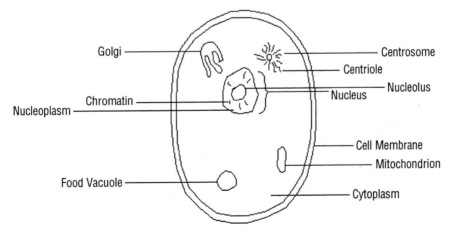

Figure 2. Diagram portion of a model of information. The diagram represents descriptions and relationships which might be difficult to express verbally.

Table 1. Information table for the "Cell" model of information.

Component	Information	Occurrence
Cell membrane	Creates boundary for the cell. Holds cell contents in. Keeps foreign matter out. Filters passage of all materials in and out of cell.	Completely surrounds cell on outside.
Cytoplasm	Holds all cell contents—liquid and solid. Enables cell chemicals (nutrients and wastes) to move within the cell. Stores some chemicals for time of need.	Fills the cell from the outer membrane to the nucleus.
Nucleus	Contains genetic code-bearing chemical, DNA.	A space within the cell enclosed within a membrane.
Nucleolus	Place for the building of parts which will later be assembled into ribosomes.	Located within the nucleus. Shows up as densely-packed chemical matter.
Nucleoplasm	Performs same function for nucleus that cytoplasm does for the whole cell.	Fills the space within the nuclear membrane, except that taken up by nucleoli.
Chromatin	Holds the DNA structure used in cell replication.	Shares space within the nuclear membrane with the nucleoli.
Food vacuole	Stores nutrients and other chemicals which can be used by the cell. Can be used to increase the size of the cell.	Fills most of the space inside the cell between the cell membrane and the nuclear membrane. Does not include the nucleus.
Mitochondrion	These break down carbohydrates in order to release the energy stored inside. Help form ATP, which hold energy in a form usable by the cell.	Oval-shaped body within the cytoplasm.
Golgi body	Participate in the creation and modification of chemicals used within.	Stacks of flat bodies shaped like pita bread, found within the cytoplasm.
Centrosome	Functions during cell division to help separate chromosomes into the dividing halves of the cell.	Dot-like body within the cytoplasm.
Centriole	Gives rise to cilia and flagella.	Hair-like lines arranged in a star star pattern.

What does this represent? It certainly does not represent everything known about the subject, nor everything the student will know by the time instruction is finished, *but it does represent the core of facts that the developer has targeted for learning* and which the developer will plan for instructing and testing. Each column has information of different logical types within it. For instance, the "Occurrence" column contains information of at least two logical types: (1) location of the component, and (2) appearance of the component. One of the steps in constructing a table of information like this one is to identify the categories of information that it will contain relative to the subject being instructed.

By specifying the content in this way, the developer sets the expectations for the instruction and defines an area of responsibility or scope and depth of coverage. The model defines the minimum quantity of information that is expected to be learned and therefore brings focus to the designer's work. However, guard against the assumption that the designer or a subject-matter expert must be the one to fill in the table during instruction. In making this table and diagram, the designer is not committing to instructional strategy, and it would be premature to assume that this information represented the message content of instruction. The real use of this table during instruction may be for the student to fill it in from his or her own observations. The table only represents a scoping of the information and a key to it.

A model may be constructed for abstract and conceptual systems as well as for physical ones. Figure 3 and Table 2 represent a model of information for the abstract model Republican Democracy. Chapter 18 on Message Management describes in some detail the use of tables for capturing instructional content—not only for memory instruction but as a useful technique for preparing for other types of instruction as well.

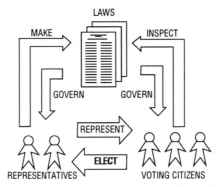

Figure 3. The diagram for the system of information "Republican Democracy" describes process relationships.

Table 2. Information table for "Republican Democracy."

Component	Information	Function
Voting citizens	Citizens registered to vote within a voting precinct. To register, certain requirements for age and citizenship must be met.	(1) Study proposed laws and judge their soundness and fairness before they are passed, (2) Observe laws once passed, (3) Identify laws in need of revision or repeal.
Representatives	Citizens elected by other citizens to represent the citizen group during the making of laws.	(1) Poll the wishes and opinions of voting citizens, (2) Study additional information available from other sources, (3) Propose new laws or modification of existing laws, (4) Vote on proposed laws, (5) Report back to voting citizens on results.
Laws	Regulations made by elected representatives to govern the country.	(1) Provide protection to citizens from dangers within and without, (2) Regulate government operations, (3) Regulate the process of making laws.

Criterion in memory network instruction

When the focus of instruction is a larger body of facts, rather than an isolated list or collection of them, the problem of criterion becomes more important. That is because with the list there is no question exactly what is to be recalled or to what level of performance. But when a network of information is the subject of instruction, it becomes impractical to practice and test the entire fabric of the network exhaustively, and the developer must make some simplifying decisions.

There are generally two criterion levels which may be applied during memory network instruction. The first and least demanding level is commonly called the *familiarization* level. The familiarization criterion does not require complete knowledge of a memory network and concerns itself only with the most important core parts (as determined by the designer). In familiarization instruction, no exhaustive tests are given. Instead, testing and practice both take place at relatively superficial levels, and that only for the most important facts. The second criterion level for memory network instruction is the mastery criterion. At this level, students are expected to give flawless or nearly flawless performance in recalling the associations and node names of the networked information. The memory level selected by the developer depends on the real-world demands which will be placed on the students.

Instructional strategy for networked memory

There are a few differences in the way the basic memory instructional strategy is applied to networked memory because of the somewhat different nature of the content to be learned.

Network mnemonics

The mnemonic types which have been introduced to this point are what you might call obvious. They have all the subtlety of a mackerel in the face. There are other types of mnemonic which are not so visible and which tend to blend in with the facts they are intended to assist students in remembering. These mnemonics are often subtle enough that we do not look upon them as a separate instructional tactic.

These help us remember structured networks of information—systems or models of information which may have complex inner organization. It is the bodies of information as well as their inner structures which the mnemonic must help us recall. The mnemonic therefore serves a unifying function, drawing the separate elements of knowledge together into one organization. Here are a few examples of this type of mnemonic:

Metaphor or analogy mnemonic: This type of mnemonic compares the model that is being learned to an object or model that has already been learned and is familiar to the student. Because the student knows all of the objects in the known model and their relation to each other, there is a ready set of associations which can be borrowed and used to decode and remember the objects and relations in the new model. The student can use the metaphor model to anticipate nodes and relationships in the to-be-learned model and can become an active participant in inquiring after information.

> EXAMPLE: *In the course of instruction on biological subjects, we often use metaphors to explain and to promote memory at the same time. We say, "The heart is a pump," "the skull is a helmet," "the immune system is a defense against intruders from outside the body," and "the skeleton is the structure which supports the body like the inner steel structure of a skyscraper."*

The more that student knows about the metaphorical system—a pump, for instance—the more help it supplies to the student—who begins to look for fluid-holding chambers, valves, compression and expansion cycles, use of vacuums and pressures, and a host of other things associated with pumps.

The downside of this type of mnemonic, and one which must be actively protected against, is incorrect and unwarranted extrapolation by the learner within the domain of the newly-learned model. If the student knows a great deal of detail about the model being used as a mnemonic device, the he or she may incorrectly extend properties or structures from the original model to the newly-learned one, concluding through inference something about the new model which is erroneous. The designer must be aware when this is a danger and establish safeguards against it.

Generative principle mnemonic: This mnemonic asks the student to remember one fact which is stated in the form of a rule. By executing the rule, the student can reproduce the information in the memory network, even if it has been forgotten. The benefit to this type of mnemonic is that if the student can remember one fact, then he or she is carrying the key to numerous other facts as well.

> EXAMPLE: *In order to remember the rule for Ohm's law, a circle is sometimes used like the one shown below. This circle represents the three forces used in basic electrical circuit calculations—voltage, current, and resistance.*

The circle itself is a mnemonic that allows a student to remember the formula for computing any one of the three from the other two: Simply cover up the element you want to compute, and the other two are left in the appropriate computational relationship. If one remains above the other, then division is used. Two side by side means multiplication. Therefore, to compute voltage (E), you divide current (I) by resistance (R).

This mnemonic is a fact which has been designed specifically to summarize a great deal of information. Not only does it hold the key to formulas for computations, but it can also be used by students to remember the dynamic relationship between voltage, current, and resistance: "As resistance increases, voltage decreases, current being constant," and so forth.

This type of mnemonic is a very powerful one. However, using this specific example permits one of the difficulties of this type of mnemonic to be illustrated. It is, in a sense, the same type of error which can be induced by the previous type of mnemonic—incorrect generalization. This circle is capable of conveying incorrect understanding of the relationship between the three forces. As the forces are shown on the circle, they are not subordinate to each other: it appears that each one may freely influence the others simply by changing value. Barbara White, however, has shown that this is not an appropriate sequence of cause-effect reasoning for real electrical circuits and that many people currently reason incorrectly about electrical circuit relationships because of this mnemonic. You must pick mnemonics carefully.

Episodic mnemonic: One mnemonic which has already been discussed, the Event Sequence mnemonic, capitalizes on the heavily ingrained patterns of memory—episodes—which our mind is very good at remembering. We use sequence patterns to remember things, even abstract things. We are thoroughly familiar with certain action sequence patterns—everything from the operation of physical laws ("...the apple drops when released...") to the operation of social interaction patterns ("...she said something confusing, so he is hesitant...") and even to the tracing of intentions ("...he did it to amuse her..."). The episodic mnemonic takes advantage of our ability to remember stories (event sequences) and uses the everyday experience patterns to help us remember what comes next in a sequence to be learned. Often in the process, we give personality and intention to inanimate objects so that their pattern of behavior can be understood and recalled.

> EXAMPLE: *"...then the messenger RNA decides that it needs to share this information with the...."*

> EXAMPLE: *"The Iron atom is wandering around at this point, missing a few electrons, so when it bumps into the Oxygen atom which has a few extra...."*

A sufficiently dramatic instructor can turn the DNA replication process into a very understandable and memorable process with a little of this sort of humanizing. Many master science teachers communicate otherwise difficult process sequences understandably in this way. The noted scientist Richard Feynman used this technique very effectively to explain complicated scientific phenomena.

By creating episodic scenarios as mnemonics, we link into the student's vast store of event-oriented memory and use parts of it to supply structures and recall cues for new information.

All of the above mnemonic types can be combined with all of the other types described up to this point. As you introspect on your own methods for recalling factual material, you will see that you use many of these techniques in personal recall processes, as well as others which we may have missed.

Network drill-and-practice

Drill and practice for memory instruction does not need to look like drill and practice. This is especially true for networked memory instruction. The function of drill and practice is to give the student experience in recalling information which has been learned. There is something which causes us to begin forgetting immediately after we have learned something. Recall of the learned information, however, temporarily reverses the forgetting.

In networked memory recall, there are usually a high number of relations which the student has learned. An exhaustive drill and practice of each fact individually would not only be impractical for the designer, it would not be tolerated by the student. Then how do you perform drill and practice for networked memory instruction? Here are a few suggestions:

Drill in proportion to the importance of the facts: Not all of the facts in a network are of equal importance or value to the student. As a developer, you must make some decisions about how completely you want each fact committed to memory. You may want to define classes of facts within the network and specify a different level of mastery for each one. You may require one class of facts to be recalled without hesitation and without error, while a second class of facts may be recalled at a much lower criterion. A third group of facts may be treated as an optional or extra credit group, with credit for remembering but no penalty for forgetting.

Drill on the use of the mnemonic: In network memory mnemonics, there is great generative power. You may want to concentrate on whether the student recalls the mnemonic and how to use it. You may assume that if the student can use it to generate a sampling of facts, he or she will be able to use it to generate all of the key facts. To emphasize the mnemonic, you may structure questions in such a way that you are sure the student has had to use it to answer the question. You can also provide wrong answer feedback which is phrased and illustrated in terms of the mnemonic.

You may ask questions which require use of the information in a deductive or inductive way, but be careful not to include the answers in the score for the memory objective being taught. Keep a separate score for these kinds of answer, and realize that there is a formal strategy for instruction of principles which is much more robust than just making inferences during a memory drill.

Instead of making drill questions look like drill questions, try placing them in the context of a real-world, everyday problem situation to which the student must respond.

These ideas, when integrated with the drill and practice ideas already presented, will give you a wide variety of options in dealing with both networked and discrete fact recall instruction.

The wording of memory objectives

A sampling of memory objectives of the various types is given below. Note that the verbs used in the objectives are not a reliable classifier of objectives. Under the categories below, objectives of the same type often use different verbs to describe the action to be taken by the student.

Fact recognition objectives

- Recognize a picture of any of the American presidents when it is presented.

- Recognize the names of three composers from the Baroque period.

- Recognize the smell of a ketone when it is presented.

Isolated fact recall objectives

- Name the New England states.

- Write the names of the phases of the ISD process in any order.

Ordered fact recall objectives

- Name the stages of cell division during mitosis in correct order.

- State the steps in radar set calibration in correct order.

Associated fact recall objectives

- Given a state name, touch the state on a map of the USA.

- Given a picture of a carburetor part, name the part.

- State the defining characteristics of a cold front.

Networked fact recall objectives

- Tell what will happen after the honey bee returns to the hive.

- Explain the how a bill may become law even after it has been vetoed.

- Explain why the piston moves downward after the ignition step is completed.

- Name the three means which the government can use to regulate the rate of inflation.

Self-directed activities

- Measure as many of your mind's memory characteristics and abilities as you can by doing the following:

  Have someone slowly read to you a list of numbers. Repeat back the list after a certain number of numbers have been read to you. Vary the length of the list on different trials. Record how many numbers you can recall. Note whether your performance on list recall improves over time (that is, whether there is any learning how to learn going on). Record which numbers in a list tend to be recalled most often: the first numbers in a list, the last ones, or the middle ones. Note the effect of patterns of numbers on your ability to recall them.

  Perform the same kind of memory tests using words instead of numbers. Try several varieties of lists:

  - Lists of totally unrelated words
  - Lists of words having a common theme
  - A list of 26 words which have initial letters starting with "A" and proceeding in order to "Z."
  - Lists of words which can easily be pictured
  - Lists of words which are hard to picture
  - Mixed lists of both easy and hard-to-picture words
  - A list of words made from the jumbled words of a long sentence. Test the effects of minor rearrangements in word order against major reordering of words.
  - Lists of nouns, verbs, adjectives, and adverbs

  Have someone read you a fairly long story:

  - Try to repeat portions of the story verbatim.
  - Try to re-tell the story in detail in your own words. Which details did you recall?

  Have someone collect a huge number of pictures of all kinds (photos from news magazines will do, and try for about 1,000). Have this person show you 800 of the pictures very quickly. When you are finished, have the person show you all 1,000 of the pictures in random order. Record the number of pictures you recall seeing correctly, the number you recall seeing but did not see, the number you saw but did not recall, and the number you did not see and correctly said you had not.

Further reading

Anderson, J. R. (1995). *Learning and memory: An integrated approach*. New York: John Wiley and Sons.

Baine, D. (1986). *Memory and instruction*. Englewood Cliffs, NJ: Educational Technology Publications.

Bartlett, F. (1932). *Remembering: A study in experimental and social psychology*. Cambridge, England: The University Press.

Neisser, U. (1982). *Memory observed: Remembering in natural contexts*. San Francisco: W. H. Freeman and Company.

Norman, D. A. (1976). *Memory and attention: An introduction to human information processing (2nd ed.)*. New York: John Wiley and Sons.

Ormrod, J. E. (1989). *Using your head: An owner's manual*. Englewood Cliffs, NJ: Educational Technology Publications.

Sylwester, R. (1995). *A celebration of neurons: An educator's guide to the human brain*. Alexandria, VA: Association for Supervision and Curriculum Development.

11

PROCEDURE-USING
INSTRUCTIONAL STRATEGY

Chapter Objectives:

   1. *Describe the succession of steps in procedure learning.*
   2. *Design a presentation strategy for a specific procedure.*
   3. *Design a demonstration strategy for a specific procedure.*
   4. *Design a practice strategy for a specific procedure.*

Procedures are everywhere

A procedure is a sequence of steps or actions, mental or physical, which we perform to achieve a specific purpose. Procedures are a main avenue of human action, and without them we could not function. Just how much we depend on them becomes clear to us whenever something in our life changes.

For instance, if you buy a new car with the ignition key slot in an unfamiliar location, you will probably attempt to put the key in the wrong place many times before you begin to remember the new location. Without thinking, you are trying to apply an old, automatized procedure in a new setting where it doesn't work. This mistake will continue until you learn a new procedure—one containing a step where you place the key into the real slot.

Enough people have made the mistake of trying to start a car while it was in gear that for safety purposes auto makers have created interlock systems which prevent a car from starting unless it is in park (for automatic transmissions) or the clutch is depressed (for manual transmissions). This major modification to automobile designs occurred because we use procedures so much in our daily behavior that their automatization becomes, in some situations, very dangerous.

Not all procedures we perform become as automatic as starting a car. For many procedures, it is necessary that we concentrate on each step as we perform it, even after we have performed it many, many times. Building a model sailing ship, painting a house, and using a word processor are activities heavily loaded with deliberate, carefully-performed, non-automatized procedures.

We generally progress through three stages as we learn a procedure:

- An initial stage, in which the steps in the procedure are learned consciously (often verbally) and performed slowly and deliberately.

- An intermediate stage, in which we transform the procedure into a fluid, somewhat automatic decision-and-behavior sequence.

- A final stage, in which the performance of the procedure becomes more or less automatic, with the main improvements occurring in the areas of speed and automaticity of performance.

Procedure instruction atempts to supply the right kinds of information and student-system interaction during each of these stages to support the student who is forming a new procedure capability.

The major burden during procedure-using instruction is on memory. The student's task is to remember lots of things: steps, orders of steps, decision criteria, warnings, indication states, and sometimes technical data. These things must be remembered at key moments and in key orders during the execution of the procedure. This coordinated recall of the right information at the right moment comes with practice, but it requires some support in the early stages of procedure learning.

Having considered memory behavior, one might be tempted to say that procedure performance was just another form of memory behavior, but that is far from correct. There is no doubt that memory is heavily involved in procedure behavior, but memory is heavily involved in all forms of behavior. There are many parts of procedure behavior which are not strictly memory recall steps, and the execution of a procedure may call for both mental and motor acts coordinated within a framework of decision-making and information processing which carries it far beyond memory behavior.

This chapter describes the support you can provide to the student as a designer by structuring a procedure instructional strategy appropriately. You are already somewhat familiar with the procedure-using strategy pattern, having seen it dissected in Chapter 9. Moreover, in Chapter 21 you will see it in an extended example of the tutorial design process. The focus of this chapter is creating appropriate strategic variations for different kinds of procedures. Figure 1 diagrams an instructional strategy pattern which applies generally to the teaching of procedure-using. Let's examine its parts separately.

Presenting the procedure

The first stage of the procedure-using strategy is to present the information related to procedure steps. This part of the strategy is included in all procedure instruction. In practice, however, it often omits information which the student needs, or sometimes it presents information in a confusing way, which has the same effect. Below are some suggestions for designing good procedure presentations.

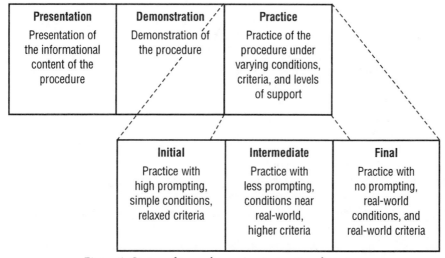

Figure 1. Stages of procedure-using instructional strategy.

1. Make sure you present complete basic information for each step of the procedure: A surprising number of procedure-using instructional scripts are missing basic information that the student needs in order to perform the procedure.

This may be hard to believe, until you recall that most scripts are written either by subject-matter experts or by designers who are not subject-matter experts. Subject-matter experts are usually very close to their content and very far away from the days when they themselves learned as students. They see the content through an expert's eyes, and details which are critical to a new student's understanding have become second nature and are no longer even noticed by the expert.

The designer, on the other hand, often has only a passing and academic acquaintance the procedure. Often he or she does not realize the full importance to the student of certain procedural or technical details, never having performed the procedure under realistic conditions.

There is a core of procedural information that a student must be given, regardless of the procedure being learned:

- When to begin a particular step (step starting cues).

- What action, physical or mental, to perform.

- When to stop doing a step (step ending cues).

- What indications will be seen as a result of the step (primary indications).

- What other ignorable indications may be experienced (secondary indications).

- Cautions to be observed during performance of the step.

This information is relevant to the student learning to compute freezing point elevations in physical chemistry, the student learning to add fractions in basic math, and the student learning to dock a cargo ship in the merchant marine. It represents an essential core of procedural information which the student must have in order to perform the procedure—and, by implication, to learn it. It is not required that all of this information be presented verbally, but it is essential that the student know it or have access to it. Techniques for obtaining this information from a subject-matter expert and capturing it in a documented form that can be used by other development team members are described in Chapter 18, Message Management.

In addition to this essential list of information, there are other categories of information which may be of particular importance to certain procedures. This information also must be captured and presented to the student. These additional information needs are usually determined by the examining the qualities of the procedure and the setting in which it is performed.

For instance, if a procedure demands that the judgment and insight of the performer play an important role, you must gather information on the intent or purpose of each step, along with a description of what the step accomplishes (e.g., "When you press the lever, gasoline is sprayed into the throat of the carburetor, which carries it into the combustion chamber, and the engine can begin firing."). Without this information, which helps the student build a simple cause-effect process model of the system to which the procedure is applied, the student has no information upon which to base judgments. Moreover, you probably should include information which will aid decision-making during the procedure if decisions are to be required of performers (e.g., "If the starter motor is beginning to overheat, you will smell a faint burning odor. Stop cranking for thirty seconds in order to give the motor a chance to cool down.").

For procedures in which steps are difficult and occasion frequent errors, it is highly desirable to include information on the indications which signal that something has gone wrong (e.g., "If you notice oil leaking from the pan at this point, you may have failed to tighten the drain plug sufficiently. Stop and tighten it at this point, before proceeding."). Perhaps you ought to capture information for motivation purposes in such cases as well (e.g., "Failure to do this may result in an empty oil pan and a seized engine."). Call these implications.

In cases such as you would find in the control room of a large electrical ditribution grid, where numerous indications are visible to the student during a procedure—some very relevant and some irrelevant to the procedure itself—it may be necessary to provide information on secondary and tertiary indications. Secondary indications are those which occur during a procedure and are related to the procedure but are not used as cues for the beginning or ending of a step; tertiary indications are those which occur during a procedure but are not influenced by the procedure. Secondary indications can act as correlative evidence that a procedure is proceeding correctly; their absence may in some cases also be the heralds of a fault. Tertiary indications are indications which may occur contemporaneously during procedure execution but which have nothing to do with it. Such indications can confuse things if the student does not realize that they can be ignored (e.g., "If a small amount of sediment forms and collects at the bottom of the beaker, it can be overlooked and will not affect your experimental results."). You must judge whether a procedure for which you are creating instruction requires the gathering of these elements of the presentation.

2. When presenting the steps of a procedure, present them in sequential order, unless you are following a specific plan which causes you to do otherwise: Except for the strategy example involving mathetics which was described in Chapter 9, it is not usual to find procedure instruction in which steps are presented out of order, but when the procedure allows a branching of the action path into alternative paths, an orientation problem can occur for the student. The best approach in such situations is to instruct the most frequent procedural path and then to return to instruct the alternate paths as special cases. You must be sure to also provide demonstrations and practice opportunities for the alternate paths.

3. Clearly define the boundary between steps: Don't let steps run together. This can happen when you fail to identify the ending point of one step and the beginning point of the next. During procedure instruction, you cannot harm things by giving extra emphasis to the fact that the instruction is moving on to a new step, but you can cause problems for the student if you fail to give enough emphasis to it. As you provide information on a step, there should be no question in the student's mind which step you are referring to.

It is worthwhile in most cases to be sure that each step in a procedure is clearly defined—even to the point of assigning a name and a number to each one. This provides a means of clearly communicating the procedure to the student in concrete and readily understandable terms. It also provides a terminology by which steps can be called during interactions and feedback.

4. When it is appropriate, provide a mnemonic for the steps in the procedure: This should be strongly considered for procedures which the student must recall from memory: the more critical the procedure, the more important the mnemonic. The phrase "stop, drop, and roll" is such a mnemonic. It summarizes a procedure which even children can use to extinguish clothing fires. It is a procedure which must be recalled instantly when it is needed, and with no mistakes. Chapter 10, which deals with memory instructional strategy, lists several types of mnemonic which can be used.

5. Combine the presentation stage of procedure-using instruction with the demonstration stage when possible: It is common and beneficial to combine the presentation and demonstration stages of procedural instruction. One benefit of combining is that the abstract terms in the presentation of the procedure are given concreteness by the demonstration. Instead of having to remember what a butterfly valve looks like, the student sees one and observes the step of removing it as it takes place. This is a good example of the interleaving of instructional intents within an instructional strategy, described in Chapter 9.

When the presentation and the demonstration must be separated for some reason, it is useful to refer ahead to the demonstration as you present steps and identify specific things which the student will see and should watch for as the demonstration takes place (e.g., "As you view the upcoming demonstration, be sure to note these special precautions that the technician takes to avoid receiving a shock from the power supply wires.").

6. **Consider breaking long procedures into "blocks" of 10 or so steps at natural division points:** Long procedures are difficult for students to deal with because of the memory burden they impose. However, most long procedures can be broken into natural "blocks," each of which accomplishes some major purpose of the procedure (e.g., "These eight steps prepare the specimen for the gram stain to be applied.").

Dealing with five of these blocks, each containing ten steps, is easier for the student than dealing with a list of fifty individual steps which seems to have no internal organization. A step sub-division defines a group of steps which can be presented, demonstrated, and practiced as a somewhat independent chunk. At the same time, it gives the student a type of generative mnemonic (see Chapter 10) which will allow him or her to recall many more steps than if the fifty steps were recalled individually.

When blocking is used in this way, the order of instruction should begin with an overview of the blocks and the logic which binds them together into a higher-level sequence before proceeding to the details of the steps within any block.

Demonstrating the procedure

Procedures are normally demonstrated during procedure-using instruction, and there are many ways that demonstrations can be enhanced to communicate a better, more useful message to the student. Below is a list of recommendations.

1. **Be sure that graphics and video used to demonstrate a step do in fact contain enough information to adequately demonstrate it:** It is very common to see demonstrations which are unclear, incomplete, and misleading. For instance, demonstrations are common in which the text or audio refers to a component while fifty components—all unlabelled—appear at the same moment in the visual. Demonstrations are common which verbally warn about the difficulty of a step or prescribe special techniques for performing it but which then provide demonstration visuals taken from ten feet away with a shoulder and two arms blocking the view. Even when pointers are used to direct attention, it is frequently difficult to be absolutely sure just what is being pointed to.

- It is a bare minimum requirement that visuals provided in a demonstration show all relevant objects and actions.

- It should show them at a level of detail which allows each object and action to be seen clearly and unambiguously.

- It should do so with unmistakable visual and verbal emphasis that points the student's attention to the key observation point.

- It should do so with labelling of parts when it is possible that students have failed to memorize part names by the time of the demonstration (this can perhaps be optional, student-requested labelling).

- When motion of a peculiar kind is an essential part of a step, the motion should be shown.

These provisions ensure that there is no ambiguity in what the student sees and understands. Additionally, there is a basic information requirement for a demonstration in the same way that there is for a presentation. The items of information for the message accompanying a demonstration include:

- Identification of the object being operated upon at a given moment of the demonstration.

- The name of the operation being performed.

- Explanation of each specialized technique movement or step in the operation which is shown visually.

- Varieties in technique which are being demonstrated.

- Observable relevant and irrelevant indications.

- Identification of beginning and ending points of each step.

It is important that these items of information be visualized, verbalized, and emphasized in an unmistakable way.

2. Give students control over as many of the visible, verbal, and timing elements of the demonstration as possible: There are many ways in which student curiosity and need for information can be satisfied on demand, using the power of the CBI system. For instance, at points in the demonstration where details of the procedure are important, students can be allowed to zoom-in for a closer look at what happens.

Whether zoomed-in or at normal viewing distance, students can be given control over the pace of the demonstration and its direction. This means that after any step in a procedure is shown, the student can be given the power to stop the demonstration, reverse it, and replay any part of it at normal speed or in slow motion.

3. Mix as many elements of the practice as you can with the demonstration—blend strategy stages where possible; have students perform as soon as possible: Presentation and demonstration do not need to be spectator activities. The computer makes it possible for students to do the demonstration themselves, performing steps even on their first exposure to the procedure.

After telling the student that Step 4 entails turning on a power switch, and after supplying relevant cautions and warnings, have the student operate the switch by touching it and watching it change positions on the screen, along with the other normal indications. By doing this, you not only reduce the spectating the student has to do and increase the level of beneficial interaction, but you also verify that the student knows where the power switch is.

4. Make the invisible visible: It is characteristic of many procedures that much of the "action" is invisible, being performed as a sequence of decisions which take place in the performer's head. For steps which are not seen as they are performed, it is most important to find a way to represent to the student the actions which are taking place. This is true whether the step is part of completing a balance sheet or using a word processor to create a table.

5. When the presentation and demonstration are given separately, match the order and grouping of steps in the demonstration with that of the presentation: This advice is especially important when you have decided to break a long procedure into blocks while maintaining the presentation and demonstration as separate entities. This seems like an obvious point, but it is ignored with surprising frequency by designers who do not realize its impact on the student.

As a student experiences the presentation of a procedure, sequence knowledge begins to form in memory that represents the steps and the order(s) in which they are rightly performed. This memory is fragile at first. It is not forgotten as readily as short-term memory material is forgotten, but neither is it a robust and strong memory. When the student encounters a part of the instruction which in any way conflicts with this newly-forming memory, it often results in long-term effects. Not only can the memory structure be thrown into disorder, but the student's confidence in recalling it can be challenged. Is the memory correct? Is it in error? Which recalled version of the steps is correct? This crisis of confidence can have serious consequences for future learning and performance. It is possible that such effects can persist long after the student has re-learned the correct step order. If the procedure for long division is uncertain knowledge, then everything that uses long division will also be uncertain to a degree.

Not only should divisions of the procedure be maintained the same way between presentation and demonstration, but overviews, reviews, and summaries must also be constructed using exactly the same list of steps and blocking of steps.

Practicing the procedure

The diagram in Figure 1 shows that practice is a multi-stage process for procedure-using instruction. Multiple stages provide a bridge to help the student transition from the deliberate, step-by-step performance of the procedure which is typical of early stages of learning to the more automatic performance which is possible in later stages. The ultimate target of instruction is practice that is as realistic as the designer can make it. CBI systems are not always capable of providing practice which has all of the characteristics of the real world, but they are capable of providing practice over a range of realism from very low (for initial stages of training) to very high (for later stages of training).

As a designer, you may elect to provide the staged practice as two or more separate versions of practice, because that is the structure that existing authoring tools will allow you to construct with the least complication. Emerging authoring tools will allow for the adaptation of support during procedural instruction to become continuous and transparent to the student.

Learning a procedure consists of much more than learning just a set of verbalized steps. It is true that some simple procedures can be learned simply through verbalization from one person to another, but we tend to overestimate the number of procedures that can be learned this way.

Harken back to your own experience as you first learned to drive a car or, better yet, to ride a bicycle. Your early attempts were tentative and halting and were only taken after careful mental rehearsal of all of the steps, factors, and possible outcomes. As your experience increased through practice, your performance became more automatic. You found fewer and fewer situations in which you had to deliberately think through what you were doing.

All of this, of course, changed when you rode a bicycle having more than one gear or travelled to a country where automobiles were driven on the opposite side of the road. At that point, you reverted to an earlier stage of performance—to careful rehearsal of individual steps until you became confident your decisions were not going to lead to harm. Do you remember mentally rehearsing the procedure for a right-hand turn from the left side of the road several times before you actually attempted one in a car?

There are several instructional factors related to the practice of procedures which vary during practice: prompting/coaching, criterion setting, selection of practice problems, feedback, and review and re-testing. The consideration that must be given each factor varies from procedure to procedure, as discussed below.

Prompting/coaching: During prompted or coached practice, a student is expected to perform steps of the target procedure following supportive cues or prompts of some sort. Prompts may be given for several reasons: to temporarily reduce the memory burden placed on the student, to reduce the anxieties associated with a step, or to allow the student to direct his or her attention toward some detail of performing the step. Prompts may consist of:

- Supplying the name of a step to be performed. ("Step 3: Insert four panel mounting screws.")

- Providing display cues which point out relevant control or action points. (Screen arrows point to the mounting holes.)

- Providing suggestions, hints, or reminders on technique before the step is performed. ("Remember that the screws turn counterclockwise.")

- Providing reassurance or feedback while the step is still in progress. ("Very good, you are seating the screws in the correct order.")

- Providing the opportunity to go back immediately and re-perform a step which was done incorrectly in some respect. ("You placed one screw in the panel out of order. Go back and try this step one more time, remembering that the correct order is 1–4–2–3.")

Over a number of practice attempts, prompts should vanish (or fade) in a systematic way, causing the student to become more and more personally responsible for adequate performance. Ideally the speed of fading is controlled by improvement in student performance. In addition, it can depend on the characteristics and experience of the student, the properties of the procedure, and the historical difficulties which the target population has with the procedure. There is no absolute guideline for removing prompting support, and it is unlikely that the same levels of prompting and the same rate of prompt withdrawl will be appropriate for all students.

For example, in the instruction of new pilots who are learning to fly their first aircraft, the designer may find that a slow retraction of the prompts is in order, with an automatic re-introduction of prompts if student performance shows signs of falling off. However, for experienced pilots transitioning into a new aircraft from an old one, the speed of withdrawing prompts can be much faster, if they need to be used at all, which they may not. Student performance during benchmark testing and student comments to the designer are probably the best guides to follow in making this decision.

Criterion-and-condition setting: The performance criterion set for students may vary, depending on the stage of practice. In early stages, requiring full criterion performance is often unreasonable. In later stages, full criterion performance is essential.

If timing in the performance of a procedure is critical, early stages of practice may relax the time constraints, giving the student an opportunity to practice execution without the normal pressures of time, gradually enforcing timing as student performance improves.

The same principle applies to other conditions and standards, such as accuracy or completeness criteria, and the inclusion of conditions which make the procedure more difficult to perform. Early during prompted practice, the stringency of the performance requirements may be relaxed, with increased emphasis being placed on them as performance improves. Selective relaxation of standards is not a form of prompting, but it is a variable which can be used by the designer in much the same way.

Designers should bring students by degrees to a level of practice which is as real-world-like as possible. The progression toward realism should take place in optimally-sized (for the student) steps. The size of each step can be determined by experience with the student population itself and should neither overwhelm nor bore the student. The adaptive instructional system of the future will be able to make adjustments of this type tailored to the individual student.

Selection of problems: For strictly sequential procedures, there is little question about the selection of problems for practice. There is really only one version of practice, and that is to execute the procedure. For procedures which are not strictly sequential, however, such as those with decision points resulting in multiple path sequences, there must be deliberate and careful selection of practice items. This selection must take into consideration the number of decision-making (branching) points in the procedure, the criticality of correct performance, and the frequency with which different branches of the procedure are required in real-world experience.

A procedure with few decision points may be practiced in such a way that the student is exposed to all possible variations of the procedure. In such cases, the student may be required to practice the procedure a certain number of times to ensure that all of its varieties are encountered and mastered.

For procedures with numerous decision points, the designer must identify those points which are critical and where the consequences of incorrect performance are costly. These variations of the procedure must be encountered by the student as a minimum and practiced to mastery.

If the number of potential varieties on this list is prohibitive and would produce more practice than is reasonable, the designer has three choices:

- Break the instruction on the procedure into smaller lessons, each covering only a part of the larger procedure.

- Break out the decision points for isolated instruction, including decision-making practice to the mastery level.

- Identify those decision points which are of low consequence and low frequency and make the decision to omit them from training. If this is done, the decision should be documented and its effects on performance and safety should be calculated and reported.

The second choice assumes that a variety of problems will be presented to the student during instruction on the procedure. These problems must be selected in a way that tests either by direct evidence or by inference that the student can in fact perform the procedure under all required conditions.

Feedback: Feedback during prompted practice should be corrective feedback. When an error is made, the error should be recognized, and the correct response should be either told or demonstrated to the student.

It can be argued that the forms of presentation used during feedback should echo those used during original presentation of the procedure or step. This may include mnemonics, or any category of information from the presentation or demonstration. The strength of this is that it reminds the student of something which was forgotten but which is most likely still within easy reach in memory. However, if the original presentation was inadequate in some way, it is logical that showing it again to the student won't help any more than it did the first time. To cover for this contingency, some designers use an alternate form of presentation during feedback.

Review and re-testing: Procedures are forgotten over time if they are not used regularly, and the designer should provide opportunities for review and re-testing, beginning during training. In deciding the pattern of review to use, several things must be taken into account:

1. The time since the last opportunity to perform the procedure, either by itself, or as a part of a larger procedure grouping. Some procedures will be reviewed automatically as training progresses to more complex levels. Some will not be seen again unless the designer includes a review of them in the course.

2. The varieties of the procedure which will be practiced as a normal part of training. The designer may need to identify only certain esoteric varieties of the procedure

to be reviewed. Other more common varieties may be encountered naturally as training progresses.

3. The criticality of performance. If a student must be able to perform the procedure from the first without error, then the need for review increases rapidly.

4. The degree of help available in the real world in performing the procedure. If the environment provides many helps to performance of the procedure, review may not be necessary.

5. The frequency of performing the procedure. If the procedure is critically important but only infrequently performed, the need for review and re-certification are increased—sometimes to the point of requiring a periodic renewal after the student has entered the work place.

Implications of procedure variations

Procedures are not all the same, and many of the differences between them have significance during instruction. For instance, procedures can differ in:

Sequence: Some procedures are performed in a sequence of steps that never varies. Some procedures have decision points in them which lead to alternate paths of action, with the result that these procedures are seldom performed the same way twice in a row.

Strictly sequenced procedures are quite common. We learn, for instance, from a cranky lawnmower that one and only one starting procedure will work. Once the procedure is learned, to vary from it is to risk an unmowed lawn.

Sequence invariance is also found in certain high-risk environments, such as the electrical power industry, where throwing a switch at the wrong moment can cause injury or death. It is also common in aircraft flight (checklists are procedures), manufacturing equipment operation, and in academic subjects such as chemistry (lab work) and mathematics (long division).

Procedures which vary are also quite common. Most often these procedures involve a great deal of problem-solving or at least decision-making. Though problem-solving activity is not the same as execution of a procedure, experienced troubleshooters often use procedures to accompish repair goals that used to require intense problem-solving. Realizing this helps us to relate problem-solving to procedure-using. Procedures may be seen as memorized solutions to frequently-occurring problems.

Starting an old car engine provides an example of both sequential and decision-heavy procedures. On a warm day, the procedure for starting is normally short and unvarying. On a cold day, however, the procedure becomes quite a bit more complex, and includes a set of hard-start tricks which sometimes work right away, but can turn into a series of mini-procedures linked together by decision-making.

During instruction, increased variability in a procedure leads the designer to increase the amount of attention given to the decision processes which link step sequences. This may result in: (1) stress being placed on decisions during the presentation of the procedure, and (2) a flexible practice structure which requires the student to exercise each critical decision repeatedly—and in isolation if needed. Once procedure-related decision skills are well-learned, practice can widen to include major segments of—and eventually—the whole procedure. This should be done in a way that is proportional to the practical importance of the decisions being made.

Degree of interference: Sometimes we must learn procedures which resemble ones we already know. Sometimes the already-learned procedures get in the way. Rappelling is the technique climbers use to descend from high places. Nothing in the procedure is completely new, but many of the sensations (e.g., leaning back on a rope) and actions (e.g., walking backwards over a cliff) clash with strong safety habits learned early in life. The same thing happens when someone learns to use SCUBA equipment: Most of us have been trained by experience not to breathe underwater.

In both of these cases, people not only have to learn new procedures, but they have to unlearn some old ones at the same time. For this reason, the learning of such procedures has to include deliberate over-learning. The new version of the procedure has to be learned so thoroughly and so automatically that it eclipses the earlier procedure and becomes as strongly a part of the habit pattern as the old procedure was.

In addition, new procedures for which there is likely to be interference must not only be learned well once, but there must be continued opportunities to practice them frequently over time, because of a heightened tendency to forget and revert to previous habit patterns.

Degree of novelty: All of us can remember a procedure which was so totally new to us that it took great effort and concentration to learn it. Reading is a complex set of procedures which challenged most of us because at one time it had a high degree of novelty.

By the time of maturity, most of us have left behind situations which force us to learn procedures which are completely new. We begin to think that we have become fast, easy learners, when in fact we have become learners of things with little novelty and little challenge.

However, there is still plenty of novelty left for the adult who never learned to ride a bicycle as a child. The challenge is still there, and the less training in physical activities that person has had, the more novel the procedure of riding the bicycle will be.

Several factors can increase the degree of novelty of a procedure.

New equipment can introduce novelty. The introduction of sophisticated electronics and computer systems into the aircraft cockpit is changing the role of the pilot from that of a "driver" to that of a "manager." Experienced pilots attempting to change from the old role to the new one find that they must learn new procedures for acting, planning, and reacting in the cockpit. Learning to perform in the newer cockpits presents to them a real challenge due to novelty.

This is true not only for pilots trying to change from one role to another, but for new pilots as well. Training pilots "ab initio"—or from the beginning—is an exercise in the training of novel procedures.

New motor skills can introduce novelty. One fighter pilot was unable to simulate the firing of weapons in the air during a mock combat due to his unfamiliarity with the physical procedure of setting up a control panel—which had to be done without looking and in rapid order. Though the procedure had been learned and practiced in the classroom and on low-level simulation equipment, it had never been performed with gloves on and without looking, as was required in the air.

New information processing habits can introduce novelty. It became apparent with the introduction of radar that a new skill was demanded of operators—vigilance. Vigilance was a complex of information processing procedures, that required special training, since it was not one that most operators brought with them to the job. One of the novel skills for beginning pilots is to learn the procedure for scanning the cockpit instruments periodically: a cycle of scanning performed in a sequential sweep around the cockpit. Early in training, this new skill must be prompted by an instructor pilot, and each step of the scan must be done deliberately, but after automatization, it is a skill which occurs without notice by the pilot who performs it.

The designer's response to novelty usually includes: (1) learning of novel behaviors in isolation before combining them into more comprehensive complexes, (2) careful, incremental addition of complexity during the practice of newly-learned procedures, and (3) extra practice in areas of novelty as procedures are combined with other procedures into more complex sequences.

Degree of physicalness: Some procedures are very physical and require timing, precise muscular coordination, and steadiness. Other procedures are performed without moving a muscle. During Olympic training, athletes use computerized tools to improve the precision, force, or timing of their procedures. Golfers at certain training locations are able to use video and computer tools to improve their swing. They are training in procedures with a high degree of physicalness.

A wide range of technological devices is used to train highly physical procedures. Their main function is to provide the precise feedback which the learner can use to increase physical control and coordination. The challenge of highly physical procedures for CBI systems is that the system must be able to monitor performance and prescribe changes in practice exercises which will improve control and coordination as rapidly as possible.

Criticality of timing and coordination: Some procedures involve precise timing and coordinated actions. Others are done without that constraint. Landing an airplane, for instance, is a precisely-timed activity, as are gymnastics and certain phases of chemistry lab work. In these procedures, timing of the performance can make the difference between wearing a gold medal or a leg or arm cast.

Training for such precision in timing often begins in a forgiving environment—an environment in which the procedure, or parts of it, can be practiced beyond the limitations of timing and without normal consequences. This environment is most often a simulated environment (an aircraft simulator, a chemistry lab simulator) or one in which there are sufficient supports (such as the safety belts used in gymnastics, or nets and padding) to remove the penalties for slow performance.

When the procedure and its parts have been learned thoroughly, the simulation's consequences and timing regimen can be traded for the real world's, and the safety equipment can be gradually removed.

Length: Some procedures are done in an instant. Others require days, or even weeks to perform. Laboratory tests in microbiology often require the culturing of bacterial growth, isolation of specific types of growth, preparation of specimens, and examination through a number of possible viewing devices. Some procedure have many steps, and some have few.

Instruction in long procedures is normally broken into parts before training takes place. Individual parts of the activity are instructed and practiced in isolation. Then, when individual parts have been mastered, practice can take place with all parts combined.

If there is a typical problem in the training of long procedures, it is the common practice of training parts of the procedure without ever offering an opportunity to practice the whole procedure in its entirety, a stage of instruction which is called integration. One good example of this is found in the training of instructional designers. Some of them are trained to do the separate parts of the development process but fail to get practice in the entire cycle of it.

The problem created by this omission is that feedback for certain kinds of decision are systematically denied the student. Decisions with short-term consequences receive adequate feedback, but those which are long-term do not, and students experience rude awakenings when they reach the real world and make the same kinds of decisions they had been making in school.

Difficulty of individual steps: Some procedures are uniformly easy or difficult. Others have steps which raise special instructional challenges. One training problem involved a technician's job of operating an electronic sensor. A paper tape which issued from the sensor had on it a squiggled line. Certain patterns in the line told the operator when a metal deposit had been found.

The operator's job was a simple procedure. Interpreting the marks on the tape was the single difficult step, however, and it was causing a performance problem. The answer was to train the single difficult step in isolation first. Since the step involved making a discrimination (yes-no decision), the instruction for it required a separate concept-using lesson. After training in the single step, students learned the entire procedure quite easily.

Difficulty of a procedural step can arise from several sources: heavy memory load, a requirement for complex problem-solving or mental computation, intricate motor actions, precise timing, novelty, or requirement for making difficult discriminations. Very often we refer to such procedures as requiring "expert judgement," or the "master's touch." In fact, they very often only require adequate amounts of practice, in isolation, with feedback in order to produce a master.

Number of performers: Some procedures are performed by one person alone. Others are performed by teams of people. The training of team procedures employs the same set of principles as the training of single-person procedures; however, there is an element of team coordination and communication which adds a new degree of challenge. Not only must individuals perform their own procedures correctly and promptly, but they must act as a part of a larger unit which acts as a whole.

Problems are encountered in team training when two important guidelines are forgotten: (1) individual team members must be trained thoroughly in their own procedures, and (2) communication and coordination procedures must be trained deliberately and in accordance with sound principles for procedure instruction.

The tendency in team training is to forget that the coordination and communication activities are themselves procedures—novel ones for many students—and to expect that these behaviors will just automatically materialize as students are thrown into the team environment.

Wording procedure-using objectives

Procedure-using objectives are simple to identify by their wording, as the examples below show:

- Power up the "Little Wonder" grass cutting machine.

- Calibrate the BL-5A laser levelling instrument.

- Perform long division problems with 2-digit divisors and 4-digit dividends without borrowing.

- Assemble the "Little Hot Shot" tricycle.

- Periodically scan the power control panel for readings which are out of safe limits.

Conclusion

Procedures as a major component of human behavior come in a variety of forms, sizes, and types, as described in this chapter. Because they are so numerous, and because we spend so much of training time learning them, we sometimes relax the instructional rules, but as we have tried to show, that can lead to problems in learning. We recommend that careful attention be given the preparation of instruction on procedures so that they can be learned quickly, moved to the desired level of automaticity, and then performed reliably as components of the more sophisticated and integrated performances which are a part of our daily activities.

Self-directed activities

- In addition to teaching a student the correct way to perform a procedure, some designers say that a student must be taught what can go wrong during a procedure and how to back out of errors. Take a position on this issue and support your position by referring to the consequences it would produce in a number of different training situations: teaching mathematical computation procedures, teaching surgical procedures, teaching the procedures for operating a lawnmower, teaching the procedures for solving a problem, teaching the procedures for piloting an aircraft.

- Besides teaching a student how to perform procedural steps, there are other items of information which must be taught with respect to the procedure as a whole. Suggest what this knowledge might consist of.

- Design a piece of instruction which teaches a procedure entirely without words. In addition to other things, this instruction should engage the student in practice with feedback.

- Describe the effect of decision-making on procedure instruction. What if a procedure has no decision points? What if it has only one? What if it has several? What are the implications for the design of the presentation, the demonstration, and the practice?

- Describe the special instructional provisions that are necessary to instruct a procedure which is carried out invisibly, within a student's head. How does the presentation of step information differ? How do demonstrations differ? How does the practice with feedback differ?

Further reading

Anderson, J. R. (1993). *Rules of the mind.* Hillsdale, NJ: Lawrence Erlbaum Associates.

Reigeluth, C. M. (Ed.). (1987). *Instructional theories in action: Lessons illustrating selected theories and models.* Hillsdale, NJ: Lawrence Erlbaum Associates.

Resnick, L. B. (Ed.). (1989). *Knowing, learning, and instruction: Essays in honor of Robert Glaser.* Hillsdale, NJ: Lawrence Erlbaum Associates.

12

PROCESS-USING INSTRUCTIONAL STRATEGY

Chapter Objectives :

1. *Discriminate process-using from memory, procedure-using, concept-using, and principle-using.*

2. *Explain how processes originate through the accumulation of everyday event-pattern experiences.*

3. *Describe how processes are revised to provide greater explanatory power.*

4. *Describe the difference between memory for processes and process-using behavior.*

5. *Design process-using instruction for a given instructional goal.*

What is a process?

A process is a pattern of events. There are two types:

- *Natural* processes—which occur in nature and are not planned or designed by humans.

- *Artificial*, manufactured, or procedural processes—which describe patterns of events planned, designed, or controlled by humans.

Procedural processes describe the influences and effects of a procedure as it is performed, from a third-person point of view. As a driver turns the key in the ignition switch, a procedural process describes what happens within the car's ignition system that results in starting. When procedure and process instruction are combined, a student learns to perform the procedure while at the same time learning how the procedure affects the environment in which the procedure is performed. This kind of instruction often imparts enough cause-effect understanding to enable students to perform the procedure under conditions requiring decision-making or response to unusual or unexpected events. In effect, learning the process becomes a kind of amplifier that makes the procedural learning more useful, flexible, and powerful. Because procedure and process instruction are so often combined in this fashion, process instruction is frequently omitted from behavior taxonomies and lists of instructional objective types as a separate type. This is surprising, considering the enormous amount of process instruction which we actually carry out. The interest in episodes and schemas in the field of cognitive science and work by M. D. Merrill in Instructional Transaction Theory have placed much greater emphasis on the instruction of processes.

Natural processes consist of all event patterns which can be observed or experienced which were not designed by humans. You might call these the natural processes because they are found in nature. This type of process is both concrete and abstract. There are physical mechanisms in nature which take part in processes, such as the Venus Flytrap. There are also systems of invisible energy transfer. We do not see the cycles of energy transfer between the convection cells in the atmosphere until they produce the weather patterns which we experience. The operation of these cells, however, can be described as a process. The year progresses through a seasonal process: Spring, Summer, Autumn, Winter. A human life progresses through a growth-maturation-aging process: fetus, infant, toddler, child, youth, young adult, middle-aged adult, elderly adult. Butterfly lives have similar life process that include a different pattern of events: egg, pupa, cocoon, adult. Much of biology and science education knowledge consists of processes. Cell division, DNA replication, and propagation of nerve impulses are all examples of processes which have been described in great detail by scientists. One of the major activities of a scientist is to uncover and expose to our view nature's ongoing processes.

Organizing events together into sequences or patterns that we call processes helps us bring a kind of temporal cause-effect order to an otherwise chaotic world of experienced events. Processes give us terms with which to name and describe observed patterns of experience. As we reason using these patterns, we can use them to describe specific occurrences and extend our knowledge of them through study. Processes also provide us with rich metaphorical thought tools, creating our most evocative forms of expression: "the blooming of algae," "the gestation of a plan," "the war on homelessness," "the technology explosion." *Blooming, gestation, war,* and *explosion* are all terms that denote processes. By using these terms, we automatically evoke a large corpus of process-related knowledge. Speech and thought would be impossible without the process patterns which we constantly press into the service of value-laden reasoning and expression.

Processes and time

The temporal dimensions of a process can be very short or very long. Build a time-continuum and place all processes on it. At the short end of the continuum you will find nuclear fission—atom-smashing—whose nuclear particle scatterings take only the smallest fraction of a second. Normal explosions, which take from one to three seconds, are extremely long by comparison. Normal workaday processes can take minutes (hard-boiling an egg), hours (freezing an ice cube), days (growth of a lawn to mowing height), weeks (turning and falling of autumn leaves), months (eruption of a volcano), or years (graying of your hair). Even longer sequences can take decades (re-forestation), centuries (rise and fall of a civilization), millennia (fossilization), ages (advancement and retreat of great sheets of ice across a continent), and longer periods of time for which most people don't even have a name (creation and destruction of stars). The study of history, archaeology, paleontology, sociology, political science, and geology are in one sense the study of different kinds of processes.

Processes and levels of detail

A single process can be viewed at different levels of detail. Advancements in process knowledge for both individuals and societies consist for the most part of adding detail to already-existing process event structures. Early in life, we normally learn at a general level how our body carries out its basic processes. Then we spend the rest of our lives learning in more detail how the body processes work. We get this additional knowledge from reading books and articles, seeing film and video documentaries, listening to news reports, talking with friends and hearing about their operations and sicknesses, and by seeing doctors ourselves about specific ailments. It is unfortunate that so much of our process knowledge about the body comes from discussions of abnormal function and breakdown. Much of our process knowledge of cars is learned in the same way from auto mechanics who impart this knowledge to us at great cost.

Processes do not just exist at one level but at several levels. We explain events at one level in terms of events at a deeper level. For instance, we explain shortness of breath or labored breathing in terms of the binding of or inability to bind oxygen to red blood cells. We explain the binding of oxygen to red blood cells in terms of the presence of hemoglobin within the red blood cell. We explain almost everything in terms of levels in this way. In order to explain things at one level, we describe an event structure at the next lower level of detail. Physicists trying to unravel the nature of the atom pursued their answers in terms of events at the atom level, then the electron-neutron-proton level, then the muon, pion level, and have come to the quark and charm level where they are finding it difficult to proceed further. The main point is that like advancing science, humans: (1) organize processes at multiple levels, and (2) try to explain observed events at one level in terms of the next lower level.

Changing processes

From time to time, we also replace old process descriptions with newer and more powerful ones which account for and explain more of our experience. As we exchange the new process for the old one, we reorganize the detailed knowledge connected with and supporting the old process structure around the new one. Science does this continually as old theories are cast aside in favor of new ones. Theories are often expressed as a form of event structure, which means they are in some cases process descriptions.

A good example of a new process-structured theory is Plate Tectonics, which was introduced early in the twentieth century and was accepted near the midpoint. Plate Tectonics describes the major historical and future events in the motion of the earth's landmasses by describing the process of continental drift. Plate tectonic theory overturned the conventional wisdom of its time but now explains more of our observations of the earth—more events—than the old theories it replaced.

There is a close relationship between processes, theories, and principles. As we observe the world and have experience with it, processes are discovered, and we use processes at one level to predict what will happen. However, diverse processes which are similar (that is, which seem to share a common cause) lead us to higher, more abstract statements with predictive value. These are principles, and principles are an important ingredient of scientific theories. Therefore, processes are stepping stones to theory but do not become obsolete as soon as theories are formed, because new processes are also used to test theories and determine when their predictive value has decreased, which tells us when a new theory is needed.

Episodic memory and processes

Our memory finds it especially easy to remember the structure of individual life experiences—episodes. This memory for episodes (which are just patterns of events) is called episodic memory. As we accumulate repeated experiences with very similar episodes, we are able to notice their general pattern similarities, and a process is born.

It is not hard to detect the importance of both similarity and contrast between episodes as an influence in the learning process. One frequently-used example of an episode pattern is the experience of restaurant dining. When we dine out once, we can remember the events of the experience. When we dine out the second time, we remember the events of both experiences and are able to compare the two experiences for their similarities and differences. Certain parts of the experience are duplicated, while others are not. Over the course of several dining experiences, we begin to notice a common pattern in the events. Cognitive scientists, who are very interested in how people learn and remember, call the distilled memory structure that is thus formed a schema of the dining experience. The event structure—or process structure—of our experience is closely related to the basic functions of memory, and processes are one thing that we remember very easily.

Process-using versus process memory

Just remembering the event structure of a process is simply a memory behavior. But a process can be instructed at two levels: the memory level, and the level of process-using.

Memory-level process instruction: Most of the process knowledge we acquire through casual instruction is at the memory level. This level might be called the "gee-whiz" level, because memory-level process knowledge is not as useful as it is interesting. It is interesting to record in memory the stages in the birth or death of a star, but without going beyond mere memory of those stages, the knowledge does not allow a student to generate new understanding of stars, to interpret information about particular stars, nor to predict the outcome of a particular set of circumstances surrounding a star.

There are different degrees of memory-level process knowledge. We have described the process as a set of states or events which are related together by varying causal conditions. This means that process knowledge is comprised of several possible event paths which events might follow depending on how conditions vary. The most superficial degree of process knowledge consists of memorizing the steps in a process. For example:

> *The remote-control telescope operates this way:*
>
> *Step 1: Light from the heavens enters the mouth of the telescope and strikes the mirrors at the telescope's base.*
>
> *Step 2: The light is reflected by the base mirror back to a secondary mirror near the mouth of the telescope.*
>
> *Step 3: The light is reflected back through a hole in the center of the base mirror and strikes a digitizer.*
>
> *Step 4: The digitizer changes the light patterns into bit patterns and stores them in a computer memory.*
>
> *Step 5: Remote users request images in the computer's memory.*

Sometimes the delivery of this level of process instruction does not even separate things into steps. This instruction is most often delivered in the form of paragraph prose:

> *The T-cell contains glutathione, an anti-oxidant, whose function is to seek out and neutralize harmful free radicals within the T-cell. Special molecules in the blood tell the T-cell when the body has an infection, and the T-cell responds by making free radicals. Glutathoine removes these free radicals in a normally functioning cell, but prolonged exposure to messenger molecules eventually exhausts the cell's supply. At this point the T-cell stops responding to the infection and through its own internal dysfunction, dies.*

This instruction requires the student to keep a lot of process threads straight and to absorb a lot of new information in a short space of time. Moreover, it presents only two event paths out of many and presents only a limited amount of information that the student can use to determine other paths that might occur.

This is the second major shortcoming of memory-level process instruction: It eliminates information that is useful to the student and in so doing creates the feeling of understanding when in fact there is little. It is common for a student to resonate to the presentation of process information and gain the impression that much has been learned, only to find that attempts to practice are thwarted by missing bits of information. This pattern is characteristically related to homework and may be a major motivational stumbling block for many students.

Missing information may include missing events, incomplete description of the mechanisms for transition between event-states, confusing presentation of the mechanism, lacking specification of the conditions under which state-transitions take place, or lack of linkage between condition causes and event effects.

Process-using instruction: For process-using behavior to occur, a student must not only predict an outcome, but also must be able to supply a rationale for it. The student must be able to explain through a chain of reasoning why and how the outcome occurred. The strategy described in this chapter assumes that the goal of instruction is process-using instruction and not simply memory for process steps.

When an event pattern occurs, it is because some force, energy, or signal has been applied and a natural element has responded in a lawful way, causing some observable result. The result is the *state* that we call an *event*. The force, energy, or signal is the real but invisible *driving power behind* the event. Humans have the ability to note events but also to reason in terms of the forces which drive event patterns and make predictions based on them. When we observe an event sequence created by forces acting on natural elements, we infer a process. Reasoning about the forces as well as the observed events is called process-using behavior.

We have been careful to describe a process as a pattern of events and not a sequence of events; now it is possible to see why. As natural elements are acted upon by all kinds of forces, energies, and signals, there are many forces acting at once, and so there are many possible outcomes depending on the forces acting, their magnitude, and their balance. Any set of circumstances can thus result in a large number of outcomes, depending on the final resolution of the forces. That means that a process as we experience it is not a fixed, rigid, unchanging sequence of events but a possibility with numerous outcomes—numerous possible event sequences. Process-using means being able to predict from a given set of elements and acting forces one or more likely or possible outcomes. Process-using behavior deals in the cause-effect linkages between events and explains them in terms of force, energy, or signal transfer between related elements. The student is not only able to predict the result of several forces converging, but is also able to name and describe the action of those forces.

Let's look at the process of volcanic rock formation as an example. This description draws upon a geology text by John Shelton entitled *Geology Illustrated* (Freeman, 1966) for its factual content.

There are several types of volcanic rock: obsidian, a whole family of lavas, ash, welded tuff, basalt, biotite, granite, and others. These types do not resemble each other very much, and that is due to the process by which they are made—with the resolution of the forces that form them.

The source of volcanic rock is molten magma, or melted, rock. Heat in excess of a thousand degrees liquefies rocks within the interior of the earth. The molten rock contains water vapor and several mineral components, many of which are in the form of ions which are free to move about in the liquid medium of the melt. This chemical brew is often under great pressure, and when it finds an exit route, it streams through the opening just as thick water would. If the opening vents all the way to the earth's surface and out into the atmosphere, then the melted rock is ejected into the air, where it cools rapidly under conditions of lowered pressure. This results in a rock which solidifies just as the compressed water vapor and other gasses are boiling to the surface, and the resulting rock is either lava or ash, both of which are pocked all over with holes called vesicles. Which of the two rock types is formed is determined by the speed of cooling and the speed of depressurization. In ash, the vesicles grow into large, glass-like structures before shattering into a powdery form. In lava, the vesicles boil out more slowly, without disturbing the integrity of the rock.

If molten rock remains confined, it remains under pressure. The type of rock formed from the cooling of this molten mass depends to a great extent on the rate of cooling. A rapid quenching of the heat will result in a clear, dark, glass-like rock called obsidian. The glass contains embedded crystals, but they are so small that they cannot be seen with the naked eye, and their main effect is to impart a dark color to the otherwise mostly clear rock.

If the confined mass of hot magma cools more slowly, then the rock remains molten for a long period of time—perhaps thousands of years. Within this liquid environment, the chemical substances in ionic form are free to move about. As they encounter compatible ions, they form crystalline structures which continue to grow as long as the rock remains liquid. The longer the rock is liquid, the larger the crystals grow, until at some point, the ions are no longer able to move about. At that point, the rock solidifies as a glass matrix with embedded crystals. The differences between volcanic rocks formed underground is in the size of the crystals embedded within the glass of the rock. If the crystals grow very large and it is hard to see the glass component of the rock at all, then we call the rock granite. If the crystals remain small and the glass is more visible (normally under a microscope) then we call the rock basalt or biotite. In welded tuff, the crystals are large and the spaces between them are filled with much glass. If the rock is ash, then the glass portion shatters away from the crystals, leaving only small chunks of lava (which we call ash) and an underlying layer of glass splinters which is covered by the ash and therefore not normally seen.

This little bit of geology instruction illustrates how forces acting on natural elements in varying balances produce different results. The process of magma solidification described here is one with a number of possible outcomes. A student can learn to *predict* the type of rock (that is, specific rock characteristics) that will result from a particular balance of forces. The student may also be asked to *explain* the blend of forces and the process that produced a specific rock. This is process-using behavior.

The learning of processes

Learning a processes involves learning: (1) a central event structure, and (2) the generative rationale for each event occurrence.

Event structure: Process learning requires the formation of a central event structure for the process. If students have never experienced a process like the one they are learning, they must learn a new event structure. If an event structure similar to the process they are learning already exists, the learning of the new event structure can be accomplished by copying it and modifying its details.

For this reason, we sometimes explain the process of the heart's pumping action by copying or borrowing the existing process structure of the water pump or the bicycle pump and drawing parallels. Interestingly, as we encounter students who have never seen, used, or repaired pumps, this borrowed structure itself has to be taught first, before it can be used to teach about the heart.

An event structure consists of a number of observable states and the paths between them. States represent events—observable outcomes. The paths between the states represent the balance of forces acting upon states that promote or cause conversion to a new state. Event structure information can be represented in many ways. One way is a state-transition diagram like the one in Figure 1. This is a simplified version of the event structure which might be appropriate for middle school or early high school instruction. Clearly this information as diagrammed does not represent "truth" as far as the subject of magma cooling is concerned, but it does represent the level of content useful for a targeted level of instruction.

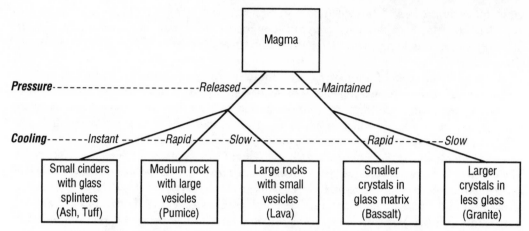

Figure 1. State-transition diagram form of process event structure.

Instead of two states of two input factors (pressure and cooling time), this diagram could as easily have accounted for more (such as several gradations of pressure and cooling time), producing twenty, one hundred, or one thousand outcome states—events, or types of rock, in this case. Sometimes this state-transition information can be represented in a table, as shown in Figure 2.

A more precise and complete version of the event structure—usable for advanced instruction—might take the form of data tables, or a family of graphs from which a continuous range of event outcomes could be determined. Figure 3 shows a graph for determining the size of crystals, given cooling time and cooling pressure conditions. This same type of graph could be built for determining the number of vesicles, the size of vesicles, and the glass-crystal ratio from the same two conditions. Given this family of graphs and a volcanic rock scenario, the student could predict the nature of rocks formed at various places, such as deep underground or at the mouth of the volcano.

	Very rapid cooling	**Relatively rapid cooling**	**Relatively slow cooling**
Pressure Released	Small cinders with glass splinders (Ash, Tuff)	Medium rocks with larger vesicles (Pumice)	Large rocks with smaller vesicles (Lava)
Pressure Maintained	Obsidian	Smaller crystals in glass matrix (Basalt, Biotite)	Larger crystals in less glass (Granite)

Figure 2. Tabular representation of state-transition information.

Generative rationale: In addition to identifying the possible states or events, process learning requires identification of the rationale or cause behind the movement from state to state. This consists of: (1) the name(s) and values of the trigger force(s) for the state change, and (2) a description of the mechanism behind the change.

The line labels in the Figure 1 diagram and the row and column headings in Figure 2 name the trigger forces for the magma example—temperature and pressure. The forces are also evident in the graph in Figure 3 in the form of dimension labels. However, none of the figures describes the mechanism behind the state change. For this, instructors most often appeal to

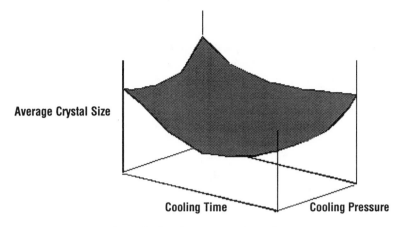

Figure 3. Graph representation of process event structure.

principles or mechanical explanations. For instance, larger size and greater number of vesicles (the holes) in volcanic rock is related to more rapid depressurization and more rapid cooling. The familiar mechanism that explains this is *boiling*. Consider very hot water under pressure and the rapid release of that pressure. What happens to the water when pressure is released? It boils vigorously, sometimes turning to steam. The same kind of thing happens when the pressure is released from a carbonated drink. The gasses boil out of the liquid vigorously (and all over your hands). As the pressure on liquid rock is released, it too *boils*, as the gasses and water vapor trapped inside by the pressure escapes, and as the boiling rock-liquid cools rapidly, the rock solidifies, capturing the shape of the boiling liquid in a solid form. Boiling, then, is the mechanism that explains the vesicle structure of volcanic rocks. Other mechanisms (ion migration and crystal formation) explain its crystalline structure and the size of the crystals formed. It is not surprising that these mechanisms are often themselves processes.

Processes occur in two ways. Either one element of a process transfers energy or signal to a second, modifying the properties of the second, or a force operates upon one element and its own properties change. The former case is represented by a bat hitting a ball: the bat contacts the ball, transfers energy to the ball, and therefore a process takes place. The latter case is represented by the melting of a solid into a liquid: Heat applied to a solid excites the atoms or molecules of the solid, and eventually the movement of the atoms is such that they can no longer remain in their orderly arrangement within the solid. As they leave their former positions, the substance melts. In either case, describing a process is like telling a story.

The nature of the explaining mechanisms used during process-using instruction is of great interest and import, because there are several types of explanation, and they vary in their ability to afford the student predictive power. If a student is instructed using low-power mechanisms, then the knowledge itself will not be as useful as if a mechanism with greater amplification value were used. Below is a list of several types of explanatory mechanism. Many of these were suggested by the work of Othanel Smith, an early pioneer in the structural strategy approach.

Mechanical. This explanation form describes an outcome in terms of the physical operation of process elements on each other. When parts of a reciprocating engine strike one another, one of them must move. This is the mechanism that delivers force to the wheels and makes them turn. When the wheels don't turn, it is often because one of the links in this physical-mechanistic chain of cause and effect is broken.

The elements mechanically interacting in a process may be things human eyes have never seen but which we still presume to have physical reality in some sense. The interplay of atoms and molecules during chemical reactions is often described using a mechanical explanation. We speak of atoms of one type "replacing" atoms of another in a bond during a reaction, and we speak of the effects of heat on a substance by explaining how its atoms begin to vibrate more rapidly, bumping into each other more frequently.

Force. We often describe the influence of process elements on each other in terms of invisible, amorphous forces. We have difficulty representing energy in any of its forms: heat, sound, waves of any kind. But frequently it is these forces which transfer energy from one element to another during a process. Gravity pulls on objects and they fall; heat causes objects to change color. Wind strikes the windmill blade and causes turning.

Sequent. These are explanations in terms of more detailed processes (or sequences, hence the term *sequent*). This is illustrated by the explanation of crystal growth (itself a process at the eyeball level) in terms of molecules taking their place in an orderly and crystal-shaped structure at the unseen level.

For processes which involve the interaction of abstractions, we sometimes give sequent explanations in single-word terms, and in order for a student to understand the explanation, he or she must find and invoke the processes associated with those terms within his or her own existing knowledge. Historical explanations are often of this sort. We explain peasant uprisings in terms of feelings of resentment brought about by oppressive actions of the king. If we use the single-phrase term "oppressive actions" as a shorthand explanatory mechanism, and if the student does not have past learning of this schema, or has not observed the influence of oppressive actions in the affairs of humans, then this process cause and its importance will not be understood by the student. As instructors, we are often oblivious to the vast array of process memories that we call up in the student's mind through the use of single words or phrases. This type of explanation, frequently but unwisely used, and without auxiliary student supports, probably accounts for a lot of student failure to understand.

Procedural. This type of explanation accounts for an outcome in terms of transformations that result from the application of a procedure. Mathematical explanations are often of this type. The x-term disappears from the left side of the equation because of subtraction from both sides, which is at the same time the name of a procedure, but also (observed as if by a third person) a process. Procedural explanation is often used to describe to a student why the electrical motor he or she built does not work, while the instructor's did.

Teleological. In a teleological explanation, the propagation of force, energy, or signal from element to element in the process is due to goals, values, wills, plans, or presumed destinies. Historical and psychological explanations are often couched in teleological terms. Much of the explanation in this book uses teleological explanation, including especially the discussion of goal types during instruction in Chapter 8. We also use teleological explanation sometimes in scientific explanations, and they do the student little good. When asked why the butterfly comes from the cocoon, if we answer "Because that is the next stage of the butterfly's life cycle," we have used teleological explanation, but we have given the student little new knowledge and no amplification power at all.

Normative. A normative explanation for the cause-effect relationship in a step appeals to an accepted standard, law, or rule as the reason or force behind a state-transition. The conjugation of verbs in a foreign language is a process when observed in the abstract, and a student asking why a verb was conjugated in a particular way would receive an explanation for each step of the transformation of the verb in terms of a rule for conjugation, applied to the root verb and taking into account the issues of agreement, number, tense, mode, and other verb-ish dimensions.

Principle. Principles are used as the explaining mechanisms for process events (see Chapter 14). If we observe a drop in the current of an electrical circuit that attends an increase in the voltage, the process which has occurred may be explained in terms of Ohm's Law, which is the principle relating voltage, current, and resistance within circuits.

Using these explanatory mechanisms (which are themselves process descriptions) is what creates the *generative rationale* for the event. It is also an important factor in distinguishing process-using behavior from memory behavior. A student does not have to recall from memory the explanation for a process event. He or she need only recall the principle or mechanism involved, and from it generate the remainder of the detail of the rationale. The full explanation given by the student is generated, not memorized.

Explanations are couched in terms of processes. As we attempt to describe why something happened, we are often supplying an answer in smaller and smaller terms. A curious student (or scientist) can ask after every explanation, "Yes, but why is that?" This exposes the designer to the problem of *infinite regress*, which means that there is no end to the more detailed explanations possible. Nuclear physicists, in their quest to explain the nature of matter, are encountering this problem. As soon as they discover the mechanisms operating at one level of detail, they immediately discover that there are mechanisms within the mechanism. Where this will lead, no one can imagine. It is, however, interesting to note that despite our society's huge technological base, we are still unable to provide fundamental explanations for electricity, for magnetism, for light, or for gravity, all of which lie at the foundation of our technologies. Eventually, the only rationale we can supply our students is, "Because that's the way it works!" There has always been a limit on our ability to explain.

Process-using instructional strategy

The computer allows the student to become involved in process-using instruction as no other medium can. Figure 4 provides a diagrammatic outline of the stages in process-using instructional strategy. The sections which follow suggest guidelines for implementing this strategy.

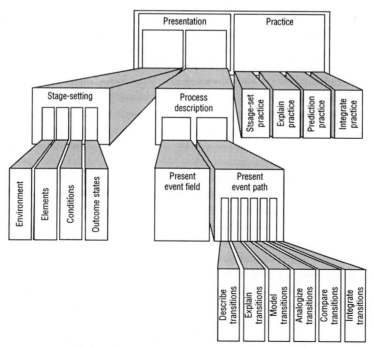

Figure 4. Process-using instructional strategy.

As with other strategies, the process-using strategy is divided into Presentation and Practice portions. Also as with the other strategies, the events of the strategy are not fixed in their order; consider them functions to be carried out in either the student's or the instructor's chosen order. The strategy as a whole appears more complicated than the other strategies in this book. This is perhaps because there is more information exchange involved in a process strategy and because there is a type of integration connected with process learning that is not present in the other strategies until a later stage of instruction. This integrative function first instructs the influence of single forces and secondly combinations of forces on the outcomes of processes. We sometimes study the effects of cooling on lava formation and then study the effects of lowering pressure on lava formation. Then we study the combined effects of both cooling and lowering pressure.

Stage-setting

The nature of process instruction requires—perhaps more than other forms of instruction—much stage-setting. The instructional message must convey information not only about the process, but also about the forces motivating the process, the natural elements upon which the forces act, and the many relationships between the elements themselves. The stage-setting phase of the instructional strategy supplies this prelude to the actual description of the process.

Perhaps the stage metaphor is a good one for process instruction, because learning about processes often places the student in the position of a beholder, and much of process learning comes simply from observation and self-initiated exploration. The image which we wish to convey about process instruction is that the student is sent on a voyage into the process environment. He or she is taken into a natural or human-made world as a spectator—one able to move and look around the world in order to observe close-up and in detail what happens. The student is also given controls over this world which make time and space plastic and allow events to re-occur at will. The stage-setting phase of process instruction is the first act on this stage, and during it the actors introduce themselves, assemble themselves for the drama, and tell how they are related to each other. These introductions can involve a great deal of extremely important information, but they also greatly simplify the description of the process itself. The subdivisions of stage-setting are described in the sections which follow.

Environment description

Process instruction must describe the stage upon which the process is enacted. It may be a space as large as space itself (for instruction on star birth) or as small as the interior of a cell or a molecule. The designer must supply information to describe the extent of this stage. That extent is in some degree decided by the designer; it is not an absolute. In process instruction, what to describe of the environment depends on the assumptions the designer is willing to make about the student's prior knowledge of the environment. For instance, if the process to be instructed includes the operations of a computer's hard disk drive, the amount of description necessary may range from a complete description of the structure and components of the disk drive for novice students to mere mention of the name of the schema-connected environment—hard disk—for experts. Novices have no knowledge base for the hard disk, so the dimensions of the stage must be deliberately and carefully drawn for them. Experts are expected to have a robust and perhaps detailed model of the disk drive in mind, so the only environment description needed is a description of the exceptions to that commonly-held model.

This difference in the requirements for environment description for novices and experts is the key to an important principle for all of process instruction. Process instruction, more than any other type of instruction, is prone to great compression. For process instruction, the instructional message can sometimes be compressed into a few words if the audience for the instruction is experienced and already has a great deal of knowledge in the content. For novices, the explanations must be detailed and explicit—sometimes painfully so—up to a point. But even novices at some point during instruction begin to accelerate their learning speed in process instruction. The rate of new information intake increases dramatically, and understanding crystallizes suddenly. This characteristic of process learning poses difficult challenges to designers of process instruction. It requires them to design the instructional message: (1) so that it is influenced by student control, so that the level of information is appropriate to the speed of the learning, and (2) so that the message is available at several levels of explanation, each correlated with the types of knowledge structures possessed by the student working at that level. We are speaking here of an ideal case, and not one that is standard practice among designers. Our point is, however, that the computer makes this adjustment of the strategy to the student possible if the designer can systematically identify the levels of explanation and the paces of explanation that are appropriate to the target audience.

The designer often artificially delimits the scope of the environment for process instruction. In order to describe the processes for reading from and writing to a hard disk drive, the designer may choose only the platter-actuator arm-head portion of the hard drive for the described environment and ignore the rest of the hard drive and its controlling software. Alternatively, the designer may choose to review the entire drive and the disk operating system. Once again, this decision is related to the level of prior knowledge assumed in the learner. When the environment is limited, it is sometimes necessary to treat outside forces which contribute force, energy, or signal to the process as unnamed ghost elements of the process. This constitutes a kind of *deus ex machina* approach to instruction, but it frees the instruction of a lot of otherwise necessary stage-setting.

This is exemplified by the designer who decides not to describe the involvement of software in disk processes, but must somehow describe how data arrives at the head to be saved and how the actuator arm positions the heads over the platters. This is normally done by simply omitting mention of the source of the data and the control signal, but that constitutes limiting the environment. This limitation influences the student's ability to maintain orientation within the environment. It also has implications for the limits of practice and testing. Only if the instructor can safely assume that students have prior knowledge of the environment beyond that explicitly provided in the instruction can any of it be assumed during practice and testing. Instruction which omits mention of the disk software cannot fairly require that knowledge to be supplied by the student unless the student has already demonstrated accountability for it earlier.

Though establishing the environment sounds complicated, involved, and intimidating, it can be simple. The principle of compression already described suggests that the designer can prepare multiple versions of the message to allow students to receive instruction at a pace and level of detail comfortable for them.

The designer must exercise care in deciding what is and is not included within the scope of the process description. Natural and human-made systems both connect with a larger world in what one philosopher described as a "seamless" way. To describe a hard disk function, it is possible to invoke the environment of the entire computer, including the power supply. The designer must make decisions concerning where to tear this seamless fabric of system and process knowledge, but should do so with care for the needs of the student for orientation, and the decision should support the student's need to later integrate process knowledge into larger wholes. Therefore, there is likely to be need for overlapping environment definitions, reviews, and even exploration of connected environments not directly related to the immediate process.

Element identification

A description of the actors—the natural elements or parts which take part in the process—and their assembly on the stage constitutes a second major stage-setting task for the designer. In the disk drive example already referred to, the actors are the disk platters, the read/write heads, the actuator arm, and other connected parts as far back as the designer has chosen to include within the environment. Once this suite has been defined and outlined for the student to see (or experience), then information about each one's individual characteristics and its relationships with others must be made available. This aspect of process instruction is often shortened considerably, and the student's needs for information are sometimes greatly underestimated, leading to poor performance.

Consider an individual learning through direct experience about the structure and process of a clock. That learning takes place as the self-directed student disassembles the clock. Does the student simply tear the mechanism apart as rapidly as possible? Or is there some method and order to the exploration that occurs during this learning? What does the student learn by taking the clock apart? Here are some knowledge items of element identification which have implications for designers.

Names. The student may feel inclined to ask an expert—if one is present—the name of each part, as a means of cataloging future items of information about it.

Numbers and similarities. The student may take inventory to see how many of each part is present in the environment. One gear? Three? Are they the same or different? Are they interchangeable? The student will try to determine the number of elements. If there is more than one of a part, the student may try to draw inferences about their arrangement and the commonality or synchronization of their function.

Physical appearance. The student not only observes the appearance of the part but may question why it is shaped as it is. The student may feel inclined to ask the relationship between the form of the part and its function.

Location in the environment/relation to other parts/fit. The student may hold the part close to the point where it was taken from the clock, even holding it in same orientation it had while still in the mechanism, to study its fit with the general structure and with other parts. The student will look for contact points, holding points, stress points, points where force might be applied, and points where the part might apply force to other parts. When part interfaces are detected, the student might look especially closely at the point of contact for clues as to how wearing or stressful the contact is. The student may look for clues as to how force or signal is transferred across the part-to-part interface. The student may hold two parts close together independent of the framework of the whole mechanism, moving them with respect to each other to see how they alone might behave with respect to each other.

Analogues and comparisons. Elements of other, familiar, process may be analogized to the present element. The student may say, "This looks just like a...," or "This seems to do the same as...."

Sensations. The student may turn the part over in the hand, sensing its characteristics, boundaries, and qualities. The student may smell it, or even subject it to destructive testing to find out more about it—biting it, bending it, scratching it, dropping it, tapping it. This experience provides the student with information on the properties of the part which may be important in understanding part operation or behavior.

Action and range of action. The student may study the type and range of motion, action, or the sphere of influence of a part. How far does this arm extend? What stops its forward motion? How far does it retract? What causes it to retract? The student may be interested in terminology which refers to actions or motions.

Though all of these items of knowledge are relevant to the process, they alone do not disclose the process; they are only bits of information that are part of the process knowledge that ultimately becomes organized around the central core of the process description. Very often the presentation of some of these items takes place during the description of the process itself, to avoid the student's having to hold a body of unconnected information in memory. This information may be supplied verbally, but in many cases it can be conveyed more readily through direct experience, insofar as that can be supplied to the student.

Conditions

Conditions include all of the environmental forces, energies, and signals which bring about state changes—that is, they are the forces which cause events. In the lava example described earlier in this chapter, the conditions involved in event creation were pressure and rate of cooling. Between them, they accounted for all of the variations in the events (or *outcomes* or *states*) of the process, the various varieties of volcanic rock. Every process has a set of conditions which vary. A condition may be a force or signal which is applied to the environment and its contents, bringing about a change, or it may be simply a change in the value of an already-applied force or signal which triggers the transition from one state to a new one.

A condition can be expressed in one of three ways: binary, qualitative, or quantitative. Binary treatment of a condition means that it will be treated either as present or not present. Either the wind is blowing on the windmill, or it is not. Qualitative treatment of a condition means that it will be treated at two or more levels of value. The wind is at low, medium, or high velocity. There may be several qualitative gradations, and they need not be arranged along a scale of magnitude. The temperature may be falling, rising, or steady. These are non-scaled qualitative expressions of a triggering condition. Finally, quantitative treatment of a condition means that an exact value is attached to the condition (for example, pressure=35 millibars) and that changes in the value are linked to changes of state, or events.

Students of processes need to know: (1) all of the conditions that can precipitate (now there's a process word!) a change of state, and (2) the range of values those conditions can take on. They also need to know conditions (forces) present in the environment which do not influence events. This is necessary because many confusions occur as we witness processes and then assign incorrect causal conditions. For instance, a doctor may assign the cause of our headaches to noise until we leave the noisy environment and find that we still get the headaches. By pointing out factors which do not influence the path of events, we help the student avoid this kind of incorrect assignment of cause during instruction.

During the description of the process, which normally follows stage-setting, the student will observe the value of conditions and try to link condition values to outcomes. This implies that the values of conditions must be visible to the student during instruction. During stage-setting is an ideal time to create a standard informational format for reading momentary condition values. This format can continue into the process description as a familiar landmark and information source. Since students may be able to control or give values to these conditions in later stages of instruction, it is also useful to present the controls to the student during stage-setting and demonstrate their use so that the learning of controls does not compete for attention later during exploration of the process itself.

Outcome states

In many cases, there is benefit for the student in knowing in advance the outcome states, or events, that are within the event field of the process. What kinds of volcanic rock are going to be identified as outcomes of the volcanic process? Instruction which provides this information in a pre-familiarization sequence can refer to the outcomes as known quantities later, rather than as more facts to be learned at a time of already heavy information processing when the process itself is being learned.

One possible use of this pre-familiarization is to involve the student in observational interactions in significant ways. To familiarize the student with the range of volcanic rocks, and instead of just presenting the information, the student might be asked to study carefully several rock samples (grossly represented as well as microscopically), noting their characteristics on an evaluation form (supplied on-line) and comparing them rather than just evaluating each separately. ("Which of these two rock samples seems to have larger embedded crystals?") This approach increases interactivity and involvement of the student, improves the quality of student observations and focuses attention, and can be used as a stimulus to interest, especially if a few well-placed hypothetical questions are asked during the inspection-evaluation. ("What kind of force could have caused this solid-glass obsidian rock to form?")

Process description

Process description consists of: (1) presenting the event field in schematic form as an organizing tool for the student, and (2) describing the individual paths within that field separately.

Present event field

The event field for a process consists the complete range of states (events, outcomes) which the process can produce. An example of a very simple event field is shown in Figure 1 of this chapter. Figure 3 is also a representation of an event field, as is Figure 2, but in a form more difficult to recognize as a family of paths related to one process. Some event fields are best represented as cycles, because they take place as cycles in nature. Life cycles are a good example, as are chemical cycles in human metabolism, such as the continuous ADP-ATP cycle that is basic to human energy use in the muscle.

The purpose for showing the student the entire event field is that it supplies a map of the process which allows the student to organize the large amount of detailed information which process instruction provides access to. The event field can either be presented to the student in advance and then used as a guide or table of contents (or menu), or else it can be built step by step during the presentation of the event paths.

Present event paths

The field of events for volcanic rock creation (Figure 1) channeled the magma (the element acted upon by the process) down five paths. Each of these paths was described individually in the text that narrated the figure. This is the process of presenting the event paths. However, for process-using instruction to be complete, there must be more attention to presenting each path than was given in that short section of text. One of the shortcomings of most process instruction is that it presents only one event path and does so in a way that requires the steps of the process to be memorized. Moreover, as was the case in the presentation that we gave, the information is often delivered in textual, paragraph form. Did you notice the value of the diagram in organizing your interpretation of the text? There is a lesson in that observation regarding the use of non-verbal messages in process instruction. Another shortcoming of the verbal presentation of process description information is that the individual condition influences are seldom integrated at a later time to present a more accurate view of the larger scale of the process to the student and to give an idea of the interrelatedness of systemic processes. The sections which follow give some suggestions for presenting event paths.

Describe transitions

A transition is a change from state to state. In the volcanic rock example, the change was from magma into a variety of volcanic rocks: the specific end-state being determined by the conditions of pressure and rate of cooling. One combination of conditions sent the magma down one event path; different conditions sent it down another. In Figure 1, only one level of transition was shown in the event path, but in some processes, such as the life cycle of the jellyfish Aurelia or the infection cycle for bacterial plague, there are junctures in the event path at multiple levels. This can create an event path with several levels of branching, each of them responding to different condition values, and each leading to a different event destination. For the purposes of instruction, each transition from one state to another should be treated as a single event path, even in multi-juncture event fields. In a different stage in this instructional strategy, the manner of integrating these with each other is provided. To describe a transition from one state to another, the designer must first name it as an event for the student. This is as simple as noticing and emphasizing its occurrence either visually or verbally.

Explain transitions

Having marked that an event has occurred, the designer should explain why it occurred. This includes describing the initial state of the element acted upon, the initial values of the conditions acting upon it, the principle or process explaining the change, and the resulting state. This is the designer's explanation of why the transition occurred, and several types of explanation available to the designer were listed earlier in this chapter. The information provided at this point of the instruction forms the basis of the student's ability to reason about the process. In order to heighten the information's value to the student, it may be combined with the modeling described in the next section.

Model transitions

The designer should provide information and visualization resources for the student which show the details of the transition as it occurs. This may include time expansion or contraction as well as magnification or compression of visual scale to provide the modeling in an appropriate time and space frame. Normally, visual modeling involves some form of animation, slide progression, or live graphic modeling. This stage of process instruction not only has great impact on the student's ability to understand the process, but it can be one of the most appealing, interesting, and involving parts of the instruction as well.

Transition modeling information can be provided in an interactive form. The student can be given controls that allow the transition to be played, replayed, viewed from different angles, looked at in greater detail, or the student can be given the ability to ask questions about what is happening. In some cases, the use of a simulation is more efficient than a frame-based approach and can give the student a better quality, more varied experience. For instance, in the model-centered instructional metaphor described in this book (see Chapter 16), the student is given an actual model of the system within which the process occurs, and is given the ability to operate the model and ask it questions. This includes the ability to experiment with the model by setting different condition values, levels, or trends and then asking the process to occur using those values. The model can also be made auto-verbose, which means that it can describe what is happening each time the process occurs.

The possibilities at this point in the process-using strategy are immense, and the computer is the medium of choice for process instruction because of its multimedia capabilities and the ability (in the near future, we hope) to generate computer-produced, 3-dimensional, modeled graphics according to formula on the personal computer. This would mean that the molecules through which the student was touring during the process description for a chemical reaction would be a representation of the reaction the student had requested, generated at the time of instruction and not canned or pre-composed in graphic form. Of course, this kind of graphic representation is limited to physical (and some conceptual) processes that lend themselves well to generated graphics and are not much use to a student learning the processes of history. However, even for historical processes, models have been constructed that allow the student to raise and lower taxes and then observe their result on public attitude. To some degree, this feature has been implemented in commercial gaming simulations.

Analogize transitions

Concurrent with the explanation and modeling functions just described, the designer might provide reference to analogous processes or transitions. The boiling metaphor, which is very useful to understanding the formation of the bubble structures in lava, is an example of an analogous process being called into use. Analogs not only assist the student in recall, but as described earlier, they can act as a generative force, allowing the student to attach a large amount of explanatory structure to a small memory item.

Compare transitions

Also concurrent with analogizing transitions, the designer should provide comparisons between transitions. The student should be permitted to see or should be shown side-by-side the results of both individual-condition transitions and combined-condition transitions. For example, students should be given the opportunity to compare microscopic sections of basalt formed under one set of conditions with the same substance formed under slightly different conditions which may vary only in one condition value. There may later be value in showing the student comparisons between outcomes from or in multiple condition values variations as well. The entire field of outcome samples should be made available to the student for inspection. They become the substance for the student to use in performing numerous comparisons and thought experiments—either self-initiated or in response to directions from the instruction. There are many instructional mechanisms for bringing the student into contact with this field of events. The totality of variations in outcome states forms the event field. We have already suggested that the event field be presented to the student. Here we are saying that the careful observation and exploration of the details of the selected pairs or groups of individual outcomes (events) ought also to be part of the instruction related to transitions.

Integrate transitions

As more and more event paths are traced in the manner described in the sections above, patterns and trends of causation begin to become evident. It is useful for the student to be shown or guided to discover these trends, because they also have the effect of compressing much knowledge into a small generative package within memory. There are several possible instructional techniques for integrating transitions. One is to review previous transitions following the presentation of each new transition. Another is to build an outcome comparison table which places the outcomes in some graphic or matrix structure with respect to each other. A summary graph of trends within the table might be shown, and to increase the involvement and discovery for the student, the graph might be constructed step-by-step by the student as he or she learns about or discovers each new transition.

Practice

Two main forms of performance are related to process-using: prediction and explanation. Therefore, both of these represent forms of practice which should be designed. Practice may also be carried out at the single-transition level or at the event field, or integrated, level. It is also beneficial for the student to have opportunity for stage-setting practice.

Stage-setting practice

For stage-setting practice, you can present the student with a system assembly (the environment and all of its contained elements) in a disassembled state and allow him or her to re-assemble them. This can include asking for detailed articulations of parts (concrete or abstract) to be constructed in their appropriate geometries. There may also be asked questions regarding the articulation of parts or the relationships between them. Any of the message elements provided during presentation may be asked for legitimately. Which ones to actually ask for depends on the specific subject-matter and the use the knowledge is to be put to. It may also depend on common errors and misconceptions to which students are prone as they study the particular subject-matter. The point of stage-setting practice is to ensure that the student knows the basic relationships between the elements which participate together in the process.

Prediction practice

Prediction practice supplies to the student an environment, a set of elements in specific states, a set of conditions, and changes in those conditions. It then asks the student to: (1) predict the outcome, and (2) explain the reason for the prediction. Two levels of prediction practice are possible: (1) single transition, and (2) multiple transition. That is, if the event field is multi-level, the student can be asked to predict the outcome of one set of conditions (predicting a one-level outcome), or to predict the outcome of a sequence of condition changes that take place in some order (predicting a multi-level outcome).

Practice must cover the important event transitions and event chains, and a minimum set of them can be specified by the designer using some systematic rule for selection. If practice is at the student's discretion, and if there is adequate time and interest to practice all possible chains, that can be desirable. Feedback following practice may be given immediately, and its content should remind the student of the explanation of processes and principles that was provided during presentation.

Explanation practice

Explanation is the second major variety process practice. It gives to the student some combination of a final event state and beginning element states and conditions and then asks the student to trace the path(s) leading to that given state, supplying the missing forces, explanations, and intermediate states. In instruction on the volcanic rock process, the explanation practice might provide the student with a microscopic section of a rock sample and ask for the story of its origin. That explanation might require a single-transition explanation, or it might require a combination of several transitions to be described. This form of practice is common in multiple choice tests for science, but the computer makes it possible for the student to manipulate graphic or symbolic representations within spatial arrangements to allow the student to express the knowledge that is asked for.

Integration practice

Integrated practice is an important step toward enlarging the scope of a student's understanding and ability to reason within a content area at above the single-event level. Integrated practice includes varying multiple conditions and the tracing of multiple event paths. An inventive designer can see ways to string single-transition prediction items together to form a type of unfolding scenario, taking a beginning condition, a beginning set of forces, and a beginning state of the process system, and following the process all the way through one chain or sequence of event states. Integrated explanation practice involves obtaining from the student explanations of multiple-event chains or explanations where multiple paths may have led to the same final result state.

Process-using objective wording

The wording of process objectives normally includes the words "predict" or "explain," or one of their synonyms.

- Given the condition of a substance being digested within the small intestine, identify the defects in the digestive process which may explain its condition.

- Given a description of a star and the forces operating on it, describe the most likely next stages in the star's life.

- Given a description of the conditions within a muscle, describe what you think will happen the next time a command is received to flex the muscle.

Conclusion

Historically, process instruction has received little direct attention, yet processes are among the most important knowledge we possess and use. By instructing them using the right elements of message and interaction, we can facilitate learning and do so within environments which engage the student in the knowledge-creation process to a greater extent. In these environments, the student will learn by experiencing and experimenting with processes through interactive process models.

Self-directed activities

- Identify the processes described in this book. Compare the manner in which they are presented with the strategy described in this chapter. What rules did we observe? Which ones did we break? How would you rewrite this chapter? How would you teach this chapter using a computer?

- You have discovered processes during your own experience. Recall a process that you have discovered on your own and recount how you discovered it. Pay attention to the types of information that you had to search for and how you conducted the search for it. Target a new process that you do not understand and observe yourself as you learn it.

- Processes are related to other processes, and the ultimate result is very large and comprehensive process structures like the one which we use to predict the rainfall in Kentucky, using the temperature of the ocean's surface off the coast of South America. Describe different ways that processes can be taught when the ultimate goal is understanding of these larger networks of interlinked processes.

- Processes are explained in terms of other processes which take place at a lower level of detail. Consider the effects of explaining a process at one level when the lower level processes are not familiar to the student. Consider the effects when the student understands the lower level processes but does so incorrectly. What is the impact on the understanding of the target processes? What are the implications for the instructional designer?

- Process learning often requires learning processes at more than one level of detail. What kinds of prerequisite learning orders do suppose are most effective? Is it better to learn the lower level process before the higher level process it explains, or vice versa?

- Examine several examples of process instruction. Identify the types of generative rationale used by each. Try to find at least one example of each of the types described in this chapter.

Further reading

Mayer, R. E. (1992). *Thinking, problem solving, and cognition (2nd ed.)*. New York: W. H. Freeman and Company.

Norman, D. A. (1993). *Things that make us smart: Defending human attributes in the age of the machine*. Reading, MA: Addison-Wesley Publishing Company.

Schank, R. C. (1990). *Tell me a story: A new look at real and artificial memory*. New York: Charles Scribner's Sons.

13

CONCEPT-USING INSTRUCTIONAL STRATEGY

Chapter Objectives:

1. *Discriminate concept-using behavior from association and network memory behavior*
2. *Design the presentation strategy for a given concept.*
3. *Define an example/non-example set for a given concept.*
4. *Select and arrange instructional examples from a large example/non-example set according to the rules for matching and divergence.*
5. *Design the example presentation format for a given concept.*
6. *Design the practice strategy for a given concept.*

Concepts

A concept is a class of things. Each of us knows and uses an enormous number of concepts. We use them without even being aware, but the concepts we know allow us to respond to statements like: "the Board of Directors is angry," "the goldfish is sick," and "the pizza is hot."

Board of Directors, angry, goldfish, sick, pizza, and *hot* are all useful concepts, even if they do not mean precisely the same thing to each of us. Either a food item is a pizza or it is not a pizza. Either it is a member of the class of things we call pizza or it is not a member of that class.

The process of making discriminations of class membership is called concept-using behavior, or classification. We classify things constantly, because classification is a prerequisite to making decisions and taking action. For instance, most of us use a principle that goes something like, "If it is a cold day, take an extra sweater." In order for us to use this principle, we first have to be able to classify the day. If it is a *cold day*, we will take a sweater; if it is not a cold day, we will not take a sweater. Once we decide—that is, once we classify the day—the path of action dictated by the principle will be clear.

How do we go about classifying the day? We examine the morning for certain attributes: the attributes for *cold day*. Each of us has our own set of attributes for the concept. Some people look for signs of frost on the grass; others look for ice on the car. Some check for the presence of cold haze against the mountain or test the air for breath vapor. Maybe we even look for two or more of these attributes to be present at the same time. Some people who are more precise and methodical in their definition of *cold day* (like meteorologists) will actually make measurements of attributes such as temperature, humidity, and wind before deciding whether the day is *cold*. Each of us has his or her own set of attributes that we use to classify the day.

This example of concept-using isn't of earth-shaking importance, but the next one is: A geologist trying to determine whether a particular set of data means that a geological fault has been found uses the same process of attribute checking to see if attributes in the data match with the scientist's formal concept definition for *fault*. Science is very much interested in concepts and concept-using behavior. In fact, one of the main activities of scientists is inventing categories, giving the categories names, and then sorting things into them.

There is no shortage of examples of concept-using in real-world applications. Doctors spend much of their time in classification activities.

Is this patient's infection BACTERIAL (or VIRAL)?

Is the growth BENIGN (or MALIGNANT)?

Is the bone BROKEN (or NOT BROKEN)?

242

Lawyers and judges also live by making classifications.

Is this a case of NEGLIGENCE (or NOT)?

Has a FELONY (or a MISDEMEANOR) been committed?

Was this a CRIMINAL ACT (or NOT)?

Is this law CONSTITUTIONAL (or NOT)?

A student can name the class of an object in one of two ways:

1. By remembering having seen an object before

   "I've seen that one. That's a Hymenoptera."

2. By applying a decision rule to determine the class membership of object which has never been known as a class member before:

   "If it has large wings and two body segments, then it must be Hymenoptera."

Only the second example above is true classification behavior, because true classification does not include just supplying memorized answers. Classification means we are able to identify a thing or an event which we have never seen labeled as a class member before. This gives some insight into the relationship between classification and memory behavior. As we classify things, we add to our store of knowledge—our memory. Once we have classified an unencountered thing, we can remember the class it belongs to and do not have to classify it again in the future.

Classification also gives us a way to teach ourselves new knowledge. If we know the definition of a class, we can identify new members of that class, even when we have not seen them before. In this way classification allows us to react appropriately in new situations that we have never before encountered.

Instruction for classification behavior must supply the student with the decision rule for judging class membership, along with a number of examples of that decision rule being applied to make classifications. It must also supply adequate practice in which the student applies the decision rule to a variety of possible class members. Figure 1 illustrates a general strategy for concept-using instruction which provides these elements. Let's describe each stage of the strategy.

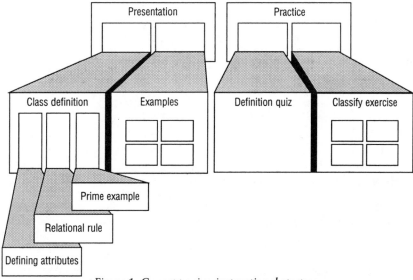

Figure 1. Concept-using instructional strategy.

Presenting the concept definition

The most important thing about a concept is its definition. A definition consists of:

- A list of defining attributes

- A rule that relates them together

For instance, the dictionary, the place where our culture publishes its concept definitions, gives the following defining attributes for the concept class insect:

> *An insect:*
>> *Is an animal*
>> *Is invertebrate (has no backbone)*
>> *Has an adult life stage during which it possesses:*
>>> *Three pairs of legs*
>>> *A segmented body with three divisions*

Other attributes of insects are listed in the dictionary which are not defining attributes. These are attributes which are not used to determine class membership. An animal may have these attributes, but it makes no difference one way or another. Some non-defining attributes for insect are:

> Are numerous
> Are normally small
> Usually possess two pairs of wings
> Sometimes bite you

The rule which relates the defining attributes of insect to each other is a simple one: An object must have all of the class' defining attributes in order to be a member of the class.

Some concept classes have much more complex decision rules and many more defining attributes to relate together. For instance, a biologist's definition of insect no doubt has many more class attributes, which are expressed in more precise and measurable terms.

During concept-using instruction, presenting the concept definition consists of:

- Listing the attributes of the class.

- Stating the rule which relates them.

In addition to this bare minimum of information, most designers accompany the concept definition with a few extra messages intended to ensure that the definition really will hook up with the student's existing knowledge and that the student will remember the definition.

These extras may include:

1. A memory aid for the definition: A memory aid may be useful for certain concepts to help the student recall the defining attributes. This is especially useful:

- When a class definition has a long list of relevant attributes.

- When the rule relating the attributes to each other is unusual or complex.

- When several concepts are being instructed at one time which are very similar and may lead to confusion.

When several concepts are instructed at once and when each one has several defining attributes, the memory burden imposed by remembering the definitions of all of the concepts at once and keeping them from becoming confused with each other is quite large. During such instruction it may seem more like memory behavior that is going on, because of the extra emphasis that must be placed on aiding the memory. For instance, seagoing people must learn to recognize a variety of ship types (classes) from the profile each one casts against the horizon. This is a classification behavior which is both modern and as old as seafaring itself. It is called *ship rigging*. ("It's a man o' war, Captain!" or "It's a Klingon ship, Captain!")

On earth there are many classes of ships, and the differences between the classes are often very subtle, but nonetheless, seagoing people must know the differences and be able to classify ships they have never seen before. But because there are so many classes of ship, and because the classes are so much alike, great attention is given during ship rigging instruction to the memory helps for each class definition.

2. Access to the definitions of the attributes, which are concepts themselves: Students may not be familiar with all of the terms and concepts used in the definition of a class. For instance, it may mean nothing to some students that an insect is an *invertebrate*, because they do not possess the concept *invertebrate*. If a student can't classify a thing as an invertebrate, then that student can't classify whether an animal is an insect either, because *invertebrate* is one of the defining attributes of insect.

A designer must ensure that students possess the concepts that are used as defining attributes for the concepts they intend to instruct. This can be handled in a number of ways, including making provision for remedial instruction within the designer's instructional event, or providing a diagnostic pretest prior to instruction which can identify students who need instruction in one or more defining attribute concepts.

3. A concrete prototypical example: The second stage in the presentation portion of the concept-using instructional strategy (see Figure 1) involves the presentation of a number of examples and non-examples to the student. All of the examples will be class members; all of the non-examples will not. During the presentation of the concept definition, it is appropriate to include one carefully-chosen example as well. This is called the prime example or the *prototypical example*. Providing one can serve several purposes:

1. It supplies an example of each of the attributes named in the definition. This makes the definition much more concrete.

2. It provides a type of mnemonic for the definition. By remembering the example, the student can recall the list of attributes in the definition.

3. It shows the student for the first time the format which will be used for presenting examples and non-examples. Chapter 19 on Display Management will underscore the importance of standard messaging formats for rapid, efficient communication with the student.

4. The manner of presenting the example will demonstrate for the student the step-by-step procedure (the rule) for applying the concept definition to a potential example. For some concepts, this mental process is non-trivial: a procedure which at first must be done quite deliberately but which becomes increasingly automatic with practice.

Presenting examples and non-examples

Part I: Defining the example/non-example set

The bulk of the instructional work in a concept-using strategy is performed by a set of carefully selected and carefully arranged examples and non-examples. These provide the student with a clear contrast between class membership and non-membership. Moreover, because they are arranged in a certain sequence, the examples and non-examples show the contrast in the most efficient way and use less of the student's time and energy.

A designer generates the example/non-example set using the following two rules:

Rule #1: Examples and non-examples are presented in pairs which look as much alike as possible:

That is, (read this part slowly and carefully):

1. The example and the non-example in the pair will have the same non-defining attributes.

2. The example will have all of the defining attributes.

3. The non-example will be missing one or more of the defining attributes.

Put into plain English, an example/non-example pair is selected to look very much alike, but the non-example will be missing one or more of the defining attributes and therefore is not a class member. This provides a contrast between a class member and a non-class member. Example/non-example pairs of this sort are said to be *matched*.

Rule #2: Subsequent example/non-example pairs will diverge as much as possible from each other:

That is:

1. The non-defining attributes used in this pair will differ as much as possible from the ones used in the previous pair.

2. The example will still have all of the defining attributes.

3. The non-example will be missing one or more of the defining attributes, but a different set than earlier non-examples.

In plain English, the example chosen is as different from the prior example as possible, and the non-example matches it as much as possible. The first example and the second example are said to *diverge*. This provides a contrast for the student between the pairs themselves. As the number of pairs presented grows, the student sees an entire spectrum of examples and will see non-examples that match. This seems like a complicated set of rules, but in fact the relationship is quite simple. Figure 2 diagrams it.

Before a designer actually creates any examples, he or she writes a prescription for the entire set of examples and non-examples. This consists of defining what is called a minimum critical subset of examples. The *minimum critical subset* is that set of examples which shows the student all of the major varieties of example which exist within the concept. That means it will cover the entire breadth of examples of the concept class. In addition, the minimum critical subset will show the student all of the major varieties of

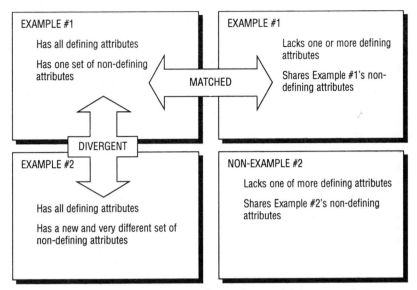

Figure 2. The example/non-example matching and divergence relations.

non-example which are ordinarily mistaken for examples. This is what is normally called a *common error analysis*.

For example, if the concept being instructed is *domesticated dog,* we can conceive a large class of quite different-looking examples: Chihuahua, Saint Bernard, Weimaraner, Scottish terrier, poodle, pit bull. These all have identical defining attributes but differ in their non-defining attributes (shape, size, profile, behavior). We can also conceive another large class of animals that look somewhat like domesticated dogs but lack one or more defining attributes: fox, wolf, coyote, jackal, dingo. These lack at least one defining attribute but share with domestic dogs many non-defining attributes (shape, size, profile, behavior) that make them resemble domestic dogs very closely.

In order to insure that the student has a complete and accurate conception of the class *domestic dog,* the broadest possible variety of examples will be selected that spans the entire range of examples in all defining attributes. Instruction will also show the broad variety of easily mistaken non-examples listed above as well. Both of these considerations taken together will define the minimum critical subset of examples which must be included in the instruction. Defining a minimum critical subset is surprisingly easy. It entails identifying the attributes of each example and non-example pair in a systematic way. Table 1 can serve as a form for performing the following steps:

Step 1: To create the minimum critical subset, you can begin by listing the examples that must be shown in order to present the broadest spectrum of examples. Since every example will possess all of the defining attributes of the class, there is no use in listing those. Instead, you will list the non-defining attributes that each successive example in the sequence will have. That is, you will list for each example the things it will possess that make it different from the previous example. If the first example dog your list is a small one, make the second one on the list a gigantic one. If the first is very hairy, make the second one bald. If the first one has long legs, make the second one squatty. Let your list contain all of the important variations in non-defining attributes of this kind. This will define for you the list of examples to be shown.

Step 2: Next you will pair up every example in your list with a non-example that matches it as closely as possible in non-defining attributes. If your example has long hair, is large, has

Table 1. A process and format for defining example/non-example sets.

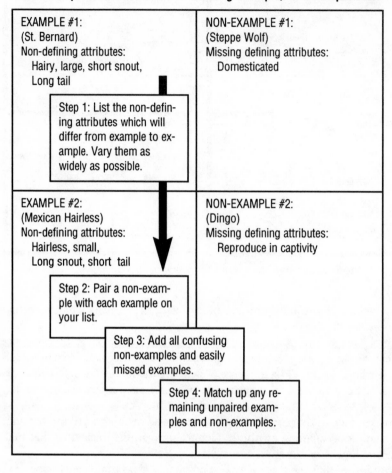

EXAMPLE #1:
(St. Bernard)
Non-defining attributes:
    Hairy, large, short snout,
    Long tail

NON-EXAMPLE #1:
(Steppe Wolf)
Missing defining attributes:
    Domesticated

Step 1: List the non-defining attributes which will
differ from example to example. Vary them as
widely as possible.

EXAMPLE #2:
(Mexican Hairless)
Non-defining attributes:
    Hairless, small,
    Long snout, short tail

NON-EXAMPLE #2:
(Dingo)
Missing defining attributes:
    Reproduce in captivity

Step 2: Pair a non-exam-
ple with each example on
your list.

Step 3: Add all confusing
non-examples and easily
missed examples.

Step 4: Match up any re-
maining unpaired exam-
ples and non-examples.

a short nose and a long tail, try to find a non-example that has the same qualities. Match up all of the examples with a non-example in this way.

Step 3: Now you will complete the list of non-examples you have chosen. This list is not complete if it does not contain every commonly mistaken non-example possible. Ask yourself the question, "What non-examples are most often confused with class members?" You will come up with a list of things that are very much like domesticated dogs but which are not them. Make a list of these and add them to your non-example list. Check the list against the non-examples that you have already chosen and paired up with an example. If the new ones are not already used, add them.

At the same time you are finding all of the confusing non-examples, you will also want to find commonly missed examples as well. Which domestic dogs are most often not recognized as dogs? Add these to your example list. Place them in the list so that they are as different from their neighbors as possible.

Step 4: Finally, you will find pairs for every example and non-example that does not have one. This completes your list of examples and non-examples.

Creating this table is a simple way for the designer to plan an example set with appropriate divergence between pairs and matching within them. Moreover, it does it without cumbersome writing effort. Although the table provides a place for the designer to enter a candidate for the example (a specific example to be used), that is not required, and the table can be filled out strictly on the basis of attributes.

The examples actually included in an instructional set and their number depends not only on this array of attributes but on practical considerations as well. There are practical size limits to an example set, and the designer often is forced to pick certain examples for inclusion which are more important than their peers, while omitting others.

The following practical considerations enter into the selection of the examples actually used in instruction:

1. The size of the instance field: This is another way of saying *the number of possible examples*. If a concept class is very small, there may be very few examples to present. Even if there are thousands of class members, there may be few unique examples, and the necessary size of the example set may be very small, depending on the other factors on this list.

2. The degree of homogeneity in the class: The class insect has a large population and is tremendously varied. The class *cocker spaniel* tends to be much more homogeneous and has less variety (at least, to the non-connoisseur). When a class is highly varied, the number of instances required to show the whole range of those variations is larger than if the class members are quite a bit alike. This is another way of saying that the number of examples is related to the number of non-defining attributes which are likely to be mistaken by the student for defining attributes.

3. Typical misconception patterns: Students learning any classification bring with them certain cultural and educational backgrounds which cause them to form misconceptions in certain predictable patterns. When these patterns are found, they often require the designer to strengthen the example set in a specific area to offset the tendency toward misconception.

4. Difficulty of the concept: Most new concepts are simple to learn because of an experience or set of experiences which has supplied us richly with a sense of the concept, even before we encounter it formally. Other concepts come to us completely unanticipated, new, and abstract, and we have no experiential base to help us comprehend them. This is often the case in the study of law, statistics, and philosophy. We may also question whether it is part of the reason why some students excel in languages. In such cases, the missing experience can be supplied by a large example set.

In current practice, concept-using instruction is typically very short on examples, and few instructional presentations have a set adequate to allow the student to truly master the concept. As a minimum, the example set:

- Should be large enough to span the range of all important non-defining attributes in order to demonstrate the full scope of variation in the concept.

- Should give additional examples concentrated in the areas of typical misconception.

- Should be created in duplicate so that a set of instances is available for practice purposes.

The ultimate judge of example set size is experience. During the development of a set, the designer estimates and makes best judgments on size and composition of the set, but the final test comes during tryouts of the instructional event with typical students. Error patterns clearly define problem areas. The next section shows how to test the adequacy of the example set using a mastery test.

Part II: Tuning the example set

Consider this way of thinking about a concept class: It is a set of things. We could draw a circle to represent the set or the class, like in Figure 3. Everything inside the circle has all of the defining attributes of the class and therefore is a member of the class. Everything outside the circle is not a member of the class because it is missing at least one defining attribute.

Examples are of different types. Some examples are very easy to determine as members of the class. They are easy to classify, and few people make errors when trying to classify them. Other examples may be more difficult to classify, and the error rate may be fairly high. For instance, a large satellite moving at high speed and reflecting the sun brightly is easy to discriminate from the stars at night, but a small satellite moving more slowly and reflecting less sunlight is difficult to tell from any other star. It takes instruction and practice to classify those latter examples.

In Figure 3, the easy-to-identify examples are shown at the center of the concept circle. The hard-to-identify ones are shown near the edge of the circle, as if to suggest that they were almost not examples. In addition to the examples, there are non-examples. Some of them are clearly not examples. A cow, for instance, is not a satellite (even though a cow was once rumored to have jumped over a satellite). However, there are things in the night sky which can be mistaken for a satellite. These are non-examples which are hard-to-identify non-examples. They are shown near the edge of the concept class circle, as if they were almost within the class.

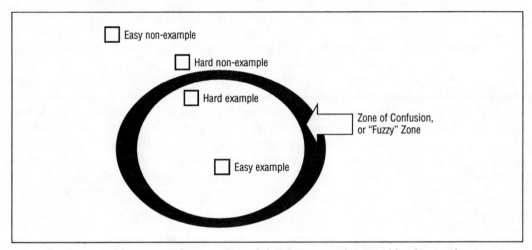

Figure 3. The concept class as a set and the placement of easy and hard examples.

The edge of the concept class circle is not a single, thin line. That is because most classes do not have a clear boundary. There are instances at the edge of every concept class that keep the experts in business arguing whether a particular thing is or is not a member of the class. For instance, in the realm of science, there are things which are clearly alive (humans) and things which are clearly not alive (rocks). There is also a class of objects which scientists have not agreed upon. Some scientists think these things are alive, and others think they are not. Even the experts don't agree.

While designing concept instruction, you may find that the concept you are instructing has a clear boundary (if it is a defined concept), but you will in many cases find that, like the satellite example, there are concept classes which are fuzzy at the edges. In the fuzzy zone, it is not clear whether an instance is a member of the class or a non-member. These instance make good subjects for debates.

Your job as a designer is to help the student establish a concept class boundary and to reduce the fuzzy zone where possible. Since many of the world's concepts are fuzzy, you should expect many of the concepts you instruct to be fuzzy also, but by using the example/non-example approach to instruction, you can reduce the fuzziness considerably. This does not mean that we all end up with exactly the same concept, but it does mean that our concepts overlap enough to give us a better chance at communicating between ourselves, relative to our classes.

You can classify examples and non-examples as being easy or hard to classify through practical experience. Simply expose the examples and non-examples you intend to use to students in the context of instruction and record the errors which are made. As you do this, you obtain data that can be used to tune the example/non-example set. You can give emphasis in instruction to examples which are difficult to classify and non-examples which are easy to include by mistake.

Part III: Presenting the examples

What does an example look like as it is presented to the student? How do examples merge into a instructional event? Some guidelines are provided below.

The first consideration in presenting examples and non-examples is to present them in such a way that all of the defining and the important non-defining attributes are perceivable by the student. This is harder to do than it sounds. For instance, in a given concept-using instructional event, you may decide to use a picture of a dog as an example of the class *mammal*. On the surface, this seems to be a good idea, since we all know that dogs are mammals. However, among the defining attributes of the class *mammal* are: (1) warm-bloodedness, and (2) suckling of young. If the picture of the dog which you show depicts neither of these attributes, a student cannot discern from the display the defining attributes of the class, so he or she cannot tell from the picture alone whether a mammal is being shown. When an example is shown, the defining attributes of the class must be discernible. This may mean that in many cases, still pictures alone will not constitute an adequate representational form for an example. It may take an extensive experience for the student in order to present one example of a subtle class. That experience may last moments or years.

If this problem seems trivial, then consider the situation with yourself as the student and the concept unfamiliar. If you are shown a picture of space and told that a particular spot of light which is slightly brighter than its neighbors is a *red dwarf*, then you too may begin to see that there are characteristics of *red-dwarfness* that you are not able to experience from the drawing.

Probably the largest single error in concept-using strategy, after the error of presenting too few examples, is failing to make attributes of an example sensible. In order to make all of the defining attributes of an example perceivable to the student, there are two things to consider:

- How to make attributes available to the senses.

- How to emphasize them as defining attributes.

Making an example's defining attributes visible requires that the designer look at an example less as a media object and more as an experience or an episode. To be properly presented, most examples require stimulation of multiple senses: the senses that a real example would stimulate with its defining attributes.

If one of the defining attributes of rose is a certain type of fragrance (it's not, but let's suppose), then the student must experience the fragrance with each example. If one of the defining attributes of *Baroque music style* is a certain type of sound, then that sound has to be heard with each example. One set of examples may require communication through several senses.

Once the designer has adopted a form for examples that ensures the defining attributes will all be sensed, he or she should make additional provisions for drawing attention to them. This is done in two ways:

1. Through the use of special emphasis techniques which point out important attributes as they occur.

2. Through adoption of a standard example presentation format.

Special emphasis used to highlight attributes can include anything from graphic techniques, to textual labels, to announcements by a commentator—any form of attention direction which is appropriate to the type of example and the instructional medium.

For examples presented as a static graphic or text, the emphasis may be any of the standard emphasis techniques employed in books, pictures, posters, or other static media. Other examples presented in a moving medium may use any of the visual or verbal emphases commonly seen in video or film presentations. Provision of this kind of emphasis in a concept-using instructional event is called *attribute isolation.* Providing it either automatically or on student request helps the student pick out the defining qualities of an example and the ones missing in a non-example.

In addition to attribute isolation, the designer can invent a standard format for the presentation of examples. This may include arranging examples for sensing in a particular sensing pattern in order to simplify scanning. Every example and non-example in the set would be shown in this same arrangement. The result is that the student is able to reduce the amount of attention spent on scanning each new example and can spend more time attending to the attributes themselves.

Such *layouts or formats* for example presentation normally also include a consistent pattern for displaying the attribute isolation. This also improves the efficiency of information transfer during instruction and can act as a subtle mnemonic, as later the student recalls the framework itself as a help in applying the classification rule.

A second major consideration in presenting examples is deciding on the sequence and timing of their presentation. Up to this point, the discussion has assumed that examples and non-examples would be presented more or less side-by-side in order to facilitate comparisons between them. However, what do you do when one example is an episode three minutes long? Or a whole portfolio of pictures?

Moreover, the assumption has been that the designer controls the sequence in which examples are presented. But what do you do when your instruction implements student control? These issues create questions about the sequence and timing of examples.

As was said earlier, the benefits of matching and diverging appear to come from the contrast they provide for the student. If this is so, then examples should be presented in such a way that the contrasts are most visible, even when the shape and size of examples prevents them from fitting nicely on one page or one screen.

If examples cannot be made to fit on the screen simultaneously, then they can be made to follow one another, and in many cases, split screen techniques can be used to show examples in an apparent side-by-side fashion—the residue of one example remaining on the screen while the non-example is shown on the other half of the screen. With such an arrangement, we can even envision multiple replays of example/non-example pairs in this side-by-side format.

Moreover, when student-directed instruction is administered, it can be done in such a way that the student is required to examine an entire set of example pairs before proceeding—in any order the student chooses. In this case, you as the designer lose control over the divergence of the set, but maintain adequate coverage of its range.

A third major consideration in presenting examples is the degree of foregrounding given to the example itself to set it off from the surrounding context of the instructional event. This consideration is somewhat like selecting the setting for a jewel. Research and experience both show that examples—and other components of instructional strategy for that matter—are more effective when they are set off somehow from the surrounding terrain of the instruction. This technique is discussed at some length in Chapter 19 on Display Management.

At this point, it is worth saying that the instruction should also somehow signal to the student that an example is being presented. This signal can consist of any number of verbal or graphic roadsigns which the student can come to recognize.

A fourth and last major consideration in presenting examples has to do with the look and feel of the instruction to the student. The approach to this strategy is very analytic. We have discussed not only the use of examples, but also the manner in which the examples should be selected and ordered. That's a lot of structure.

Does that mean that the instruction has to look like it has a lot of structure? And does the structure have to be the most obvious thing about the instruction to the student? Of course, the answer is "no." A famous novelist whose writing was considered to be free-flowing and almost lyrical once described his painstaking structural planning of each twist and turn of the plot and described the reams of paper that it took to plan one novel.

No one would have guessed from the surface of the novel that this amount of planning had gone into that author's work. The structure was there, but it was hidden under surface features. In the same way, the South American jungles look lushly green and mostly flat. It is difficult to imagine under the bumps which mark the surface of the land the ancient ruins which hide within those bumps. Not until an archaeologist cuts away the forest and scrapes away the sediment do we see the intricate and detailed design of the temples and living places of the ancients.

Your concept instruction (and all of your instruction for that matter) can have this same quality. If you use technical and analytical methods during the design of the instructional event, it does not have to be apparent to the user. Take some time to consider ways in which you can make the instruction natural and easy to follow on the surface as your design supplies structure and substance to the student.

Concept-using practice

There are two stages of concept-using practice: (1) practice of memory for the definition, and (2) practice in classification of instances. The practice of definition memory is strictly memory instruction, and the techniques for those interactions are described in Chapter 10. Practice for classification is described in this section.

During concept-using practice, students are given examples and non-examples which they have not seen before and are asked either to affirm or to supply the name of the class. An inventive mind will think of several ways to present this concept-using question. The critical feature of concept-using practice is that the student be asked to make a discrimination. Moreover, it must be made on an example which the student has not seen labeled as an example before. Otherwise, the student could be responding from memory, rather than applying the concept definition to determine class membership. This means you will create at least two sets of examples and non-examples: one for presentation, and one for practice. Some developers create even more than two, for the purposes of remedial instruction and for additional practice requested by the student.

The size of a set of practice items depends on the size of the example set. You can see that during practice, you must present examples and non-examples from the entire range of the concept class to insure that the student's application of the definition is correct across the entire breadth of the class. In this respect, the table of examples and non-examples you just created is your guide.

Concept varieties

A concept class may vary in many dimensions, and these variations have instructional implications. Consider the following dimensions of difference:

Size: Some concept classes have a gigantic number of members. The biological class *insect*, for instance, includes thousands of varieties. Moreover, it is an open class which is still growing. Other classes are comparatively small, like *Moons of the Earth*, a class of one (and not likely to grow). The small class *Moons of Uranus*, on the other hand, has recently grown slightly. The implication of class size is that a small class is almost always instructed as a memory objective. If there are only a few members of a class, then memory instruction can cover them all.

On the other hand, instruction on large classes (for instance, Hymenoptera) must recognize that all members of the class will never be seen by the student. In such cases, instruction has to train the student's ability to recognize previously unencountered members of the class. During instruction of this sort, the student experiences a broad range of examples, spanning all of the variations in class attributes.

Number of defining attributes: Some concept classes have many defining attributes. Others have only one, like the class endangered species. As you have already seen, the number of attributes of a class affects the number of examples and non-examples a student must see during instruction.

Relationship of defining attributes: Most concepts have a fairly simple definition. It usually takes the form "If the object has (attribute A) and (attribute B) and (attribute C), then it is a member of the class." The important words in this definition are the *ands*. They signal that all attributes must be present to make a class member.

Some concepts, however, particularly in the area of Law or Taxes, have definitions which relate the attributes together in a more complex way, like this:

> *If a recipient is a minor or an adult with a limited self-supporting capacity, and who depended on the decedent for the majority of his or her income, and if there is an account in the name of the decedent, and if there is no outstanding governmental claim against the account, then the recipient is a dependent and may receive payments from the account according to Rule B.*

This is a much more complex form of definition, which people like tax accountants have to deal with every day. In fact, rules like this may be the reason for tax accountants.

The instructional implications of complex definitions are three. First, for a complex definition, it may be necessary to give increased emphasis to memorization of the definition. Second, it becomes even more important to supply the student with helps which provide a step-by-step pattern for the scanning of potential examples. Third, it must be assured that all concepts which are used in the definition are themselves understood. Those which are not known by the student must be instructed separately in advance.

Measurability of attributes: Some concepts have easily measurable attributes and some don't. This makes a concept either clear or fuzzy. For instance, a basketball court is *regulation size* if its dimensions are X feet by Y feet. That's measurable. It is less easy to define the attributes of a *defensive* person in a counseling session, and it is much less easy to measure.

Many human technologies, such as management, communications, and counseling, include concepts which are somewhat unclearly defined or which have hard-to-measure attributes. The fuzziness of the definitions in these fields may be what gives them the name of *soft* skills. Surprisingly, the strategy recommended in this chapter handles the fuzzy concepts best. That is because instruction will supply a broader range of experience with the great variety of examples in a way that allows the student to isolate the important class features from experience. That is, this strategy gives the student a *feel* for that class because it supplies more data to the student from which the student can make his or her own conclusions or observations.

Coordination with other concepts: Some concepts are not defined by a definition. They are defined in relation to other related concepts. For instance, a *foreigner* to an English person is anyone not from Britain. This type of concept is sometimes called a *coordinate* concept. The implication of this type of concept is that two concepts must be taught in order to teach one concept.

Wording concept-using objectives

Concept-using objectives are sometimes hard to identify. That is because it is not just the verb in the objective which defines the behavior actually being performed. It is most important to concept-using that examples to be classified during practice and on tests must not have been encountered before by the student as examples, and this characteristic is not normally evident in the wording of concept objectives. Therefore, the designer must often ask a question or two about the intent of an objective before classifying it as concept-using.

To show the diversity of wordings used in concept-using objectives, several examples are presented below. Notice that the wording of the objective does not betray whether examples are unencountered. That is something which has to be determined by the designer.

- Identify a supernova when an astronomical phenomenon is described.

- Given a box of crabs, pick out those which are Dungeness crabs.

- Presented with several counseling scenarios, select those which show defensive behavior on the part of an interviewee.

- Given an in-flight situation on video, touch the screen when the situation reaches a point which requires ejection.

Conclusion

The learning of concepts can be made more accurate and sure if the instructional principles described in this chapter are used. Research has shown that systematic and predictable errors in learning of complex concepts can be generated by manipulating the family of examples and non-examples presented and practiced during instruction. Though not every concept will require an extensive group of examples and non-examples, the instruction of every concept can benefit from the selection, ordering, and presentation rules we have described.

Self-directed activities

- Describe the relation of concept-using behavior to what we normally call decision-making. If you find a relationship, explain the implications you see for the teaching of decision-making.
- The concept-using instructional strategy requires careful preparation. Describe the types of concepts for which it is best suited or most needed.
- Specify, if a formal concept-using strategy is not used, what the alternative might be.
- Search for examples of concept-using instruction. Analyze the extent to which the examples you find follow the strategy guidelines found in this chapter. Reflect on how difficult or easy it was to find concepts taught as concepts. Did you find it unexpectedly easy or hard?

Further reading

Merrill, M. D. (1994). *Instructional design theory.* Englewood Cliffs, NJ: Educational Technology Publications.

Merrill, M. D., Tennyson, R. D., and Posey, L. O. (1992). *Teaching concepts: An instructional design guide (2nd ed.).* Englewood Cliffs, NJ: Educational Technology Publications.

14

PRINCIPLE-USING
INSTRUCTIONAL STRATEGY

Chapter Objectives:

1. *Discriminate principle-using from fact-using, concept-using, procedure-using, and process-using behavior.*
2. *Describe the particular care required in the preparation of instruction for principles and explain why it is important.*
3. *Design principle-using instruction for a given instructional goal.*

What is a principle?

A principle is a statement of a general relationship. Principle-using behavior is an integral part of our everyday life. Not every principle is a scientific principle, and not every one is capable of mathematical expression. Most importantly, not every principle is equally well-defined and clearly expressed.

Principles in human affairs range from the very explicit and precise to the very fuzzy and probabilistic. We do scientific work using well-defined principles, and science progresses according to the quality and integrity of its principles. Professional areas of law, medicine, and design are heavily dependent upon principle-using. Unfortunately, the degree of rigor applied to principles in science is not always observed in the other areas of our lives, and so human decisions get somewhat messy and hard to explain. So far as we know, humans are the only life forms capable of principle-using behavior, so we should do what we can to be good at it, and that means teaching it better than we have in the past.

Principles and prediction

The relationship expressed in a principle always has predictive or explanatory power under a specified set of conditions. Newton's laws of motion for many centuries described all of the relationships we needed to predict the behavior of bodies in motion. These laws were considered valid, however, only in frictionless vacuums. Also, they were limited to predictions for no more than two bodies at a time. Given any set of conditions within these boundaries, Newton's laws were considered to produce correct predictions for the motion of bodies due to forces applied to them.

Newton's laws of motion fit the definition of a principle: (1) they express a general relationship, (2) they have predictive or explanatory power, and (3) they apply only under specific, prescribed conditions. In modern times, Newton's laws have been superseded by higher principles (Relativity) which make predictions not only for bodies in motion, but also involve time and gravity, and make correct predictions at conditions near the speed of light, which Newton's laws did not.

Principles are a little intimidating to most of us; many of us feel vaguely uncomfortable in the presence of principles. This may be because principles are content non-specific; a single principle can apply to many specific, concrete situations. When Newton specified his laws for bodies in motion, he did not specify the details of the bodies, their shape, size, weight, motion, or composition. Likewise, when we speak of the principle of the lever, it does not matter whether the lever is actually a teeter-totter, a pry-bar, or a crane; the principle of the lever applies generally in many specific, concrete settings. This is true of all principles: They express a relationship which is true beyond just one specific physical circumstance, and that is why principles themselves are abstract rather than concrete.

Principles are only found after much work and careful observation. When things in nature consistently act in certain lawful ways and under certain conditions, we are able to form a principle that expresses that relationship. These principles are general and constant. Sometimes we can express them in mathematical form and use them to make specific quantitative predictions about situations that before we could not predict nor interpret. Using the computations related to the law of gravity as we know it here on earth, scientists were able to make correct predictions about the thrust needed to safely settle a landing module on the moon's surface. The laws of compounding, because they are based on a mathematical relationship, apply not only to amounts of money, but in non-financial matters as well—the growth of any population— whether it is a population of dollars, buffaloes, bacteria, or fission reactions.

Most principles are not capable of mathematical expression, but that does not prevent us from using them. In fact, most of the principles we know and use daily are non-mathematical. The discussions in this chapter apply equally to scientific and everyday principles, both mathematical and non-mathematical.

Principle-using behavior

Principle-using behavior consists of applying a principle to (1) make a prediction or (2) explain a natural phenomenon not previously understood by the principle user. This stipulation that the explained phenomenon be previously unencountered is important. If we were to try to explain why bubbles form in cooling lava, having read Chapter 12, we would not be exhibiting principle-using behavior, because Chapter 12 explains in detail how bubbles form in cooling lava. It would not be an unencountered situation for us; we would be simply recalling something we had been told. However, if we were presented with a rock whose origin we did not yet understand and if we were able, through principled reasoning, to explain its form and texture in terms of the boiling principle, then we would be using a principle. Likewise, if we were trying to accomplish a goal, such as sending a rocket to the moon, and we had never done it before ourselves, and if we were to apply the principles we knew to predicting the amount of thrust required to escape the earth's gravity, then we would be using a principle to make that prediction.

Principles are powerful forms of knowledge. All of our technology is based on the constancy of principles. Scientists search for new principles. When a principle is found, it can be used to discover other principles, to make predictions, and to explain phenomena that have never been explained before. If it were not for principles, we could not explain the orbits of the planets, the boiling of water, the energy production of our bodies, or the reactions of chemicals. Principles are an important means by which humans expand their knowledge, and principle-using behavior is how we accomplish it. This is as true at the individual level as it is at the societal level.

Compared to the elemental forms of behavior we have considered thus far, principle-using behavior requires a far greater degree of self-awareness and planning of mental processing. Sometimes this self-directed executive mental function is called "thinking about thinking," or *metacognition.* Principle-using behavior involves a high degree of problem solving behavior. This is why metacognition is required: Problem solving can be a conscious, deliberate, goal-directed process. Principle-using behavior is more than simply recalling information or applying a procedure's steps. It is more than simple interpretation of a process and more than discriminating class membership. In fact, it incorporates all of these behaviors. It is a sustained chain of both metacognitive and content-specific reasoning and problem solving. Generally, its stages include:

- Recalling the principle itself, often in exact wording.

- Isolation of principle elements of interest to the present problem.

- Analysis of the elements of the problem situation.

- Matching of problem and principle elements.

- Identification of missing links in the chain of reasoning.

- Setting of goals to fill in the missing links.

- Reasoning to achieve the link-filling goals.

- Self-checking of the solution through alternate knowledge paths.

If anything, principle-using is a more complex, integrated behavior made up of other more atomistic forms of behavior. In this sense, it shows how the atomistic approach to behavior classification exemplified by Gagné and Merrill relates to the more integrated approach exemplified by Bloom (see Chapter 8 for a discussion of these behavior classification systems).

Principles and memory

Principle-using behavior depends on the novelty of the situation presented to the student. Once a principle has been applied by a student to a specific concrete situation, it is not possible for that person to apply that principle to the exact same situation again and have the performance be authentic principle-using. That is because the experience of applying a principle is recorded in memory, along with the situation, and if a student encounters the situation again, his or her response to it can come from memory rather than from the activities of principle-using. When asked to explain why an apple falls from a tree, we normally do not perform a complete cycle of principle-using behavior. We simply recall the causal principle "gravity," because we have answered the same question many times before. Indeed, it is possible that once having learned the memorized answer, we never really have to apply the principle of gravity as a principle.

Principles and concepts

It is also possible for students to memorize the name for a principle and the defining characteristics of a set of stock situations to which the principle applies. By identifying the stock situations, the student can give the impression of performing principle-using behavior without ever really engaging in it. For instance, asked if a screwdriver prying open a paint can is a lever, a student can recall that almost any prying situation involves a lever and answer correctly only on the basis of that recalled class of applications of the principle. This counterfeit principle-using is really concept-using behavior which uses the stock situations (themselves concept classes) and the ability to identify them in daily experience (classification behavior) as the key components of their performance. It is a useful form of behavior which saves us much time and mental effort, but if it is the only form of principle application that we require of our students, then they are being cheated.

Principles and processes

Principles differ from processes in important ways.

First, principles do not deal in specific content, whereas processes are almost always content-specific. Newton's laws apply to all body-motion problems and are principles. The field of events by which a space shuttle is launched and flies to the moon, though explained in terms of Newton's principles, is a process.

Second, principles can apply to many specific content areas, whereas processes are most often restricted to one content area. The compounding law is a principle which applies in many fields of study. Photosynthesis is a process particular to one area of biology.

Third, principles are often provided with no explanation—no rationale for the observed outcome. Processes require a rationale explaining the cause effect relationship involved in the transfer of force, energy, or signal from one natural element to another. Many of the principles of science as yet have no explanation. We do not know why gravity and magnetism work; we simply know that they do.

Defining principle-using more carefully

We might ask ourselves if much of our teaching of scientific principles in the schools is not really the teaching of principles as memorized solutions or as concepts. Though this allows the student to understand and interpret to some minimal degree the world of experience, it also robs the student of the ability to decode new experiences that have never been encountered before and to create new knowledge and new understanding in the process. Therefore, we need to exercise care in how we teach principles. Though some principles may be taught through simplified instructional methods, some principles do need to be instructed in the context of authentic principle-using performance, if for no other reason than to introduce the student to the systematic thinking required for authentic principle-using.

Principle using is a subtle and complex form of behavior. It is seen often in daily behavior but frequently is not carried out with care, which can easily lead to inconsistent and incorrect conclusions. Principle-using includes a careful matching procedure between the characteristics of a situation (where the principle might apply) and the definitions and boundary conditions of the principle (the rules for applying the principle, which are an important part of the principle). If the principle matches the situation, principle-using can also include a careful analysis of the problem and the principle and one or more procedures for predicting the outcome of applying the principle.

The detailed description of principle-using behavior of Frederick Reif and Sue Allen sheds useful light on the nature of principle-using and instruction for principle-using (see "Cognition for interpreting scientific concepts: A study of acceleration." F. Reif and S. Allen, *Cognition and Instruction*, Vol. 9, No. 1, pp. 1–44). For their description, Reif and Allen isolated a principle—acceleration—which is essential to understanding much of basic Newtonian physics. Not only is it a scientific principle, but it is commonly used as well in everyday thought. For instance, we speak of *accelerating* a car.

Reif and Allen show how the principle *acceleration* in science and the principle *acceleration* in everyday usage differ in an important way. In science, where it is intended to lead to new understanding and the precise interpretation of phenomena, the principle is carefully defined and carefully bounded. In everyday usage, it is used much more loosely. In their research, Reif and Allen found that not only did the application of the principle challenge the average student who had already been thoroughly instructed in it, but in some cases, the experts as well, who had taught the principle to the students.

Reif and Allen asked both students and experts to apply the principle to fifteen problem situations. They asked them to determine at a qualitative (non-numerical) level the existence of acceleration in the situation (present/absent, positive/negative). They also asked the students and experts to answer questions about the relative size and direction of acceleration (if present) and to explain their answers by describing aloud their reasoning as they solved each problem. Only if they reasoned correctly about the principle did they receive credit for a correct answer.

When the tests had been administered to students and experts both, the results were surprising. The students, who had been instructed in the principle over a several-week period, only answered about 33% of the questions accurately, and even among the experts, who had done the instructing, there were errors. One instructor scored only 11 out of 15 correct, and three others missed one problem each.

What made this principle so hard to apply? Why did not the experts score perfectly on every problem? Does this tell us something about the nature of principle-using behavior?

Certainly one factor in the difficulty of the problems was the scientific nature of the principle versus its common usage with a different meaning in everyday discourse. When we say "accelerate" in everyday speech, we normally mean that we pushed the gas pedal with our foot. A scientist means something different by "accelerate." This factor might account for some of the misunderstanding of the students, but it does not account for the errors of the experts, who are expected to have divorced the daily meaning of the principle from its scientific meaning.

Why did some of the experts have difficulty applying the principle? Reif and Allen explain that it is because applying a principle to a situation and interpreting the future behavior of the situation requires a careful matching process which has many steps, as well as several kinds of knowledge which are required to reach correct conclusions through reasoning. If the reasoning process is not followed carefully, errors can result, even for experts.

First, they explain, the terms of the acceleration principle are very clearly defined. An acceleration involves:

1. A change...

2. ...(positive or negative)...

3. ...in the velocity...

4. ...or...

5. ...the direction...

6. ...of a particle.

Moreover, these qualities may occur under a wide variety of circumstances:

Trajectory: object moving in a straight line, object moving on a curve.

Direction of change: velocity increasing, velocity decreasing, velocity constant.

Plane: object moving on horizontal plane, object moving in vertical plane.

Moreover, many of the irrelevant elements of a situation can distract and confuse the student attempting to solve a problem: the object as a car, the object as a sled on a hill, the object as a rock swung round on a string, the object as a clock pendulum.

In order to apply the principle *acceleration* precisely and accurately to a specific situation with all of the above dimensions active, a student must have a systematic procedure for verifying that all of the terms and conditions of the principle are met. Then the student must have a similarly systematic method for making predictions or explanations using the principle. Reif and Allen identify several specific kinds of knowledge which the student must have in order to reach a reliably accurate conclusions using principles. Importantly, in their study, they were able to show how the absence of certain elements of knowledge or the failure to apply them in a systematic way led to the types of errors observed in both novices and experts.

To apply the principle of acceleration to a specific unknown case, a five-step procedure is described, which involves:

1. Identifying the velocity of the object at one instant in time (using vector notation), which includes showing not only the speed of the object but its direction as well.

2. Identifying the velocity of the particle at a slightly later instant in time (using vector notation again) showing its (possibly changed) speed and (possibly changed) direction.

3. Finding the difference in velocity between the two samples velocities (through vector arithmetic).

At this point, if the two vectors obtained are identical, then acceleration is zero, and it is not having an effect on the situation. If the vectors are not identical, then the procedure continues and applies the principle to find the value of the acceleration by:

4. Finding thé ratio of change in velocity to change in time.

5. Repeating the calculation with values of time chosen closer and closer to the original time (a calculus technique), until the time is infinitesimally small.

Why is all this work necessary to determine whether acceleration is occurring and to determine its value? It is because acceleration is very precisely defined, and because it is easy to be fooled by a situation in which there *seems* to be acceleration but is in fact none. It may seem like hair-splitting to apply principles with such care, but to the astronaut whose life may depend on accurate acceleration determinations, it is very important, and perhaps this contrast emphasizes the looseness in applying principles which leads us everyday to accept incorrect conclusions and make errors in reasoning.

Perhaps we should also recognize the value of more disciplined use of knowledge to our students. Equipped with this method of determining the occurrence of acceleration, a student is free to approach virtually any physical situation and decode it—determine whether it involves acceleration. Without this procedure, a student is at the mercy of memorized solutions and analogous cases. The application of this procedure, then, is one of the marks of authentic and robust principle-using behavior.

Reif and Allen identify several other forms of knowledge which the student must possess in order to exercise authentic principle-using. They are evident in the instructional strategy outline presented later in this chapter, and because of their importance we will also take time to define them here. Note that some of the forms of knowledge are not directly related to applying the principle as much as they are additional knowledge which allows the student to confirm that the principle has been applied correctly to a given situation. This ability to self-check principle application by arriving at the same conclusion through alternate paths of reasoning is an important part of principle-using behavior. It is one of the things that allows the principle-user to proceed with a conclusion with some confidence that a correct or acceptable one has been reached.

The forms of knowledge related to principle-using according to Reif and Allen are:

Definitional: The definition of a principle includes a verbal expression of the principle, along with its symbolic expression, if there is one. The wording of the principle's verbal expression must be precise. Terms used in the definition must be themselves clearly defined, either within the principle definition or in some external authoritative source. In the acceleration example given by Reif and Allen, not only the definition of the principle, but also those of component concepts, like velocity, must be clear and unambiguous. Many of the errors made in their study came from failure to use exact definitions.

The importance of this definitional knowledge is that students can return to the definition time and time again (not only in the classroom but in real-life situations) in order to note its exact wording (or symbolics) as the basis for making inferences which might provide a clue to applying the principle to a particular situation (see Entailed below).

Entailed: Entailed knowledge for a principle is knowledge which can be derived from the definition (or related symbolic expressions) through inference. Entailed knowledge is very useful in solving a new principle-using problem; it is the product of analysis of the problem situation and the principle to derive as many true statements from them as possible. These statements, if linked properly, often supply the path to the solution. In the case of the acceleration principle, Reif and Allen show that useful entailed knowledge includes breaking the motion of an object into two components (as in vector analysis), one which describes the forward motion of the object, and one which describes its motion at right angles to that forward motion. By dividing the object's motion into its forward and side-ward components in this way, the problem is amenable to easy solution.

Entailed knowledge is not the same as prerequisite knowledge. Most principle-using problems can be approached through more than one line of principled reasoning. Therefore, it cannot be said that splitting the motion components is a prerequisite behavior to solving acceleration problems. However, some types of entailed knowledge do lead to specific solution paths, as in this case.

Supplementary: Supplementary knowledge for principles is knowledge which cannot be derived from the definition, but which is related to application of the principle to a situation. Supplemental knowledge is often the key to an alternative approach to a problem. In the acceleration example, Reif and Allen show that Newton's motion law, F=ma, can be used to solve the problem as well as the main approach of splitting the motion components and using vector arithmetic. A student identifies the supplemental knowledge by recognizing linkages between it and the present problem. F=ma represents the principle, "Force equals the mass of an object times its acceleration." The student, recognizing that this principle also deals with acceleration, may use it to construct an alternate path to solution. This is an approach to solution based on supplementary knowledge.

Case-specific: Case-specific knowledge is knowledge of memorized cases to which the principle has been seen to apply in the past. This knowledge can sometimes lead directly to the application of a memorized solution or can suggest to the student a case similar to the one he or she is working on and thus supply ideas about how to apply the principle to the present one. Case-specific knowledge can provide a shortcut to the student for applying principles to previously-seen cases, but it is also often used as a substitute for authentic principle-using behavior. When case-specific knowledge is supplied during principle-using instruction, the reasoning behind its application must be made clear in order to prevent the student from applying the case-specific solution to situations where it does not really apply.

One form of case-specific knowledge which is troublesome to students is that which results from inaccurate observations or conclusions based on everyday experience. In the classroom the student will see correctly-obtained case-specific knowledge, but every student brings from outside the classroom a body of intuitive knowledge, much of which is incorrect or applied without care. This knowledge must be neutralized through re-learning of correct knowledge, and a list of common misconceptions should be a part of the designer's catalogue of principle-using knowledge. Students must encounter these difficult cases during practice and learn that they can be deceiving.

Sometimes closely-held intuitive knowledge is retained by a student even after much instruction in a principle which conflicts with it. Retaining intuitive knowledge can destroy the effect of good principle-using instruction. This is a common and puzzling finding. It may occur because formal application of a principle takes many steps and is a slow and painstaking reasoning process, whereas application of memorized or intuitive knowledge is quick and easy, even if it is often also often inaccurate. Students tend to prefer the easier approach. Moreover, research is showing that principles, since they are used by people to explain and understand so much of their daily life, are closely held by people to the extent of being personal beliefs—basic keys to evaluating daily experience. This high personal value of principles implies that as we ask people to exchange a new principle for an old one, we may be asking them to give up or change a personal value. This non-trivial issue can lead to resistance to the learning of new principles. It implies that principle-using instruction should be approached by designers with sensitivity, humility, and thoughtfulness.

Applicability conditions: Applicability conditions knowledge helps a student determine when a principle does or does not apply. Newton's laws of motion technically apply only to bodies in a frictionless vacuum. Acceleration technically applies only to an object whose position can be described as a single point. Application conditions knowledge takes the statement of boundary conditions supplied in the principle definition and places it in a form which is ready to use. Therefore, it is appropriate to say that applicability conditions knowledge is derived at least in part from the definition. Another part of applicability knowledge is the procedure for determining whether the principle is active in the given problem situation. Steps 1 through 3 of the 5-step procedure given earlier constitute applicability knowledge.

Application methods: Knowledge which tells students how to apply the principle. An example of an application method for *acceleration* is given as the last two steps of the 5-step procedure just mentioned. The statement of an application method as a step-by-step procedure is useful because it causes the student to use data derived from the specific problem to reach a carefully-reasoned conclusion. It also ensures that the student performs reasoning steps in an appropriate order. When students are not given an application procedure, then they work one out for themselves. Many of the mistakes students make during principle-using instruction have the effect of debugging these idiosyncratic procedures.

These several types of knowledge are all necessary to principle-using because principle-using is a complex behavior. It is possible that our problems instructing students in principle-using center around: (1) failure to teach students the full range of knowledge needed to apply principles, and (2) the lack of adequate practice in applying principles to previously unencountered situations. The strategy for principle-using instruction described later in this chapter is structured to supply these needs.

Reality check

Are all principles like the principle of acceleration? Does every principle application require a painstaking and procedural application of steps to determine that the principle is appropriate to a situation and to apply the principle? The answer is probably, "Yes." If that is a surprising answer, it is probably because: (1) principles are seldom taught as principles, and (2) they are seldom taught in a way that fully empowers the student to use them as principles. There are forms of behavior which seem to be principle-using but which are in fact abbreviated forms or shortcuts to it. If we teach those behaviors rather than true principle-using, then we are teaching incorrect knowledge and limiting the future performance of the student. To review these shortcuts:

> *Application of principles from memory:* Remembering a specific instance to which a principle has been seen to apply and using that instance to predict or explain the current situation.

> *Example:* Remembering that apples fall because of gravity.

> *Application of principles by classification of cases:* Remembering several cases in which a principle has applied and selecting the case which is most like the present case, then making the necessary correspondences between the elements of the selected case and the present case.

> *Example:* Application of acceleration to problems where only the horizontal plane and turning on a curve within that plane are involved—problems which can be solved by imagining oneself in a car.

The procedural approach for applying principles, described by Reif and Allen and also in this chapter, equips the student for independent performance in principle-using. Whereas the two shortcut methods mentioned above limit the student in some way within the boundaries of previous experience, the procedural approach does not, and it allows the student to approach and successfully interpret a wider range of life experiences and gain new knowledge from them. This is the power of principle-using. It also explains why principles are more complex to instruct.

In addition to the subject-matter of science which has been used as the main example so far, it is possible to see much principle-using behavior in the areas of architecture, all forms of engineering, all forms of science, medicine, political science, economics, and law. Principle-using behavior is important to our students and our society. If students are to get real benefit from the principles we instruct and be able to extend their own and our society's knowledge using them, then they must encounter the method of principle-using in its most precise and demanding form in at least some of their studies. Students may not always use the method in daily activities and personal lives, but they will find many occasions when they need to reason on the basis of principles, and it will be easier for them to use a skill that they have already acquired when that need arises than it will be to discover the method on the spot.

The symbolic expression of principles

Equations are symbolic expressions of relationship. Therefore, they represent principles.

$C = \pi d$

...can be expressed as...

"The circumference of any circle is equal to the diameter of the circle times the value of pi (3.1416)."

...and also in an IF/THEN form...

> IF there is a diameter of a circle
> THEN the circumference has a length of pi times the diameter

This relationship between diameter and circumference is a principle, and the basic operations of algebra allow us to use the relationship to determine any variable value in the relationship. For instance,

$d=C/\pi$

A chemical formula is also a the expression of a principle. It shows the change relations between a particular group of molecules, atoms, and ions as they change from one combined state into another. In the expression of chemical formulas, two levels of principle can be demonstrated—the specific, and the parametric.

The specific principle states a reaction relationship for one and only one set of reacting chemicals. For example, sodium hydroxide and hydrochloric acid react to form sodium chloride (table salt) and water:

$Na + Cl \rightarrow NaCl$

Chlorine (Cl) belongs to a family of chemicals called *halogens*. All of the halogen family can participate in this same reaction. A parametric principle form gives the reaction relation for a whole family of reacting chemicals. The halogens (fluorine, chlorine, iodine, bromine) are usually represented by an "X" in parametric formulas:

$Na + X \rightarrow NaX$

This reaction formula therefore represents the principle of a family of chemical reactions—those involving any chemical from the halogen group.

Qualitative and quantitative differences

Can a person understand the principle of acceleration without being able to make computations? Clearly so, and this means that principles may be used at two levels: the quantitative level and the qualitative level. The quantitative level of principle use involves precise and numerical answers to principle problems, which are derived through symbolic expressions—normally mathematical equations.

At the qualitative level, no symbolic expression of the principle is used. The number of principles that we use in daily life which have no mathematical expression is probably greater than the number that do. For these principles, only the direction of the outcome and some relative assessment of effect size can be determined. Virtually all principles are capable of use at both the qualitative and quantitative levels. The fact that a mathematical expression of a principle exists does not mean that that expression must be used in order to apply the principle.

The qualitative use of principles is coming to be recognized as a major issue in principle-using instruction. Most of our principle-using performance is in terms of non-computational principles, and our conclusions are normally expressed without numbers. This appears to be true of scientific principles as well, where it seems there are two levels of principle-related thinking: one a qualitative level, and one a quantitative level. The most important level is likely to be the qualitative level.

In addition to varying in the qualitative/quantitative dimension, principles also vary in the precision of their expression or completeness of expression. Some of the different knowledge types related to principle-using may be missing for a given principle or may less than complete or expressed in ambiguous (ill-defined) terms. Many principles which we use in everyday activities have no clear expression of where they apply and where they do not. Others have no procedure to guide their application. Still others come to us without case-specific knowledge. Some come to us only in the form of specific cases, from which we are left to generalize the principle ourselves.

Principles cannot be applied casually without the risk of reaching incorrect conclusions. In principle-using, the reasoning and method applied to reach an answer is as important as the answer itself.

Principles and prerequisites

Principles are seldom instructed in isolation. One reason is that many principles rely on prerequisite knowledge and skill for their application. In many cases, this prerequisite knowledge becomes either the source for or a part of the entailed and supplementary knowledge described earlier in the chapter. The acceleration principle, for instance, requires that a student know the component principles of speed and velocity (and the distinction between them) as well as being able to draw velocity vectors, perform simple vector arithmetic, and execute limiting functions using calculus (or at very least be able to discern that any difference between the two velocity vectors represents an acceleration). This suggests that the context within which principles are instructed is as important as the strategy for instructing the principle itself. This, in turn, should cause the designer to pay careful attention to the analysis of tasks and content which is normally carried out prior to instructional design. As our vision of instructional strategy grows, our realization of the importance of the analysis stage of instructional design will no doubt grow as well.

Principle-using instructional strategy

Table 1 lists the stages in an instructional strategy for principle-using. According to the practice adopted in earlier chapters, the activities of the strategy are divided between presentation and practice, but equally important with that dimension, the table shows stages through which the student progresses in order to be capable of independently applying the learned principle. You may note that some of the stages of this strategy are very much like entire strategies described in earlier chapters. For instance, the *expression of principle* stage below corresponds in many (but not all) respects to the strategy for recalling verbal information from memory. The *applicability* stage shares many of the characteristics of a concept-using strategy.

The remainder of this chapter describes the principle-using instructional strategy. As it is presented here, this strategy's focus is on the use of principles for prediction (either qualitative prediction, or the computation of a quantitative predictive value). The emphasis of this strategy is not on instructing the student on how to use principles to explain unfamiliar phenomena, because the explanatory use of principles takes place beyond the scope of instruction for a single principle.

In order for explanatory use of principles to take place, the scope of instruction must be centered around an unexplained phenomenon, and the student must already have a set of several already-learned principles to be applied for the explanation of the phenomenon represented by the problem.

Table 1. Principle-using strategy outline.

Stage	Presentation	Practice
Expression of Principle	1. Present the exact wording of the principle	1. Practice exact recall of principle wording
	2. Present symbolic expression(s) of the principle	2. Practice exact recall of symbolic expression(s) of the principle
Applicability	1. Present boundary conditions of applicability	1. Practice verbalization of boundary conditions
	2. Present procedure (if any) for determining applicability	2. Practice verbalization of the procedure for determining applicability
	3. Present stepwise examples of application (using the procedure), including non-examples	3. Practice judging the applicability of the principle to a range of appropriate and inappropriate situations
Preparatory Analysis of Problems and Principle	1. Present the reasoning procedure for problem analysis (deriving problem knowledge through analysis)	1. Practice applying reasoning procedure to problems (emphasis on process)
	2. Present examples of correct and incorrect reasoning during problem analysis, including rationale and goal structures during reasoning	2. Practice problem analysis (emphasis on reasoning and goal selection)
	3. Present reasoning procedure for principle analysis (deriving entailed principle knowledge)	3. Practice applying reasoning procedure to the principle (emphasis on process)
	4. Present examples of correct and incorrect reasoning for principle analysis	4. Practice principle analysis for specific problems (emphasis on reasoning)
	5. Present related principles and techniques (supplemental principle knowledge) for this principle	5. Practice identification of related principles and techniques
	6. Present examples of application of related principles and techniques (supplemental knowledge) to problems as well as common reasoning errors	6. Practice applying related princi- and techniques (supplemental knowledge) to problems
Qualitative Application	1. Present a procedure for structuring a qualitative problem solution from analysis elements of problem and principle, as well as inappropriate structurings (common errors)	1. Practice the application of qualitative problem solutions (emphasis on process)
	2. Present examples of struturing a qualitative problem solution from analysis elements, as well as inappropriate structurings (common errors)	2. Practice the application of qualitative problem solutions (emphasis on reasoning)

(Continued)

Table 1. Principle-using strategy outline (continued).

Quantitive	1. Present a procedure for structuring a quantitative problem solution from analysis elements of problem and principle, as well as inappropriate structurings (common errors)	1. Practice the application of the quantitative problem solution procedure (emphasis on process)
	2. Present examples of structuring a quantitative problem solution from analysis elements, as well as inappropriate structurings (common errors)	2. Practice the application of quantitative problem solutions

If this type of exercise were carried out within the scope of single-principle instruction, then the correct answer would be only too apparent to the student, and there would not be a field of principle alternatives from which to select an explanatory principle. That would short-circuit the behavior for this form of principle-using.

Multiple encounters, multiple surface forms

Principle-using is not normally learned in one encounter in the same way that a simple memory structure, discrimination, or procedure might be. Instruction in one principle normally takes place over a period of time through several encounters and across multiple instructional activities.

During that sequence of instructional encounters, examples and problems must be selected which represent the full range of specific problem settings and contents to which the principle applies. If in one encounter the principle lever is treated in the abstract, then in a second it should be treated as a discussion about teeter-totters. In a third, it should be treated as a construction crane problem. By providing a complete range of surface applications of the principle, the instruction can keep the student from focusing on the surface representation related to one type of problem. An instructor could instruct the principle only using abstract problem settings, but there is a penalty for doing so: The student does not receive practice in applying the principle in the presence of irrelevant and sometimes confusing problem specifics which are supplied by the various concrete surfaces chosen to embody the problem.

Not only should the surface features of problems vary over the complete range exhibited by real-world problems, but the designer must be careful to supply a complete range of structural problem cases as well. Reif and Allen are careful to identify the dimensions along which an acceleration problem can vary and to specify the set of variations represented in their test problems. Rather than being random or capricious in their selection of problems, they selected them from a structured field of problem possibilities defined by the dimensions listed earlier in this chapter, which are repeated below:

Trajectory: object moving in a straight line, object moving on a curve, object moving in pendulum fashion.

Direction of change: velocity increasing, velocity decreasing, velocity constant.

Plane: object moving on horizontal plane, object moving in vertical plane.

Note that only problems in two dimensions—either in the vertical or the horizontal plane—are included in this set of problem types. Three dimensional problems, such as airplanes turning and descending at the same time in a three-dimensional spiral are not included. Perhaps Reif and Allen decided that the number of problems this would generate were unnecessary for the scope of their research. In a similar manner, the instructional designer must decide the scope of problems which constitutes the focus at any given point during the instruction of a principle. In many cases, it may be desirable to focus on a limited set of problem structures and then systematically expand the set through multiple exposures. Once the structured problem field is designed, it should serve equally as the basis for the generation of presentations, demonstrations, and practice items. Lack of balance in this respect will cause demonstration of one type of problem and practice of another. But that would not be fair.

Presentations

Several kinds of presentation are made during principle-using instruction, and each is related to a specific stage of the strategy. It is important to keep in mind that those presentations described in Table 1 are not restricted to traditional presentations in which the core of the message is simply told to the student. Several avenues are available for supporting the establishment of new information and knowledge structures within the student's thinking, and direct telling is only one of them:

- A student may be brought to discover information through questioning or highlighting of details.

- A student may be asked to apply a particular reasoning process to a given set of facts or observations which are arranged in a way that suggests their order to the student.

- A set of activities can be arranged which lead the student to conclusions in a certain order which leads to yet further pattern recognitions or conclusions.

An excellent instructor uses many of these techniques, but none exclusively. The interplay of initiative between student and instructor in this respect is delicate but very important, and this should remind you of the important (we think) discussion in Chapter 9 of performance and strategic goals and the sharing of initiative in their selection.

As a reward for working in harmony and with shared goals, the student not only obtains a new principle, but the capability for self-directed learning as well.

Practice

Practice, likewise, is of several types within the principle-using strategy. As the application of a principle is either demonstrated or practiced, the designer must ensure that the full range of possible applications is represented there in appropriate proportion. Problem sets have subtle effects on misconceptions in students, and the designer must be sure to show the student a balanced variety of problem settings during both presentation and practice.

This includes also structuring into the problem set a number of problems to which the principle does not apply and a set of problems which represent common misconceptions and common errors. Instruction must help the student attain a clear definition of those problems to which the principle does not apply as well as those to which it does. This is the main purpose of the *applicability* stage of the instructional strategy, but even once that stage has been completed by the student, it is not wise to omit inclusion of further problems outside the scope of the principle. All problem sets must contain some problems beyond principle scope, and the student must be asked to determine the applicability of the principle each time it is applied.

Certain common misconceptions can be anticipated within a student population and can be avoided through prior identification and inclusion within the set of problems and examples. Their use is to fortify students against the misconceptions through greater emphasis (provided by greater proportional visibility) and straightforward warnings.

In principle-using instruction, the opportunity for discouraging the student is greater than in any of the strategies described so far. Problems which are difficult, if presented too soon and with little support in the form of prompting and hinting, can be demoralizing. The selection of a graded set of problems and the analysis of student progress within that problem set is of much importance. Problems must be arranged in an order of ascending difficulty, and students should progress from easy to hard problems with renewed levels of support at each transition to a higher level. Students who continually fail because they are encountering problems above their level of immediate ability will lose hope of learning and therefore lose their motivation. If problems continue to frustrate the student and the student does not maintain a satisfying level of success in attempts to apply the principle to new problems, then desire to continue learning will wane. This does not mean that the problems should be chosen in an order that removes all challenge, for this will lead to boredom and decreased motivation. The difficulty of problems encountered by students is a variable which must be adjusted for individual students to achieve the best level of challenge.

Stage: Principle expression

The goal of the *expression* portion of the strategy is to help the student establish recall for the exact wording of the principle. This is an essential part of principle-using, because the expression of the principle embodies not only the defined terms on which the principle is based, but their relationship as well. The principle is a law, and as the student interprets the law, he or she must know what the law says.

Presentation: The presentation of a principle must supply an exact and invariant wording for the principle. This wording will be referred to again and again until its expression becomes almost automatic for the student. Much explanation of the principle will eventually be given during the presentation, but the principle's expression itself must be made to stand out as the undeniable centerpiece. To establish this contrast between the representation of the principle's expression and its explanation, the physical (spatial) and stylistic (fonts, sizes, boldness, etc.) representation of the principle may be made to differ from the surrounding material whenever it is seen.

It is worthwhile to point out to the student specific features of the principle's expression and their implications. These may consist of specific phrases or even single words. One means of highlighting elements of the expression is to call out individual words and to give each definition in turn, at the same time calling out the implications of the specific wording. This linkage will assist memory and is echoed later during the feedback given during all of the practice forms. The expression of the principle is the central point that all corrections and instructions should lead back to.

Mnemonics are often not as useful during principle instruction as they might be for other memory instruction. The student will come to be able to express the principle through repeated repetition and reference to the exact statement of the principle, and a mnemonic is of limited value for this purpose. Mnemonics can also be misleading regarding the operations of the principle.

It is useful during presentation of the principle expression to model the general implications of the principle in physical terms. Every principle has some pattern of operation. As the principle operates, forces are applied and are translated into observable outcomes. The interplay of these forces and the outcomes should be modeled in a generic way for the student during the presentation of the expression. Even a non-concrete principle can be given a physical manifestation which can be used to show the forces and elements which the principle relates together and the generic nature of that relationship. Living diagrams may be useful in this respect. That is, the student should be given a model of the system within which the principle operates as well as controls to vary the values related to the principle. The student should be allowed, encouraged, or led to explore the effects of varying the parameters of this model.

While the description of the operation of the principle is being given, keep in mind that it can be given at several levels. In the pursuit of rigor and exactness, many instructors are unwilling to express the principle in easily understandable terms, and the student is left to wrestle with mathematical expressions or prose which have the clarity of the Gordian knot. The principle should be expressed at a level at which the students have knowledge tools to understand it.

Expressing the principle in only an exact expression or only a simplified expression also has drawbacks, whereas expressing the principle in both forms has benefit for the student. If the instructor feels there is danger in presenting a simplified-wording explanation of the principle, then it may still be presented if accompanied by sufficient caveats to avert its improper application. Everyday metaphors or prime examples are useful in this respect if ones can be found which do not lead to erroneous conclusions or applications of the principle. For instance, the principle of acceleration in two dimensions can be related to the movements of a steering wheel and a gas pedal while driving a car. In fact, this description of the principle precludes one of the common misconceptions of acceleration, which equates acceleration only with pressing the gas pedal. By using a homely example and explaining it carefully (in this case, explaining that only movement of the pedal or the steering wheel in either direction causes acceleration), a designer can not only make the principle more easy to understand but eliminate erroneous conceptions at the same time.

Practice: Practice for the exact expression of the principle requires asking the student to reproduce from memory the expression itself. "Fill in the blanks" drills are a useful vehicle for drilling the student in exact wording. These should be spaced over time, even after the student has achieved mastery of recall once. This ensures that the recall of the principle will continue to become automatized. Any hesitations to recall the principle expression during problem solving will result in cognitive blockages, as other processes are set aside to allow the ill-learned recall to proceed.

Several forms of practice for exact recall should come readily to mind. One that may not, but which is effective, consists of a fading drill in which individual words and phrases are systematically deleted in increasingly larger chunks from the wording of the definition. The student encountering multiple deletion variations becomes focused on different key words of the definition in each one. Other forms of drill and practice are appropriate, and each one should be accompanied by decreasing support in the form of prompts and increasingly larger amounts of memory performance required, until the point when the student can reliably recall the target material on multiple, time-separated occasions.

This expression phase of instruction can be and should be combined with the applicability stage. As with other strategy types we have described to this point, the stages of the strategy are not expected to be separated by distinct boundaries. Instead, the stages intermingle in interesting patterns which may appear distinct in the student's mind or which may blend with each other so fully that they are unrecognizable as different stages of instruction.

Stage: Applicability

During the applicability stage of the principle-using strategy the student is learning to answer the question, "Does this principle apply to this problem?" or "Is the principle operating in this situation?" The behavior asked of the student here is not a problem solving behavior; it is a form of classification. The applicability of a principle is a matching procedure in which the attributes that are matched are: (1) the requirements of the principle for applicability, and (2) the characteristics of the problem.

Presentation: A procedure for determining the applicability of a principle in a given situation can be formed for most principles, which serves as a stable guide for the student learning to apply the principle. This procedure itself should be memorized in order to be maximally useful. The memory for this procedure is in most cases as important as the memorization of the principle definition itself, because it is this procedure that will guide the student to apply the principle only to those situations where the principle is operating.

For the principle of acceleration, the procedure provided by Reif and Allen is a three step (of five total steps) procedure. Three steps determine whether there is acceleration in a given situation, and two actually calculate the value of the acceleration. In our strategy description, we will consider the applicability procedure and the application procedure as separate instructional issues.

The presentation of the application procedure may be very structured and should involve application to a full range of examples (situations in which the principle is operative) and non-examples (situations in which the principle is not). Failure to present the non-examples isolates from the student knowledge of the bounds of principle application and prevents clear identification of situations in which the principle is not operative. In this field of examples and non-examples, there should also be emphasis given to those situations which are most likely to cause misconceptions in students. For this stage of instruction, the concept-using strategy supplies much of the structure and guidance needed by the designer.

Practice: Practice for applicability should consist of structured application examples. The procedure for determining applicability is the central focus of the structure, and through exercise of the procedure repeatedly in a structured way, with equally structured feedback, the student becomes aware that the procedure is an important part of principle-using. The same range of example and non-example situations used during presentation should be used for practice (and testing) as well in order to guarantee that the student is capable of performing anywhere within the boundaries of the principle in previously unencountered situations.

Stage: Preparatory analysis

In the presentation of the easiest principle-using problems to students, the key elements of the problem are presented in such a way that they are readily apparent to the student and ready to be matched with the elements of the principle. Perhaps the motion vectors in an acceleration problem are readily discernible because they are already identified or provided in drawings in the problem presentation. In later problems, however, the student is expected to analyze the provided problem situation without such pre-analysis, and the student must perform the analysis in order to identify the elements of the problem that are useful in a solution. In some problems, elements are left to the student to derive. Therefore, the student has to draw the velocity vector at different points along the motion path for himself or herself and perform many other analyses that were originally supplied by the instruction. This constitutes the slow dismantling of a scaffolding originally provided but withdrawn so that the student begins to supply it instead.

Many skills may be brought to bear on the analysis of a problem or of the implications of a principle in order to render it solvable. The final goal of these analyses is to derive from the principle and from the problem situation a set of elements which correspond and show the student a path to the solution of the problem. This analysis is necessary for either a qualitative or a quantitative solution to a problem, and may in some cases be a necessary precursor to the applicability stage as well. In the case of acceleration, if the velocity vectors are not supplied with the problem statement, then they must be provided by the student in this way.

The analysis of the principle and the problem is probably the most important stage of principle-using. It is the stage during which the student determines whether there is a path to solution, and both presentation and practice must show the student not only how to make the determination that there is a path, but also how to determine when there is none.

Presentation: The analysis of problems is not a performance that the student will learn for the present principle only. It is a skill which the student must learn for the application of all principles. Therefore, in one respect—the non-content-specific one—this analysis is a separate instructional goal from the principle-using goal, and the principle-using goal is just one of several presentation and practice opportunities for the larger goal of learning to analyze a problem situation. This points up the importance of seeing every instructional goal in the context of more inclusive, higher-order goals. That higher goal is achieved through numerous examples of the analysis of problem situations for specific principles.

Instruction on analysis of problems is carried out through the modeling of reasoning processes. It focuses on helping the student apply what is already known to building a bridge of relationships between the principle and the problem. From the student's point of view, this may include such component activities such as:

- Recognizing a new identity for or re-naming a problem element.

- Recognizing an alternative expression for a problem element.

- Deriving new information through inference or deduction.

- Transforming known relationships into new forms.

- Plotting computational or inferential paths to a solution.

There is no procedure that will lead a student unfailingly through the analysis process. For each problem, the considerations are slightly different. Even though problems tend to be analyzed using the same basic approach and steps, the specific information given with each problem modifies the student's analysis task, making it, from the student's naive and uncertain point of view, a new analysis task. The instructor's most powerful tool for this instruction is to carefully model, within the student's view, the thinking and reasoning process which goes on during analysis. Not only must the steps of the reasoning be apparent in this model, but the reasons for each step being chosen in its order must also be evident for this instruction to be effective and pleasant. The student is learning the skills of setting goals and of calling up from memory knowledge representations that can be linked together into a chain that forms a bridge between the problem and a solution. Though this sounds dry, if applied with imagination this stage of instruction is actually the most interesting and rewarding of principle-using instruction. It is the heart of principle-using itself.

In a sense, the student is an apprentice in the presence of this model of reasoning. To the extent that the steps in analysis can be made systematic, or to the extent that the student can be given a checklist of considerations or "don't forgets," the student is given tools which can be used for constructing novel paths in future problems. It is especially important for the student to become aware of goals and goal structures which are used during problem analysis, since it is a process directed primarily by setting and then achieving a sequence of problem solving goals. The model of analysis provided should therefore be able to express its momentary goal to the observation of the student, along with the reason it was the goal selected, the actions taken to satisfy it, and the reasoning for either persisting with it or abandoning it.

This stage of instruction benefits from heavy interaction with the student, and the student can be involved in the demonstrations of reasoning modeling even before formal practice begins. In problems where there are multiple solution paths, the multiple paths should be demonstrated, but separately.

Practice: The normal *range of problems* considerations are effective here as everywhere in this strategy, and the student must experience the spectrum of problems and problem solving approaches.

As the student begins to encounter difficulty solving a problem, it is desirable, rather than to permit floundering and de-motivation to occur, to provide a system of hints which lead the student toward a solution goal or step without being direct. Hinting systems have been constructed with two or three-deep hints available. The hinting may be generic to the problem type or specific to the problem. Giving a hint can benefit from knowing what the student has already done, though that is not essential. And though constructing a hinting system sounds like a difficult undertaking, it need not be complicated at all. As students advance in their ability to solve problems, the level of hinting may be reduced to a single-level hint which summarizes the steps toward problem solution.

Technically, this stage of instructional strategy is trying to establish only the performance of being able to analyze a problem in order to establish a solution path. Achieving a solution is a separate consideration, and the issues for that phase of practice are described later. However, in practical terms, the analysis of the problem and setting it up for solution are often more complicated, involved, and interesting than actually applying the solution. If analysis is performed properly, final solution is done rapidly and easily. You may wish to combine the practice for the solution with that for the analysis, but heavy emphasis must be placed on the analysis rather than on the solution.

Two approaches are possible for the feedback to accompany practice in problem analysis: (1) feedback can be given at the first moment that a student strays from a useful path, and (2) feedback can be saved for review with the student following the last problem solving step. Both approaches have been taken in effective products. Providing immediate feedback for a step taken away from the desirable path of solution requires a complex monitoring and decision-making system. Such feedback systems have been constructed, but they require technical skills for programming in order to implement them. Simpler approaches are possible at two levels. The first level provides a step by step analysis of the student's solution path with a comment on the usefulness of each step. This kind of system can be constructed, but still requires some programming in expert systems languages. The most simple approach to feedback after a complex series of steps is to record the steps executed by the student and contrast them with the steps taken by an expert problem solver in an item-by-item comparison list. This can be relatively simple to construct and yet can help the student identify steps which are consistently being left out of solutions.

It is important that the feedback should evidence the same pattern of *visible* reasoning as the presentation. Even if the only feedback provided is an account of the problem solving steps of an expert (with no student step comparisons), the reasoning of the expert is valuable, and providing only a description of the steps without it leaves the student with questions which most students are unable to answer on their own. These comments on feedback apply as well to the following stages of qualitative and quantitative solution.

Stage: Qualitative and quantitative application

The analysis of the problem and the principle are the complex part of problem solution. The qualitative and quantitative solutions are often relatively simple. They normally involve applying the solution path that has been constructed to predict or calculate the direction, size, and nature of the effects of the operation of the principle on the problem elements. Once it has been determined that acceleration does apply to the situation, and once the problem situation has been analyzed to provide information concerning the velocities (if any) of the elements within the problem at different points, then determining the direction of the acceleration and its relative size requires only the application of a few interpretive rules of thumb (for qualitative solution) or making a few formula computations (for quantitative solution). For instance, acceleration along a curve is always toward the convex or inner side of the curve. This rule of thumb answers one of the questions for a qualitative solution.

During quantitative solution, the monitoring of student steps during solution is an important detail for determining the location of difficulties in performance. Structured, stepwise *worksheets* for recording solutions step-by-step may be used during early practice to scaffold the students' information processing and decision making during solutions. Of course, the instruction is not complete until this scaffolding has been removed and the student is able to perform reliably without it.

Wording principle-using objectives

Principle-using objectives are easy to spot because of their wording. The words *predict, infer, deduce,* and *determine* are often used:

- Predict the effects of heating a metallic carbonate in the presence of a weak hydroxide.

- Given the results of the experiment described below, deduce what the chemist saw at each stage of the procedure.

- Determine whether the force of gravity acting on an object of given mass moving at a given velocity at a given distance from a planet of given mass will pull the object to the planet's surface.

Conclusion

Principle-using behavior lies on the border between simple, insular forms of behavior and integrated behaviors which combine the simple behaviors into larger complexes of performance. Principle-using is the last of the fragmented behaviors for which we consider strategies separately in this book. At this point, the book begins to shift emphasis toward performances that are more complex and integrated, and toward strategy considerations for instruction on performances which are longer and which integrate individual behaviors into patterns of performance.

Self-directed activities

- The steps by which a student applies a principle are spelled out in some detail in this chapter. This contrasts with the other objective types described in previous chapters; for them the method of applying the behavior was not nearly as important. What additional instructional implications does this fact have for the instruction of principles over the instructional principles for other behavior types? Which of the other strategies we have described between Chapter 10 and this chapter comes closest to having to teach the method of applying the behavior?

- It seems more difficult to instruct principles. In your opinion, is this extra effort justified in terms of results in student ability?

- To what extent should a student be taught new knowledge at the principle-using level as opposed to the other levels described in earlier chapters?

- We are used to thinking of instruction on one objective requiring only a single instructional encounter. The instruction for principles seems to call for multiple instructional encounters. Can you think of other kinds of learning that require multiple encounters? What are the implications for the instructional design process? What are the implications for the structure of the curriculum?

Further reading

Reif, F., and Allen, S. (1992). Cognition for interpreting scientific concepts: A study of acceleration. *Cognition and Instruction, 9*(1), 1–44.

Resnick, L. B., and Klopfer, L. E. (1989). *Toward the thinking curriculum: Current cognitive research*. Alexandria, VA: Association for Supervision and Curriculum Development.

Resnick, L. B. (1987). *Education and learning to think*. Washington, DC: National Academy Press.

15

INSTRUCTIONAL STRATEGY III: FRAGMENTATION AND INTEGRATION

Chapter Objectives:

1. *Contrast the concept of micro-strategy with the concept of macro-strategy.*

2. *Describe the shortcomings of the fragmentation approach to instruction when it is used without a corresponding integration approach.*

3. *Describe the implications of learning stages for the formation of macro-strategies.*

4. *Contrast the terms instructional scope, instructional event, instructional challenge, and simulation scope.*

5. *Describe the influence of the concept of increasingly complex microworlds on curriculum structure.*

6. *Describe the function of work models as a mapping intermediary between learning tasks and instructional events.*

7. *Describe the role of work models and simulations in the creation of an integrative curriculum.*

Enlarging the view of strategy

The last five chapters have dealt with instructional strategies for single, specific classes of instructional goals. Each strategy consisted of designed support for the student while he or she was learning a specific type of performance: concept-using, process-using, memorization of factual matter, principle-using, or procedure-using. In this chapter, we will try to put those individual strategies into a larger perspective and expand our definition of instructional strategy. We will show how instructional strategy is applied to different forms of instruction and explore how to implement strategy when instruction is aimed at multiple or grouped instructional goals.

Instructional strategy is given considerable attention in this book. We feel that attention is proportional to the importance of instructional strategy as an issue for instructional designers. Strategy serves as the skeleton of an instructional product: It donates structure and form to the student's instructional experience, it allows the student to exercise initiative during instruction, and it provides the central organizing structure for the designer's plans.

As we continue our discussion of strategy, keep in mind that we have carefully separated the notion of strategic structure from the notion of instructional control. If a designer provides a structured instructional strategy, it does not mean that the designer will assume control of the instruction as it is delivered. Providing strategic structure means providing experiences and events—possibilities—for the student to use while learning. The issue of who controls the use of the strategy is a completely separate design question. We emphasize this because many designers assume that strategic structure automatically implies instructional control. This view is an impediment to investigations into varied applications of instructional strategy.

In this chapter, we shift our attention away from direct and tutorial forms of instruction and toward forms which are less direct, though they still consist of a set of structured experience opportunities for the student. We will continue to emphasize the importance of instructional strategy, but we will begin to speak of strategies which—rather than corresponding to just one instructional goal and the boundaries of one instructional event—correspond with groups of two or more goals and patterns of integration across many separate instructional events. We turn our attention now to instruction which integrates individual performances into larger performance capabilities.

Integration of learning

Imagine several students learning to ride an 18-speed mountain bike. Each of the students arrives at instruction with varying degrees of past experience and learning. One has ridden a 15-speed mountain bike, one has ridden a 3-speed bike, one has ridden a bike without gears, and one has never ridden a bike.

Clearly the learning and instruction needs of each student are different. Each one has different levels of experience in performing the integrated activity of riding and shifting. Each student requires different learning content, and each one faces a different set of tasks to learn and integrate.

The non-rider has many new sensations and coordinated actions to learn and to integrate into a performance capability. The experienced riders will each learn less that is entirely new, and so they will have more energy and attention to devote to combining the fewer newly-learned tasks into an integrated performance. The no-gears rider will have a somewhat heavier challenge because he or she does not possess the skills, timing or decision-making related to shifting gears. Although an experienced rider shifts almost automatically, this learner will go through a stage of performing each shift deliberately, and each shift will use up a given amount of the student's energy and attention until the process becomes automatic.

During learning, the precious mental resources of all of the learners will be divided between performing tasks, monitoring the quality of their performance, and correcting mistakes in knowledge. The amount of new knowledge being learned will vary widely among the students. The amount of integration necessary—the number of lower-level tasks to be combined into a higher-level performance ability—will vary widely also. The designer's task for this instruction will be to adjust the type and amount of strategic support to each learner's needs, best learning rate, and prior knowledge.

How are instructional strategies applied differentially for different learners in such a way that each is challenged within his or her best range of growth? Should the experience be different for one student than for another? If instructional strategy supports a student's information processing during learning and performance, then different students learning the same task will need different levels of that support if they begin from different levels of previous learning and experience.

The 15-gear rider has much skill and knowledge which will transfer readily to the new task. Many of the components of already-learned tasks will apply directly to the new performance. There will be a much lower level of new information processing and integration for this rider, which will influence the amount and type of practice he or she needs. On the other hand, the non-rider has little relevant skill and knowledge to transfer to the new task. Therefore, the non-rider will probably require a much greater degree of strategic support in the form of additional practice, additional prompts and feedback, and perhaps even specialized types of practice which give extra support for the integration of skills the student is attempting to make.

The important design question is how to adjust the instructional strategy so that it meets the support needs of the individual student without overwhelming or boring the other students. Many aspects of a strategy can be adjusted: the amount of information supplied, the amount of coaching support, the amount and type of feedback, and the amount of practice. In addition, several levels of practice can be defined for any performance, and different students may encounter different combinations of these levels. These are the issues that we need to discuss as we consider instructional strategy from the broader perspective. Whereas before we were discussing strategy within one instructional event, called *micro-strategies*, we now want to consider the structure of strategies which operates between events. These are called *macro-strategies*.

Fragmentation and integration

The single challenge which faces all of the bike riders in our example is the integration of separate skills (balancing, steering, pedaling, and shifting) into a single, unified skill. In recent years, instructional designers, including designers of computer-based instruction, have been criticized for creating entire courses of instruction which teach fragments of performance without ever teaching their integration. This is the problem of *fragmentation*. Using our bicycle example, it is as if many courses—in both education and training—were built on the philosophy that you can teach students to balance, pedal, steer, and shift in isolation and then expect them to form these separate skills into a single integrated performance ability on their own. It is possible for people to learn in this way, but it is inefficient, frustrating, and sometimes dangerous and costly to do so. Young people, already able to windmill their arms, kick their legs, and breathe as separate acts, are sometimes taught to swim by being thrown into the water, but most who learn by this method of instant integration do not like swimming afterward.

There is much evidence that the fragmentation problem is real, both in training and education. We produce math students who can solve word problems from the textbook but who cannot apply their math skills to new problems presented in a slightly different form. Their knowledge is said to be *contextualized*. That is, they can only apply that knowledge within the narrow context within which it was originally learned. Contextualization is one by-product of fragmentation.

The villain most often singled out as the cause of fragmentation is the systematic instructional design process, with its emphasis on task analysis—a process which decomposes larger tasks into smaller tasks of more learnable size—and on objectives analysis—a further fragmentation of tasks to identify prerequisite knowledge and skill elements to be taught. We suggest, however, that the real villain is not fragmentation by analysis, because analysis is essential to sound designs.

We name as the real villain the lack of a decontextualizing synthetic or building-up process to follow task analysis and synthesize analyzed fragments into instructionally-useful, integrative instructional events. Using task analysis, designers have, over several decades, built a bridge toward improved instructional designs, but by performing only analysis, they have stopped construction half-way across the river. Designers are now in need of a complementary, synthetic technology which will allow them to design instructional event sequences which integrate fragmented performances.

We feel that it is important for designers of computer-based instruction to pay more attention to integrative levels of instruction than they have in the past. Not only does the computer help the designer create integrative instruction better than the traditional media forms, but the creation of integrative learning environments for practice and assessment is something at which the computer excels. It is one thing which computers do with relative ease that other media find quite difficult.

Failure to integrate: Reasons

We may speculate several reasons why a designer would omit integration-level instructional experiences:

1. Failure to recognize the value of integration experiences: Many designers do not recognize the magnitude of the burden they place on the student by failing to supply adequate integrative experiences. They have no accounting of the personal and organizational costs which result when a student makes errors due to inadequate practice at integrated levels of performance. Some designers believe that the student benefits from the experience of being challenged to make the integration on his or her own, and for some types of instructional goal this makes perfect sense. However, when these students make serious errors in the workplace or in public because they failed to make the appropriate integration on their own, the designer is not there to share the responsibility or the consequences.

2. Inadequate budget to cover the additional design and development required to provide integrative experiences: Integrative instructional experiences have tended historically to come at a higher cost, and designers often lack additional funds for designing integrative experiences. This is because design budgets are normally based on past experience, and the past experience in most instructional settings is that integrative experiences are denied. When the consequence of performance errors is great enough, however, the additional funds required to design integrative instructional experiences are normally found. The training of airline pilots, brain surgeons, shuttle astronauts, and lawyers includes multiple levels of integrative experience—sometimes to the extent of what is called *overtraining*. In the case of doctors, this integrative phase of training lasts for years.

3. Inadequate budget and resources to provide integrating practice environments to students: Not only has it been historically more costly to design integrative practice environments, but it has been more costly to build them as well. An integrative practice environment is more complex than the one in which fragments of performance are learned. It begins to resemble the real world in ways that are important to the practice of the integrated performance. Budgets which do not include funds for the design of these environments normally do not include the funds for implementing them, either. Therefore, designers must discover ways to lower the costs of designing and producing integrative practice environments.

Computer-based learning environments have tremendous potential in this respect. The aircraft simulator which is used for the training of pilots is a form of computer-based practice environment for performing integrations. Despite their very high individual cost, aircraft simulators are still less expensive to build and operate than the aircraft they simulate, so they represent an example of reducing instructional costs through the use of the computer. We believe this same pattern of reduction is possible at many levels of integrative instruction if a way can be found to reduce costs through the use of the computer and tools for designing integrative environments efficiently.

4. Inadequate design tools for defining levels of integrative practice appropriate to a particular audience of students: Instructional design is still a very young technology. Design tools are still evolving as our conceptions of instructional forms evolve. Techniques for identifying integrative instructional events have not been well-defined in the past. One of the important tasks of this chapter is to describe new techniques you can use as a CBI designer to design curricula which provide instructional opportunities for the joining of fragmented performances into an integrated performance capability.

To lay a foundation for talking about integrative instruction, we need to define several basic concepts.

Basic concept: Stages of learning

Several learning theorists describe learning as a process that takes place in stages. The important common thread running through the writings of these theorists is the idea that a new learning task is difficult for a while, but the longer a student practices the learning task (followed by appropriate feedback), the easier it becomes. This means that the student's performance ability increases up to a certain point, then levels off, at which point the student is ready for a more challenging learning task. These plateaus of performance ability are not absolute. In general, however, learning theorists identify plateaus which are common to most learning tasks.

Plateau #1. Basic knowledge: First, there appears to be a stage of learning in which the student is committing to memory certain basic information, semantic, or declarative knowledge related to the performance. If a student is learning a concept, this may consist of learning the defining attributes of the concept; if the target behavior is procedure-using, then the learning may involve the steps, their names, and their order. This knowledge does not consist simply of verbal knowledge. The ability of humans to learn by imitation shows us that it consists—at least in part—of knowledge which can be learned just by observing a performer. Until the basic knowledge is learned, however, performance of the target behavior is not possible. You can't, for instance, apply a concept definition to make a discrimination if you do not already know the definition, and you can't execute a procedure whose steps you have not captured in some form of knowledge.

Plateau #2. Basic proficiency: Once basic knowledge of a performance is learned, the performance itself can be executed, but initial attempts tend to be halting, poorly-timed, and somewhat error-prone. This is not unusual, because the learner is going through a period of intense information processing in which new memory recall habits are being established, ordering of steps is taking place, and decisions are being practiced. Some learning theorists go so far as to say that a new form of knowledge is created during this stage. In any case, the primary task at this point is the coordination of memory activities as they interact with decision-making, discrimination, reasoning, and sometimes motor activities. Eventually, with repeated opportunities to practice the new performance, new levels of capability emerge, and performance becomes smoother, better-timed, and increasingly error-free.

Plateau #3. Automatization: Beyond the level of basic proficiency, if a performance continues to be practiced under appropriate conditions, its speed and automaticity increase. In addition to performing the once-challenging task more easily, the student becomes able to carry out competing tasks at the same time. The newly-learned task consumes less of the student's attention, and the steps are executed with steadily improving timing and skill and in better coordination with other tasks. If a piano player during an earlier stage of learning has to concentrate carefully in order to avoid making mistakes while playing a particular piece of music, once the playing is automatized, it becomes possible to answer questions, carry on a conversation, and even have creative thoughts while playing it. Dr. Will Kessling, a notable musician from the West, was once invited to sit in the orchestra pit of a Broadway theater while the orchestra played the 6,142nd performance of a popular and long-running musical. He was amazed by the bass viol player's ability to work crossword puzzles while playing perfectly and the percussionist's ability to read a book without missing a cue.

Theorists differ in their explanations of why these stages of learning exist, but they do appear to exist universally among humans. Instructional designers must take these stages of learning into account as they devise instructional macro-strategies. They must provide support and practice opportunities for each stage. These stages also figure in maintaining the right level of challenge.

Basic concept: Instructional event

Instruction is subdivided into parcels of time. A learner can stay on one learning task for only so long before the questions occur, "When will I be done? When do I reach a stopping point?" A course of instruction, whether it is measured in terms of hours, days, months, or semesters, is divided into parts having a beginning and an end, and there are several reasons for the division. Purportedly, the school instructional day is divided into parts because humans need variety and convenient break points just as much as the school needs a manageable schedule. Since the schools have invented no other basis for dividing instructional time, it is broken into equal parts—*periods* of equal length.

In less rigidly structured instructional settings, we still divide the instruction into parts. We may call them *presentations, lessons, modules,* or *math time.* The terminology is not so important as the reason behind the division. There is a need for closure with humans; there must be some point at which a learner stops to survey the learning which has been accomplished, measure progress and attainment, and consolidate new learning more fully with the old. There must also be breaks during which the learner can rest from the intense activity of learning, renew energy, and clear out the cobwebs that result from intense concentration. Moreover, there is some evidence that learning is consolidated after a period of rest for the mind, such as the passing of time or a period of sleep.

The breaks in instruction can be chosen on several principles. School days are divided on an administrative basis; whether instruction has reached a plateau of completion or not, when the bell rings, the class ends. In other instructional settings, the length of the instructional period is determined by the content or the goals of instruction. When a goal plateau has been reached, there can be a break before the next one is initiated. In this view, instruction is like eating an orange: the size of a performance to be learned is almost always larger than a student can handle in one bite, so the orange is divided up into parts to be eaten. At any given moment during instruction, it is possible for a student to attack one new instructional goal at a time, or maybe two, but it is not likely that more than that number can be handled at one time if the goals are entirely new, so we divide complex performances into parts which can be learned and then integrated.

Whatever principle is used, every designer must select some basis for breaking a course of instruction into manageable, instructable parts. We will refer to these parts in this book as *instructional events.* As you will see, the term instructional event refers to an unbroken length of instructional time which: (1) is used to pursue a specific composite instructional goal, (2) proceeds to some appropriate breaking or ending point, (3) can be scheduled separately within a larger instructional plan without affecting the intentions of the plan, and (4) uses one instructional medium or combination of instructional media. Let's explore the implications of this definition.

An instructional event has internal coherence if stopping the event means full instructional effect is not achieved. Consider the common frustration of the English teacher when leading a classroom discussion of a novel through which the teacher is trying to guide the class toward conclusions about the author's art. If the bell ending the class rings before the discussion reaches a good closure point, then the intended instructional event has been interrupted and left incomplete. A scheduled administrative terminus has been reached before the terminus of the instructional event. This example makes clear the difference between the administrative definition of an instructional event and one related to instructional goals. Clearly, the designer is most interested in the definition of instructional events in terms of instructional goals.

Basic concepts: Instructional scope and challenge

The goal or objective of an instructional event defines its *instructional scope,* and every event has a scope. Instructional scope specifies a performance level that a student is expected to reach during one instructional event. One of the most important decisions a designer makes is the selection of instructional scopes and their sequence.

In fragmented instruction, individual instructional events normally have an instructional scope the size of one task or one objective. Chapters 10 through 14 describe instructional micro-strategies (strategies used within one instructional event) which can be used for instruction whose scope is one objective in size. However, as single-objective fragments of performance are learned and students possess skills and knowledge that are ready for integration, the instructional scope necessarily broadens. It begins to encompass gradually-expanding numbers of individual tasks and objectives in various combinations, sized appropriately for the learning abilities and readiness of the students in the target population.

Instructional scope is closely related to a complementary concept called *instructional challenge*. Whereas instructional scope describes a specific performance level to be attained, instructional challenge describes the level of difficulty which that scope represents to a given student at a given moment. Scope describes the attainment in absolute terms; challenge describes it relative to its difficulty to the student.

Students vary in the size of the instructional step they are ready to take at a given moment—the level of challenge for which they are ready. This seems to depend on several factors, including: the existing skill and knowledge level of the student, the student's state of confidence, the student's level of interest and motivation, and the number of new to-be-learned knowledge elements and performances included within the scope. Interestingly, it depends also on the type and degree of micro-strategic support which the designer provides.

One of the designer's tasks is to supply the possibility for a succession of instructional events for students, each possessing its own instructional scope, such that the level of instructional challenge is constantly maintained within the student's ability to achieve. This must be done without the challenge level falling below what the student finds interesting and worthwhile. That is, the level of challenge must be fitted to the student: neither too difficult nor too easy. This is an example of a strategic issue which influences motivation.

To adjust the level of instructional challenge, the designer must not only consider the characteristics of the individual instructional event but also the relation between events. The size of the step between events is selected carefully. The designer's decisions concerning the scopes selected, the size of the steps between them, and their ordering is called the designer's macro-strategy.

Consider an analogy to stair-climbing. The height of stairs in a staircase is calculated according to a standard formula which ensures that the size of step is comfortable for an adult of average height. An infant climbing a staircase built for adults finds it to be considerably more challenging, just as the average adult finds climbing the pyramids—where the average step size is chest-high—more challenging. A designer of computer-based instruction must be deliberate in making macro-strategy decisions and must adjust the level of challenge to fit the student population receiving the instruction.

Simulation, instructional events, and instructional scope

As instructional designers attempt to use simulation, there is often a confusion between the scope of the task being learned, the instructional event, and the boundaries of the simulation. Sometimes the designer is not sure whether to begin designing the instructional event or the simulation first, and the relationship between the simulation and the task analysis becomes confused as well.

The important thing to remember is that an instructional designer must try to prepare the *best sequence* of instructional events. Therefore, the events are the first concern. The events themselves are defined in terms of tasks and objectives from an analysis process. Tasks are the basis for event definition. The designer's job is to select one or more tasks or objectives to define the scope of each event.

A simulation is merely an instructional vehicle to create an interactive practice environment for one or more instructional events. One simulated environment may be suitable for the practice related to *one* or *many* instructional events, depending on the tasks the simulation is designed to support. Finally, it is possible for one task to require more than one instructional event for learning, and it is further possible that one of those multiple events will require simulation, while the other does not.

Figures 1a and 1b illustrate the relationship between tasks, instructional events, and simulations. Figure 1a shows that it is possible in some cases that the task, event, and simulation boundaries will coincide exactly, that the instruction for one task or goal requires exactly one practice event, and that one simulation program is created to supply the practice environment.

Figure 1b illustrates the more likely situation where the learning of one task requires multiple instructional events, some using simulation and some not. As a designer creates a curriculum which involves the use of simulation as an instructional means and which is based on task analysis and objectives analysis, it is very useful to recognize these relationships. Doing so keeps the designer focused on the primary goal, *which is the construction of the best sequence of instructional events for the population of students being instructed.*

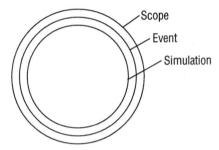

Figure 1a. The case in which scope, event and simulation boundaries coincide.

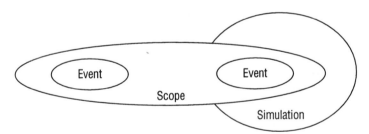

Figure 1b. The case in which scope, event and simulation boundaries do not coincide.

Structure, order, and choice

We are describing such a structured view of things that it may appear we are promoting single-path, lockstep curricula which march the student along toward mastery. This is the opposite of what we intend, and we feel we must pause to describe our point of view on structure, order, and choice as they relate to curriculum-building.

The standard organization of curriculum most commonly found in both education and training today is, in fact, the single-path, lockstep variety. All students follow the single path of instructional events through a syllabus which is the same for all students. In some cases, designers of CBI, trying to appear to be more flexible and adaptive, will place a menu of instructional events before students from which they may select an instructional order. When possible, classroom teachers provide experiences prescribed for the needs of the one student, but neither the training world nor the educational world—even with computer-based tools—

has yet learned how to adapt instruction to the individual while still moving the individual along within a general curricular stream leading to accomplishment within a common set of knowledge and skill competencies. As we described in an earlier chapter, the dream of adaptive instruction is still only a dream.

We know that it is possible to create single-path curricula because instructors and designers have been doing it for centuries. In this chapter we are describing technological concepts which allow the CBI designer to create curricula adaptive to the individual student. It is possible for designers to break free of the lockstep conceptions of curriculum which have been the staple fare of the past. We have surfaced the issues of *instructional challenge* and *size of step* because these are the parameters which must be measured and adjusted in order to adapt the curriculum to the individual. We describe the differences between the boundaries of the scope (goal), time frame (event), and method (simulation) of instruction because it is in part the confusion of these things which has led to retaining the lockstep conception of curriculum.

Our thinking regarding curriculum has been overly simplistic. We do not maintain that making things more complex will necessarily improve our curricula, but we do feel that we must invent a few new definitions and conceptions which allow us to make thinking which is now rigid and inflexible become more adaptive to the individual. If we realize that the level of challenge is a thing which can be adjusted, then we can begin to look for techniques which allow us to design practice interactions which differ in their level of challenge while advancing students toward a common educational or training goal. If we are lucky, we may find that providing different levels of challenge for different students is neither as difficult nor as costly as it seems.

Curriculum choices within a highly-structured curriculum may be placed under the choice of the instructor or the student; similarly, the site of control does not have to remain fixed during the entire course of instruction. It is possible for the control over curriculum choices to be computed moment by moment and given either to the student or to the instructor, based on the wisdom of choices being made.

We believe it is the duty of the designer to provide a set of curricular events for instruction. How students move through the events presents a design opportunity, and the options are many, but only if we go beyond the over-simple thinking of the past and begin to speak of different structural and pathing options. We feel that curriculum structure options is an especially important issue in instructional design because it is becoming increasingly apparent that each instructional session is an opportunity for instructors to teach students not only academic or skill-directed content, but to teach them how learn how to learn as well—by letting them participate in higher-order instructional choices. One step in that direction is for designers to understand the structural features of the curriculum, and that is our purpose in this chapter.

Macro-strategy and curriculum structure

At this point, we want to relate the basic concepts which we have been describing into a coherent view of instructional macro-strategy and the structure of instructional curricula in which the desired end-product is integrated performance rather than fragmented performances. Since simulation-based instruction is often used in curricula as a tool to promote integration, it means that we are also interested in knowing how simulation participates in this macro-strategy. The design of integrative sequences of instruction is a technology which has not been well-developed within the world of formal instructional design. Interestingly, it is well-developed in many areas of practical and applied instruction: sports, music, law, aviation, medicine, and theater.

The purpose of a curriculum is to help a student move from some level of entry performance to some level of real-world performance capability, as shown in Figure 2. The real-world capability which is the target of instruction can consist of any human performance: from operating machines, to philosophizing, to performing artistic acts, to designing and constructing new tools and products. Therefore, the principles of curriculum construction are not restricted just to either simple conceptual knowledge or performance knowledge.

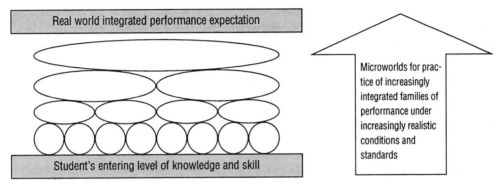

Figure 2. The microworld structure of an integrative curriculum.

A curriculum of instruction leading to real-world performance moves the student in steps which are sized according to the student's abilities, readiness, and motivation. It does so by constructing a sequence of performance microworlds within which the student can perform tasks in realistic settings, under increasingly realistic conditions, and to increasingly realistic standards of quality. This conception of the curriculum has been named the principle of *increasingly complex microworlds* by Richard Burton, John Seely Brown, and Gerhard Fischer, who first described the concept. In this view of the curriculum structure, determining the size and nature of the steps provided for students to reach as intermediate waypoints is the essential challenge of curriculum design.

Figure 2 shows movement through a curriculum of gradually-expanding performance steps which by degrees approximate and finally reach a real-world performance threshold. This model, as we have already pointed out, is applied to some degree in a number of professional fields.

A musical example

Let's use an example from music instruction to illustrate this integrative structure of a curriculum. Our main goal will be to illustrate how a sequence of instructional events can lead to integrated performance. In this example, we will try to show how the macro-strategy created by this ordering of events helps the student move from a condition of incomplete or absent performance capability to a target level of capability. This journey will take place through a sequence of widening (increasingly complex) instructional scopes which provide practice for fragments of the performance, leading eventually to practice of the integrated performance.

In our example, we will observe a master choir director teaching a complex choral work to a group of singers who are assumed to have already learned the basic skills of vocal control and basic music reading skill. We will also assume that the choir members have neither heard nor sung this music prior to its introduction by the director.

Having shared with the choir the end goal of being able to perform the musical work at a high level of proficiency, the director may play through the piece to give the students an orientation to its parts and their relation to each other. The same work performed by another choral group may be played as well not only as a model but in order to set some quality expectations.

At some point, the director will select one section of the choral work to begin instructing. This constitutes the first scope, or task grouping, of the instruction. The director will keep the choir practicing within this scope until some quality criterion (which the director has in mind) is reached or until it is clear the choir cannot reach that criterion.

As practice is accomplished within this scope, the director will systematically and temporarily vary the size of its component scopes both upward and downward, focusing on parts of the section and on details of the parts and then enlarging the scope as the choir's performance permits. The director will also vary the quality of performance expected for each scope and the conditions provided to support performance within each scope. This will define *a series of instructional events* which build upon each other, each one moving the choir closer to the largest target performance scope and performance quality level.

At the completion of each instructional event, the director will select a new scope (larger, smaller, or the same size), a new set of conditions, or a new quality standard based on the performance of the choir at that point in time. It is the change in scope, conditions or standards— or a combination of these three—which will define the ending of one instructional event and the beginning of another. There will be many potential paths toward the final desired performance level, *and the path actually chosen will be selected by the director as instruction proceeds, based on moment-by-moment assessments of progress.*

When the choir reaches the full quality standard for the performance of the original target scope, the director will simply repeat the same processes which led to its attainment within a new target scope until the target scope has widened to include the entire choral work, performed under the most realistic concert-level conditions, and to the concert-quality standard of performance. The complete succession of instructional events will take place in short practice sessions spaced over weeks or months and will include the repetition of many of the practice levels for review purposes over the course of these sessions.

Let's follow in some detail a portion of the exact sequence of scopes selected by a real choir director during an actual practice session.

The sequence of instructional events is shown in Table 1, along with a commentary which describes how the immediate event relates to the previous event. The musical piece being learned by the choir is divided into four main parts, labeled A through D. Within each part, there are numerical symbols above the music which indicate convenient beginning and ending points for practice purposes. The musical piece is written to be sung by the four standard vocal ranges: soprano, alto, tenor, and bass.

As you read through the description in Table 1, note that all standards of performance can be expressed relative to the highest standard of performance. Each standard will consist of some degree of relaxation of the highest real-world standard. Conditions in every case will be standard (piano accompaniment), except when special provision is made for extra support during a practice or when the standard piano support is removed for a specific purpose (such as to allow the singers to hear more clearly what they sound like as they sing a specific note sequence or certain words).

The purpose of this example has been to illustrate that the integrative curriculum—illustrated here being used by a classroom instructor—consists of a sequence of instructional events, each with a specific scope for its instruction and practice and each with its given conditions of practice and hoped-for standards of performance. The distance between instructional events—the size of the learning step—is a direct result of the designer's (or instructor's) systematic manipulation, moment by moment, of these three factors: scope, conditions, and standards, as shown in Figure 3.

Table 1. A sequence of instructional events at choir practice.

Scope, Conditions, and Standards	Commentary
Scope: Section B of the choral work, subsections 1 through 9 (in other words, the entirety of Section B). **Conditions:** Piano accompaniment as usual. **Standards:** Lowest possible standard. There will be no corrective feedback following this instructional event because it is intended to be diagnostic.	The director asks the choir sing through one section of the larger work in order to become familiar with it. As they do so, the director uses a diagnostic ear to observe spots that will require extra practice. These are remembered, and they will become the basis for selecting future instructional events. The quality standard for this attempt is very low—any level of performance will be acceptable—because the instructional event is for orientation and diagnostic purposes. No special conditions or assistance are provided for this attempt.
Scope: Numbered passage 2 of Section B of the choral work. **Conditions:** One-note piano accompaniment of each vocal range separately, playing only the targeted range's notes. Only one vocal group will sing at a time, so there will be no auditory cues from the other vocal groups while one group is singing. **Standards:** Each vocal range will be expected to sing the correct notes played for it by the piano twice through in a row. The standard for the holding and releasing of the notes will be relaxed, as will the standards for diction and dynamic.	The director now selects a numbered passage from Section B which sounded quite muddled during the first sing-through. This numbered passage now becomes the temporary target scope, and the director's temporary performance goal will be to get each vocal range in the choir to sing its part of this passage correctly—at a low standard of quality, but distinctly hitting the right notes. Therefore, each of the four vocal ranges will sing through the passage with one-note piano accompaniment while only that group sings its part. Each vocal group will repeat this practice in solo until it is capable of singing the right sequence of notes twice in a row.
Scope: Numbered passage 2 of Section B of the choral work. **Conditions:** Relaxed tempo. The passage will be sung slightly slower than usual. All parts will sing together. **Standards:** Each vocal group will be expected to hit its correct notes in two successive sing-throughs. The standard for the holding and releasing of the notes will be relaxed, as will the standards for diction and dynamic.	The director, having brought each vocal group to the ability to sing its part separately, will now select as a temporary scope getting the vocal groups to sing their parts together, but more slowly than usual.
Scope: The scope is narrowed to include only one note within the passage. **Conditions:** Same **Standards:** The single note of interest must be sung with the correct time value in order for performance to be acceptable.	The director now chooses a more narrow temporary scope and focuses on one note which is not being given the correct duration. Choir members are dropping the note too soon in order to take a breath.
Scope: Same **Conditions:** Same **Standards:** Same as the previous event, only the passage is to be sung with correct diction.	Having reached the point where the vocal groups can sing the correct notes together as a choir and with the correct timing given each note, the director next chooses to keep the scope the same but increase the quality standard. After a short modeling session in which the correct pronunciation of the words is demonstrated (sometimes with comical exaggeration), the choir will be expected to sing the correct notes in the passage and with correct diction.
Scope: Same **Conditions:** Same, with the addition that the piano will now play at normal tempo. **Standards:** The choir is expected to sing the passage with each vocal group hitting the correct notes, singing the words with correct diction, and singing at the normal tempo.	The final step toward full-standard performance of this isolated passage (scope) is taken as the director asks the choir to sing the passage with correct diction, hitting the correct notes, giving each one its correct time value, and at the normal tempo. If the choir reaches the expected standard during this event, it means that the choir will be singing this one passage at a level approaching real performance quality.

The remainder of the learning of this piece of music consists mainly of a repetition of this general pattern of instructional events. The pattern described in Table 1 can best be described as an integrative pattern. The notion of integration does not require that instruction begin with the smallest fragment of skill or knowledge. The choir director used a relatively high-level scope as a diagnostic to gauge the size of steps this choir was ready take. Following that, he focused on points of need by selecting specific sub-scopes to practice. But the selection of events did not follow strictly bottom-up rules of ordering, and in some cases it was influenced by motivational needs.

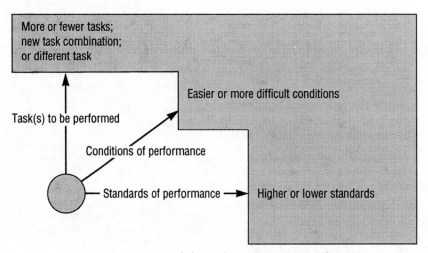

Figure 3. Dimensions of change between instructional events.

It has become a standard practice for designers to assume that they must begin instructing at the lowest levels of scope—at the lowest task of the task analysis. This principle has contributed greatly to the tendency toward fragmented instruction which lacks later integration. It also tends to deny to students a kind of orienting knowledge that would be helpful to them in taking more responsibility of their own learning.

The quest of the instructional designer during curriculum-building is to construct one or more sequences of instructional events suited to the needs and abilities of the target population. This means selecting, grouping, and ordering tasks within instructional events to be practiced together, and then arranging the groupings themselves into instructional sequences which are either set beforehand or decided at the time of instruction.

The designer's creation and ordering of events controls the level of instructional challenge. This is true just as much for the invisible cognitive skills as it is for the visible physical skills. It is also as true for ideational or conceptual content as it is for performances. Recent research is showing how progressions of performance capability are involved in the learning of both conceptual and performance structures.

Work models

The technology by which tasks and objectives are grouped into instructional events is called work model synthesis. Work model synthesis is the synthetic process we described earlier for building an integrating bridge of instructional events between fragmented learning and integrated learning. Each unique grouping of tasks and objectives used for instruction and practice, with an accompanying set of conditions and standards, is called *a work model.* Changing a task, a condition, or a standard creates a new work model.

The name for the work model comes from the function it performs: It defines a model of work or performance which the student is expected to reach through (1) instruction and (2) practice with feedback. The instruction given may consist of didactic messages, demonstrations, discoveries, observations of models, questioning, or any number of techniques. The practice is accompanied by feedback because the feedback allows the student to correct misconceptions and establish the ability to monitor and self-evaluate personal performance.

The work model itself is not the instructional event, but instructional events are patterned by work models in the same way a cookie cutter patterns cookies. Work models provide a template of performance which can be made to create either one or multiple instructional events, all based on an identical performance specification.

The work model synthesis proceeds like this: Work models are created, and then instructional events are defined from the work models. The work model is only an intermediary because instructional events covering identical tasks, conditions, and standards may occur more than once in an instructional curriculum. A work model is a combination of the three elements that only occurs once. A work model is conceptual, but an instructional event is an actual, schedulable thing. Instructional events are created using work models as their pattern (see Figure 7).

The work model, then, is just a mapping entity. Figures 4 through 6 show how tasks and objectives are mapped onto work models. There are only three patterns of mapping possible, and each one is used for certain purposes.

One-to-one: A one-to-one mapping (see Figure 4) is used when a single task or objective requires instruction and practice in isolation (or you might say, in fragmentation) before being combined with other tasks and objectives for integrative practice. It is a common thing today for instructional designers to create one-objective or one-task instructional events. In fact, the fragmentation problem arises mainly from the failure of designers to specify work models containing more than one task or objective.

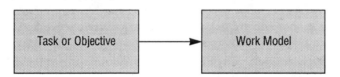

Figure 4. One-to-one objective to work model mapping.

One-to-many: In many cases, a single task will appear in a number of work models (see Figure 5). For instance, a complex performance may be practiced in several simulated settings, each more realistic than the last. Each successive simulation constitutes a different set of practice conditions and therefore a new work model. Successive levels of criterion also define multiple work models. Most importantly, tasks are learned within one performance context, and it is important to give the student practice of the task outside that context, so that the task becomes free of the original context in which it was learned. *Decontextualizing* task performance is achieved by allowing the task to be performed in different settings and in combination with different sets of accompanying tasks. This is the reason that just one or two practice problems is seldom sufficient to give the student the ability to perform well in unfamiliar task settings.

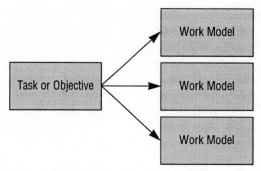

Figure 5. One-to-many objective to work model mapping.

Many-to-one: In many cases, multiple tasks are combined within one work model for integrated practice (see Figure 6). When tasks have been learned separately, they are combined into larger groupings for integrative practice. The higher the level of integration, the more tasks are included within the scope of the work model.

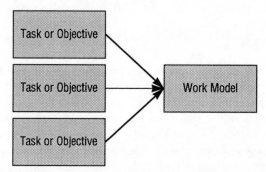

Figure 6. Many-to-one objective to work model mapping.

Multiple instructional events can also arise from a single work model as shown in Figure 7. This is true particularly when one experience of practicing a performance is not sufficient to bring a performance to the standard of quality specified within the work model.

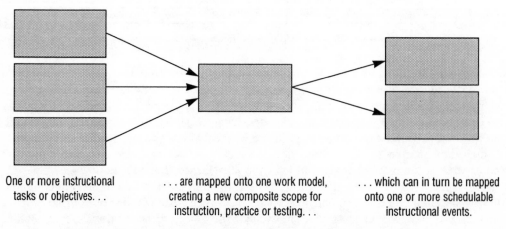

One or more instructional   . . . are mapped onto one work model,   . . . which can in turn be mapped
tasks or objectives. . .   creating a new composite scope for   onto one or more schedulable
                                 instruction, practice or testing. . .   instructional events.

Figure 7. Work model mapping from objectives and to instructional events.

A complex performance improves with practice and feedback, and multiple, spaced practices under the same conditions and with the same criterion of quality are sometimes a good strategy, but it also leads to the creation of more than one instructional event from the same work model.

Variations in grouping

Tasks can be combined in any variety to form work models which represent some partial real-world performance. New tasks can be introduced into work models incrementally, with each introduction bringing the scope of performance one step closer to the real world scope. This can result in a large number of work models if the incremental changes to tasks, conditions, and standards are small.

New tasks need not be introduced in a particular order. The order in which new tasks appear within work models is not necessarily fixed by their hierarchical position in a task analysis. Even in cases where one task is a prerequisite or component of another, the higher-order task can be practiced if the instruction fills in the performance of the missing subtask for the student. This is called *scaffolding*, and it allows the student to practice simplified versions of the higher task without being required to perform the whole task.

This principle is illustrated in the following excerpt from an account of the training of a neurosurgeon taken from Mark Shelton's *Working in a Very Small Place* (Vintage Books, 1990). After describing a specialized operating microscope used for neurosurgery, Shelton writes:

> *Generally, the attending surgeon will watch the resident's work through this [the microscope] until the resident reaches the limit of his experience; then they switch places and the attending surgeon operates while the resident watches and learns. The process is accretive; no resident suddenly performs an operation from start to finish, but rather does a little bit more each time. "I remember vividly the first time I did a case all the way through," says Dr. Mark Dias, a senior resident on the neurological service. "I was going right along, just concentrating on what I was going to do next, and I realized that I was doing it without anyone telling me what to do. The attending was just sitting there very quietly at the side of the microscope, not saying anything, and I thought, 'That was it; I'm there.' It is an eerie feeling the first time to recognize that you've just done an operation without any help." (pp. 61–62)*

The work model is a very flexible container which expands to fit the momentary capacity and performance goals of the student. Each work model is in effect a meta-instructional objective that combines performances together for practice purposes (or splits them, according to the need). Sequences of work models can be used by designers to define one or more paths of learning challenge which move the student from novice to proficient behavior. The work model can also be used by the designer to define a complete *field* of problems which may be used by students to progress toward integrated performance, each student taking a path through the field particularly suited to his or her learning speed and trajectory. We call this the "field" theory of curriculum design.

The incremental introduction of increasingly complex tasks is described as an essential feature of the cognitive apprenticeship model of learning described by Collins, Brown, and Newman. This model of the instructional process brings to the schooling of the invisible cognitive functions the same level of structure that has been used for ages to train craft skills. Just as the visible skills are learned through a stepwise movement through many experiences toward mastery, the invisible skills of thinking and problem solving yield to the incremental expansion of performance scopes made possible by work models. Work models, then, represent the main element of a designer's macro-strategy.

Work models and simulation

Using work models does introduce a new step into the instructional design process, but it is not certain whether this is an entirely new step or simply the formalization of steps which designers have been taking for years without recognizing the formal process, principles, and constructs which were available to guide them. We have shown an example of the use of work models in music instruction to sequence instructional events. This age-old technique has been used in fields as diverse as sports and theater. We hope that it can become more commonly applied in the design of computer-based instructional products.

The main benefit of work model synthesis is that it brings system, order, and the capability for more precise control to the otherwise confusing and imprecise process of defining progressive, integrating sequences of syllabus events.

Use of work models allows syllabus and media decisions to be made in a rational and public manner. It also encourages more careful consideration of the uses of simulation in the curriculum and increases the chance that the syllabus will incorporate appropriate levels of integrative practice for the target population for each instructional task and combination of tasks. This normally requires the use of simulation.

Once syllabus decisions are made and tested during instruction, the syllabus can be revised on the basis of data which accumulates from use, enabling adjustments to be made with more precision than would otherwise be possible. Use of work models applies to virtually all forms of performance, and it has been applied by students to performances as diverse as Pinyin (Chinese) language reading skills, tennis serving skills, library research skills for elementary children, scientific process skills, and spoken foreign language comprehension. The more complexly integrated the performance, the more useful the work model technique has been, whether or not the performance is visible or motor-biased.

The use of work models facilitates the appropriate incorporation of simulation within curricula in several ways.

First, work models align instructional media concerns with instructional strategy concerns, then allow portions of the instructional strategy for a single instructional objective to be split out as separate designer intentions for separate media assignment. The presentation phase of instruction for an objective can be carried out in a medium that is appropriate for its strategic requirements, frequently a presentation-oriented medium, while the practice phase can be carried out in another that suits its requirements, frequently a simulation.

Second, using work models encourages definition of intermediate-level task and objective combinations which require practice as a group, and allows the selection of an appropriate instructional medium for them. Most often, the appropriate medium for intermediate-level instruction is some form of simulation.

Third, using work models encourages the notion of incrementality in designing paths toward real-world performance. Instead of thinking of simulation as one level of practice on the single path toward real-world performance, it suggests that a progressive family of simulated environments may be used, each distinguished by its level of fidelity (conditions), scope of task and objective inclusion (behavior), and level of expected performance (standard).

The variation of these dimensions should suggest that a syllabus or curriculum can be a multi-dimensional field of possible work model stepping stones. The designer's task becomes one of selecting the best path for the student to move across the field—not stopping at each point on the path, but only those which optimize progress for the student.

Conclusion

The more complex the performance being trained, the greater the need for the work model as a design structure and simulation as an instructional vehicle. If work model synthesis is performed, it increases the likelihood that simulations or whatever form of instruction is used will be well-integrated with other instructional forms into a coherent curriculum.

Self-directed activities

- Recount from your own life an instructional experience in which you learned fragments of performance but never had the opportunity to integrate them into coherent abilities at a higher level of performance. What kinds of experience did you feel you needed that you didn't get? How did you finally arrange to have the experience you needed? What was the cost?

- Recount from your own life an instructional experience in which you were asked to learn at an integrated level of performance without adequate experience at a more fragmented level first. What problems were caused? What kind of preparatory experience did you need that you did not get? How much of that experience did you need? Did you ever finally obtain the needed experience?

- Identify several performances that you have learned to the level of automaticity. Identify several that you have learned to a basic level of proficiency but not to automaticity. What will it take for you to reach automaticity in those performances? How much time? What type of activity or instruction will be needed?

- Examine several instructional products. On what basis is the product partitioned into instructional experiences? What degree of uniformity do you see in the relative size and difficulty of the steps the student must take in moving from experience to experience? Does the size of the step taken accelerate toward the end? Is this good or bad?

- Identify educational experiences from your own life that exemplify the use of increasingly *complex microworlds*. What was satisfying about this experience? What was not satisfying? How could the learning experience have been improved?

Further reading

Bunderson, C. V., Gibbons, A. S., Olsen, J. B., and Kearsley, G. P. (1981). Work models: Beyond instructional objectives. *Instructional Science, 10*, 205–215.

Burton, R. R., Brown, J. S., and Fischer, G. (1984). Skiing as a model of instruction. In B. Rogoff and J. Lave, *Everyday cognition: Its development in social context* (pp. 139–150). Cambridge, MA: Harvard University Press.

Collins, A., Brown, J. S., and Newman, S. E. (1989). Cognitive apprenticeship: Teaching the crafts of reading, writing, and mathematics. In L. B. Resnick (Ed.), *Knowing, learning, and instruction: Essays in honor of Robert Glaser* (pp. 453–494). Hillsdale, NJ: Lawrence Erlbaum Associates.

Gibbons, A. S., Bunderson, C. V., Olsen, J. B., and Robertson, J. (1995). Work models: Still beyond instructional objectives. *Machine-Mediated Learning, 5*(3/4), 221–236.

Lepper, M. R., Woolverton, M., Mumme, D. L., and Gurtner, J. (1993). Motivational techniques of expert human tutors: Lessons for the design of computer-based tutors. In S. P. Lajoie and S. J. Derry, *Computers as cognitive tools* (pp. 75–105). Hillsdale, NJ: Lawrence Erlbaum Associates.

O'Neil, H. F. (1978). *Learning strategies.* New York: Academic Press.

Pappo, H. A. (1998). *Simulations for skills training.* Englewood Cliffs, NJ: Educational Technology Publications.

Reigeluth, C. M., Merrill, M. D., and Bunderson, C. V. (1978). The structure of subject matter content and its instructional implications. *Instructional Science, 7,* 107–126.

Reigeluth, C. M., and Stein, F. S. (1983). The elaboration theory of instruction. In C. M. Reigeluth (Ed.), *Instructional design theories and models: An overview of their current status* (pp. 335–381). Hillsdale, NJ: Lawrence Erlbaum Associates.

Shuell, T. J. (1990). Phases of meaningful learning. *Review of Educational Research, 60*(4), 531–547.

White, B. Y., and Frederiksen, J. (1990). Causal model progressions as a foundation for intelligent learning environments. *Artificial Intelligence, 24,* 99–157.

16

INSTRUCTIONAL SIMULATIONS

Chapter Objectives:

1. *Identify the barriers to the increased use of instructional simulations.*

2. *Give the identifying characteristics of the instructional simulation and differentiate instructional simulations from path and visual simulations.*

3. *Describe the working relationships between simulation and other forms of CBI.*

4. *Describe the trade-off between the fidelity and resolution level of a simulation on the one hand and instructional focus and development cost on the other.*

5. *Identify three main types of instructional simulation.*

6. *Describe the pattern of learner interactions characteristic of model-centered instruction and identify the functions carried out during instruction using this model.*

7. *Describe the experience-centered curriculum and contrast it with the message-centered curriculum.*

8. *Name six major instructional features of an instructional simulation and describe the appropriate use of each feature.*

9. *Define object-oriented development tools and describe their impact on the designs used for computer-based instructional products.*

10. *Describe the change in management systems which will necessarily follow the use of experience-based curricula.*

The challenges of simulation

Simulation as an instructional tool has historically enjoyed a special status. It is widely appreciated as a powerful tool for instructing higher-level principles, procedures, and cause-effect relationships. The ability of simulations to grab and hold the attention of learners is an effect so common that it is seldom questioned. Instructors frequently desire to use simulations but are prevented by one or more of the many barriers which simulations present to the designer:

- The high cost of developing simulations.

- The specialized technical skills required to develop simulations as opposed to more sequenced or scripted forms of instruction.

- The difficulty of the tools—often specialized programming languages—used to create computer-based simulations.

- The non-sequential and non-linear modes of designer thinking required to design instructional simulations.

- The difficulty of making simulations instructional in a strategic sense as well as in an experiential sense.

- The problems of integrating simulations within the larger curriculum structure.

The combined effect of these factors is reduced reliance on simulations for instruction, reflected in the low relative proportion of simulations to other instructional forms. This creates the ironic situation where one of the more powerful forms of computer-based instruction is also one of the least widely used.

A few highly-technological areas of instruction have benefited greatly from the use of simulations. Large and expensive aviation simulators which are used to train flight crews have become an indispensable instructional medium. If they could no longer be used, the training of aircrews would be more expensive, more dangerous, and would take more time.

One of the main challenges facing the computer-based instruction industry is making instructional simulations available to a large population of designers without the requirement for specialized tool skills, and at an affordable cost. This goal is being achieved. In this chapter we will describe principles for the design of instructional simulations which are moving within the reach of the average CBI designer.

Instructional simulations

Instructional simulations must be distinguished from simulations which are created for other purposes. Independent of the instructional world, simulations have been developed and used since the beginning of the computer age to support the creation of complex designs and for scientific inquiry. Architects can know before a building is constructed how it is expected to respond during an earthquake, high wind, or other natural calamity. Scientists can predict the effects of colliding atoms and colliding galaxies because simulations allow them to create models of real-world systems, put them under stress, and observe their behavior. Progress in both science and technology would be severely limited if we did not build simulations.

Once it became evident that simulations could teach scientists and technologists, the next logical question was whether they could be used to teach the general population of students. Early general purpose simulations were sometimes used for instructional purposes with generally satisfactory results. They allowed students to observe things directly which before could only be imagined. Through direct manipulation over repeated experiences, they allowed the student to observe nuances of system behavior that would otherwise require enormous amounts of verbal communication to convey or long spans of time to observe. This information became available to all, and not to just those who understood the special symbolic languages of mathematics and logic.

However, simulations used by scientists and technologists differ in important ways from those tailored for instructional purposes. Scientists use simulations to explore an unknown phenomenon, but when simulations are used for instructional purposes, specialized *instructional functions* often are used to guide and support learning. The instructional simulation can be a subtle force, active and sometimes directive in its interactions with students, nudging or leading them in certain directions, helping them to discover and explore the extent of the otherwise hidden knowledge which they contain. In many cases, a simulation will present a carefully selected problem to a student to be solved, and in many cases, the simulation's goal is to lead the student in self-directed learning, fostering the development of cognitive habits and skills which enable the student to become an independent learner.

For these reasons, instructional simulations must be outfitted differently from technological or scientific simulations. They must allow the designer to target specific instructional goals, and they must possess instructional features in addition to their ability to simply model something. Designers of instructional simulations must realize that their task includes the design of the *instructional* aspects of a simulation as well as its *modeling* aspects.

We define instructional simulations by four characteristics:

1. An instructional simulation has **modeling capability**. It truly simulates something: a solar system, a car engine, or an economic system. It may model either a system or an environment. It does not simply play out pre-planned scenarios or display sequences; it actively models a system by computing and maintaining a record of the system's internal states and inner locations and by displaying a representation of them to the student.

2. An instructional simulation engages the student in interactions. These **interactions** challenge the student to make discriminations, perform decision-making, apply principles, and exercise dynamic control, leading to the achievement of a specific learning goal.

3. An instructional simulation reacts to the learner in two ways during interaction: (1) it provides the **natural responses** of the modeled system to manipulation, and (2) it provides one or more **instructional features** beyond the modeling of the system which have intentional and designed instructional value.

4. An instructional simulation does not guide the student along a sequenced path of interaction except to achieve a temporary strategic goal. It allows the student as much **freedom of choice** as possible and minimizes restraints on student movement and inquiry.

Instructional simulation look-alikes

Not everything that looks like a simulation is a simulation. Two commonly-produced forms of instruction seem very much like simulations but differ from real simulations in important ways.

Visual simulations: A visual simulation is often an animation, video sequence, or sequence of still graphics which runs like a movie for the student to view. Every time a visual simulation is played, it appears identical to the previous playing. The benefit of a visual simulation is that a good one can convey enormous amounts of information to a student in a short time.

A visual simulation might show the process of photosynthesis, DNA replication, or some aspect of plate tectonics. It can show how blank paper rolls through a printing press to become a newspaper. All of us have been exposed to numerous visual simulations in our educational careers. As designers, we come to appreciate the talent of an artist who can conceive and execute colorful, motion-filled visual sequences.

More recently, these skills of the artist have been enhanced and extended by powerful 3-dimensional animation and rendering software, which allow the artist to create wire-frame polygon structures and then render surfaces onto them so that they can be rotated, moved about, and viewed from multiple perspectives. Much of the visual appeal of virtual reality comes from the ability to *walk* through 3-dimensional spaces which have been created by this kind of tool.

The major difference between a visual simulation and a real simulation is that the visual simulation has no underlying model of the system or environment. It is merely a sequence of recorded visuals which can be played like a movie by the computer. A real simulation may produce views which are identical to those played by a visual simulation, but the real simulation has the added capability to respond dynamically as the student manipulates controls and influences the underlying model, leading to changes on the visible surface.

Path simulations: A path simulation is even more like a real simulation than a visual simulation, because it appears to respond just like a real simulation to control by the student. However, underlying the logic of the path simulation consists of a very narrow logical path of expected correct answers which must be given in a prescribed order. As long as the student's responses to the simulation are on this path, it is impossible to tell the path simulation from a real simulation, because the path simulation acts just like a real simulation would act. For this reason, path simulation is sometimes called *pseudo*-simulation. However, as soon as the student makes a response which is off the path of correct actions, the result is a corrective feedback message which prescribes the action for getting back onto the narrow path. A logical description of the path simulation can be found in Chapter 5: a simple chain of multiple choice question frames.

Path simulations are very useful for the early stages of procedural instruction, where performance centers on step-by-step execution and when the student's performance is still newly learned and needs the close attention that immediate feedback can give. However, as the student's performance capability matures, a path simulation can become confining because it does not allow for self-correction of errors by the student. Moreover, for procedures which involve decision-making or where there are multiple correct step sequences, path simulation very quickly becomes difficult to implement.

The fact that path and graphical simulations are not what we call instructional simulations does not imply that they are not valid and useful instructional forms. It does mean that they do not possess some of the characteristics of the more versatile instructional simulation. Many things can be learned from both visual simulations and path simulations. These are both important forms of instruction, but in this chapter we will focus on the model-based instructional simulation—one that is somewhat more complex and far more powerful and versatile than the others.

Relationships between instructional forms

Simulation blends with all other forms of computer-based instruction and can be used in many instructional contexts. In the future, we predict that all of the traditional forms of instruction will incorporate simulations to a greater extent. We find it highly plausible that simulation will become the preferred mode of computer-based instruction and that other forms will become secondary to it or incorporated within it.

Simulations can function within the context of tutorial instruction. In fact, some forms of tutorial instruction are difficult to carry out without the use of a simulation. It is difficult, for instance, to carry out the practice related to procedural instruction for procedures which contain multiple decision points and alternate execution paths. For these procedures, a path simulation does not suffice as a practice vehicle, because it is too complicated to try to anticipate all of the possible correct and incorrect student action sequences and provide appropriate feedback for each one. What is needed is the ability of the student to perform procedural steps in varied orders, being able to observe the normal indications after each step. Only a model simulation allows that degree of freedom and that kind of responsiveness during practice.

Simulations are also used within tutorial instruction for process-using (see Chapter 12). When a process takes place, changes may take several paths, depending on the conditions present. Volcanic ash and obsidian both begin as magma and only become different end products as temperature and pressure conditions surrounding them magma change. In order to demonstrate processes and allow students to observe the effects of varying conditions on their outcomes, a simulation is often the most flexible tool. A process simulation embedded within a tutorial allows the direct presentation of instructional message but also can allow the student to manipulate and explore all of the dimensions and variations of the process.

Simulation can function in the context of a job aid/performance support system. Our thinking about what constitutes a good performance support system is expanding. They are no longer simply lists of job steps to be performed. During the use of a performance support system, a worker may use a simulation to test the possible outcomes of various courses of action.

The simulation can function as a tool to support decision-making in situations where the purpose is to maximize the outcome rather than to do the one correct thing. In business, finance, and science, it is not difficult to conceive of a performance support system that consists of no more than a suite of simulations bundled together into one package, able to share data and report their outcomes to each other, and therefore to assist the worker to progressively solve a problem and arrive at the best decision. An architect testing an evolving building design may "play" the design on such a simulation-based performance support system in order to observe the effects of design modifications on the structural integrity.

In Chapter 2 we also described an approach to instruction called the Learning Coach. A learning coach is a very smart type of performance support system which begins to be used before a student leaves instruction. Some parts of it move with the student into the real world of job performance. A Learning Coach performs a job with the student, guiding and instructing along the way. The job may be performing maintenance on a piece of equipment or balancing the books of a large corporation. Whatever the specific content, since its real function is instruction, the learning coach may find it useful to pause during the task and either demonstrate something conceptual to the student through the means of a simulation or allow the student to explore the outcomes of several possible courses of action.

Simulation can function as a stand-alone instructional method. In this chapter we will focus mainly on the use of simulations as a stand-alone instructional tool. We do this for several reasons:

1. If you understand the principles for designing stand-alone instructional simulations, you can adapt those principles easily to the design of ones which are embedded in other instructional forms.

2. We feel that though simulations have been used for instruction in the past, there has been inadequate emphasis on the design of simulations for instructional purposes. Particularly, we want to talk about the auxiliary instructional features of a simulation which change it from just a simulation into an instructional tool.

3. We want to demonstrate the possibility that simulations can provide the backbone of a curriculum in the same manner as direct instruction through tutorials now does—changing the look and feel of the curriculum, the manner in which students move through it, and the manner in which progress is marked and measured. Before we do that, however, we must describe a few additional characteristics of instructional simulations.

Some simulation characteristics

Let's review some terms already introduced with respect to instructional simulations and introduce some new ones which are important to designers. These terms describe the main characteristics of instructional simulations.

Instructional scope: The instructional scope of a simulation consists of the task or constellation of tasks and objectives toward which the simulation and its instructional features are directed. The scope of a simulation may be as limited as one procedure or one process or as broad as a complex, hour-long performance. The instructional scope of a simulation is important because it identifies the tasks which students must be enabled to perform within the simulated world. It also identifies the task or set of tasks which the simulation's performance judging capability must be able to produce data that describes the quality of the student's performance. This data must be recorded, analyzed, stored, and used later for decision-making by or on behalf of the student.

Simulation scope: Simulation scope describes the outer boundaries of a simulation's simulating capabilities. *Instructional scope is momentary and changes as instruction advances; simulation scope is a property of the simulation itself and therefore does not change.* A particular momentary instructional scope may use only a fraction of the simulation's full capabilities. Therefore, it is possible for one simulation to provide the basis for numerous instructional-scope experiences for students. A single simulation may thus reveal new capabilities to students as performance improves and grows.

The notion of simulation scope is important because designers sometimes confuse the simulation experience in the curriculum (one instructional scope) with the simulation program itself (the simulation scope) and fail to see the benefits of creating more comprehensive simulations in which several tasks can be mastered over time through repeated visits to the simulation.

Fidelity: The fidelity of a simulation is the level of detail at which it models the real world. Fidelity can be reduced by simplifying displays and controls, leaving out details not relevant to the current instructional scope. Fidelity is a source of inaccuracy—not introduced by erroneous computations, but by an intentional and temporary "rounding" of the features of the real world in order to simplify the performance environment.

Resolution: The resolution of a simulation is the precision or exactness with which it models the real world. Since a simulation is a model of some part of the real world, it is possible for the model to be highly accurate in some parts which are of most importance to instruction while being less accurate in others. Most models have some functions which are portrayed less accurately than others. Exactness is decreased by rounding errors and by errors from estimation, such as from extrapolation, interpolation, or curve-fitting. In a famous simulation modeling the sales of lemonade at a lemonade stand in response to cloud cover and temperature, both the fidelity to real world cause-effect relationships and the resolution at which those relationships portrayed were both lowered considerably. The purpose of the simulation was to teach a handful of central economic principles, not to make the students into lemonade marketers.

Fidelity and resolution are easily confused. The importance of these dimensions of a simulation are seldom disputed, however, because the designer selects fidelity and resolution levels deliberately in order to focus the attention of the student on aspects of the learning task which the designer judges to be of most importance.

Fidelity and resolution levels are frequently mixed within one simulation. In the terminology of model-centered instruction, the lowering of fidelity and resolution levels for instructional purposes is called *denaturing*. One part of the interaction with a performance environment may be modeled with high fidelity and high resolution, while other parts of the environment—ones less directly connected with targeted performances—will be handled at lower levels of fidelity and resolution. Thus an office in-basket simulation might have high fidelity and resolution with respect to the letter, memo, and report communications coming to the student during the problem but place low priority on the details of operating the telephone used to make calls to imaginary persons during the problem. The fidelity and resolution of the communication contents (which are directly relevant to the target performance) is high, while that of the phone system (which has low relevance) is low. This technique of simplifying the simulation where possible is virtually everywhere: Even high-priced aircraft simulators have only photographs (rather than real controls) attached to panels which are not involved in simulated exercises. For example, the ejection seat controls in military jets are sometimes handled in this fashion.

The importance of fidelity and resolution are heightened by their close linkage with the costs of simulation development. Just as every frame of a frame-based tutorial adds its incremental cost to the product total, every detail and functionality of a simulation has its cost. The assignment of fidelity and detail to the different parts of a simulation influence cost, and the designer must be aware of their impact.

Instructional features: The instructional features of a simulation are extra functions provided by the designer to be used in conjunction with the modeling functions of the simulation. These added functions extend the simulation beyond mere mimicry of a real-world phenomenon or environment. By providing extra support and assistance, they help the student who is attempting to learn from the simulation in much the same way a live instructor would. A designer may provide several types of instructional feature adjunct to the simulation's modeling function. We describe instructional features in detail later in this chapter.

Basic instructional processes and instructional simulations

Instruction consists of certain functions which are intended to support student learning directed toward a learning goal which is selected either by the student or by the instructional system. Instructional functions are normally described under three headings: (1) presenting information, (2) demonstrating (a specialized form of presentation), and (3) providing practice with feedback.

The instructional simulation is lacking a feature normally present in other forms of instruction: a sequenced message. Whereas other forms of instruction often require a script, there is no strand of continuous message in a simulation, because a user can take almost any action at any time. Therefore, the simulation designer must learn new techniques for presenting, demonstrating, and interacting with the student.

The messages of a simulation come from two sources: (1) the natural responses of a simulation model, and (2) the instructional features provided by the designer. The designer must make a plan for the coordination of these message sources and how they will complement each other during instruction. This is made especially challenging by the unsequenced nature of simulation instruction. And remember, most simulation messages do not consist of words.

Simulation types

Though most people commonly picture a simulation as a model of some system like the stock market or an atomic reaction, there are really three types of instructional simulation, and they can combine together to form a fourth type. The basic types are: (1) the modeled system, (2) the modeled environment, and (3) the modeled expert behavior. The fourth type is called a "hybrid" simulation, because it combines the other types.

The modeled environment simulation

A modeled environment simulation provides the student with a set of *locations* between which he or she may move. A location is any place to which the student may navigate in order to obtain information. Students use a set of movement controls to navigate from location to location. A great variety of control systems are possible, and often part of the interest of an environmental simulation comes from the operation of the controls to zoom around the environment: a solar system, a planet, an island, a set of rooms, the inside of an atom, or the inside of a building.

Physical environments come most readily to mind as subjects for an environmental simulation, but it is equally possible to conceive an environment as any conceptual space: the parts of a musical piece, the parts of a novel or play, the elements of an art work of any kind, the components of a theory, or periods of history. Consider that a famous painting can be accessed in three dimensions, providing views of the underlying layers as well as its visible surface. As well, an archeological dig supplies locations at each level of downward motion through layers of time. The task of the art student might be to reconstruct the various surface versions of the final art work over time; the task of the archeology student might be to reconstruct each level of civilization.

Time and location are combined as *travel* dimensions in an environmental simulation. This might result in a simulation of the Battle of Gettysburg or the Second Continental Congress, in which locations and persons could be accessed at specific moments in time and physical locations. This would allow the study of changing opinions over time and the influence of specific events on those opinions. This provides a way to explore history and understand the forces working behind events.

The environmental simulation requires that there be some form of sensory information at each location—not necessarily visual information. The sensations at a location may be auditory (the notes played by one instrument within an orchestra, the animal sounds heard within one section of a wooded area) or even tactile (locations presented to blind students by description through a Braille display interpreter). It should be apparent from this that the virtual reality environments which can be seen or (at some time in the future) felt by the student constitute a sophisticated environmental simulation—one in which the locations form a continuous stream rather than being discrete experiences. Therefore, to the extent that virtual reality systems can be coupled with good instructional principles, they can become powerful tools for learning, as well as being powerful sensory experiences.

The main requirements for a location or environmental simulation are: (1) that every location be defined in terms of the new information it provides, and (2) that there be a set of paths defined for moving between locations. The method of issuing navigational commands can vary widely. A keyboard may be used, as may be a mouse, a touch panel, a motion glove, or a voice recognition system.

One early environmental simulation used the videodisc—then a cutting-edge technology—to provide *surrogate travel* through an environment. It allowed the student to explore the town of Aspen, Colorado by moving down streets, making turns at intersections, and entering buildings and rooms within buildings. This constitutes a set of locations and connecting paths, and we should ask whether it is an instructional simulation of the environmental type. According to our definition of instructional simulation, an instructional simulation has an instructional goal and judgeable interactions with the student to assess progress toward the goal. In its native form, the Aspen experience does not qualify as an instructional simulation. What could be added that would make it instructional in the sense we have defined?

An instructional goal: The goal might be, "Use sources of information within the city to find out whether the owner of the Gold King Mine was murdered."

Judgeable interactions: By defining the instructional goal, all movements within the environment become judgeable, because each one either moves the student closer to important information or not, based on the information obtained there. Locations which might contain information relevant to the problem become positively valued, whereas others are of less value.

Other additions are possible in the form of instructional features. We will see how the Aspen simulation could be given instructional features later in the chapter. Without any changes, the Aspen experience would still be able to convey information and would be a very useful and interesting instructional tool. However, if it was used for other than its original exploratory purposes, it would need a few extra features. We will describe them also.

Indirection: This description of the location simulation highlights an interesting aspect of some instructional simulations. We call it *indirection*. Indirection is a technique of instruction where the specific content of the instructional messages does not relate directly to the underlying instructional goal. Location simulations are often used for instruction by indirection. The real goal of the Gold King Mine mystery is not just to get the student to learn the places in Aspen which contain important crime clues; it is to help the student learn which places in the city provide relevant information for the solution of a particular type of problem—one of many different problems that the student might be given over time, set in many different environments, to promote problem solving ability through indirect instruction.

Indirection is a technique that promotes the student's ability to generalize. The student learns principles from the problem which he or she discovers later can be applied in other problem-solving situations. By asking the student to solve structurally similar problems presented within very different environments (a pyramid, a castle, a factory, and a space capsule), a designer helps the student to *decontextualize* the knowledge. Environmental simulations are very good vehicles for this instructional purpose. A student may be given a range of problems covering all of the practices of the scientific method (observation, hypothesis formation, data gathering, etc.), but the problems are given in different settings. This helps the student avoid attaching the practices to only specific problem settings.

One important characteristic of a location simulation is what we term the *interpretability* of its locations. Interpretability means that certain locations within the simulation have been designated as the place where the student can obtain specific problem-relevant information—one of the many pieces needed to assemble the whole puzzle. If the locations in a simulation are interpretable, a visit to a location informs the designer that the student is in possession of the specific information obtained there, and a critique of the student's performance is possible through an analysis of the sequence of locations visited. Information in one location may lead the student by deduction to the next location. If this location-to-location movement sequence is missing from the student's movement record, then it can be determined that the student had difficulty with the specific line of reasoning, and that knowledge has diagnostic value for the designer.

Environments which are made up of interpretable locations allow the designer to interpret performance patterns, misconceptions, and missing skills. The structure of the environment, therefore, may be made to correspond in some significant way with the structure of the problem the student is expected to solve within it. We have tried this approach and found it to be very useful in creating realistic problem solving situations and then afterward, analyzing or reconstructing the performance of the student for feedback purposes.

The modeled system simulation

A modeled system simulation is one which models the internal cause-effect interactions of some natural or human-made system. Because it mimics the responses of the real thing, the simulation responds to a student's manipulations of it as if it was the real thing. System responses are modeled by a family of "if...then..." rules, or by computations using mathematical equations which describe the behavior of the system under different conditions.

A model simulation is the most frequently encountered type of simulation. The history of CBI is full of modeled system simulations, from the very simple to the very complex. At the high end of the simulation spectrum, aircraft simulators are capable of providing convincing simulations—not just of the aircraft's flight in response to the controls, but the view of the ground and the sky outside the aircraft's window as well. At the low end, simple simulations provide the opportunity for young students to solve a problem, run a small business, or watch the change in the value of the dollar fluctuate as the daily news changes.

Models are quite versatile. They can duplicate the behavior of natural physical systems, like volcanoes, natural force systems such as planetary attraction by gravitation, human-built systems of all kinds, and even conceptual systems, allowing the modeling of individual and societal human reactions to events.

By equipping a modeled simulation with instructional features (such as set problems to solve, and feedback following solution) and by designating instructional goals which the simulation can support, the simulation becomes more than a simple model which the student can observe; it becomes an instructional simulation—a combination of both modeling and instructional functions. This gives the model the power to instruct: It improves the knowledge of the instructor about what the student does and doesn't know, and it gives focus to the student's activities with the model, increasing the amount that can be learned without taking from the student the initiative or responsibility for learning.

The expert behavior simulation

An expert behavior simulation is one which models the performance of an expert (1) within an environment and, (2) acting on one or more modeled systems within that environment. Expert behavior is most commonly modeled using "...if...then..." rules. Expert behavior simulations are not common in instructional simulations nor in tutorial instruction, perhaps mainly due to the unfamiliarity of most instructional designers with their planning and construction. We believe that unfamiliarity is more of a factor than complexity, because many small-scale instructional experts can be constructed using readily-available standard authoring tools and incorporated into both tutorials and simulations.

The value of the expert behavior model is that it provides an example of the behavior students themselves are trying to learn. In this sense, the model program creates the model performance, which the student may observe, interact with, and eventually emulate.

Though it is common to think of expert behavior programs as monolithic, special-purpose, independent, and complex products, small experts can be written fairly easily that deal with a specific set of decisions and operations. The thought logic and (in most cases) the programming logic are both written to reach the average computer-based instructional designer.

A simulated model of a system can be accompanied by instructional features that help to interpret its actions to the learner—supplying necessary instructional images in the process. Likewise, expert behavior models can be used in conjunction with instructional features that describe the actions of the expert, their relation to existing performance goals, the strategy and principles used to generate actions, and the expected outcomes of the actions. This provides a commentary on the expert's behavior that makes the combinations instructional.

The hybrid simulation

A hybrid simulation results from combining the three model varieties; that is, some combination of modeled environment, modeled system, and a model of expert behavior. This is perhaps the most useful and interesting type of simulation for instruction and performance assessment, and it is appearing much more frequently today than ever before.

In a hybrid simulation, students are provided with an environment made up of individual locations throughout which they can move along location-to-location paths. In different locations, one or more models are made visible by either controls or indications of the model placed within locations. An expert behavior model demonstrates, coaches, and provides feedback to the learner in practice attempts to solve a problem. For instance, a student learning about electrical distribution grid control may move through several control room locations, reading values from indicators, and adjusting controls which influence a model of the grid. In turn, through the computations of the model, the influence of the controls on the indicator values in that location can be displayed immediately to the student. An expert companion can show appropriate solutions to control room problems and then support the learner's attempts to do the same.

In the same manner, elementary science students may find themselves inside the "Science House," a set of graphically-displayed rooms, encountering in different rooms projects which they set in motion on previous visits to that location: a corn growing experiment, a temperature-recording experiment, a chemical reaction experiment, or an evaporation experiment. As students return to the rooms containing experiments, they find there things just as they left them on the previous day, including notes taken, experiments in progress, and data recorded or charted. The rooms (or visual counter-top areas) containing the experiments are locations, and the experiments themselves are simulation models (of growing corn, of an evaporation, and so forth) which exist within the location. A science companion suggests experiments and supports the learner in interpreting the results.

From these two examples, it can be seen that the relationship between models and locations may be arranged however the designer wishes. A system model may be entirely contained within one location, or it may be manifest (and controllable) at several locations. More than one model may be linked with more than one location. Models of the electrical and water systems of a house can be hooked to many different rooms. Both electrical and water system controls (switches, faucets, etc.) and indications (lights going on, water flowing, etc.) will present in some rooms, such as the kitchen and the bathroom. There can also be multiple expert models, each illustrating a particular type of thinking or approach to problem solving.

Virtually all simulations are actually hybrids, because at least one location is needed by every system model simulation and every expert model in order to display the otherwise invisible indications, controls, and decisions of the model. A stock market simulation may have a "big board" display from which the user can obtain current stock prices, and the lower part of that display may be used for placing buy and sell orders. This single display constitutes a location, even though the designer may make no provisions for making it look like an actual room or place. The same display may have an area devoted to the reporting of expert judgments, recommendations, or instructional commentaries. The location is used by the model as an interface at which the model reports its current values (the location's information) and from which it obtains control inputs from the student.

The hybrid simulation is becoming quite popular in the form of educational games and entertainment software. An avalanche of recent software titles are hybrid simulations which have been given so interesting an outer appearance and such an engrossing problem and set of subproblems to solve (for the target audience) that users spend hours and days solving them. Industrial and commercial training systems are also adopting the hybrid simulation technique. Students in training find themselves diagnosing patient ailments, planning cross-country airplane flights, solving complex business problems, reacting to emergency situations which require judgment, and controlling water flow within river drainage systems.

Model-centered instruction

We want to begin now to describe the potential impact of simulations on the look and feel of the instructional experience and eventually on the structure of the curriculum itself. To set the stage for that discussion, we want to examine how instruction is carried out today in both live and CBI settings. We also want to explore some of the possibilities that are not common in current instructional practice.

Figure 1 below depicts the interaction between a human and the either natural or manufactured systems which exist in the world. This interaction promotes learning as the learner (L) acts upon the system and the system responds in some way that the learner can sense. As sensations are analyzed, results and patterns are compared with prior knowledge, reasoning takes place, conclusions are reached, and learning takes place. Knowledge has been created in the mind of the learner.

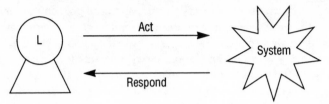

Figure 1. The natural process of learning through experience.

Humans gain much if not the majority of what they know through this natural path of learning, which involves experience with the world and its natural, human, and human-made systems. We learn to walk, talk, get along with people, and how to think, mostly through carrying out small experiments—with ourselves, with other persons and objects, and with natural and human-made forces.

As much as we learn from this type of interaction, the learning produced has limitations. It is often incomplete, since there are always some useful learning experiments that we do not think to perform. Moreover, it is easy to misinterpret sensations and experience, and that can lead to erroneous, even superstitious, knowledge. Some mis-learning is always likely when the learner is alone and unsupported in the learning process. A good solution is to provide each learner with a *companion-in-learning* capable of supporting and aiding the learning process in beneficial ways. Figure 2 shows the relationships produced when this companion (C) is introduced. We have deliberately avoided terming this companion *teacher* or *instructor* because we feel the possibilities go well beyond the narrow definitions we currently assign to those roles.

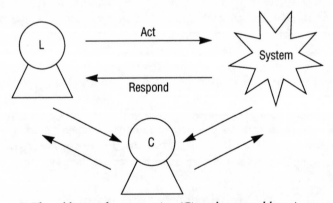

Figure 2. The addition of a companion (C) to the natural learning process.

Just like the learner, the companion is capable of acting on the target system and observing its responses. As learner and companion communicate, additional knowledge can be gained from experiences with the system, depending on: (1) the knowledge and skill of the companion, and (2) the skill of the learner in using a companion as a resource. If the learner and the companion-in-learning are roughly equal in their previous learning, then they learn together from their common experiences, supplementing each others' knowledge in a *group* learning situation.

At some point, the knowledge limitations of the companion, combined with those of the learner, make it difficult to extract reliable and accurate knowledge from new experiences, and a companion with a greater degree of knowledge becomes necessary. As this substitution is made, if the new companion-in-learning (and there may be more than one at one time) is only slightly more knowledgeable than the learner, some form of peer tutoring or teaching takes place.

If the companion is *much* more knowledgeable, then some form of teacher-student relationship is formed, but that relationship need not conform to the standard teacher roles with which we have become so familiar from our own experience.

Most of the arrows in Figure 2 are left unlabeled because of the great variety of possible messages, functions, interactions, and initiatives they represent. It is the specific functions assigned to these arrows which determines the exact nature of the companion-learner relationship and therefore the type of instruction being employed. The role of the companion may vary from being controlling and directing to merely being responsive and non-directive. These two possibilities represent the opposite ends of a continuum of possible initiatives for sharing information, questioning, answering, suggesting, acting, observing, analyzing, leading, and concluding.

Live classroom teachers working within the current educational system find themselves located at various points along this continuum, depending on their instructional style. Some teachers take a controlling role during the learning process, and some allow themselves to become more peripheral to the learner's own efforts. A teacher's style may vary from moment to moment—at one moment placing the teacher in a controlling role and at another moving the teacher to the periphery. The control of instruction moment by moment depends on the constantly changing assignment of roles to the learner and the companion-in-learning. It is this changeability that is one element of *adaptive* instruction.

Figure 2 describes a learning relationship in which a significant amount of the student's experience comes from direct interaction with the target system, with the companion role being secondary to direct experience and observation. Historically, several forces—most of them economic—have led to a drastic reduction in the amount of direct or even simulated experience which can be given to students. This has resulted in a replacement of direct experience with a surrogate and much less immediate form of experience provided through verbalizations, visualizations, or demonstrations—usually by the companion-in-learning acting as teacher, as shown in Figure 3.

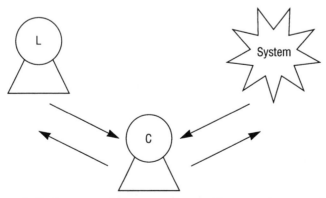

Figure 3. Replacement of direct experience with companion-as-teacher.

This modified relationship greatly reduces the student's ability to learn from direct acting, observing, and interpreting. It emphasizes learning by receiving information, remembering it, and becoming facile at manipulating and translating it into different semantic forms. The student is lucky if the teacher in this arrangement has had direct experience with the system which is the subject of instruction (as also shown in Figure 3). However, too frequently, the teacher has had little or no direct experience and is himself or herself reliant on knowledge which was gained from the verbalization-centered model of instruction shown in Figure 3. This forces instructors and instruction into the "lexical loop," which is instruction based on verbal instructional goals, even when the ultimate purpose is to create a performance capability.

As teachers with less direct experience themselves are employed, the abstraction level of the verbalizations becomes greater, and it becomes harder and harder for the learner—no longer an active participant in the educational process, but its passive ward—to understand the relevance of the knowledge to his or her own life. The interest and vitality of the knowledge and its learning is lost, and the process of instruction becomes one of force-feeding verbal knowledge to marginally motivated recipients.

The direct-experience varieties of learning (shown in Figures 1 and 2) which are so natural to humans have been almost universally replaced in our culture with a verbal-propositional variety of instruction. Though some degree of direct experience learning takes place in almost every classroom, the amount which comes from direct experience is proportionally minuscule, and our learning institutions for the most part deal in verbalizations of experience.

This view of the teaching-learning relationship is useful to demonstrate the value of simulations as an instructional tool, and it explains why instructional simulations are capable of promoting a revolution in the curriculum. Experience with a simulation does not supply all of the realism (and therefore learning potential) that can be provided by experience with a real system, but simulations can supply much. The extensive use of simulations on many areas of high-tech training shows that the simulator is effective as a substitute for real experience and that it often makes possible a reduction in training costs. Figure 4 shows the simulation model as a replacement for real-system experience with the balance between the learner, the system, and the companion-in-learning restored. This change restores experience-based natural learning by using a simulation model to supply direct experience for the student. The learning companion is restored as an auxiliary function rather than as the main instrument of instruction.

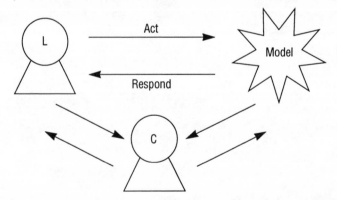

Figure 4. Restoration of experience as the source of knowledge using models.

Implications of model-centered instruction for CBI

This view of instruction, which places the model and direct experience back at the heart of the learning process, is what we call *model-centered instruction*. Provided that ways are found to reduce the cost of developing simulation models of real-world phenomena and systems, this learning/ instruction metaphor has enormous implications. It changes not only the way we think of CBI but also the way we build it.

However, we must first change the mindset by which we judge instruction. What constitutes good instruction? Much of today's CBI still tries to imitate the style of other instructional media: books, lectures, slide/sound presentations, videos, and audiotapes. The advent of multimedia—welcome as it is to those who know how to use it in instructionally appropriate ways—threatens to prolong this confusion for those who do not see the computer as a new instructional medium in need of a new metaphor of instructional delivery. The computer as a tool is the preeminent supplier of interactive models to our culture, and for us to use it to use it perpetuate a dated paradigm of message-centered instruction when a model-centered alternative is available does not make sense economically or educationally.

The shift toward the increased use of simulated models in CBI is due to several trends:

- The falling cost of simulation model construction due to new object-oriented programming tools and specialized simulation construction systems.

- Changing conceptions of instruction and instructional functions arising from research on cognitive processes.

- The realization among CBI designers that CBI up to this point has largely neglected the power of the computer to instruct through direct experience.

Just as early books, motion pictures, video, and audio had to establish their own paradigm for instructional use, CBI is breaking from its imitation of those media forms and establishing its own. We believe that new paradigm for CBI will be model-centered.

Some of the more intriguing implications of this shift are described in Chapter 24. Our immediate interest, however, is in the implications of model-centeredness in the near-term. We are interested in the following:

- The shift from a message-centered curriculum to one that is model- or experience-centered.

- The development of principles and guidelines for augmenting simulation models with instructional features.

- The growing availability of object-oriented authoring tools.

- The shift which must take place in the way we report and use the data resulting from instruction.

The remainder of this chapter deals with each of these issues in turn.

The experience-centered curriculum

The experience-centered curriculum is an educational reform which visionaries since Dewey have hoped for, but for which there were no affordable instructional tools. Dewey converted his school into a type of factory where children could experience the processes which turned raw materials into fabric and fabric into usable items, and when the children had produced those items, they further experienced the process of marketing them. This type of schooling is neither economically nor logistically feasible, given the number of children we educate today without the use of both live and computer-simulated experiences.

Consider, for instance, an example of instruction which is already heavily experience-based today in both high schools and technical colleges nationwide: the electronics shop. It was long ago realized that even the highly conceptual subject of electronics could not be properly instructed without large doses of practical, hands-on experience to accompany theoretical discussions.

Today, in school electronics shops across the nation, the main fare of instruction includes lectures accompanied by hands-on exercises which are considered an auxiliary function or complement to the main flow of instruction. The lecture is considered to be the "real" instruction; it is there that theoretical ideas are introduced. The primary instructional method in the average electronics classroom is still message-centered. Experience with real systems is introduced to support or confirm the content of the lecture. This formula could easily be reversed, however. Students could learn theory through a carefully selected sequence of hands-on exercises which introduced principles and skills in an ascending order of complexity and sophistication.

Barbara White, a learning researcher, has found that a succession of electrical circuits provided in this way not only moves the student along a path toward the understanding of increasingly complex circuit principles, but it does so without introducing the misconceptions and incorrect oversimplifications into the student's knowledge that most lecture-delivered knowledge tends to do. It is a long-accepted but erroneous assumption that hands-on instruction, including simulation-based instruction, is only useful for teaching trade skills and for providing concrete experiences to demonstrate or confirm abstract theoretical principles after the fact. Those who make this generalization fail to recall that those abstract principles were originally derived through practical hands-on experiments by scientists who had questions on their minds or problems to solve. We also fail to realize that every student can duplicate the discoveries of those scientists. And given the appropriate simulation support, they can do it efficiently.

When experience is placed at the center of instruction, the key decisions faced by the instructional designer center on the family of instructional events that will allow the student to move from a novice entering state to a state of proficiency in steps that are learner-sized. This path toward performance ability was described in Chapter 15 as the technology of *increasingly complex microworlds:* a path made up of work models of increasing scope.

The instructional features of simulations

Instructional features are one of the elements that set instructional simulations apart from general purpose simulations. General purpose simulations are used in research or design work; instructional simulations are designed specifically for an instructional function. General purpose simulations may be adapted for instructional use by a live instructor who provides the instructional intent and additional instructional messaging which the general purpose simulation is not constructed to provide. But without this supplementing function, either from an instructor or a computer program, the general purpose simulation is not an instructional one. A student may learn through observation from a general purpose simulation, but instructional features support the student by guiding, catalyzing, and informing the learning process, and by so doing, they amplify the instructional value of the simulation.

The role of instructional goals in an instructional simulation is of primary importance because any measurement of student performance which is based on the simulation will take place relative to the instructional goal. Moreover, *the substance of the messages provided by instructional features can only be determined relative to the momentary instructional goal—* one which has been selected either by the student or by the system.

Under the traditional programming language approach to simulation development, the addition of instructional features is difficult because the operation of the features sets up a parallel line of processing which it becomes difficult to integrate with the functioning of the simulation model itself. Using frame-based authoring tools, the addition of instructional features is equally or more difficult, due to the essentially sequential execution of frames and the lack of provision for monitoring the state of a simulation model.

For these reasons, simulations with instructional features are still relatively hard to find. However, if a simulation is constructed using object-oriented programming tools, many of the instructional features can be constructed modularly, being switched on or off without disruption. (Though some instructional features are difficult to modularize in this way because they involve inherent qualities of the instructional message itself—particularly visual qualities.)

We define six classes of instructional feature:

- Coaching systems

- Feedback systems

- Representation

- Control systems

- Scope dynamism

- Embedded didactics

Coaching assists the student to form a plan, prepare a response, or discover an option; *feedback* helps the student to evaluate a plan or judge a response which the student has made and can also suggest types of correction or methods for improvement to the student; *representation* determines the manner in which information is presented to the student and can influence both the channelization of information and its formatting; *scope dynamism* involves the selection and sequencing of instructional scopes and therefore influences the order of instructional experiences and the regulation of instructional challenge; *embedded didactics* are instructional means which are incorporated within the fabric of the simulation. The sections which follow describe these instructional features in more detail.

Coaching systems

Coaching is in reality at least three functions: (1) support for student memory processes which are just forming, (2) proportioning of the instructional message, and (3) mapping of learning opportunities for the student.

Coaching as memory support: As a student is first learning a performance, there is a heavy load on memory while performing. New actions must be remembered, as well as new sequences of actions, new decisions, new decision criteria, and new self-evaluation criteria. The content of a new learning is not normally absolutely new to the student; the student usually is learning to place already-familiar steps, decisions, and judgments into a new order, which may also entail new rhythms of action or new timing constraints. Recalling this new arrangement of already-familiar things can be difficult, and in the early stages of learning, it is often very productive to provide some level of assistance in the form of coaching. This coaching disappears as the student continues to practice the new performance. It provides temporary support for the student's evolving capability.

The function of coaching is to lighten the student's information processing load during performance at a time when it is especially heavy, giving the student extra energy and attention to devote to the execution of individual steps. A coaching message may help the student with directing attention, observing, analyzing patterns, making judgments, making decisions, selecting goals, selecting steps, executing steps, or self-evaluating. Each of these types of support implies potential content for the coaching message. Each support possibility in effect asks a question for which the coaching message may provide an answer. Consider the following questions:

- Where should I be watching? (Directing attention)

- What should I be watching for at this point? (Observing)

- Is what I saw a cause for action? (Analyzing patterns)

- Is the indication strong enough for me to take action? (Making judgments)

- Is it time to act? (Making decisions)

- What should I try to do now? (Goal selection)

- What should I do next? (Step selection)

- How do I do this step? (Executing steps)

- Am I doing this correctly? (Self-evaluation)

The designer may provide any or all of these types of support and make them available automatically according to some schedule, or else the student may be given the ability to request that a particular class of help (one type of information) be made available. As you can see, the number of options available for the coaching message is enormous. Moreover, good coaching is not delivered on the principle "more is better." The best coaching is very selective in what it says, and sometimes the best coaching is to say nothing and let the student learn from experience. Timing is certainly a factor. The coaching decision must be guided by the student's motivation level, the degree of difficulty of the task presented to the student, and the student's learning tendencies (fast/slow, bold/tentative, etc.).

The opportunity for coaching appears on the spur of the moment and passes equally rapidly. Coaching systems which have been devised to date tend to use a formula approach and are often called *hinting* systems. It is possible that a live coach is also acting from an inner formula, knowing in advance that certain kinds of message are likely to be useful in a given situation for a given type of student, and being ready to help when the degree of challenge reaches a certain critical point.

Coaching as proportioning: As a performance capability forms within a student, it becomes clear to the student that certain actions are critical to success and safety, while others are of less import. Coaching messages are often used to establish this sense of proportion and importance in students. Since coaching is provided prior to action, the proportioning message may take the form of a warning or a last-minute urging to watch for a particular indication or to avoid a particular type of action. Mariners are coached to watch for the boom—the large and often heavy pole that secures the bottom of the sail—during turns in a sailboat. Those who disregard this coaching often learn why it is called a boom.

Coaching as opportunity mapping: Etienne Wenger (1987, p. 124) describes the final function of coaching. It is to help those who:

> ...*overlook learning opportunities and get stuck on plateaus of proficiency. Making them aware of further possibilities is the task of a coach: his purpose is not to lecture but to foster the learning inherent in an activity itself by pointing out existing learning opportunities and by transforming failures into learning experiences.*

This role of coaching functions at several levels of learning. It can promote awareness that a single important conclusion is being missed by the student during an interaction, or it can promote awareness of the importance of the study of mathematics as a whole. It also functions at all of the levels in between.

Coaching summary: Our technology for coaching constitutes a largely unexplored and unformalized field of instructional technology. A great deal of research is needed before we can speak with any authority about how or when to coach, or what type of coaching to offer in a given situation. At the same time, many educational disciplines use coaching as a main technique for nurturing and improving performance. Coaching technique is the mainstay of orchestra conducting, choir direction, drama direction, and athletic coaching. Tutors use coaching constantly as they conduct sessions with their students. As the non-computerized instructional world becomes more aware of the principles that guide coaching, we who are interested in technology-based instruction must learn them as well.

Feedback systems

In virtually all instruction, there occurs the opportunity or demand for decision or action by the learner. When the student responds, it is the responsibility of the instruction to judge the response and decide whether to provide feedback. If feedback is given, the content of the feedback message must be selected, and the message must be composed and delivered—either verbally or non-verbally.

Feedback is an instructional message which follows and is in some way conditioned by the actions of a student; it is based on a higher degree of prescription than other instructional messages. During tutorial instruction, after every response it is customary to provide students with some form of feedback, even if the response is no more than a menu selection. Even from this simple feedback the student learns: (1) that the computer recognizes the student action, (2) that it is evaluating the action, and (3) eventually, that the evaluation is complete and further actions are in order. This rudimentary feedback is provided in the form of an hourglass or wristwatch cursor in popular operating system software. During instruction, the feedback becomes more complicated than this because the range of information that is useful to the student following a learning interaction is greater and the message must be composed with more care and specificity.

Failure to provide feedback has the same effect on a learner as failing to answer during a conversation: There is a feeling of having been snubbed or ignored. During simulation, there are two types of feedback: *natural* and *designed,* or *artificial.* Natural feedback comes from the simulation model. When the student's actions influence the model of a system, its states change, and if the designer has made provision for it, that becomes visible to the student. When the student's actions take him or her to a new part of a simulated environment, that is shown the student also. These constitute natural feedback—the natural results of actions.

Designed or artificial feedback consists of any feedback which is not a result of the re-computation of a model's states or movement through an environment. It is feedback which does not exist in non-instructional settings. It is feedback for which the message has to be constructed somehow, based on instructional principles.

In this chapter, we are more interested in designed feedback than in natural feedback because simulations—even general purpose ones—give natural feedback to the user. Instructional simulations go beyond natural feedback and provide many different kinds of message calculated to assist the student in self-correction and in establishing the capability to self-monitor and self-judge performance.

Designed feedback systems normally require: (1) a mechanism for recording the student's response, (2) a mechanism for analyzing and judging the student's response, and (3) a mechanism for constructing the feedback message according to the designer's principles. In the early days of CBI, feedback systems tended to assert themselves after every student response. In the short term this helped the student to correct misconceptions, but it did not allow the student to form self-monitoring and self-correcting habits. Therefore, in later stages of instruction, feedback must become less and less apparent and should follow longer and longer sequences of performance. It fades from the student's view in the same manner that coaching fades over time, as student performance improves.

Instructional simulations may vary widely in the *when* (timing), *what* (message content), and *how* (delivery method) of feedback. As with other instructional features of simulations, we must assume that feedback is a dynamic principle and that it must be related to the conditions that exist during instruction. Just as other instructional features, feedback is derived relative to the immediate instructional goal. What constitutes good feedback early during instruction may not be good later.

We assign five general functions to feedback:

- Providing knowledge of right/wrong

- Supplying corrective information

- Supporting recovery and resumed instruction

- Establishing self-monitoring

- Dealing with attitude and motivation

Providing knowledge of right/wrong: When simulation is involved, the feedback principles used in tutorials become overly simple. Simulations require a broader and deeper conception of feedback, one with a few new dimensions.

To begin with, it is not always clear from the natural feedback of a simulation whether actions taken by the student are correct or incorrect. A student may not yet be familiar with an outcome and may not be able to interpret the natural indications by themselves. One need only remember the last learning encounter with a word processor to recall how easy it is to become disoriented as the system provides its natural feedback to inputs, disregarding the information needs of the learner. ("Why did the screen just go blank...?")

Second, the thing judged may be either a process or a product. Both of these require not one but many judgments. There are many aspects of a product, and they defy being summarized into a single, simplistic judgment. A process has equally many evaluatable parts. This means the judgment of a performance cannot be simply "right" or "wrong." In some cases there are multiple correct action paths during performance, each of which is right or wrong in degree. Moreover, parts of a performance may be acceptable, but not all. The judgment of a response recorded during a simulation includes judgments of right, wrong, and shades in between. It requires a message which offers praise for excellent performance and information and support that allows the student to make corrections of erroneous performance patterns.

To make things more complicated, what is acceptable performance on one occasion during early learning may not be acceptable in a later stage due to an accelerating criterion. This implies that response judgment and formation of the feedback message should be dynamic processes. Canned or pre-set sequences of messages, though they are the general style now, become impractical when an extended sequence of actions and decisions is being judged.

Supplying corrective information: Current instructional trends treat the student as a decision-maker, responsible to some extent for self-managed learning. The feedback message is given at a point where the student has been informed of an error, which may be based on misconception or faulty knowledge. Content can be supplied during feedback which allows the student to amend knowledge structures. This content can be supplied in several forms:

- Descriptions and demonstrations

- Modeling of expert performance

- Comparisons with other performances

- Simple replay of the student's performance

- Commentaries on and self-evaluation of replays

- Enumeration of error points

- Reconstruction of error-thinking

- Restatement of instructional content

Some of these forms resemble very closely elements of instruction which might be provided in a traditional tutorial instructional presentation. This leads us to believe that the difference between tutorial instruction, with its prominent presentation, and simulation-based instruction, with its diffuse presentation, may be to some extent a matter of message massing as opposed to message distribution across interactions with a simulation model.

Supporting recovery and resumed instruction: The forward momentum of learning can slow at the feedback point unless something pushes it forward again. The selection and initiation of a next instructional activity must be considered a part of the feedback process, because the types of error detected in a student response may change momentary instructional needs with regard to a particular scope, as may excellence reduce the need for further instruction within certain scopes.

Following feedback, which often contains some negative content, the need to move the student toward a success experience becomes more acute. A sufficient number of negatives can harm and eventually kill motivation in the average student. Though there are a few students who are stimulated by an elusive goal, not all students are so motivated, so the feedback mechanism must help to select a next experience which restores the positive momentum to instruction.

Establishing self-monitoring: The most neglected function of feedback in the past may well be the most valuable: self-management and self-evaluation by the learner. Designers have assumed that the feedback message should be directed from the instruction to the learner, but it may well be that the most effective form of feedback involves students in the review of their own performance or review from peers.

There are many ways in which self-review and self-critique can be facilitated. Students may be asked to rate a replay of their own performance prior to the system's evaluation; students may be told there is an error without being told where, and may be assigned to detect and correct the error; students may be asked to express how certain they are about the correctness of each step of a problem solution; students may be asked in one form of practice to check the work of other students, creating an evaluative habits which can be expected to transfer to their own work.

Dealing with attitude and motivation: At the point of receiving feedback, especially negative feedback, the student is in a somewhat different frame of mind than during instruction. The student's performance is judged, and there will be consequences. Will forward motion be halted? Will there be remediation? If the student felt confident in the answer, will that confidence be overturned?

A student may be either certain or anxious, and when a judgment is adverse in some respect, it can create feelings of frustration, anger, impatience, or lowered confidence. In many cases, the negative effects of feedback are minor, but in some cases, students may be approaching the end of their patience with the instruction. The feedback message must help the student place bad news in perspective.

One way to do this is to compliment the good portions of the performance before noticing the faulty ones. Positive feedback has been largely ignored in practice other than to provide messages like, "Good job," or "That's right." Designers tend to take the "glass half empty" view of feedback and fail to realize that the positive things a teacher says to a student, if they are insightful and personalized, may provide enough motivation to overcome hundreds of future negative experiences. Perhaps this is one element of the inspirational aspect of instruction to which technologists have paid little attention.

Another technique for giving a positive motivational bias to feedback is to involve the student in the evaluation process as suggested in a previous section. Doing so creates a kind of indirect feedback which involves students in the reconstruction of their own knowledge, rather than placing them in the role of the victim or the transgressor. Most student faults are relatively minor and result from inattention, hastiness, memory faults, or timing errors. The student in many cases knows the right thing to do to correct a fault and can reach a correct answer through directed questions.

Representation

The representation of information to the student is an integral part of any form of instruction. For instructional simulations, however, the importance of representation is multiplied manifold by the fact that instructional simulations are denied the luxury of the connected stream of informational message that is the mainstay of other forms of instruction. An instructional simulation must communicate to a much greater degree through means other than prose sequences, and so the designer must be aware of the alternatives for communicating through all of the sensory channels: graphic and motion graphic, tabular, verbal and non-verbal auditory, tactile, kinesthetic, and olfactory. We do not have an olfactory computer terminal yet, but don't bet that there won't be one.

Representation is a central issue for instructional simulations because representations differ greatly in their ability to convey information efficiently and understandably, yet they constitute a highly controllable design element. The representational principles used by a designer either enhance or limit the instructional ability of a simulation. Learning from a simulation places large but possible information processing burdens on the student. Poor representations only add to this burden, restricting the amount of learning in a given period of time. Good representations not only accelerate information intake and therefore the rate of learning, but they also suggest re-organization of the original problem data that often constitutes a subtle hint toward a solution. In a probem based curriculum, this is a powerful instructional strategy.

Time and *space, location, motion,* and *value* are the main elements of representation, and contrast is the main principle. The information available from a simulation is frequently represented in tables, charts, diagrams, pictures of real things, and sounds. Often the information from a simulation must flow to the student through two channels simultaneously, and the timing and coordination of the information can be of prime importance.

Focusing and scanning are the two main techniques by which a student obtains information from a simulation display, and so the techniques of drawing attention and providing global views are very important. The simulation display must provide a global perspective to orient the student but at the same time provide access to great detail and highlight or emphasize detail that is especially important. The controls for zooming in, out, and around the display must be intuitive and economical in the effort and attention they require. Since a student may be required to track the development of several threads or trends of information simultaneously from a simulation display, these must be represented clearly and without interfering with each other.

We feel that four main aspects of instructional simulation representations bear detailed examination:

- The representation trace
- The focus of representations
- Timing and channeling of information elements
- The structure of information frameworks

The representation trace: The representation trace is the historical dimension of the display which allows the student to see trends and changes as the simulation progresses. The historical trace of changes over time is especially important, because simulations are used specifically to model change and dynamism for the student. The representation trace consists of new display information combined with a residue of information from previous displays in a way that allows the student to observe and compare changes which take place (that is, contrasts).

Everyday experience provides us with numerous static representation traces. Magazines and newspapers provide charts, graphs, and tables of data which record historical trends in everything from economic indicators to earthquake frequency. These traces are usually annotated with historical events thought to be correlated with changes in the direction or magnitude of some outcome indicator. It is the rare issue of a magazine or newspaper that does not have one or more of these.

The student gains the simulation's most important and useful information from the representation trace, yet despite its value, the trace frequently receives the least designer attention, and it is too often omitted altogether. A student studying the effects of rainfall on vegetation must be able to compare vegetation states relative to the history of cumulative rainfall. A student studying the effects of air temperature on snowpack depth must be able to run experiments which involve adjusting the air temperature at different rates and levels and then observing the rate at which the snow melts.

If a student could learn from static representations alone, we could simply add more tables and charts to our instruction and not worry about simulations, but there is something valuable in having the student participate in preparing the trace, and there is something missing from the static traces which are provided in the non-interactive media. When the student participates in constructing a historical trace of trends, there is an element of curiosity aroused which is not present if the trace is simply viewed. Moreover, the student can be asked to predict how a trend will unfold step-by-step and to assign causes. This strengthens the student's processing of the information and sets up anticipations which are not present when a completed representation is viewed.

What is missing from a static representation? Dynamism. The melting of a mountain snowpack does not take place in just one way. Gradual increases in temperature over longer periods of time melt the snow slowly. Rapid increases in temperature over short time spans melt it rapidly, and flooding can result when the volume of water produced reaches certain critical levels. Mud slides can also occur when the runoff is produced at a rate greater than the ground can absorb. What are the patterns of heating which produce dangerous conditions? Which ones produce high water flow but no danger? These are the kinds of question a simulation allows the student to explore, and the variety of experiences a student may try using a simulation are not adequately represented using static trend diagrams.

The focus of representations: The manner in which information is presented greatly influences how easily and rapidly it can be taken in and used by the student. In effect, the manner of representation focuses the attention of the student on certain structures or trends within the information. Since most information can be represented in multiple ways, how the designer chooses to represent it is of much importance.

Larkin and Simon have illustrated the importance of representational focus by suggesting that we consider a set of points in a Cartesian coordinate system—the x-y function system we all used in high school algebra to plot the points of mathematical functions. There are two ways to represent these points. One way is to plot them on an x-y grid and connect them with one or more lines. The second way is to list the functional pairs of x and y points in a table. As it turns out, each of these ways of representing the information has strengths, and one representation might be chosen over the other depending on the user's purpose. If the purpose is to determine the shape of the function (i.e., linear, hyperbolic, parabolic, etc.), the graphical representation of the points would be used because it provides that information readily, while the tabular representation makes it difficult to determine shape. On the other hand, if the purpose is to determine the exact value of the x-intercept, the tabular form of the information gives that information readily and unequivocally, while the graphical form requires the user to perform an interpolation which produces at best an estimated and therefore possibly erroneous value.

The manner in which information is represented does make it either easier or harder to use. Designers selecting a representation for the information produced by a simulation must wrestle with the question of whether detail and accuracy are more important than shape, form, and trend. They must decide which are the critical elements of information the student needs most readily and supply that information in the form best suited to the goals of instruction. If the goal is for the student to make mental transformations of numerical data into visual form, then the representation must supply numerical data. However, if the goal of instruction is to use the data to make decisions, then providing it in a form which requires extra transformations may be adding unnecessarily to the student's already heavy information processing load, and the graphical representation may be more appropriate. As with all other instructional features, the way representation is used depends on the goal of instruction.

Timing and channeling of information elements: Research by Richard Mayer and his associates has shown that the timing of messages coming to a student through different sensory channels is a critical factor in understanding the messages and using the information contained in them. In this research, the timing of arriving visual (seen) and auditory (heard) information to the student influenced how well a student could learn process information. By delaying the information in one channel, these researchers could systematically increase or reduce understanding of the process.

The timing of sensory input—information in all of its forms—to the student is an important simulation design issue. It is so important that computer-based development tools have been created specifically to give the designer precise control over the timing and ordering of display events, including visuals, animations, and sound. The metaphor of such tools makes the designer in effect the producer of a movie which will be administered by the computer. The strength of these tools is that they allow the designer to control the timing of the various representation channels. Their danger is that they focus the attention of the designer on the movie-like properties of CBI, and if designers do not move beyond that restricted metaphor, they will produce only movie-like CBI and fail to use the full instructional power of the computer.

The structure of information frameworks: The details of a display (and remember that a CBI display consists of all of the sensory channels to the student) need not be simply independent bits of information. They can in most cases be placed within a larger pattern or organization which makes sense to the student. It is no mistake that many personal computer operating systems use an organizational scheme like the top of a desk, the tabbed sections of a notebook, or the folders in a file cabinet as a central organizational scheme.

These organizing frameworks help the user transfer familiar functions to an otherwise unfamiliar computer environment. They suggest to the user appropriate actions, and they greatly reduce the amount of training necessary to use the computer. In contrast, the early command line operating systems make much greater demands on the user, because nothing in their display helps the user to select actions or implement them easily.

In the same way, simulation designers can use existing frameworks to help the student understand the sometimes-complex displays and control systems of simulations. One student management system for CBI was designed along the lines of the student's study desk. The information normally needed by the student to make self-directed instructional decisions was available through the means a student might normally use while working at the desk. Historical data on past instruction was provided in file folders placed in a file cabinet. Pending assignments were listed in an assignment book. Deadlines were shown on a calendar, and various support tools and information were found in the desk's drawers or in the volumes placed on a book shelf.

Simulation interfaces are becoming increasingly realistic, and these realistic performance environments are providing an organizing framework for presenting information generated by the simulation. The authors were involved together in the design of a simulation which placed the student inside a typical airline maintenance shop at an airport gate. The graphical environment contained all of the information sources normally consulted by the aircraft maintainer, including manuals, phones for making calls to supporting organizations, computers containing maintenance reports, and a microfilm reader containing the aircraft maintenance manual.

The use of this environment by the student is intuitive, because it represents an environment with which the student is already familiar and within which the functions to be performed suggest themselves. In such an environment, a few simple directions to the student are all the training that is needed to allow the student to begin solving problems. Not only is the use of the simulation made more simple, but the patterns of action a student would normally use in real-world performance are practiced as part of the instructional problem-solving process.

Control systems

When a designer creates the interface for a simulation—the display conventions—one of the major concerns is to make the controls by which the student moves and acts as simple and easy to employ as possible. It is critical that no more energy and attention than necessary be required for the student to operate the simulation. This can sometimes present the designer with a considerable challenge. The controls which the designer provides determine the amount and types of information a student can derive from a simulation. They define the student's options and therefore the student's opportunities.

Some tough trade-off decisions face the designer of a simulation control system. By presenting too many controls and too many choices the designer places the student in a difficult position. The controls themselves and the range of options they present becomes a major learning task and memory load. On the other hand, by restricting the control set and range of functions the designer prohibits the student from conducting self-directed explorations and prevents access to certain kinds of information that might be useful to the student. This takes some of the initiative for learning from the student.

We treat control issues under the following headings below:

- Range and type of controls number of controls

- Relation to data structure

- Alignment with instructional goals

- Control transparency

Range, type, and number of controls: Instructional simulation controls fall into four main categories, as listed below. It is not hard to define several potentially useful controls in any of these categories.

Controls which are related to simulation problem administration:

- Select a problem to solve

- Restate the problem to be solved

- Restate solving directions

- Describe the use of problem controls

- Exit the problem

- Save the problem for later re-entry

- Restart the problem

- Restart the problem at time X:XX

Controls which influence the representation:

- Zoom-in, zoom-out

- Focus on specific detail

- Re-orient the object being viewed

- Change the viewing perspective

- Adjust the position of the light source

- Eliminate details or objects during replay

- Provide (tailored) commentary

- Provide/hide historic trace representation

Controls which influence the simulation model:

- Set a system model to specific initial values

- Initiate system model activity

- Halt system model activity

- Reset a system model to initial values

- Set termination or "stopper" values

- Modify system model rules

- Increase/reduce system model cycle speed

- Move between environment model locations

- Perform actions within environment locations

Controls which influence the instruction:

- Restate the instructional goal

- Add/remove emphasis graphics or messages (where)

- Add/remove model action commentary (what)

- Add/remove rationale descriptions (why, how)

- Add/remove object labels

- Provide comparison model

All of these controls are within the realm of possibility, given today's powerful programming and graphical tools, and a good case can be made for providing any one of them (and others which have been omitted to keep this list from becoming too long). The designer's challenge is to select the subset of controls which will actually be provided, because if all of the controls which are possible are implemented, the total number will be staggering to the learner. In this case of over-choice, rather than using a larger number of the controls, the student will be more likely to use fewer.

Certain standard simulation problem controls from the areas listed above must be provided. Students must be able to enter and exit problems, submit problem solutions for final evaluation, and pause problems. They must be able to replay a simulation from the beginning, and depending on the specific nature of the models provided, they may have to move about the simulated environment. Beyond these basic requirements, a designer must carefully select which controls to include. Each one chosen will have cost implications during development and information processing implications as the student tries to learn from the simulation while controlling it at the same time. In the ideal case, the activities of controlling the simulation and learning from it should complement each other as much as possible and reduce information processing conflicts in which attention is diverted from learning to control problems.

Relation to data structure: Many of the controls of an instructional simulation have the effect of allowing a student to explore data fields, charts, tables, or graphics created by the simulation. By examining these data fields the student reaches conclusions, and these become the basis for learning. Examination of the fields is made possible through controls which allow the student to scan its extent, its trends, and its details. Using the controls is analogous to turning one's head in order to get a better view. It is also analogous to moving to a better vantage point. Data may be displayed for the student in several forms, sometimes two-dimensional and sometimes in a three-dimensional.

The designer designs the data display to convey the maximum of relevant and useful information in a form most readily applicable to the performance being learned. As the data display is designed, so are the controls which the student will use for navigating the display and orienting it to the momentary need. The controls must be designed in a way that maximizes their intuitiveness and minimizes the amount of direct attention the student must pay directly to them to obtain the information desired. The design of the display and the controls for navigating the display comprise some of the most important design decisions of an instructional simulation.

Part of the great attractiveness of the head-mounted display associated with virtual reality is its intuitiveness. In everyday life, in order to see what is to the left of our visual field, we turn our heads to the left, and this same deeply-learned motion is the one used to actuate display change using the helmet. The user pays hardly any attention at all to the act of seeing to the left. The great mass of instructional simulations, however, are not virtual reality environments. Though they may become common after several years of additional technology development and design tool building, they are not common now. So designers are faced with how to design two-dimensional graphic and video displays which represent system and environment model output and which have controls for scanning, changing perspective, and zooming which are intuitive enough to be nearly transparent to the user's attention.

In this respect, many current computer-based recreational titles supply ideas for moving about environments and moving about the conceptual spaces of a model. Even these, however, represent a technological step beyond what the average CBI designer will find possible, and so static displays equipped with directional motion controls, zoom controls, and perspective controls may be the best approach. These are easily constructed using available frame-based or object-based authoring technologies. Virtual reality can be to a great extent achieved on a two-dimensional screen.

Alignment with instructional goals: Chapter 9 described the multiplicity of goals active during and influencing the course of instruction: designer/instructor goals, student goals, performance goals, and strategic goals. Figure 5 reviews the simple matrix of goals created by crossing these dimensions.

	Designer/Instructor	Student
Performance Goals		
Strategic Goals		

Figure 5. Relationship between designer and student goals for performance and strategy..

The control set designed for an instructional simulation must allow students to express those goals which are assigned to student control. Designers sometimes jump to the immediate conclusion that instruction should be controlled by the designer or the instructor. By making this decision, they fail to explore the great variety of instructional forms possible when the student is given greater choice in guiding the instructional process. The sharing of control during instruction has been treated in the past as if it were a single all-or-none decision. However, a great variety of strategic decisions are being made constantly during instruction by a live instructor, and the same potential for instruction-time decision-making exists in computer-based instruction. Designers are learning how to turn many of these decisions over to the student, and this implies that controls will be supplied for the student to express whatever choices are shared.

Instructional simulation is often used when the goal of instruction is a higher-order form of knowledge or problem solving ability. Instruction of this type often demands that a student make choices moment-by-moment because it is the ability to make intelligent or well-informed choices which is being learned and therefore which must be practiced. In such instructional settings, the design of the control set to allow the expression of goals, intentions, and action plans is of paramount importance.

There is a growing tendency among designers to allow students to express action plans as a part of the instructional interaction. The action plan may be a set of actions selected and sequenced by the student which he or she expects to solve a problem and which the student may then "play" or have executed to see the result. The LOGO programming tool and teaching environment is but one example of this use of externalized goals. Alternately, the action plan may be a set of steps which the student proposes to take in order to solve a problem, and the expression of the action plan may be for the purpose of allowing a feedback critic to detect mismatches between the student's stated intentions (conceptual plans) and the student's actions (operations). This is a very useful diagnostic technique to use when students are experiencing performance problems and a cause must be identified. The use of either of these goal-expression patterns of instruction requires the ability of the student to express action goals, which implies a set of controls with which to do so.

Control transparency: The effort and attention required of the student to operate an instructional simulation must be minimized. Every bit of attention focused on the controls themselves subtracts from the learning process. The control set supplied with a simulation must be as transparent to the user as possible.

Two principles dominate the designer's attempts to maximize control transparency:

Use familiar metaphors where possible. A simulation designer can take a clue from the designers of operating system interfaces. Some interfaces are made to resemble a filing system and file folders. Others are made to look like the tabs of a notebook. These interfaces are easy to use because they contain structures and actions which are already thoroughly familiar to users. An examination of existing simulation interfaces can help the designer identify useful and intuitive control sets which have worked best in the past. However, the evolution of instructional simulations in the future will require that new features and user controls be implemented which are not now available in simulations.

Designers should constantly search for new metaphors which readily suggest control possibilities and actions which are natural. One approach to this is to use settings as part of the interface. As already described, one computer-based management system design uses a student's study desk as the setting for an interface which allows the student, among other things, to retrieve historical records of instruction (from a file drawer), use standard reference works (supplied on a bookshelf above the desk), review deadlines for course completion (from a calendar on the wall), and to obtain instruction (through a book atop the desk). A setting related to the instructional content may supply ready controls if it is used as the backdrop or context for the student's choices.

Maintain control consistency between simulations as much as possible. The days where CBI designers felt the necessity of making each CBI interface new and creatively different are gone. Extensive experience with computers has shown that control transparency results from control familiarity. New control sets pose a learning problem to the user, and if a student must learn a new control set with each new instructional simulation, then a considerable amount of energy and attention is being diverted from the intended learning. Moreover, if simulations differ in their use of a standard control convention, then confusion is the result. The familiar right and left arrow symbols which are virtually everywhere in CBI have been used in so many different ways that their meaning is beginning to become uncertain.

Scope dynamism

Scope dynamism, as an instructional feature of instructional simulations, consists of adjusting the size of the performance challenge as an instructional technique. We have already discussed scope dynamism extensively in this chapter and in Chapter 15. We have referred to it mostly using the phrase *increasingly complex microworlds*, and we have discussed a technique which designers may use to accomplish scope dynamism: the work model.

The use of simulation as the first-choice instructional technique within instructional curricula means that designers must be able to provide for the student an appropriate sequence (either student-selected or system-selected) of learning tasks. Whereas tutorial instruction does not concern itself as much with scope dynamics, simulation-based instruction *must* do so. The designer must provide for either: (1) a single, designer-chosen sequence of progressively challenging learning tasks, (2) a designer-provided field of tasks through which the student may choose a path, or (3) a designer-provided field of tasks through which some instructional algorithm can choose the best path for the student based on performance on prior tasks.

The past practice of providing only one version of the course syllabus—only one set of instructional events which all students experience—will begin to change as designers discover ways to create families of problems, each differing in a calculated way from the others, and each representing a specific level of difficulty or challenge. As this happens, we should expect to see the technology of problem selection mature and begin to supply more guidance to designers.

Embedded didactics

Embedded didactics are instructional messages or presentations which are embedded within a simulated environment. They are a form of direct teaching which can take place during the solution of a problem.

Bringing the instructional message closer to where performance is taking place is a concept that is drawing increased interest. It is, after all, the basic principle behind the popularity of electronic performance support systems, or job aids. When students perceive a need for learning, there is greater likelihood that learning will take place. As a student encounters a problem for which a solution path is not known by the student, resources can be placed within the problem environment which guide and support the student toward finding the path. Embedded didactics place the role of the instructor back into perspective—not as the sole deliverer of instructional message, but as a companion-in-learning.

There are many ways to implement embedded didactics within an instructional simulation:

Direct instruction: The most straightforward way is to create an instructor function which can be invoked by the student at any time and which can supply to the student on demand instruction on any task selected from a menu. If a student does not consult the instructor function and persists in making errors or failing to solve the problem, then the instructor can impose itself on the student, supplying instruction that is designed to correct the errors.

Personalities within the environment: Embedded didactics can be placed within the simulation environment in the form of personalities which might normally inhabit the environment. If a problem is set within a maintenance shop, then the didactic function can be supplied by an instructor which takes the form of the shop supervisor or a shop assistant. This personality can be made to instruct only in the case of need, or on an automatic basis, it can provide a commentary on the student's solution of the problem—complete with suggestions on how to proceed. Other personalities can be introduced through phone calls from outside sources of help or the ability to make phone calls to an environment personality. For this reason, many current environmental simulations include a phone somewhere in the environment.

Personalities may supply a range of instructional functions, depending on the designer's principles. They may provide messages as simple as short suggestions or as involved as lengthy presentations or demonstrations. All parts of the instructional message can be delivered in one way or another through environment personalities.

Embedded resources: The authors were involved in the design of a simulated environment in which the student had the option of using manuals that were available on a simulated shelf on the simulated wall of the simulated work room. The problems within this environment were intended to be test problems, so there was little help offered on how to use the manuals. However, in an instructional version of this work room, the manuals would have contained one additional section—the "how-to-use-this-manual" section. A student unfamiliar with the manuals could learn to use them from a quick look inside the front cover. Providing this resource would not only provide instruction just at the time of its need, but it would perhaps increase the likelihood that students would consult the instructions in other manuals in the future as a means of learning to use them—even real ones.

Perhaps the most important aspect of embedded didactics as an instructional technique of instructional simulations is that it helps designers to change the way they think about instruction. Many designer minds are captured by the metaphor which views instruction as a direct, sequenced message to the student. Though this has been proven in the past as a useful instructional technique, it is a limited technique which too often excludes the student as an active agent in the learning process. Embedding instruction within simulation environments poses a greater technical challenge to the designer, but it also carries with it benefits to the student and to the broadening view of instruction as a process.

Simulations, objects, and tools

We have placed great emphasis in this book on objects, object-oriented design and development tools, and their transforming role in the future of CBI. We believe that object-oriented tools remove many of the barriers which have hindered the development of CBI technology without creating significant new barriers. We believe this in general concerning all forms of CBI, but we believe it especially with respect to the evolving concept of the instructional simulation.

Several benefits accrue to the CBI designer when object-oriented design and development tools are used:

Freedom from the confining frame metaphor: The frame metaphor and its incorporation into CBI authoring tools was responsible to a great extent for providing access for greater numbers of designers to the CBI medium. Frame-based authoring removed the requirement for programming. But it also imposed on the CBI product certain limitations. Some types of logical structure became easy and efficient to create, but other types of structure, like simulations, remained quite difficult and still required recourse to programming—this time using the arcane programming language of the authoring system.

Object-oriented development tools supply, if nothing else, a new set of thought tools, beginning with the elimination of the frame as a basic structural unit. We need no more think just in terms of frames and their appliances, but are free to imagine structures which before this have been costly and required difficult technical skills. This release from the frame limitation is good news to many, but for others it produces a troublesome void where the comfortable frame structure used to reside. This is because designers think in terms of structures.

What will the new structures be which designers build together to form their products? Models? Problems? That question has not been answered definitively and will not be for several years. However, we would like to suggest some interim answers. For one thing, the object mechanism shows its power by being able to perpetuate the frame metaphor. That is, frames can be objects. It is interesting to note that early object-based systems tend to select the "frame" (Quest 5.0 for Windows) or the "page" (ToolBook) as their central organizing structure, while providing the capability to extend and to create new structures. This reliance on the old structural metaphors may be intended as a conceptual bridge for designers who must use the tool, and as our conceptions of the new generation of computer-based instruction mature, these early structures will be joined by new and more varied ones.

Compatibility of design and programming structures: The frames of frame-based systems and the subroutines of authoring languages have dominated our development tools, so designers have had to convert or transform their ideas into frame or subroutine structures—despite the fact that the designs are rarely conceived in that form naturally. A frame-based designer thinks in terms of sequences of visual elements, message elements, and interactions, but not all forms of instruction are readily sequenced. Designs for non-sequential instruction are constructed from different thought primitives, and object-oriented tools provide thought structures appropriate for conceiving those types of design.

Ability to create independent knowledge and instructional structures: Designers have long though of their instruction as a combination of message content and instructional strategy woven together. The work of David Merrill and others has shown that message content can be separated from the underlying strategic structure and that the structures can be generalized and reused with minor, parameter-driven changes.

This realization means that instructional engines can be created as separate mechanisms from content structures and that the two can be mixed at the time of instruction, rather than having to be pre-planned and pre-sequenced by the designer. The separability of instructional content and instructional mechanism was a dream which the artificial intelligence community pushed toward realization.

One of the most interesting elements of Merrill's work is the conviction that the core elements of the instructional message can be supplied by a knowledge base and that the message itself can be generated using slotted, formatted message structures. The knowledge base can consist of a collection of static knowledge objects or, as work by Anderson and Gibbons has shown, the fresh knowledge generated by a simulation. Whatever knowledge mechanism is used, the separate instructional mechanism, independent of environmental or model simulations, is a reusable asset, and this suggests the idea of the instructional *player*.

The instructional *player*

The instructional player concept promises to reduce the cost of CBI by permitting multiple uses of simulation models for different instructional purposes. Figure 6 shows how this might work.

A single simulation can supply message elements for a variety of instructional surfaces: tutorials, simulated problems, interactive reference works, or job-aids. What differs between

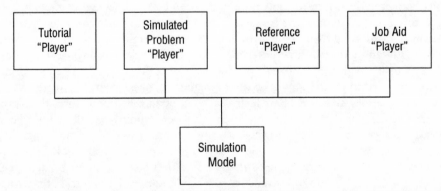

Figure 6. The "player" concept, which bases multiple products on a single simulation model.

these separate players is the manner in which the fresh content is placed into a message context for the student, the controls given the student, and the message contexts available within each one. Of course, the student need not even be aware that a different player has assumed control of the messaging function. The players allow the student to interact with the experience-producing mechanism, the model. And recall that it can be experience with an environment model, a model of a system, or a model of expert behavior. This is the spirit of model-centered instruction, which we described earlier.

The evolution of CMI

Just as CBI instructional forms have tended to mimic the instructional forms of the past, so have the tools by which we monitor progress using CBI. We are referring to instructional management tools. In the classroom, the teacher records learning in terms of completion of assignments and marks down a numerical score for each one as a sign of how well the student is progressing.

We have become used to single-score reports of achievement just as we have become used to single-score reports of intelligence. But the feeling that intelligence must be represented by more than a single number is growing, and so is the feeling that achievement within any domain of performance must be reported by more than a single score or index. Any performance is a complex of behaviors, each individually performed better or less well under varying conditions. One element of a larger performance may be weak, and the indices which are used to report performance capability must capture this information in order to permit instructional prescriptions which target the weak area.

For this reason, as instruction becomes increasingly performance-oriented and situated in realistic performance contexts through the use of simulations, we should expect the nature of the performance recording and reporting system—the instructional management system—to change also. It must be capable of reporting performance relative to specific tasks and combinations of tasks. This will make performance data useful in selecting problem sequences which gradually increase in difficulty relative to the individual student's capabilities at a given moment.

This concept of task-centered management is not only possible, but it is being used increasingly in instructional systems which adjust the syllabus to the student, rather than the other way around.

The traditional model of CBI management has been what might be termed the "crane" model. The management system built this way acts like the loading crane at a wharf, picking up one lesson at a time and placing it before the student. The student studies the lesson, and a single score from the lesson test (either a number or a pass/no-pass) is carried away with the lesson by the crane when the lesson is completed. The crane records the number in a data base just as a number might be recorded into a teacher's class record book for one assignment. Then the crane gets the next lesson and places it before the student and the cycle continues.

The alternative to the crane model of management is what may be called the adaptive model. Early CBI pioneers envisioned computer-based instruction as an adaptive process, in which each response of the student was used to determine the computer's next initiative. If this vision existed at the individual response level, then we must assume that something like it existed at all levels of instructional management and decision-making above the response level, including the level of selecting of lessons, or as we have been referring to them, instructional events.

The price for getting away from the crane model and the monotonic reporting of performances is that designers must establish a profile of the tasks or skills which they expect skilled performers to be able to accomplish. This is often done using an analysis process called *cogni-*

tive task analysis. Progress toward expert-level performance must then be marked in terms of each task, as well as in terms of task complexes, sequences, and combinations which the student is able to perform at a given moment. Though this notion of management is more demanding of the designer than the crane model, it increases the designer's ability to design instructional systems responsive to the student and capable of advancing the student through an appropriate succession of instructional experiences until expertise is achieved. Most remarkably, this approach to management and reporting of capability will eliminate the need for meaningless grading curves and allow each student to approach some recorded level of mastery.

Conclusion

We have tried to broaden the traditional conception of computer-based instruction by recommending that the simulation and direct experience be placed at the center of instructional experiences. Though simulations are not rare in current CBI products, the notion that simulation-related instructional features can support learning instead of tutorial presentations is a departure from the trend in today's CBI products. We believe that the computer as an instructional device has yet to be used with even a fraction of the power that is possible. We therefore point the designer in this new direction, realizing that not all of the answers have been formalized, but confident that inventive designers will solve problems and share their learning, bringing about the simulation revolution in CBI.

Self-directed activities

- Collect as many simulation and simulation-like products as you can. Separate those which are instructional from those which are not. Separate those which are simulation look-alikes into a third group. If possible, determine the effectiveness of the programs in each group. Determine the possible applications of each and the limitations of each.

- Divide the instructional simulation programs in your collection into four classes: environment simulations, model simulations, expert behavior simulations, and hybrids. Which group is largest? Which type did you have the most difficulty finding?

- Write a defense of "indirection" as an important instructional technique. Describe the types of learning it promotes and explain why you think they are important.

- Make as large a list as possible of the things you have learned unaided through interacting directly with natural or human-made systems without a *companion in learning.* Then make a list of the things you have learned from such experiences where there was a companion who was not formally a teacher or instructor. How satisfactory was the learning under both conditions?

- Within the group of instructional simulations resulting from the second activity above, classify for each simulation the instructional feature(s) combined with the model or environment simulation. Begin to keep a record of different instructional features and how they are implemented by different designers within different products. Look for categories of instructional feature not described in this chapter.

- Imagine what the teacher's grade book will look like when the single-score version of computer-managed instruction is replaced by one that is based on competence in the performance of tasks and task combinations and sequences. Design such a grade book or describe what it will be like.

Further reading

Anderson, J. R. (1993). *Rules of the mind.* Hillsdale, NJ: Lawrence Erlbaum Associates.

Burton, R. R., and Brown, J. S. (1979). An investigation of computer coaching for informal learning activities. *International Journal of Man-Machine Studies, 11,* 5–24.

Butler, D. L., and Winne, P. H. (1995). Feedback and self-regulated learning: A theoretical synthesis. *Review of Educational Research, 65(3),* 248–81.

Gagné, R. M., and Merrill, M. D. (1990). Integrative goals for instructional design. *Educational Technology Research and Development, 38(1),* 23–30.

Gibbons, A. S., and Anderson, T. A. (1995). *Functional description for the design of automated authoring for tutorial-based simulations.* Apple's East-West Authoring Tools Group, CD-ROM, Apple Computer, Inc., Advanced Technology Group, Authoring Tools Program, Cupertino, CA.

Gibbons, A. S., Fairweather, P. G., Anderson, T. A., and Merrill, M. D. (1997). Simulation and computer-based instruction: A future view. In C. R. Dills and A. J. Romiszowski (Eds.), *Instructional development paradigms* (pp. 769–804). Englewood Cliffs, NJ: Educational Technology Publications.

Gibbons, A. S., Trollip, S. R., and Karim, M. (1990). The expert flight plan critic: A merger of technologies. *Educational Technology, 30(4),* 32–35.

Larkin, J. H., and Simon, H. A. (1987). Why a diagram is (sometimes) worth ten thousand words. *Cognitive Science, 11,* 65–99.

Lesgold, A., Chipman, S., Brown, J. S., and Soloway, E. (1990). Intelligent training systems. *Annual Review of Computer Science, 4,* 383–394.

Lesgold, A., and Lajoie, S. P. (1989). Apprenticeship training in the workplace: Computer-coached practice as a new form of apprenticeship. *Machine-Mediated Learning, 3,* 7–28.

Loftin, R. B., Wang, L., Baffes, P., and Hua, G. (1989). An intelligent system for training space shuttle flight controllers in satellite deployment procedures. *Machine-Mediated Learning, 3,* 41–51.

Mayer, R. E., and Anderson, R. B. (1991). Animations need narrations: An experimental test of a dual-coding hypothesis. *Journal of Educational Psychology, 83(4),* 484–490.

Mory, E. H. (1996). Feedback research. In D. H. Jonassen (Ed.), *Handbook of research for educational communications and technology.* New York: Macmillan.

Newman, D., Grignetti, M., Gross, M., and Massey, L. D. (1989). Intelligent conduct of fire trainer: Intelligent technology applied to simulator-based training. *Machine-Mediated Learning, 3,* 29–39.

Ram, A., and Leake, D. B. (1995). *Goal-driven learning.* Cambridge, MA: MIT Press.

Reigeluth, C. M., and Schwartz, E. (1989). An instructional theory for the design of computer-based simulations. *Journal of Computer-Based Instruction, 16(1),* 1–10.

Snow, R. E., and Lohman, D. F. (1989). Implications of cognitive psychology for educational measurement. In R. E. Linn (Ed.), *Educational measurement (3rd ed.).* New York: American Council on Education and Macmillan Publishing Company.

Wenger, E. (1987). *Artificial intelligence and tutoring systems.* Los Altos, CA: Morgan Kaufmann Publishers.

17

SIMULATION LOGIC PATTERNS

Chapter Objectives:
1. *Describe why frames are often not the best vehicle for constructing simulations.*
2. *Define the two main types of environmental simulation structure.*
3. *Describe the advantage of a shell structure in the design of location simulations.*
4. *Describe two approaches to model simulation structure.*
5. *Identify the benefits of object-orientation in the design and development of instructional simulations.*

Introduction

In Chapter 5, we described patterns of logic commonly used as the understructure to support a great variety of tutorial surfaces and interactions. The patterns in Chapter 5 were constructed of frames, a convenient logical structure which exists inside the CBI authoring tools most widely used today. These basic tutorial building-block patterns do not *require* frames for their construction; they can be created using *any* programming or authoring tool. We introduced the concept of frame to give you a glimpse into the logical details of tutorial CBI programs and to show you how standard frame-based authoring tools can create a variety of tutorial structures easily and rapidly.

In this chapter, we will introduce a set of basic logic patterns which can be used in a similar way to construct simulations. Frame-based authoring tools can be used to build some simulation structures, but we do not use frames to describe simulation logic patterns, because the frame has some shortcomings when it comes to simulation that limit the choices of designers. The frame does not make it easier to build simulations and can make it harder. When you construct a simulation, you also must construct or attach its accompanying independent instructional functions. These important adjuncts to the simulation model can be added with greater ease if object-oriented tools are used. Moreover, an object-oriented tool will normally give equal or greater efficiency, and if objects are constructed in a generic fashion, they can be transplanted into other products as well.

In Chapter 16, we described four types of model: environmental, systems, expert, and hybrid. In this chapter, we will describe the inner logical structures which can be used for their construction.

Environmental simulation structures

An environmental simulation consists of a group of information-bearing locations and a lattice of paths connecting them. Each location is provisioned with movement and action controls which allow students to move between locations and to perform actions within them.

Locations within an environmental simulation are organized according to one of two basic structural motifs: the hierarchy and the network. Figure 1 shows both of these organizations. Paths between locations allow movement one-way or in both directions, depending on the environment being simulated.

Hierarchical environments have one or more *starting* or *initial* locations at the top of the pyramid from which the student begins problems. Lower locations in the hierarchy are accessed by moving down one level of detail at a time. This often creates a "zoom-in" effect as

A. Hierarchical Location Pattern   B. Networked Location Pattern

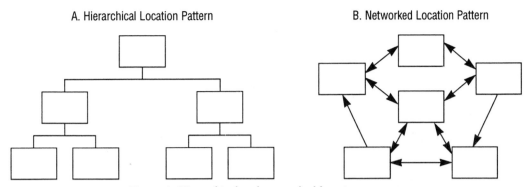

Figure 1. Hierarchical and networked location patterns.

the student moves to increasingly detailed views of the environment. Exiting a location means either zooming out one level of detail or express-zooming back to the initial location.

We have designed several hierarchical location simulations. One of them was for training fault isolation within electronic equipment housed within a small metal room. In this simulation, from an overhead view of the room (which had electronic gear attached to all four walls), the student could zoom in to a specific wall, then to a specific piece of gear on that wall. From there, it was possible to zoom-in to a part of the item, such as the front of the control panel or the back of the control panel. Below that level, additional zoom-ins brought the student to see individual controls on the control panel, indicators, and voltage measurement points behind the control panel. Just as students could zoom in level by level, they could zoom out using the same steps or use an "express" zoom out which took them back to the bird's-eye view of the room.

Another simulation depicted an airline's maintenance shop at an airport gate. From the full view of the shop, the student could zoom in to several locations: manuals on a shelf, a computer terminal, a microfilm reader, or a telephone. Zooming to (by selecting) a manual showed its cover and title. Further zooms showed the manual's table of contents, a section, and eventually, individual pages. A door leading from the shop led to a parts room, and through the window, an aircraft, (made up of many locations) could be entered. The shop was one hierarchy of locations, and the aircraft was a second hierarchy of locations. At the top level, all roads led to the shop, the initial location in the simulation.

Networked environments do not have a main central location. Though there may be a initial location into which the user is placed at the beginning of the problem, that location offers paths to many locations, and the user may wander away from the initial location, never to return. The paths of a networked location simulation are not arranged in a hierarchy.

There are several varieties of hierarchical and network structures for environments. Figure 2 shows some varieties of hierarchical environments, and Figure 3 shows some networked environment variations. Note that the linear variety of networked environment is no more than a single path of locations, each supplying the student with some amount of information—the defining characteristic of a location. The information within a location may take any form: video graphic, textual, auditory, kinesthetic. It should be clear by now that a standard linear tutorial presentation is no more than a highly specialized, linear environment adapted to presenting messages in a set sequence. However, a linear environment could easily be made into a guided tour of one of the long hallways within the Louvre and therefore represent an environment simulation rather than a tutorial.

The concept of an environmental simulation is broader than that of a tutorial. It allows the presentation of information in any form (literal, figurative, symbolic, or verbal), and it of-

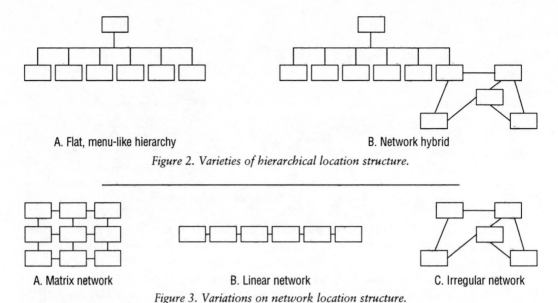

A. Flat, menu-like hierarchy   B. Network hybrid

Figure 2. Varieties of hierarchical location structure.

A. Matrix network   B. Linear network   C. Irregular network

Figure 3. Variations on network location structure.

ten implants information within the context of a problem scenario. This allows it to carry out instruction by indirection. When this happens, the focus may be on higher-order behavior in addition to specific domain knowledge.

Beneath the surface of locations

The hierarchy and the network are surface forms which a location simulation may take. They soon become apparent to the user simply through use. There are at least two main schemes for organizing the logic which underlies these surface types, and the user can never detect which of the two schemes is being used. They are: the pre-compiled location and the location driver. These schemes of invisible (to the user) logical organization differ not only in their structure, but in their economy as well.

The pre-compiled location is the most often used scheme, but the location driver is more economical. The pre-compiled location is best done using a commercial authoring system. The location driver, which somewhat more complicated to create, can be built using an authoring system or just about any standard programming tool. Both logical schemes can be created using object-oriented tools as well.

The precompiled location

The precompiled location, as the name suggests, is created as a self-contained location by the authoring tool, normally in the form of a CBI frame to which all of the media resources used to construct the location are directly attached. In its most primitive form, the pre-compiled location can be created by hooking together a family of menu frames—each one representing one location. Menu choices, instead of being textual entries on the screen, are made to correspond with graphical features of the display. When a user selects one of the graphical features, the scene branches to the new location, contained in another menu frame, which is associated with that choice. Both hierarchies and networks of locations can be created in this way.

If an object-oriented authoring tool is used, the basic structural component of that tool (the page, or some other object) is used as the base for constructing each location, and location media resources are attached directly to the element. When the pre-compiled approach is used, regardless of the type of logic tool used, the structure of logical elements corresponds closely to the structure of the locations.

We have used the pre-compiled logic approach to create environment simulations. Since each new location adds new graphical and logical resources to the authored file, files can grow to an unreasonable size when larger environments are modeled When this happens, authoring becomes difficult and slow. Moreover, the amount of frame logic to keep track of grows large, and the product becomes difficult to maintain. Finally, it becomes complicated to add global simulation functions, such as problem controls and action controls, because these functions operate across locations, rather than within them. Therefore, we recommend the pre-compiled approach to locations mainly for small and uncomplicated simulations. This approach is excellent for creating numerous small, inexpensive problem worlds which children can use to solve "mysteries" and develop their inquiry and problem solving skills at the same time.

Some designers are misled into taking the notion of location too literally. They assume that each *location* must correspond exactly with some real-world physical place. Recall that the term *location* is defined in terms of information which it provides. To simulate conversational interactions in some location simulations, the designer will provide a menu of questions to be asked. Each menu should itself be seen as a location, and each answer to a question is also a separate, information-bearing location.

The normal structure of locations used for asking questions of a simulated personality is: (1) select the character and the "Ask" or "Speak" control (the character is the first location), (2) a menu of questions appears (this is the second location), (3) a question is selected, and (4) the user hears or sees the answer to the question (at the third location), following which (5) an instantaneous branch from the third location returns the user back without delay to the second location (the menu) to select another question to ask or to zoom out to a higher location.

The location executive or driver

A second major approach to the logical structure of location simulations combines the virtues of relative simplicity, relative compactness, reusability of program logic, and much more rapid and simple authoring. It involves the construction of an execution cycle capable of *executing* or *interpreting* locations using data supplied from some source, normally a designer-constructed data file, but also possibly including computed values. We have used both frame-based and object-oriented development tools to create the location executive or driver mechanism. The mechanism itself is reusable program logic. The same location driver can be used to create a multitude of location simulations.

The executive itself consists of a cycle of program logic which is executed once following each action or choice expressed by the student. The executive performs the same cycle of events for each location. As it does, it *constructs* the location using location-describing data and media resources, in effect "moving" the student to that location. Some controls within an environment simulation carry out an action—like speaking to a simulated personality or picking up a portable object—which are carried out the same regardless of the current location. These actions are carried out as independent subroutines, after which the student is returned to the location from which the action was performed.

An example of the executive cycle for an environment simulation is diagrammed in Figure 4. This particular cycle assumes that data to describe each location has been placed within a data file (or else that the necessary data can be computed somehow, which is an interesting concept to think about). As this cycle executes, it consults the data file to determine what media-based informational experience(s) to execute for the student (i.e., graphic, animation, video, audio, etc.). The cycle then uses the remainder of the data to configure and display student controls, define and activate control or choice areas, specify branching destinations for each control or choice, and other necessary functions. Then the cycle returns to the waiting state, ready for another response from the student, following which it repeats the cycle.

The amount of data used to describe each location can be extensive for highly detailed and interactive location, but the fact that the data is accumulated and maintained within a file rather than within a precompiled program file makes the creation of the simulation easier and faster and reduces the size of the file. This data-executive simulation mechanism makes a special demand of the authoring tool: The tool must be able to draw media resources from a library of resources *at the time of execution* by name. While the precompiled approach binds media resources directly to separate logical structures, this driver approach merges logical structures and media resources only at the exact moment of execution.

This means that a single bundle of logic (a frame, or an object) can be used to execute *any* location as soon as it has the name of the file(s) or library item(s) which constitute(s) that location's media resources. In our own personal experience we found this one feature of authoring tools (the ability to reference rather than pre-bind media resources) to have an enormous impact on the costs of simulation design and production, amounting in one case to two orders of magnitude in cost. The location data describes the initial state of the location at the beginning of the problem, but it also stores the changed or current state of the location as the problem progresses.

The functions illustrated in Figure 4 are described in more detail below.

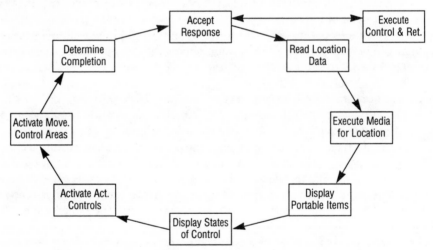

Figure 4. A location execution cycle.

Accept response: The computer waits until the student takes action. The response accepted at this point consists of selecting a new location to move to, operating an action control, or operating a problem control.

As soon as a response is accepted, the cycle begins to execute the student's request. The cycle may at this time also send a notification to some other part of the simulation (such as an instructional feature) describing what the student has chosen. The feature may then use its own internal logic and data to determine whether an intervention is advised and at the very least will probably record the student's choice for later analysis. This exemplifies the communicating link between the simulation and the instructional features adjunct to it.

Execute control subroutine and return: If the student has selected one of the specialized actions (like picking up a portable object) or a general problem function (like obtaining a restatement of the problem), a message is sent to the appropriate object (or program subroutine) responsible for executing that function. The function is performed, appropriate data (if any) is recorded, and the cycle returns to waiting for the next student response.

Read data for the new location: If the student has requested movement to a new location, the data which describes the new location is found in the file (or computed) and made available to the executive cycle, which then uses the data to carry out the remainder of its steps. In doing so, it constructs the new location. The data describing a location can include (but is not limited to):

- The names of media library objects or media files which contain the background visual for the location, as well as media files which contain information unique to the location

- The coordinates for the placement of "portable" elements of the location— things which can be picked up, carried or moved, as well as the name of the library object or media file which contains the representation of the object itself

- The names and states of the action controls available to the student at the location. This is necessary since some actions may be denied the student in some locations (such as picking up an object in a location where there is no object to pick up)

- The coordinates which define the click-sensitive screen areas for movement to new locations and the name of the destination location associated with each area

If the student has requested to exit the simulation, a close-out process is initiated which normally consists of taking a data snapshot of the current location to allow its later re-construction.

Execute media for new location: The graphic or bitmap file named in the data for the location is displayed if there is one. If the location includes or consists of audio, then the audio file associated with the location is played.

Display portable media items: Some location simulations include portable objects which can be moved from location to location during problem solution. Most often these consist of "tools" of one kind or another which the student uses in solving the problem (such as a portable calculator for math or science problems, a journal for recording findings, or a manual of instructions for operating some piece of equipment). Since these cannot be represented as a permanent part of the location backdrop, they must be represented separately. They are displayed at this time.

In addition to portable objects, a location display may include the controls or indicators of a model which are visible at the location. Since controls can be set by the student and left in any position, and since the value of the indicators is computed by the model based on the control settings, neither control nor indicator graphics can be static. In order to display them, the executive cycle consults the model data, determines the objects related to models, and then displays them in the correct configuration or value.

Display states of controls: Many location simulations provide on-screen controls used to perform actions (pick up, put down, speak to, etc.) or to carry out problem administrative functions (review the problem statement, exit the problem, save this state of the problem for later return, etc.). The availability of these controls may vary between locations, so each must be placed on the display separately at this time. The data that drives this placement may come from the data file or may be computed.

Activate action controls and movement areas: As the immediate precursor to beginning to wait for a student response, the response-sensitive areas of the display (or the keys used for legitimate responses) are activated. If frame-based authoring is used, the data defines the upper left and lower right coordinates of a mouse-sensitive area. Object-oriented tools normally allow objects themselves to recognize when they have been selected, which is a nice built-in feature.

In addition to the cyclic functions described in this section, the location executive cycle may contain a timing function which constantly increments a problem time clock while the student is idling at the accept response point. For many problems timing is an important factor. Moreover, the designer may want the student to feel realistic time pressures during problem solving. Some problems also change the content of locations on a time-determined basis. Not only can the information (media) resources at a location be changed on a timed basis, but additional new locations may become available for exploration as well.

Model simulation structures

A model simulation consists of: (1) a set of *rules* or *formulas* used to compute the (2) *property values* for a group of related system *elements*. To make things simple, consider a model simulation consisting of an electrical switch and a lamp. Assume a constant supply of electricity to the circuit (so that we don't have to monkey with the battery). When the switch is turned on, the lamp illuminates. Another way of expressing this is to say that "...when the value of the switch's *position* property changes to on, set the *illumination* property of the lamp to *yes*." Using rules, we have modeled or simulated the action of the lamp and the switch.

There are several varieties of model simulation. You can model a natural system, like the tectonic forces of the continental plates of the earth's crust or the blood system of the human body. You can also model the artificial systems created through design and manufacture, such as light systems, mechanical systems, or even abstract idea systems.

As a bare minimum, to define a model simulation, you must specify: (1) the *components* which make up the system, (2) the *properties* of each element which may take on a value, (3) the *ranges* which those values may take on, and (4) the *rules* or *formulas* which relate the property values of one element to the property values of other elements. In our simple switch-and-lamp example, here is the model specification:

Components: *Switch, Lamp*
Properties: *Switch (position), Lamp (illumination)*
Possible values: *Position (on, off), Illumination (yes, no)*
Rules: *If Position=on, then Illumination=yes, else Illumination=no.*

Two major tool approaches exist for creating simulations. Therefore, there are two parts to our discussion of logical structures for modeled simulations. The two approaches are: (1) the traditional modeling program, and (2) the object model.

Traditional modeling: The simulation cycle

For years the *simulation cycle* has been the favored method for constructing model simulations. The tool most often used to construct simulation cycles has been the standard programming language, which executes program commands and subroutines in a linear, cyclic sequence.

To construct a simulation cycle using standard programming languages, you design a comprehensive, repetitive cycle of computations that is executed over and over again. When the computation sequence reaches its end, the cycle is ready to begin again, needing only a new input or an incompleteness of the computations to cause it to continue. Figure 5 shows this kind of sequence.

When this type of cycle is executed, new values are normally computed for every property value of every system component which is affected by the computation rules. This

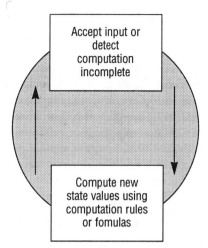

Figure 5. The model simulation cycle.

cycle has two main varieties. The *discrete* variety executes the cycle only once or until stasis (no further changes in computed values) occurs. Then the cycle waits for fresh input from the outside before beginning again. The *continuous* variety executes continuously, never reaching stasis. Flight simulator programs perform their computations a continuous cycle, never waiting for new input to begin the next round of computation. Many natural system simulations are the same. Many natural processes, such as the flow of blood through the circulatory system, continue on regardless of input. Both of these systems are able to respond to input or influences from the outside, but the systems continue to function even if there is no input. On the other hand, a computer (which can be simulated from the user's point of view) only responds when we touch a key or operate a power switch. This is a discrete modeling cycle.

Modeled simulations also vary in the form of their computations. Some models have *rules* in the form of computable, *quantitative equations*. As the equations are solved, new values are computed for component property values. Other models consist of *logical rules* in an "If...then..." form, as we have already seen with the lamp and switch example.

Finally, modeled simulations vary in the *types of values* they compute. There are *qualitative* models and *quantitative* models. A *quantitative* model computes numerical values: the wind is blowing at 10 knots, the temperature of the acid is 20 degrees C, the heart is beating at 60 beats per minute. A *qualitative* model computes qualities rather than quantities: the wind speed is "low," the acid temperature is "moderately high," and the heart beat rate is "rapid." Qualitative models are very useful in modeling a variety of systems even though they are less precise in the values they produce. Person-to-person interactions, for instance, can be modeled very usefully in a qualitative fashion: the boss is "receptive" to your proposal, the client is "nervous," or the chairman is "happy" with the sales figures. These qualitative states can be computed by using rules rather than formulas to define the model.

Model simulations, from the very most simple lemonade stand to the most complex aircraft simulation, use the simulation cycle or some variation of it to achieve their modeling effect.

Object-oriented simulations

An alternative to the cycle structure for constructing model simulations is to use groups or communities of objects. Object-oriented programming was originally invented to make the design and creation of simulations faster and easier. The mechanism of object-oriented programming is really quite simple, and the action of an object-oriented program is easy to understand. Those who seem to have the most trouble with objects are those used to traditional imperative language programming, which produces long, sequential lists of commands.

To understand how objects work, envision a group of people assembled in a room. Each knows how to respond to the sound of his or her own name and knows certain basic social actions and how to perform them. In order to get this group of people interacting, you need only send a message to one of them. We could send a message to the object (person) John, a message called "say hello to" Sally. At that point, since John knows how to "say hello to," he could carry out the action without help. To do so, John would send a message to Sally—a message called "hello." As Sally received the "hello" message, she would respond appropriately, since she knows the actions to take upon receiving a "hello" message.

Now consider the objects in an object-oriented program as if they were these people. A program object knows how to send and receive messages. When it receives a message, it knows just what to do in response to the message, because the routine that makes the response is a part of the object. Moreover, just as each person knows his or her name, each object in an object-oriented program knows certain information and data about itself. This data resides within the object, not in a common pool of program data as in traditional computer programs. The messages each object can receive and send may vary from object to object. Wally may know how to react to some messages that Sally does not know and vice versa.

In an object-oriented program, objects are created, and each one is given messages which it can receive and send. Each object is also given certain data about itself. If we were to create an object called "switch," it could be given a property called "position," and that property could be either "on" or "off." The switch would be capable of remembering its position as part of its personal data. Likewise, when the switch received the message (from some other object) "change to on," it would know how to respond to the message and could change its own data from "off" to "on."

An object knows the messages it can receive because of several small program subroutines which are attached to it. These subroutines are called *methods* or *handlers* in object-oriented terminology. A programmer gives an object new message capabilities and new behaviors by adding new handlers to it. Most object-oriented development systems make this fairly easy, so the construction of objects can proceed quickly.

To create an object simulation, we create objects which correspond to the components of the real system, give them properties, give them messages to send and receive, give them handlers (methods) so that they know how to behave, and then allow them to interact with each other naturally.

The rules contained in the handlers cause property values to change as objects interact. This is where the model rules are kept in an object-oriented simulation. For example, we could create the objects "switch" and "lamp." "Switch" would have the property "position," with possible values "off" and "on." "Lamp" would have the property "illumination state" with possible values "off" and "on."

For these objects to interact, the switch must send a message to the lamp whenever it changes its position. To do this, we would attach a handler to the switch to "handle" the message from the switch when it arrives. The switch does not cause itself to change its own position; someone or some thing has to flip the switch. Therefore, the switch must also be able to receive messages from an outside source that tell it to turn on. A handler called "turn on" would allow the switch to receive such a message from any other object and enable the switch to carry out appropriate actions in response, such as passing an appropriate message on to the lamp, telling it that it has just "received power."

Simulations are seldom as simple as the examples we have been using. Most simulation models have tens or even hundreds of components to be modeled. Moreover, these components are usually organized from groups of sub-components. Think of your car engine: It has a functional group of objects called the carburetor, and the carburetor is nothing but an assemblage of several objects, each of which can act properly (your engine runs) or improperly (it doesn't).

To handle this property of real-world systems, object-oriented programming systems allow objects to be combined into groups. Single objects have their own handlers and their own data, and in the same way, these grouped objects have their own as well. This means that messages can be sent to a single object to prompt it to perform an action or to grouped objects to prompt them to take action at the appropriate level.

There are lots of choices the designer can make in designing objects, properties, messages, and message handlers. This creates an opportunity for the designer to create models of many kinds which behave in a way that suits the need. We have illustrated very simple models, but they are not too far removed from the types of models which might be employed to enable grade school students to experience and learn about simple electrical principles of cause and effect.

Benefits of objects: Among the benefits of objects is the fact that objects are often reusable. Once the switch and lamp objects are created they can be replicated to create many switches and many lamps to be connected by students into circuits which behave just as real circuits would.

Another nice feature of objects is that many object tools allow the objects to manage their own display and disappearance from the screen automatically. This removes a huge display management burden from the designer/programmer.

Yet another benefit the object-oriented approach is that objects with special instructional functions can be included alongside the model and can be added to and subtracted from the simulation with relative ease. This is possible because objects, their behavior, and their related data are self-contained. These instructional feature objects can observe the operation of the model from a third-person perspective. They can watch for key values of key properties of key simulation components, or they can watch for patterns of values or patterns of student events. At the right moment, that is, when they spot a pattern or value of interest, the instructional feature can perform its designated function, which may include articulation of knowledge to the student, providing an explanation, providing feedback, coaching an action or memory, shifting the instructional initiative either toward or away from the student, modifying the level or type of information-bearing representations to the student, or adjusting the difficulty of a practice problem. In a non-object programming environment, adding these features can be quite difficult. Using objects, doing so can be made relatively easy (though not without some effort), and the functions can be made switchable. That is, they can be made to be turned off or on at the student's or the designer's will.

Perhaps you can see that the structure of an object-oriented model depends on the structure of the thing being modeled. This is one of the best advantages of the object-oriented approach: It allows you—the designer—to express a design in terms of the elements which will interact within the simulation model. There is no need to convert the design into computer program terms first. This saves you a good deal of time and design energy.

It also makes objects an ideal vehicle for creating rapid prototypes of simulations. Designers can create an essential core model—along with a simplified interface and simplified instructional features—in order to test the functionality and feasibility of the final product before committing too many resources to an unworkable design. In addition to testing the product surface concept, this approach also allows the designer to test the organization and the communication patterns of the principal objects and object groupings. Once the core functionality has been tested, the original objects can either be further developed (if the first organization worked well), modified, or scrapped in favor of a better approach. Both surface and structural plans are thus tested and corrected at an early stage, reducing the cost of correcting them later.

Object-oriented programming tools: The use of object-oriented tools for developing CBI is a fairly recent trend, but it is one which can be expected to accelerate. Frame-based authoring systems have been popular for nearly two decades. Until recently, object development systems within the reach of the average designer's personal skills and the power of the personal computer were not available. However, several development tools suitable for CBI uses and relatively easy to use have emerged or are in the process of emerging. Response to these tools has been quite strong, and we predict that they will help us change how we think about and design computer-based instruction and reduce the cost of our products.

Conclusion

We have tried to supply several basic structural approaches to the creation of environment and model simulations. We have especially tried to point out ways in which the cost of simulation development can be reduced through: (1) use of driver structures, and (2) use of object programming technologies. Though simulations have been used for a long time for instructional purposes, the concept of the instructional simulation is yet in its early stages of development, and the tools for building simulations are quite primitive compared to what is needed for rapid design, effective development, and low cost. The next decade promises to be one of the most exciting in the field of simulation-based instruction. We believe that the ideas we have discussed here will be important to progress in this area, and we look forward eagerly to the great variety of products and instructional approaches which is sure to emerge.

Self-directed activities

- Create a simple location simulation consisting of 5–10 locations using: (1) the pre-compiled approach, and (2) the executive cycle approach. Create the first versions of the programs with few complicated features. Compare the cost of creating these simulations in terms of time and programming skill required. Next, create a second problem using each of the approaches and compare the costs in terms of the learning curve generated by each.

- Plan how you might add instructional features to the simulation created in the previous exercise. Which simulation approach makes this easier?

- Create a simple model simulation using: (1) an object programming tool, and (2) an traditional programming tool. Calculate the cost of development for each. Once you have created the model, add a new component to it. Calculate the cost of making the addition as well as describing any unexpected problems you encounter while doing so.

- Begin a list of simulation development tools of the following kinds: (1) packaged simulation development systems, (2) object-oriented development tools. Begin to collect information about each one, concentrating on costs, range of applications, and limitations of each system.

Further reading

Cezzar, R. (1995). *A guide to programming languages: Overview and comparison.* Boston: Artech House.

Choi, W. (1997, Sept./Oct.). Designing effective scenarios for computer-based instructional simulations: Classification of essential features. *Educational Technology, 37*(5), 13–21.

Keegan, M. (1995). *Scenario educational software.* Englewood Cliffs, NJ: Educational Technology Publications.

Sethi, R. (1996). *Programming languages: Concepts and constructs.* Reading, MA: Addison-Wesley Publishing Company.

Towne, D. M. (1995). *Learning and instruction in simulation environments.* Englewood Cliffs, NJ: Educational Technology Publications.

SECTION IV

PRINCIPLES OF INSTRUCTIONAL DELIVERY

*Specific practices to improve the instructional power of the message,
the interactions, and the CBI display.*

18

MESSAGE MANAGEMENT

Chapter Objectives:

1. *Describe the differences in CBI instructional messages compared to messages for delivery in other media forms.*

2. *Describe a path of activities leading to final message creation for CBI which avoids bottlenecks for the designer.*

3. *Construct a content table for an instructional objective.*

4. *Describe the benefits of using content tables in a development team situation.*

5. *Design appropriately-formed visual message elements for CBI.*

6. *Write appropriately-formed verbal message elements for CBI.*

7. *Describe the effects of pace and density of new information on student message processing.*

8. *Describe how a message table is created from a content table.*

What is message management?

Message management is two things: (1) capturing instructional content, and (2) forming it into an effective, efficient instructional message: one that communicates with the least amount of unnecessary information processing by the student—one that does not block the flow of traffic along the student's information highway (see Chapter 7).

Computerized instruction communicates its message through many sensory channels: text, audio, graphics, animation, video, and touch. Its messages must convey a maximum of information in a minimum of time. Often as much can be conveyed non-verbally in CBI as is communicated verbally. CBI messages must be information-rich, yet compact; therefore, faults in CBI communication show up more readily than in other media. Let's consider the characteristics of the CBI message which make special demands on the developer:

1. CBI messages are focused: Good CBI instructional products tend to be lean and focused. We have already explored how to achieve focus using the lens of instructional strategy. In this chapter, we study techniques for focusing the instructional message, when a message is needed.

The number of sensory channels available for the communication of messages has been expanded by multimedia, but we cannot allow this to create a storm of sensation for the user, so the challenge of message focus requires carefully orchestrating the use of the sense channels and carefully planning message content.

2. CBI messages are display-limited: The CBI learning station has undergone radical changes in the past five years. It has gained million-color capacity, high resolution, and blinding speed. It has also become capable of serving up motion video and audio. Many of the severe limitations which existed ten years ago are now gone.

However, some limitations persist. The average CBI terminal still looks like a terminal: It is used on a desk top, it is not portable, and it is bulky. Moreover, the visual screen is space-limited, and audio and video are time-limited. So far, attempts to make the display more compact have only led to smaller, somewhat harder-to-read displays. The "windowing" metaphor releases some of the restrictions on screen space by stacking message areas on top of each other, but the more screen capability we have, the more we seem to want. In reality, the "desktop" is nowhere near the size of a desk; that's why we have to stack things. CBI developers spend much design time figuring out ways to get more performance out of a limited display.

The physically limited CBI display area leads to psychological limitations. Trying to preserve space, developers normally fail to provide users with the ability to keep their orientation. These are easy to obtain from a book because a reader can scan through the pages at any time. But with a CBI display this is harder top do. Some users feel "hemmed in" by the CBI medium, a response somewhat akin to claustrophobia.

In addition to screen real estate concerns, there are user posture concerns. Students are restricted to a small number of postures while learning from CBI. Options are restricted by power needs and computer portability. The number of comfortable positions at a CBI display are limited, and it is not recommended that you take your CBI terminal with you into the bathtub like a good book.

The pressure of these space and use limitations requires that the CBI message be: (1) succinct and to the point, (2) perceived as relevant and useful, and (3) engaging. CBI messages must have a high—but appropriate—information density and active pace without overpowering the student's ability to process and store. Not only must the verbal parts of instruction do their work quickly and well, but as much as possible, the burden of communication must be shifted from the verbal modes into more visual modes which can carry a more dense message within the same space.

3. CBI messages are dynamic: Though we have used a book for comparison, the nice thing about CBI is that it is not a book. Neither is it a slide/sound presentation, nor a video. At its best, the CBI message has a dynamism and plasticity which makes it a learning environment more than a traditional medium. The ideal CBI display demands that the user take some part in shaping it. The power of CBI is to create an engrossing, surrounding presence for a student, which changes as the student acts, enabling the student to interact and accomplish things not possible with traditional media.

This quality of the CBI display places different demands on the message designer. A CBI developer must shed the static image of the instructional message and envision it as a dynamic, constantly changing, adaptive response to student actions. The computer can present many messages, and the student can respond in many ways, so the developer can no longer be content to prepare a single linear message. Instead, a field of harmonious and compatible message elements must be contingent upon student choices, all of which support the attainment of an instructional goal.

Implications

It is the students who suffer from poor message management—the chief symptom of which is the students' inability to process the instructional message efficiently and without accidents. Students often erroneously blame themselves for the failure to learn, without suspecting that in many cases the real culprit is the incomplete message, the poorly written message, the unclear message, the imprecise message, the too-technical message, the too-academic message, the poorly organized message, the unreadable message, the misleading message, the surplus and distracting message, or the inaccurate message. These faults are the rule rather than the exception, not only in CBI but in the world of instruction as a whole.

But the effects of poor message management do not fall solely on the student. CBI designers and writers also suffer from poor message management because they are forced to work harder. The writer's task is to create the instructional message. When writers ignore the fact that message creation is a multi-stage process, they find themselves caught in a bottleneck caused by carrying out several complex writing sub-tasks at the same time:

- Gathering, mastering, and organizing technical content (often in an unfamiliar subject area).

- Writing a clear, efficient message.

- Creating multiple channels (audio, video, text, graphics) of message which are balanced and work together in harmony.

The attempt to do all of this at once often produces a frustrating bottleneck for the designer/writer. In its initial stages, message management is a process for obtaining and organizing instructional content—a commodity as slippery as fish. Only after it has been obtained and prepared can it be structured, organized, completed, channelized, made accurate, and placed in a form ready for rapid uptake by students, and it is best to do these things in an orderly, stepwise manner.

A case study in message management

CBI designers and instructors are sometimes slow to admit that problems with their messages may be contributing to their own and their students' difficulties. We worked once with an instructor who had taught the same subject—electronic troubleshooting—for almost twenty years. As designers, we were responsible for writing a body of CBI messages and simulation plans in a highly complex and technical area, and this instructor was our subject-matter expert.

We consulted all available training materials, other instructors, and technical manuals as sources of message content, and as we examined this mass of technical content, we were forced by the size of the task and the complexity of the content to devise some simple techniques for dealing with it, organizing it, and assessing its completeness.

Upon applying these techniques (described later in this chapter), we found to our great surprise (and the even greater surprise of our subject-matter expert) that even after exhausting the full range of content resources available to us, there were still large and important gaps in the content. We discovered from this that for many years the content had been taught in an incomplete form. There was no possible way that students could have been getting all of the information required to perform their jobs from the training, because all of the sources used during instruction put together could not supply it. In fact, we found that many sources contradicted each other in important details.

We discovered that rather than detecting and correcting these content deficiencies, the sponsoring organization had decided to implement a large and expensive on-the-job apprenticeship program for the graduates of the training program. This work experience was being used at least partly to make up for the message problems inherent in the training.

Since that experience, and through several similar experiences, we have come to the conclusion that when some students fail, it is often not the fault of the student: *it can be a fault of the message*. Over a decade of reviewing messages and instructional material from all content areas in the military, education, and industrial worlds has only strengthened this conviction. Most instruction suffers from a message deficiency of some type which can be remedied by a process of more thorough and orderly message planning and preparation—the process which we call message management. Message management is a two-stage process which includes:

- Capturing the instructional content in an accurate, complete, and organized form.

- Structuring that content into a channelized message, which communicates efficiently, supports the student's information processing efforts, and harmonizes with strategy guidelines.

The remainder of this chapter outlines the message management process.

Capturing the content

The commerce of the designer and writer of instruction is in ideas, relationships, and meanings. Because they have no concreteness, these idea units are slippery and can squirt away as the author tries to grasp them. Because they have no constant form nor shape, ideas are difficult to inventory and account for. Yet conveying these intangibles to student minds is what we pay designers and writers to do.

How do you capture content in such a way that it cannot escape and in a way that allows for its public inspection and use during design? The best way is to identify a form for holding the content. This form must be capable of collecting elements of content within categories which have consistent logical, semantic, and sometimes instructional properties.

When content has been collected within such a form, it can be dealt with in a systematic way. The goal is to capture all that is needed and only what is needed. We call this first step in message management a *content table*, and it is a useful tool for the forming of instructional messages related to simulations just as much as it is for tutorial instruction.

The solution to the missing content in the electronic troubleshooting problem we just described was to create a content table. We sat with the subject-matter expert and drew a table on a large sheet of flip chart paper. We invented the table headings appropriate to the type of instruction we were designing—both tutorial and simulation in this case. Then we proceeded to ask the expert questions which would fill the cells of the table. In the beginning, the expert was doubtful about where this was leading, but willing to go along with the process. As the work progressed over a matter of a few hours, the expert became more and more interested and involved in the process, until a point when we were about half way through, when the subject-matter expert asked if he could have the table when we were finished with it. He said, "This is all of the information that I need to give to the students—all in one place!"

We continued the content tabling process to its completion. The expert found it easy to understand and became quite involved in it. Toward the end of the session, he volunteered to fill in the remainder of the table himself, which he did at home that evening. We were excited to get so much useful and focused information in such a short time, and the expert was excited by the insight that he had gained into the internal organization of his content—insight he had not reached in nearly two decades of teaching it. We found that as the project progressed, we and our development staff referred constantly to this basic document; we maintained it and it became a central element of our development process.

As we examined the completed table with the expert, something became readily apparent which none of us—especially the subject-matter expert—had suspected: There were open cells in the table. They were not open because the information to fill them was not needed; they were open because the expert did not have the ready knowledge to supply. Moreover, as we went to the manuals and documents provided as a reference for the students, we found that some of the open cells could not be filled by them either and that in some cases, there were conflicts between sources over the contents of some of the cells. From this we learned that the first and necessary step in the preparation of the instructional message was to form a content table as a standard and a reference source for the development team.

Tables and objectives

Over time we have used the content table notion repeatedly, and each time we have found that it provides focus and efficiency to our activities and acts as the basis for evaluating the soundness and completeness of the content. We have found, however, that content tables are sensitive to differences in the type of instructional goal. Content does have its own inherent structure, and that is further influenced by the type of performance being instructed—in which the content will be used. There is one form of content table appropriate for procedure instruction and another for concept instruction.

We have created examples of content tables for different objective types. We include them here to illustrate our point. The first example is for procedural instruction.

Procedure-using content table

Procedure-using content tables capitalize on the fact that a procedure is made up of steps and that all steps are pretty much alike—including the steps in long division and the steps in repairing a bulldozer. In order to perform a step in any procedure, the student requires a certain core of information. Figure 1 shows the categories of information which form this core, and the content categories are described in the list below Figure 1.

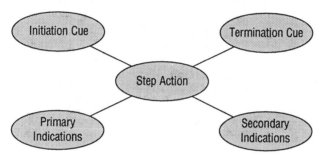

Figure 1. The core of content related to one procedural step.

- **Step action:** The name and description of the action itself.

- **Initiation cue:** The signal to the performer that it is time to perform the step or that it can be performed.

- **Termination cue:** The indication which tells that the step has been successfully completed and that the action can be stopped.

- **Primary indications:** A description of the indications which occur that signal that the step is successfully proceeding. These indications are a direct result of having taken the step and indicate its progress.

- **Secondary indications:** A description of the indications which may accompany the performance of the step (always or intermittently) but which are not to be taken as indicators of step progress.

In addition to these categories of content, there are many additional categories which may be important to include in a procedure content table, depending on the nature of the procedure being performed and the instructional intentions of the designer. For procedures which involve risk, *cautions* or *warnings* may be included to moderate the performance of specific steps. Occasionally, *special techniques* information is required for steps which must be executed with finesse or timing, or which might involve unexpectedly complex actions. In many cases, *decisions* are made at the end of a step, and information on *decision criteria* must be included in the table.

During some procedures a system is operated, and there may be a need to explain to the student the internal responses of that system's processes to each step. (This actually means incorporating a portion of the Process content table for that system into the Procedure content table.) An important category of information may be a goal rationale, which declares why or for what intent each step is taken in terms of the larger purposes or goal logic of the procedure. There are still many more categories than these which a designer may include in a Procedure content table. The headings of a table are not absolute; they are adapted by the designer to reflect the instructional goal and the characteristics of the procedure. And they are made to correspond where possible to message slots in the instructional strategy which will be used.

These content categories are used as column headings in the content table. Since each category of information potentially applies to each step of the procedure, the steps of the procedure become the rows of the table. The result is like Table 1, which has been filled in with content from the first few steps of a simple procedure.

Table 1. Content table for a simple procedure.

Step Action	Init Cue	Prim Indic	Sec Indic	Term Cue
Insert the key into the ignition	None	Sound of key moving into ignition; key stops	None	Key does move in any further; key head is against ignition faceplate
Turn the key fully clockwise and hold, then release at	Key in ignition	At first detent dashboard lights illuminate; at second detent, loud cranking sound is heard from engine	Radio or other electrical devices which have been left on may begin to operate with key at the first detent but will go silent when the key reaches reaches the second detent	Release key at sound of engine beginning to fire
Press accelerator to give gas to the engine	Sound of engine beginning to fire	Rising sound comes from engine, denoting faster idling	Radio and other electrical devices which went off during cranking will come back on	Release gas when engine is running smoothly

Some cells of a content table may be empty, either by design or because of a lack of information. By monitoring the content table as it grows and by using a consistent notation and symbol system, an entire development team can share in the development of content tables, including subject-matter experts, who find this approach to development satisfyingly concrete and well-defined.

Memory content table

The "Ten Classes of Supply" strategy example from Chapter 8 was originally built from a content table which was ultimately expanded to include elements of strategy as well. The rows of the content table, which normally correspond to repetitive structures within the content, in this case represented items in the list of things to be recalled—the ten classes themselves.

The memory association of interest in this instruction was the name of a class, the number, and the contents of the class. These, therefore, supplied the headings for the table. Since it was clear from the strategy selected that a mnemonic was going to be used, the content table was expanded to include that mnemonic. (Frequently, strategy elements are included in a later step in which the content table is converted into a message table.) The result of this effort was Table 2.

Table 2. Memory content table.

Class	Class Content	Mnemonic
1	Food items	Graphic, See Ch. 8, Table 3.
2	Footwear	(Same)
3	Petroleum products	(Same)
4	Construction supplies	(Same)
5	Clothing items	(Same)
6	Sundry supplies	(Same)
7	Repair parts	(Same)
8	Medical supplies	(Same)
9	Precision tools	(Same)
10	Agricultural supplies	(Same)

You must be careful not to let the table become an end in itself. You may structure it any way you find useful—any way that assures you that you have captured the complete content. More importantly, since you most likely will design CBI as part of a team, your team must jointly participate in setting and observing standards and conventions for the content tables it will participate in building and using.

We often use content tables which include graphic material (or references telling where it can be obtained) mixed with verbal content. In a tutorial describing the path of a signal through a circuit, a diagram of the portion of the circuit affected at each step is highlighted and placed in the appropriate cell of a content table. A content table can contain any type of content that will aid the writer in organizing and controlling instructional content. Chapter 10 has already shown how content tables (there referred to as "models of information") can be created for memory network instruction.

Concept-using content table

The content table for concept instruction includes a summary of the concept definition and a table defining the example-non-example field to be used for instruction. In this case, the information of import to the instruction which is captured does not consist strictly of verbal information or even graphics. It consists of the information created when two examples are contrasted with each other. Therefore, the concept-using content table is influenced more than the others by the structure of the instructional strategy, but the purpose of the table—to capture the information relevant to message formation—is the same.

The content table for concept-using is actually two tables—a main idea table which merely lists the defining attributes of the class, and an example table. An example of such an example table can be found in Table 1 of Chapter 13. Instead of literal examples, this table contains a set of *formulas* or *specifications* from which specific examples and non-examples can be generated at the time of writing. The benefit of having the table is that the writer does not have to decide at the time of writing how to structure the entire example-non-example field. Instead, attention is devoted to the selection and expression of individual examples. Making fewer decisions at one time simplifies the writer's work and allows both writer and designer to contribute to the eventual message.

Principle-using and process-using content tables

Chapter 14 describes a set of information categories for principle-using instruction. Those categories can be used to structure tables for that type of objective. Process-using content tables are structured in terms of the events of the event field which make up process-using content. The headings of the table consist of Event Name, one column for each of the Predisposing Conditions that brings about a state change within the process (for recording the combination of conditions producing the state change), and Explanation, (for recording the rationale for the state change).

These examples of content table formats for different objective types show different influences at work in content table construction. Some influences come from the inner structure of the content itself, and some come from the structure of the strategy used for instruction.

Utility of content tables

Content tables have a high payoff for the designer:

1. Content tables give development team members a tool with which to publish and review message content before it is placed into the message.

2. The content table serves as a public record for development team members to use during actual product development. They give system and order to questions of message content. Changes in content involve changes first to the table: deletion of unwanted columns, addition of new columns, or changes to specific table entries in order to correct them or add or subtract detail.

3. Content tables allow and even promote division of labor among members of a development team. Development teams are rarely composed of just one person. Development team members, including writers, artists, subject-matter experts, and designers, must review and use each others' work. The use of content tables encourages and facilitates communication to that end.

4. Content tables involve subject-matter experts fully in the development process at precisely that point where they are most badly needed. Content tables are a non-technical tool that can be easily completed, edited, and reviewed by developers and non-developers alike. Once they have seen a few examples, most subject-matter experts feel comfortable creating tables themselves.

5. Content tables are not limited to gathering content for single-behavior objectives. They may be used with equally rewarding results for gathering information for integrated objectives and therefore in the design of simulations. The electronic troubleshooting example given earlier in the chapter involved both tutorial and simulation instruction. The content tables for simulations are used in several ways, depending on the type of simulation being created.

It is important to keep in mind what content tables *don't* represent as well as what they do. They *don't* represent instructional messages at this point. The remaining stages of message management modify the content table material into instructional messages, not only by disciplining and channeling the expression of the table contents but also by adding to the table other messages of an instructional nature which are not a direct result of the content structure but which are required to support practice interactions and feedback.

A content table is also a useful tool for reverse-engineering existing instruction and reference material. Existing instruction can be analyzed in terms of content used in its strategies. This makes them a useful tool for product evaluation. It is especially useful to apply this analysis to principle-using instruction, often the least adequate in terms of strategic help for the student.

Expressing the content

There are two parts to message expression: (1) expressing the message in message units which correspond with the logical organization of your instruction, and (2) expressing the message in a form that will travel over the student's information highway without causing roadblocks.

Content tables, once approved by subject-matter experts, are the raw material from which the instructional message can be derived. However, in the form the content table exists, it is not ready to translate directly into instructional message. That is because: (1) a content table is almost completely verbal when it is first gathered, (2) a content table is normally filled out in haste during a subject-matter expert interview, so the entries in the table are rough and not worded appropriately for instructional purposes, and (3) a content table gives no attention to the media channel through which a particular item of content will be conveyed. A content table is only a raw dump of content *ready to be transformed* into instructional messages, much like the raw lump of clay which a sculptor begins to transform into a statue.

The final product of message management will not be simply the verbal message we are most familiar with, but it will rely heavily on the visual and audio message channels—if those are ones you have selected to use—and on the coordination of message channels to increase communication and reduce interference between channels. Message expression for CBI includes creating a message which is both *clear and efficient.*

Assigning message to verbal and visual channels

One of the main tasks of message expression is to assign channels for expression to each part of the message. That decision most often equates to a choice between visual expression and verbal expression. Some messages are better expressed visually than verbally, and vice versa. One of the main tasks of message management is to select which form of expression to use for different parts of the message content.

Some decisions, of course, require little thinking. Instead of describing a physical object to students verbally, you will probably choose to visualize the object if you can. Graphics and video are excellent for showing shape, form, general spatial relationship, and motion patterns. You may even find yourself trying to visualize abstract structures to the student—things like idea systems which have no physical form but which can be pictured symbolically.

On the other hand, there are elements of the message which require a greater degree of precision in expression or a type of expression which is not easily accomplished with graphics. Graphics and video are less adept at displaying certain kinds of detail. For instance, though we often show graphically how two parts of a car engine exert force on each other, we normally resort to verbalization to describe the precise nature of the forces at work and to explain why they occur. The nature of language is that it gives explicit expression to detail where graphics give suggestive expression to it, and so language is normally used to express details and reasoning processes, often complementing a graphic or video.

Visual expression

As a society, we have become much more visually oriented, perhaps because those who convey messages to us through the mass media have discovered the technological value of the old saying, "A picture is worth a thousand words." But a picture is only worth that much if you make it so. Some pictures are worth 500 words at best, some are worth one, and some actually detract from learning.

Visual expression is a field of study unto itself. Entire career fields center around the design and creation of visual expressions. The principles and techniques for expressing visual ideas clearly and concisely are well-developed. They are important enough to merit some level of independent study by the CBI designer, and certainly the designer is well-advised to seek associations with competent visual specialists who can help to develop messaging concepts for CBI products. We can't summarize the entire body of artistic wisdom and experience in a few paragraphs, but we can give some general guidelines to help the CBI designer make some basic messaging decisions.

Organization

Chapter 19, Display Management, describes how to organize the display (both visual and verbal) for rapid scanning and comprehension. In this chapter we are discussing the organization of individual video or graphic elements of the display, but the same principles which pertain to whole displays can be applied also to the elements of the display. The principles in Chapter 19 derive from the designer's overall desire to minimize information processing which is not directly related to the instructional goal and, in so far as possible, to focus the processing of information to support that goal.

How can you organize graphic and video message elements to enhance their "readability?"

Make the relevant content visible: One of the hallmarks of badly-made instruction is that the visual material provided has the look of being reused thoughtlessly and produced without care for the user: graphic and video material looks "borrowed." Frequently in such instruction, the details you are supposed to notice are not even visible, sometimes because they are lost in a sea of other details, and sometimes because the resolution level of the reproduction is not capable of showing the detail legibly. Excellent instruction uses carefully created or selected graphics or video, ensuring that the detail that needs to be noticed and studied is clearly visible to the student. Clip art is not a good solution for instructional visuals.

Make it clear what is being pictured: Every graphic or video image (including motion) is a study in contrast. One of the keys to making images readily "readable" is to provide contrast between the foreground of information that the designer wants to be noticed and the background of contextual information which is not so much important for its details as for the broader canvas it supplies.

You will see later in this chapter that the same principle applies to verbal message material, both spoken and written. The principle involved is called "new information." Originally the notion of new information was proposed as a linguistic principle, but we have adapted it for use in instructional design. Every communication which we receive through the senses contains both new information and information which we already know. By providing contrasts as we structure the communication, we can make it more readily clear to the student what part of the message is new and what is context.

Emphasize structural elements that you want noticed first: New information is most often set off from the rest of the message through emphasis of some kind. Many forms of emphasis are available to the visual designer: perspective view, contrasting level of detail, use of light and dark, use of motion, use of building sequences in which the full graphic appears one part at a time, and other techniques. These techniques are used to delineate a structure of information which the designer wants noticed. By helping the student notice this structure upon first exposure to the visual, the designer provides an organizational motif to the message which can then be used to decode the remainder of the message.

Ensure that the visual provides the entire message: In some cases where visual materials were created in haste or with too few tools, the interplay of relationships which is a vital part of the message is not made visible to the student. This is especially apparent in some video materials which, though they show details adequately, are unable to overlay graphics on the image to show interacting components, forces, or hidden events—the normally *invisible* part of nature which instruction is trying to make *visible*. Visual material which is provided in incomplete form in hopes that the student will be able to supply the missing portion may be wasted and may in some cases provide more of a hindrance to instruction than a help.

Capitalize on familiar patterns of scanning: We normally scan the contents of a large message surface in a certain order. When you look at the front page of a newspaper you notice the top of the page first and tend to notice the left side of the page more readily. You might say that this is a function of the bold headlines at the top of the page, but as you open to the inner pages of the paper, you also tend to look toward the top of the page and to the left.

We develop habits of scanning message surfaces. We not only tend to scan pages in a certain spatial pattern, but our attention is drawn to sections of the message space which appear to be busy, highlighted, or structurally interesting. As designers, we should capitalize on scanning and noticing habits, not only for entire message surfaces, but for individual elements of the visual display as well.

Relate the content to its surroundings and show context: Designers are sometimes so intent on showing the details of interest in a visual that they forget to show also the context of the details. What connects to what? What influences what? What is beyond this small part of the mechanism that I can see? These are questions a student is likely to have, and providing a small amount of context behind detailed graphics and video shots allows the student to have the answers.

Label things on demand: Though it may not be difficult for an expert to label the contents of a visual, it can be very frustrating for a student to see a detailed visual and not be able to pinpoint the element of the visual that the verbal is talking about. A student can be given labels to every graphic on demand. Moreover, those labels can be menus themselves, providing the student access to descriptions and other information concerning the visual. We also suggest that in many cases a visual can be made explorable. A less detailed view can be provided with student controls used to explore details of the view more closely. In this sense, if the designer wants it, every visual can become a "living" visual, capable of exploration and inquiry by the student. Costs for this type of visual can be minimized if one master set of visuals is created for the entire CBI product and then used in multiple locations. Points on these visuals can even be given hypertext-like qualities which allow each visual to be "toured."

Provide video controls: Students may not capture all of the information they want or need from a single playing of a linear sequential medium like video or audio. Designers should provide controls that allow the student to replay, stop, and otherwise control video and audio segments used during instruction.

Verbal expression: Writing clearly

Despite the fact that the field of writing is as large and well-developed as the field of graphic and video production, we also want to provide some general principles to guide the formation of verbal message elements for CBI.

First, a word in general about clear written communication. When most of us graduate from school, we have had enough practice at writing to feel like adequate writers. However, for any writer, writing for instructional purposes takes much practice and includes many humbling experiences.

The problem is that few of us were trained to write for a student audience. When we wrote in school, it was for our teachers. We were writing to someone who had already some understanding of what we were likely to say. Moreover, we were usually trying to impress the teacher, trying to sound erudite, and bluffing when we really didn't know what we wanted to say. Most of our writing experience did not concentrate on the writing of clear, simple, readily understandable prose for the purpose of conveying clear meaning in one reading. We were not particularly rewarded for that.

Good instructional writing and good CBI writing are hard to achieve. Very often they are mistakenly confused with good technical writing. We offer here several principles for good CBI writing.

General message organization and presentation

The CBI message must be skillfully crafted in order to attain the level of communication of which it is capable. CBI writing is different from writing for more traditional media. Successful ex-text writers tend to write CBI as if it was a book; ex-video writers write as if for videotape. However, most messaging techniques do not transfer well from medium to medium. Some media, like prose, are mainly sequential in their presentation. Sequential development of ideas is an important principle. However, the computer medium sometimes denies this element of message structure because CBI messages can be administered in different orders. Therefore, the CBI message can profit from being less sequential, and more holographic or omni-referential. Moreover, CBI writing often must complement visual message elements, making the writing the less conspicuous part of the message, yet still requiring good communication from the verbal element.

We have several suggestions to help you structure verbal messages appropriately for CBI:

Get used to writing message elements in chunks of 25 to 30 words or less: During one period of the history of CBI, writers used to fill the CBI display with text in imitation of a book page. For audio, these writers used to create long narrations. The increased emphasis on visual message brought about by videodisk and multimedia technologies has reduced this tendency, but it is still apparent in some products. Textbooks and professors may be verbose, but computers may not be. CBI demands verbal brevity.

Pace the instructional message so that each change of message represents one item of new information: A writer must control as much as possible the rate of presentation of new information. The flow of processable material to the student should be at a rate which the student can process in a sustained way, without having to stop to untie dense knots of poorly-written information.

Instructional messages have two elements: the part the student already knows (the "old" information, or background context), and the part student needs to learn (the "new" information). "Old" and "new" here do not refer to specific words in the instructional message, but to the ideas and relationships behind the words. All new information (a new fact, relation, principle, example) imposes a certain information processing requirement on the student. The processing burden should be placed on the student at a relatively steady rate or pace during informational presentations. This avoids processing bottlenecks as the student executes continuous processing of the incoming instructional message.

This pacing of the message is difficult to discuss, because instructional designers have invented no technical terms to describe it and no units with which to measure idea density. Try to imagine, however, several varieties of poorly paced message and their possible influence on the student's intake of new information.

Consider the message in which packets of new information arrive too slowly: The student is able to process the message efficiently—too efficiently—and much of the time is spent waiting for something which is recognizable as significant and new. Attention is relaxed. This is a waste of the student's time.

Consider the message in which packets of new information arrive too frequently: The student is like an overworked juggler, trying to keep too many plates in the air at once. While trying to decode one message to find its "new" part, another packet arrives. Placing this in a temporary memory splits the student's attention. This only complicates and slows down the decoding of the first message. Eventually, a point is reached where enough new messages have arrived that temporary memory cannot hold any more. The student gives up trying and empties memory altogether.

Consider the message which combines the worst features of both too sparse and too dense packets of information: For long stretches of time no new information arrives, which lulls the student into reduced attentiveness, and then a large mass of new information arrives all at once, causing a processing overload.

The term *new information* used here does not refer to linguistic units like sentences or phrases, it refers to ideational or semantic units, knowledge interrelationships within the instructional message which the student can recognize as being new. A student may listen for minutes at a time and not detect one new item of information because the message contains no knowledge relationships which are new. On the other hand, a single short message can provide new information enough for many minutes of decoding and sorting.

The rate of presenting new information affects the processing of that information by students. An instructional message can be said to have a certain new information density and a certain new information pace. Density refers to the amount of new information knotted up at one new information location within a message. Pace refers to the rate at which new knots are encountered in the incoming message stream.

Within certain limits, a student can adjust to a developer's rate of delivery by hurrying up or slowing down his or her normal intensity of processing. Students may say that the instruction "moved ahead too slowly" or "moved ahead too rapidly" but still be able to learn from it. Certain extremes and irregularities in pacing and density, however, interrupt the smooth inflow and processing of information and make it very difficult for students to learn and store the new material. Developers should avoid those extremes by writing relative to their audience.

Pace and density problems are signaled by differences in reading speed and the need to go back to re-read certain portions of the message repeatedly. Subject-matter experts may find a message clear and easy to read from their perspective, but that is no guarantee that students will. Careful examination of a problem passage often reveals too rapid a pace or too dense a new information knot.

In some cases, an author who has been proceeding toward a conclusion at a steady and manageable rate will abandon the measured pace and try to complete the student's understanding all at once. The result is a conceptual lump which is hard for the student to swallow and digest, and that only at the expense of repeated reading of the message. The remedy is to realize that once a paced presentation is begun, it is wisest to maintain a more or less steady pace, even if it means using a few extra words or message elements to do so. In this case, more (words) can be less (difficulty) for the student.

Ensure that main new information structures are securely in place before adding details: Technical people drafted as message writers sometimes try to present both main idea structures and details at the same time. In the thinking of experts this is a reasonable thing to do, since the technical details and their central, uniting structure are so closely related in their minds. But to a novice the task of separating structure from detail and holding it all in working memory until it can be organized properly is quite difficult.

Maintain the main message's focus: The previous principle emphasized that details of the message should be left until after the main structure of ideas is in place. Now we encourage you to identify elements of information which can be left out of the message altogether because they are irrelevant. Some things that can be said during instruction do not answer any part of the instructional question in the student's mind, and so they constitute excess informational baggage.

Authors frequently insert extra information into messages because they recognize a compelling beauty in the ideas. But when students deal with such an instructional message, they are not always sure which parts are structural, which parts are details of the structure, and which parts represent interesting sidelights. This sets up a guessing game where the student tries to "psych" the mind and intent of the writer, which wastes time, attention, and energy unnecessarily.

If information is important enough to spend instructional time on, then it should exist within the scope of the instructional objective. It should be included within instruction whose objective it fits. If objectives do not provide any place for this information, and if the designer deems it important, then perhaps the objectives themselves should be revisited and perhaps restructured or extended.

Provide informational roadsigns for the student: Behind every item of information an author includes in a message stands the question from the student, "So what? Why are you telling me this?" This question is asked continuously by the student, as moment-by-moment the student's own self-management of reading and learning seeks to process the incoming message, derive its meaning and intent, and consolidate the new knowledge.

This process in the student must measure, sort, and prioritize new information elements in order to determine what to do with them. Only by asking the "So What?" question is the student able to maintain focus on the intention of the instructional message, reduce the load on memory, and organize new knowledge for storage. If the developer is kind enough to place clues to the answer to "So What?" within the instructional message, then the student is not left to his or her own devices to determine the labeling and sorting of incoming information. Authors frequently leave subtle roadsigns that help the student decode the writer's intent.

Roadsigns take several forms:

An instructional objective, a sample test item, or both. Objectives and sample test items focus the student's uptake of the message by showing him or her the behavior that is the goal of instruction. Once apprised of what is expected, the alert student is able to discern the structure of the information to follow and assign it due proportion and place in relation to other information given. By this means, each student is given an increased degree of control over his or her own learning, and the processing of incoming message is more efficient.

Within-text roadsigns. An author can provide labels for instructional strategy elements which enable students to sort through tutorial messages more efficiently. Such messages as "...consider the following example..." or "...here is the main idea..." flag critical information and make it stand out from the rest of the text. In addition, transitions are critically important as roadsigns which point out for the student when one element of a the strategy has ended and another is about to begin.

Some designers place formal labels within displays which identify for students the type of information contained therein. Labels can include: *Objective, Main Idea, Example, Simplified Explanation, Demonstration, Prompted Practice,* or other strategy- and content-related information labelings. Within these larger units of message, a writer can send additional signals early on which allow the student to anticipate the rest of the upcoming message structure. "Notice the five key differences between Lepidoptera and Hymenoptera," is a signal to the student that five items which follow are to be recorded. The student can attend to them as organizing points in the message.

Labels act as roadsigns which enable students to anticipate upcoming message texture and prepare in advance for its intake and processing. Labels also allow students to control to a greater extent the order in which they seek information and make possible a greater degree of learner control.

Labeling by physical placement. Chapter 19, Display Management, will describe how screen or temporal positioning of messages can provide a subtle clues to the student which act as a type of label for incoming information. For this reason, tutorial designers may use one area of the screen for examples and another for main ideas.

Authors often label instruction with elements of their own style without even thinking about it. Our experience has been that students welcome consistent roadsigns, intended or not, subtle or direct. Research also suggests that students benefit from roadsigns.

Adopt a clear, consistent style: Time once was when designers felt that each CBI instructional message had to be unique. The challenge was to approach the writing of each message with a new and creative twist. A good deal of experience in CBI has shown that this is not a fruitful application of creativity. Designers have learned that a writer's consistent style (among other things) can be a powerful tool in the student's favor. In fact, the wide variations in style and presentation once thought to draw interest and motivation from the student have been found only to make extra work for the student—requiring him or her to re-orient to a new set of subtle roadsigns and expressive habits with each new tutorial.

Sentence structure

Instructional messages can be made more readily understandable at the sentence level by attention to the following principles:

Keep sentences short (8 to 15 words): Long sentences like those we are used to seeing in printed media most often look clumsy and out of place on a computer display. We indulge the writer in the printed medium and allow him or her to use a few extra words without criticism. The limited dimensions of the CBI display surface (audio and visual), however, do not allow this.

Most instructional sentences are not long because they need to be; they are long because the writer has not taken the time to weed out inessential words. Up to 50% of the average instructional message can be excised without damaging meaning. The result of deleting the unneeded words is leaner, more readable text. Notice the difference between the two sentences below:

Long sentences like those we are used to seeing in printed media most often look clumsy and out of place in a computer display.	Long sentences usually look clumsy in a computer display.

As a general rule, use one word if you can and two when you must. Keep sentences on the average of eight to fifteen words long. Compute the price of reading and processing each extra word.

Avoid complex phrase structures: Compound and complex sentence structures are the result of combining the ideas from separate sentences together into one sentence. There is normally a benefit to the student if these ideas are expressed as separate sentences instead. Doing so reduces a processing burden. Research in verbal learning and comprehension has shown that there is a measurable processing tax of time, attention, and effort associated with each added complex sentence structure. This subtle and unnecessary tax adds up over time to a major reduction in information obtained and constitutes a lost learning opportunity.

Choose nouns and verbs with action, concreteness, and dynamism: This is really four separate pieces of advice:

- Choose active verbs over passive verbs.

- Choose concrete nouns and verbs over abstract nouns and verbs.

- Use simple rather than complex verbs.

- Avoid conditionals when possible.

Research in verbal learning indicates that an extra processing burden, measurable in time units, is added when sentences use passive verbs, abstract nouns and verbs, and complex verbs. When you avoid these things, sentences may be read more rapidly and require less processing. Direct, active, concrete, and uncomplicated prose benefits the student.

Language

Language decisions influence the communication ability of an instructional message. The following principles can be used to maximize language choices:

Use simple words in place of complicated words, even for sophisticated audiences: When college students write, particularly for essay exams, the trick is to be as glib, vague, and noncommittal as possible. Long words with nebulous meanings are friends in this environment, as are special academic-sounding words which most of us were taught to use—especially in research reports. With them, the writer maximizes impressiveness and can make broad implications of knowledge without being held responsible for details.

In instructional writing, there is no professor to impress. The purpose is to inform precisely. A policy of using simplified wordings where possible pays off for the student by making prose more readily digestible and by leaving energy for other processing tasks. Instead of a twenty-five cent word, learn to use two dimes and a nickel instead.

Introduce technical terms carefully and with gradually fading support: Training and educational materials are full of technical terms and acronyms, which it is part of the student's job to learn. Instructional writing should introduce them carefully and with support. Each should be clearly and unequivocally attached to its meaning at the first introduction.

When introducing terms and acronyms, depending on the audience, it may be desirable to: (1) highlight the term's meaning or acronym's full expression by drawing special attention to it, (2) use these associations several times in the message, rather than just once, and (3) provide some form of query capability by which the student can relearn the definition of a term or acronym in the text. This may be done by providing a ready-access glossary or by using a hypertext arrangement which allows direct query of a word for its meaning.

Message summary

Though the advice in the preceding sections has focused on verbal and visual expression rules, forming a message means more than just forming words and symbols:

- It means assigning elements of the message to either verbal or visual expression, providing appropriate levels of redundancy.

- It means providing cues in the message which signal information context, location, and structure.

- It means embedding explicit informational roadsigns within the message.

- It means using emphasis techniques and timing to direct the attention of the learner.

- It means signaling the proportional importance of message elements.

- It means supplying special elements of the message which help the student decode and organize the remainder of the message.

Messaging involves designing the structural framework of the message and the sequence(s) of message events. Too often, in the haste to arrive at a finished product, message formation processes are jammed together without considering separately and in a proper order the requirements for a clear and an efficient message. The result is often a message which is neither clear nor efficient.

The message table

The message table helps the designer and writer move from the raw information contained in the content table to a final instructional message without experiencing this compression of decisions and the attendant quality failure in the message.

A message table contains:

1. Content from the content table translated into message elements.

2. Channelization of message elements in a systematic way.

3. Additional non-content message elements required for instruction.

A message table is *not* a content table, but much of its substance is derived *from* a content table. The message table evolves through a series of decisions from a content table.

A content table contains *categorized expressions* of *raw content* from a subject-matter expert or other knowledge source. A message table contains the *exact expression* of the verbal portion of the instructional message and specifications for the non-verbal portion. It contains the instructional message for all message channels, expressed as it will be delivered to the student.

A message table is related to—but not synonymous with—the popular notion of a *script* or *storyboard*—documentation formats which are used to express the message for sequential media like film, video, and slide/sound. The usual assumption of linearity associated with those media does not always apply to CBI, because CBI is often a non-linear medium, even in the tutorial form. Its message can occur in different possible orders. Therefore, the message must be expressed as non-ordered packets of message (which we call *message elements*) which do not have to be used in a particular sequence to make sense.

A message table is channelized. It specifies the messaging channel that will be used to deliver each element of the message to the student: audio, video, graphics, animation, or text. It can specify timing when that is an important quality of the message.

Finally, a message table matches elements of the message with the elements of computer logic that will be used to present them. For one logic element of a tutorial, such as an authoring system frame, there may be one or more corresponding elements of a message designed to be conveyed by that logic. This means that the logic must be known before the message table is written. Frequently, instructional logic and the message table are developed together.

Message table creation

Chapter 21 provides a complete example of the generation of both logic diagrams and the related message table. Here we will only provide a brief description of the stages by which a message table is created from a content table. For a full concrete example of this procedure, see Chapter 21.

Stage 1: Use logic functions to define message element table headings: For every type of computer-based tutorial, basic logic patterns are used to execute the instruction, either to deliver a message or provide an appropriate interaction. These logic patterns consist of variations of the frame patterns described in Chapter 5. With the linking together of these patterns, the entire instructional product takes form. Each frame that takes part in one of these patterns may deliver an element of the message. For those which do, the first step in message table construction is to identify them and create a column in the table to contain the messages for that logic element (frame). In some cases a single frame will deliver two elements of message, and so two columns are created in the table.

Stage 2: Channelize message elements: When the message elements delivered by each logic element have been identified, a media channel is selected for each one. The message elements in one column of the message table may be selected for delivery through text. Another column may be designated for audio delivery. Another may be assigned graphic expression.

Stage 3: Create exact message content or message specifications: When the channel for each message element has been selected, the content from the content table is used to express the entry of each cell in the message table. This will consist of writing either a specific verbal message or a graphic or video specification.

Stage 4: Add non-content instructional messages: The computer logic for presentation and practice portions of the instruction require messages which cannot come directly from the content table, either because they are general directions or because they are interaction-specific. For example, the content of feedback messages following incorrect answers often require tailoring to the specific interaction they follow. Once these indirectly-derived messages are added to the message table, it is complete, and the message is ready for production.

Conclusion

The principles for message capture, organization, and expression which have been presented in this chapter help the designer create a message that is focused, clear, and concise, yet adequate to convey a complete message to the student. This method also improves the efficiency of message creation. Chapter 19, on Display Management, deals with the display or presentation of the message and tries to identify the principles which govern the use of the various communication channels, both singly and in tandem. Moreover, it deals with the use of the display, regardless of the channel used, as a dynamic and changing surface. It will describe how to manage that change, maintaining focus and supporting the processing done by the student.

Self-directed activities

- Take several instructional products of several different forms (textbook, lecture, video, CBI, etc.) and examine their messages for regularities. Create one or more content tables for each one capable of capturing in a regular structural format the main elements of the message. Why are some products more difficult to tabularize than others? Are there any products that you have selected which defy tabularization? Why?

- Take the message from any instructional product (including this book). Cut the verbiage in the product by 50%, but be sure that the final product is as easy to read and understand as the original and that the full and correct meaning of the original message is preserved. Are there any products for which a second 50% reduction can be made on the same terms?

- Take a textbook passage which is particularly confusing or difficult to understand. Re-express the passage in an easier-to-understand form and ask a friend to judge which of the two is better.

Further reading

Fleming, M., and Levie, W. H. (Eds.). (1993). *Instructional message design: Principles from the behavioral and cognitive sciences*. Englewood Cliffs, NJ: Educational Technology Publications.

Horn, R. E. (1997). Structured writing as a paradigm. In C. R. Dills and A. J. Romiszowski (Eds.), *Instructional development paradigms* (pp. 697–713). Englewood Cliffs, NJ: Educational Technology Publications.

Marsh, P. D. (1983). *Messages that work: A guide to communication design*. Englewood Cliffs, NJ: Educational Technology Publications.

Pettersson, R. (1993). *Visual information*. Englewood Cliffs, NJ: Educational Technology Publications.

19

DISPLAY MANAGEMENT

Chapter Objectives:

1. *Design the use of multimedia message channels such that information processing by the student is enhanced.*

2. *Define the needs for information and control at the interface with the student.*

3. *Design instruction in a manner that maintains interface continuity.*

4. *Design interactions which are easy to use, support instructional goals, and fit cost constraints.*

5. *Explain the importance of an interface which does not assert itself any more than absolutely necessary into the student's attention.*

What is display management?

In the beginning, CBI terminals could only place text characters on the face of a monochrome display screen. CBI was then almost entirely verbally-oriented. Over time, terminals gained the ability to display simple graphic shapes, high resolution graphics, and then color. Now the graphic capabilities of the average CBI terminal are so sophisticated that artists can use them as a medium to create dazzling and complex works of art. The use of computers in motion pictures creates scenes so realistic and yet so fantastic that they cause us to suspend disbelief. During all these changes, the definition of "display" relative to CBI has been changing, and it continues to change.

Today's average CBI terminal has high resolution video and graphic animation capabilities. CDs or videodisc players are common equipment at CBI work stations. Sophisticated software controls these media to supply motion and still video mixed with graphics which are overlaid to modify, mask, or otherwise enhance the base image.

Independent of the monitor screen, there have been developments which can also be said to be part of the CBI display. Audio from digitized audio files and digital synthesizers is used extensively to accompany or replace visual elements of the display. Can you imagine a totally-audio CBI instructional event? How many uses can you think of for such instruction?

The use of the tactile and motion senses as part of the display is also increasing. Air and spacecraft simulators, which are forms of CBI, have long used these channels as an important part of the training experience, and these are only the beginning of the fields which are using this capability.

Recently, the use of three-dimensional, simulated equipment boxes and panels that sit beside the CBI monitor have been increasing in number. These small simulation boxes can create simulation exercises which are very realistic—sometimes indistinguishable from real equipment. These boxes must be considered a part of the display. Lest you think that only hardware boxes can be used to support training in this way, consider the plastic dummy used to provide practice and feedback for students learning cardio-pulmonary resuscitation (CPR). There are clearly several elements to the CBI display beyond the CRT screen, and science fiction fans realize that most of the really interesting possibilities haven't been tried yet.

We can define the CBI display as the sum of the communication channels to the student from the computer which are used during instruction. Of course, there is a complementary and equally interesting set of channels—called controls—that the student can use to communicate back to the computer. Joysticks have long been a staple of video game controls, touch panels are today found on copy machines, and keyboards have always been an option. The simulator boxes described earlier normally provide realistic controls which connect with the simulation program to produce realistic results. And for less than $50 today you can purchase toys for children which use voice control for playing educational games. Properly conceived and executed, the CBI display and related controls form a dynamic "surface" at which the student and the CBI system meet to exchange information and interaction. In computer parlance this is called the *interface*.

Display Management is all about how to design the CBI interface to provide maximum support for and minimum interference with the learning process. Display Management includes a lot of issues. As we treat them here, the decisions made during display management fall under four main headings:

- Displaying the message for rapid communication.

- Providing information and control for self-management.

- Ensuring message continuity.

- Designing clean interactions.

We have divided the remainder of this chapter into sections which correspond to these headings in order to discuss the principles in each of these areas. Remember during this discussion that a display consists of all of the channels by which message information is conveyed to the student—the visual, audible, olfactory, tactile, and kinesthetic channels. Don't allow your conception of the display to narrow to include only the CRT screen. Also, realize that the sections which follow deal with the guidelines and standards for display management which are unique to CBI. This chapter is not a complete review of the extensive body of media design principles which CBI shares with traditional media. With that in mind, let's consider each of these areas of display management, one at a time.

Displaying the message for rapid communication

One of the major goals of display management is rapid communication of information. This is an important element of excellent CBI. In our society we are afloat in information. Even if we wanted to we could not keep up with each day's new developments in current events, science, the arts, and politics. There is too much to be conveyed in the time available. The media constantly search for techniques that will speed the transfer of information. Instruction is not just information transfer, but that transfer is an essential step in instruction, and because other steps in instruction compete for time and energy, the transfer of information should be carried out with minimum effort and attention.

The thirty seconds that used to be too short to contain an advertising message is now all that is needed to stage a small dramatic production promoting cars and taco sauce. National weather news which once took columns of fine print and 15 minutes to read now appears in color graphic form. It can be read in half the time, conveys both big picture and details, and makes the information more memorable. For many areas of our society, more efficient communication is not just a nice idea, it is an imperative which allows more information on topics from aardvarks to zygotes to be accessible to an informed public. Instructional displays (graphic, textual, and audio) benefit from this trend toward more efficient information transfer.

As a CBI designer, you should be alert to anything you can learn from the way in which the popular media economize the time required to process their message yet maximize the amount of information transferred. However, you must mix these techniques with the interaction demands of the instructional strategy and the required content of the message. We have assembled a set of guiding principles for making CBI displays communicate rapidly yet effectively. They are presented in the sections which follow. We refer you also to the readings at chapter end.

Text and graphics displays

The materials written by the average CBI designer for the remainder of this decade will be presented on a system with a high resolution graphics screen, including a huge palette of colors and the capability for sophisticated graphics and video. How does a designer use these graphics tools to simplify and shorten communication? Here are a few principles:

1. Construct displays with a general scan structure that is top-down or upper-left to lower-right: This principle is true if you are designing CBI for western hemisphere students whose language follows the top-down and left-to-right reading pattern. A more generalized wording of this principle would be: Build displays structured so that the scan pattern follows the general scan pattern of the student's native language.

The idea is to take advantage of the student's habitual scanning patterns through the structure of your displays. The scan pattern signals to the reader the writer's hierarchy of structure in the message. In most of the world, large size and boldness of text signals a headline or title. A good deal of reading instruction has habituated those in Western society to looking for headlines and titles at or near the top of a display, whether printed or electronic. Although this rule is sometimes violated for artistic effect or variety, as a general rule, people look for and expect headlines and titles at or near the top.

Another Western reading habit equates size or boldness of text with relative importance. Headlines of more importance or generality or those intended to be read first are larger; those of less importance or generality or which are intended to be read later are smaller. The placement of the smaller text is usually below and to the right of larger text. In some cases, smaller text titles or headlines are used to subdivide the ideas of the main headline and are positioned in such a way that they direct the reader's eye to that fact and signal as well the structure of the division.

These principles are not new to most of us. We read the front page of the newspaper and see these principles at work every day. We also see them on bus advertisements, magazine ads, the sports scores on the evening news, and on cereal boxes. They are principles which help us scan and extract the essential information in a display quickly and without extra effort. They are so much a part of our world and our reading habits that we only notice them when they are violated.

The placement of graphics in relation to text is much more flexible but has a set of conventions nonetheless. Blocks of text can be placed above, below, to the left of, or to the right of a graphic, but they are usually retained as blocks. This is to make line scanning while reading easier on the reader, among other things. Labels used in graphics are normally connected to the portion of the graphic they represent using some standard technique, which may include proximity, arrows, or keyed symbols.

The structure of a display which includes graphics and text must still retain the basic scanning pattern structure, regardless of where the graphic is placed. Once a reader has observed the graphic, the size and boldness of text will still be the key used to interpret the text, and most often the pattern of top-down and left-right will still be observed.

CBI designers can use society's reading habits to minimize the effort of reading CBI displays as well. Certainly a creative designer can design alternative display patterns, but it should not be done if it increases the student's reading effort by an appreciable factor.

2. Make sparing but intelligent use of emphasis techniques to draw attention to key parts of the display: Many graphics techniques can be used to draw the eye to important new information and do it within the scanning structure of the display. Emphasis devices may include motion, blinking, color, capitalization of text, or pointers. Use of these things should be sparing.

In the early days of color CBI displays, the temptation to use the new tool (color!) was too great for many designers, and displays tended to look like a rainbow factory. Not only did this interrupt and compete with the normal scanning pattern of the display, but it produced a situation of overemphasis that made it hard for students to decide which of the seemingly random splotches of color was the most important and which was meant to be noticed most.

CAPITALIZATION and *italicizing* are other EMPHASIS *techniques* which have been OVERUSED *at times* by CBI *designers*. However, BEFORE LONG, it became APPARENT that their OVERUSE was *distracting* the ATTENTION of STUDENTS from the MAIN STRUCTURE of the *display* and SLOWING *processing* of the DISPLAY.

Most experienced designers have learned that when using emphasis, well-choreographed understatement is a powerful technique. Understatement means that the emphasis will become noticeable because there is so little of it. Its appearance on an otherwise uniform display is readily detected and cannot help but draw the eye to wherever the designer chooses. Well-choreographed means that the designer has carefully selected the timing and order of giving emphasis—often over the course of several changes to the display.

3. Phrase-block text for easier comprehension where that is possible: Most CBI systems do not right-justify text, which means that there is a ragged edge where the text is broken to begin a new line. When it is possible, a small boost in readability can be obtained by selecting a phrase boundary as the breaking point.

> There is one way
> to put text on the screen
> so that breaks at the end of lines
> come at natural phrase boundaries,
> so that a line of text
> corresponds roughly to an idea unit.

> There is another way to
> divide lines of a text message so
> that there is a slightly larger processing
> burden placed on the student while
> reading.

Where possible, break text messages at a phrase or idea boundary.

4. Limit the amount of text on the screen at one time: It was common in the days when CBI was trying to look like an on-screen book—and still is in the work of novices—to see pages and pages literally filled with text. This practice opposes almost all of the unique strengths of the CBI display and is neither effective nor popular with students. We do not recommend it as a technique.

Instead, pick your words carefully, and then display them on the screen in idea units which relate to the purposes of your instructional strategy. This may cause some of your screens to have much text, which is not a problem if: (1) there is a clear reason for it, (2) it doesn't happen all of the time, and (3) doing otherwise would break up a strategic element.

Graphic messages—dynamic graphics

In addition to static graphics, one of CBI's real strengths is its ability to produce dynamic graphics. By *dynamic*, we do not mean graphics which are animated. We mean the ability of the CBI screen to build a graphic one part at a time over a sequence of frames. In this type of dynamism the screen changes stepwise to add either new text or new graphic material or to change emphasis on existing text or graphics. In this way, a graphic which begins as a simple representation on one screen may grow in detail or size to be much larger or more complete. In addition to this growth of the display, parts of it may move, and portions of it may show some marks of emphasis such as color filling or flow. What are the guidelines for using this dynamism? A few suggestions follow below.

1. Start simple and build to complexity: You cannot tell from looking at a single CBI screen whether or not it is too complex. To make that judgment, you must see the screens which preceded it; you must see the sequence of steps by which the screen evolved to that point. The problem with complex displays is that they take extra time and effort to decode. However, a screen which is initially very simple can build in small steps—meaning the addition of short, single-idea messages and minor graphics additions and changes—to a very complex screen, full of detailed graphic material. If the building sequence is handled with care, it can occur without causing a processing problem for the student. In fact, the transition at the addition of each new element of the display can actually carry extra information over and above the actual screen contents.

Someone entering the room and seeing the filled screen would express concern that the graphic was too complicated, but the student who was there for the step-by-step evolution of the message and the graphic might find it an advantage to have the "big picture" available, with all its detail. Used wisely, such sequences can have good instructional effect.

2. Take small steps during graphic building: This is the visual correlate of the verbal principle we proposed in Chapter 18, which said to keep the pace of presenting new information reasonable and more or less consistent. We restate it here because it applies to the presentation of new visual information as well.

3. As incremental additions are made to a growing graphic, make it clear what part of the graphic is new and what is old: The powerful graphic software and monitors we use today are so fast that they can add graphics to an existing display faster than the student's eye can follow—especially if the student blinks or looks away. Then the student is left in doubt about which part of the graphic is new and which was old. The more complex the evolving graphic, the more acute the problem. There are several ways to overcome this problem:

- Add the new graphic addition slowly enough that the student can see it appear, examine it, and compare its old and new parts. It is ironic, after years of demanding faster graphics software and hardware, that we should now have the problem of slowing down and controlling graphics. However, for the student to have precise control of the intake of the graphic information, that is what is needed in many cases.

- Reserve graphic additions until the student is ready to attend to them. Consider adding them after the student gives a predetermined signal.

- Add new graphic material in a different color or line pattern when it is first added, then re-draw it in its normal color and line pattern when you are ready to advance to another graphic addition.

- Blink the new graphic addition on and off a few times when it is first presented.

- Designate the size and location of new graphic content by outlining it or by pointing to it.

- Form a consistent pattern for adding new information to graphic displays. Every time you add something, use the standard method. Over time, this will begin to signal to the student what is happening, and students will be able to read the syntax of signals as if they were reading words.

4. Match the text precisely to the graphic: In a best-selling book written to explain science to the average reader, we came across a graphic drawn in great detail and labeled, but with names which could not be found anywhere in the text. We were surprised to find this in a well-known, popular publication, and the strength of our own negative reactions taught us what to expect from a student having the same experience.

Another faulty technique is reference in text to details of graphics which are not actually visible on the graphic. In printed materials this problem often occurs when the sharp photograph the author sees in the printable master is taken down a generation or two during printing or is printed at a much lower level of resolution, blurring or destroying the original's details.

Beginning CBI designers sometimes do not understand the problems they create for students when a mismatch occurs in graphic text and content. Ensure this coordination in your own products by: (1) avoiding graphics which show either too much or too little detail with text, and (2) by matching labels on the graphic exactly with those supplied in the text.

5. Time text and graphic events to avoid distractions: This means to avoid the common timing problems of CBI graphics:

- Avoid the use of time-outs which change the display automatically after a designated period of time unless you are creating a kiosk presentation or a conference demonstration loop.

- Avoid putting complex graphic and text changes on the screen at exactly the same instant unless both changes are somehow signaled to the student.

In timed sequences of frames which are not under student control, the author has to decide how much time the average student needs to read the display. Even if the estimate is right for the average student, it will be too short for those below the average reading speed and too slow for those above. Regardless of the care used in choosing the timing, it will be wrong for the majority of students.

The solution is to place the changing of screens under student control where possible. The only exception to this is in the presentation of a sequence where the timing of a transition between system or process states is the idea being illustrated. One way to place screen changes under student control is to provide replays possible so that stopping and looking at changes is easy and repeatable.

Complex graphic and text changes which take place simultaneously are confusing. If the text comes on first, followed by the graphic, the student is in the middle of reading the text as the graphic begins to appear. This causes a crisis in reading. The student tries to read the text and monitor the change in the graphic at the same time and finds that this doesn't work. The result is a big traffic jam on the information highway and frustration for the student.

The best way to handle graphic and text changes is to bring them to the display separately—especially if they contain complex content. This leaves the designer some choices:

- Put text on, then graphics, separated by the student's advance signal. You can also reverse this order: graphics and then text.

- Put the graphics and text on, separated by a short pause, and always put them on in the same order—graphic-text, or text-graphic.

- Use audio with graphics instead of text, being careful not to cause the two channels to compete.

It is important to develop a *style* in your communications which involves standard practices and timing during the modification of displays. When you talk to people face to face, you realize that every person is different and adjust your communication to them accordingly. The adoption of a style for display management is a substitute for the ability to adjust communications to the individual: Your style can be recognized and used by the student to anticipate changes and to interpret them.

6. Provide adequate detail to fully illustrate the thing being described: One frequent problem is "crunching" graphics in an attempt to get more and more on the screen. During the simulation of a computer's control panel, for instance, a designer is likely to find that in order to get adequate numbers of controls on the screen it is necessary to reduce the size of the graphic to such a small scale that the individual controls are neither clearly visible nor manipulable.

Many designers, discouraged by this dilemma, conclude wrongly that they must trade CBI for a medium that allows higher-detail representations. With a little creative thinking, however, this problem turns into a demonstration of the strength and flexibility of CBI. There are at least two solutions to the detail problem: (1) zoom-in, and (2) windowing.

Zoom-in allows the student to designate a part of the control panel (or any other large visual surface, such as a map) and zoom closer for a detailed look and for action. The designer supplies the closer look for the student by presenting the graphic or video image at closer range. From the close-in position, the designer may move even closer, zoom out, or explore from side to side. This approach has worked with maps, equipment panels, and tours of cities.

Windowing is a familiar form of zoom-in that does not destroy the original view as the detailed image appears. The window closes when the inspection or use of its contents is complete, and the entire reference image is restored.

7. Avoid unnecessary or irrelevant graphics, particularly the trivial use of animations and distracting scenes: Even in a mature audience, most people experience a kind of delight or heightened interest the first time they see an animated train move across the screen bearing the message "Press Return." The second time they see it, they register recognition. The third time they see it, they show an indifference or impatience that grows with each subsequent train. The level of impatience is directly proportional to the time it takes for the train to traverse the screen.

Youthful audiences have a great tolerance for—even a desire for—graphics effects, and some instructional events use graphics as a feedback device to tell students how they did. If they do well, they get a little reward in the form of some graphics fun. This is a positive use of graphics as long as it does not cost more in design or instructional time than it is worth—and as long as it does not backfire.

One piece of mathematics instruction used graphic feedback for both right and wrong answers. Right answers caused the drawing of a happy face. Wrong answers caused the drawing of a crying face, complete with graphic tears running down graphic cheeks. The problem arose that the graphic designers were more inventive in the design of the sad face than the happy face. Children liked the sad face more and after a while were deliberately supplying wrong answers so that they could see it.

In the final analysis, the use of graphic effects depends a great deal on the level and likes of the audience, as well as on the quality and interest-getting properties of the graphics. Remember to adjust the quality and interest of graphics consciously as a part of the display design process. Also remember that even in high-productivity multimedia authoring tools, a large part of CBI cost is still in the preparation of display content. This means that each special effect you use has a cost.

Graphic messages—motion video

Recent advances in video technology have expanded the display capability of CBI immensely. Equipment for recording, editing, and playing video have been available for some time, but today's tools are better than ever. However, the digital disc (CD and videodisc) and new hardware and software technologies have made the instant selection and displaying of video images and sequences by the computer a commonplace thing where they used to be luxuries. Moreover, these things can be presented in any order the designer or student requests.

This development has turned the computer display into a magic image machine, capable of bringing the entire visual world under control for instantaneous display. The video images can be still, slow motion, normal motion, forward or reverse.

Video images can be overlaid with computer graphics to enhance them or to make up for their lack of detail or emphasis. Audio may accompany the video also. This adds up to a lot of possible combinations. There are guidelines which can help you get more from motion video:

1. Use the same care in selecting and preparing video motion sequence as you would use with graphics and still video: This means that the principles covering scanning patterns, use of emphasis, visibility of detail, building toward complexity, timing, adequacy of detail, avoidance of distractions, and matching of the text and video all apply equally to motion video as to still graphics.

2. Combine motion with still video: Electing to use some motion video in a CBI interaction does not mean that everything must be in motion. There are many times when still video is preferable to motion video in a CBI interaction.

3. Don't use motion for motion's sake: The positive version of this guideline is, "Choose carefully the places where you will use motion video and know why you are using it." There's no denying that motion video, when it is expertly prepared, can be a very forceful message-bearer. At the same time, that power is diluted when there is too much of it or when it is used for purposes which obviously don't require it.

It has been mentioned before that new instructional media often are used in the manner of older ones. This is apparent in the way video motion is used by new CBI designers. Occasionally you will see a computer-based video presentation that is no more than the transfer of existing videotape material to a videodisc, with the insertion of an occasional menu to provide a (false) sense of interaction.

This is an excellent approach for certain non-instructional uses of video, and it is also economically attractive for organizations which have large libraries of videotape stock which need repurposing. But this approach does not challenge either the capacity of the CBI system or the ingenuity of the designer, and often this approach carries over the instructional limitations of the originally non-computerized video.

Since the cost of professional-quality interactive motion video is still relatively high, designers should avoid its indiscriminate use. Usually its use requires a strong justification to the sponsoring organization. What kinds of applications justify the use of videodisc and motion? The question actually has two answers—one of them purely instructional, and one of them somewhat promotional.

The instructional answer is that motion videodisc should be used when the characteristics of the behavior being instructed or the content being communicated require the presentation of motion which cannot be presented adequately in any less costly medium. What are some examples? All media questions are relative to the budget, but here are some ideas:

- Consider motion in the training of physical and social skills, where there is often a need for motion video as a source of demonstrations or to show subtle cues. Many trainers also use video recordings of student performances for review and feedback purposes.

- Consider motion in the training of skills in which subtle movements or techniques have a part. Video can supply demonstrations and raw materials for interaction.

- Consider motion in the training of content where it is important to see things happen first-hand and where it is important to interact with the ongoing process, especially where doing so would be costly or dangerous.

The training of laboratory technicians who must work with highly dangerous materials may be best initiated in an environment where mistakes cannot cause harm to the student. Dangerous industries profit from the use of interactive video by allowing their students to practice delicate and emergency skills safely. Cost savings is realized when expensive equipment is replaced by motion video. One excellent example is found in the welding trainer created by David Hon in which the student, using a light pen in the shape of a welding torch, actually "welds" two pieces of metal—again and again and again at no extra cost.

The more promotional answer to the question of when to use motion video says that it should be used whenever there is likely to be a strong favorable impression to be made on a student, a client, a public, a board chairman. We are a video-oriented society; quality video material has a magnetic effect on most of us. Coupled with even a moderate degree of interactivity, computerized video can have enormous effects on attitudes, even when it only has marginal effects on real competence.

Many designers find it useful to look for opportunities to use motion video (budget allowing) for the benefit of students. Most courses have at least some relevant content which admits the use of video, and many organizations have accumulated material which can be used effectively without great expense. When video is used in this way, it should be done professionally and in instructionally relevant ways. Students are quick to spot the gratuitous use of flashy material when it is intended merely to amuse.

Audio messages in the display

Audio use in CBI is very common. A combination of higher speed computers and better software has combined to lower production, duplication, and storage costs of audio. Audio can be used profitably in a number of applications. Consider the following practical justifications.

- Consider audio when the student's attention must be on a part of the display which must be examined or manipulated. Consider, for instance, the use of audio in training on human anatomy for beginners in which the student takes a guided tour by listening while at the same time poking about in the cadaver with free hands. The cadaver may be one of plastic and rubber, and there may be pressure points which tell the computer when the student has touched the spot under discussion.

- Consider audio when students are for one reason or another disposed to the audio channel by habit, preference, or lack of other channels. Students with visual impairments can enjoy all of the interactivity and instructional benefit that fully-sighted students can through audio-presented CBI. Accountants may express a preference for audio, particularly in early stages of training in which they are consulting legal reference manuals and large sheets of figures.

- Consider audio when the content or skill being taught involves sound. Music instruction must make extensive use of the audio channel and does not always require video to accompany it. Language training makes extensive use of audio CBI. Training mechanics to service engine problems which involve variations in engine sound is a reasonable use of audio, as is training crews who must work at large equipment consoles and respond to aural as well as visual stimuli.

There are some principles for the use of audio in CBI that will improve the experience for student and designer alike:

1. Keep audio messages short and crisp: Audio loses its punch when the narrator drones on for long minutes at a time while the student stares at an unchanging screen. Short messages work for the audio channel just as they do for text. That means that the designer should have a good reason for any audio message which lasts more than ten seconds.

2. Be careful to pace the introduction of new ideas and the density of technical terms: It is relatively easy to process and remember an audio communication whose contents you anticipate, for instance:

> *Tell Tom that the City Cat Inspector phoned*
> *and would like a return call at 224-5555.*

In this phone message (which most of us barely remember long enough to write down) there are items of information which we anticipate, which makes it easier to process and store. On the other hand, something like:

> *The radial dial pointer indicates the direction to*
> *the homing beacon when the frequency selector is*
> *set to the beacon's temporary operating frequency.*

This message is not as easy to anticipate. Consequently, several such messages densely packed with technical terms and one or more new pieces of information in a row can easily cause a momentary but defeating information overload.

If anything, it is more critical to pace an audio presentation carefully than it is to pace a text presentation of the same information. Once a student hears the audio, it is gone, with nothing left behind to re-read. With text, at least the student can re-read the text if necessary. You can replay audio, but you have to listen to the whole message to retrieve one bit of missed information, which reduces the likelihood that the student will do that often.

3. Provide a repeat control: One way to soften the problem of the vanishing audio message is to provide a control that the student can use to request a repeat of the audio passage. With this control, a student has plenty of opportunity to absorb even difficult passages.

The frequency of repeats by the students also serves as an indicator of trouble spots. If only one student is having a high frequency of repeats, then the student can be helped. If a specific message has a high frequency of repeats, then the message can be repaired.

One problem the designer has to deal with when an audio repeat control is used is whether to repeat the graphic changes to the screen as well. Each designer has to deal with this question in the light of project priorities and cost. Graphic repeats may be easy to accomplish or difficult, depending on the technique used for displaying graphics, the capabilities of the authoring tool being used, and the type of instruction underway.

4. Avoid the temptation of slipping into page-turning; remain interactive: The flowing form of an audio presentation, where one idea leads on to another in an unbroken sequence, is a great temptation to turn the interactive CBI medium into a one-way slide/sound presentation. Developers must be extra cautious when using audio to observe the need for frequent, significant interaction.

5. Avoid echoing text with audio: One technique frequently used by novice CBI designers is the reading of screen text in audio. There is little benefit in this technique unless the instructional goal is related to reading skills. In fact, experience shows that the dual channeling of the message actually interferes with the student's uptake of it.

The rationale most often provided for audio echoing of screen text is that if information through one (sense) channel is good, then information through two is better: The more senses involved, the more is learned. This principle does not hold up under close scrutiny. If it were true, then the ultimate instructional message would be an audio and visual cacophony.

6. Work for a natural tone in audio: Audio projects a personality to the hearer along with its information. This personality has an influence on student attitude. Most of us have at one time or another had difficulty with the forced tone of an announcer who does not understand the material and whose voice and inflection show it.

In selecting voices for audio, it is a good idea to audition several narrators and select the one who is most capable of reading the material confidently, with the right inflection, and with a comfortable, natural tone—almost as if an instructor were speaking, or someone who understood the material. Radio announcers are not the best choice. The drama department of your local college may be more helpful.

7. Provide variety and facilitate revision by compartmentalizing: One of the weaknesses of audio becomes apparent as revisions are made to instruction. New audio for revisions is almost always recorded in a noticeably different voice from the original—even when the same narrator is used. Revisions become embarrassingly apparent, and the quality of the product becomes patchy.

The solution to this problem is compartmentalization—breaking the total audio narration into blocks which represent a portion of the total message. Blocks are then recorded using a different voice for each one. Then, when revisions are made within a block, only the block has to be re-recorded rather than the entire script, and it is not possible to detect the changes.

The sectioning of scripts into blocks coincides nicely with a concept which will be introduced later in this chapter—continuity. Consider matching audio continuity blocks with visual continuity blocks during script planning.

8. Establish a pattern for channel use when mixing audio with other channels: Select communication channels consistently for specific message content. For instance, you may choose audio as the carrier of the main information and use text to provide only directions and feedback, or you may choose audio to direct the student and put the main message in text. You have several options. What you choose probably does not matter as much as being consistent in the pattern that you do choose. The use of communication channels according to a consistent pattern becomes a roadsign that can help the student process the message.

9. Use audio creatively and in new ways: Our mental picture of the proper use of audio comes from the highly linear traditional media—videotape, and slide/sound. Developers of CBI use a medium with greater sophistication in the audio realm and should be ready to use the audio capability in inventive ways, unfettered by past habits.

CBI audio opens up new possibilities for the use of audio in constructed dialogues, drills involving sound, and the use of sound effects and music. With the new capability comes the challenge to experiment with audio to find out what can be done.

3-Dimensional physical objects in the display

The use of 3-dimensional physical simulation objects *connected to the CBI system* to provide a more realistic student interface can be effective. Sensors and controls imbedded in a 3-D object (a dummy, a control panel, even a map of the world) allow students to interact directly with and obtain responses from realistic equipment or object models and their attached instructional systems. Consider a student walking through a large physical atom model and conversing with the model while doing so, asking it questions and asking it to perform different actions for observation, such as bonding with another atom.

As we look at the future definition of the CBI terminal, we can see not far off something which does not look like a computer at all and which does not betray the presence of a computer, but which is a powerful interactive computer-controlled environment. As the size and visibility of the computer diminishes, we also see today's monolithic, box-shaped terminal shrinking to the vanishing point. In its place, we see specialized interfaces in which the now-invisible computer connects with a variety of solid, real-appearing input-output surfaces.

Earlier we mentioned a computer-based welding trainer designed by David Hon. The (invisible) computer in that system was connected to a (visible) display screen and a (visible) light pen which had been covered with a plastic shell exactly resembling a welding torch. On the torch-pen were two potentiometers, fashioned like the acetylene and oxygen knobs on a real welding torch. When turned, these were connected through the computer software with the display on the screen which showed a welding flame whose size and intensity varied with the adjustment of the knobs. When held close to the screen, the torch produced a bright "bead" of molten metal which followed the torch across the screen as the weld was completed. This is an example of a 3-D CBI interface.

Hon, famous for trying to scuttle the traditional sit-here configuration of the CBI terminal, also invented the CPR dummy. Once again, the (invisible) computer was connected to a display screen and, in this case, a plastic human torso and head. Pressure sensors within the dummy could tell where and how much chest pressure was being applied, and during the breathing phase, how much air pressure was applied to the realistic plastic airway. The display screen summarized these variables over time to produce a real-time feedback system capable of self-training CPR.

Currently, CBI stations which include a 3-D object as part of the interface normally use a monitor display screen for the purpose of supplying directions and feedback. Probably the best advice for those who use 3-D objects is to design the terminal layout carefully, even to the extent of creating prototypes and using them with several users.

During the testing of the terminal prototype, if the designer has created prototypes of the CBI products as well, they can be tested for another factor—their rhythm. When the CBI terminal incorporates more than one display surface, the student is forced to attend first to one and then the other. Sitting close, as most students do, the attending process can become a major activity, requiring a degree of attention and decision making which under bad conditions can lead to confusion and frustration.

A well-designed product for use with a 3-D object will fall into a rhythm of alternating between display surfaces. To aid in the establishment of this rhythm, the designer can use tones, bright flashes, motion, voice messages, or other obvious roadsigns to attract or direct the student's attention to the appropriate place.

Using off-line materials

Off-line materials include printed tables, diagrams, manuals, objects, references, or other materials such as photos, slides, video, or film which are not placed directly under the control of the computer. In this form, they constitute a lifeless but important extension of the display. Such materials are often necessary and desirable, although there is sometimes an unexplainable reluctance among CBI designers to use them. Perhaps in our passion to use the computer for all it can do, we find ourselves showing an unreasonable bias against off-line materials.

Here are some examples of the use of off-line materials to supplement a CBI display:

1. Reference or job-aid material which the student will use in the real world: Students learning a complex decision-making process may be practiced in the use of non-computerized reference or job-aid materials in the form they will show on the job. In some cases, overzealous CBI designers try to put reference materials and job aids onto the computer, even though the materials will be used on the job in a non-computerized form. This does not make sense, since part of the desired learning is learning to use the tool itself—off-line. Not only is computerizing it an unnecessary expense, but it competes with one of the main purposes of the instruction: mastery of the tool.

2. Existing media resources which are appropriate for use in your instruction but over which you do not have computer control: Before using CBI, many organizations accumulated a wealth of media material which, with a little adaptation, is suitable and desirable for use with computerized materials, either for enrichment or to provide detail not found in the computer materials. Using these materials is usually beneficial in several ways. It provides another point of view of the content being learned, it provides a change of pace from looking at the computer screen, and it saves money for the organization.

3. Material that needs to be presented which is too large or too finely detailed to be presented on the screen of your system: Despite the increasing use of very high-resolution and detailed display formats, despite the versatility of the computer screen, and despite our best inventive efforts, some things just do not fit on the computer screen and still provide the "big picture" perspective that is needed. In such cases, it is wise to provide an alternate, off-line media version.

4. Materials for the student which are intended to get the student started at the terminal for the first time and keep the student's personal records and notes: There are certain materials which are intended to aid the student in getting started with your CBI. We usually put such material in the form of a student manual, and this can contain several sorts of information and space for records. Student manuals contain outlines of the course, course rules, instructions for logging on to the computer, and instructions to follow when things go wrong. This constitutes a kind of non-computerized security package. In some cases, designers choose off-line materials such as this as the location for HELPS of all kinds. It can reduce CBI design time to use off-line materials in this way.

An additional use of off-line materials is a carry-away package which contains summaries and diagrams which the student can use for review purposes off-line. Materials that the student is intended to carry away from instruction should be carefully planned and should remind the student of what has been learned.

Providing information and control for self-management

Up to this point, the chapter has been concerned with structuring the display for rapid communication. It has presented guidelines for using each media channel and suggests ways to multiply and manage the number of channels active at one time without causing interference.

Now we turn our attention to another dimension of the display: the manner in which it interacts with the student's efforts toward self-management. We have tried to create an image of the student as an active agent in the learning process. As students learn from CBI, they execute a constant cycle of trekker decision-making activities, as illustrated in Figure 1. Not all of these activities are directly related to information intake and message processing. Many of them have to do with the students' efforts to manage learning. In one sense, these activities correspond to the activities of a hiker in the wilderness.

The wilderness trekker examines the map, searches for recognizable landmarks and asks, "Where am I?" This is *seeking orientation*. Then the trekker measures the distance between landmark and current position. That is *status evaluation*. Next, several goals are considered with respect to the landmarks. How far can I hike today? That peak? That river? This is *goal formation*. A goal is selected and a *plan of action* is made for reaching the goal. Then the *execution of the plan* takes place, which means pursuing the trek.

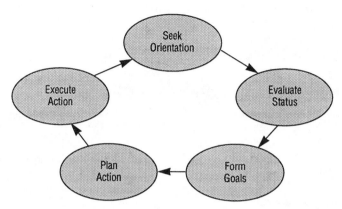

Figure 1. A student's cycle of self-management activities during learning.

Self-managed learning is no different in principle. Part of a student's instructional time is spent in specific learning, and part of the time is spent in more administrative functions that lead to strategic plans for learning, as shown in Figure 1. How much of a student's time is spent on self-management, compared to learning? No one professes to know, but one of the tasks of Display Management is to provide information and controls at the student interface which allow the student to perform efficient learning administration, leaving greater time and attention for specific learning. This is an important part of an instructional design that allows the student to be an active, decision-making participant in the instruct-and-learn process.

This element of design has been viewed in the past from a more narrow point of view. There is often an assumption that the designer will provide the strategies and the goals that the student needs, but the broader view of instructional goals and intentions described in Chapter 9 requires that we seriously consider causing the student to take a much more active part in the goal-setting and strategy-selecting process than we have in the past. This means that we must provide more information than we have in the past that the student can use in making instructional decisions and then provide controls for expressing both goals and plans.

This opens up a host of new questions. What information should/could we provide at the interface that would be useful to the student? What kinds of controls can/should we make available? In order to summarize the issues, we have identified three important factors which must be considered:

- The student's information and control needs *within* and *between* instructional events differ. The questions that are relevant within instruction are not exactly the same as those that are relevant when one instructional event has just been completed and another is being selected. Another way of saying this is that the information and controls for micro-strategic decisions are different from those for macro-strategic decisions.

- The student's information and control needs differ across the stages of the self-management process pictured in Figure 1. What is needed during orientation seeking is not what is needed during action planning.

- Information must be provided, along with a capability for expressing the choices that the information has supported.

These three factors create a design space, which we have shown in Figure 2. A designer can (should) make deliberate decisions within each of the cells of this figure. The following sections try to name and illustrate specific issues and options within the cells. These issues and options guide the design of the student interface for instruction.

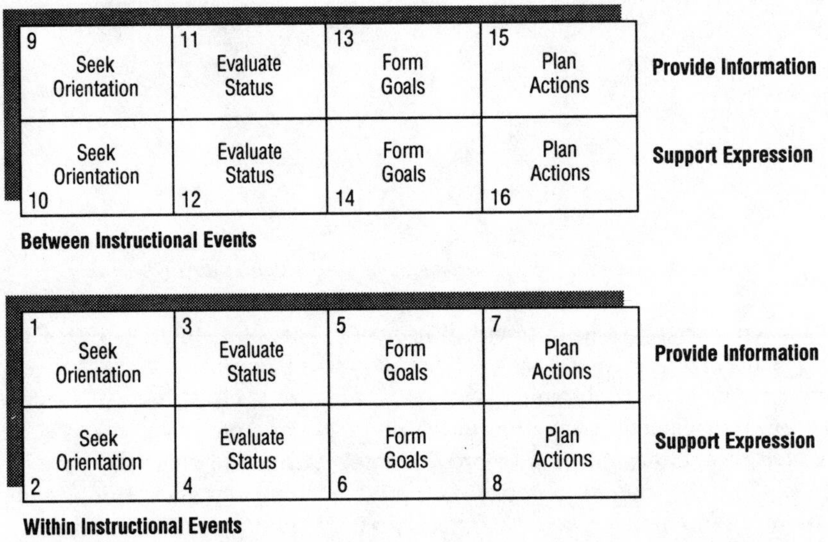

| 9 Seek Orientation | 11 Evaluate Status | 13 Form Goals | 15 Plan Actions | **Provide Information** |
| Seek Orientation 10 | Evaluate Status 12 | Form Goals 14 | Plan Actions 16 | **Support Expression** |

Between Instructional Events

| 1 Seek Orientation | 3 Evaluate Status | 5 Form Goals | 7 Plan Actions | **Provide Information** |
| Seek Orientation 2 | Evaluate Status 4 | Form Goals 6 | Plan Actions 8 | **Support Expression** |

Within Instructional Events

Figure 2. The dimensions of interface design that support learning management.

More about instructional objectives

Before we begin to detail the cells of Figure 2, we feel it important to make one additional point about instructional goals relevant to design of the user interface. Some instructional products make all of the choices for the student. Others at the opposite end of the scale require the student to choose everything. We do not, without reservation, support either of these radical positions. Instruction is a cooperative exercise between *two* wills: the instructor's and the learner's. Both participants must assume some degree of choice during instruction. This is especially true when one of the stated goals of instruction is to help the student become an increasingly self-directed learner.

Though designers tend to treat instructional goals as if they were unitary and one-leveled, all instruction has goals at different levels. We identify four levels which are useful to the designer—levels that roughly parallel those recommended by cognitive apprenticeship.

Goals at the specific knowledge or skill level: Instruction normally has a target body of knowledge or skill to be learned. This is the level of goal most frequently expressed in instructional objectives. These are the immediate and most visible goals of instruction. But there are other goals during instruction which a designer must keep in mind.

Goals at the integrated knowledge or skill level: Most instruction also has the goal of relating new knowledge and skill to that previously learned by the student. Designers should design for knowledge and skill integrations which they expect to occur to unite otherwise fragmented learning.

Goals at the discipline tools and skills level: Instruction often attempts to promote certain discipline-specific ways of thinking or information processing. Science students are encouraged to think like scientists, while aviation students are taught patterns of observing and attending which will keep them safe in moments of crisis. Mathematics students find the subject difficult until they begin to think like mathematicians, and language students are encouraged to think and form ideas in the foreign language instead of trying to think in their native language and then speak in the foreign one.

Goals at the learning skill level: Students are expected to learn how to learn. Most instruction has the goal of helping the student to become an independent learner.

All four levels of goal are addressed by instructional designers. They are inherent in virtually all instructional activities. If a designer makes no provision for them, then that is a strategic decision by default.

The attempt is often made to pursue the higher level goals through direct instruction; for instance, by providing direct instruction on the scientific method or how to solve a problem. But the results of such direct instruction are often disappointing. When this type of instructional goal is pursued across several instructional events in an indirect manner, better results are obtained.

Therefore, these goals must be supported not only by the strategies organized within instructional events, but must be supported by the user interface as well, between instructional events. Some levels of goals, especially those at the discipline tools and skills and learning to learn levels have implications for the design of the student interface. The designer should keep these multiple levels of goals in mind during interface design, looking for opportunities to engage students in decisions and actions which advance those goals as well as the subject-matter related goals.

On splitting things up

Figure 2 shows the functions of instructional management as if they were carried out separately and one at a time. This is not normally the case. We have separated these functions for this discussion so that their implications can be examined more closely by CBI designers, not because we feel that they should be carried out by separate parts of the interface. The best interface combines information-giving and control in a simple, easy-to-use way that allows the interface itself to seem almost transparent to the user. With this emphasis in mind, let's begin to consider the cells of Figure 2, exploring the information needs and controls that support student self-management during instruction.

Cells 1 and 2: Within-event orientation

The first and most immediate need of the CBI student is orientation. When a student picks up a textbook to read, he or she may turn the pages looking for headings, titles, pictures, and other landmarks. This becomes a mental map of the book. As the student reads, the landmarks are used to gauge progress, bolster motivation, and manage energy reserves. But this familiar form of orientation is only *one* of *three* types of orientation students normally seek.

During instruction, and within an instructional event, orientation can be sought relative to three kinds of landmark: (1) strategic structures, (2) goal structures, and (3) physical event structures.

Physical orientation: The book example we have just provided is an example of a student maintaining orientation in the physical sense. Students want to know how far they have come in the instructional event and how far they have yet to go. In CBI there is not really a physical dimension. But in the student's mind there is something analogous to a physical dimension, and it is most often measured in terms of *time*. How long, the student asks, until I am finished? In a book we count pages to obtain a time estimate. In CBI, it is more difficult, but a designer should provide for some estimate of time remaining for students when they request it, even if it is a very rough estimate.

Strategic orientation: Orientation with respect to strategic structures means that the student: (1) understands the kinds of strategic elements that are available for use, (2) how much or how many of each kind are provided, and (3) the learning function that each kind supports. In addition to knowing this, strategic orientation consists of knowing what type of structure is presently in execution and what its intended purpose is.

Strategic orientation is especially important during practice exercises, where a student may want to know: (1) the structure of the exercise (e.g., types of items, type of problem), (2) the extent of the exercise, and (3) the identifier of the practice element or phase of practice currently under execution (e.g., item number, location within the problem, etc.).

Goal orientation: Orientation with respect to goals means that the student understands what the goal(s) of instruction are—for all of the multiple levels of goal we have described previously. These goals may have been selected by the designer or by the student. In either case, there must be a way for the student to return and look once more at the goal that currently pertains.

The most common information support for orientation in CBI is the graphic or verbal map describing variously the size, shape, and consistency of the instructional event, depending on the interest of the designer. Maps vary widely in the type and amount of useful information they supply students and in their appearance. They range from one or two sentences of information to elaborate, multi-color, dynamic diagrams. Most frequently they supply information to support one of the three forms of orientation we have described here, without supporting the others.

Even if a designer can devise a way for all three types of orienting information to be supplied at the interface at once, the display is likely to be quite hard to interpret. Therefore, it may be the best approach to supply the most directly interesting orienting information to the student automatically—perhaps the physical orientation—and reserve the other types of information to be supplied upon student request.

Here the importance of deliberate design of this part of the interface for a particular audience becomes apparent. Not all students need the physical orientation. An instructional event may be so short or so interesting that the student has no need or interest in it. Moreover, not all students are ready to use information to support the other forms of orientation (strategic and goal), even if it is supplied on request.

Students who were established self-managers might be given the strategic and goal orientation information on request, but for students just learning to be self-managers, it might be volunteered at important waypoints in the instruction as a means of showing the student its importance and usefulness. Such intrusions would, of course, need to be accompanied by an interpretation of some kind for the student that modeled how an accomplished self-manager would use the information.

Information supplied constantly during instruction through standard page formats are a frequently-used orientation technique. This is especially true when portions of the instruction contain multiple parts. Example or practice sets are sometimes extensive. A standard notation showing that the current item is "3 of 15" can be provided textually or graphically.

In addition to this, labels on the display can be used to provide orienting information on a continual basis to tell students where they are and what portion of the instructional event (physically or strategically) they are currently using. These, in combination with clear transition messages upon leaving and entering parts of the instructional event keep students aware of where they are, what instructional function they are experiencing, and what goal they are working toward.

Content summaries are another technique for maintaining student orientation. A student can be oriented to the extent and structure of the content covered by instruction. Content summaries can perform several functions: (1) they can signal the endpoint of one section of an instructional event, (2) they can summarize the message in a structure that aids the memory, and (3) they can echo their format in off-line study materials. Their important orientation function, however, is to provide a retrospective view of the amount of content covered up to a given point during instruction.

Orientation controls: Controls to support orientation include ones by which the student can request information for any of the three types of orientation we have described. These controls may take any form which fits within the style and format of the interface. Since information and controls for the self-management functions are closely related and tend to be used in conjunction with each other, a unified set of controls which facilitate several combined functions may be desirable.

Cells 3 and 4: Within-event status evaluation

Status evaluation within an instructional event reports completion and achievement. *Achievement* is the measurement and certification of a performance. *Completion* is the experiencing of all of a component of instruction without certification of performance. Students are interested in their achievements and their completions within an instructional event. The same physical, strategic, and goal landmarks used for orienting the student are used for evaluating and reporting student status.

Physical completion status: Completion status is frequently reported for instruction which is divided into blocks of experience, as are most tutorials. It is common for tutorial menus to check off or otherwise mark sections of instruction which have been only entered or entered and completed.

Strategic completion status: The reporting the completions of physical instruction elements is fairly common; the reporting of completions to the student in terms of strategic structures is much less common. Nonetheless, if a student is expected to become proficient in self-managing learning, then an understanding of strategic structures and personal strategic needs is an important tool, and awareness of those structures can be awakened by using them to report progress. A student should be able to find out which available strategy elements have been used and which yet remain to be used for the first time.

This includes especially a survey of the practice. Students should be aware of the varieties of practice included in one event of instruction. They should be able to see how varieties of practice relate to tests which must be passed. They should be able to see the number of each variety which have been encountered. In addition, the student should be able to examine a sample of the practice/test content, criteria for acceptable answers or performance, and conditions of performance such as time limits.

Goal achievement status: In addition to surveying the usage of practice elements and examining a sample, the designer should provide data on the status of the student with respect to goal achievement. Traditionally, progress reports contain scores for the most recent test (usually) or practice session (rarely) and little else. This does not give the student adequate information on which to base plans for improvement or remedy, so the student is left without the ability to self-manage.

A summary of achievement respective to goals should be supplied at the completion of each practice and test. If practice and test events can be challenged more than once, then students should be able to obtain a historical trace of previous attempts. The details of this trace might include:

- A review of specific responses for individual items (both correct and incorrect).

- A review of performance on each attempt when the test is a performance test.

- A summary score comparison across multiple attempts for both practice and test.

Some designers object to providing detailed analyses of past practice and test performances. Most frequently this objection is based on the fact that the tests are memory tests whose answers can be memorized. If there is no alternative to memory tests, and if there is a limited pool of test items, then there may be no real option to review past performance. However, if the majority of instructional events are targeted toward such memory tests, the designer might well consider increased performance-basing of instruction and the use of performance tests—whose answers cannot be memorized.

The key principle behind providing more complete reviews of past performance is the maximization of useful information to the student which can be used for self-correction and improvement. Football teams make films of each game and use them for review and improvement. It is reasonable for an instructional system to keep adequate data to recreate practice and test events for the purpose of supporting self-directed student learning.

Status evaluation controls: Just as for orientation, the controls required to support status evaluation include controls for obtaining the information saved and made available for student review.

Cells 5 and 6: Within-event goal formation

It is more difficult to write about support for goal formation (or selection) during instruction because it is a practice mostly absent from our current instructional metaphor. Instead, we have settled for pre-set sequences of designer-chosen goals: one set for all students. Perhaps because we are so new at the game, our tools for constructing instruction with flexible goal sequences and for allowing students to become involved in goal structuring and selection are almost non-existent.

Freedom for students to participate in goal selection or creation is desirable: How else can students learn to select their own learning goals in future situations where there will be no instructor or designer present? Clearly, there are many instances where goals should be selected for the student, but the designer must be able to turn control by degrees over to the student, as the student demonstrates readiness to handle increased levels of self-direction.

With some imagination, it is possible for us to devise systems that allow the student to understand different kinds of goal structures and participate in decisions affecting those the student will actually be required to navigate. Designers should spend some creative energy in the near future, first identifying the varieties of goal structures, then inventing ways to inform the student which ones are being used or which ones are available in a given product. It would not be difficult from there to find ways to invite the student to participate in goal selection and make selections possible through appropriate control systems. Doing so would be an appropriate step in providing increased opportunity for self-direction to the student.

There is some evidence that CBI will in the future allow students to take a greater part in goal creation and selection. In this book, we have tried to describe technologies which will lead to this type of instruction, including a more detailed conception of the function of goals during design and instruction, and a vision of the curriculum as a "field" of potential instructional events from which either the student or an expert rule may choose the specific ones which are best suited to the student's readiness and capacity.

What are the designer's present options for student participation in selection of goals within an instructional event? And how does the need for goal-setting participation influence the design of the instructional interface?

Providing goal information: The interface can provide students with information on the structure of the available instructional goals and on the student's options with respect to those goals. As we demonstrated during our discussion of instructional strategy in Chapter 9, every instructional goal is decomposable into smaller and smaller instructional goals. The recognition of those goals allows the designer to provide instructional resources more flexible to the student's need or interest. An instructional interface should be able to describe to the student what goal system the designer has made accessible to the student and identify the choices the student has relative to those goals.

Providing for goal selection: When goal options are presented to the student, it is necessary to provide at the same time a means by which the student may express a goal plan—one that names the goals which have been selected and the order in which they will be challenged. Today, with the exception of advanced laboratory systems, such plans are made only by the designer and provided alike to all students, with too little explanation to allow the student to understand, let alone participate in the goal setting process.

Cells 7 and 8: Within-event action planning

Having selected an ordering of instructional goals and sub-goals to pursue, the student must finally be able to form and plan action sequences, instructional interactions, or strategic moves which will lead to the fulfillment of those goals. This is what is represented by cells 7 and 8 of Figure 2.

Information for action selection: As with goals, students must be informed of available or enabled strategic actions which are contained within the instructional resources that can lead to the fulfillment of the goals selected or created. More than one strategic action may be made available for each goal. It is this unfulfilled prospect of multiple resourcing for goals to which designers have pointed for years as the ideal for individualization of instruction.

Controls for action selection: Controls for the selection and ordering of actions are also requisite if the student is to make or participate in instructional action plans. One benefit of identifying these normally-missing elements of the interface will be that students will not only become aware of the opportunity for participation in control over their own instruction, but will have afforded to them the tools with which they can, through practice, become proficient in specifying effective plans.

The remaining cells

The last four sections describing cells 1 through 8 of Figure 2 define information and controls provided to the student by the interface so that decisions can be made and expressed *within* the instructional event. The second half of Figure 2 defines information and controls that allow the student to make or participate in instructional decisions *between* instructional events. The decisions which are supported by information and the controls made available for student choice-making in this second half of the figure mirror those in the first half, only now the decisions are not micro-strategic decisions, they are macro-strategic ones.

The primary information requirements and controls required at this level of goal and strategy formation relate not to the sequence of instructional interactions but to the selection and sequencing of instructional goals. At this level, the student is orienting, evaluating status, forming goals, and planning actions of a curricular nature. If we can put aside the antiquated notion of the "lesson" and come to understand curricular decisions in terms of increasingly challenging problems which the student will participate in and solve, then we can see that through the information and controls at this level, the student is able to participate in the selection of competencies to pursue and their integration into larger complexes in the manner described in Chapter 15. This is in contrast to the decisions made in cells 1 through 8, which were more closely related to the contents of Chapters 9 through 14.

This extended discussion of the functions of the interface has departed from the usual course of such discussions because if we focus alone on the visible surface design of the interface, we obscure the important instructional functions which it alone can carry out—the function of allowing the student to practice self-direction in learning. Having digressed for a while into this new area, we would like now to return to the more familiar and expected grounds of describing the surface of the interface, which is less directly instructional and tends more to be the stage on which instructional activities take place.

Providing control information

There is a kind of helpless feeling that comes over you in the middle of a CBI instructional event when you realize that you want to:

- Go back a few displays.

- Quit the instructional event.

- Have a word defined by a glossary.

- Look at the objective again.

- Skip ahead to the test.

- Review a previous instructional event.

But you can't recall the control to use, and you don't know how to find it. It is also annoying to confront a screen cluttered with symbols and text intended to remind you how to obtain these non-strategic support services, especially if there are many services and each one has its own icon (with no text label, of course!). Every CBI designer has to arrive at a control style for each designed product that moderates the control problem somewhere between these two extremes.

There are really three parts to the control design problem:

- Deciding what controls to make available to the student.

- Deciding how to make them available to the student during instruction.

- Deciding how to let the student know that they are available at a given point in the instructional event.

On the one hand, designers want to supply the needs of the student. On the other hand, anticipating and filling too many needs creates a decision-making overload for the student, leading to a decline in the number of services used by the student. There are also costs to be counted for providing controls to the student. During both design and production, the designer can spend more time and effort creating support services than creating the main elements of the instructional strategy.

Control questions are a major decision for the CBI designer. Let's take a look at some of the non-strategic controls and options which designers tend to offer. Later, we will consider ways for making them available to students during instruction.

Must-have controls

There is one non-strategic controls which is pretty much required, regardless of the student group or content being taught:

QUIT: The *Quit* function is important for obvious reasons. It is the student's escape hatch and safety valve. If a student is having a bad experience (and there can be many reasons), providing an exit can give the student reassurance that he or she is not trapped by the computer's logic. *Quit* should be available without penalty to students, except at points where the student has been warned before entering that it will not be available, such as during a test. *Quit's* level of use provides valuable evaluation data. Its frequent use by large numbers of students almost always points to problems in the design.

Quit may mean, "quit this instructional event and go to another," or "quit this instructional session and go home," or "quit long enough for a drink and a break," or "time out, I need help from a human." It is hard to tell which one the student means, and the most logical way to find out is to ask the student. *Quit* can use a menu to determine the student's reason for quitting before executing the requested exit. One of the options on that menu should be "Oops! I clicked by mistake." *Quit* options can be presented in a pop-up window that does not interfere with the ongoing instructional event.

Other useful controls

In addition to the must-have controls, designers may select from numerous nice-to-have controls. Some of the more common ones are described below:

BACK: Students will sometimes accidentally move ahead before they intend to and will want to reverse the effects of a forward-moving control within a sequence of messages. They may in some cases (heaven forbid!) need to re-read a poorly-written message that was difficult to process. It isn't always easy to provide a *Back* option. CBI instructional events, with the exception of "page-turning," normally have displays that have been "built" piece by piece by addition over the course of several display changes. In good CBI, the screen seldom refreshes entirely. Normally, only portions of the display change at once. Therefore, recreating a display the way it was just a moment ago can sometimes be extremely difficult. One solution is to design sequences of instructional message with specific re-entry or screen refresh points. At these points, re-entry from a *Back* control or from a fresh restart can be made easily. The more complex the instructional event logic, the more difficult the *Back* command is to implement. In some cases, *Back* is simply infeasible. In a simulated environment whose displays are designed to be non-sequenced, *Back* has less meaning than another control, *Undo*, but in a simulation, *Undo* can be complicated to implement.

AHEAD: Ahead is a must-have control when some portions of the instruction consist of sequences of messages. *Ahead* is normally given one of several names: *Next, Return, Continue,* or *Page*. It frequently takes the form of a right-pointing arrow, a hold-over from the old book metaphor. *Ahead* is the control that moves the student ahead in a sequenced presentation when no other interaction is required. *Ahead* is normally easy to implement; it is so easy that designers can be seduced into using it as an alternative to real interaction. The result, of course, is the dreaded page-turning.

COMMENT: A student can supply valuable evaluation data about an instructional event through comments offered spontaneously. This data is best if it is captured while the problem is still fresh on the student's mind. A *Comment* control records a student message to the instructional system along with the context (location, time) in which the comment was made. The message may be in text, or it may be a simple marker code inserted into an event record which the instructor can discuss with the student.

MAIL: Some CBI systems are connected to networks which allow the students to communicate through electronic mail without the need for an Internet connection. A message on the system can be automatically relayed to a receiver at log-on. The *Mail* function is often included as part of a computer-managed instruction (CMI) system. When it is made available, its control has to be integrated into the instructional interface.

The cost of *Mail* can be high but *Mail* can have great benefit when used to facilitate collaborative activities. The instructional computer is recently being used more frequently in group communication modes. *Mail* can also be linked into the internet to connect students located anywhere for collaboration.

TEST: Students can become good at predicting when they are ready to be tested. Performance and even objective-item tests may be constructed so that students can take them multiple times, encountering a slightly different test each time. It is necessary to build in some safeguards to avoid the abuse of self-initiated testing, but if it is used wisely, it can shorten instruction time and increase student self-direction.

GLOSSARY: A glossary of terms used within an instructional event is usually appreciated by students. A *Glossary* need not be duplicated, because most authoring tools allow them to be accessed from within multiple instructional events. As a part of the Glossary, it is good to include a list of acronyms also.

RECAP/REVIEW: Consider providing reviews and summaries of content covered within instructional events. A *Review* can be created as an independent module, just like the *Glossary*.

Learner control

We have expressed the opinion that students can benefit from increased participation in decision making during instruction. Turning control or choice over to the student during instruction has historically been referred to as the question of learner control. There are two questions pertinent to learner control:

- How much control CAN the learner be given?

- How much control SHOULD the learner be given?

How much control can be given? With modern programming tools and computer systems, the practical limits of student control are set mainly by designer imagination. Experience in the field of CBI, as in other areas of computer technology, has shown that even our zaniest ideas come true. Just about anything you can dream these days can be done. Instructional computing problems are difficult ones, but research systems today are showing remarkable responsiveness, adaptability, and intelligence.

How well does heavy emphasis on learner control work? For some students it works quite well, but for others, it does not. Research shows that there are practical and personal considerations influencing the success of a heavily learner-controlled system. Individuals differ in their understanding of learner control, in their ability to use it, and in their desire to use it. There are controls students are not sure how to use because their prior educational experiences have not taught them how; a learner must learn to use learner control.

Even after learning to use controls, we might conclude that not everyone will want to use them. Each learner brings a set of learning habits and preferences to the instructional encounter. We must design systems to reach these students also and not just the ones who share a particular free-wheeling, self-directed instructional style. However, as we instruct, we are teaching the student on many levels. We are not just teaching academic content, thinking ability, or problem solving; we are teaching students how to learn. Therefore, it seems we must require some degree of student decision-making and initiative-taking during instruction, and we must help students learn to use control to take charge of their own learning.

Even more important, we need to teach students to share initiative during learning, and the computer is capable of creating collaborative environments—both as the substrate for student-to-student collaborations, and as a collaborator itself. The principle that all students ought to have full control at all times during learning is simply not supportable. There are too many moments when a student may need a nudge, an idea, some encouragement, direction, help, advice, or support. Therefore, we suggest that designers think not only of their content-related instructional goals, but also about a parallel set of goals which target the degree of self-determination they would like students to reach and sustain. Those goals will provide guidelines for the design of control systems.

Making controls available

Once a designer has determined the set of controls to make available, the question remains, "Under what circumstances will each control be made available?" This is not only an instructional question but a cost-benefit issue as well, to be answered by the designer for a given course, because each option carries a price tag for development.

Regardless of the final decision, the designer should make a table which places in one dimension a list of each of the course event types (e.g., test, quiz, presentation, practice, etc.) and in the other dimension a list of the controls selected (e.g., Back, Quit, etc.). Into the cells of this table the designer should write the rules controlling the availability of each control available during each type of event. During some events, students will have access to all controls but only at specified points. During other events, such as tests, some controls will be restricted or made available in a modified form.

Once these guidelines are prepared, the designer turns to another important display management issue, "How will control options be presented to the student?" This is in reality two questions:

- How will the control option first be presented to the student?

- How will the student be reminded during the instructional events which ones are available at a given time?

At the first exposure to a new or modified set of controls, students are benefited by a short, interactive presentation about them. The fewer words and the more interactions this introduction has, the better. Two common mistakes made when introducing controls for the first time are:

- Telling the student (in lots of words) about each control and all of the complicated modes and sub-modes for its use without any chance to practice using the controls.

- Providing only a single-page summary of the controls and their function without a chance to practice using them.

When we write "How to Use the Controls" instruction, we take it as a challenge to write as few words as possible, while providing multiple opportunities for the use of each control in a realistic context. In one case, we found that the controls for a simulation were readily learned when students saw and used them in a set of tutorials which preceded the simulation. The controls were never addressed directly, except in short messages like "Click ZOOM to see more detail." But by the end of the tutorials, the controls had all been used in their normal usage in familiar-looking contexts, and the students had no problems using them to control the simulation. Other students who did not receive the tutorials, however, had difficulty with the simulation, partly because of not knowing how to issue commands to get things done.

Once a student has been introduced to a set of controls, two provisions are usually sufficient to keep the student familiar with them. The first is to associate a specific icon or symbol with the control consistently. When a control is available to the student, its icon should be visible in a specific (and consistent) location. When a control is not available, its icon should be masked but not necessarily removed from the display.

A second provision for control awareness is to make a review available to the student at all times. This resource may take several forms:

- A printed reference or job aid near the workstation.

- A keyboard template.

- A Help menu icon always available.

You can also standardize a set of controls and their functions for all of the products your organization generates. This must take into account the needs of all of the courses you teach now or expect to teach later, but it greatly simplifies instructional event design, since it allows some of the instructional event functions to be templated and used many times. Standardization also makes moving between instructional events and courses much easier for the student.

Ensuring message continuity

One of the best examples of the need for continuity is the typical beginner designer's CBI product. With every control action by the student, the entire display changes, erasing the familiar roadsigns which were on the screen. This type of CBI is much like a slide show, and by the twenty-fifth frame of this type of instruction, there are normally two results:

- The student's eyes start to tire from processing whole screens of new information, and the student begins to look away from the screen for short periods of time to give the eyes a rest.

- Students realize, that like Hansel and Gretel, they are moving further and further into a dense forest where they can see neither ahead nor backward, making them feel confined and lost, since they have not had the luxury of dropping bread crumbs along the way.

The early authoring efforts of most CBI designers are characterized by a particular technique we have already described called *page turning*. Page turning is the effect produced when a instructional event advances from frame to frame, covering each display completely with the next one. We call the opposite of page turning *continuity*. Continuity is the retention of orienting features during display changes. It helps the student identify quickly what new information has been added to the display and what remains from the previous messages. This provides the student a useful contrast, which contains rapidly-absorbed information.

Using continuity, a multiple-display sequence can be created which gives the student the sense of minor successive changes to a single display. The key to solving the page turning problem—and the key to increasing continuity—is to realize that page turning is mostly in the perception of it. The sense of page turning comes when the student *feels* that everything is always changing. This feeling can be reduced by using some of the principles below:

1. Seldom change the display completely, and then only to punctuate idea or environment boundaries: The end of one block of ideas or one activity and the beginning of the next is an appropriate place to create the psychological break which accompanies a complete or near-complete screen change. The "blocks" of the instructional event created by this technique are called *continuity blocks*, a technique discussed earlier in this chapter in the section describing the principles for using audio.

2. Allocate screen locations for the placement of specific categories of information from the content table: Minimize the change perception by using consistent screen locations for certain message elements. Interestingly, recent progress has rediscovered this principle. Web pages were originally structured in the form of scrolling documents. Web tool makers have recently invented the *frame*. This type of frame is not a logic element for the creation of CBI building blocks like the frames we described in Chapter 4, but a display structuring device. A Web frame allows portions of the display to remain constant while other parts of the display change around it. It is a very useful technique that soon will become a standard, used to promote the feeling of continuity and to overcome the Web's version of page turning, eternal scrolling.

3. Erase only portions of the screen at one time: Old display content is changed by overwriting it with new material. Only overwrite one or two sections of the display at one time. The student does not sense an erasure when this is done; instead it seems like the arrival of new information.

4. Use building sequences of graphics wherever possible: Especially when the presentation of a complex graphic is the goal, it is wise to present it in increments which build the graphic in stages. There are many specific effects that can be used to accomplish this.

5. Insert interactions when they are relevant: When you are presenting information, it is sometimes desirable to emphasize specific items by asking the student a question about them. This not only accomplishes the emphasis, but it breaks up the regular pattern of change that can be detected as page turning. The question need not require a verbal response and may relate your verbal message to the graphic elements of the display.

We can best illustrate the application of these principles for defeating page-turning with a few examples.

To *defeat page-turning: Example #1*

Example #1 shows how a long sequence of messages can be presented without appearing to be page turning. The underlying logic pattern for this example is the *Menu with Linear Limbs* described in Chapter 5. Because this pattern has linear sequences in it, it is an invitation to use page turning. We will try to defeat the feeling of page turning by using three techniques: building sequences, formatted screen locations, and inserted questions.

The messages for this example will be a description of the six main features of a new automatic mail-handling product—an attachment to the user's postal box. The display during the instructional event is formatted as in Figure 3. It is divided into four main areas:

- A *Menu* area to accept student content choices.

- An *Information* area to present the requested information (including any graphics used).

- An *Interaction* area in which to present questions and accept answers.

- A *Control* area for the placement of all controls.

In this example the instruction is really promotional and instructional, and the questions asked will be the kind intended to help a potential customer select the product.

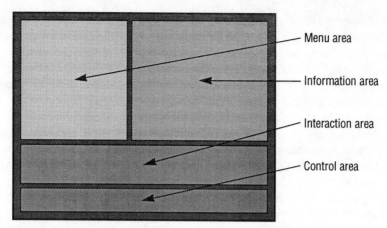

Figure 3. Screen format for defeating page-turning.

The message elements which will be displayed in each of these areas are shown in Table 1.

Table 1. Message elements for the screen format in Figure 1.

Feature Name	Emphasis	Descriptive Text	Questions
Auto Answer	Highlight the small box on top of the product	The Auto Answer feature automatically answers any incoming letter that looks like a job offer. It works in coordination with the Auto Resumé feature.	None
Junk Mail Detect	Arrows point to the Junk Mail Detect Slot	Junk Mail Detect spots junk mail, regardless of wrappings and devious markings used to disguise it. JMD recognizes names of talk show personalities and bills for magazines you never subscribed to.	None
Turbo Discard	Circle around the Turbo Discard chute	Turbo Discard automatically throws away any uninteresting looking mail: expired pizza coupons, county newspapers you didn't order, and transmission shop advertisements. You may set Turbo Discard for specific types of mail you wish to avoid.	How long has it been since you received a 5-year subscription offer from *Popular Geology*?
Junk Mail Return	Arrow points to Junk Mail Return indicator	The new Junk Mail Return feature sends two copies of any junk mail received back to the sender, C.O.D. This feature has been very popular. One company obtained a 48% reduction of junk mail using this feature within a one year period.	How many pieces of junk mail do you receive each year?
Address Security	None	Address Security prevents your address from being added to mailing lists. It does this by changing your address periodically, whether or not you have moved. This may mean that you miss receiving some of your mail occasionally, but your address will not be on new mailing lists.	None

Once the base display has been created, consisting of the areas themselves, an initial graphic, and a menu of features, a sequence of informational frames begins, controlled by the student's choices from the menu area. At the end of one choice, the student makes another selection from the menu, which of course changes the display again. As each feature is selected, some indication mark is placed on the menu to indicate that the selection has been viewed. This helps the student maintain orientation.

The large blocks of message from the third column will be broken into smaller chunks, resulting in more than one screen change per feature. Messages will be shown in a sequential order in their designated display area, and only that area of the screen will change that is required to change. The student will soon realize that certain screen areas are used for certain types of information, so this psychological labeling will convey additional information without increasing the effort of scanning or interpreting the display. At any point, only about 30% of the screen's area will change. That makes this instruction seem only one page long—a single dynamic page that the student never completely leaves, and one that only a computer could create.

To defeat page-turning: Example #2

The second example of defeating page turning using the principle of continuity emphasizes how a "building" sequence of graphics and a graphical menu can make a long stretch of page turning seem very interesting.

In this example, the designer is faced with giving a name and a short description of 30 or so parts of a boiler system. The screen-building sequence begins with a black-and-white outline drawing of the boiler system on the screen. In this case, the entire graphic is a menu, and the student is instructed to touch or click one of the outlined components in order to learn about it.

When a component is touched, it appears in detail and in color, along with its label. A two-line message in a message area at the bottom of the screen gives the name and a brief description of the component. The screen then reverts to being a menu, waiting for the student to touch another part of the diagram. In this way, the diagram is filled-in piece-by-piece, and the student learns about 30 items which normally would have been covered in a linear sequence, but the unchanged continuity base of the display helps the message avoid the sense of linearity.

Continuity

The principle of continuity can be used in conjunction with the content and message tables described in the Chapter 18 (Message Management) to create a very interactive instructional event out of an otherwise long and linear sequence. Continuity is one of the most important yet invisible (until violated) principles of CBI event design. It has two effects. First, it radically reduces the amount of display scanning and re-orienting that the student has to do. Second, it provides the maximum information to the student by using the subtle context and screen location cues. Displays designed with continuity in mind contain a great deal of information that does not appear on the screen in written or graphic form due to the use of contextual cues. Sometimes the message and emphasis conveyed by what is not changed can be as great as that is conveyed by what is changed. As continuity is employed skillfully within instructional events, the unity and focus of the instructional event improves, as does its efficiency of communication.

Designing clean interactions

Interaction design is the design of the give-and-take which occurs between the student and the CBI system during instruction. CBI is the most interactive instructional medium. It gets much its power from its ability to interact immediately and adaptively with the student. The designer must ensure that all of the features of the interaction contribute to the effectiveness of the experience and that none of them detract from it. Where does a student interact with a CBI system? In many places. Interaction happens:

- When the student exerts control over the course of a instructional event.

- When the student seeks and requests information.

- When the student moves straight ahead through an expository sequence.

- When the student is responding to questions.

- When the student is making menu selections.

- When the student is interacting with simulated controls and indicators.

Earlier sections of this chapter have suggested techniques for providing easy access to instructional support features through standard controls. This section offers suggestions for designing interactions beyond the standard menu of controls.

Menus and questions

Here are some guidelines to make menu and question interactions easier for the student:

1. Make it clear that a choice is expected: Occasionally when reviewing a CBI product you will come upon a display which is intended to be a choice point (menu or answerable question), but it will not be readily apparent as such until after you have made a careful study of the wording and have done some decoding of the screen. In one instance, we found a question hidden within a paragraph near the bottom of a screen that was full of text.

To make it apparent that a menu is a menu or that a question is a question, you probably should establish some standard graphical, structural, or locational roadsigns that say "menu" or "question" to the student without words. These roadsigns may include: a standard display heading, a standard symbol which appears prominently whenever an menu or question is presented, a standard page format which is common to all menus and/or questions, a standard screen or cursor action which takes place whenever a question or choice appears, or some combination of these.

2. Make it clear what the choices are: To choose between options, the student must first know what they are. Options must be visible as options, and they must to be readable and understandable. With surprising frequency you will find menus and questions where the choice or the question is not clear. This is most often true when options are embedded in a paragraph of prose or when there is nothing to distinguish options from other text or graphics on the screen. Options should somehow stand out from the surrounding display. All options should stand out using the same style of emphasis so that the student can readily identify them all.

Different designers use different techniques to make options stand out: isolation on the screen, bolding, larger text size, boxing, platforming, lettering or numbering. Standardization of display formats throughout an instructional event is very helpful.

Brevity is also an important principle in presenting options. Some menu items or questions are worded as short paragraphs. Wording of options should be concise, easy to understand, and unambiguous. If explanations are necessary, they may be offered in one or more preparatory messages which lead up to the selection point.

3. Make it clear what kind of response is expected: How is the student to respond? Arrow key, then ENTER? Mouse click? Touch the screen? Where? Type a letter? The display should make clear what kind of response is needed and where. Standardization helps the student know these things, but once you standardize, be wary of deviating from that standard, because the student will tend to respond out of habit.

4. Keep instructions visible, clear, and brief: Instructions given to the student should be brief. They should be placed on the screen in a location where they will readily catch the eye.

They should be unambiguous. You will probably spend as much time and care writing good instructions as you spend writing the question they pertain to. The nice thing is that standard instructions need only be written once for many uses.

5. Display the results of the student's choice: As the student makes a choice from a menu or question display, the acceptance of the choice and the choice itself should appear on the screen, even if only momentarily. Typed responses should be echoed to the screen. Touch and other locational responses should show screen response by marking or highlighting the area selected. This is especially true of situations where feedback or response will be given to the student without erasing any of the question. Retaining the response on the screen in these conditions allows the student to make comparisons and examine his or her answer in the light of the feedback.

Designing extended interactive exercises

CBI designers can create simulated environments in which students can live and act temporarily. Several chapters in this book describe how to design such products. Simulated environments consist of displays of data and visuals to the student and channels of input and control between the student and the computer. Properly designed, a useful portion of the world can be represented to the student for a few minutes or a few hours which will result in an increased capability to perform in the real world.

While designing environments, the designer must make a series of trade-off decisions between the desire for sensory and interactive realism and the ability of the selected hardware and software to create it. Most importantly, the designer's goal must be two-fold: (1) to create a world with as much useful realism as possible, and (2) to create controls the student can use which do not distract from the behaviors being practiced and which do not introduce unwanted behaviors that are an artifact of using the environment. Creating exercises on two-dimensional CBI systems with these qualities and using the available authoring tools can require great imagination in display management and almost always exacts some degree of compromise.

Useful realism

Realism is the interactive or sensory quality of an exercise which makes it resemble the real world, real objects, and real experiences in some way. Useful realism is the level of realism which can benefit a student in some way during an exercise, and it is a varying quality as training progresses. That is, there is not a direct and unchanging relationship between the *absolute realism* of an exercise and its *useful realism*.

An illustration will show why. In the early stages of learning any given task, it does not take a high degree of realism to create an environment for the student which can provide useful practice. During early learning, students are learning the environment of the task and its gross features. Moreover, the student's expertise in behaving in that world is shallow and lacks precision and speed. To present a student in this learning condition with a highly detailed and complex set of visual displays and an ultra-responsive and sensitive set of controls can actually produce negative learning effects—such as confusion, visual overload, and anxiety.

On the other hand, later stages of training for the same task may require a sophisticated visual and interactive system in order to produce a useful level of realism for the same student. This is because the student's knowledge of the task world is much greater, and the student's behavior in that world is performed at a much higher level of skill and precision than before. If the practice environment is to add anything to the skill already there, it must be able to respond with at least the level of precision the student's performance has already attained. It is difficult for a student to regress to an earlier stage of performance. In designing an exercise, the designer must show great sensitivity to the student's knowledge and experience levels at the beginning of the exercise and design accordingly.

Consideration must also be given to the action and display requirements of the task. In an environment for practicing equipment-related tasks, such as operating a telephone console, both visual and control realism are important. For non-equipment related tasks like diagnosing a disease, visual realism may be vital, but control realism (signing the prescription form) may be secondary. Ideally, a designer will provide optimal levels of complexity and realism, both visual and interactive, to suit the student's performance levels and matched to the peculiarities of the task is being trained. Stated in other words, the details of the performance environment should be sensitive to the task or task complex which is being learned, de-emphasize tasks already learned, and simplify, supply, or scaffold tasks yet to be learned.

The concept of useful realism as it is described here implies that a sequence of carefully graded performance worlds probably is the most direct, efficient path to mastery in the training of one task and the larger family of tasks to which it is related and with which its performance must be integrated (see Chapter 15). This realization on the part of a CBI designer is one of the keys to creating successful, integrative training products.

In the early days of pilot training, there were no intermediate steps between the lecture on the ground and taking the controls of a real aircraft. That was when aircraft were comparatively simple systems. Increasingly sophisticated aircraft systems have placed a greater burden on the student, and experience has shown that a less abrupt introduction can prevent overloading and confusing the student through the use of a graded sequence of practice environments, each with its own level of "useful realism." In pilot training today, a student works through a graded family of increasingly complex training devices, each of which represents a slightly closer approximation to the real world, and each of which polishes and refines the student's skill and precision within a certain range.

There are several dimensions to realism in an interactive CBI exercise. The skillful designer will adjust each of these: (1) to an appropriate level, (2) for a given student population, (3) for a given training task, and (4) at a given stage of training.

Consider the following dimensions in which realism can approximate the real world:

- *Visual detail*—The level of detail present, including highlights, dimensions, clarity, and level of resolution.

- *Visual proportion*—Relative size and shape of objects depicted.

- *Visual arrangement*—Relative location and arrangement of objects depicted.

- *Visual exactness*—The exactness of coloring, shading, etc., which makes a visual appear realistic.

- *Visual timing*—Occurrence of visual changes and events in a realistic timing sequence.

- *Non-visual or proprioceptive exactness*—The exactness of the feelings of motion associated with an action.

- *Control speed*—The rapidity of response to control action, and the response of controls to frequent or continuous activation.

- *Control action*—The "feel" of the control as contrasted with the feel of a real control.

- *Control proportion*—The degree of response to a given sized input to a control.

Selection of an appropriate blend of these elements for a given exercise can make the student's task of learning much easier. In many cases, it can also produce an economic benefit for the training system by practicing skills to a higher degree of perfection on less expensive training devices, thus ensuring less wasted time and less total time in more expensive training devices.

Unfortunately, the setting of these levels and the design of environments is an inexact technology, and designers have a great deal to learn about what constitutes the "best" sequence of worlds for a given task of given complexity. The best guide at present is the designer's own experience and data gained through testing on a variety of task types at varying levels of complexity. Developers should be encouraged to build a fund of ideas and judgment by constructing different worlds for a given task and evaluating the effects produced by each one. As a general guideline, designers realize that on every dimension above, early stages of training require low levels of each dimension, while later stages of training require high level representations.

An important implication of the principle of graded practice environments is that simulated visual presentations and control modalities may be supplied by CBI up to a point, beyond which a CBI system cannot meet the need for realism. CBI is only one of several levels of device which may be required to train a given family of tasks to real-world performance levels. Keeping this perspective of the place of CBI in the spectrum of training devices is very important for designers, who might otherwise come to see their favorite training medium as the one solution to all problems.

Striking a compromise

Creating interactions in CBI exercises which have useful realism is a process of fitting, during which you are always asking the questions:

- What are the essential parts of this task that the student must perform?

- How close to the real world can we make this interaction?

- How effortless can we make interactions and responses?

- What is the cost of each functionality we intend to model?

Your design of interactive exercises will require you to modify the real world somewhat. The extent and type of modification depends on the hardware of your delivery station, the demands of the task, the stage of the training, and your imagination. Your goal will be to maximize the amount of beneficial interaction for the student and minimize the problems where your interaction differs from the real world. What choices do you have when attempting to create the most convincing, most useful approximation to reality?

1. Use real controls and indicators: Advancements in CBI authoring systems allow some of them to interface with relative ease with peripherals other than the normal video screen, mouse, keyboard, light pen, etc. This means that a "black box" can be created which has as its features a set of real or very close to real controls and indicators for the student to use. These controls can be operated as if they were real controls, and the indicators can provide readings as if they were real and connected to real equipment.

In the past, systems of this type have not been considered a part of CBI's world because of the specialized engineering and production tasks required to assemble and program them. The connection of such trainers was looked upon as its own special field. Today, however, CBI authoring systems have made the programming task much more simple, and the use of this type of black box will become much more common in the future where it is needed. With the black box becoming an extension of the CBI system, it will be possible to provide directions, guidance, coaching, hints, feedback, correction, scoring, and remediation for the tasks of operating it in a way not previously possible.

2. Use simulated controls and indicators: When you cannot use a black box, you must compromise reality somewhat, selecting a display and control mechanism that is within your resources. This entails representing the controls and indicators on a 2-dimensional screen in some way (graphics, video, or a combination of the two) and simulating their use.

The traditional feeling persists with some trainers that training must be done on the real thing. This opinion is often held by well-intentioned trainers who have not as yet seen a better technological alternative. The "real thing" for them may represent real equipment being used as a training device, or real-world situations used as training situations. ("Come with me to make this sales call and I will show you how to close a deal.")

Some interesting research and experience with the use of simulated, 2-dimensional displays challenges this traditional idea, both in the area of equipment-related training and in non-equipment related training. But rather than quoting research, we want to give one or two representative examples to illustrate the point.

Years ago, the training for a particular piece of aircraft equipment was performed using over 12 hours worth of workbooks, followed by 4 hours of practice in expensive part-task trainers of a non-CBI variety. An additional four more hours of testing then followed in the same trainer. As an experiment, some CBI advocates decided to test how much of the sophisticated trainer was really necessary by implementing the same instruction on a computer. They used a touch panel to improve the realism of interactions, since the target performance involved programming a computer using a set of keys on a panel.

The instruction was constructed so that students used their knowledge as soon as they learned it. Good display management practices such as continuity were followed, and a graphic of the equipment controls and indicators occupied one area of the display, while text messages were presented in another designated area. The displays provided to students during interactions were realistic only to a moderate degree, since these were the days of the low-resolution monochrome display. The responses of the panel to input were accurate, but not identical in every respect to the real equipment. For instance, some of the panel keys on the real equipment were colored. Those same keys on the computer terminal screen were monochrome.

The results of the experiment were startling at the time but have been repeated in many other education and training content areas since. Students were able to *master* the operation of the panel using the computer display representation, despite its lower level of realism. Mastery was achieved in only 8 hours of CBI instruction, instead of the 12 hours required when workbooks were used. Students were able to move directly to the final performance test in the trainer, eliminating the need for the additional four-hour practice period in the trainer. In summary, the 2-dimensional interactive CBI exercises alone were able to replace a considerable amount of time in the trainer—4 hours worth—and were able to reduce the overall instruction time by 8 hours. This difference occurred despite the fact that the 2-dimensional trainer did not look and feel *precisely* like the real thing. The difference in realism from the real world was not a hindrance to instructional effectiveness in this case.

To illustrate our point with a second example, an early CBI designer, Fred O'Neal, created a family of interactive exercises which differed greatly from the details of the real world and yet excelled in training effectiveness. The learning task was the diagnosis of complex medical problems by doctors—at that time considered almost impossible using computers as the instructional medium, but now using computers quite commonly.

While creating the interactive exercises, the designer formed a hypothesis about those parts of the world that needed to be represented with accuracy and detail and those parts which did not require high fidelity. Then he worked out the best compromise, given the characteristics of the delivery system and the costs involved. Controls in the case of the medical diagnosis were determined to require only a low level of realism—exactly the opposite of the aircraft example. Five control instructions were created which students could ask for by pressing a key on a special keypad: Take Medical History, Perform Physical Exam, Examine Patient Records, Perform Laboratory Tests, and Manage the Patient.

Some of the indications, on the other hand, were decided to require a very high degree of realism, which was directly the opposite of the aircraft example. Doctors do much of their information gathering from X-rays or by looking at the results of test procedures—or by looking at and listening to the patient. The X-rays and certain other test results are highly graphic and very detailed. Fred decided that those indications requiring high fidelity should be administered by the videodisc image. Others were presented where possible using text.

The 2-dimensional interactive exercises created were highly successful in providing the level of useful realism that students needed. For indications which required high realism, students could see the indication. During the initial complaint, and during the answering of history questions, the patient's words and energy could be experienced directly through a videodisc motion sequence. The patient was seen undergoing the physical examination. Key test results appeared on the screen just as they would appear in real life. The results of the whole simulation were, as expected, very good. The exercises were capable of engaging the interest of doctors (who used them for refresher training in complex problem-solving).

This family of exercises demonstrated that for non-equipment related interaction, two dimensions can be as effective as three when the right judgment was used to determine the student's realism needs.

Designing interactions

While designing interactions, whether 2-D or 3-D, care must be exercised in designing the interaction itself to ensure that the product is easy to use and that it meets the instructional goals of the exercise. Some suggestions are given below:

1. **Select modes of student control which are easy to use, intuitive, and that have as much as possible in common with what the students will do in the real world:** Most often a 2-dimensional screen will be unable to duplicate the real world precisely for the student. Even 3-dimensional systems differ to some extent from the real world in look or feel. This means that the designer must always negotiate a deliberate scaling-down of an interaction from what the real world delivers to what the hardware and software can deliver. As was shown in the previous section, this scaling-down by no means requires that the designer scale-down the expectations of the benefit that can be obtained from the training.

In making this compromise of reality, the designer should invent control mechanisms which are as close to a sense of real-worldness as possible, yet which are easy to use and remember. We emphasize the "sense" of real-worldness, because it will be possible to create input mechanisms which are more exactly like the real world but which are clumsy, time-consuming, confusing, or otherwise difficult and attention-gobbling. Although they are more precise and accurate, they will also require more of the student's attention than is worth the extra degree of precision.

If possible, control mechanisms should be invented which retain the principles of the real operation but which are simplified versions, easy to perform on a 2-dimensional screen, not requiring many steps, not requiring delays, self-explanatory and intuitive, and usable by a novice without special instruction. Practice of real behavior with real controls can come after the student leaves the 2-dimensional system.

This advice must be balanced by a contrary instruction: Do not create interactions which, however simplified, will be misleading or confusing to the student later. The goal of simplifying the controls is not to teach the student patterns of behavior which are antagonistic to the learning of real control behaviors. The purpose of simplifying is to provide the student enough control over an exercise to be able to practice sequences of steps which make up a real world procedure.

2. **Ensure that your system can support the speed and volume of the display and interaction requirements:** Interactive exercises can place demands on CBI systems that for one reason or another (e.g., heavy graphics demands, heavy computational demands, heavy interrupt processing, etc.) make the system unable to support the load. Since every CBI system has its limit, you can plan exercises which will max out your target machine. As you plan exercises, you must make an assessment of the processing burden you are creating and plan within your delivery system's limits. Otherwise, you may produce a fine exercise which runs at the speed of a snail. In making this assessment, you may find it useful to try out ideas in a prototype.

3. **Avoid creating false habits:** As emphasized earlier, you must design interactions which do not teach students misconceptions about the real world. Controls given to students should be the best possible blend of ease of use and realism.

4. **Compress time if necessary:** We learned an interesting lesson while creating a set of exercises for pilot training. In one exercise, the pilot's job was to make one or two control adjustments and then watch the resulting instrument indications change. In the real world, the changes took as much as ten to fifteen minutes to occur. The first version of the exercise we created was faithful to this timing reality, and for ten to fifteen minutes students were asked to watch a set of indications move slowly down or up, exactly as they would in an aircraft.

This turned out to be boring and unnecessary. Even to us as designers, it was boring. Accordingly, we compressed time by excising long stretches of indication changes which contained little new information for the student. Student and client appreciation increased, and there was no adverse impact on student performance.

During exercises, time can be expanded or compressed for students as long as it is clear to the student what is happening. This is one of the beneficial features of simulation over the real world training.

5. **Design prompt and feedback messages so that they blend with and do not compete with the exercise:** A real benefit of CBI exercises over real equipment is that feedback and coaching can be provided, along with the realistic interaction.

Provision of these functions is part of your instructional strategy plan—the plan for instructional features of the simulation described in Chapter 16. If your plan calls for prompting, provide prompting, and do it in a way that observes good principles of display management.

6. **Provide the capability to review the goals and data related to the exercise:** Interactive exercises normally have a goal that the student is trying to reach as well as special data items which must be used in the problem (e.g., "Tune VOR frequency to 116.40," or "Your task is to identify the proper treatment for this medical condition by typing its name."). In problems where these data are numerous or where there is a chance they might be forgotten due to the complexity or length of the problem, you should make them accessible in some way to the student during the problem. It is usually possible to allow students to halt a problem, consult review data, and return to the problem.

Preparing the student for interaction

In addition to these ideas for designing interactions, realize that much can be done to prepare a student for an interaction:

1. **Give clear instructions and adequate warm-up practice on the interactions students will engage in:** We have found that students can pick up the moves necessary during an interaction very easily if you provide a short introductory instructional event which requires them to

practice each interaction once or twice until it is certified that the student knows it. Such introductory instructional events need not be long and can be very simple in nature, first commanding a student to execute a control, letting the student exercise it, showing typical results, and then allowing the student to practice a few times, while the system records the requisite number of successes.

2. Provide a review of interactions, controls, and their operation: During an interactive exercise, students can profit from having help available which reviews for them the rules of the road for the interaction. This constitutes the same kind of help on control options that you normally would include in a tutorial instructional event or job aid.

Conclusion

This chapter has covered a lot of territory on the management of the instructional display. Interface design is one of the key competencies of the good CBI designer. These principles applied to the design of interactions will speed the uptake of information, will make it easier for students to interact with the computer during instruction, and will reduce the time and energy spent on the interface itself, leaving more to be applied to the learning process itself.

Self-directed activities

- Collect examples of several CBI displays. Try to improve each display by rearranging, simplifying, adding, changing proportions, changing emphasis and salience of display elements, or by changing the timing of display events. Ask a friend to judge whether your revised display is better in a blind test.

- Begin to observe and critique the timing of multimedia events. Notice examples of: (1) poor synchronization, (2) competition between sensory channels, (3) content mismatch, and (4) message overload. For each problem that you find, derive the positive principle that would correct the fault. Begin to record the new principles you discover.

- Critique several CBI products in terms of the information and controls which they supply or withhold. Design improved versions of particularly bad interfaces.

Further reading

Fleming, M., and Levie, W. H. (Eds.). (1993). *Instructional message design: Principles from the behavioral and cognitive sciences (2nd ed.).* Englewood Cliffs, NJ: Educational Technology Publications.

Gayeski, D. M. (Ed.). (1993). *Multimedia for learning: Development, application, evaluation.* Englewood Cliffs, NJ: Educational Technology Publications.

Jones, M. K. (1989). *Human-computer interaction: A design guide.* Englewood Cliffs, NJ: Educational Technology Publications.

Laurel, B. (1990). *The art of human-computer interface design.* Reading, MA: Addison-Wesley Publishing Company.

Norman, D. A. (1993). *Things that make us smart: Defending human attributes in the age of the machine.* Reading MA: Addison-Wesley.

Schweir, R. A., and Misanchuk, E R. (1993). *Interactive multimedia instruction.* Englewood Cliffs, NJ: Educational Technology Publications.

Wileman, R. E. (1993). *Visual communicating.* Englewood Cliffs, NJ: Educational Technology Publications.

20

CBI BARNUM: HOW TO USE SHOWMANSHIP
WITHOUT BECOMING A CLOWN

Chapter Objectives:
1. *Evaluate special effects from the point of view of the student who is serious about learning.*
2. *Identify the pros and cons to using special effects in computer-based instructional products.*
3. *Identify complementary versus competitive uses of special effects in CBI.*

Special effects and motivation

How much should designers rely on special effects—which CBI is so good at—to produce student interest? This is part of the riddle of motivation for learning. We begin from the premise that humans desire to learn and that they enjoy learning. We feel that instruction which supports efficient learning is inherently motivational. The feeling of having learned—having discovered—is exhilarating to humans. We feel that although you may find special effects used with great benefit in good instruction, the special effects themselves are not the source of learning, and if improperly used, they can be distractions to the student. Therefore, we recommend that special effects be used with care and planning.

A great deal depends on how special effects are used. To be truly beneficial, special effects must not only be interesting but integral to the instructional experience as well. Some designers rely on the mere presence of special effects for motivational benefits, but this is wrong-headed. The student response to this is illustrated by the experience of one large corporation which created a series of videotapes for training. The subject matter was mechanical and technical (manufacturing computer circuit boards), so in order to promote motivation for the student, each videotape was given its own lead-in sequence, which lasted approximately one minute. These introductions had swimmers, beaches, palm trees, boats, upbeat music, and narration. The reasoning was to awaken the interest of the students, preparing them for the (dull) instruction to follow.

The tapes were sent to the field for use in training. Old tapes, when outdated, were sent back to the developing organization for recycling. Often the tapes were returned with a note still attached: "Start the tape at 00:01:28." Students had passed their own unfavorable judgment on the upbeat, entertaining introductions and found them irrelevant. The note (which we believe was made by students and not by supervisors) told students that the useful information began *after the glitzy introduction.*

A second example of the superficial—and unsuccessful—use of special effects was experienced by an industrial training organization which developed a long course on a very technical subject. The student population consisted mainly of high school dropouts. The medium of instruction chosen, by a distant governing board, was a form of programmed instruction. The course materials were extensive, and it became apparent that the students—most of whom had poor reading skills—were going to face a mountain of reading in complicated technical material over a twenty week course.

A disaster seemed inevitable, but the governing board would not change the medium of instruction. To soften the pain for these students and give them relief from the heavy regimen of reading, local designers inserted interesting (but unnecessary) video and slide presentations at appropriate points in the course syllabus. Since these presentations already existed, and since video and slide delivery systems were already in place at the training site, there was little additional expense incurred from using them, and it was reasoned that they would break up the monotony of the reading.

When the course began, the students, as expected, encountered the difficulty that their reading skills would have predicted. The video and slide shows did provide some relief at first. As the course continued, however, an unexpected change occurred. The students discovered that the real learning came from the programmed texts, and they happened to be very good programmed texts. As students discovered this, they discovered as well that they were learning and mastering a complex technical subject. Motivation grew out of the perception of learning; student pace accelerated; and reading skills grew as measured by reading tests. Students who had originally welcomed the slide and video presentations eventually found themselves disliking them as irrelevant intrusions, and asked to have them withdrawn.

These two examples—two of hundreds—suggest that special effects are an optional feature of instruction. Too-heavy reliance on them for motivation is almost always an admission that the substantial elements of the instructional event—the strategy, message management, and the display management—are weak. Moreover, the examples also show that when special effects are used they must be incorporated into the instructional product in a way that they are integral to the operation and effectiveness of the product.

Does this mean that instruction should avoid the use of special effects—those extra touches intended to "grab" or impress the student? That position is equally unreasonable. The question is not *whether* we should use special effects, but *how* we should use them.

Some designers are conscious of a strong but non-instructional pressure to use special effects. These pressures come not from student considerations but from the need to have a good demonstration for the Boss, the General, or the Dean. We have seen in our own experience several development projects which had special designs (and budgets) in addition to the main product design (and budget) specifically for the production of one or two "demonstration" products. These demo products were to have an extra loading of bright lights, loud noises, and sudden movements for the benefit of those who like to see that sort of thing and were in a position to influence funding. The bulk of materials for these projects were normally produced according to an effective—but less-showy—design. The demonstration materials were for just one purpose: demonstrations. The designer is often in the position of adding extra features in order to please decision makers which are not only economically unwise but undesirable from the point of view of the normal user as well. In this chapter, we want to concentrate on the use of special effects for instructional purposes.

Some special effects

What are the classes of special effects that CBI designers use? They constitute a broad class of very simple to very complex techniques. Here are a few:

- Popular or interesting images showing attractive activities or life-styles such as beaches, cars, attractive people, rank, success, wealth, recreation, etc.

- Humor, from subtle to slapstick.

- Special video or graphic effects showing glitter, polish, attractive textures, speed, detail, exciting motion, unexpected or surprising sights and sounds, etc.

- Interesting interactions between the student and the medium, including games, timing, visible results of student actions, realism, etc.

What are the pros and cons related to the use of special effects in CBI—*simulations* and *tutorials?*

The pros

The *positive* side of special effects seem to be:

1. The potential for building the confidence of the learner toward the instructional event. If a student finds an attractive image in the materials, interest can be created.

2. Potential for attracting the interest of students who might otherwise not find interest. The attention of unmotivated students may be caught by special effects just long enough for learning and motivation to be kindled.

3. Potential for re-energizing students whose determination is flagging. Since learning is work, a break from it can renew low energy levels.

4. Potential for increasing student attention at key instructional event points.

The cons

The *negative* side of special effects might be stated:

1. Most varieties of special effects in instructional events have a measurable development cost, and some have very high cost. Once a developer begins to use special effects, costs can multiply rapidly if the developer attempts to keep up a consistent level of them.

2. Special effects are often designed as additions to the strategy rather than as an integral part of it and often seem artificial. Some special effects are noticeable as late additions and reveal the developer's motives too clearly.

3. Special effects which are very good can become more memorable than the message itself. Advertisers have learned that humor in commercials is not enough and that there is a distinct difference between humor and memorable humor.

4. Special effects can offend. Some images and attempts at humor are offensive to students, and you can always count on losing a certain number of students to this cause.

5. Effects can lose their appeal as familiarity sets in. What was entertaining a few moments ago may not be amusing at all now. Even arcade games soon lose their appeal for all but a die-hard few. There is some reason to feel that if artificial excitements have to be depended upon to attract students, then the designer is placed in the role of providing ever-larger doses as the student becomes inured to the older thrills. We may take a hint from the history of video games, which began as innocent ping pong games and comic dot-gobblers but have become physically violent and threaded with frightening and occult themes.

A middle ground

Obviously, policy on the use of special effects in instructional events has to be based on considerations of cost and potential for effect. The policy will vary with student age, education, culture, interests, and personal taste. There are principles which designers can follow to prevent unnecessary expense, avoid offenses, and yet add another dimension of interest to instruction. Principle #1 is what we call the Seasoning Principle. It can be stated:

Consider special effects as the salt of the instructional event.

This metaphor works well, because student taste for special effects resembles student taste for salt. This should lead designers to the following conclusions:

1. Too much should be avoided.

2. Too little is preferable to too much.

3. The seasoning should never overcome the taste of the other ingredients of the dish.

4. The taste of the seasoning should blend with and enhance other tastes.

5. Seasoning should be consistent throughout the dish.

Principle #2 works in harmony with principle #1. It is:

Use effects which are organic to the instructional event and avoid superfluity.

Stay away from special effects which do not actively participate in the strategy and intention of the instructional event. We often see instructional presentations that use cute illustrations which do not act in harmony with the instructional event and are potential distractions. A clown is seen, for instance, carrying a sign which presents one of the messages of a instructional event—not because the clown is in any way integrated with the purpose or strategy, but because the clown is a decoration: an irrelevant trifle.

On the other hand, a clown with a mouth and nose in the shaped of an "O," juggling "O"-shaped balls may be an integral, organic, and perfectly natural vehicle in an instructional event whose objective is learning letters of the alphabet. In this case, the clown not only entertains but can have instructional value and actively advances the purposes of the instructional event. What can we do to achieve balance in the use of special effects and to focus their use on instructionally important things?

Do's

1. DO use impressive effects which also advance the instructional goal when you can afford to do it and when it can be done without negative side effects: Special effects must: (1) advance the idea or the strategy, (2) be affordable, and (3) have no negative side effects. Of these three, affordability is the drawback most often overlooked. We live in a visually-oriented society and have come to view special visual effects as an everyday occurrence—simply watch one commercial break during a televised athletic event and you will see a constant fountain of them. Video and graphics techniques today can cause us to float in a submarine in the blood stream, zoom through the universe aboard the Enterprise, and observe the opening of a rose in fast motion. In advertisements, humans walk through walls, animals talk, and the face and shape of one person dissolves into the face and shape of another as they speak the same sentence.

...And the lighting and focus are always perfect.

There is almost nothing that is impossible to show graphically or with video. But CBI designers sometimes forget that these special effects have a special price—one which can be far out of proportion to their instructional benefit. One of our colleagues, Olin Campbell, points out that thirty seconds of commercial-quality video (an advertisement) can cost hundreds of thousands of dollars to make and can take months. We realize that movies cost in the millions of dollars—thousands of dollars per minute—but still we imagine having loads of movie-like effects in our instructional material, failing to realize the cost attached. And frequently the justification for the added cost is not better learning, it is great-looking product.

2. DO cause delight and surprise when it is appropriate: When it can be done without detracting from the purpose and strategy of the instruction, extras can be dropped into instruction which unexpectedly delight, surprise, amaze, or otherwise practice plain old showmanship on the student. Such extras may include:

- Special graphics effects which are so sudden and well-timed that they take the student by surprise.

- Creative, affordable graphic or sound effects which use the basic capabilities of your system to produce unusual or unexpected sensations.

- Touches of personality that show the student that someone human and intelligent is behind the computer.

- Especially attractive layouts of the screen which show a touch of artistry in their composition.

3. DO use perceptive, insightful feedbacks where appropriate, avoiding the evils of the geometrically expanding instructional event: There is a feeling of delight and motivation that occurs when students realize that the computer has not just responded to them but has responded with understanding—with some degree of analytical insight.

We were impressed by the perceptive, intelligent-seeming feedback which Fred O'Neal and his development team constructed for a set of medical simulations as early as 1980. During the simulations, it was possible for students to choose from a list of five major activities (e.g., perform physical examination, perform tests, etc.). Within each of these categories, it was possible to ask numerous questions, perform a large number of tests, or prescribe any of several treatments—in any order.

The feedback, given at the end of the problem for each simulated patient, was constructed in such a way that it could comment on whether the student doctor had done the right things, the wrong things, unnecessary things, or too much or too little of anything. It could also detect the order of student choices and was aware when the student performed tests which were unnecessary, redundant, or expensive, or when the tests were performed in an unwise or illogical order.

The feedback was very precise and seemed as if it could have been given by none other than a very proficient, insightful human. Most interestingly, this feedback was provided by a relatively simple program. It is difficult for some kinds of learning problem to provide this level of responsiveness to the student, but it is greatly rewarding. We have had opportunities to develop and design several feedback systems of our own and have found that there are techniques for building fairly sophisticated feedback systems at relatively low cost. In future CBI systems, this is one area where the computerized instructor should be expected to excel.

There is a negative side to the feedback issue. Sometimes in order to provide the kind of feedback which evokes a positive response from the student, a designer may construct what we call a *geometric monster*. This is the kind of instructional event that tries to anticipate every right and wrong response the student could possibly make and create messages and logic to meet all possible contingencies using fixed, frame-based logic.

The geometric problem arises as the student makes one erroneous response, to which the instructional event gives corrective feedback. But what if the student makes a second erroneous response after receiving the feedback? The instructional event must anticipate right and wrong responses and provide feedback. You can see that the principle of giving feedback to the student for each possible contingency could create a instructional event in which the feedback messages and logic far out-size any other part of the instructional event.

The answer to this dilemma is not to cut back on the plans for feedback but to create alternative, non-frame-based forms of feedback logic. On work performed for the airlines, our development team found that one standard logic engine for providing feedback could be used for a variety of location simulations. This is described at greater length in Chapter 16.

4. DO use interactions as a special effect: One product we created had an unexpected motivational side effect and taught us a valuable lesson. The product was a laboratory exercise for electronics training in which the student was expected to create a circuit using components made available for selection at the bottom of the screen. Normally, this type of exercise is carried out using real components and a breadboard—a special board with connectors on it for connecting electronic components together into a circuit.

The CBI version of the breadboard we designed used a touch panel as the input device and divided the graphic screen into two areas. In a small lower area, the symbols of electronic circuit components were pictured, each in its own square. The larger upper area (the breadboard area) was divided into squares of the same size. This upper area looked like a blank checkerboard.

After directions to the student, a problem was presented. The problem said something like, "Construct a circuit consisting of a lamp, a switch, and a battery which will cause the lamp to illuminate when the switch is closed." Then the student was presented with the components and the breadboard.

The student was expected to touch a component and then touch a square of the breadboard, at which time a graphic of the component would fill the breadboard square. In this way, the student could touch all of the components needed, one at a time, then the location where they were to appear. When the circuit was complete, the student would touch the word "DONE" at the bottom of the screen. This was a simple interaction; not difficult to design.

What surprised us most was the delighted response shown by most of those who tried out this simple mechanism. In addition to providing a convenient interaction for accomplishing circuit building, there was something more present. Somehow the interaction itself was inherently interesting and pleasing. The interaction turned out to have that element of *seasoning* which added enjoyment to the use of the instructional event.

Designers can sometimes see ways to turn otherwise mundane interactions into something with a little pizzazz. In doing so, a prime consideration is that the interaction must act in harmony with the primary learning thrust of the instructional event. It cannot become a star in its own right.

5. DO deliberately form and project a consistent persona for your product: Behind every piece of instruction there is a personality. In some cases the personality is very visible. This is particularly true in the case of lecture presentations. In some cases, the instructional personality is more subtle, bland, and hard to detect.

The personality projected by instruction depends on either: (1) deliberate choices by the designer, (2) serendipity, chance, or (3) the personal style of the designer, as manifested in a series of design decisions. The personality of instruction can influence student confidence in the source of instruction as well as desire to learn, so it is worth the developer's time to be deliberate in choices which influence it.

Where is the personality of the instruction visible? In virtually every decision the designer makes. In the tone of every piece of text, in the style of every graphic, in the sharing of control, and in the feel of the instruction, the personality of the instruction talks with the student between the lines.

Some examples of this are provided in Table 1.

Table 1. Messages sent to students by the product.

Feature	Value	Message to student
Appearance and finish	Polished, clean consistent	"This is nice stuff"
	Rough finish, careless, uneven	"This didn't cost much"
Control given to student	Few constraints, many choices	"We trust you to make wise choices"
		"You know how to manage your own learning"
	Many constraints, few choices	"We know better what you need"
		"You don't know how to learn on your own."
Options and helps available	Useful options, broad range	"We thought of your needs"
	Ho-hum options, narrow range	"Take it or leave it"
Verbal tone	High energy, controlled pace, disciplined style	"Energetic, disciplined source"
	Low energy, irregular pace, loose style	"Careless, inexpert source"
Feedback	Complete, helpful, perceptive, insightful	"Careful, thoughtful designer"
	Lean, obscure, not helpful	"Mechanical, thoughtless designer"
Management tone	Generous, trusting, open	"You are a self-directed learner; participate in your own instruction"
	Closed, suspicious	"You need to be watched"

Students size up the personality of a piece of instruction and probably react to that personality even before they react to the instructional message or its content. Some personalities are easy for a given target population to relate to and can have a positive net effect on learning. Other personalities are difficult for certain segment of a target population to accept and trust, and for some populations, certain personalities are offensive. The offense may come from an image which is unpopular or which the student does not match the image of the student's group. In a product called the Physics Tutor, Bowen Loftin provided students with a choice in the delivery of feedback. They could receive feedback from an unknown male figure or from their own teacher (identical feedback messages in either case). Interestingly, they overwhelmingly chose the familiar teacher figure.

We cannot produce here a style manual for designing CBI product personalities, but designers must be aware that their instruction will project one, and they should deliberately design an attractive or at least a neutral personality for their intended population. Designers must also realize that images which appeal differ across student populations, just as clothing and music styles do. Most importantly, designers should avoid the trap of designing instructional events and courses using a given style just because it is the easiest style to maintain or because it is a natural product of the particular development technique being used. Frequently an organization which does considerable training will deliberately design a style or an image which it wants its instruction to project.

6. DO trust the sound and clean design of your strategy to motivate: Some designers inject motivational elements into an instructional event because they secretly fear that their instructional event is not adequate to hold the student's attention otherwise. It is hard to review an instructional product that you have created and form a clear picture of its effectiveness and interest-holding ability. What gives it appeal? Is it the "look" of the material? Is it clear or cleverly crafted wording? Is it good graphics? Good practice interactions? Actually, they must all be present to create an instructional event of excellence.

Perhaps it is the word *event* that best describes the kind of design thinking that is needed. As designers, we tend to look at an instructional product as a static, physical thing—a nice looking workbook, a set of well-drawn or photographed slides, a videotape. To the student, the value of a CBI encounter is the experience that takes place. Long after instruction is over, students can still re-create the feelings they had as they were instructed.

How do we know when a piece of instruction has the ability to create a satisfactory and motivating experience? It is impossible to judge by examining the product itself, so we follow the best principles available and then try the product out with real students. From this tryout we verify our principles and gain insight for the design of future products. The thing we must avoid is the temptation to add baubles and bangles to the surface of our product in hopes of making it attractive to students. We must trust the soundness of our technology and the appeal of good instruction.

Don'ts

1. DON'T create unnecessary image problems: We discovered this pitfall by mistake—literally. While developing a course for some military officers, it was necessary to illustrate certain characters using drawings. The course was for reserve officers who were not on active duty. This means they were business people serving a short period of military duty during the summer. We assumed that there would be a relaxation of self-image in the students and that a relaxed style like the one used by Bill Mauldin (a writer and cartoonist during World War II) would be viewed favorably. Consequently, we encouraged the staff artist to develop that sort of approach, which she did superbly.

We expected that the effect of these drawings would be a heightened student appreciation of the course, but the real effect was just the opposite. The students found the drawings quite offensive. There was an image line which we had unknowingly crossed. The students had a professional self-image which ran counter to the relaxed drawing style in almost every particular, and the drawings offended the students. One of us still keeps a picture from that experience on our desk as a reminder.

We could have saved ourselves from this problem by testing sample illustrations with typical students. Had we seen their dislike for a few drawings, we would not have produced the rest. At the same time, the experience taught us a valuable lesson about the image that a course of instruction projects, and we have tried ever since to consciously pick the image that we would project and control it for the benefit of our courses.

2. DON'T assume a false friendliness or intimacy with the student, and be careful of the implications of keeping data on students: We have spoken to many people who have expressed a dislike for computers that try to call humans by their first names and try to address them in a personal way. One person expressing a dislike of this technique says that instead of typing his name, he always types something comical when asked for his name. He then enjoys watching the computer say completely ridiculous things.

Even in this, the computer age, interacting with a computer has a negative —even threatening—connotation to a surprisingly large number of people. Many people feel quite comfortable with computers because they use them as tools at work daily, but there are also many who seldom have cause to come into contact with computers and others who purposefully avoid coming into contact with them. Many of these people experience some degree of anxiety when asked to use them.

Some of these people can be swayed by a non-threatening approach into discarding their feelings of reserve, but others find their feelings of concern heightened by what they perceive to be an over-friendly computer. Therefore, though the use of personal names may be good for some users, be aware that it is not good for all users.

Also, be judicious in what you ask the user to tell the computer about himself or herself. This principle extends beyond just giving of names to computers and their use in verbal interactions. It includes the giving of any personal data to a computer, which to some students is a threatening experience. Some students are concerned, and perhaps rightly, that information given to a computer can be used against them or against their wishes. The fear of "big brother" is in the back of many minds.

We were surprised to find this reaction very strong in one highly-paid professional area. Training in this area required that we keep scores on student performance. At the end of instructional events we reported scores to students as a normal matter of course, assuming that students would find it useful and interesting. Instead, they found it threatening, expressing concern that scores recorded in early, error-prone stages of training could be used against them legally in future professional situations—even in a career-threatening way. After considering this issue, we agreed with them and removed the scorekeeping during early instruction.

The moral of this story is that designers should be aware of the sensitivities of their population of students to name and data collection issues. This is an area that may come to have legal implications. Interactions should be designed and results should be reported in such a way that reassures these concerns, rather than heightening them. Moreover, designers should ensure that any data collected is secure against unintended use and that it cannot be used to harm the student by uninformed management.

3. DON'T use silly, irrelevant, or overdone effects, especially in humor: The positive way to state this principle is:

Make sure that the special effects you use are adjusted to the needs, interests, and tastes of your target population.

We had at one time a strong reaction against a piece of instruction which used video motion sequences for feedback. In the feedback sequences, people dressed as vegetables would jump up and down, clown around, and act happy in response to a correct answer and cry and look sad for a wrong one. We still remember vegetable people crying, jumping for joy, and doing other things which seemed very much overdone.

For some time we held the opinion that this was a misuse of special effects. The humor, it seemed, was overdone and silly. However, we have since decided that our judgment was hasty, since the target population for the instruction is very likely to appreciate these vegetable shenanigans. To us, the humor used in the feedbacks was not humorous, but to the target population it may be just what is needed. We can only hope that the developer had a clear and correct perception of the population. If not, then there is another designer somewhere in this world who has sitting on his or her desk at work the framed picture of a human dressed as a vegetable....

Certainly, the humor element of instruction is one which can be tried out with a sample of the target population with little risk.

4. DON'T entertain for entertainment's sake: Make every element of the instructional event count instructionally. On economic grounds alone, this is sound advice. Designers are aware that every element of an instructional event has a production cost. Moreover, during instruction, every element has a cost in student mental processing. Each element used, especially special effects, should be carefully weighed.

5. DON'T use techniques which are so engaging or so diverse that they distract the attention of the student from the main learning task: We have already given the example of the mathematics instruction whose graphic crying face was more interesting than its graphic smiling face. The flaw in this plan was that the frowning face was more elaborate and entertaining than the smiling face. The smiling face only smiled, but the frowning face displayed animated tears which appeared and rolled down the graphic cheeks. This caused students to prefer the frowning face, and they began deliberately missing items just to see it.

In this example, a special effect backfired—succeeded too well—and distracted students from the main learning task. This story illustrates the need for balance in the use of special effects to ensure that they enhance rather than distract.

6. DON'T repeat the use of special effects to the point where they become commonplace or annoying: We have also described the instance in which a small, detailed animation was used to deliver the message "Press RETURN." Each time the graphic appeared, it took 5 to 10 seconds to complete its cycle, and there was no way to circumvent it. After several presentations, students began to view this touch with apathy and eventually with scorn. Perhaps they saw it as too much of a good thing, or maybe it wasn't that good to begin with.

Conclusion

This book has concentrated on establishing excellent instruction as the main motivating factor for students. Though motivation has been seen in the past as a special, attractive appendage to instructional plans, we believe that motivation and interest are the natural result of good instruction. Learning itself is motivating. When good instruction is detected by a learner, the problem is not getting the learner to learn, but just the opposite. This discussion of special effects, normally seen as a major tool in motivation, reflects our view that the designer's first task is excellent instructional design and that special effects which are not harmonious with or do not promote the effectiveness of that design should be seriously questioned. However, when a designer finds the opportunity to employ special effects to amplify the effectiveness of a strategy, it is important to do so.

Self-directed activities

- Begin to keep a record of: (1) appropriate uses of special effects which don't wear out their welcome and act in harmony with instructional goals, and (2) inappropriate special effects which do work out their welcome or conflict with goal attainment. Keep a record also of special effects which are so out of proportion with their host product that they distort, overshadow, or otherwise harm the overall effectiveness of the product.

Further reading

Dempsey, J. V., and Sales, G. C. (Eds.). (1993). *Interactive instruction and feedback.* Englewood Cliffs, NJ: Educational Technology Publications.

Keller, J., and Burkman, E. (1993). Motivation principles. In M. Fleming and W. H. Levie (Eds.), *Instructional message design* (pp. 3–53). Englewood Cliffs, NJ: Educational Technology Publications.

Laurel, B. (1992). *Computers as theater.* Reading, MA: Addison-Wesley Publishing Company.

Schwier, R. A., and Misanchuk, E. R. (1993). *Interactive multimedia instruction.* Englewood Cliffs, NJ: Educational Technology Publications.

SECTION V

HOW TO DESIGN CBI

Design processes for tutorials and simulations, including key structural elements, the order of design, and principles to guide the design process. Examples of two different approaches to the design of CBI products.

21

CREATING TUTORIALS

Chapter Objectives:

1. *Identify the beneficial reasons for documenting tutorial designs.*

2. *Distinguish situations which benefit from rapid prototyping from those which don't.*

3. *Identify CBI design and development team members and describe their contribution to and use of the data on production sheets.*

4. *Design and produce a CBI tutorial.*

5. *Describe several ways for incorporating a subject-matter expert into a design/development team successfully.*

Bringing it all together

Designing CBI tutorial tutorials can be easy or hard, depending on how you approach it. What it will be for you depends on your methods and degree of organization. By organizing properly in advance and using well-defined procedures, you can make the design task the most interesting and exciting stage of development.

The greatest challenge during tutorial design is disciplining the creative process in a way that produces consistently good, consistently interesting tutorials. This chapter draws together principles and techniques which have been described in earlier chapters and shows how they operate together to form a unified design process.

The design process

Everything in this book to this point has focused on the principles and techniques that can be incorporated *into* a design. In this chapter and the next one, we deal with the process of *design itself*: the steps and activities used to blueprint a product that embodies those principles. Before we plunge into a description of the design process for CBI tutorials in this chapter, we want to place design itself in perspective.

Design is a fascinating process, and because it is one of the most valuable forms of human creativity, it defies being reduced to a simple formula. Rather than trying to do so, we have included two chapters on design in our book, each modeling a different approach to the design of a CBI product. This chapter demonstrates a highly structured and stepwise process for designing CBI tutorials. The next chapter demonstrates a much less sequential design process for an instructional simulation. Neither process is the *right* or *wrong* way to design. The two demonstrations merely show two different styles or approaches to design, both typical of approaches taken by successful and innovative designers.

What differs between the two methods is the number of pre-made assumptions about the characteristics of the final product. The tutorial design process can be expressed more sequentially because more is known at the outset about the form and features of the final product. There is structure supplied by the tutorial form itself and by the central instructional strategy the tutorial will employ. In the case of the simulation, the design of which is described in the next chapter, there are fewer pre-made decisions about the final product from the outset, and no central instructional strategy, so there are more structural decisions to be made during design, and the process is much less sequential.

By showing these two examples, we hope to illustrate the idea that design is a very complex process and that the way you approach a design task can vary from project to project, depending on a number of factors, including pre-existing decisions, time constraints, resource constraints, and product goals.

We have been careful to designate design as a technological and not a scientific process. Rather than being the search for the *one right thing* to do, design is a search for *possibilities* which weighs each potential design feature for its *relative benefit*. There are many designs, each with its own consequences. We need to remind ourselves once more—at the beginning of this description of a design process—that there is not just one right way to design. You can use this chapter's design process as a thought tool to create widely divergent products, depending on the instructional principles you use.

Documentation

One of the most important choices you make in designing a CBI tutorial is the choice of documentation method. Surprised? For projects of any size, CBI tutorials are designed and documented on paper before they are created on the computer. There are several good reasons for this:

1. To permit reviews of the evolving tutorial by others: If you document a tutorial, you can review it with members of the development team. Subject-matter experts, fellow developers, project managers, and production personnel all have a vital interest in the content and treatment in your tutorial, because they will be responsible for helping to produce it. Documentation is essential to any kind of organized team effort.

2. To ensure consistent quality throughout the entire tutorial: If you document a tutorial, you can better control its consistency from beginning to end and ensure that a product which starts strong will end strong. There is a tell-tale look to tutorials which are not documented before production. They begin with energy and enthusiasm but end on a much lower key.

3. To integrate the design of the tutorial with a larger systematic design process: This chapter shows the design steps for a CBI tutorial, but tutorials are seldom designed by themselves. There is almost always a larger instructional context into which the tutorial fits, consisting of other instructional events in other media. All of them must be designed as a suite of products targeted to fill a specific need. This larger instructional product will probably be designed using a systematic instructional design process which relies heavily on documented plans in order to maintain the focus of each product and clearly define the functions of each instructional component. The mass of data produced while doing this can only be managed through documentation of each component's design.

4. To allow staff specialization: The day of the renaissance person in CBI development is a thing of the past. Today we are obliged by schedules, product quality expectations, and product size and complexity to work with development teams, each member of which specializes in playing a particular part during tutorial creation. In this new work environment, documentation is indispensable.

5. To facilitate revisions: Revisions to tutorials may come after weeks, months, or even years, at a time when everyone connected with the original product is gone. Documentation is the key to making revisions to tutorials in a fraction of the time it would otherwise require. If you do not document a tutorial when you first create it, you or someone else will most certainly document it when it is revised down the road. Documented tutorials make revisions much easier, faster, and safer.

6. To guide and speed the production process: If you document a tutorial, you can almost automatically create shot lists and other production documents for use by your media production people—both those who create the computerized portions of the tutorial and those who will create multimedia and supplemental off-line materials. Without documentation, there is a significant risk of inadvertently omitting to produce one or more important elements of media.

CBI design is like an engineering or architectural process. When buildings are designed, it requires piles of documentation—paper, computer files, or both—to capture the data which defines the design. Documentation is not just wise, it is one of the tools of choice for the professional.

Automated design as documentation

Paper documentation is not the optimal choice for documenting a design, but it is better than no documentation at all. The tools really needed by the instructional designer are CAD/CAM-like systems which assist and support the design process and its accumulation of data from decisions *from the very first step*, through all of the decision-making and data generating steps, to the last step where the data is poured automatically into an authoring system which automatically creates the tutorial. Such systems have been dreamed about for decades.

Those long-held hopes are turning into reality as automated design systems are beginning to become available to CBI designers generally. *Designer's Edge™* from Allen Communication is one example of what will eventually become a designer's tool chest of design products. In several research laboratories, automated design systems are being explored, and within the next decade there is little doubt that an avalanche of new products for the designer will make an appearance to reduce the work load associated with a design, permitting increasingly complex, interesting, and useful designs to be imagined and executed by the average designer.

As these tools emerge and come under review, designers should keep in mind the key principle that the tool should not constrain the design. One of the leveling forces which has acted upon designers in the past was the constraining influence of available tools on the quality, quantity, and sophistication of the product that could be produced. As automated design tools become increasingly available, there will be two types, and it is important that designers discriminate between them. One type will be a true design system which invites the designer to express a design without pre-determined limits—a design which assumes no particular approach to instruction, no built-in metaphor—and then helps the designer move the design through successive stages of decision-making toward a complete, programmed product. The second type of design product will provide the designer with a specific approach to instruction that will be implicit in the tool's structural elements and processes. This second type of product will confine designs, and none will be constructed outside of the structural metaphor that was in the tool maker's mind.

An automated design system for CBI designers must be an open system that allows the designer to link conceptual elements to structural program elements of many kinds, creating building block-like compositions that were never imagined by the tool maker.

Rapid prototyping

The CBI world is quite interested in a technique called *rapid prototyping*. How does it fit into the CBI design process? And how does it relate to the *documented design* principles we have just described?

Rapid prototyping is an extremely useful technique. It relies on new authoring tools, like *Authorware, Quest,* and *ToolBook,* which have very user-friendly interfaces and are capable of assembling samples of program logic and display material rapidly. Rapid prototyping allows the designer to experience a design, as opposed to merely imagining it. The designer can form and test several designs in a short period of time, selecting the best features of each one to retain. Clients can also be exposed to prototypes created in this way to see how their product will look and feel.

Rapid prototyping has an important role in the evolution of designs. The industrial world in general considers prototyping an important stage in the design of any new product. Cars, television programs, and computer chips are all prototyped before they are manufactured in quantity. Prototyping is a method for arriving at a mature design concept for any new product. It is a valuable technique which can be used in coordination with the design process described in this chapter. Rapid prototyping is a means of on-the-spot testing for design ideas for frame logic, instructional techniques, and production methods. The information gained from prototyping in all of these areas is of value in controlling the quality and cost of the final CBI product.

If there is a danger in the excitement about rapid prototyping, it is that the prototyping step has been seen by some as a replacement for well-thought-out designs and stable documentation methods. When prototypes are used in the design of an automobile, their construction is preceded by much analysis and pre-planning to identify promising approaches. After tests of the prototypes have been conducted, data is analyzed and final design decisions are made. Design decisions and revisions are then captured in some form of document for use by an entire production team. Then procedures and mechanisms are formed for the production of the product in quantities greater than one. Rapid prototyping is but one of the players on the larger field of product design, development, and production. To omit either end of the design process—rapid prototyping or design capture—would be short-sighted.

The words and the music

As you create a CBI design, what do you write down, or *capture*? And how? In answering this question, you face precisely the same dilemma that musicians faced in the 8th century—before many of the conventions of our Western music culture had evolved. At that time, there was a great ferment in the musical world; change and innovation were the order of the day. One of the challenges facing musicians was capturing their ideas in writing so that they could be remembered and performed by groups of musicians.

There was no five-line staff as we know it today. Instead, there were many types of scales which had been imported from different cultures, and new systems of musical notation were being invented. There was one, for instance, just for writing Gregorian chants. Some musical notation systems used three lines; some used ten lines; some used the dot symbol; some used dots to mean one thing and squares to mean another. Some very unusual squiggle shapes were tried, and the result looked like anything but music. The house of musical documentation was in disarray, and musicians lacked a system for capturing ideas in a way that preserved their freshness and dynamism, as it had originated in the composer's mind.

This was a documentation problem. It made it difficult for a composer to create lengthy or intricate pieces, because it was hard work to use the existing complex and inadequate notation systems. Much of the composer's energy was spent trying to figure out a way to write down the simplest musical ideas.

Over time, a standard was formed; the twelve-tone scale we use today was generally adopted, and a set of common musical notation standards evolved. The result was a blossoming of Western music. The scale and notation system were inventions of great worth. They provided the basis, the vehicle, and the drawing board for all of the music we now enjoy. Without them, Beethoven, Bach, and Mozart would have been only music teachers.

A lot of things occur in the CBI developer's mind during the design of a CBI tutorial, just as they do in a composer's mind during musical composition. Who is to say that the dynamics of a truly excellent CBI product do not or could not call forth from the CBI designer a degree of subtlety and complexity rivaling some musical compositions?

Today's designer, however, faces the same problem faced by the composer of the 8th century: the lack of a simple, standard means of representing complex and dynamic events in a way that allows them to be molded, stored, revised, and shared, and which does not interfere or compete with the designer's thinking.

For CBI, in order to produce one product, there are many workers who must take the designer's theme, elaborate it, create a part of it, add details and variations, suggest improvements, and do so in a way that does not destroy the original intent, freshness, and focus of the design. It's like a symphony composed by a team.

Table 1 shows how the members of a design/development team use and add to the information of the design documentation for a CBI tutorial. The documentation which is created by and shared by this team must communicate completely but cannot be allowed to become a hindrance. Whatever tools are used, they must aid work, not slow it down.

Table 1. Team use of and contribution to tutorial design information.

Team Member	Information Obtained	Information Added

Lead Designer	Production progress info
	Material for review
		Seed information:
		Name of tutorial
		  −Instructional objective
		  −Production guidance
		  −Strategy guidance

Writer/Designer	Lead designer guidance
	Seed information
		Branching logic:
		  −Menus
		  −Controls
		  −Learner options
		  −Accessories (Glossary)
		    Screen plans
		Display/Message content:
		  −Text content
		  −Graphic content
		  −Animation content
		  −Video content
		  −Audio content
		Tutorial structures:
		  −Introduction
		  −Presentation
		  −Practice
		  −Test

Subject-matter Expert	Reviewable material:
	  −Message content
	  −Visual content
	  −Technical content
	Strategy elements (problems)
		Raw content (table)
		Corrections, reviews problem content

(Continued)

Table 1. Team use of and contribution to tutorial design information (continued).

Team Member	Information Obtained	Information Added
Project Manager	Production progress Labor expenditures	Special production Instructions
Computer Artist	Graphic art specs Art production list Raw resource information	Completion status info Filenames for completed art Labor expenditure data Production notes to other team members
Audio Specialist	Audio specs Audio production list Sound EFX specs	Completion status info Raw tape data Edit tape data Master tape data Audio filenames Labor expenditure data Production notes
Narrator	Narration script content	
Video Producer	Video specs Video production list	Completion status info Raw video data Edit video data Master video data Location data Video filenames Labor expenditure data Production notes
Programmer	Logic template requirements Template connection info Template modifications Special routine requirements	Tutorial filename Completion status info Labor expenditure data Production notes Test plan name Special testing instructions

Entry Person	Raw entry data
	Tutorial filename
	Production info
	  −Art names, filename
	  −Audio names, filename
	  −Video names, filename
		Completion status info
		Labor expenditure
		Production notes

Tester	Test plan name Special testing instructions	Bug sheets Completion status data Labor expenditure

The documentation system for the CBI developer must arise naturally from the development process itself, with each step of the process supplying a little more data to be documented, until the product is fully designed and ready for those who will produce it. Then, once production has occurred, production specialists must contribute information produced during their steps to the documentation, telling those downstream, who will assemble the product, where the product's separate elements are to be found.

A design and development process

Let's begin now to define a tutorial design process that automatically creates its own useful documentation. This process causes the designer to make decisions about the tutorial in a logical and consistent order. Each decision adds slightly to the documentation, and the documentation is structured to provide the necessary inter-worker communication of data which later will sustain the production process. At the end of the design process the following products emerge in turn:

1. A diagram relating strategy functions to blocks of frame logic.

2. A table containing raw subject-matter content.

3. Diagrams of all logic blocks within the tutorial.

4. A logic diagram relating the frames in the tutorial to each other.

5. A table containing all instructional messages and their media channels.

6. A production sheet for each frame, which contains display, logic, and production details.

7. A built-in production status record.

A designer's first use of this process requires additional time for learning, but subsequent uses will speed and streamline design and provide documentation as well.

This tutorial design process assumes that some larger program of systematic instructional design has gone before. That larger sequence might include task and objectives analysis, profiling of the target population, media selection, and syllabus creation. That systematic design process sets the stage and provides the context for the design of the present tutorial.

Figure 1 gives an overview of the tutorial design process. It is performed once for each class of objectives in your instructional product. That is, it is performed once for procedural objectives, once for concept objectives, once for process objectives, and so forth (or for whatever categories of objectives you have chosen to use). Designs created can be applied to all objectives within their class with minor adjustments.

The design process includes several activities you may relate to earlier chapters. The list of steps below is keyed to Figure 1 (for steps 1 to 10):

Step 1: Select an appropriate strategy pattern.
The designer selects or designs basic strategy functions.

Step 2: Subdivide the strategy into blocks.
The basic strategy functions are subdivided to provide a more detailed breakdown of instructional functions.

Step 3: Divide strategy blocks into content-related blocks.
The structure of the content is applied to the strategy blocks created so far to subdivide each instructional function one step further.

Step 4: Shuffle content blocks into instructional order.

Either (1) strategy blocks are arranged into the order in which they will occur during instruction, or (2) the menuing system for student selection of blocks is planned, or (3) the system for computer selection of block order is planned.

Step 5: Create content tables.

Raw content is obtained from subject-matter sources to be used as the foundation for formation of the final message.

Step 6: Add auxiliary features.

The tutorial organization at the highest level is completed by defining the auxiliary support features to be included in the tutorial and by diagramming the logical flow between tutorial elements.

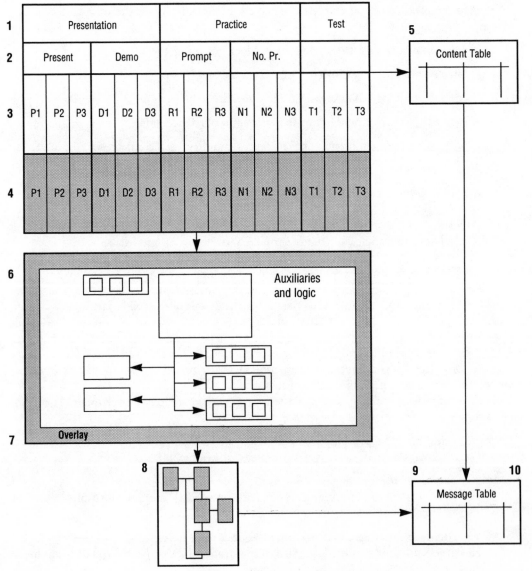

Figure 1. Overview of the tutorial design process.

Step 7: Design the creative overlay.
The surface context of the tutorial is designed as the setting for the execution of strategy elements.

Step 8: Diagram logic blocks using authoring tool logic.
Authoring system logic is diagrammed to capture the interaction plan for each tutorial block. The effects of the logic design on message and representation blocks is given detail.

Step 8A: Diagram test logic.
Test logic is defined.

Step 8B: Diagram unprompted practice logic.
The logic for the least supportive form of practice is defined.

Step 8C: Diagram prompted practice logic.
The logic for the most supportive form of practice is defined.

Step 8D: Diagram demonstration logic.
The logic for presenting demonstrations is defined.

Step 8E: Diagram presentation logic.
The logic for presenting the core information of instruction is defined.

Step 8F. Diagram auxiliary function logic.
The logic for branching within auxiliary functions is defined, and tutorial-level logic is updated and drawn together.

Step 9: Create message tables.
The content of messages is distilled from the content table into real instructional messages.

Step 10: Channelize messages, specify continuity blocks, design screens.
Each class of message content is assigned to its media channel, and designs for the use of the screens is created.

Step 11: Create production sheets.
Production sheets are created to hold the data which will accumulate as design decisions continue and to coordinate communication between development staff members during production.

Step 12: Review by the SME and designer.
The subject-matter expert and the designer review the emerging product at several points in the design and development process.

Step 13: Add production sheet details during production.
Data accumulates in the production sheets as production activities go forward.

Step 14: Produce authoring logic and integrate message.
Tutorial logic is created using the authoring tool, and the produced elements of the message are attached to it.

Step 15: Test and debug.
The integrated tutorial is tested to ensure that it meets design specifications and that it runs without bugs.

Step 16: Pilot test with students.
The product is tested with students who are representative of the target population of the product.

Step 17: Archive and begin configuration control.

The computer files which contain the product and its raw materials are placed under an accounting system which ensures that the latest version is the correct version, that the product will be maintained, and that nothing will get lost.

Step 1: Select an appropriate strategy pattern.

Instructional strategy is the backbone—the inner structure—of your tutorial. It is the first decision you make about your tutorial. The structure of your strategy will influence all of the other decisions you make during design. Chapters 10 through 14 provide a set of strategy prescriptions for tutorials for our chosen objective types. The objective for our example tutorial will be *Start a Diesel Engine*. This is a procedure, so we are designing a procedure tutorial, and we will use the procedure strategy pattern as a framework with which to begin.

The design of the tutorial starts with drawing the strategy pattern in the form of a simple block diagram containing the major stages of your intended strategy. This is represented by circled item "1" on Figure 1. A procedure strategy normally has a Presentation stage, in which information is given to the student, and a Practice stage, in which the student is asked to perform the behavior expressed in the instructional objective. This generalization will almost always be true. The exceptions are when the CBI is intended to provide only the practice portion of the instruction (with the presentation taking place through some other means), or when the intention of instruction is presentation-only (for familiarization purposes). According to the definition of instruction we have been using in this book, since that would not include practice with feedback, that may be *informing* but not *instruction*.

Step 2: Subdivide the strategy into blocks.

You have expressed the strategy so far as merely *presentation* and *practice* blocks. You must now break those functions into their varieties or their stages before going further.

You may have in mind that there will be more than one type of presentation or more than one type of practice. You may also have in mind that there will be more than one stage of either presentation or practice.

If the objective being instructed does not fit neatly into one of the objective types we have described in this book, that is not a problem. Chapters 8 and 9 discuss principles which allow you to define your own strategy. To accomplish the present step of tutorial design, you need only specify the main strategic functions you want to be carried out for your particular objective. This will normally consist of one or more phases of presentation and one or more of practice. These you will represent in a simple block diagram just as we have done here. Subsequent steps in this chapter apply to strategies you have designed in this way as well as they do to the ones we have described in this book.

For the purposes of our sample tutorial, we want to present the information for each step. We also want to present a demonstration of each step being performed. Since we consider these both parts of the presentation function, we have split the Presentation block of Figure 1 into two sub-blocks—Presentation, and Demonstration—opposite item "2" in Figure 1. Moreover, we would like two levels of practice and one level of test in our tutorial. Therefore, we have split the Practice block of Figure 1 into two parts: Prompted Practice, and Unprompted Practice. We have also added Test to the strategy block diagram, because we will want to test the student to certify learning.

These divisions of a strategy should be familiar, except for the modifiers Prompted and Unprompted used with the practices. Prompted Practice will consist of practice in which the student is prompted when or how to perform, step-by-step. Following performance of the step, the student will receive either confirming or corrective feedback, depending on whether the action taken was right or wrong answer. Unprompted Practice will consist of practice with feedback but without any prompting in advance of the step for the correct action. The Test will consist of an Unprompted Practice with only brief corrective feedback.

If we wished, we could add a verbal quizzing function within the Prompted Practice which tested memorized details for each step. This would give the student a chance to identify and correct misinformation and would provide the assurance that those details had been mastered. The quizzing could cease once factual mastery had been demonstrated. At this point in strategy design, we are free to add those high-level functions that we desire to have performed, and there is no restriction to what we can add, including perhaps a pre-test, a review of previous tutorials, or an attention-arousing prologue.

Step 3: Divide strategy blocks into content-related blocks.

The instructional strategy and the content are integrated in this step by dividing the strategy blocks into smaller blocks corresponding with the natural divisions of the content. In Chapter 18 on Message Management, we described how the content for each type of objective has a repetitive structure of some type. Procedures divide naturally into steps; processes are characterized by events in an event field and the transitions between them. Concepts are structured in terms of the examples and non-examples they delineate. Principles are also structured in terms of examples and non-examples—examples of the application of the principle. There are regular patterns in virtually all instructional content.

At this stage of tutorial design, you must subdivide each strategy block from the previous step in terms of these content divisions. Since we are designing procedure instruction, our blocks will be divided into parts corresponding with steps in the procedure. This is shown opposite item "3" on Figure 1. There are three steps in our procedure, so each block is divided into three parts. The codes within the blocks created by this division represent the three Presentations to be made (P1, P2, P3), three Demonstrations, (D1, D2, D3), Prompted Practice for each of three steps (R1, R2, R3), Unprompted Practice (U1, U2, U3), and Testing for each step (T1, T2, T3).

Step 4: Shuffle content blocks into instructional order.

Chapter 9 described how many varieties of surface experience can be created for students using the exact same strategic primitives if the primitives are shuffled into different orders. This is possible because at this stage of design, each block of the strategy represents only a function to be carried out. The strategy at this stage is still in the abstract, and its surface features have not been defined yet. While it is still abstract, you define the orderings in which you want the stages of the strategy to be experienced.

You actually have three options which you may choose from:

1. You may place the strategic functions in a specific order which every student will experience.

2. You may place the choice of ordering in the hands of the student and merely supply the student with a menu from which to select what comes next.

3. You may create a routine capable of computing at the time of instruction what will come next.

Actually, you have a fourth option as well. It entails any mixture of the three above choices. Some portions of the strategy you may wish to be experienced in a prescribed order; others you may wish to place under the student's choice; others you may wish to be invoked by the value of a computer variable, only if it is deemed necessary or deserved, according to some rule you have formed. As CBI designers, we have fallen into the habit of creating tutorials in which the control of strategy is all-of-one or all-of-the-other. You should be aware that you have a choice, because it opens up to you so many alternate tutorial structures and textures of experience.

It is at this point of tutorial design that you make this ordering decision. It is made early in the design process, because it is a structural issue; decisions after this one will add detail to the structure but will not change it.

You may want to make a rough sketch of your ordering ideas at this point, along with some amplifying notes. A later step (Step 6) will make a formal diagram of the paths of movement through the tutorial, but a few additional structural elements must be added before you are ready for that step. Once you have decided on the ordering of the content blocks, you are ready to proceed.

Step 5: Create content tables.

At this point, the content blocks that you have designated lead you naturally to creating content tables into which you place content from the subject-matter experts (SMEs) and other authoritative sources. Chapter 18 describes this step in detail; it is the first step of Message Management.

For our sample tutorial, we have created a content table. Its headings are appropriate for procedure content. As we described in Chapter 18, the headings of a content table vary, depending on the nature of the procedure. The headings chosen for our content table represent a group common to most procedures. These headings are described in Table 2. The filled-in content table for our procedure is Table 3.

Getting complete content for one tutorial can be difficult. Filling out a content table is not inherently hard, but it is hard to find a subject-matter expert who has all the facts you need.

Table 2. Content table headings for the sample tutorial.

Table Heading	Meaning	Rationale
Step name/number	The name and number of the step for identification.	Steps don't really have numbers, but you will want to number the ones in your procedure so that they can be referred to without confusion by developers and students both. The use of a step number alone can cause problems if a procedure has branches, so we will give each step a verbal name as well. The verbal names will actually be used during instruction.
When	The initiation cue for the step.	The step is performed correctly only if it is performed after the initiation cue signals that it can be or must be performed.
What	A description of the action performed in the step.	A verbal description differs from the name of the step. Frequently the name will identify what is accomplished by the step: "Provide power to the dialysis machine." The action description names the exact action performed: "Turn the POWER KNOB to ON." If two specific actions occur in one cell of the content table, the designer may consider splitting the cell into two cells.
Where	The location of any control activated or indicator read.	This is gathered in order to inform the student and also to inform the developers.
Why	The intention of the step.	Why is this step performed? In order for students to perform the procedure under conditions which require decision-making, they must know the purpose of each step. What is intended to occur as a result of performing the step? With this knowledge, students are capable of telling in many situations whether to perform or withhold the step, depending on their intention at the moment.

(Continued)

Table 2. Content table headings for the sample tutorial (continued).

Table Heading	Meaning	Rationale
See, Hear, Feel	The indications which occur as a result of the step.	Three kinds of indication accompany the execution of a step: (1) critical indicators of step effectiveness, (2) caused indications which are correlated with the step but are not success indicators, and (3) non-correlated and accidental indications. All of these must be identified if they will influence flexible performance of the procedure.
Meaning	A description of what has happened inside the system being operated as a result of the step's performance.	This is really two items of information: (1) naming of the effect of the step on the system, and (2) description of the implications of the effect. The implications can be stated in terms of impact on equipment states or readiness for continuing the procedure.
Warning	A description of varieties of action associated with the step which will lead to adverse effects.	Several things can occasion a warning: technique-connected effects, order-connected effects, correlated activity-related effects, or effects from omission of an action. If any commissions or omissions can lead to damage, injury, cost, or inconvenience, then the student must be warned against them.
Technique	Special mannerisms to be used for performing the action.	Technique can include physical action modifiers (speed, manner, force, timing) or non-physical action modifiers (timing, frequency, extent, duration).
Emphasis	Emphasis placed on the importance of the step for overall procedure completion or success.	It is sometimes more important for some steps to be done correctly than others to be successful in completing a procedure.

Table 3. Content table for the sample tutorial.

Category	Content
Step 1	
Step name/Number	#1: Prepare to start
When	N/A
What	A. Place the gearshift lever into Neutral
	B. Set the parking brake
	C. Insert the key
Where	N/A
Why	To prevent car from moving while it is being started.
See, Hear, Feel	N/A
Meaning	N/A
Warning	While being started, car has no power assist to steering or brakes, so if motion should begin, the car will be largely out of control and very dangerous. Do not overlook this step.
Technique	N/A
Emphasis	N/A
Step 2	
Step Name/Number	#2: Heat glow plugs
When	When ready to start
What	Turn key in ignition to second detent.
Where	First detent is the "Accessories" detent. Second detent is on click beyond that.

(Continued)

Table 3. Content table for the sample tutorial (continued).

Category	Content
Why	To prevent damage to the glow plugs.
See, Hear, Feel	Two lights on the dashboard illuminate:
	Water in fuel and Glow Plugs.
	You will also hear a buzzing sound until the glow plug light goes out. When it goes out, you are ready for the next step.
Meaning	The water in fuel light goes on in order to test the light and prove that it is working, It is a very important emergency light, since water in diesel fuel can cause major engine problems. The glow plugs light goes on to show you that the glow plugs are warming up. Until they are finished warming, the engine will not start, so turn the key to start the engine before this light goes off will only hurt the engine.
Warning	Do not turn the key full on until the glow plugs light goes out. You can damage both the glow plugs and the starting motor, both expensive repairs.
Technique	N/A
Emphasis	N/A
Step 3	
Step Name/Number	#3: Start engine
When	After the glow plug light has gone out.
What	Turn the key to the third detent until the engine starts, then release the key.
Where	N/A
Why	The engine will start now.
See, Hear, Feel	You will hear the normal cranking sound of the engine.
Meaning	N/A
Warning	N/A
Technique	Do not press the accelerator. Do not hold the key on after the engine starts.
Emphasis	Do not put your foot on the accelerator pedal until the engine starts. Your engine has fuel injection, which means that it is able to give itself adequate fuel to start. If you press the pedal, too much fuel will enter the engine, and you can place the engine in a condition where it will not start.

Before you are through filling out the typical content table, you will probably consult several sources, including one or two subject-matter experts, the existing technical manuals and reference manuals.

It is a good practice to consult a variety of sources of information when completing a content table. When you have an arrangement to meet with a subject-matter expert on a particular topic, you may even want to consult the other sources before the interview and fill out what you think is a reasonable content table beforehand. It will save interview time if you are right, and if you are wrong, you will at least know the subject well enough to ask intelligent questions and move the interview ahead swiftly.

The timing of content table construction is not fixed. At any time after the instructional objective has been determined (and therefore the type of the instructional strategy), content tables can be created and filled.

Step 6: Add auxiliary features and define tutorial-level logic.

Up to this point we have concerned ourselves with tutorial parts which will accomplish core strategic intentions, but there is nothing in the design yet to connect the tutorial with the real world. There is nothing that links the content blocks together and prepares them to be used by students.

For instance, nothing in the design to this point helps the student transition from one part of the strategy to another gracefully. No menus present choices to the student at option points, and nothing introduces the tutorial or performs any of the other basic housekeeping functions of instruction, like recording scores and reporting them to the student and to a management system. There is also no definition of the paths students may travel between strategic and content blocks, except for the general notes you made in Step 4. In the present step, these auxiliary functions are defined and given detail and the top-level logic paths of your tutorial are defined.

Specifying auxiliary functions: Auxiliary functions which are added at this point frequently include the following kinds of things:

- Introduction to the tutorial (Title Page, Objective, etc.).

- Transition points between stages of the tutorial.

- Specification of all possible entry and exit points to the tutorial (points at which control is delivered to the tutorial by the management system and at which control reverts back).

- Menu points at which the student or the system expresses an option.

- Branch points where the outcome of one stage of instruction influences the choice of the next stage.

- Transition messages which describe the path to the student in cases where the system is choosing the next instructional move.

- Points at which students can obtain a progress report and select a next event (or find out what has already been selected).

- Auxiliary services to be provided with the tutorial (Glossaries, Summaries, Reviews, Overviews, etc.).

- Reports of variables and scores to a management system.

The diagram you draw as you add these events to the strategy blocks becomes the top-level road map for the tutorial. It shows how and under what conditions students may move from one element of the tutorial to another.

Standard movement paths can be an important factor in maintaining student orientation within the instruction. If the same pattern of paths is shared by all of the tutorials within a group of tutorials, the student is not required to learn a new structure and a new set of conventions on entering every new instructional event.

The present step is only one of two that will contribute to the arrangement of the tutorial at the top level. The present step contributes the names of general support services and identifies major choice points within the tutorial. The step which follows this one will contribute a *setting* or *context* to the tutorial which gives the tutorial its personality and *plot*. Together, these steps define the top-level structures and the experience the student will encounter in the tutorial.

Figure 2 shows that the following events have been added to our sample tutorial as a result of this step:

- A tutorial introduction, accessible at any time.

- Designation of an exit point.

- A menu seen after each strategy block (whose ordering will be under student control).

- A progress report combined with the menu to show the student's progress toward completion.

- Two auxiliary services—a glossary and a tutorial summary—also provided on the menu.

- No pre-test (assumes that the content of this tutorial will be new to the student).

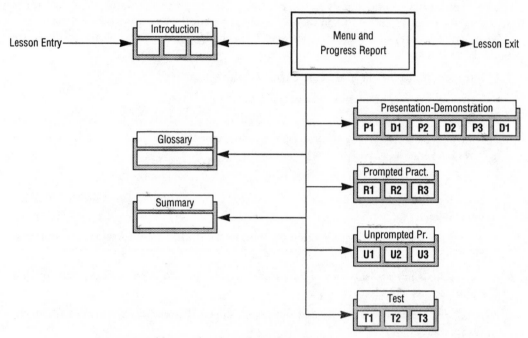

Figure 2. Addition of paths and auxiliary features to content blocks.

These items can be added to the evolving diagram of our tutorial. Notice that individual content blocks (P1, U3, etc.) are not accessible from the menu individually. In this design, once the student selects the strategic blocks Presentation-Demonstration or Prompted Practice, all of the content blocks within the strategic block will be delivered in sequence. A different structuring of this tutorial might make the individual content blocks available on request. To do so would require only a minor modification of the menu and the specification of some new paths.

The separate strategic and content blocks of the design begin in this step to blend with the larger context. If the designer desires it, that blending can obscure the edges of the strategy and content blocks, which will nonetheless continue to form the backbone of the tutorial, even if they are not clearly visible. The visibility of the blocks to the student is a variable under the control of the designer, and this step of tutorial design and the one following are where that decision is made.

The arrows and lines in Figure 2 represent paths the student can take; arrows with two ends indicate paths which return from the block back to the menu. In our design, the menu is the center of activity. That is not absolutely necessary; it was a design decision. The designer could create an arrangement of blocks in which the student progressed from one to the next without being offered any options at all—or perhaps being offered only a few options. (Example: "Are you ready for Unprompted Practice, or would you like to try Prompted Practice?") At the other end of the spectrum, each individual content block could be given to the student separately on demand, or the computer could decide at the time of instruction which one to execute. In either case, it is at this point that you finalize the ordering decision you began in Step 4.

Note that the underlying pattern created by our design (in Figure 2) is the same as one of the standard frame patterns from Chapter 5 (Menu with linear branches and return). Chapter 5 treated the patterns as frame patterns, but here you can see that they can be used as high-level organizational patterns for entire tutorials as well. If you were inclined to spend some time thinking about it, you would soon realize that all of the patterns can be (and are by different designers) used to supply the structure for tutorials well as tutorial parts.

With the tutorial organized as in Figure 2, the student is given control over the order of major strategic events in the tutorial. Some students may begin with the presentation; others will go directly to the unprompted practice to get a taste of the upcoming test.

Designers normally ask how much choice a student should be given during instruction. They express concern that students might pass through tutorials in which they did not see everything and emerge from instruction lacking proficiency or knowledge. This can only happen if the test which is used as the exit gate from the tutorial is incomplete. The designer must ensure that the exit from the tutorial occurs only when the student has proven him or herself proficient in all of the *intended* performance and knowledge. In some cases, this will lead the designer to include both a performance requirement (to test proficiency) and a knowledge quiz requirement (to test key items of knowledge which might otherwise be missed but which are essential) at the exit to the tutorial. Each of these provisions would, of course, add an appropriate strategy block to the design.

Detailing the auxiliary functions: The diagram of our tutorial at this point (Figure 2) identifies all of the elements which must be created. Some of them are very simple elements and only consist of a few items of information or a menu. Others are still quite large and include considerable information and interaction.

Before we proceed to the next step, we will break the auxiliary features into informational units in a fashion similar to the breakdown of the strategic and content blocks. This will prepare the auxiliary features for the step of authoring logic definition, which occurs in Step 8 for both the content blocks and the auxiliary features.

Let's examine which auxiliary tutorial functions are ready for further detailing.

Introduction. The tutorial introduction can be broken down fairly easily. To do it, you list the functions that you want the introduction to perform. Some functions commonly assigned to the introduction include (but are not limited to):

- Identification of the tutorial title.

- Introduction of the purpose of the tutorial.

- Description of the size and texture of the tutorial.

- Identification of the goal of instruction.

- Overview of high-level knowledge about the tutorial.

- Provision of sample test items.

- Review of the controls used during the tutorial.

- Identification of materials (books, supplies, equipment) needed during the tutorial.

- Identification of the authority for the tutorial (the sponsor and a reference which contains technical or authoritative content).

- The creation of an anomaly (a puzzling and unexpected fact that shows the student there is something important to be learned).

The contents of an introduction are not fixed and are based on the designer's policies and style. Your own circumstances may dictate needs in addition to those listed above. They may require disclaiming messages, instructions on management or scheduling, instructions on how to obtain help from instructors, marketing messages, or other administrative concerns.

The last item on the list—creation of an anomaly—requires explanation. An *anomaly*, as intended here, is a feeling within the student of unrest about the status of his or her knowledge. It is a realization by the student that something is not known that needs to be known. A live teacher will sometimes attempt to create an anomaly by presenting an interesting problem that the student cannot solve or a tantalizing question the student cannot answer. As the student wrestles with the anomaly, the realization occurs to the student that there is something that is not known that should be, hopefully increasing the likelihood of motivation, attention, and the student's active and willing participation in learning. Creating an anomaly is an important stage of any instruction—computerized or not—and it is often provided within the introductory part of a tutorial.

For the sample tutorial we are designing, we will have a simple front-end. The introductory part of the tutorial will consist of:

- Tutorial identifier (Title Page)

- Tutorial objective

- Duration information

- Materials list

- Authority (sources)

- Tutorial geography

- Procedure overview

- Summary of procedure steps

Tutorial Geography will consist of a map of the tutorial for the student to view (which will be able to show the student's progress through the tutorial), and a brief on the contents of each part of the tutorial. The designer should create a list or diagram showing these functions inside the Introduction block.

Glossary. The Glossary is relatively simple for a short tutorial. The Glossary will contain a list of technical terms from the instructional message which may be unfamiliar to the student, along with a definition of each term. At this point, there is no breakdown of the Glossary into blocks, because it is either a simple list or menuing function, either of which are detailed when the authoring system logic is designed in Step 8. There are no major functional divisions of the glossary.

Summary. A Summary for a tutorial is normally a synopsis of the core content presented by the tutorial. The Summary for our sample tutorial will consist of the presentation of a cleaned-up version of the content table to the student. This will provide a complete summary in verbal form of key procedural information.

Having added several auxiliary features to our design and the pathways between tutorial elements, we are ready to continue to the next step.

Step 7: Design the tutorial overlay.

The tutorial overlay is the surface structure of the tutorial. To this point in the design process, we have concentrated on the inner structural elements of the tutorial. Beginning with the previous step we began to work outward, toward the surface of the tutorial which is actually experienced by the student. First, we defined the network of services which would accompany the core of strategic functions and then related them together with movement paths and movement rules. Now we will define the *surface* of the tutorial as it will appear to the student.

This does not mean that we will design screens, select fonts, and arrange visuals. It means that we will define the *unifying theme* of the surface. Several words convey the intent of what is designed here: dramatic context, setting, rationale, plot, personality, location, story. Because the surface and inner structures of a tutorial may differ, we now need to design the surface structure. This is one of the interesting and creative steps of tutorial design. It is the step during which the tutorial is given its personality and unity as the student will experience them. It is the step which makes one tutorial (for technicians) businesslike and straightforward while making another (for children) seem more like the telling of a story.

We have several choices open to us for the design of a procedural tutorial. We may decide to set the tutorial in the context of ABCD Motors, where a customer has just paid for an expensive repair to the ignition system of a diesel engine (in the family pickup truck, perhaps). The repair was necessitated by improper starting, so the owner is motivated (by several hundred dollars worth of repairs) to learn how to start the engine in the correct way. The procedural information and demonstration could be presented in the context of Lynn, the mechanic at ABCD, training the owner how to start the truck.

This is one possible overlay design. You should be able to see that all of the strategic and content blocks included so far in the design could be fit within this context, which would include a character, Lynn, in a dramatic context, wiping her greasy hands on a wipe rag, explaining how to start engines step-by-step and then inviting the student to try it while providing audible feedback.

An alternative to this dramatic approach to the overlay might be a simple, straightforward presentation of all of strategic elements in an unadorned and undisguised form. This may include clear labeling of the strategy and content blocks for the student as they are executed. In this approach, there is almost no overlay at all to design.

Still other alternatives for the overlay exist. One might be a diagnostic approach, where the student was given a performance test directly upon entering the tutorial. Subsequent instruction might be predicated upon the results of the test, being directly referenced to it and provided within the context of a review of the results of the test. For this overlay, you might create an instructor character who spoke to the student at key junctures.

At this point, the designer must select the approach to overlay that will be used for the tutorial. Some approaches may modify the paths in the diagram produced in the previous step, as a different overlay may change the roles assigned to the student. Once these modifications are made and a brief outline of the overlay design has been described in the form of designer notes, the tutorial is ready for the next step of design. For our sample tutorial, we will stick with a simple overlay but incorporate Lynn, the mechanic, to give our demonstration and feedback messages.

Step 8: Diagram logic blocks using authoring tool logic.

This step will define the program logic used to implement the functions which have been included in the design. This is the *implementation logic* level of strategy design described in Chapter 9. It is a critically important step in tutorial design because of the cost factors it influences.

The design of logic begins with the selection of the authoring tool that will be used to produce the CBI product. All logic designs from this point are specified in terms of the structures your selected authoring tool can create. Since the popular authoring tools for CBI are frame-based, the logic will probably be expressed in terms of frame logic. Because the frame metaphor so dominates the thinking of CBI designers today, even if one of the more object-oriented tools available is selected, the probabilities are high that the design for a tutorial will still be expressed in a frame-based way. For instance, *Quest* offers object-orientation, but an easy expression of that orientation is in the form of frames and frame functions, which are among the main objects in *Quest*. Even *ToolBook*, which has robust object-orientation, is structured in terms of *pages,* the most simple incarnation of which resembles the frame.

We shall proceed in this chapter on tutorial design as if a frame-based approach were being used, because the frame metaphor is good for expressing tutorial designs. Frame-oriented authoring tools were, after all, originally designed to facilitate the creation of tutorials. Moreover, we will use the four basic frame types described in Chapter 4 to create our logic, since we know that is a common design language in this book and we cannot assume that you know any other.

This design method uses what is called a *top-down* approach. We have so far divided higher level functions of the tutorial into successively smaller units of function. Now we will continue the breakdown to the finest level of logical detail—the frame. There are several benefits to this top-down approach:

- The designer can give equal attention to the details of every part of the tutorial, each in its own turn.

- The process automatically directs the attention of the designer to areas of the tutorial which need more complete definition.

- The process leads almost automatically to very clear specification of logic details.

- When the logic for separate tutorial blocks is combined, it will automatically create a flow diagram of the entire tutorial.

The process for defining logic is of great interest to designers. It is here where the designer makes the most direct use of the tools that are available, and it is here that detailed knowledge of the tools and their capabilities pays off the most.

From this point we will describe the steps in logic design for each major subdivision of the tutorial separately, for there are lessons to be learned about the efficient design of reusable, or templated, frame logic.

Step 8A: Diagram test logic.

We begin logic design by attacking one of the harder parts of the tutorial: the test. The test is the defining element of the tutorial. It is the interaction during which the student demonstrates performance ability. The test is the gate which measures and certifies student progress.

The design principles to which we personally subscribe dictate that: (1) practice and test should both ask the student for the same performance, and (2) both practice and test should reflect the performance described in the instructional objective. If this is true, then designing the test logic first should provide a useful basis for designing practice logic as well, since they will be quite similar.

A good place to begin logic definition is to diagram the logic of the test interaction for one content block. In a procedure, the content block equates to one step, so we will design the testing interaction for one procedure step. (For the other objective types, this principle also holds: You define the test interaction for one content block—one example pair, one process event, one memory element, one memory network, or one principled example.)

To design the test interaction, consider what things will look like to the student and what performance you expect from the student. This will tell you the functions that have to be performed by both student and computer.

For our sample procedure objective, the performance we expect from students is that they *perform* the step. Therefore, we must reproduce for the student the conditions which exist when it is time to perform the step, and we must provide controls which allow the student to perform the step. When a response has been made, we must judge the response and then react on the basis of the judgment—whether the step is performed correctly or incorrectly.

Let's list those functions in slightly more detail, because they are the very functions which have to be carried out by the frame logic we are constructing. They are the functions which have to be matched with frame capabilities:

- Display the environment in which the procedure is performed.

- Display the system upon which the procedure is performed.

- Display the current state of that system just prior to step performance.

- Display the controls which the student must use to respond.

- Display indications or cues that it is possible or necessary to perform the step.

- Accept the student's input.

- Judge the student's input.

- Respond to acceptable input (show realistic system response).

- Respond to unacceptable input.

- Branch appropriately following both acceptable and unacceptable input.

This list of functions is generalizable to virtually any procedural test item. The mention of the *system* in the list above should not be interpreted to mean that procedures are applied only to hardware or equipment systems. *System* used here refers to any organization of controls, cause-effect relationships, and sensed indications. Procedures include things as diverse as performing addition, executing a buy order in the stock market, performing an acid-base titration, or tying a knot. Each of these procedural environments has its own set of controls (for performing actions) and indications (for observing the results). Therefore, the system being manipulated can be either a physical or a conceptual system.

Figure 3 diagrams a relatively simple frame logic that carries out these functions. The frames of the diagram are labeled according to the functions they perform:

(X-1)RES: This frames creates the display which the student will respond to. It is actually is associated with the previous step, as you will see. It displays the results (RES) of the action from the prior step. The "X-1" in the frame name means that the frame belongs to the prior step, since the current step is Step "X" (which could stand for Step "5" or Step "2").

Example 1: If the prior step consisted of turning on a power switch, and assuming this was the correct action, this RES frame might show a light illuminating as a result, providing the (X-1) cue for performing Step X.

Example 2: If the previous step consisted of telling the person in a counseling scenario to relax, and if that was a proper thing to do, the result shown might include a video segment showing the client relaxing back in a chair and beginning to smile slightly, providing a cue for the next step of student action.

(X)INP: This frame presents an opportunity for the student to perform the current step. The only thing the student sees at this point is the left-over display from the prior step. There is no prompt to perform the current step (since this is a test) and there are no hints as to what the proper step might be (except perhaps standard controls present on the screen which allow the student to express an action). It is assumed that the student knows what to do once he or she has been directed to perform the entire procedure and has learned during Prompted and Unprompted Practice how to express an action. The student must determine both the correct step to perform at this point and the correct control action to perform it. Once an action is taken, it will be judged by this frame.

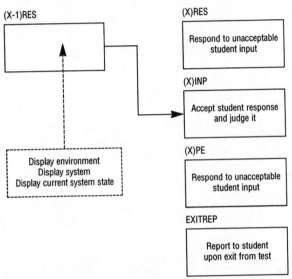

Figure 3. Frame logic for one step of test interaction.

Example 1: The student, looking at the illuminated light displayed by Step X-1, may now decide that the next step is to adjust its brightness. To do so, he or she selects the brightness adjustment control, which is also visible on the screen.

Example 2: The student, having gotten the client to relax, may now decide that the right thing to do is to ask a non-threatening question and so selects the ASK control icon at the bottom of the screen. This brings up a list of questions, some appropriate, and some inappropriate.

It should be apparent from the example that some responses may require more than one student action. That may require inserting one additional response frame after (X)INP, creating an (X)INP2 frame. It may also require a similar related set of associated feedback frames as will be connected to (X)INP.

(X)RES: If the student's decision to act has produced an acceptable performance for the step (or steps) anticipated at this point, then the result is shown by this frame, completing the cycle for one step, and the (X)RES for this step becomes the (X-1)RES for the next step. No artificial or designer-created feedback is presented, since this is a test.

(X)PE: If the student's action is unacceptable, then that is made known to the student through a message on this frame. Since this is a test, and since it would be prohibitive to continue with the test (and have to model all of the possible system actions following an incorrect response), the test in our sample tutorial terminates following any incorrect response. Notice that in accordance with the tutorial-level logic depicted in Figure 1, this means that the student will exit from the test block of the diagram and return (automatically) to the Main Menu to make another choice.

EXITREP: As the student leaves the test, following a report of the specific error, we have decided to give the student a report of how well the procedure was performed up to this point. This could include (as in this case) a report of the number of steps which were correctly performed. If this report is presented in a standard format and visually, it gives the student a goal for improvement of performance the next time around.

The above logic provides the testing interaction for one complete procedure step. Importantly, it does so in a way that tries as closely as possible to model the performance that would occur in the real world, excepting for the termination of the test due to error. No prompts are given to aid the student, and when correct responses are made, no artificial feedback is given, only the natural feedback which would normally follow an acceptable performance.

Because this logic serves for testing one step, the natural question is whether it might serve for testing *all* of the steps in the procedure. The answer is "yes," but with a qualification. This same bundle of logic can be repeated multiple times to allow the testing of several steps in sequence, as shown in Figure 4.

Templates

By creating a standard logic pattern for the test interaction, we have come across the templating issue of CBI design, and since it is an important productivity issue, we should spend a moment discussing some of its implications, before resuming our step-by-step treatment of the tutorial design process.

The logic pattern created for the test is a repeatable logic pattern (see Figure 4). A repeatable logic structure can be captured in reusable form in what is called a *template*. Using templates has some advantages and some drawbacks:

Advantages: Templates can be constructed once in an authoring tool, duplicated, and linked together with relative ease. This reduces the amount of logic construction at the keyboard and creates the logic more rapidly. Moreover, writers can write a templated message more easily, since its structure is regular. Communication with production staff as a whole is also easier, since a template makes it easier for them to understand the designer's intention and produce work that supports it. Templates are debugged before multiple copies are made of them, and so there is a lower likelihood of bug occurrence in the finished tutorial product using templates. Since the logic pattern is more regular, testing and the writing of test plans are easier, and product maintenance is easier.

Drawbacks: Templating requires that the expression of the instructional message fit within a logic pattern having certain dimensions, which can be confining in some cases and stretching in others. Little inconsistencies in instructional messages begin to introduce irregularities into the logic, and after a certain number of exceptions have been made, the benefits of templating disappear. It is almost more work to use a template which has multiple exceptions. Some subject-matter experts find templated thinking about their subject matter easy, and some do not. To some SMEs, templates are a welcome tool, but to others they are an annoyance. To yet others, they are an insurmountable obstacle, so some SMEs refuse to use them.

You must decide whether to use templates on a project-to-project basis. Templates are a very good idea in some cases and not in others. Designers faced with the requirement for high-volume development of a quality product, especially a highly interactive one, find templates to be very useful and to increase the productivity of their teams to a significant extent.

Path simulation versus model simulation

Another important digression from our step-by-step treatment: The logic pattern that has been designed for the test creates what is called a path simulation. It is described in Chapter 5 as the linear question frame pattern. To the student this pattern seems very much like interacting with a real system as long as no errors are made and the student stays on the path. (This is the pattern of **bold** frames in Figure 4.) When the student makes an error, however, the tutorial steps in to correct the error, and the feeling of a simulation disappears.

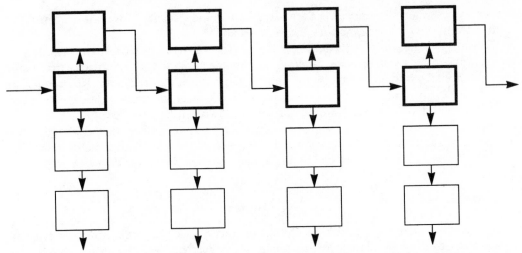

Figure 4. Chaining of identical step testing logics to form a complete test.

The alternative to this form of logic is called a *modeled* simulation. Modeled simulation is true, computed simulation, whereas path simulation is a type of pseudo-simulation. Once the student enters the interactive environment of a modeled simulation, any action within the bounds of the simulation can be performed at any time, with natural feedback (system indications) showing the student accurate consequences of both correct and incorrect actions. The implications of a modeled simulation are two-fold:

1. The modeled simulation does not automatically correct errors as they happen. It produces realistic responses to controls (natural feedback), but an instructor's corrections (artificial feedback) must come from a source other than the simulation model. This implies that a record of the student's actions may need to be drawn off and either monitored by an instructional program or examined following the simulated practice and used to generate a feedback message.

2. The logic preparations for a modeled simulation are more extensive and complicated than those for the preparation of a path simulation. They not only include the creation of a *model* of the environment which must be somehow programmed, but in order to include instructional functions, they also require an external feedback mechanism.

The modeled simulation and the feedback generator are described in Chapter 17 in more detail. Instructionally they represent a more flexible performance environment for the student, but they also give the designer more challenge in planning interventions which guide the student back to the correct path of performance once errors occur.

The choice of whether to use a path simulation or a modeled simulation as the unprompted practice vehicle is influenced by the following factors:

1. **The nature and complexity of the procedure being practiced:** Does the procedure have a complex branching structure (several points at which any of several actions are appropriate)? Modeled simulation for this procedure may be the only reasonable choice for creating a realistic practice environment due to production complexities (and therefore cost) for the alternative approach.

2. **The level of expertise of the student at the time of this practice:** Has the student practiced on more confining forms of practice to the point where no errors are being

made? Is he or she now ready to practice in an environment which, rather than paying attention to the individual step, can attend to decision-making and judgment aspects of the performance?

3. **The resources and skills available to the designer:** If the designer does not have access to a skilled programmer with some experience in creating simulations, or if the designer does not have those skills personally, then a modeled simulation can be a risky and (possibly) costly decision.

4. **The designer's desire for reusable practice logic:** The path simulation uses a set logical pattern to achieve its realistic interaction with the student. A modeled simulation will require the creation of logic routines of a different type. Both types can be created in a way that makes them reusable, but they will be reused in different ways.

5. **The importance of placing feedback close to the performance:** In the early stages of procedure learning, there is some evidence that allowing students to perform a procedure incorrectly can cause the formation of erroneous patterns of action which are later difficult to overcome. If the student is in the early stages of learning, a path simulation is probably preferable. However, in later stages of learning, a wider scope of action can allow the student to perform under more realistic conditions, including those in which an error has been made and must be corrected before proceeding. For this type of instruction, a modeled simulation is more suitable.

Drivers and superframes

Finally, before resuming our step-by-step treatment of the tutorial design process, we now want to describe two further mechanisms for logic which may have some attractive economic consequences. We call the first mechanism the driver or shell mechanism, and its main benefit is that instead of creating multiple instances of the frame logic—one for each step—a single set of the frame logic is created which is capable of executing all steps, being reused by each step.

Creating a driver is accomplished: (1) by creating individual frame logic elements without attaching them to specific display resources such as graphics or audio files, and (2) by creating branches between logic frames whose precise value is not specified to the logic until the movement is to be executed.

The exact display resources and frame to frame branch data, instead of being bound to the logic at the time the logic is created, are bound to the logic at the time it is executed. The names of the display resources and branching destinations are given to the empty logic by a data file which contains the specific data necessary for each frame.

This data supplies the name of one or more graphic or audio files to be used in the display, the location of selection (mouse click) areas of the display, and the names of the destination frames related to each selection area. As a frame is executed, the driver asks the data file for that frame's data and then uses it to execute the frame. As mouse-clicking and branching lead to a new frame, the old frame's data is discarded, and the new frame's data is requested, and the driver's cycle executes that frame.

When a shell structure is used, the main activity of designing frame sequences consists of: (1) building the shell itself, and (2) building the data file that describes each frame to be executed.

The second economical logic variation goes beyond the driver and requires the creation of only one frame for the entire tutorial. This might be called a *superframe*. It consists of the shell structure carried to its extreme, with all of the frames in the shell being collapsed into a single frame whose content and behavior are governed at any moment by the content of a data file.

A superframe is simply a single frame which turns on or turns off frame functions in response to data from a data file. It is a one-frame shell.

The idea of the superframe is easier to grasp if you return to Figure 3 of Chapter 4. This frame logic could serve as a superframe if data were supplied to it which functions to execute and which to ignore. Therefore, in addition to the display and branching data required for a regular shell structure, the superframe requires only the additional data defining which frame function switches to turn on or off. In this book we do not treat the details of the superframe, but we suggest that you look carefully at the frame construction technique used by *Quest*, considering whether you could build a superframe using *Quest's* basic frame-building elements. Whatever tool you use, the shell and the superframe can in most cases greatly reduce the cost and complexity of design.

Step 8B: Diagram unprompted practice logic.

Let's resume our construction of logic for the sample tutorial where we left off on page 435. Unprompted practice is a very test-like practice; it does not give any help to the student. Students can use it as many times as they wish to prepare themselves for the test, and since there is no score recorded for this practice, they can do it without any penalty or stress. They can concentrate strictly on learning the procedure.

The interaction for unprompted practice is almost identical with that for the test (see Figure 3). The difference is that the test records a score as the student exits (either successfully or unsuccessfully), while the unprompted practice may or may not, depending on the designer's choice of which would be of more benefit to the student.

No new logic structures are created for our sample tutorial in this step. This is an important discovery. By beginning with definition of the test logic, we have simplified our design task greatly, and as you will see, the remaining logic definition, including those parts which make presentations of information, will consist of further elaborations of and additions to this central core of practice logic.

Step 8C: Diagram prompted practice logic.

Prompted practice provides much more support for the student than unprompted practice. As we have designed it, it will provide a prompt before each step and feedback following each step. We have designed this way in order to support the student's still-weak recall of the procedure.

Just as we made a list of functions to be carried out by the test logic, we will begin the same way to define the prompted practice functions. They are listed below. *Italics* indicate functions which are already found in the test logic and which we may reuse.

> *Display the environment in which the procedure is performed.*
> *Display the system upon which the procedure is performed.*
> *Display the current state of that system.*
> *Display the controls of the system which the student must use to respond.*
> *Display indications that it is possible or necessary to perform the step.*
> Present a quiz item testing step-related factual knowledge.
> Accept the student's input to the quiz item.
> Judge the quiz response.
> Respond to an unacceptable quiz response.
> Respond to an acceptable quiz response.
> Prompt the student with the name of the step (but not the action).
> *Accept the student's performance input.*

Judge the student's performance input.
Respond to acceptable performance input.
Respond verbally to acceptable performance input.
Prepare the display to move on to the next step.
Respond to unacceptable performance input.
Inform the student of the correct response in cases of error.
Prepare the display for a second response.

Figure 5 shows the frame logic which carries out these prompted practice functions. The new functions from the list above are shown as unshaded frames. Functions carried over from the test and unprompted practice logic are shaded in Figure 5.

The frames and functions shown in Figure 5 operate as described below.

(X-1)RES: This frame performs the same function it did in the test logic: It prepares the screen for the present step by displaying the results of the previous step.

(X)QUIZ(N): This new addition to the logic inserts a quiz question into the prompted practice. Sometimes step performance does not cause a student to use certain key facts of knowledge while performing a step, and the designer may feel it important to confirm that the student possesses that knowledge. (For instance, knowledge about a safety factor which must be considered.) A quiz question is one way of ensuring that. The (N) placed at the end of the frame name indicates more than one quiz question may be inserted per step of the procedure.

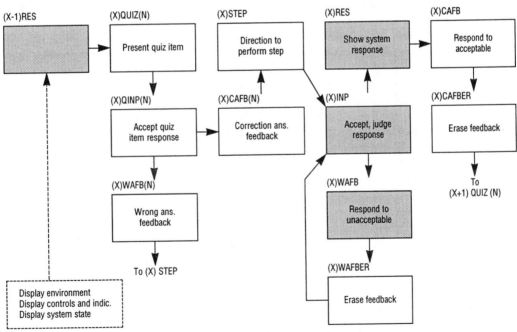

Figure 5. Frame logic for prompted practice.

(X)QINP(N): This frame accepts the student's answer to the quiz question and judges it.

(X)QWAFB(N): This frame provides feedback when the student's answer to a quiz question is incorrect. We have it designed not only supply the bad news but also to correct the misinformation that led to the student's error. The feedback placed in this spot can include anything the designer feels will help student. This may be a single statement, a short sequence of frames emphasizing the corrected information, or a complete re-teaching of the step. We have designed for a single statement to be provided for our sample tutorial.

(X)QCAFB(N): This frame provides correct answer feedback for a quiz question. It does not need to say very much. It can be something as simple as a sound effect.

(X)STEP: This is an instruction to the student to perform the step of the procedure. It is placed following the quiz questions. After this message appears, the next event in the logic is the opportunity to perform the step. Just prior to this frame, it is possible that the display may need to be cleared of the correct or incorrect answer feedbacks which follow a quiz question. If that is the case, just insert an additional clean-up frame before this one or use this frame's display to erase the excess from the previous frames.

(X)INP: This input frame is a direct carry-over from the unprompted practice logic. It is the frame where the student performs the step. It also judges the student's action.

(X)RES: This carry-over frame displays the indications (the *results*, the natural feedback) which follow correct step performance.

(X)CAFB: This frame is new. It displays feedback written by the designer that tells the student that the step was correctly performed. This message can be short and may consist of simply, "That's right." However, it can also be used to give emphasis to the indications which have appeared by enumerating them and drawing the student's attention to them.

(X)CAFBER: This frame clears the display of any unneeded correct answer feedback messages or highlighting effects prior to moving to the next step.

(X)WAFB: Following an incorrect step action, this element of the logic presents a feedback message informing the student that the step was wrong. It probably also names the correct action so that the student can perform the step correctly. Figure 5 shows that after cleaning up the display, the logic takes the student back to the input frame to try the step again. Without some information regarding the correct step to be taken, the student could end up in an endless loop, not knowing how to perform the step correctly and so not knowing how to move ahead.

(X)WAFBER: This frame erases wrong answer feedback and makes the display ready for the student to attempt the step again.

The logic in Figure 5 gives the student an opportunity to practice procedure steps in a guided, feedback-rich environment. It is a suitable form of practice for a student in the early stages of learning a procedure. It is good preparation for the unprompted practice which withdraws these supports.

It is important to draw attention to the quizzing function embedded within this logic. It is an optional feature of this practice logic. Because we are instructing with a computer, we can design practice interactions carried out in very realistic practice environments. This practice is action- or performance-oriented rather than information-oriented.

However, in our enthusiasm for interactivity we must recall that performance of a procedure requires an individual not only to be able to perform a sequence of steps but to use facts and information which make decision-making possible. If the student were to perform the procedure under all possible and relevant conditions (thus making use of the full range of information in decision-making), we could exhaustively test the student's ability to perform the procedure. But there would be a high price in instructional time for this type of instruction, and since it would be highly repetitive, students might find such practice and testing to be an ordeal.

If we are not content to assume that the student knows all necessary procedure-related information, as well as the steps themselves, we can insert one or more quiz questions into the prompted practice logic. This allows us to check and correct errors in the student's memory. If errors on quiz questions persist during unprompted practice, the tutorial can be designed to take note of it and append an additional information quiz to the unprompted practice or to the test.

The new logic added to provide prompted practice incorporates within itself the heart of the logic of the unprompted practice. This reuse of logic between instructional functions is an additional benefit of templating of logic. It makes possible the design of several versions of practice and several versions of presentation and demonstration for a fraction of the otherwise high logic cost. Simplified, reusable logic is a worthwhile design goal.

There is benefit for the student from templated logic as well as for the designer. The message incorporated within a generic logic pattern is easy for the student to apprehend, since it is placed within a consistent context of information and interaction *roadsigns*. This means that the student can pay less attention to decoding and understanding each display and pay more attention to the instructional message itself. This reusable logic is one of the techniques for keeping information moving freely on the student's information highway.

Step 8D: Diagram demonstration logic.

For procedure instruction, a demonstration demonstrates steps being performed. Such a demonstration has multiple purposes. It clarifies verbal descriptions and provides an immense amount of additional information, much of which is simply impossible to verbalize. It can demonstrate technique, it can demonstrate timing, it can demonstrate complex actions, and it shows the environment and the implements associated with the procedure.

One critically important but often overlooked purpose of a demonstration is to make visible to the student the *internal* thought processes of a competent performer as each step is selected and then performed. If appropriate commentary is supplied with the demonstration, it can be the vehicle for modeling the *invisible* thinking of an expert performer that leads to the *visible* performance and the *visible* result.

Virtually all strategies use some form of demonstration as a technique because most performances, whether fragmented or highly integrated, need to be modeled within the student's view. During concept-using instruction, the demonstration includes not only presentation of a prime example of the class, but an example of the expert's thought process as an example is being examined and classified.

Most of the demonstrations found in common instructional practice are superficial and neglect to model the expert's thought process, ignoring the fact that it is the critical activity that lies at the heart of performance. There is reason to believe that modeling is one of the most efficient, powerful, and frequently-used learning techniques applied by humans as they learn without teachers and from their own experience.

For our sample tutorial, we decide that the demonstration will be provided as motion video and that the performer (Lynn the mechanic) will narrate each step and each decision that is part of the performance. We also decide that each step of the performance have a clearly visible beginning and ending point and that they will be verbalized as well. In this way it will be possible to divide the demonstration into steps so that the video for each one may be played and replayed separately, as well as being played as an entire procedure.

We must decide how this type of demonstration fits within the logic of the tutorial. For the purposes of our sample tutorial, we have decided to combine the demonstration with the presentation for each step. Therefore, let's move to the next section and design the logic for both at once.

Step 8E: Diagram presentation logic.

It may seem strange to talk about presentation "interactions," but they are not only possible, they are desirable. The computer is as good as any medium at presenting information. This is mainly because today's multimedia computer *incorporates* the other media.

However, when we use the computer as just a slide viewer or a text book, or even as a non-interactive video system, it becomes an added expense without added effectiveness. Computers are ideally suited for providing interactivity. One of the hardest types of new thinking required for the proper use of the instructional computer is to conceive of *useful interactions* rather than thinking just in terms of glittering presentations.

For our sample tutorial, we will look for ways to make the presentation of step information interactive. One way to keep a presentation active and participatory is to give the student control over the information sequence. This is the technique we will use for our sample tutorial, mainly because it is the easiest. The core of information to be presented for each step has been captured in the content table. It is categorized there under several headings. We will provide the information to the student under some of those headings. We must therefore design a menuing system that places the order of information in student hands.

Before we do that, however, we must decide on the headings to be used for the delivery of the message. The content table has too many separate headings for students to choose from, so we will consolidate them into a message table which has only three or four columns. We will also add the demonstration as a category of information which can be requested.

How shall we make the information available? Figure 6 shows how on a simple menu, logic can incorporate the presentation and demonstration into a generic logic structure which can be repeated for all steps. Notice that in addition to observing the step in a demonstration, we have also added a description frame for each step, (X)BY, which tells the student the actions to use to perform that step. This is especially important when the controls supplied by the computer differ from the controls used in the real world to perform the procedure.

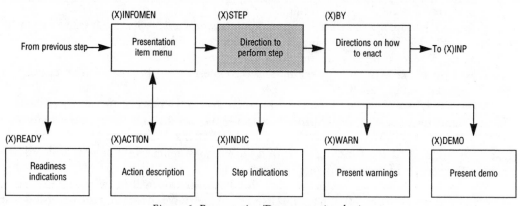

Figure 6. Presentation/Demonstration logic.

The unshaded elements of Figure 6 represent the new additions to the generic logic. They consist of the following frames:

(X)INFOMEN: This menu frame presents a choice to the student of the available presentation messages for each step. There will be five choices. The double-headed arrows leading from this menu and back indicate branching to one or more display frames and then back to the menu to make another choice. The video demonstration will be one of the choices. There will also be a selection by which the student indicates that he or she is finished and ready to move on to the self-demonstration. The heading of this menu will come from the "Name/Number" column of the content table.

Although the action of this logic is to branch out to an information item and then back to the menu, screen design techniques will be used that combine the visual aspects of the menu with the information given in each menu item. It will seem to the student as if the same single screen was providing all of the information and menus, even though there are many individual frames involved in creating the display.

(X)READY: This frame or group of frames describes the conditions that exist before the step is performed which indicate that it is time to perform the step, that the step may be performed, or that it is possible to perform the step. Any of the frame patterns from Chapter 5 may be placed in this position, though the most likely is a single frame or short linear sequence. Source content for the messages of these frames will come from the "When" column of the content table.

(X)ACTION: This frame (or group of frames) describes the action performed in order to execute the step. Its content comes from the "What," "Where," and "Technique" columns of the content table and includes also the demonstration, which will be a video segment that incorporates the content of many of the columns. If we wanted to, we could also incorporate the demonstration video here.

(X)INDIC: This frame will describe the indications which result concurrent with and following step execution, including the terminal cues which indicate that the step has been completed. This frame will be accompanied by a repeat of the demonstration video sequence with the indications highlighted.

(X)WARN: This frame or sequence of frames provides the information from the remaining columns of the content table: "Why," "Meaning," "Warning," and "Emphasis." This will be a sequence of frames, marked with the categories of the information being supplied.

(X)DEMO: This frame will simply play the demonstration video. The student will be able to play it independently, viewing it as many times as desired.

(X)BY: This frame is considered a part of the self-demonstration. It begins in the frame named (X)STEP, which directs the student to perform the step by naming the step. (X)BY names the specific action for carrying out the step. It says, "Carry out the step by (doing some action)." This is an important message, made necessary by the use of the computer, because the computer interaction for carrying out the step will differ in some ways from the real world. The student will not actually turn a knob; during instruction he or she will mouse click a knob or mouse click a setting for it. This is a somewhat artificial control action necessitated by the medium. Since it will not always be apparent to the student what kind of action is expected, the (X)BY message tells the student what is expected.

Following the (X)BY frame, the logic continues with the inclusion (not shown in Figure 6) of an instance of prompted practice logic. Having been instructed to perform the step in a self-demonstration, the student is thus able to perform it. The inclusion of prompted practice logic within the presentation function not only increases the amount of content-relevant interaction, it also places the first performance of the step very close to the point of the instruction.

Our choices for providing the presentation to the student included options other than menuing. We could simply have placed the information for each step into a pre-set sequence and made that sequence the same for each step. This would have been page turning. Our choice to menu the information was motivated mainly by the desire for more interaction. We realize that this interaction does not inherently ask the student to process new knowledge and therefore represents a less than ideal quality of interaction. Nonetheless, it does cause the student to be aware of the classification of new knowledge and represents an improvement over mere presentation of information in paragraph form.

It is also an option to insert questions into the presentation. Carefully chosen, they could be a means of helping the student to think critically about the cause-effect linkages in the procedure. For instance, as a particular step was described, the student might be asked (before being told) what kind of reaction was expected from the system in response to the step action—a noise? a movement? Such questions can be non-judged and therefore non-threatening. This type of interaction is more content-relevant.

Step 8F: Diagram auxiliary function logic.

At this point, the inner workings of the auxiliary features (Introduction, Glossary and Summary) are defined. The Introduction will consist of a simple page-turning sequence of frames. The Glossary in our tutorial will consist of a simple menu with glossary words listed. Upon clicking a word, the definition will appear in a window over the face of the menu list. This surface appearance is achieved through the use of a simple Menu pattern from Chapter 5—a menu with a very large number of choices.

The Summary for our sample tutorial will consist of presentation of the content table for the procedure and controls with which the student can scan it. This will consist of a family of menu frames which present one portion of the table and allow the student to move laterally or vertically to the next section of the table. The sections displayed by each frame will overlap sufficiently to allow the student to maintain orientation. Figure 7 illustrates this logic, which is a type of closed menu tree with only one level.

At this point in logic design, all of the separate elements of logic have been defined, and it is possible to link them together into a complete tutorial. Most frequently, this would require such a large area that a single diagram for the entire tutorial is not created. Using the top-level logic diagram created in Step 6, however, it becomes easy to see that the logics defined to this point fit into the small boxes within each of the strategic blocks. This automatically connects the separate logics together and defines the branch-in and branch-out points where transition is made from one group of logic to another.

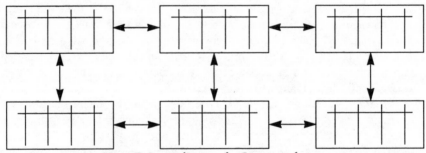

Figure 7. Logic diagram for Summary feature.

Step 9: Create message tables.

Decisions made during logic creation have automatically structured the message table. There must be messages to fill the message slots created in the logic. Where there are feedbacks, the feedback message must be written; where there are step descriptions, they too must be written; where there are pictures, they must be described in detail. In this step, those messages will be identified, and a message table will be constructed to hold them. A main source of message table messages will be the content table constructed in an earlier step.

A message table is much different from a content table, and the two must not be confused. A message table contains the *exact wording* of the instructional message (and descriptions for graphic, audio, and video portions). Some (not all) of these elements are already included within the content table, but they are in the rough form in which they were originally recorded, not in a form ready for consumption by the student. Creating a message table converts all of the content table elements into a form ready for consumption by the student and detailed enough to guide the work of the production staff, who will turn them into media elements.

To create a message table, we study the logic which has been created, identifying the existence of message slots. A small portion of the message tables for our sample tutorial—covering the prompted practice—are provided in Table 4. They contain some message content not included in the content tables: (1) transition messages and directions to the student, (2) feedback messages, and (3) descriptions of non-verbal portions of the message. This last category of message elements can be large.

Table 4. Message table for the sample tutorial.

Message category	Message
(2)QUIZ(1) contents (Step 2, first quiz question)	**Visual:** Inset visual of the dashboard, Water in Fuel light illuminated. **Verbal:** What does it mean when this light is illuminated during starting but then goes out? (A) There is water in the fuel, (B) The lamp and its circuits are functioning properly, (C) It is not safe to start the engine.
(2)QINP(1) contents	**Visual:** No change. **Verbal:** Select by clicking an answer.
(2)QWAFB(1) contents	**Visual:** No change. **Verbal:** If the light illuminates and then goes out, it means that the lamp and its circuits have been tested and are functioning properly.
(2)QCAFB(1) contents	**Visual:** No change. **Verbal:** That is correct.
(2)STEP contents	**Visual:** Erase remnants of all Quiz question messages. **Verbal:** Now perform Step 2.
(2)INP contents	**Visual:** No change. **Verbal:** No change.
(2)RES contents	**Visual:** Water in Fuel and Glow Plugs lights illuminate. **Verbal:** Buzzing is heard.
(2)CAFB contents	**Visual:** No change. **Verbal:** Good.
(2)CAFBER contents	**Visual:** Water in Fuel light goes out. Glow Plugs light goes out. **Verbal:** Buzzing stops.
(2)WAFB contents	**Visual:** Freeze on visual. No change. **Verbal:** Buzzing stops. Sorry. You should turn the key in the ignition to the third detent now to start the engine. Click this message and try the step again.
(2)WAFBER contents	**Visual:** Erase feedback screen additions, if any. **Verbal:** No change.

The message table can take several forms, depending on the preferences and resources of the designer. Ultimately the design process will result in the creation of a complete and detailed design for the tutorial on production sheets (which will be described in a later step). The critical task for now is to record all message elements in an exact form at some place where they can be gathered to the production sheets.

The forms a message table can take include:

1. Preliminary notations on the logic diagram: Designers who are trying to move very rapidly capture messages first as notes scribbled on copies of the logic diagrams. After noting message content, the designer can later create production sheets which contain the exact and final version of the message, as well as production specifications for the non-verbal message elements.

2. A separate message table: In some cases (such as in development over long distances by a fragmented team) it is worthwhile to create a formal message table. This table is often not in a standard columnar table form. It can be a structured list of messages, including their names and exact content. This is the method we have used for Table 4.

3. Production sheets: A designer may decide to record the messages directly onto production sheets (see Step 12). This approach is essential for very large projects or projects for which there is a staff with diverse production skills.

Step 10: Channelize messages, specify continuity blocks, design screens.

In this step, the issues of display management become important. Details of displays and the manner of representation of the message elements are determined. These detailed decisions have been awaiting the completion of the logic structure of the tutorial. They are as important and as powerful in their influence as logic decisions, but attempts to design the details before deciding major structural issues leads to confusion, wasted time, and an inferior product.

It is difficult to separate this step from the previous step. The previous step supposedly created message tables. However, until the decisions of this step are complete, the message tables cannot be fully completed. So far, only a general division between visual and verbal channels has been specified for the delivery of messages. Now the details must be added to indicate which verbal (text? audio?) and which visual (video? graphic? motion? still?) channels will be used for each message.

In a design, every decision influences other decisions. Suffice it to say that many of the decisions of this step—specifically those on channelization—are already presaged in the message tables constructed in the previous step, since the visual and verbal channels have been separated there.

The decisions made at this point will include all of the decisions described in Chapter 19 on Display Management. They can be grouped under three tasks: channelizing the message, specifying continuity blocks, and designing screens. Two of these—channelizing message and defining continuity blocks—interact closely, another example of design steps which influence each other.

Channelizing the message: Channelizing the message means assigning each message element to the media channel that will be used to communicate it. This may be a visual channel (graphic, video, text), an audio channel (spoken language, sounds), or any other communication channel which the chosen delivery system can support.

Message elements, represented by *columns,* or message categories, on the message table, should be assigned consistently to a single channel. A designer may choose to signal correct answers on a quiz to the student with a "boing" sound effect rather than with words. This decision is a channelization decision. All hints may be given as audio messages, all corrective feedback may be given in text, and all examples may be represented through motion video. This is channelization.

In addition to selecting the delivery channel for each message element in a standard way, the timing of elements must be determined as a standard also. On some occasions, two channels will be used to convey parts of the same message (e.g., a visual emphasis, accompanied by an auditory verbal message explaining it). When two channels are used, carefully coordinating their timing can be critical to avoiding confusion and miscommunication. Timing of multiple-channel communications is one of the less-researched areas of display management, but the research that exists points to the importance of timing as a factor in student understanding.

Channelization is the means by which consistency of message delivery is ensured. The student recognizes in this consistency the message roadsigns which increase efficiency in processing the instructional message.

Specifying continuity blocks and designing screens: A continuity block is a sequence of frames within a tutorial executed without a complete screen erasure. Within a continuity block, successive logical elements may change a portion of the screen, but significant portions of the screen remain unchanged, establishing a kind of visual continuity for the student. As long as the screen does not change entirely, the student feels he or she is still in the same psychological location within the tutorial. The designer also benefits from the use of continuity blocks. They make the writing of certain sections of the tutorial much more structured and straightforward.

Each continuity block is associated with a screen format which designates geographically how the areas of the screen will be used to present visual message and interaction elements. Each screen layout designates areas to be used by specific message elements: presentation messages, feedback messages, directions to the student, graphics, video, and other things which become psychologically tagged or labeled for the student by their location.

The goal of defining continuity blocks is to reduce the number of complete erasures of the screen during instruction. It is also to provide re-entry points for the student who opts to use one of the tutorial's auxiliary functions (such as Summary or Glossary) and then return to the instruction. Instead of trying to re-enter a block in the middle, where the screen may be incompletely built and difficult to manage, the student can be placed at the beginning of the continuity block, the point at which the screen does erase or refresh completely before beginning another building sequence.

How are the continuity blocks and screen designs used in our sample tutorial? Our tutorial consists of an Introduction and four strategic sections: the Presentation/Demo, Prompted Practice, Unprompted Practice, and Test. The introduction has two sub-divisions, and the strategic sections are divided into blocks corresponding to procedural steps. Each of these is a continuity block and requires a screen format to be assigned.

Figure 8 diagrams the screen format for the Glossary and Summary continuity blocks of the Introduction.

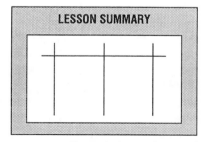 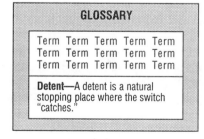

Figure 8. Screen formats for lesson summary and glossary.

For the strategic sections of the tutorial, we will assign the screen format diagrammed in Figure 9.

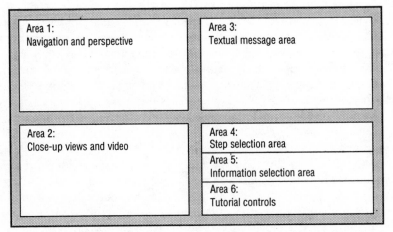

Figure 9. Screen format for strategic portions of the tutorial.

This screen format is flexible enough for use during presentation and practice both. The screen is divided into four main quadrants, and one of the quadrants is subdivided into three smaller areas. The areas are used for the following functions:

Area 1: This area provides a visual navigation ability to the student. It will contain the major orientation visual for the entire procedure, consisting of a far view of the interior of the diesel vehicle being started. Using this area, the student will be able to see the larger context for close-up views, which will be shown in Area 2.

Area 2: This area will present close-up views of controls and indicators. When the Water in Fuel light is the subject of informational presentations, it will appear in this area, while Area 1 will still contain the general perspective view.

Area 3: This area will be used for textually-delivered messages, such as those obtained through selections from (X)INFOMEN see Figure 6.

Area 4: This area will contain controls for step selection during presentation if the tutorial design provides for that. Due to the difficulty of managing the display, the student will not be given control over practice step order. If the student is not given choice over step order during presentation, then this area contains only information (in this case a title and perhaps a set of numbered buttons) showing which step is being presented.

Area 5: This area presents controls to the student for information selection. It is the area in which the (X)INFOMEN choices are expressed.

Area 6: This area is reserved for general tutorial controls which allow the student to exit the tutorial and obtain all of the auxiliary services provided with the tutorial.

Table 5 shows the correspondence between sections of the display and logic elements diagrammed in Figures 3 through 6. Bold names are frames with message elements to display. This table shows all messages channeled through screen text. If the audio channel is used for messages, the table is changed.

Designing screen layouts requires judgment about the placement, size, and readability of graphics and video as well as the placement of controls. The look of the screens has a major impact on the student's impressions of the tutorial. Experienced designers frequently involve the skills of an artist or graphics designer in the creation of screen formats.

Table 5. Assignment of message elements to display areas.

Logical Function	Screen Allocation
Presentation—**Infomen** and its subordinate frames except **Demo**—(see Figure 6)	Choices: Area 5 Information: Area 4
Presentation—**Demo**—(see Figure 6)	Choice: Area 5 Information: Area 2
Prompted practice—**Step**—(Figure 5)	Information: Area 3
Prompted practice—**By** (Figure 5)	Information: Area 3
Prompted practice—**Input**—(Figure 5)	Interaction: Area 2
Prompted practice—**Result**—(Figure 5)	Information: Area 2
Prompted practice—**CAFB**—(Figure 5)	Information: Area 3
Prompted practice—**WAFB**—(Figure 5)	Information: Area 3
Unprompted practice—**PE**—(Figure 3)	Information: Area 3

Step 11: Create production sheets.

The best vehicle we have found for the capture of CBI tutorial design details is the Production Sheet. Figure 10 is an example of one of these. A new production sheet form is tailored for the needs of each CBI project.

Some people mistakenly use the terms *script* and *storyboard* to refer to production sheets—terms inappropriately borrowed from the design of other forms of media such as video or film. Production sheets are much more than a storyboard and much more than a script. They are the appropriate vehicle for the expression of CBI tutorial design details.

Each production sheet contains the graphic, audio, video and text specifications that are necessary to describe changes made to the display by one frame. It also specifies the logical behavior for one frame in terms of timing, click areas, branching destinations, and so forth. One production sheet provides the tutorial *script* for one authoring system frame.

The production sheet is needed for the design of CBI tutorials because CBI is a non-linear medium. In a highly interactive tutorial, you cannot predict where the student's actions or choices will cause you to branch next. Linear systems for representing CBI—such as scripts or storyboards—are not sufficient to express all of the details—particularly the branching—of the design. When scripts and storyboards are used by CBI designers, the result is always either an incomplete expression of the design (which makes production difficult) or, more frequently, a linear form of CBI which reads sequentially like a video script. The production sheet is ideal for the expression of non-linear designs, because it provides a form for the collection of data for one authoring system logic element—frame or icon, and in CBI, that is the element which is actually produced.

The entries and uses of the production sheet require some explaining. Remember during this discussion that the production sheet should be tailored to the individual project; it reflects the characteristics of the authoring tool and the specific media forms being used. A production sheet for an *Authorware* user is different from one for a *Quest* user.

DISPLAY Frame Name _____ Logic template _____

Message table cell _____

Graphic spec _____

_____

Graphic source _____

Graphic filename _____

Video spec _____

_____

Video source _____

Raw video location: Tape_____ SMPTE begin_____ SMPTE end_____

Intg video location: Tape _____ SMPTE begin_____ SMPTE end_____

Final video location: Tape_____ SMPTE begin_____ SMPTE end_____

Audio spec _____Integrated? Yes No

Audio content _____

_____ Audio filename_____

Sound efx _____

Raw audio location: Tape_____Begin _____ End_____

Final audio location: Tape_____Begin _____ End_____

Text spec _____

Text content _____

_____

Text filename _____

Check Vdisc frame numbers: Begin_____ End_____

Final Vdisc frame numbers: Begin_____ End_____

LOGIC Next frame name_____Back/Bookmark frame_____

Text menu? Yes No   Area menu? Yes No   MC Question Yes No

Selection/Area	Destination	Variable change
_____	_____	_____
_____	_____	_____
_____	_____	_____
_____	_____	_____
_____	_____	_____
_____	_____	_____
_____	_____	_____
_____	_____	_____

Figure 10. Sample production sheet.

A project may specialize its production sheets so that there is more than one variety of sheet. Since there can be different types of authoring frame, there can be different types of production sheet, each one collecting the data relevant for a particular type of frame or icon. The Production sheet we have provided as an example is generic; it is not specific to one frame type. It is capable of capturing data for any of the types described in this book.

There are three main areas of our generic production sheet: the display description, the logic description, and the media production data. The display description may contain specifications for an entire screen full of material, or it may specify the change of only a small fraction of the screen. It may add to or subtract from the pre-existing display or both. This means that as you read production sheets, you must also keep in mind what may already be on the display. Only then can you interpret how the new frame will modify it and what the resulting experience will be like for the student. Remember also that the display consists of several forms of visual content (video motion, graphics, text, etc.) as well as non-visual audio and possibly other input and output channels. Only by imaging the totality of all of these channels and their timing and orchestration can you interpret a set of production sheets.

Let's explore the sample production sheet in Figure 10 geographically. The upper half is the display data, and in the upper right corner is a rectangular area devoted to the sketching of display contents which are added (or subtracted) by this production sheet. The display description requires several entries:

Frame name: The name by which this frame can be referred to. There must be a unique and permanent identifier for the frame in order to keep track of it. You can see that by using templated logic and by devising a naming system, we have given names to every frame in our sample logics.

Logic template: The name of the logic template (e.g., prompted practice, presentation, etc.) is useful information which helps to locate the frame more easily.

Message table cell: This refers to the specific cell(s) from the message table containing the messages to be used with this frame. The messages may be delivered through one or more media channels. For this entry, you may reference a table cell rather than copying the exact contents of the cell if you wish. This, of course, implies that you have a system for naming each cell, which may be something as simple as "C-4."

Graphic spec, video spec, audio spec, text spec: These entries consist of *descriptions* of channelized messages. They can *describe in words* a graphic which is sketched into the display rectangle, a video motion sequence, an audio message, or the manner of presenting a text message. The blank rectangle to the right can be used to capture a sketch of the intended graphic.

Audio content, text content: These entries may contain the exact wording of a text or audio message.

Sound efx: Non-verbal signals are described here, such as the sound of an engine starting or a bell to signal a correct answer.

Graphic source, video source: If the designer has in mind a specific existing piece of graphic or video, or if there is a graphic or video which is being produced for another production sheet, that can be referenced here.

Graphic filename, audio filename, text filename: Frequently, if multimedia is being used, there will be computer filenames associated with audio messages, graphic content, or even text strings. Those entries are recorded here.

Integrated audio: Audio may be produced as a separate entity or as the sound track of a video source (such as a computer movie or videodisc motion sequence). Integrated audio is audio which is produced in conjunction with another source. Checking here alerts the production specialist of that fact.

Raw, integrated, and final video location: As new video is produced, it is produced first in a raw form, then it is integrated into production forms ready for transfer to either a videodisc or a computer file. The video production staff uses the production sheet to record the data showing where these various forms exist. This makes the data public and available to all of the production staff.

Raw and final audio location: This area is used for cataloging and tracking of the various production versions of audio messages.

Check and final Vdisc frame numbers: If a videodisc is being used, the tracking of locations of various message resources is important. It is so discouraging to lose a single frame of video on a videodisc filled with tens of thousands of other frames and not be able to locate it.

The logic portion of the production sheet has equally important entries:

Next frame name: If the present frame has only one branching destination, and if the branch is an immediate branch (no action required by the student), then that destination is recorded here. If there is a delay before the branch is made, its value is also recorded here. If the branch requires some student input to initiate it, then the data for the branch is recorded under "Selection/Area."

Back/bookmark frame: If there is a frame at the beginning of a continuity block which is branched to when the BACK control is used by the student, then the name of that frame is recorded here.

Text menu: The text menu places choices on the screen for the student to pick from. The choice will be expressed as a keyboard entry. A check here distinguishes the frame from the Area type of menu described below.

Area menu: If the student response to a menu frame is to select an area of the screen by clicking or touching, then an Area menu is being used and a check would be placed here.

MC Quest: If the student's choice is judged, as in a multiple choice question, then a check is placed here.

Selection/Area: There may be many responses gathered by a frame from the student. The legitimate ones—ones to be noticed and responded to—are recorded here. The last entry in this list should be an *unexpected* response, so that inputs can be handled which are not anticipated.

Destination: The destination frame for each response is recorded here.

Variable change: If a change in the value of a score or some other variable is to accompany a particular selection by the student, then that is noted in this column, along with the increment (in points) to be added to the variable for this question.

This production sheet is only a generic sample. It is a leftover from one of our own previous projects. A little examination will show you that it is missing entries for display event timing, acceptance of textual input from the student, and on-frame feedback messages following questions. These things were not required by the project from which we borrowed the production sheet, but they may be for yours, so you will want to modify this basic sheet idea to fit the needs of your project.

Though a project may begin by using the production sheet from a former project in order to get started, the old production sheet will soon evolve into a form unique to the new project. As you will see in a later step, the production sheet is for the whole *production team* to obtain and record production data for individual media or message elements.

Step 12: Review with SME and designer.

Once the first draft of the message table has left the writer, it must pass an examination by the subject-matter expert. Sometimes the translation from content table to message table does violence to accuracy. The subject-matter expert must approve the message table. He or she should be carefully briefed on the scope and intent of each review as it occurs. There are certain things for him or her to pay attention to (like accuracy and terminology), but there are others that are beyond the pale of subject-matter expertise, and you must clear these issues with the SME in advance.

The best way to discipline reviews with a SME is to provide a review checklist which enumerates the main concerns of each review. As the SME sees all of the review checklists together, he or she should be able to find comfort in the fact that all of the relevant questions have their moment for consideration and that nothing the SME might wish to contribute will be neglected. The alternative to disciplined reviews is reviews late in development which try to overturn or revise decisions that were made early in the design process and should have been reviewed then. When the script has passed the SME's test, its message is formed, and it is ready for the next stage of development.

Step 13: Add production sheet details during media production.

Once your tutorial design is captured on production sheets, you have completed most of the design task, and production begins. Surprisingly, there is probably more data added to the production sheet after production begins than before. This is because the development staff obtains information from the production sheet that allows them to perform their job, but as they do their job they also produce new data. This has to be recorded on the production sheet for use by yet other production staff members in their work.

For instance, the audio person on your staff will be tasked with producing several audio clips. The content for these is provided in the production sheets. Once recordings have been made, the location of the audio segments actually selected for use has to be recorded. You do not want this done on the back of an envelope or a scrap of paper that may be lost, especially if your audio person is likely to come down with a cold just when you need the data the most. The audio person records the data on the production sheet, along with the other data about that audio clip. As production proceeds, the name of the file for the audio clip is entered by the person who digitizes the audio, or perhaps the audio goes onto a master tape. This new location data must be recorded as well.

Every production worker adds to the production sheets in this way. It is to the benefit of a project leader to be sure that entries are being made. Though time pressures will encourage staff members to cut corners and forget to record data, it is important, and it can save much more time than it takes, since later you do not have to search for or re-create data that has been lost.

Step 14: Produce authoring logic and integrate message.

The production sheets are now complete, and the tutorial is ready to be entered into the computer. Worst case, you (or someone else) will be programming in a computer language. Best case, you will be using an authoring system which eliminates some or all of the programming. Such systems tend to be efficient for products like ours that use a standard logic pattern, which do not include the use of simulations, and which do not make requirements beyond the capabilities of the authoring system. Whatever system you use for entry, you should organize the effort carefully to minimize the level of effort required, since the entry process can be the most costly part of CBI development. It can be even more costly than procuring CBI workstations.

This fact surprises most designers, but it is correct. CBI development costs include hardware and software costs, plus facilities and furniture costs. Normally, these are one-time costs with a yearly maintenance residual, which is some fraction of the basic system cost. Once the system has been obtained, the big costs for hardware and software diminish. On the other hand, once the system is installed, the development costs begin, and once they begin, they tend to increase, rather than go down.

For each hour of CBI material created, there is a predictable development cost to your project. That cost is related directly to your media design and your data entry and testing process. Over time, these costs increase as employee costs increase. Moreover, having developed the first version of a product does not terminate its costs. Maintenance of the product begins, and that has predictable costs also. What most designers fail to realize is that cost is very sensitive to the authoring tool, templating system, and entry technique that you decide to use.

There are ways to lower these costs: (1) Make sure the authoring system you are using has high-productivity features, so that it creates the maximum amount of material in the minimum amount of time, (2) organize the entry effort for the maximum possible productivity (without injuring product quality), and (3) use a method of entering the tutorial data into your authoring system that has the lowest initial and re-authoring costs attached to it. What kinds of things can you do to increase the productivity of the entry process? Here are a few suggestions:

1. **Adopt a complete set of standards and procedures for entry:** Make as many decisions as possible before entry begins concerning the details entry personnel will need to know. Publish these standards and policies in a product design document to be read by your production staff, and keep the document updated as changes are made by you.

2. **Centralize resources as much as possible:** Identify those things which can be done once and then made available to all entry people. Some authoring systems allow graphic work to be created once and then made available to all enterers through libraries. Some allow the duplication of logic elements in the same way. Notice, for instance, that the design of our tutorial uses common patterns of logic which can be replicated again and again. Take advantage of all of the features of the authoring system you are using to avoid duplication and make commonly-used resources available to all the entry people.

3. **Divide the tasks to be done in a way that takes advantage of specialized skills on your staff:** You may have an artist on your staff who can do wonders with certain kinds of graphics. It seems logical to let the artist do the kind of work that he or she does best and fastest. You may have other entry people who do other parts of the entry process best. You can speed up entry if you use people for their special abilities. That way you can also increase the quality of the product. If you do not have an existing staff but must form one, you may want to talk to several users of the authoring system you intend to use and find out what types of staffing patterns worked most productively. Then as you create a staff, you can divide the labor among a staff of specialists for the best effect.

What can you do to lower the costs of revising your product? You can pick an authoring product that does not require all of the data for your product to be entered through the keyboard. The notion of the instructional designer sitting down to the keyboard to enter a great and complicated piece of CBI is as far-fetched as the notion of Beethoven sitting down to the keyboard to compose all at once the final version of the 9th Symphony. We know now from historical studies that the 9th actually emerged gradually in its details rather than all at once. Your CBI products will be no different. As parts of your own music emerge, capture them in production sheets, then use a flexible authoring tool that allows you to add this data to a data file rather than to a dialogue box.

One of the problems Beethoven faced, and maybe the reason we don't have more symphonies from him, was a transcription problem. Every change required some degree of rewriting of the music. Pretty soon the amount of rewriting required a fresh consolidation of all of the changes to the music into one score. This must have taken Beethoven a considerable amount of time and trouble to manage, and that was not necessarily creative time.

As you design a CBI product, you can be almost certain that the design and the content will change over time. During the development of the product, reviews and try-outs will necessitate changes to the product in order to correct bugs and content inaccuracies. Even after the product is complete, when you would normally think that the changes would cease, you will find a constant and predictable level of maintenance changes required as well. In some products, this level of effort will be quite high.

If you have to re-enter your product through the front door of an authoring system each time you want to make changes (possibly introducing additional new errors each time), then the cost of maintenance will be very high. If on the other hand, you have an authoring product which allows you to generate new authoring automatically after changes to the production sheets and the data files which result from them, then the changes can be inserted to the product at a low cost and without introducing new errors into the product.

Step 15: Test and debug.

Once a tutorial is entered into the computer, it naturally follows that it should be tested to make sure it works properly. Most developers can't wait to test a new product that they have designed to see what it feels like. Of course, rapid prototyping solves this problem. However, the kind of testing a new product needs is that which ensures that the product is "bullet proof"—that is, that it won't crash or produce the wrong message while a student is using it. Most people are surprised at the effort that is required to bring a CBI product to this level of dependability.

It is difficult to give a reliable metric for how much of your development effort to devote to product testing. Products simply differ too much in their complexity, and different development techniques, such as logic templating, can cut the time of product creation, giving testing a much higher proportion of the work effort. However, in either case, testing can easily represent half your effort.

There are usually enormous numbers of possible paths through a tutorial or exercise. Each of these must be tested. Nothing can be assumed about the stability of any part of a tutorial.

Testing normally requires careful running of the tutorial or exercise *numerous* times in order to find all faults and then numerous *additional* times to verify that faults have been corrected. Just running the product eats up considerable time, in addition to the time eaten up by documentation of faults as they are found and the time required for correcting them. This may seem like a big price to pay, but it is required to achieve dependable products. You can also see how valuable error-proof production techniques really are.

Testing a CBI product is an art, and it takes a special kind of person to do it. While hiring testers, look for the malevolent grin, the ironic sneer, the doubtful brow. The tester you want must deliberately look for ways to break your product and must be creative in finding bugs. If your testers do not find them, the user will, and that is not good for your product's reputation.

It is not enough that the product be able to make it through one or two trials safely. It must be able to handle any unexpected combination of events at any point. In the real world, where your product must live, things just happen to CBI products. Wrong keys get pressed accidentally or intentionally. Wrong answers, even unexpected ones, are given—answers that make no sense at all. If your product cannot weather all of those storms and others that your testers will devise, then the product will fail for users in the field.

As testing uncovers faults, you must debug them. With different authoring systems, this can be either an easy process or one which requires much work. In addition to picking a good authoring system for debugging (or for error-free development), you can do some other things to make this step easier:

1. Design products with a high degree of structural consistency: A set of CBI products (tutorials or exercises) is most often repetitive in some respect. If you design the logic of the tutorial to be identical at each repetitive point, you can reduce the amount of time that it takes a debugger to figure out how a particular error is originating and what might be wrong. This is one of the benefits of using templated logic.

2. Plant debugging aids within the tutorial: Some authoring systems have debugging aids built in to help find faults. For those that do not, it is possible to build them yourself. If you employ user-defined variables in your product, you can debug them by printing variable values to the screen as the tutorial is run. You may also be able to slow down the execution speed of the product by temporarily placing gates in the product which stop the user and allow the variables to be checked before going on.

3. Keep structural components of the tutorial simple and easy to work on: Programmers like elegant and clean solutions. To create these, they often compress several functions into one component of a product. This is good from a programming point of view, but it causes problems when it is time to make changes. If several functions of a tutorial are bundled together into one frame structure, it is difficult to change one without affecting the others adversely. Therefore, we always make it a policy to design things internally in a simplistic way that separates functions and keeps them independent. Then when it is time to make changes, they can be made with a minimum of collateral problems being caused.

Once a product is entered, tested, and debugged, it can be exposed to another SME review. The review at this point should confine itself to accuracy of interactions and messages. If you have had a good policy for SME reviews up to this point, there should not be major changes in instructional message resulting from this review.

Some people question whether it is important to test and debug tutorials before the SME review. Our personal experiences have taught us that this should always be the case. In development teams which are functioning properly, a certain degree of informality exists which makes it possible for members to work together productively. When it comes time to review products, however, informality and relaxed judgment is dangerous. Reviews must be honest and complete.

The problem of using un-debugged material for reviews is that there are emotional undercurrents in a serious review. Reviewing products which fail in the middle or which have glaring or even minor errors that could have been corrected bears negatively on this emotional situation and can do a great deal of damage to SME confidence. SMEs will beg you to show them uncompleted or undebugged products. They will assure you that they will not be critical when things go wrong. But it doesn't work that way, and the best policy is to debug before showing the product.

Step 16: Pilot test with students.

It is almost inconceivable that any clear-thinking developer would place a CBI product into regular use which had not been tested first with a small sample of target users. Doing so is asking for trouble and possible embarrassment.

The purpose of a field test is to try out a portion of the product (one tutorial or one exercise) with typical users to see how well it works and where it needs to be modified or corrected. Some developers in their haste to reach a finished product rationalize away the need for a field test of individual products on the grounds that the product faults will surface anyway when the whole product is first used.

The problem with this position is that if there are enough faults in the product when it is tested in this way, the negative feelings toward the product can build and create a reputation that will never be overcome, regardless of how much modification follows. On the other hand, a product in which the individual elements have been tested and modified separately is normally a very good product, since the problems have been worked out in advance. The only question unanswered in the full-scale employment is how well all of the parts can function together.

What kinds of problems get detected during a field test of individual products? There are a range of problems, including logic bugs not detected during testing: poor communication with the student due to language, image, or strategy problems; interface problems; conflicts with student taste or style; pace and timing problems (too much or too little); capacity problems for the computer; and problems in the organization of the learning situation and environment.

In order to discover these problems in private before they become public news, there are some common sense guidelines that you should follow while conducting field tests.

1. **Use typical students for try-outs:** Do not attempt to use SMEs or professional experts to test a new product. Do not use people who are familiar with the product. These people cannot look at the product with fresh eyes and see it from a student's point of view. They will not be looking at things the same way a first-time learner would.

2. **Try out products in a setting like the one that will be used by regular students:** The environment for training does make a difference. In your project office, the chairs may be very comfortable. In the learning area, they may be too hard or otherwise bothersome. To learn this, you have to use the actual training location and equipment or something very similar.

3. **As students try out materials, you may choose to be present, but you, the designer, must remain silent:** A tryout of materials which is augmented by your running commentary is not a fair trial of the product. You are an expert persuader. You can smooth over rough spots to the extent that they are not noticed. You can talk students out of thinking that there are needs and problems in the product. Students using your product in the real world will not have you there to carry them over the rough parts. In a tryout, the conditions should be the same, and you should remain silent. Let someone else conduct the tryout, and you watch.

4. **Listen to *everything* the user has to say after the tryout:** If you go into a tryout with preconceptions about what the outcome will be, you stand a chance of seriously influencing the results in the wrong direction. You may have specific questions to ask the user following and perhaps during the tryout concerning the product, but don't let these be the only source of information you use for evaluation. Given a chance to speak freely about the tryout experience, the user will often point out to you qualities of the product you had not considered as problems, and things you were worried about may not attract any notice at all.

5. **Don't confuse a tryout with research:** In trying out a product, you are not assuming the role of a scientist, although you might use some of the procedures of a scientist. You are trying out a real product in a real-world setting. If anything, this type of activity is properly called action research. The end goal is not to announce scientific findings. You are just trying out one product in one setting to see if it works. If there are glitches as you try out the product, don't despair, but gather additional data to see how general the problem is, then make changes to eliminate the problem and test the product again.

Step 17: Archive and begin configuration control.

This point in the design and development of a tutorial is both an ending and a beginning. It is the end of the tutorial creation process, but it is the beginning of an equally-important tutorial maintenance process that will continue throughout the lifetime of the tutorial.

The requirement to maintain instruction is not a new one brought about by the CBI medium. It has always been necessary for instruction in any medium to be maintained. Outlines for lectures are revised when needed; slides in a sound/slide presentation are replaced as the visual content of the training changes; the audio itself is revised as needed. Doing otherwise would lead to an instructional system which disseminated false, misleading, and potentially dangerous or costly misinformation.

To avoid this, tutorials which have been approved for use should be regularly reviewed and maintained when necessary. The first step to enable this is subjecting the tutorial to a process called *configuration control*. Configuration control refers to the process of:

- Ensuring that any and all changes to a product are properly made, documented, and tested.

- Ensuring that the product being distributed for use is the most current version and that older versions have been either destroyed or removed from circulation.

- Ensuring that unauthorized changes to the product are not allowed.

Configuration control is not a difficult process when you alone are the dispenser of tutorials and when the number of tutorial versions is small. As the number of tutorials grows, however, and when several staff members have access to tutorials and assignments to modify them, the configuration of a course can get out of hand quickly and can cause time-consuming, frustrating problems. Before long, you find that:

- There are revised versions of tutorials which have not been tested which have slipped out of the development shop and are being used with students (you normally find this out in a panic call from the learning center telling you that a tutorial which has never crashed before just crashed).

- There are tutorials which need revisions and have needed them for some time but have been neglected.

- You have two versions of a tutorial in your archive which appear to be identical but you know that one has been updated and don't know which copy is most current.

Configuration control is both a protective process which guards your course(s) from unauthorized or unwanted changes, and a positive maintenance process which ensures that your course(s) are updated and accurate. To support both of these outcomes, you need to approach configuration control as you would any periodic maintenance program. You must:

- Originate a system for identifying each version of each tutorial and tracking the location of each authorized copy of each file.

- Organize monitoring of authorized content sources to identify changes and their effects on existing materials.

- Define procedures for examination and revision of materials.

- Specify a process for the testing and release of modified materials.

With adequate configuration control procedures in place, the life of your course is extended. Materials retain their currency and accuracy. The work of course revision is reduced overall, and control of your development activities is greatly simplified.

Subject-matter experts

The topic of working with subject-matter experts is somewhat new to instructional technologists, because it is a need which has been created by the more widespread use of formal instructional development procedures by design professionals.

In early days, subject-matter expertise was provided in one of two ways: (1) a subject-matter expert in an area would study instructional development, or (2) an instructional developer would study the discipline which needed training and try to become a subject-matter expert.

Both of these approaches assumed that the instructional developer was not only the center of development activity, but that he or she had pretty much absolute control over the product. In fact, as often as not in those days, the developer was the *whole* staff of the development project. Those were the days of the renaissance person in development.

The need for a better division of labor and for more carefully yet efficiently developed products led to formal instructional development processes being specified. It became apparent that the attempts to convert subject-matter experts into developers and vice versa were not working. Too often the resulting instruction lacked content depth and integrity, or else the instructional techniques used were inadequate.

The distribution of development labor is much better today and tends to produce better quality instruction. In this process, the subject-matter expert supplies accurate content according to a set of procedures which the developer is responsible for defining. The developer is responsible for integrating that content according to a pre-specified plan into an instructional sequence. The developer and the subject-matter expert share the responsibility for the product, but they can do so only because of the explicit and public set of principles and procedures which they share.

This is a nice theory, but making it work in the real world is a challenge. Subject-matter experts come in many varieties, and the working climate of development projects varies widely. Problems encountered may center around allocation of SME time, division of his or her attention among multiple duties, acceptance of the development process by the SME, SME preconceptions about how the product should look or act, or personality differences. Not all SME-developer relationships turn out to be successful, but there are a few things you can do to give them the best chance for success.

1. **Make expectations (procedures, duties, responsibilities) clear on both sides from the very outset:** Most SME/developer relationships cross some organizational boundary. This removes the customs and habits of the organization as the common ground for working together, and developers and SMEs must find some other basis for forming expectations of each other. In this situation, it is important for the developer to clearly specify the steps in the development process and the rationale behind them for the SME. For each step in which the SME will be involved, there should be a clear statement of quality and completeness standards and estimates of the time required to complete each step. This will help the SME manage time and provide a way for measuring normal progress.

2. **Train staff members to work with a SME:** The SME's confidence in the development staff depends on how the staff conducts its business. If development staff members are trained in the development process and the techniques for interacting with SMEs, it is easier for the SME to have confidence in the developer's competence. This in turn can be a key to SME productivity. Staff members should be taught how to act professionally. They should realize the importance of respecting and not wasting SME time. They should understand how common courtesies and interpersonal skills make it easier to keep SME support. Finally, they should realize the devastating effect of dumping hard or unpleasant jobs on the SME without adequate technical or moral support.

3. **Make progress visible:** The development staff often has a clear picture of progress toward a finished product. The SME, on the other hand, is normally unfamiliar with design and development steps and has no way of measuring progress. Whatever method you use for showing progress, its visibility will increase the motivation of the SMEs as they see the job getting done.

4. **Treat the SME as an integral part of the development team; don't allow we/they thinking:** Gulfs can form between the SMEs and the developers. Each group has its own pro-

fessional world, jargon, and social customs. If separation becomes a pattern for a project, it normally spells disaster. SMEs must be encouraged to see themselves as part of a development team. They should know their skills and knowledge will be respected and that they will be influential. Most important, when they do well, they should be recognized within their sponsoring organization.

Conclusion

We have tried in this chapter to introduce a systematic procedure for designing CBI tutorials. This approach begins with the objective and defines the central structure of instructional strategy. It proceeds from there to define the details of logic, message, content, use of media channels, and content representation.

The procedure is sufficiently sequential to separate main design functions to avoid their interference with each other. It also recognizes that one stage of design is often not complete until the next stage is at least begun. Therefore, the user of this procedure should expect steps to overlap and interact significantly.

We believe that through this process designers can speed designs, improve product consistency, increase productivity during writing and assembly, reduce errors, speed testing, and improve instructional focus while achieving the broadest range of interesting and attractive surface contexts.

Self-directed activities

- Begin to collect the documentation systems used by the best CBI designers you come in contact with. Get to know some commercial product developers or find articles about them which give case studies of their design and documentation process. Contrast the work of those who document with that of those who don't.

- Use the process described in this chapter to create a brief CBI tutorial. Critique the process as you use it, adding steps where necessary and dropping others. What could be done to increase the productivity of this process?

- Test an automated design system and critique its ability to remove from the designer the repetitive and uncreative steps of design. Does the design system do all that is advertised? Are there more steps which could be automated? Have some design decisions been removed from the designer? What kinds of designs does this prevent? What is the real increase in design speed using the system? Which steps of design and production are supported?

Further reading

McCarthy, J. (1995). *Dynamics of software development.* Redmond, WA: Microsoft Press.

Greer, M. (1992). *ID project management.* Englewood Cliffs, NJ: Educational Technology Publications.

Hales, C. (1993). *Managing engineering design.* Essex, England, UK: Longman Scientific and Technical.

Head, G. E. (1994). *Training cost analysis: A how-to guide for trainers and managers.* Alexandria, VA: Association for Supervision and Curriculum Development.

van Merriënboer, J. J. G. (1997). *Training complex cognitive skills.* Englewood Cliffs, NJ: Educational Technology Publications.

22

CREATING SIMULATIONS

Chapter Objectives:

1. *Contrast the design process for tutorials described in Chapter 21 with the levels and ordering of design for instructional simulations described in this chapter.*

2. *Defend the importance of the problem in the design of instructional simulations.*

3. *Explain the reason for approaching the design of instructional simulations in waves rather than steps and define the main goal of having at least two waves of design.*

4. *Describe the interaction between decisions made at different levels of an instructional simulation design.*

Overview

The purpose of this chapter is to define a pattern for the design of instructional simulations. A swarm of issues must be juggled as a simulation goes through several stages of design, and this chapter tries to provide some guidelines for the relative timing and importance of design decisions.

We carefully avoid speaking of this chapter as a *procedure* for designing simulations. The activities of simulation design are not really stepwise; in fact, one of the main activities of the designer at any point is to decide what to design next. This seems to be the essence of simulation design; we speculate that it is a pattern for design in general, but that is a subject for another book.

As we write about designing simulations, we are conscious that entire books are devoted to the subject of designing simulations for industrial and scientific use. We realize that we cannot possibly be exhaustive on the subject of designing instructional simulations—simulations which incorporate not only a model or an environment but instructional features as well. Nonetheless, we feel that we can give some important insights into the design and creation of instructional simulations.

The simulation we will use as an example is a relatively simple one which contains an environment made up of locations through which students can navigate. Our simulation will also incorporate a model whose dynamic values and controls will surface within at least one simulated location. We have selected a simulation which illustrates several important design issues, including the model-location relationship and the incorporation of instructional features. We will assume the use of an object-oriented programming tool, which will allow us to illustrate some of the benefits of object-orientation that we feel are important to designers.

Levels of design

In Chapter 21, the more stepwise tutorial design process took place mainly at three levels (see Figure 1): the strategic-structural level (Steps 1–4, Chapter 21), the level of software or frame logic (Steps 8A-8E, Chapter 21), and the level of the dramatic surface overlay (Step 7, Chapter 21). We also showed how a designer places the instructional strategy at the core of the design, building outward from there in both directions toward the surface design that creates an interface with the student and toward the logic design that relates the strategy to the computer's logical actions.

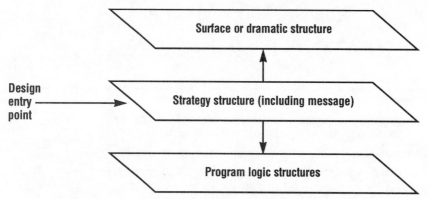

Figure 1. Sequence of design for CBI tutorials described in Chapter 21.

A simulation can be embedded within a tutorial or can stand alone as an instructional tool. Tutorial-embedded simulation is dominated by the tutorial's strategy, and the design process originates there. However, stand-alone simulations do not fit within the context of a tutorial strategy; the simulation's strategy is most often one of indirection rather than direction (see Chapter 16). Therefore, a different core structure for the design has to be used.

In Figure 2, we show a simulation's design taking place on four levels. Design begins with a problem structure and moves outward to the design of an environment and its associated system models. These provide the structured setting and tools for the student's problem solving. From there design proceeds toward surface features and interface, But the environment and model designs also provide the basis for the computer program logic design. The problem structure thus lies at the core of the designer's instructional intention, and all other elements of the design are made to serve that intention. Normally, if something in the design has to change, the last thing changed is the problem itself.

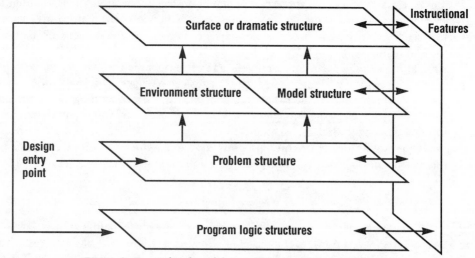

Figure 2. General order of design for instructional simulations.

The design of an instructional simulation also includes the design of the instructional features which will accompany the model. These features are the source of the instructional power of the simulation, and their design must correspond at each level with the simulation's design.

In model-centered instruction, the system or environment model is the central source of the student's experience. Auxiliary instructional functions (the ones carried out by the Learning Companion described in Chapter 16) may be supplied to accompany the experience and make it more instructional. But the experience itself—an experience which can only be provided by the model—is the first concern of design. The design of instructional functions is treated in this chapter, but it is placed in the perspective of designing a function to be used in conjunction with the model.

Some simulations are built to be non-problem centered or multi-problem-centered. The core of such simulations, since there is no single problem from which to derive structure, must contain the sum of all environmental locations and all models which the designer has identified for all of the problems. These may either be constructed into one large simulation program or as multiple smaller programs capable of supporting one or more problems each.

Describing design as a multi-level activity does not mean that the design of one level is completed before the design of another is started. Design of simulations is at all levels highly interactive and parallel, with decisions at any level potentially influencing decisions at the other levels. This, of course, means that each decision at any of the levels must be tested for its impact on previous decisions and for its impact on potential future decisions on the other levels to ensure there is no conflict.

The design process

We have been careful to avoid proceduralizing the design process in this chapter in order to provide a contrasting approach to the stepwise design process described in Chapter 21. As we recount our design actions, we will refer to them not as steps but activities. The design of different problems under different constraints and with different goals in mind might require these design activities to be performed in a slightly different order and might make some of them more critical. As we select each new activity to pursue, we will try to explain our reasoning for the order of selection.

In general, our activities will follow the order suggested by Figure 2. Basic problem structure and model concerns will take first priority, and surface and computer logic concerns will follow, mainly influenced by the problem structure.

Overview of the process

We will describe the simulation design process in three stages, or waves:

- High-level conceptual design

- Design testing

- Design detailing

We describe these waves separately, realizing that there is no clear line between the first and third stages and that the second stage really goes on constantly, following the making of each separate decision. Nonetheless, there is a wave of structural design which is and must be pre-eminent, and the details of the surface design must adapt to it, so the general direction of design is from inner structures toward outer surfaces, and there is a respite following the first wave of structural decisions where smart designers pause to review the design in its entirety for conflicts.

The simulation example

As an example, we will describe the design of a simulation consisting of a problem, a simulated environment, and a model which place the student into a role which requires complex, multistage problem solving and planning. This problem will use the instructional approach of indirection (see Chapter 16) to exercise and at the same time form and focus the students' skills in planning, information handling during decision making, prioritizing, and activity scheduling. This problem will be one of a family of similar problems which could use the same environment, models, interface, and logical structures. The specific dramatic context, the story told on the problem's surface has not yet been chosen and is secondary to the instructional goal.

We will perform the design of one simulation problem as if it were to be used by students ranging from bright 8th graders through high school. The problem will require the use of a variety of skills in a setting that is not specific to any particular discipline. We presume, therefore, that the problem will be usable within the context of any of several school courses and in conjunction with many themes of instruction, from social studies to biology, and from mathematics to ethics.

Wave 1: High-level conceptual design

Figure 3 shows the relation of Wave 1 design activities. These activities result in a broad structural outline of the simulation product and its major components. Decisions are made regarding the instructional goals of the simulation, the place of the simulation within the larger instructional context, the simulation's general appearance and functioning, its instructional features, and the general structure of its program logic. These decisions are not made in any particular order, and ideas in one area may lead to implications in another. Only the centrality of the problem is a given.

Activity: Specify the instructional goal(s) of the simulation.

The goal of our simulation, as we have already stated it in general terms, is to give the student exercise in problem solving of a particular type—the type involving data gathering, prioritizing, and allocation and scheduling of resources. If we haven't done so up to this point, we must make a statement of the objective so that we know specifically which skills are to be exercised.

Unfortunately, many designers begin by focusing directly on the creation of an environment or a model to be simulated and bypass the specification of an explicit goal. These designers make the assumption that if they design a reasonably good environment it will automatically call forth from the student an appropriate and generally worthwhile performance. But this is not necessarily true. Recent experience with cognitive task analysis in the design of instructional simulations indicates that the performances most often left out are the very most important ones from an instructional point of view.

Instructional goals are determined through analysis. In most cases the early stages of instructional design include a task analysis to inventory in detail the performances and mental processes to be learned. If no analysis has been performed, then the simulation designer must do at least enough to define the simulation problem. The problem will be used as the starting point to define everything else.

There are some schools of design which hope to minimize the importance of instructional goals, but we emphasize their importance. We do this because: (1) goals provide the rationale for determining what to include and what to exclude from the design—a decision which is oth-

Primary Decisions

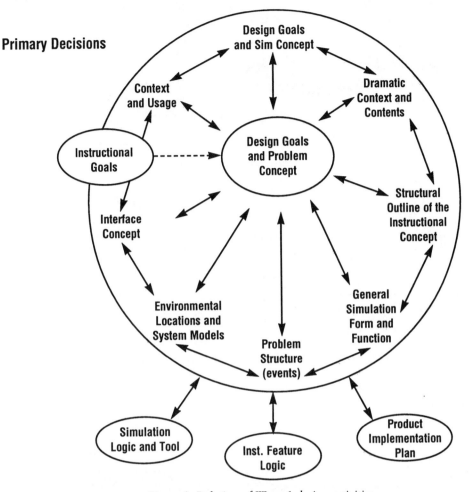

Figure 3. Relation of Wave 1 design activities.

erwise foundationless and subjective, and (2) goals provide the basis for accounting for the skills and knowledge of a student at any given point. They are therefore the basis for selecting subsequent learning activities which do not duplicate the student's previous experience unnecessarily and which do not move ahead so far that they leave gaps in the student's knowledge or performance ability.

Analyzing the task for our simulation requires that we walk through the steps—both the observable ones and those that are internal mental steps. Our list of tasks includes the following:

- Verify and define the problem and the required solution.
- Verify that a problem exists.
- Identify symptoms of the problem, their extent, and their seriousness.
- Link symptoms to causes within the problem environment.
- Define specific end-states or results which constitute solution.
- Identify possible paths to solution.

- Define sub-goals whose attainment will lead to problem solution.

- Define the end-action or results to be accomplished for each sub-goal.

- Continue to break sub-goals into further sub-goals.

- Select a path to solution for each sub-goal.

- Eliminate infeasible solution paths within problem resources.

- Determine the resource cost of each solution path.

- Determine side effects of each solution path.

- Determine internal consistency of each path.

- Select a path to be followed.

- Plan the implementation of the solution.

- Allocate resources to solution steps.

- Set criteria for solution steps.

- Schedule solution sub-goals.

- Perform scheduled steps.

These are steps any problem solver might use, and they are the steps for which we will make provisions for information and responding for the student who encounters the problem. As we move forward with the design, we will become aware of other tasks which we overlooked, and as the specific character and details of the problem emerge through the design process, we will find many more detailed and specific tasks. We will add these as we find them, expanding our analysis gradually toward completeness. This analysis will be very useful to us.

Having begun to analyze the problem solving task in this way has not fully solved our instructional goal problem. Next we must delimit the scope of the tasks which are of interest to the present design. That scope may include all of the tasks we have identified or some subset of them. A lot depends on the larger instructional design of which the present simulation is but one part. That design may call for a group of increasingly complex planning problems, and our present problem may be only one of those. That would cause us to define the scope of the present design as one subset of the analyzed tasks. A designer must consult the larger plan to see which tasks from the analysis fall within the scope of a simulation.

Activity: Take into account the larger instructional context and usage factors

The larger instructional context within which our simulation problem will be used has implications for the design, so we must take it into account. We will pay attention to decisions which have already been made about the total instructional product. These decisions may have been imposed by a client or may have been necessitated by resource levels for the project.

The factors of interest to us at this point will include the manner in which the total product is to be used: the instructional strategies being employed elsewhere within the larger product, the setting and manner in which the product will be used, the computer configuration which will be the platform for instruction, the interface and control conventions used in the larger product, the plan governing media use in the larger product (use of off-line materials, role of the computer, etc.), and the look and feel which have been adopted in the larger product. At this time, we will gather as much of this information as possible to influence later decisions.

We already know or can infer the following about our example simulation: It will be a part of a larger instructional product intended for use in educational settings. It will consist of one problem within a family of problems, designed for use over a period of time as a series of problem solving exercises. The problems must be enjoyable but also have specific instructional focus on skills for solving a specific planning/allocation type of problem.

In addition to these decisions given to us as constraints, we learn the following:

- The larger instructional product will be delivered using a standard multimedia computer configuration.

- It will have the most current chips, boards, auxiliary input/output devices, and speeds.

- It will use a standard screen resolution of 640 by 480 pixels.

We also learn that the entire product (of which our simulation is one part) will be distributed on CD-ROM. This releases us somewhat from file size constraints which would otherwise limit us.

The plan for the larger product places no constraint on the time allotted for work on individual problems. But we are aware of the practical time constraints imposed by the typical classroom period within which our product is to be used. If problems take longer than the average class period, we will have to provide a bookmark capability. Here is a design issue in one area which may have implications in another area, and we record this in our design notes.

Our product must be usable either by individuals or by groups of students, including full class groups using a projection device. Problems must be non-grade specific. We already know that they should be usable by students from bright eighth graders through average high school students. Since the instructional goal is broad problem solving skill, problems used instructionally must be varied in terms of content. The content may not require any special learning before the student begins work on a problem; we must use the kind of problem content which can be found in any community setting. We must design problems to be related to many parts of the curriculum: math, science, and social studies. Finally, a problem may not require specialized or advanced techniques (such as trigonometric solutions), which would eliminate a large portion of the target population from using them.

With this knowledge of the pre-made context of decisions in hand, we will jump to another design activity, but we will keep our decisions tentative for a while—probably until we have a complete high-level design concept—because we know that information or decisions in other areas may alter some of these decisions or cause us to revisit them. We will also continue to be alert to new or changing information relative to the larger product context.

Activity: Define design goals and the simulation concept

In this activity, we will use the information we have gathered to design the general concept of this product and to set some design goals which set the standard by which we will evaluate our design as it emerges.

What are *design goals* and how do they differ from *instructional goals*? Design goals express the *qualities* we want our product to have and the *priority* we place on those qualities. At the highest level, design goals are broad expressions of quality, such as:

"I want the product to seem friendly and non-threatening."

"I want the product to be easy to use."

"I want the product to have a professional image."

"I want the product to be enjoyable to use."

Though these goals seem vague and hard to quantify, they will have an important influence on design decisions. Note the difference between a "professional image" goal and a "fun" goal. One of these ("professional image") will be given higher priority for serious training where high performance levels are required of graduates, and the other ("fun") will be more typical of products designed for school or home use.

For our current example, the design goals to which we give the highest priority are "fun," "engaging," "relevant," "challenging," and "usable anywhere." As we continue with the design, we may encounter the necessity of balancing one of these qualities against another. We may find ourselves trading fun for relevance or making the problem more engaging by making it somewhat less challenging.

The concept for our product will be a high-level, low-detail structural pattern which describes the major elements, functions, and characteristics of our product. The concept will consist of several parts:

- A unifying dramatic concept

- A control and interface concept

- An instructional concept

- A logical structure concept

Dramatic concept: We will place the problem in the context of a challenging and exciting response to a planning problem of some kind. The problem must be one with some urgency. This type of circumstance usually draws the best out of people, stimulates a sense of immediacy, and helps the student feel that the activity is worthwhile. No special content knowledge will be required to solve the problem, making the problem usable by all students, but that means the problem content must be familiar to students from prior experience.

Control and interface concept: We will provide student problem solvers with controls enabling them to move about within the problem environment, accessing information that leads to a solution. The interface will provide realistic graphical views. We will also provide a capability by which solvers can record information as it becomes available to them—to be used later in solving. Since this is a planning and scheduling problem, there will not be a single answer. It will require a plan which the solver will create in tabular form that embodies schedules and resource allocations.

Instructional concept: Our simulation problem is not meant as a test, though it will supply data on performances from which inferences may be made. The problem is intended to teach through problem solving and experience. We will structure the problem and provide problem solving support (sometimes called *scaffolding*) in such a way that the student is afforded or reminded of things to do that will lead toward a solution. In addition, we will provide coaching and hinting functions within the environment in some form to help students move past troublesome spots without reaching dangerous levels of frustration. Though this problem will provide instruction rather than a test, there will be much data accumulated during problem solving to show where the student is proficient, indicating areas where growth is occurring and where it still requires support.

Logical structure concept: At this point we must deal with the logical structure of the product. Only by doing so can we tell exactly what the product is that we must program. Is it a single-problem simulation program or a single program capable of supporting multiple problems? If it is one program of a family of programs, what does it share in common with the other problems in the family? We must distinguish between the instructional goal, the problem, and the simulation program for this problem.

Our range of choices is outlined in Figure 4 below. If our product requires both unique logic and a unique interface for every problem we create, then it will be more costly to produce. If either or both of logic and interface can be shared with other problems, then production costs can be reduced—somewhat if an interface is shared, and much more if logic can also be shared.

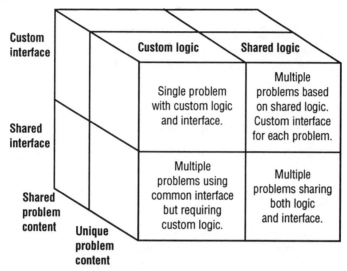

Figure 4. Simulation/simulator relationship options.

Our example problem will differ in content from the other problems in its family of problems, so there will be no benefit from sharing content in our sample case. This is done for a reason: A variety of planning problems from many content areas will help the student focus on the planning process rather than on specific problem content.

However, we will receive benefit from the use of a common problem interface. Our problem can be made to share general interface and a set of control standards with all of the others. This will make the problems somewhat less costly to produce, while at the same time simplifying the student's learning of interface conventions and operation.

We suspect (a suspicion that will be confirmed or disconfirmed by later design decisions) that the family of problems can also be made to share much of its programming logic, simplifying our programming task and reducing the overall cost of the product. We will see how this works in a later section.

The decision that we have reached is tentative. Some degree of uncertainty is common in almost all design decisions. As higher-level design decisions are made, nearly all of them represent a kind of technological hypothesis which will stand only as long as factors of cost, time, skill, and resources do not render them undesirable or unattainable. The decisions we have made tentatively here will be confirmed or discarded through continued planning. This is how the design process works, and this is why all design decisions, as they are made, must be compared and correlated with all previous design decisions and with other tentative plans.

Our problem falls within the shared-logic, shared-interface area of Figure 4. This decision about the logic lays the foundation for many more decisions to follow. The decisions we have made so far will begin to serve as a boundary within which subsequent design decisions will be made to fit, unless something indicates to us that the boundary is impractical, infeasible, or can be improved. Continued decision-making will successively narrow the range of uncertainty until a complete self-consistent, practical, and feasible design is achieved. If, however, one of the early design decisions is found impossible or undesirable, it will be changed, and all design decisions based on it will have to be reconsidered.

Having defined the concept of the product at a very high level of generality, a process now begins which will add successive amounts of detail in several areas: dramatic concept, interface concept, instructional concept, and logic concept.

Activity: Define details of dramatic concept and select content

Because our simulation is being constructed for instruction by indirection, a dramatic concept is required. A dramatic concept is a statement which describes the story or dramatic conflict of the simulation and usually takes the form:

> "You are a (role)."

> "You are in an (environment description)."

> "It is your job to (problem statement)."

Dramatic concepts are required for simulations using indirection. They are also important for many simulations using a direct strategy as well, because the dramatic concept is not always a fiction. A student may be placed in a qualitative chemistry lab, the vice-president's office of a bank, or the cockpit of an aircraft.

We know that our problem is a planning/scheduling/allocation type of problem. What dramatic situations present this type of problem? We might brainstorm a short list:

- Scheduling and dispatching trucks and trailers for a large trucking firm.

- Scheduling students, classes, and teachers for a make-believe high school.

- Dispatching life-support supplies following a natural disaster.

- Supplying material and personnel to an army during a battle.

All of these dramatic concepts are credible and would suffice. They all require planning, scheduling, and resource allocation, which is the form of the underlying problem we want to create. We may select a problem from the list or extend the list. We can begin working by elimination to shorten the list. The truck concept we might consider mundane. The high school example, though familiar to students, might not have as much appeal and as much incidental instructional value as something more inherently interesting. After some consideration of the dramatic concept in this same vein, we come up with the following, which we like:

Problem dramatic concept: We will place the student in the role of Disaster Relief Coordinator (DRC) in a town just damaged by an earthquake. The student must determine the extent of damage to the different areas of the town and the related need this creates for certain basic life-sustaining and health-supporting necessities—water, shelter, food, and sanitation facilities in the form of portable outhouses. The solver's task is to compute the size of the need from reports of damage to the town's infrastructure and to use resources which are available within the town environment to satisfy those needs. The solver must allocate the proper amount of each resource to each sector of the town and schedule its transportation so that it arrives before a shortage creates a crisis.

This concept seems good to us because it meets the criteria we set earlier: It consists of a set of functions familiar to students, it has elements which can be integrated with study units in many classes, it has an inherent public-service motive, and it contains interest and high drama. It is likely to be interesting to most students and most teachers.

With these details of the dramatic concept decided, we can proceed to other areas of the conceptual design, realizing that as other decisions are made— particularly those about underlying logic and interface—missing details of the dramatic concept will be filled in by interacting decisions and trade-offs.

Activity: Define structural outlines of the instructional concept

The instructional concept is not quite as much fun to plan as the dramatic concept, but it is very important. It represents the part of the design that will carry out the instructional purposes of the product.

An instructional concept describes the operation and interaction of the instructional features which will be included in this instructional product. Which functions need to be supplied? How and when will they be available? When will they be withheld? How will they operate? What principles will they follow? During the design of the instructional concept, the theoretical bias and beliefs of the designer are applied to the design.

Before defining the list of instructional functions, the highest-level instructional decisions concern:

- the manner in which the instructional goal will be applied; and

- the sociological environment that the product will create—that is, people (teachers and students) and their roles, and the use of non-computerized resources as part of the product.

Use of goals: Instructional goals can be used by designers in different ways by giving them different functions. In some cases, goals are used as gates to student progress, and students are not allowed to pass beyond them until a specified degree of mastery has been reached. In some cases, it is important to know how the student solved the first part of a problem before proceeding to the second part of the problem. In such a case, it is necessary to divide the goals of the simulation problem into two sets, one pertaining to the first part of the problem and one to the second. The answer the student gave to the first part of the problem would actually be checked before the student was allowed to proceed, because the answers to the second part would depend on the accuracy of the answers to the first.

If goals are used differently, students can pass through instructional experiences without being blocked by substandard performance. In those products, perhaps levels of attainment on specific tasks are recorded. In such a system, records of past attainment might be used to determine when and how much to intervene with volunteered instructional features.

Our example design will be of the first type. The problem will not have any intermediate checkpoints for determining whether a correct solution has been made for part of the problem, but at the end of the problem we will check to see that the answer falls within certain criteria: adequate food, water, shelter, and sanitation for the number of people who need them and at the right places. We will not look for an exact right answer, but we will check to see that the answer is within certain acceptable tolerance limits.

Consider how easy it would be to add immediate checkpoints if we wanted them. We might check certain key values at specified points during the problem. This would allow us to make corrective suggestions.

Whether goals are used as end-problem checkpoints or mid-problem checkpoints is really a matter of how far you have decided to let the student go, working under self-monitoring and self-evaluation. That decision can only be made relative to the student population for your problem: students' prior history of self management, their experience with this type of problem, and their levels of motivation and engagement with the problem. Over time, your support for the student during problem solving must fade out so that the student can experience being self-directed.

One implication of the use of goals for getting progress is that performance at gating points can be used as data during the choice of subsequent problems. If one area of a problem is troublesome to a student, then future problems and their levels of support can be selected to provide additional supported experience in the area of need.

Sociology: When a student uses our simulation, will it be alone or as a member of a group? What is the social environment created by our instruction? We subscribe to the principle that peer interaction during problem solving is instructionally desirable. However, the design goal we have causes us to make the product usable anywhere, and that may mean by individuals. Therefore, we will design the product mainly for individual use, but we will also try to make it easy to use with student groups. Your own favored principles for instruction may differ from the one we have chosen. This possibility illustrates the interaction between the design process and the principles applied as it proceeds. Designers should try to keep design process and instructional principles independent to give themselves the most latitude to implement new ideas through innovative designs.

What will be the role of the instructor as the product is used? Will additional non-instructor personnel be needed, such as a subject-matter expert to consult?

For our sample design, we will decide that no instructor will be required during problem solution to support the "usable anywhere" design goal we have set for ourselves. This implies that subsequent design decisions will be made to support the student in unmonitored use of the product. There are several reasons for our decision. None of them are based on a belief that instructors or teachers are unnecessary. We believe the teacher role in technology applications is very important, but we want this particular product to be usable without a teacher's constant monitoring so that: (1) an independent group of one or more students can use the product to the side without drawing the teacher away from other class activities, (2) students can use the product at home (perhaps with parents), (3) teachers can have several groups of students working on the same problem at the same time on different computers, allowing each group to come up with its own solution to be reported later to the whole class. Designers with different design goals will come up with a sociology which differs from the one we have chosen for our problems, but we have arrived at these decisions and have explained our rationale.

Having dealt with the use of goals and the sociology of our instructional concept, there are several other issues which we turn to, which are described in the sections which follow.

Use of off-line elements: Non-human elements of the instructional system are part of the instructional concept. The designer may prescribe the use of off-line elements such as physical models, calculators, manuals and documents, notebooks, worksheets, handouts, or lab journals during instruction. For our example we will use none, because we want the product to be simple and portable—hopefully self-contained on the CD-ROM.

Instructional features: The definition of a simulation's instructional features is at the heart of the instructional concept. In Chapter 16, we outlined a set of six instructional features: coaching, feedback, representation, control systems, scope dynamism, and embedded didactics. This list can be augmented by other valuable instructional techniques such as *articulation* (getting students to verbalize what they have learned from a non-verbal experience), *reflection* (getting students to think about what they have learned and articulated so that they can knit or integrate their learning together and decide what value they place on it), *scaffolding* (arranging the task environment in such a way that it suggests an appropriate path to problem solution without giving directions to the student), or *modeling* (showing the student how something is done or how it works). These are all features of the instructional approach termed *cognitive apprenticeship*.

On what basis does a designer make choices about when and how to include these features? The choice is ultimately based on the designer's (or design team's) own (or shared) philosophies and theories of instruction. One theoretical point of view may lead the designer to specify that errors by the student will be corrected immediately every time they occur. Another point of view may lead the designer to delay feedback on mistakes under certain circumstances until the student is completely finished with a problem, and can receive feedback on all errors at once. A third designer may decide to correct errors immediately in the early stages of instruction and lengthen the span of feedback delay as the student progresses, placing the student increasingly in a self-monitoring role. Your personal theory of instruction governs what type of feedback you will select, when, and how you will apply it. There is no single manual of correct and approved instructional techniques. The best the designer can do is become as informed as possible about the myriad of alternatives and then apply techniques according to the best judgment possible. Design is not a science.

A good source of guidance and ideas can be found in current examples of instructional simulations being produced by reputable instructional research laboratories around the U.S. and the world. In looking for models, it is best to be careful in examining products and to ask for data on their demonstrated effectiveness and productivity. Reputable laboratories collect this data and publish it in professional journals. It is easy to mistake a nice looking product for an effective one. The glittery surface of multimedia has the power to make an instructional sow's ear look like a silk purse, but data from product tests can provide a more sure guide for a serious designer.

Therefore, we recommend that you become familiar with numerous examples of simulation-based instruction—both good and bad—in order to see the wide range of instructional options and how they are applied. We also recommend that you test pilot versions or inexpensive prototypes of your own products with real students and learn from your own experience what is effective and under what conditions.

At this point in the design process, you need to select the features to employ and the general rules that will govern their operations. What happens when each feature is invoked? When is it invoked? What invokes it? What does the feature do? What actions is it capable of? What order does it follow internally? What data does it need to select or compose its message? You can write and sketch the general design of each feature at this point. As with other design decisions made to this point, this decision will be tentative, to be confirmed or modified by other design decisions and later by tryout data.

- For our example problem, the instructional feature design will include:

- Coaching or hints on request.

- Feedback following the completion of the problem.

- Embedded didactics in the form of procedural guides.

- Scope dynamics in the form of a family of problems.

- We will define those features generally in the sections below.

Coaching/Hints: As students work on a problem, they may reach a point with no idea of how to proceed. We will supply hints to guide them into a beneficial path of action. Hints will not give explicit directions to solvers but will merely direct attention of solvers to resources within the problem environment.

We do not know for sure as we make this decision how computer logic will be made to supply the hints, but our initial estimate of the problem and our past experience convince us that a dependency chart approach (described later) will probably provide the necessary logical basis for giving the right hint at the right moment. This is a design hypothesis which we will have to test before we make a firm design decision on hinting. However, it would be very daring of us, even foolish, if we made a design decision at this point without *some* idea of a proven or possible logical mechanism for making it happen.

This design decision about the hinting feature has implications for the interface design, so we might also pause to reflect on how the present decision will influence the interface. We not only need a control to make hints accessible by solvers, but we need some idea of how the hints will be delivered. Will it be a dialogue box which appears, containing a hint? Will the voice of a side-kick chime in with a timely reminder? This type of interplay between decisions in different areas of the design only serves to underscore the interdependence of design decisions which is especially true of simulation designs. While we are pausing to reflect on interface impacts of our decision, we might also want to reflect on considerations in all of the other areas as well.

Feedback: We will delay feedback until after a problem is concluded. We do this for specific reasons. What we are instructing is problem solving ability, not procedural action. There are several correct paths to a problem solution, and solution actions may be taken in many orders.

What counts in our case is whether reasonable actions were taken in a generally acceptable and reasonable order. During problem solving, we expect there will also be some false starts and some uncertain beginnings. Since our problems are intended for learning as well as for practice, false starts may have instructional value, and the student can learn from them. By intervening too soon after an erroneous step is taken, we deprive the student of the learning that can come from detecting and then correcting one's own mistakes.

We are willing to assume that feedback messages can be generated from the same type of dependency chart structure that will be used for generating hints (which supplies us with a logical mechanism). Having built something similar in the past makes us fairly certain that an existing tool can be modified to suit the needs of the present task. In fact, we may use this opportunity to add a few new features to the prior logic to supply better feedback.

Embedded didactics: The hinting system will be capable of guiding solvers to resources embedded within the problem environment which suggest courses of action. For realism, these resources will take the form of memos and plans stored in a file cabinet within the Disaster Relief Coordinator's office. The specific resource suggested by the hinting mechanism will depend on an examination of the steps toward solution which the student has already taken.

A solver may also discover the embedded didactics within the problem environment without hints. In fact, we would prefer that the solver do some searching within the office environment to see what might be available to help in the solution before taking too many decisive steps. If solvers fail in this survey activity in one problem, the feedback at the end of the problem will point this out, and the next problem will be selected such that survey of the resources is an important factor in reaching a solution.

Scope dynamics: We have already planned the use of scope dynamics by specifying that the problem we are designing is part of a larger family of problems of increasing difficulty. Scope dynamics is not planned at the time of problem design; it is planned as the set of problems is created. Through the judicious selection of problem features, a sequence of problems can be constructed which builds solving capability from basic performance levels to sophisticated ones in steps suited to the escalating ability of the student. We have alluded to techniques for achieving scoping dynamics in our discussion of work models in Chapter 16. The problem we are designing constitutes one rather large work model.

The sections above contain our wish (hope) list for instructional features, and in a later activity, as we define the tools and logic for their creation, we will verify whether these features are feasible to implement. Later, pilot tests will verify which features are effective.

Activity: Define general simulation form and function

Instructional simulations present a specific problem for the student to solve. The problem is solved as the student navigates the environment, gathers information, and interacts with the models placed within the environment. Before going too much further, we must decide something about the form in which our problems will be presented and administered. This will include specifying a problem's beginning point, its ending point, its major phases, and a high-level outline of paths or gateways through which the student passes during problem solving. The result is a diagram of problem stages like the one shown in Figure 5. In drawing this part of the design, we do not include content-specific paths of the solver, only the general pathways which lead from the "hello" of the introduction through to the "good-bye" following the last words of feedback and scoring.

As shown in Figure 5, after an introductory title screen of some kind, the entry point to a problem is normally through a problem statement which informs the student what is expected and provides initial problem information. After a problem is announced in this way, the solver is normally placed in an initial location within the problem environment. In the case of our current problem, that will be the Disaster Relief Coordinator's office. Recall that every simulation— even if it consists of only one model—has also at least one location where the student obtains information from the model and exercises control over it. The initial location is the one from which you want the student to begin work on the problem. The initial location may be a central location to which the student returns again and again as the problem is solved, or it may be a peripheral location which serves as nothing more than a convenient door through which to enter the problem environment.

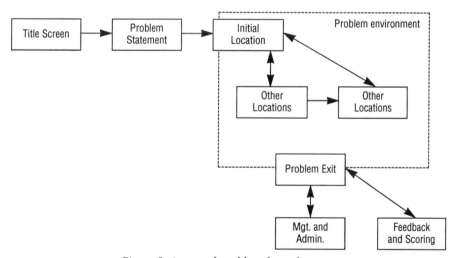

Figure 5. A general problem form diagram.

The problem exit point is the point at which the solver arrives as the problem ends or whenever the solver requests an administrative break in the problem. The end point may be the result of an action by the student (which solves the problem) or the result of the simulation detecting that a solution has been reached and automatically terminating the problem. Both types of exit are appropriate under different conditions. At this point, you should decide which to use. For our disaster relief problem, the end point will be signaled by the student because the solution to the problem does not consist of a single terminal action. The answer to this problem consists of several entries in a spreadsheet-like form that will capture the solver's plan for distributing commodities to citizens in need.

As you plan the problem exit point, you must also plan what happens upon exiting the problem. Though it sounds like the exit point should be the finale for the entire simulation, it is really only the exit point from work within the simulated environment. After work on a problem is complete, there are still several activities a designer may want to specify, such as a score computation, a detailed feedback debriefing for the problem just completed, options for further work on the problem to modify the solution, or any of several other possibilities.

As design progresses, you should begin to collect and maintain design decisions in a public and sharable form. Diagrams, tables, and written descriptions can be used, and there is no standard method for representing simulation designs as there is in architectural drawings and specifications. What is important is that you capture decisions and the data they produce so the design can be shared with others and built by a team.

As design continues, other high-level features may be added, and any design document which begins to evolve must reflect them as well.

(Note: As features are added to a design, it is important that the designer have some idea of how they can be implemented in computer logic, how messages and interaction will be created, and how much time and effort will be involved in developing the features. Simply adding services without thinking through these issues often leads to disappointment later. This constitutes a preliminary feasibility check which prevents going too far before discovering a roadblock.)

Activity: Define the problem structure

Recall at this point that the simulation design activities as we describe them in this chapter are not arranged in any strict order of performance nor in their order of importance. These design activities are most often carried out in parallel fashion, influencing each other at each step. In real practice, a designer will work on one activity for a while, then stop and work on another as ideas in one area lead to ideas in the other. If we were describing the activities in order of importance, then the present step would certainly be placed very near the front, because it is a step closely related to the instructional goal: defining the problem structure.

The problem structure consists of the following: (1) one or more events designated as solution events, (2) one or more paths of connected events which lead toward the solution events, (3) one or more *decoy* paths of connected events which do not lead toward the solution events, and (4) one or more events not connected into any path structure.

The problem structure is the structure of events which a problem solver must or might perform in an attempt to reach a solution. It is an ordered list of solving events which must be made possible within the problem environment. An event is defined as either: (1) a single item of information which the solver can obtain, or (2) an action which can be performed by the solver during problem solution. The design of the problem environment's locations and models cannot be completed until this problem structure, made up of solving events, is completed first. The locations of the problem environment will be designed deliberately to conform to the structure of the problem—its items of information, and its action points.

A problem structure is unique to a specific problem, so it is influenced by the problem's dramatic concept and can't proceed far until that concept is beginning to firm up. It contains the steps which a solver will take to express a solution, all of the correct and allowable steps toward a solution, all of the steps that lead away from a solution, and all of the neutral steps which neither help nor hinder a solution.

For simple problems, particularly those which do not involve dynamic system models, the problem structure can be expressed as in a simple diagram called a dependency chart. For more complex problems, the problem structure can be more complex to create, and for problems involving models of systems, the problem structure can become so complex that it is only capturable in the form of an expert system which is capable of solving the problem itself. This normally takes the form of a number of "...if...then..." rules which capture the expert's knowledge and allow it to be recreated dynamically.

The value of the problem structure is that it defines the steps which the student must be able to perform within the problem environment and the individual items of information which must be obtainable from the environment in order for the solver to structure the appropriate solution. It is a direct bridge between the instructional goal and the design for the environment in which the goal will be pursued. The problem structure should be an expression of the tasks to be performed during problem solving. The structure places tasks and the information in the order which they depend on each other during problem solving. The result is a diagram which we call a dependency chart.

Figure 6 shows a portion of a dependency chart for a library search problem. In this problem solvers are learning to follow threads of reference from various beginning points which converge upon the solution of a problem. Though the students are looking up information on an epidemic, the real performance being learned is the process of using information to decide the type of search to conduct next to arrive at a particular item of knowledge. Remember that this problem is set within the environment of a library which has been carefully constructed. The resources the student finds available have been structured so that each event in the solution can be interpreted in terms of what the student knew or didn't know at a given moment. We call this an *interpretable* chart, and it can be used as the basis not only for designing details of the environment and models, but is a kind of knowledge structure which can be used by many instructional features.

Events to the right in the diagram are closer to the solution events. Those to the left represent events which should lead the problem solver toward the solution events if good logic and problem solving are employed. Entering this search in the middle, we find that something has led the library researcher to read (in Event #7) an article which has been placed in the problem's model of a library. This article happens to contain the name of an author who has written a book. From the contents of the article, the researcher can tell that the book referred to in the article contains key problem-related information. The reading (Event #8) of a second source, a book, reveals the title of the book written by the one author of interest in Event #7. These two events (7 and 8) thus lead to finding of the book itself (Event #9) which when read (Event #10) contains the information leading to a problem solution (presumably in Event #11).

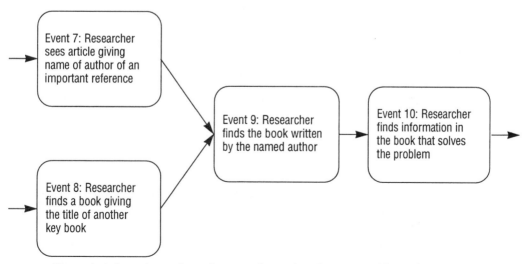

Figure 6. A dependency chart, showing relationships between problem solving events.

This problem structure—a structure of events leading to a solution—helps the designer to structure the complete "library" for this simulation problem. It not only identifies the actions the solver must be able to perform (look up a book by author, look up a book by title, etc.), but it identifies key items of information which must reside somewhere within the library. If the complete set of events leading to a solution were identified (Figure 6 gives only small section of the full dependency chart), as well as false trails which represent major error patterns and individual distracter events which lead nowhere, the content of the simulated library would be almost completely defined.

Let's examine a more complex problem—one where the problem solver is trying to determine the contents of a set of six mystery boxes by building circuits around them consisting of lamps, wires, and batteries. By observing the brightness of the lamp in different circuits, the solver can make inferences about what components are hidden within each box. This problem has more complex structure, and the set of event dependencies is therefore more complex. In this case it also can take more than one form.

The problem structure for this problem can take the form of a dependency chart. The same chart is applied in discovering the contents of each of the six boxes under examination (see Figure 7). The events on the chart name actions a solver can take with respect to any box. In order to determine the contents of a box, a subset of these events must take place, depending on the outcome of early steps, as represented by the labels ("light," "no light," etc.) on the paths between events.

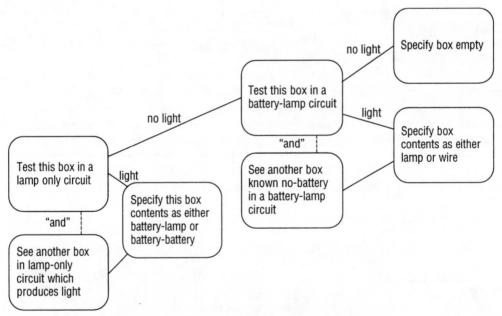

Figure 7. Dependency chart for the mystery box problem.

This same set of events can be represented in the form of a rule set capable of producing events and making judgments on the basis of their outcome. Here are the rules:

- If Box N has not been tested in a lamp-only circuit, do so.

- If the lamp-only circuit produces no light, conclude Box N contains no battery.

- If the lamp-only circuit produces light, conclude Box N contains at least one battery.

- If the lamp in the lamp-only circuit glows dim, conclude Box N contains a battery and a bulb.

- If the lamp in the lamp-only circuit glows bright, conclude Box N contains two batteries.

- If Box N has not been seen in a one-battery circuit and if it produced no glow in the lamp-only circuit, then test it in a one-battery circuit.

- If the one-battery circuit produces light, then conclude the box is not empty.

- If the one-battery circuit produces bright light, then conclude the box contains a wire.

- If the one-battery circuit produces dim light, then conclude the box contains a lamp.

These rules can be used create a set of events which are necessary and sufficient for problem solution. The rules can be crafted into a simple expert system capable of solving the boxes, providing hints, and providing feedback—either immediately or following problem completion. Because they can create a set of events, these rules also define the problem structure and can be used as the basis for specifying the environment itself—its locations and actions.

Note that the mystery box simulation (suggested by the work of Richard Shavelson) is in fact a model simulation which has only one location—the laboratory where the experiments are carried out on a realistic circuit board. The problem structure defines actions and location requirements for system models as well as for environments.

Activity: Define environment locations and system models

Creation of the problem structure makes possible the design of the locations that make up the environment of the simulation. It also leads to the design of the models which exist invisibly behind the walls of the environment, manifesting themselves through controls and indicators placed within locations. Recall that a location is defined not as a geographical spot but as a place where new information may be obtained through any of the senses.

During the design of locations the surface of the visible simulation world takes form. This surface world must be structured as a bridge between two levels: (1) at the surface level it must be a believable and reasonable version of some part of the world, and (2) at the deeper level it must correspond with the event structure of the problem, providing a place for all actions to take place and for each information item to be found. The environment of locations must not only provide for the events to occur which are on the main solution path and all of the false paths, but it must also provide the decoy events as well which lead nowhere.

As a bare minimum, there must be as many locations as there are events. Each event in the problem structure must have its own location. This may result in a lot of locations. For instance, in the library simulation, if more than one item of problem-relevant information is contained in each article, then each page of an article must be split into separate event-producing locations. Doing so is the only way to record that a specific event has or has not occurred, when the location was visited. This creates a record of what the student can and cannot know moment-by-moment while solving the problem. This information is in turn the driving force behind the coaching, hinting, and feedback instructional mechanisms and is what allows them to choose the right message to the student at the right time. Structuring the environment so that all events can be observed and recorded is essential.

In order to create a believable surface, we realize that location design will be influenced by factors in addition to the problem structure. These additional factors include: (1) the content of the problem (the disaster relief scenario we have chosen), and (2) some of the early design decisions which have already been made at more general levels.

We will try to design an interface that is a realistic microworld, one within which the student can move and act freely and effortlessly, without distracting attention from the activities of problem solving. We will use a graphic or video representation of work-like locations in which our student Disaster Relief Coordinator can function. For many students, this may contribute to interest in the problem. However, as we design the locations, we will keep in mind that physical realism is not as important as problem solving activities, because our instructional goal is to teach problem solving, not disaster relief.

We select an office as the primary setting for solving activities, where most of the work will be accomplished. This will be the office of the town Disaster Relief Coordinator. We begin to sketch an office setting which will gradually accumulate details. We will add locations to this beginning by either: (1) creating other new rooms or places outside of this office, or (2) by creating zoom-in locations within the office—places on each of the walls, within file cabinets, and wherever relevant information may be stored.

Realizing that additional locations will be created, we start a second diagram to record locations as they are created and the paths which connect them. We will eventually define a set of control actions for moving between locations and performing actions within locations.

What does a Disaster Relief Coordinator's (DRC) office look like? More importantly, what tools and information will our students need to perform their problem solving? To answer this, we return to the problem structure. If we are designing multiple problems for use within the same environment, the list of required actions and information will change from problem to problem. By adding up all of the lists, the designer obtains a master list of actions and information places which must be designed.

One source we will certainly consult to make sure our list of locations and paths is complete is the portion of the task analysis which has been selected as the basis for this problem. We will ensure that each task is not only exercised but that the environment has some way of recording that it was. From such a trace of events we can reconstruct the thinking—correct or erroneous—of the student and activate the appropriate instructional features.

Many of the actions for our problem include obtaining information from living or archival sources. Live sources can be contacted on communication channels. Archival sources can be provided within the normal furnishings of the office. We may consider the interest that would be created if we had the student move about the town in person to survey damage first-hand. This would allow us to include realistic views of earthquake damage. Though this could have some motivational effect, it also shifts the task subtly from problem solving to assessing damage. Moreover, obtaining the video resources to show first-hand damage could be costly. Since the problem time consumed by on-site inspection could be large and does not contribute (and may detract from) the instructional goal, we decide to create a cadre of in-the-field information gatherers who will supply damage information on request. These new problem characters and the variety of information items they will supply will eventually lead to the creation of numerous locations.

But how will these "inspectors" be contacted? Phone? Video phone? There are several options. Looking at our instructional goals and the budget, we select normal phone contact. However, this decision makes clear a design temptation we will face from this point on: We will be constantly tempted to pump up the DRC office with jazzy features which have gee-whiz value but little, if any, problem value. Instead of creating a simple telephone, we will be tempted to create one with video attachments.

There is no right or wrong answer to whether we should give in to this temptation. One designer will create the problem in the 21st century, opening the need for futuristic communication devices with lots of bells and whistles. Another designer will create a normal office with a few neat tricks hidden in it. The determiners of which way to go rests with the practicalities of the situation. How much real benefit will be gained by each approach? How much will it cost in time and money to implement each of the possible designs? Will there be negative side-effects from any of the options? What will appeal to the audience?

For this design, we will choose the less fancy approach. No videophones, and no 2-way tele-screens. We hope that we can make the environment *disappear* to the problem solver, so we will include in it as many familiar items as we can, realizing that the student will already know how to operate a telephone but may have to be trained in the operation of something new.

We have a second reason for our decision. It is based on our belief that students are intelligent and perceptive and want to be treated as such—even the ones who don't seem to feel that way. If we equip our office with special effects which are irrelevant to the problem, we are treating the student as children to be amused, and we not only set an entertainment tone which we must thereafter maintain, but we risk offending students who do not find the more futuristic office amusing—those who do not buy in to our fantasy world. We risk having the students take the problem less seriously.

Hoping to cultivate a more mature relation with the student, and being willing to depend on the inherent interest of the problem and what it can teach, we select in favor of a more mundane present-day office. However, we will not be averse to adding some interest when it is relevant to the problem or when it makes obtaining information and solving the problem more easy.

At this point, we are designing people into the simulation: inspectors capable of reporting the damage caused by the earthquake to various sectors of the town. If we are going to use inspectors to relay problem information, we must know how many and what types of inspectors to create.

Suddenly, we find ourselves designing a town and a bureaucracy. The number and type of inspectors we include will depend on the town we create. Most cities have water and power departments, and each of these normally has information that would be useful to a DRC after an emergency. Are water mains functioning in different parts of the town? Where is there power and where are lines broken? Every town also has police and fire departments which can provide information on road conditions, amount and location of damage, and specific human needs, which will vary depending on the level and locations of damage. If we create the normal town personnel infrastructure, we will have a ready-made source in our problem for the dissemination of much of the problem information. We can therefore assign the information items regarding damage and infrastructure functionality to locations associated with town personnel.

The specific points of information to be dispensed by these problem characters is created as we design the town itself and assign levels and types of damage to each of its geographical areas. We will divide the town into four sections. Each section will have its own level and type of damage and, consequently, human need. We may want to write down the damage details while they are fresh in our mind.

If the town has four sectors, each one probably ought to have four inspectors, for the water, power, fire, and police functions respectively. This creates a total of 16 accessible information characters. We add these as locations to our growing location map, realizing that eventually each character will give rise to a whole family of separate information-bearing locations.

As we attempt to mark the paths between the office and these new locations, we face the question of how movement between locations is to be accomplished. Communication with these characters represents movement between locations. Perhaps the telephone is a good surface metaphor for these movements.

The telephone fits into the naturalistic problem setting and the student's existing capabilities. This argues in favor of the phone as a simulation device. However, the phone creates an interface problem and brings up the question of fidelity and its trade-off with complexity. Operating a telephone in the real world requires several key presses as well as access to a source of phone numbers. Operating phones and phone books is not directly related to our instructional goal, and programming simulated phones can be a complex and costly task. These last factors seem to argue against using the phone.

We will simplify the problem by using a type of phone which provides one-button automatic dialing. This preserves realism and yet saves much programming effort as well as irrelevant student dialing time during the problem. If no automatic phone was available, we might look for other ways to simplify the calling system, since looking up and dialing numbers has several negative costs and no real benefits to problem solving. During interface design, tradeoffs of this nature are frequent, and designers have to keep a sense of purpose and priority as they create worlds.

The movement control trade-off problem does not wait long to re-assert itself, for as soon as we have chosen the method of calling the 16 inspectors, we realize that there is not just one but several items of information a problem solver might wish to gather from each one. How do we make it possible for the problem solver to ask several different questions of each one (which equates to moving between locations)?

We could create a standard menu of questions to be asked of any character. By making the entire list available every time an inspector (of any type) is called, we could learn something about the logical processes the student is using to solve the problem. However, providing questions can scaffold or channel the student's information seeking and provide more hints than we want. As the designers, we have to decide whether this foils the purpose of our design. If it does, we search for some other control system for question-asking. For our present design, we will choose the menu-of-questions approach. There will be many questions, and if a student is mining them systematically rather than depending on good problem solving logic, that will show up as a detectable pattern of performance to be noted during feedback.

The 16 inspectors we have created seem to fill most of the need for "live" information during problem solving. If we wish to add adventure to the problem, control its difficulty, or create multiple versions of the same problem (for test security), we can make the inspectors a dynamic information source by giving them schedules. If the phone rings for the inspector and he or she is not at the phone, the solver will have to decide what to do. Call back later? Call another source for the needed information?

To provide this timing function, we will add one model to this simulation. It will be a model of the comings and goings of the inspectors. At designated times during the problem, this model will send messages to each of the inspectors, telling them whether they are at their phones and what information they have to give out. As the student calls an inspector, the result may be a busy signal, a recorded message, no answer at all, or a question menu and access to fresh information. In this way, we can not only regulate problem complexity, but we can create a dynamism for the problem which will make it more realistic. As time passes, new information will become available. This will make it reasonable for a solver to consult each inspector at several points throughout the problem.

The form of the model that regulates the inspector messages will be simple. It will consist of a message chart divided into time segments. It will define the inspectors who are available and the messages they have to give at a given point in problem time. This model will be capable of sending messages to the inspector objects (which we have yet to design logic for), telling them the resources they have to share at a given moment.

With the design of the inspectors and the paths to them, have we provided sufficient problem information resources? What other information will the student need during problem solving?

Clearly there are certain archival sources of information which will be needed during problem solving. Some of these are identified in the problem structure; others are found in the instructional features. We will need, for instance, maps of the city (archival information), and an emergency response plan describing actions following an earthquake (an embedded didactic).

Other archival information may include:

- Names of the inspectors and their town area assignments.

- Names of relief support agencies to furnish supplies.

- Per-person daily requirements for food, water, and sanitation.

These information resources (and many others) can be included within file folders in a graphical file cabinet, manuals on a graphic shelf, memos lying on a graphical desk, graphical e-mail messages, or even in spontaneous phone calls from sources outside the DRC's office. Other information may be provided by a radio placed on the DRC's cabinet or even by a TV set which broadcasts periodically updated news reports.

We will create relief agencies to supply materials for problem solution (tents for shelter, food, water, trucks for transportation). These will be created by making locations for them in the way we used locations to create the inspectors. Students will be able to find out from these character-connected locations on-hand supply levels. They will also be able to arrange delivery schedules by interacting with these characters. We add these persons to our list of characters and create question menus to facilitate dialog with them, creating numerous locations as a result. Along with these questions, we will provide action controls that order the use of resources for disaster relief.

Information-recording tools present a challenge during location design. A location can be a place where information is stored by the problem solver for later use, reference, or in order to supply part of the problem answer. Such locations must allow a student to enter data (in alphanumeric, or graphic form), examine it, and modify it as new information becomes available.

As the student works on the problem, he or she must be able to record data for memory purposes describing the condition of the town and levels of resource (food, water, etc.) available for use in a solution. There must also be recording for the expression of the plan which constitutes the answer to the problem.

As inspectors are contacted, information about numbers of people needing various kinds of assistance in each part of town will accumulate. The student's first job will be to check that the information obtained is correct and complete. Then the student will have to make decisions on the basis of the accumulated data, and record decisions to be remembered, modified, and ultimately submitted as a final answer.

We select tabular worksheets as the best mechanism for data recording by the solver. Each cell of the table is treated as a separate location. When properly labeled, a worksheet can be intuitive for students to use, and can become a scaffold which reminds the student what information is yet needed. Spreadsheet formats are suitable for expressing problem solutions as well. We will make these spreadsheets into a single wall chart within the DRC office location. As an additional source of archival information, we will hang a map on the wall of the DRC office so that the student will know the town's layout, the location of key services and resources, and can calculate distances for resources to be hauled to those who need them.

Up to this point, we have invented several furnishings within the DRC's office, and we can update our sketch of it as shown in Figure 8. We have also created many locations on the location map which we should document at this time. The design of new locations and new paths between them will continue throughout the remainder of the development process.

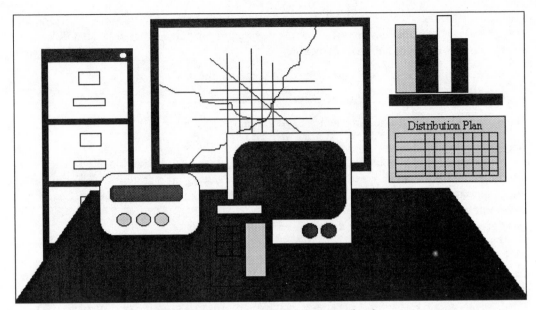

Figure 8. The updated office location sketch.

How is it possible to know when enough locations have been created? Only by careful mental walk-throughs of the problem by the designer and eventually by pilot tests conducted with real students. Some assurance can be gained when all of the actions and information items from the problem structure have been accounted for in locations, but piloting a prototype of the product is the ultimate test.

Activity: Define the interface concept

As the problem structure, the instructional concept, and the dramatic concept have taken form, we have kept in the back of our minds the possible uses of visual display area and audio channels. Our goal is to create an easy-to-use, easy-to-scan, realistic, and engaging interface between the student, the problem environment, its model(s), and the instructional features. As the dramatic concept began to evolve, we realized that the experience at the interface would be responsible for creating the students' mental image of the problem environment and even more, because the interface is also a responsive surface for the student to use in issuing commands to the simulation.

Our consideration of the interface must go far beyond dialogue boxes, radio buttons, and checkboxes. The interface design is a meeting point at which all other designs converge. All of their influence is felt there, and they in turn are influenced by interface decisions.

Movement controls: We need to consider a standard for how the student will control movement from location to location within the environment. We want to avoid the artificial feeling of pushbutton controls. We would like as much as possible to use controls which fit naturally into the environmental design itself.

We want the student to select from the displayed environment something which naturally suggests movement to a desired location. Doors naturally suggest places to go, as do phones, manuals on a shelf, and drawers on a desk. By using displayed objects as controls, we create *affordances* which invite the student to explore the environment. Instead of creating receptive learners who wait to be told information, part of our objective is to create students who will explore and probe for information in likely places that will lead to problem solution.

We will adopt the following navigation conventions:

- Objects visible in the environment will be made into click sensitive areas and used as "go there" controls.

- When a "go there" control is selected, the student will zoom or move to the location associated with that control.

We will use a small graphic icon showing a reduced image of the main office appearing constantly at a place on the display as an express zoom-back control to return the student to the initial DRC office location. Invisible "look left," "look right," "look up," and "look down" controls will be placed on the outer 1/2 inch of all sides of every display. Selecting these edge areas will move the student to the appropriate adjacent location viewpoint if one is available. As the cursor passes over a selectable object on the display, it will change shape to show a standard selectable cursor form, perhaps a pointing finger.

There are other controls we must design:

- Controls for location-independent actions.

- Controls related to problem management/administration.

Location-independent actions: It is sometimes important in a simulation's design that a student be able to perform generic acts, regardless of location within the problem environment. In an physical world simulation, it may be necessary for the student to "pick up" objects and transport them to different locations where they were "put down" or used in some task at the new location. *Pick up* and *put down* are location-independent actions.

In our disaster relief problem, there are no objects to pick up and put down, but we have mentioned one function which would be quite useful to perform at multiple locations—that of entering newfound data into an information-recording worksheet to allow the student to accumulate problem-related data and express answers.

We have already decided to place a spreadsheet as a wall chart in the main office, but we could just as easily displayed it as a chart clipped to a clipboard, available at all locations by clicking an icon. When an iconic control is unavailable at a location, a grayed or masked version of it could be shown instead of the normal one.

For in-person contact with live personalities in the environment, we might include a "speak" icon in the control area to allow the solver to address characters, make requests, or ask questions.

Problem administrative controls: We will provide a single control controls that allows students to access a number of administrative functions. These functions will include:

- Quitting the problem without finishing.

- Quitting temporarily to return (bookmark).

- Obtaining a restatement of the original problem.

- Declaring the problem solved.

- Obtaining in-process reports or summaries of activity.

We will design a single icon through which these administrative functions can be accessed. We will locate this control at the top of the display with the express zoom icon, leaving the remainder for environment graphics. In order to provide a problem time system, we will also place a small digital date and time icon at the top of the display which will show the problem day and the hour within the day.

Instructional features: The influence of instructional features must be considered before the interface design is complete. We must decide how our plans for the instructional features will be expressed through the interface. We have designed a hinting coach into our simulation, embedded didactics, and a post-problem feedback session.

Coach: We have designed so far a hinting function which can be requested by the solver. How will the hints be provided through the interface? There are several options, and we have already considered some of them. Our favorite option is to create an additional character (a *helper*) who is heard but not seen, offering advice when asked. We favor this way of delivering hints because it does not break the consistency of the office setting, it does not resort to standard artificialities such as dialog boxes, and it uses special effects in a way that supports the problem solving goal and does not distract attention from it.

A helper character can know when and what to comment by monitoring the stream of events performed by the solver and comparing it to patterns of expert performance—the dependency chart described earlier. We can also specify (if we choose) that when sufficient time or number of events has passed without productive action by the solver, the coach-helper will speak up to offer a hint taken from the expert's patterns.

When the helper speaks, a solver may wish to hear the message again, so we require a control for requesting a repeat of the last hinting message offered. There must also be a control for asking the helper for a hint. We will create a "hint" graphic icon and place it with the other controls.

Embedded didactics: The embedded didactics in this simulation do not require special interface design. Didactic materials will take the form of memos, file folder contents, manual pages, and even TV news reports. We should confirm that all of the didactics we want to provide are included in a location within the environment.

Feedback: Feedback will be presented post-problem. We have several options to choose from on how to present the feedback messages:

- A straightforward and impersonal critique given in textual messages.

- A faceless speaker giving a straightforward feedback message.

- A personality providing the feedback message in character voice.

Regardless of which option we choose, the feedback message content will be the same. Since we have already adopted the style of a hinting character, we will select the option of using a feedback character as well. We will make this character not only the source of feedback messages, but we may choose to create the person as the "mayor," who not only gives feedback and hints, but also makes the initial problem statement at the beginning.

Though our design calls for students to receive feedback at problem's end, some students may also wish to review their problem solving activities to date. We will place a feedback icon on the screen for this purpose. Creating this feedback message will simply include replaying the event file contents which have accumulated so far. If they wish for more, they can then ask for a hint.

As interface designs mature and we realize that we have created several persons and personalities to populate our simulated environment, we realize that special care must be taken to ensure that characters are both gender and ethnically balanced. Designers can use their choice of characters to show students that the community is balanced by the participation of a wide range of people in non-stereotyped roles. Care should be taken to create characters instead of caricatures, and the professionalism, good will, and responsibility of role models should be a chief consideration.

Activity: Define top-level simulation logic and assess logic tool options

We earlier defined the structure of the event or experience that this simulation will provide, so we can now define the logic of the computer program which will make the event take place. It may sound as if this is the first moment we begin to consider logic and tools, but in reality we have been keeping logic questions in the back of our minds with every design decision. We have not firmly committed to any design decision whose logical implementation we were not fairly sure how we would accomplish.

Often a designer will come to the simulation design task with a logical mechanism and a programming tool already in mind. Perhaps the designer already owns a driver program or a set of objects which has been used before and which can be reused. In such cases, the order of design is reversed, and the problem structure can be influenced by the logic, rather than the logic being influenced by the problem structure. Either direction works, and this example illustrates that the order of design decisions is not fixed. The order of design decisions changes, depending on which pre-made decision was made first or has the higher priority. Much also depends on the priorities of the designer: If software efficiency or operating speed has high priority, then logic design can easily end up influencing problem structure.

Logic patterns: The design of simulation logic frequently begins with the selection of a basic simulation logic pattern, like one of those described in Chapter 17. We have already decided to use an object-oriented programming approach. This offers two benefits: (1) potential for reduced programming time, and (2) possible reuse of objects from other simulations.

There are texts which describe general patterns of program objects, but this technology is just emerging, and none of those texts concern themselves specifically with instructional objects. Repeated experience in developing object-oriented simulations can lead to the creation of stock families of objects to carry out common functions. Over time, a tool box of reusable objects begins to accumulate, which becomes one of the designer's productivity secrets.

We will benefit much from the object-oriented approach. We have designed numerous characters with whom the solver interacts during a problem. Objects offer us the opportunity to create a generic character object which can be duplicated many times and given many unique identities through differential patterns of property assignment. This will create for us a pattern-based, economical approach to an otherwise huge programming task.

We see other benefits from reusability as well. We may be able to create the entire family of graded problems just by adding or subtracting character objects from a problem. We may also be able to redefine the properties of character objects dynamically during a problem, giving the characters a sense of development over time, giving the problem a very realistic quality as time progresses and conditions and character reactions change. These are very valuable side-effects of our tool choice.

Tool selection: Our selection of a specific, brand-name programming tool will be based on such factors as ease of tool use, speed of program creation (productivity), the available programming skills on our staff, ease of learning a proposed new tool, the nature or structure of the environment or model to be simulated, speed of program execution on the target platform, computer platform compatibility with a tool, ability to create stand-alone products, tool control of multimedia channels, and the ability to communicate data into and out of programs while they are running. The priority and relative importance of these factors will lead to a final tool decision.

Once we have tentatively chosen a tool for our simulation, we will perform a feasibility test on that portion of the design already completed to ensure that the tool can carry out the effects we have designed. If a tool is chosen early in a project, the tool strengths can help the designer create innovative effects. If a tool is chosen late, it can lead to design revisions to fit tool capabilities.

Activity: Define top-level logic for instructional features

The instructional features which were described as part of the instructional concept must be given a general logic plan. We personally consider it best to give the simulation models and the instructional features separate logical structures if possible. There are several reasons for this: (1) it facilitates the creation of driver or shell mechanisms for both, (2) it increases the possibility of reusability for both simulation software and instructional feature software, and (3) it makes the transfer of control and the division of responsibility between simulation and instructional feature clear.

A designer may make the relation between the simulation and the instructional features close, highly time-structured, and highly interactive, or more distant from the simulation, time-independent, and unintegrated. We have chosen instructional features which are close to the simulation environment (hinting) and distant from it (delayed feedback).

For feedback, we have already made the decision that it will be non-integrated with the simulation environment. The simulation problem will not be interrupted by immediate feedback messages. Instead, the simulation will produce an event file—a file containing a record of each action and movement initiated by the student. The feedback mechanism will open this file following the completion of a problem and interpret it to critique the student's performance.

The coaching instructional feature could also, if the designer desired, be isolated as a single reminding or forewarning function prior to the start of a problem. But we have decided to include coaching during the problem in coordination with movement between locations. At this point, we will try to be more specific about how this can be made to happen using object-oriented computer logic.

As problem solution proceeds, solvers perform movements between locations. We have already decided that this will in turn produce a unique event for each location, and as events occur, they will be stored in an event file for use by the feedback mechanism after the problem. The feedback mechanism will compare the stored sequence of events with an idealized pattern of expert problem solving steps in order to make judgments and produce feedback messages. These expert patterns will be represented in the form of a dependency chart which captures the expert's preferred order of solving events. The feedback driver will be capable of spotting not only the expert's patterns of solution events but several incorrect patterns as well. When it detects either a good or bad pattern, it will be capable of supplying an appropriate feedback message that matches the pattern.

With a few minor changes, this mechanism can also produce hinting messages during the problem. The dependency chart of events necessary to produce hinting messages is the same one used to produce feedback messages. For feedback, the dependency chart is used retrospectively to detect patterns that *have* happened. For coaching or hinting the dependency chart can be used prospectively to identify and recommend patterns which *should* happen.

The feedback will produce its judgments in a large batch at the end of a problem. The event stream which it judges will be supplied complete for the feedback driver to inspect at that time. The hinting function will not be able to wait until the end of the problem, however, because students can ask for a hint at any time during the problem and must receive it immediately. The supply of events to the hinting driver must be constant, as each event is produced by a student movement or action.

We will therefore design the message flow between objects so that it passes the event stream through a *coaching object* as the problem progresses. The function of the coaching object will be to read the event stream, watching for "trigger" patterns from the dependency chart—either good, productive ones or erroneous, unproductive ones. The coach will have to be able to accumulate events in order to notice patterns of them in addition to noticing the most recent event.

When the coaching object notices one event that should be followed by another specific event, it will know what to suggest when it is asked. It will suggest any of the identified, yet unfulfilled, events. With minor modifications, this hinting system could be turned into an active coaching system by volunteering the coaching messages rather than waiting for them to be asked for.

The dependency chart arrangement we have designed uses a simple pattern-detecting expert system. It could as easily be designed to detect patterns fed to it from a data file of detectable patterns, each associated with its own feedback and hinting messages. Either source of events can be used to create the basis for event-driven instructional features. From the student's point of view, there is no obvious difference between the two sources.

As we design these details of the coaching and feedback systems, we see that the object-oriented tool chosen for the development of simulation logic will serve for construction of these mechanisms, so our choice of tool has not been challenged by these decisions.

Activity: Define plan for product implementation

An implementation plan is the plan for rolling a product out of the designer's shop into the real world where it will be used. It is not a development plan which gives the schedules for product development. It is a plan for introducing the product into the real world and supplying it with the support and evaluation functions which will ensure its long-term survivability.

The plan for product implementation has a great deal of influence on design decisions. A product may have a very effective instructional approach but be difficult to implement. Teachers may require special training; schools and businesses may require special computers or special add-on equipment to run the product. Because the design profile of a product influences its usability, it is important to determine the impact of implementation questions on the design early.

At this point we are mainly interested in checking two things: (1) the product *footprint*, and (2) the product image. We will make sure these two factors are harmonious with the support systems of the user's environment and the tastes of the user. During this activity, we will use much of the context data we gathered in an earlier design activity.

Footprint: The footprint of an instructional product describes the physical, temporal, and skill space within which the product operates. This includes not only the space and time taken up by the product and its equipment but that taken up before and after use as well. The following list is suggestive (but by no means complete) of the implementation issues which can be impacted by a product design:

- Physical space requirements (physical size of the instructional area).
- Physical furnishing requirements (special work tables, carrels).
- Additional equipment requirements (headphones, speakers, projectors).
- Hardware requirements (PC type, disk size, RAM, chip, speed, CD).
- Hardware configuration (networking, peripherals, boards, settings).
- Software requirements (programs, versions, drivers, licensing).
- Software configuration (settings, networking, preferences).
- Operating service requirements (electrical, networks).
- Time/skill envelope during set-up (installation, testing).

- Time/skill envelope during preparation of instructors (new skills).

- Time/skill envelope during student use (student prep, interface use).

- Space envelope during use (noise/separation requirements, work space).

- Consumable material requirements (handouts, reference books, floppies).

- Time/skill envelope after use (data analysis, reporting, prescription).

- Operating support skill/knowledge requirements (net/system mgt.).

- Maintenance skill/knowledge requirements (repair, operational help).

The task at this point is to identify early potential problems—conflicting demands between design features and training site realities—and either eliminate them through redesign or reduce them to the point where the average user will find it feasible and affordable to use your product. Design is a great deal like packing a suitcase. Everything must fit in or be left behind, or a bigger suitcase must be used, and all of this needs to be decided before the trip begins.

The implementation task is made somewhat difficult by the lack of standards for computer installations. Designers normally find their installed base to include both very old and very new computers of various shapes and sizes. This is due partly to the rapid advance of technologies which renders today's new hardware and software obsolete within 18 to 24 months. Your best plan may be to design to today's leading-edge computer, realizing that by the time your product is ready to distribute, that computer will be an average platform.

Image: The image a product builds in the mind of the user has an enormous influence on its use and success. Our product is intended for use in a school setting with teen-agers, and so image is very critical—not just the image the students have of the product, but also the image the teachers have of it. That image will be projected by diverse elements of the product: the quality of the documentation, the visibility of instructional value of the product, and ultimately the look and feel of the box and physical package in which the product arrives.

Image begins with first impressions (packaging, documentation, finish, look, feel) and continues through detailed examination of the product (screen design, interaction, attention to detail, feel, fit, personality, and stability). In our case, a teacher will most likely evaluate the product for use by students. We would like our product to send a message to the teacher and to the student. We would like it to say: "responsible but fun," "easy to use," "inherently interesting," "worthwhile goals," and "effective instruction."

To attain these messages, we will not only carefully design the simulation itself but the physical package and documentation. We will also seriously consider providing materials for an introductory brief on the product for teachers and students, showing the product being used by real teachers and students in different ways.

The general implementation plan we will have created when we have dealt with all of these considerations is an important part of the product design—ultimately as important to the long life of the product as central instructional issues.

Wave 2: Design testing

We have described many activities so far that make up a first wave of the design process, and it may seem that there is nothing left to do. But we have only created the broad structural outlines of a design at this point. We have much detailed design to create before we can produce a product. By creating the diverse parts of a high-level design first, we have added to the overall consistency of the product and saved ourselves from many problems and delays down the road.

It may seem that considerable time has been consumed by the first wave of design activities, but the truth is quite the contrary. Though in it there are many decisions made, the first wave moves quickly. The process moves especially fast when a small, imaginative team works together in a continuous cycle of conferencing and solo work on assigned tasks.

It is important to stop at the end of the first wave of design to reflect on the integrity and focus of the design created thus far. We must consider the cost, feasibility, and unity of purpose of what has been designed before committing further effort. This is a critically important step that saves much time, money, and disappointment later on, which would otherwise result from flawed, costly, or impossible designs discovered too late.

The designer reaches the end of the first wave with decisions which are individually feasible and practical. But the whole design concept has not been evaluated in unity; the cost and feasibility of the ensemble design has not been tested. That is what takes place now.

Numerous questions exist at this point with regard to the design in its entirety. These questions include (but are not limited to):

Instructional alignment

- Does the simulation environment and model structure match the performance and knowledge goals of instruction?

- Will solving problems in the environment provide the right types and amounts of practice and the needed instructional feature support?

Technology feasibility

- Will the installed base of hardware have sufficient speed, power, and features to run this program acceptably?

- Will the software have sufficient speed and capability to support the features called for in the design?

Product internal consistency

- Will all of the separate parts of this product work together?

- Do any parts of the design conflict or compete with others?

- Is the product design complete?

User viewpoint/experience

- Will this product create a valuable and enjoyable learning experience for the target student?

- Is the interface going to be usable/learnable by the target student at an acceptable level?

- Is the learning task at the right level for the target population?

Budget/resources

- Do we have sufficient funds for personnel to complete the development of this design?

- Do we have sufficient equipment and facility resources to complete this project?

- How much will the entire development cost? Do we have that much?

Production expertise

- Will there be sufficient amounts and types of development staff expertise to complete this project?

- Will there be sufficient subject-matter expertise available to complete an acceptable product?

Time

- Do we have sufficient calendar time to develop what has been designed?

- Will the required production skills be available at the time they are needed?

Implementability

- Can the product be implemented as designed in real world setting?

- Who would be excluded/included from using our product?

- Is the product easy enough to use for the instructor?

- Does the product use the right amount of time?

These questions are more complex and encompassing than those we have had to answer up to now, but there is a lot at stake at this point. We could call this review a *fault mode analysis* because we are trying to foresee how things may go wrong if this design is used as the basis for development. The designer now turns pessimist. He or she tries to think of reasons why the design as a whole *won't* work—or if it will fail—*where* and *how* it will fail. Early iron bridge designers learned from several spectacular failures that a design that works under ideal conditions is not enough. They learned to probe their designs, looking for possible failure modes. The only usable designs are those which will perform reliably under the most adverse conditions.

The designer's curiosity should go beyond the questions listed above, but at least that list should be considered. In some cases, neither the designer nor the support staff will have enough wisdom or experience to answer them. It is advisable to halt in such cases to do prototyping and experimentation sufficient to ensure that the design is within feasible and practical limits. Designers should be happy to receive bad news during this design review, because a problem detected now is insurance against unexpected problems later, when the project's time and money have been spent.

The tools used during the second wave of design include suites of the equipment the product will operate on, the software the product will be developed in, and cost analysis methods. By far the most valuable resource during the process is the experience gained from past disasters. Once this period of destructive testing of the conceptual design is complete, the designer is ready to move on to the third wave of design and specify precise detail for every feature of the product.

Wave 3: Designing the details

The third wave of design defines every detail of the simulation product. Up to this point the design process has created the central structural elements of the simulation. Design activities at this point will add detail to those structures. The charts and diagrams sketched during Wave 1 of design now become carefully drawn diagrams and are the basis for entire notebooks of design detail collected in charts, tables, forms, and diagrams. It is these details which the production staff will use as the recipe for creating the computer graphic, audio, and logic files of the simulation. If the recipe is well-thought-out and documented clearly, production will run smoothly and economically.

In a simulation of this size there are many details. We chose our example project to be slightly on the large size to illustrate several important principles of simulation design. Before we get to those details, we should address some global Wave 3 issues.

Adding to the design team: Staff diversity

The activities of conceptual design in Wave 1 can be completed by an individual or by a small team of designers who share a product vision. But the detailed design of a larger simulation product can seldom be completed in a reasonable time by one or two people. Normally at the beginning of the detailed design process (even at the beginning of fault mode analysis), the design staff is normally increased in size.

Seldom are the newcomers to the design team the same level or type of designers as the original core. Most often the new designers are specialists in some area of production. These people will form the core of the production group. That is why it is important that they be included in the design detailing process (and even in fault mode analysis if possible).

A frequent early addition to the design team for detailed design is an art designer. This person is normally an artist with depth of training, experience, and judgment who can design jobs and standards for the other artists who will join the team for production. Other early additions to the design team may be logic tool experts and writer/designers. These people will have the same level of expertise in their respective fields as the art director has in his or hers and will perform a similar function.

The art director may not be a full-time design team member and may be shared with other projects, but the expertise of this person is a crucial issue. This person will advise decisions concerning the choice of representational standards, tools, processes, and styles. These decisions, more than any other, influence the production costs for the product. Mis-estimation or misinformation in this area can be very costly in both calendar time and money. Consider the implications if you had an entire house to paint and your painting advisor recommended a tool with the capacity of an artist's paint brush. Or what if you were told to use rollers to paint the house but advised to use a slow-drying, temperamental variety of paint.

A logic tool expert will also give very high-impact advice, and the influence on time and production costs will be comparable. The logic tool expert recommends and evaluates programming tools and must help you choose one suited to your project. The earlier you involve some portion of this person's time, the better. Not all tools are equal in their power, productivity, and ease of use, as we described in Chapter 3. Faulty direction from an art director can lead you to paint the house with an artist's brush; your logic tool expert can have you putting up the walls with an upholstery hammer or finishing the fine woodwork with a sledge hammer.

The writer/designer's task is to provide words, symbols, and information-bearing structures of all kinds where they are needed. In addition, the writer, can be a master of dramatic structure to help you detail the dramatic scenario associated with your simulation. Some simulations have strong story lines, which your writer will help you develop. Other simulations are light on story or have none at all. The great temptation of the writer will be to revert to a totally sequenced and preprogrammed story line. Simulations normally require dramatic settings which are responsive to a broad variety of student choices. The writer you choose must share your vision of this much looser, student-oriented story and must set up writing standards and processes which support a new type of instructional adventure.

Design changes and standards

As detailed design progresses, changes to the original design may be called for, either due to design conflicts between different elements of the product not spotted during fault mode analysis or due to the new and better ideas, which are almost certain to occur as the design staff becomes more familiar with the product and its potential. As changes occur, they are of three types: (1) fundamental structural changes, (2) changes to previous detail decisions, or (3) changes to detail standards.

This third change requires explanation. As you (or one of your staff) design details for the simulation, each location, its functions, and its controls will have properties in common. Some design details will be allowed to vary: the content of the location, the actions possible there, etc. But there will also be many location details that will not vary from location to location. You will want them to be the same everywhere so that the thread of similarity in location look and behavior is preserved. These similarities will be the roadsigns that enable solvers to act knowledgeably in unfamiliar locations. You will preserve these details as a standard across all locations. They will speed the user's scanning of each scene and reduce the burden of recall and figuring out controls and their operation. These standards will help to keep the interface itself secondary in the student's attention and the simulated problem primary.

Deciding what will be standard and what will be left free to vary is an important part of Wave 3 design. The standard may be constructed prior to the onset of detailed design, but the more likely case is that it will grow through an accumulation of decisions.

During the early stages of detailed design, designers will consider each decision not only as it impacts a single location or model element but as a potential standard for all locations and all models. Once two or three locations and one or two models have been designed, if designers have been recording their decisions, the automatic result will be an emerging design specification which all designers can begin to follow. Having this specification saves time in decision-making, review of design, and later modification. It reduces confusion and wasted time, and its benefit is directly proportional to the number of people working on the project at once.

Documentation

Some designers are tempted to ignore the accumulation of a standard and its documentation. This temptation is greatest when the design team for Wave 3 design is between three and six persons. A small team with a strong memory can accomplish a consistent design without documenting it. However, when product testing begins and requests for changes begin to accumulate, the value of documentation asserts itself.

It surprises many designers to discover that time and cost for modifications to a product often outstrip those for original production. Without documentation, this maintenance process becomes even more costly and dangerous, as previously-functional logic begins to malfunction following undocumented changes to an undocumented product.

The need for current and accurate documentation is greatest when two or three generations of changes have been made to the same logic or art elements. Without current documentation, it is difficult and time-consuming to determine what the current working version of the product contains—which is a prerequisite to making any changes. There is an analogue between the documentation of an instructional design and the documentation of a building design when modifications are the issue. Recently, at a large university, an extension was made to one of the buildings, and construction was delayed for two months. This was the amount of time it took to completely test the wiring of the existing part of the building. The testing became necessary when it was discovered that the electrical diagrams (part of the documentation) for the building had disappeared, and the contractor was unwilling to gamble that the electricians could make accurate guesses about which wires were connected to which switches. We strongly urge projects to perform as much documentation as they can afford, and we suggest that what you can't afford today you will most certainly be obliged to afford tomorrow.

Documentation vs. rapid prototyping

An issue which can cause conflict during simulation design is the need— primarily during the fault mode analysis of Wave 2—to build prototypes rapidly and cheaply of parts of the design for feasibility and cost studies to prove or challenge the design. As fault mode analysis ends and the detailed design of Wave 3 begins, there is a temptation to continue to build onto the successful prototypes from Wave 2, using them as the core of the real product, but failing to document the prototype. When this happens, it makes keeping documentation later very difficult. It is sometimes the justification project leaders give for keeping no documentation at all. We strongly urge either concurrent documentation during prototype development or a pause prior to Wave 3 to document successful prototypes.

Wave 3 design activities

Wave 3, Detailed Design, progresses just as Wave 1 did, and all of the general design principles that pertained there pertain here as well. This sometimes includes the parallel ordering of steps, the influence of design decisions on each other, and the order of design progressing generally from structure to detail.

The goal of detailed design is to create a body of production data which skilled production workers from all of the necessary areas can use to produce the simulation product efficiently. For single-member development teams, it is the means by which the lone designer/developer extends personal memory and ensures that details and decisions are not forgotten.

Though production and detailed design may to some extent proceed concurrently, if the design function is overtaken by the production function, then production-by-design becomes design-by-production or design-from-the-hip, and the danger of design blind alleys becomes much greater, risking time and dollars unnecessarily.

Though the detailing of the design in Wave 3 tends to require a larger design staff and takes somewhat longer to accomplish than Wave 1, our descriptions of the activities of Wave 3 will be considerably shorter than those for Wave 1. That is because Wave 3 is mainly a process of detailing the structures created during Wave 1. If Wave 1 activities are done well, then Wave 3 may be very short indeed, because many of the details will have been created by the excess energies of Wave 1. If, on the other hand, Wave 1 is performed in more haste, Wave 3 may require additional time to create some of the structures that Wave 1 forgot.

There is no way to draw a clear line between Wave 1 and Wave 3 decisions. It is not strictly a matter of deciding some issues in one wave and some issues in another. The principle is that what is not designed in one will remain to be finished in the next. Keep in mind also that the division of the simulation design process into three main waves—two for designing and one for proving the structural design—does not mean that all design efforts will correspond exactly to the three-wave pattern. Some design efforts only have time and money for one wave. Others seem to go through many more than three waves. The process is always tailored to the resources available, the skills of the designer, and the importance of the product.

Let's consider now the activities normally carried out in what we are calling the third main wave of design.

Activity: Detail problem information and locations

The source of our problem information is a town. In Wave 1 we gave definition to the town in general. Now we must finish the process, adding any details that were not invented during Wave 1.

We have divided the town into four sectors. We have created people and bureaucratic organizations within the town. We will now produce a detailed map of the town and "create" the town, including the numbers of people in each residence. We will do this in order to know the statistics of the town, its population, and the population's distribution. We will produce a complete town now—at least with respect to the four basic commodities of the problem: food, water, shelter, and sanitation.

Also during this activity, the newly-created information about the town will be allocated to locations within the problem environment where students can find it, finishing off the definition of locations that was begun during Wave 1. This information will appear as new maps on walls, new files in file drawers, new memos on the desk, new reports in the DR manuals, and other sources of information which the student will be able to discover within the DRC office.

Will the student know just where to look for this data when first presented with the problem? No, and the growing body of problem-related information can become a complexity for the student. Therefore, we will design a town, but we will keep it simple enough that the student can find the needed information with a little intelligent browsing. We want the student to concentrate on the complexities of the problem and not the complexity of the town.

Once the relevant data on the town is captured, divided, and allocated to locations, we will create the earthquake and its effects. We will identify the areas of town receiving the most damage (based on less-solid ground) and declare the residences there unlivable. We will define which water mains are out of service due to earthquake damage and which roads are impassable. We could define the number of injured persons, but the problem does not involve the student in providing medical aid, so this information is beyond the scope of our problem.

We will record the damage information, but in this case we will not store it in DRC office locations as we did the town description. The quake damage information will arrive to the student from the inspectors, each of them working in one of the four sectors of the town, and each of them having a summary of the damage to the infrastructure in their area (water, power, etc.).

In order to make the reports of damage more realistic and to add an element of interest to the problem, as well as to teach the student that all of the problem information is not always available all at once, we have already decided to make the reports of the inspectors time-sensitive. The information that the inspectors give will change with the passage of problem time.

This creates a matrix of locations (*inspector* x *specialty* x *time*), a sample of which is shown in Figure 9. One of the writer/designer's tasks will be to create exact message content for each inspector during each time slot in the problem. During some of the time slots, different inspectors will be out of office or have busy phones. This will give students the opportunity to browse the DRC's office for helpful information, learning from what is to be found there. During some time slots, the information given will be tentative and incomplete and the inspector will say so. This will be a clue to the solver to be careful about drawing conclusions from the information until more confirmed information is obtained. In later time slots, the damage data will cease to change, as it would tend to do in a real disaster.

Other sources of time-fed information will include the radio and TV in the DRC's office, which the student will have access to. Their messages will also be placed within a matrix, and message content changes over time will be planned.

Once the town and the quake damage have been designed and locations have been assigned to the message content, the resources needed for a solution may be designed. We will create various places within the town where emergency supplies (food, water, tents, and latrines) are stored. Different amounts of these supplies will be stored in different locations, creating the need for transporting them. The resources for transportation will be supplied by other organizations designed as part of the town.

	Water	Police	Fire	Sanitation
Time: 2:00:00				
Sector 1				
Sector 2				
Sector 3				
Sector 4				
Time: 4:00:00				
Sector 1				
Sector 2				
Sector 3				
Sector 4				
Time: 6:00:00				
Sector 1				
Sector 2				
Sector 3				
Sector 4				

Figure 9. Extract of a message matrix for timed access to problem information.

Activity: Define student response entry points and work surfaces

We have not defined in detail up to this point to the expression of the student's answer (the scheduling plan for transporting resources) and the student's means for data recording to capture and summarize problem data as it is discovered.

There are several reasons why this capability is important:

1. The computer must have an answer from the student to determine the quality of the solving performance. It also must have samples of intermediate performance which create events for reconstructing the source of errors. The tabular planning worksheet (which we have placed on a wall chart in the DRC office), can capture both final and intermediate answer data.

2. The volume of data the student must obtain and manipulate during this problem exceeds human memory capacity, so students must have a place to write it down.

3. If the planning worksheet can be made to resemble real-world information-manipulation tools like a spreadsheet or a data base, then another dimension of tool learning can take place during the problem. Embedded didactics from a problem character can guide the student in the use of these new (simplified and perhaps coached) tools.

4. Problem solving process can be at the same time scaffolded and recorded for analysis and feedback by asking the student to express intermediate decisions and calculations as worksheet entries.

We need to define the operation of the worksheets. We will use the worksheets in a way that teaches the student to use them by gradually increasing the performance demand. Certain preliminary worksheets will be asked for in a scaffolded exercise early in the problem. This early task of form-filling, using very simply structured worksheets, will ask students to enter a few values under coached conditions. Later in the problem, a form will be filled out for a press release, somewhat more complicated than the first one, but using the same data entry protocols. Help will be offered for this exercise on request. For the expression of the final answer, the most comprehensive answer form will be provided in the wall chart, uncoached, for the entry of the plan for distributing supplies.

Each of the cells in the worksheets presented will work on the click-and-type principle, each one will constitute a location in the simulation environment, and each one will produce a recorded event in the event stream when any entry is made or modified.

Activity: *Define model details*

The model(s) used in a simulation are given existence and general form during Wave 1; they are given detail in Wave 3. We have up to this point only expressed one model for our simulation, and it is a simple one: It sends a message to each of the information sources (inspectors, TV channel, etc.) at periodic intervals, telling the source what its current message is. This in effect creates a model of damage information changing over time—a model of a human information-gathering process. This model is driven from a table rather than by rules. Not every model is like this one, though this type of model could be used in other time-based problems which model societal or communication processes.

For most models detailed expression entails: (1) naming every component to be included in the model, and (2) specifying the cause-effect linkages between components.

To illustrate this more typical method of model design, we will invent one: a simple office lighting system with one light and two light switches. The components of this simple model include the two switches as controls and the light as the single indicator. (In practice, the lamp going on and off will be accomplished by switching between lightened and darkened versions of the lamp graphic, so there will actually be two lamp components—an "off" lamp and an "on" lamp.)

Each switch will have two positions or states: "on" and "off." The light will also have the same two states. The cause-effect relations of this model will consist of a set of if/then rules (like the set we presented earlier in the chapter) or a truth table (like the one in Figure 10). In more complex models, both controls and indicators may have multiple, even unlimited, numbers of states. In those models, the truth table and rule are replaced by formulas or equations that compute the state of model indicators.

By defining the components and (in this case) the cause-effect rules for operation, we have specified the model. A programmer will implement the rules in a set of interacting objects, making the model operate realistically.

Activity: *Define model connections with locations*

The indicators of a model must appear visibly within some location; otherwise the solver has no way of seeing them. In our office light example, both switches and the light must be visible within an office location.

Expressing model controls and indicators entails: (1) displaying the current state of each control and indicator when a location is entered, and (2) re-displaying both control and indicator states as students perform actions on the controls and changes to indicator states are computed.

To be more concrete, as the solver enters the office, the switches and the light must appear within the room. When the solver enters, it may not be for the first time, and the position of the switch may have been changed during the previous visit to the room. Therefore, as the room graphic is displayed, there must be provision not only for putting up the switch on the wall but putting it up in its current position—on or off. The same is true of the light. It must appear either on or off as the room is entered.

Moreover, whenever a model control is acted upon, the model must be notified so that it can recompute its values. Following a recomputation, the controls and indicators of the model must be immediately redisplayed to ensure that they are visible showing the latest and most correct state. Therefore, when the switch is flipped on or off during the simulation, not only the light changes state (to "on" or "off"), but the switch as well.

At this point in time, we are only designing the room and the objects in it. A programmer will later make provision for the placing of model controls and indicators on the display and for re-displaying them after model recomputation. This will be a relatively simple thing to do. Our task for now is simply to identify the changeable things in the room—those things which are the visible manifestations of a model. We will identify those things which are model-driven and all of the states or values each one can take on. This information will be gathered on a form which is described in the next section.

Activity: Create design records to store location details

At this point, a large family of locations exists in the design, and the paths between them have been charted. A mass of detail has begun to accumulate for each location. The amount of detail will continue grow for each location as design continues and production begins. We have just seen the accumulation of new detail: the names and states of model-related objects within each location. As artists, programmers, and writer/designers do their work, still more detail will accumulate in the form of file names, text segments, and logical rules. We need to begin to centralize the data about each location, because there is no way we—let alone a team of people—can hold this mass of information in memory. If we don't document, it will become impossible to produce our simulation.

- The information that defines a location comes under several headings:
- The visual design of the location.
- The model control and indicator inventory for the location (with states).
- The control and action profile of the location.
- The production detail (file names) for the location.
- The logic details for the location.

This information *unfolds* as design proceeds to produce the complete location recipe. It is actually a lot of fun to specify locations, because it is the time when the designer's imagination can be given the most freedom; the designer becomes the creator of an imaginary world. But so much data is created by this process that a form for collecting and maintaining it is a most useful and time-saving tool.

We suggest the creation of a *Location Design Record*. This record can be used to capture the data for one location. In the early stages, the information captured will be more conceptual or descriptive in nature, but as design ends and development proceeds, the information will be transformed by the production process into specific data, including numbers, text, and file names.

The Location Design Record must contain as a minimum the following kinds of data:

- Location identity
- Visual design data
- Audio design data

- Hotspot and path-out data

- Control availability data

- Portable object data

- Model object data

Location identity is created by giving the location a unique name which is used by no other location. This can be a number or a descriptive name.

As identities are assigned, it is important to keep in mind the difference between a *room* and a *location*. Many location simulations are sited within building spaces which include rooms and hallways, such as the rooms of an office or of a maintenance shop. As a solver enters a room of the office or shop, there is not just one location there, there is a hierarchy of them. Each of the walls of the room qualifies as a location, because the attention of the solver cannot be on all four walls at once.

Within the view area of each wall there may be furnishings, wall hangings, or wall features which also represent locations. A file cabinet placed against the east wall of a room, if selected with a mouse click, causes movement toward (to) the file cabinet, which is a lower-level location. Each of the drawers of the file cabinet may be visible, and if any is clicked, there is a consequent movement toward (to) that drawer and its contents. Thus, every object within a field of view is a potential gateway to many locations lower in the hierarchy of locations. This hierarchy allows the solver to move in a zooming motion, both toward and away from the details of the problem, whether they are locations where action can be taken or locations where information can be obtained.

Visual design: The visual design of a location is captured on the Location Design Record in the form of sketches and data. The physical layout and appearance of a location normally begins as a sketch. Later it includes annotations by artists and art designers. Ultimately it ends up as the name of a computer graphic file which an artist has created and stored, using the annotations, sketches and other entries as a guide.

Not every location will be information-yielding. Many locations yield no new information related to the problem. But if you design a location to contain a specific information, you must do so in a way that creates a natural-looking context. A note left in the study requires a table, a credenza, or a desk to rest on, unless the note is to be found lying on the floor.

Audio design: Since not all locations are visual in the information they supply, the Location Design Record must provide for the recording of data leading to the production of audio as well. Audio specifications normally begin as notes describing the content of an intended audio message or sound effect. From notes, the specification progresses to a narration script or a specific effect name. Finally, following production, the name of one or more audio files is recorded for programmers, data enterers, and testers to use.

Hotspot and destination data: Movement to new locations will normally be accomplished in a location simulation by selecting, with a mouse click, an area of the visual display. Selection areas are normally called *hotspots*. When a hotspot is selected, a branch to a new location is expected, so the data on the Location Design Record must not only identify the geographical areas of the screen which will be hot, but it must name for each hotspot the new location associated with it—the location which the solver will move to on selecting the spot.

Control availability: We have defined a small set of iconic action controls which will always be present on the screen in our simulation. Each control can be displayed in two forms: a masked form where it is not available for use, and an unmasked form where it is. For each location, the designer must record whether each of the iconic action controls is available at that location—whether the icon is to be shown masked or unmasked.

Do not confuse iconic action controls with model controls. The recording of data for model controls is handled below. Iconic action controls are those controls which allow generic actions ("pick up," "put down," "speak," etc.) to be carried out at any location. They are always visible. Model controls appear only within specified locations, and they have different states in which they must be shown. They are connected directly to the computations of a model behind the scenes.

Portable objects: A location simulation may have portable objects which can be taken from one location to another. A repair person may not be allowed to make a repair at a given location without the correct tool. At the beginning of a problem, certain portable objects may be placed in specific locations. Once they are carried away to new locations and dropped, these objects reside in the new location. If at the beginning of a problem, an object is to appear in a location, the name of the object and the graphic file which contains its representation should be recorded on the Location Design Record.

Model objects: Model objects (which are always either controls or indicators) need to be recorded on the Location Design Record as well. Along with the unique name of the object, the designer should record each of the states the control or indicator can manifest, and there should be room left for the recording of graphic file names which will follow production of these objects by the artist.

Activity: Define details of action icons

The routine performed when the action icons are clicked must be defined in detail. This consists of: (1) defining the syntax of actions, and (2) defining the steps which are part of carrying out the command.

The command syntax of an action command refers to the sequence of steps which must be performed by the solver in order to invoke the action. This order of steps is carried out exactly the same way every time the action is taken. One of the challenges of action command design is to make the command easy to perform so that the solver does not have to pay extra attention to giving the command. The sequence should be intuitive, and the solver should never have to ask twice how to give the command.

The "pick up" command is a common one. "Pick up" allows the solver to obtain a portable object at one location and carry it to a different location so that it can be used in problem solving. The normal syntax for this command follows the verbal command you would give if you were speaking the command: "Pick up (click the command icon) the thing (click on the thing to be picked up)." Another example of a command syntax gives the ability to address any problem character with a question. The syntax for this command is: "Speak to (click the command icon) that person (click on the graphic representation of the person)."

Sometimes a menu must be involved in command syntax. This is true when the object of the command is not visible when the command is given. For instance, the "put down" command is normally given when the objects being carried are invisible. The normal syntax of this command is: "Put down (click the command icon) (menu appears listing things that are being carried) the thing (click on the item from the list to be dropped)."

Once the command syntax has been designed for an action control, the steps (meaning the computer program's steps) for carrying out the control action can be designed. We are using an object-oriented programming tool, so we express our designs in terms of objects.

We give portable objects the ability to send and receive messages to and from the student's traveler object. When the "pick up" control is selected, it sends a message to portable objects which are visible. When an object is picked up, it disappears from the display, at the same time telling the student's traveler object that it now is carrying the portable object.

Activity: Define initial problem states

Many values can change during the course of problem solving. The solver's current location changes, portable objects can be moved to a new location, model controls can be set and reset, and indicators react to changes in model states.

Since values can change, we have specify what they will be at the beginning of a problem. Initial values have impact on how the problem appears to the student. It is one thing to enter the control room of a turbo electric generation facility during normal operation; it is another to enter the control room during a crisis. Initial values determine the difference between normal and crisis.

For each changeable object property in the simulation, the designer specifies the values for each object at the beginning of the problem. In addition, the designer specifies where the student's traveler object will be placed at problem initiation. This information is recorded in the Location Design Record.

Activity: Design details of instructional features

The details of instructional feature action must be described just as iconic action control operation had to be specified. Instructional feature specification is accomplished by: (1) defining the sequence of steps to be performed (by the computer) when one cycle of the feature's operation is executed, and (2) by specifying the structure and content of the message delivered by the feature.

We have chosen to use the feedback feature in our simulation. We have decided that post-problem feedback will be the only kind of feedback, so we will specify the sequence of steps for carrying it out.

The feedback sequence will consist of several classes of message delivered in a set sequence: (1) a prefatory message outlining what will follow and setting expectations, (2) messages that evaluate the solution attempted (assuming one was attempted), and (3) messages that evaluate the steps the solver did chose to perform. These last messages will point out positive steps taken, missed opportunities, step inversions, and other correctable mistakes. At the end of the feedback process, a summary statement will be made, and a comparison will be made between the solver's performance and the average performance, as well as with an expert's performance. These are the stepwise process for giving feedback.

If we had instead chosen within-problem, interruptive feedback, the cycle of feedback would take place (possibly) several times per problem. It would be shorter and would not contain nearly as many steps as the post-problem feedback. Interruptive feedback would take place because the solver had strayed from a path of action considered acceptable, so the conditions for giving feedback would be different. The steps in interruptive feedback would consist of delivering the feedback message and then falling silent.

In addition to the mechanics and sequence of the instructional feature, the designer must specify the content of the message(s) produced by the instructional feature. This is one of the most interesting problems in all of instructional design, because it takes the design directly to the level of the single interactions and requires the designer to specify what is the best thing to do or say under the circumstances.

Our discussion of the structure of tutorial instructional strategies in Chapters 10 through 14 showed how the instructional message can be divided into elements, each of which has a purpose or an instructional goal. In deciding what to say during feedback, the designer is creating a hypothesis about the "right thing" to do. Call it the designer's personal instructional theory, if you will.

In a feedback message, there are a number of message parts, and there are different orders in which those parts can be arranged. Moreover, there are different things the designer can do to bring the student into interaction with the correction of the fault or to practice correct responses. Here is a list of just a few message elements for feedback and a few interaction possibilities (not all of which are necessarily good instructional ideas):

Message elements:
- "You have just made a mistake."
- "Here is where the mistake is."
- "Here is how bad the mistake is."
- "Here is how you probably made the mistake."
- "Here is how to avoid making the mistake in the future."
- "Here is how to remember not to make the mistake."
- "Here is what the expert would do in the same situation."
- "Here is what your peers do in the same situation."
- "Here is why it is a mistake."

Interaction possibilities:
- "Now go back and correct your mistake."
- "Now go back and do it right."
- "Point to where you think the mistake is."
- "Point to where you think the correct response is."
- "Explain why this was a mistake."
- "Explain how to avoid the mistake."

At this point, the designer should specify the conventions and patterns for instructional feature messages in terms of structured message elements.

Activity: Define events and event-reporting

The final major design task during Wave 3 is to give unique names to all of the tasks and complete the dependency chart begun in an earlier activity. An event consists of any movement to a new location or any operation of a model control. These types of events are what make a performance trace interpretable.

Event dispatch: When an event is reported from the simulation, it may go in two directions: (1) it may be placed directly in an event file or event queue in the order it was performed, or (2) it may be sent to an event-watcher for the purpose of making an immediate assessment of its impact on the progress of the problem and possible reaction. The designer can, of course, choose to do both, since these are not mutually exclusive uses of the events.

Event form: Events take different forms when reported, depending on the use the designer expects to make of them. Some simulations report only the event name. Others report the event name and a time value that tells when the event took place. This allows the temporal distance between two events to be measured. An event which represents a model control manipulation may carry with it the value to which the control was set. This can be an important item of information for reconstructing error sequences. The alternative is to create a unique event name for each value setting of a control and report only the event name.

Finally, a complex event can be reported which represents the culmination of several smaller events. In a simulation where solvers are attempting to discover the contents of six mystery boxes, the individual events of placing separate circuit components are not of interest to the feedback system, but the completion of a circuit, the closing of the switch, and the results obtained (in terms of lamp brightness) are of interest. Therefore, the events reported by that simulation come less frequently—only at the closing of the switch—and contain the result of the circuit expressed in units of lamp brightness.

Conclusion

This extended description of the simulation design process has had several objectives in mind:

- To show that if approached methodically and step-by-step, the simulation design process is within the reach of the average designer.

- To show how dramatic settings and instruction by indirection can be employed to create learning experiences.

- To show how learning at several levels can be incorporated into one instructional event.

- To show how instructional features can be fitted to simulations, adding instructional power to environment and system models.

The best learning tool for becoming familiar with the challenges of simulation design is to actually build a few small simulations, solving problems as you go. If you can solve the problems on a small scale, you will see how the solutions apply on a larger scale.

Simulation-based forms of instruction will increase in use in the future (see Chapter 24), and we have much to learn about how to build them and how to use them for instructional purposes.

Self-directed activities

- Contrast the process described in this chapter for simulation design with the process described in Chapter 21 for tutorial design. Which process do you prefer stylistically? Which process includes more of the considerations and issues you feel are important? How well could the simulation design process described in this chapter be modified and adapted to the design of tutorials? What would be the benefits of doing so?

- Use the procedure described in this chapter for simulation design to create a simple hybrid simulation. Critique the process as you use it, adding to or taking from it as your own working style dictates. What could be done to improve the productivity of this process?

Further reading

Choi, W. (1997). Designing effective scenarios for computer-based instructional simulations: Classification of essential features. *Educational Technology, 37(5)*, 13–21.

Coad, P., and Yourdon, E. (1990). *Object-oriented analysis.* Englewood Cliffs, NJ: Yourdon Press, Prentice-Hall.

Coad, P., and Yourdon, E. (1991). *Object-oriented design.* Englewood Cliffs, NJ: Yourdon Press, Prentice-Hall.

Coad, P., and Nicola, J. (1993). *Object-oriented programming.* Englewood Cliffs, NJ: Yourdon Press, Prentice-Hall.

Gamma, E., Helm, R., Johnson, R., and Vlissides, J. (1995). *Design patterns: Elements of reusable object-oriented software.* Reading, MA: Addison-Wesley Publishing Company.

Keegan, M. (1995). *Scenario educational software.* Englewood Cliffs, NJ: Educational Technology Publications.

LaMothe, A. (1995). *Black art of 3-D game programming.* Corte Madera, CA: Waite Group Press.

Robertson, L. A. (1994). *Simple program design (2nd ed.).* Danvers, MA: Boyd and Fraser Publishing Company.

Towne, D. M. (1995). *Learning and instruction in simulation environments.* Englewood Cliffs, NJ: Educational Technology Publications.

Shlaer, S., and Mellor, S. (1992). *Object lifecycles: Modeling the world in states.* Englewood Cliffs, NJ: Yourdon Press.

23

CBI AND DISTANCE LEARNING

Chapter Objectives:

1. *Explain how the history of distance learning is influenced by the appearance of new communications media.*

2. *Describe the early attempts to span distances using computers and networks.*

3. *Identify the effects of distance learning on model-centered instruction.*

4. *Distinguish synchronous and asynchronous instruction and define the role of the computer in each.*

5. *Describe how the four legs of the CBI stool—strategy design, message management, display management, and special effects usage—are influenced in instruction over a distance.*

The Web and education

Though there are many different lanes on the electronic highway, the World Wide Web (WWW) is the most widely known of them all. The Web has expanded so rapidly over the past five years that it is fast becoming the equivalent of the village well and the village marketplace combined: a place where people meet socially and commercially. One of the growth centers of the Web is education, and the Web has become an important vehicle, providing learners with resources and interaction with other learners. That makes the Web the analogue of the village school as well.

Though distance learning can occur over *any* distance, most people associate it with video or TV signals sent over long distances to isolated outposts. This image is outdated, because it does not recognize that Web-based distance learning reverses the direction of flow in distance learning. Increasingly, it is not reaching out to remote locations as much as it is bringing resources from all over the world to wherever the learner is. It reaches over any distance, great or small, to provide contact: class-to-class, class-to-person, person-to-person.

Distance learning can occur across a nation, a state, a county, a city, or a campus. Many of the most interesting applications today occur across *short* distances—a city, a school district, or a campus. And, in many instances, the users of distance learning are located in a classroom and use the Web to reach out to centralized organizational resources—directing an avalanche of information into every classroom that wants it.

The new use of the Web for educational purposes causes concern among those who see it as a challenge to our system of schools and universities. Commercial interests are probing the educational market, and the number of commercial educational vendors doing business over the Web is increasing.

Others who have seen yesterday's new technologies enter the educational arena believe that Web-based distance learning will not destroy the universities and the schools but will expand their boundaries to embrace any location that has the requisite communications links from which a person wants to learn. As this new pattern of educational delivery unfolds, it will be as revolutionary as books and blackboards once were—changing the form of the educational institution and its practices, and helping the educational system to continue the evolutionary course it has pursued for centuries.

Growth in Web-delivered education

Distance learning is not measured in miles; it is measured, like all other instruction, in units of instructional effectiveness and experience. Distance learning obeys the same natural laws as learning which takes place in a centralized location. The rules of instruction do not change when the student is located miles instead of blocks or feet from the instructional source. What change are the dynamics of interpersonal communication and influence.

Businesses and educational institutions are finding much use for training delivered at a distance. Not only can they deliver training at less expense, but they can share scarce resources of knowledge with a larger and wider audience. Distance learning extends the learning opportunity to students who would otherwise be shut out from it. It can make instruction available at a time convenient to working students; it can allow individuals to move at the pace they can comfortably sustain; it increases the number of students that can be taught at one time; and it allows highly-specialized or low-demand courses to find students in sufficient numbers over the wider geographic service area.

It is not a question of whether the popularity and use of distance learning will increase, but how rapidly it will happen. Economic forces, along with the needs of many new potential students, are already at work. The number of totally *electronic schools* at the university level is increasing. Many states are forming alliances for the sharing of university courses and credits across state boundaries, and the Web is a media channel these institutions will rely upon heavily. Not only are universities themselves increasing their offerings of courses and degree programs over distance learning, but independent degree-offering commercial ventures which have existed for years are aggressively expanding their operations and are being joined by new competitors.

During daytime hours, the electronic media are also being used to supply specialized low-demand elementary and secondary-level instruction over a wide area and to isolated areas, and computers are involved in this instruction to an increasing extent.

Governments and businesses in most states and many countries are wiring large areas of their own territory to increase their coverage and are adding capacity as rapidly as they can afford. The electronic highways are being built, and education will become a major source of traffic for them. In this chapter, we will explore the principles of applying computers to education and training conducted at a distance.

Finally, within large organizations, trainers are finding that local webs called intranets are an efficient means of delivering both information and training within the organization. They are designing systems which bring work and learning closer together, and some day it will be hard to tell whether a user is using the organizational web for one or the other purpose, because they will be almost indistinguishable.

The computer and distance learning

The computer is a major tool for distance learning now, and it will become increasingly important in the future. The reason is not the proliferation of computers, but the proliferation of the networks that link computers. Just as the telephone system today links virtually every office, dwelling, and public place into a communication network, the future will see—is seeing even now—the expansion of much more powerful communications networks to those same places. Though their construction is now big news to us, we will eventually be as heedless of the existence of the computer networks as we are now of the telephone networks which have connected us for decades. Keep in mind that at one time they were big news also.

New electronic networks will have the capacity to carry more information at higher speeds. The transmission of video signals, once sufficient to slow a network to a crawl, will be accomplished in the future by these new networks without effort. The new networks will be able to transfer not only video content but computer programs and data on learners in both directions—to and from a central electronic schoolhouse. This school—still a place with walls, classrooms, and teachers—if designed and created properly, will have the potential of increasing the amount of individual attention a single learner may receive.

Historical perspective

Distance learning is a very old concept. It was first introduced through the technology of writing. Students could learn from written thoughts even when the sage who wrote them was not present. The distance learning movement was expanded and accelerated with the introduction of the book. Since then, distance learning has received renewed interest with the arrival of each new communication medium: the telephone, the radio, the audio recorder, broadcast television, closed-circuit television, and the video recorder. But until recently, distance learning lacked an instructional medium capable of delivering *real-time, two-way, truly interactive* instruction with effective instructional strategies which included coaching, feedback, and real-time instructional decision-making at the level of the individual.

A certain lack of immediacy, presence, and individuality, which has been historically typical of distance learning, has kept it second choice in our society, rather than the preferred mode of learning for most students. With the advent of the computer, learners now have the prospect of a highly interactive and immediate distance learning tool: computer-based or computer-facilitated instruction over the network.

The introduction of the computer has been important, but it is not alone in revolutionizing distance learning; networks have always been the most important factor in the equation. The network has taken different forms at different times. The mainframe computer and its networked terminals were once considered the best medium for distributing education because one central management and supply computer could serve numerous remotely-located users. The minicomputer, the microcomputer, and today's personal computer, each in its turn, have stimulated renewed interest in distance learning, but the strongest and most enduring interest has been awakened by the wiring of the electronic highway which connects computers of all sizes with each other. This highway has already entered businesses, schools, and homes.

Synchronous and asynchronous use

The multitude of terms associated with the electronic highway can be confusing, and the list of them is growing. Two terms of special interest to the designer of computer-based instruction for use over distance media are *synchronous* and *asynchronous*. These terms describe two of the main modes in which the computer is used for distance learning. They will be defined in more detail in a later section.

A third mode of computer use in distance learning has no formal name. We call it *off-network* or *stand-alone*. The off-network mode was probably the first one tried for distance learning. Before the days of wire and fiber networks, human networks made up of pioneering spirits mailed computer disks containing educational programs to students for use on widely-distributed computers. This was not practical until the invention of the floppy disk, and even then it created massive logistical problems: mailing and handling of disks, inevitable losses, damage, and version confusions. Early floppy disks were large—seven inches wide. The 5.25-inch and more rugged and compact 3.5-inch disks made the transferring of disks much more easy, but these innovations did not solve all of the problems. A better way was needed.

Origins of the electronic highway

Even as the floppy evolved, network-like computer systems such as PLATO were being built for the delivery of education across distances. The early PLATO system consisted of a large mainframe computer connected to many "dumb" terminals (terminals capable only of creating displays—not themselves true computers). PLATO distributed its data over existing telephone lines. The telephone lines were not capable of transferring massive amounts of data by today's standards, but they were capable of transferring the amount of data that the terminal needed to construct a display. A single PLATO computer in one city was able to provide instruction to students in many other cities simultaneously. PLATO, which is still used today in a more evolved form, was used in schools, prisons, and universities all over the U.S.

The TICCIT system was a contemporary of PLATO, and it used a slightly different system of distribution to provide learning at a distance. The name TICCIT stands for Time-Shared, Interactive Computer-Controlled Information (or Instructional) Television. TICCIT originally distributed its instructional product over broad bandwidth (high capacity) cables rather than the relatively low-capacity copper telephone lines of the day. The TICCIT span of delivery was therefore smaller, due to the higher cost of its specialized lines, but so was its computer—a minicomputer which was then the latest step in the down-sizing of computers that ultimately produced the personal computer.

TICCIT was conceived not only as an instructional system but as an information system, carrying news, commercial information, and personal messages into homes. One early TICCIT concept included the wiring of an entire town so that every home could receive TICCIT services, creating a community electronically. TICCIT systems were installed in community colleges and university test sites, where they continue to be used today to deliver effective and low-cost instruction.

At the same time that the TICCIT and PLATO systems (both funded to some extent by the government) were trying out their different schemes for networking learners and learning sources, the Advanced Research Projects Agency (ARPA), also a government agency, was constructing a new system for personal communications in the form of a network of computers stretching nationwide. This network was used for many years by scientific, academic, and military users to send and receive electronic mail messages and computer files. The network was originally called ARPANET after its sponsor, but today it forms the backbone of what we call the Internet, which has grown far beyond the ARPANET's original size, speed, and capacity.

This brief history lesson has two purposes: (1) to show that computer-based communication and instruction over distances has a considerable history of sustained interest and development, and (2) to show that today's electronic highway is really the surviving extension and result of that history. There are many today who still remember using the relatively rough and rocky roads that have become today's expressway.

Bandwidth

One of the most important dimensions of growth in the electronic highway over the years has been speed. The speed or carrying capacity of an electronic signal transmission system is called its *bandwidth*. Bandwidth is important in a network because it controls the speed with which data, programs, and resources can be transmitted from point to point, and thus the total amount of data that can be transmitted per second, per hour, and per day.

The transmission of textual material across a network does not require broad bandwidth or high speed, but today's computer-based instruction makes heavy use of visual materials (graphic and video images, audio files, etc.) of considerable size. These resources demand a great deal more than text transmission does, and therefore they are one of the limiting factors in how fast materials can be transmitted.

For the CBI designer, the speed of transmission is quite important, and therefore the designer must be aware of how large a demand his or her product will place on the transmission system—whether the product is fully downloaded to the user's computer before use or whether the product is transmitted to the user piecemeal during interactive use of the transmission system. This speed factor can lead a designer to consider one style of CBI implementation over another and is therefore one of the major influences in choosing between the synchronous, asynchronous, and off-network modes of instruction.

Instructional principles and communication at a distance

We believe that the principles for instructing over distances are the same as the principles for instructing in person or through any other technological means. However, the tools for distance learning place special constraints on the nature, length, and timing of instructional communications and interactions. They introduce new steps into instruction that otherwise would not exist, and they can erect barriers between learners, peers, and the source of instruction. It is the designer's challenge to minimize these effects peculiar to the medium and to find ways to turn them into strengths.

To illustrate these artifacts of distance instruction, let's recall the model-centered instruction idea introduced in Chapter 16 and elaborate on it. Figure 1 shows the model-centered organization of instruction in which the learner (L) interacts with a natural system or a model in the presence of a learning companion (C)—a person or program capable of noticing, deciding, coaching, providing feedback, and carrying out other instructional functions described in Chapter 16. In addition to these basic elements of the system, a student may have other resources on which to draw during instruction: subject-matter experts (E), other students or peers (P), and information resources (R). All of these may supply information, alternate models, interaction, and decision-making assistance to guide and support learning.

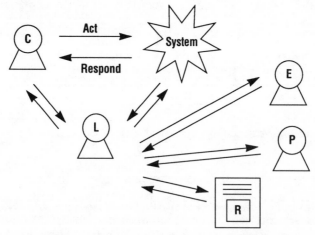

Figure 1. Model-centered instruction, showing all resources.

The effect of distance learning is to insert the network into one or more of the communication paths of this model. During non-distance (centralized) instruction, the communication between the student and the model or environment to be learned from (say a model of the atom or of a colonial village) is direct. They are created on a local computer and can be examined, manipulated, and even asked for self-explanation.

In distance instruction, the model or environment experienced may be created by a computer many states away, or part of the environment (say the graphical representation of it) may be created locally while another portion of it (say the events or objects within a location) may be created on a distant computer. Moreover, the network may be inserted into any of the links shown in Figure 1: student-to-learning-companion (C), student-to-expert (E), student-to-peer (P), or student-to-resource (R). Nor does it take much imagination to see that this same principle applies across all of the stages or major functions of the instructional communication: the delivery of instruction, the management of instruction, and the provision of interpersonal communications.

Because the network can be inserted into any part of the instructional communication, the quality of distance-administered CBI depends to a degree on the tools used to bridge the distance. A lot also depends on the designer's decisions on how to select, use and place these tools: close to the student, far from the student, or in both places. Therefore, the main concerns of distance learning on CBI—over and above the basic instructional issues—tend to be in the areas of *timing* and *access*.

Timing: Can the student be assured that responses from the distant portion of the instruction will not cause unreasonable delays? Can the student be assured that elements of the instructional event which are intended to be synchronized in their occurrence will in fact be so?

Access: Can the student be assured that the needed resource will be accessible when it is needed? Can the student be assured that the resource will be in a form which is practical and reasonable for the student to use—one which contributes to the speed of learning rather than retarding it? A form which the student is capable of using?

How is the computer used for distance learning?

It will be useful now to define the terms synchronous and asynchronous and to examine how these terms influence the answers to these questions. When the student and the instructor use the communication medium at the same time—both being present at the time the message is sent—communication is called *synchronous*. Communication is said to be *asynchronous* when only one of the two must be present when the message is sent or when it is received. The message sent is not immediately received, and because of this asynchronous communication, systems require some form of memory storage at both ends of the communication channel to capture and hold messages, resources, or programs, to await the arrival of the recipient.

Synchronous communication forms include a telephone conversation, a live two-way or one-way live video connection, or a "chat" session using two computers and an Internet link. Asynchronous forms of communication include e-mail messages, books or manuals, messages left on a bulletin board, conventional mail, a recorded video, or a computer program or data file used by a student at a work, home, or school computer.

Historically, instruction over distances has been asynchronous, because there was no widely-available, affordable medium over which instructors and students could be involved simultaneously. Even when communication was synchronous, it was only one-way synchronous—normally an instructor broadcasting over a one-way medium to listening students (radio or TV). The important reverse link that would allow student and instructor to communicate immediately in both directions was not available. Recently, two-way video systems installed in many states and countries (made possible, by the way, by computer controlled systems) and the electronic highway becoming available everywhere have opened the important path from the student back to the instructor, making synchronous instructional communication possible.

The use of the computer as a communication device and as a stand-alone instructional source is an important development in both synchronous and asynchronous instruction. During the remainder of this chapter, we will explore the uses of the computer in both types of instruction and try to identify their implications for the CBI designer.

Revisiting the four legs of the stool

The analogy used in this book likens CBI to a four-legged stool. To be stable, the stool must have all four of its legs. The legs are: (1) appropriate instructional strategy, (2) message management, (3) display management, and (4) appropriate use of special effects. It will be useful at this point to return to that analogy to see how CBI carried out over distances changes things in these areas.

Instructional strategy at a distance

We have talked about two approaches to instructional strategy in this book: *direction*, in which a direct message related to the performance being learned is the main vehicle of instruction, and *indirection*, in which the content or performance to be learned is not formed into a message. Instead, the student is expected to participate in experiences which can supply the required knowledge or allow the student to construct it. Whichever type of strategy is used, it forms the central architectural structure of the instruction, and almost all other design decisions will support and result from the strategy decision.

Are certain strategies either more or less effective when used over a distance? Are certain parts of a strategy better suited for distance use? The answers to these questions rest on the factors of timing and access. A strategy requires only that certain information and experience be available to a student at the moment it is needed. If poor timing due to distance causes unreasonable delays, or if access to a needed strategy element is denied, then the strategy must be discarded, changed, or implemented in a way that improves the timing and provides needed access.

It is likely that some indirection strategies are even more suited to distance use than for local use. Indirection strategies normally provide students with a problem, a simulated environment, a simulation model, or some combination of these in the presence of one or more instructional features. Under some conditions and for certain instructional goals, the ability to interact with other students cooperatively may be facilitated over a distance. Students from different classrooms, schools, states, or countries can work together within the same simulation or resource environment to solve a problem, to use a particular scarce resource cooperatively, or to carry out an experiment which crosses territorial lines.

Message management at a distance

Message management consists of the capture of instructional content and its organization into a message for expression. The form of content of the message is not influenced by the interposition of distance, so message management is the least influenced of the four legs of the stool.

One way that message management *is* influenced is that some of the restrictions on message form and content are removed. The World Wide Web provides access to a wide range of resources which individual designers could not previously afford to incorporate into their products due to production or size limitations. The electronic highway provides access to new forms of message and a greater variety of messages at no extra development cost. So long as the electronic highway is not turned into a toll road, this will continue to be true.

Display management at a distance

Display management is the expression or representation of the sense-able elements of the instructional strategy—the creation and maintenance of the display. Display management is quite sensitive to the timing and bandwidth of the communication links and software tools used in distance learning. It is safe to say that the principles already discussed in Chapter 19 for Display Management still hold over the network, but there are additional concerns for which the designer of distance learning must make provision.

Timing/synchronicity/coordination of resource arrival and display: Display management during CBI is much like stage management at a play. Actors must enter and exit the stage at the right times. One of the main elements of display management is the coordination and timing of display events. The ability to control timing depends on two things in distance learning: access to resources, and timing of the arrival of resources at the student's computer.

The designer has no way to predict where and when traffic jams will occur on the electronic highway and therefore must synchronize the downloading of resources to be used so that the user experiences no delays. Many of these resources will have to be downloaded behind the scenes, without the visible fanfare typical of today's net software, so some new tool features will be required in the future.

Form/format of resources: The software tools for distant communication using computers are still in their infancy. As in any rapidly changing area of technology, there are still few similarities and many differences in the formats used to store and transmit data, whether it is a bitmap graphic, or a data file. Until more standards emerge, the designer must be aware of conversion software, its capabilities, and its limitations so that resources appear to the user seamlessly.

Special effects at a distance

What we have said about the computational and attentional costs of special effects in CBI holds for distance CBI as well. If anything, the importance of respecting the network and its overuse bears emphasis. Though the networks of the future will have broader bandwidth (higher carrying capacity), they will still have finite limits.

The logistics of CBI at a distance

In addition to being an instructional problem, the practice of CBI at a distance is a logistical problem: all of the needed resources must arrive at the right place at the right time. The strongest tools the designer has today to deal with net logistics are: (1) the download, and (2) the partial download. The download consists of an entire CBI product (tutorial, simulation, resource, test, support system, etc.), which is downloaded to the user's computer and run from there. The partial download consists of a computer program downloaded to the user's computer and run from there, which communicates with either centralized or diffuse resources or users to complete its function.

A Web browser is a partial download. In a larger sense, we can envision the download of a university department's offices or a science laboratory as "virtual" environments. By running the environment programs locally, a user may open links to the department's computer or to the laboratory computer in order to find out who is present at the moment, what they are doing, and to engage in instructional, exploratory, or administrative interactions, the details of which are supplied from the distant computer.

The benefit of this structure of program allocation is that it minimizes the use of the net and maximizes timing and access factors for the user, while still providing the essential links to time-limited resources, experts, and peers.

Conclusion

The pursuit of distance learning using CBI has just begun, and the growth of this area is best compared to an avalanche or a wildfire. This is a typical stage in the growth of any new and powerful technology. Distance learning CBI today might be compared with the auto in 1900–1910, the airplane in 1920–1930, or the personal computer in 1980–1992. What you see today will look primitive in five to ten years, just as the monochrome, low-resolution screen does now. As the changes occur and the hype mounts, it will help to remember that the principles of instruction remain the same, regardless of the medium.

Self-directed activities

- Specify for several CBI products any modifications or additions that would be necessary to make the product suitable for use at a distance. Describe how each product would be used and the cost, personnel, and logistical implications. Take into consideration ownership and licensing issues.

- Identify the characteristics of CBI that give it the advantage when applied to distance learning over other forms of instruction. Make a similar list of the weaknesses of CBI.

- Design an adaptation of an existing CBI product for delivery over the World Wide Web. Which types of CBI product adapt readily and at low cost? Which types of product are more difficult to adapt, and what is the cost of adaptation? Are there any CBI products whose cost of adaptation or delivery would render them unsuitable for delivery at a distance?

Further reading

Barron, A. E. (1996). *The Internet and instruction: Activities and ideas.* Englewood, CO: Libraries Unlimited.

Giaquinta, J. B., Bauer, J., and Levin, J. E. (1993). *Beyond technology's promise: An examination of children's educational computing at home.* Cambridge, UK: Cambridge University Press.

Hackbarth, S. (1996). *The educational technology handbook.* Englewood Cliffs, NJ: Educational Technology Publications.

Hackbarth, S. (Ed.). (1997). Web-based learning. *Educational Technology* (special issue), 37(3), 5–71.

Harasim, L., Hiltz, S. R., Teles, L., and Turoff, M. (1995). *Learning networks: A field guide to teaching and learning online.* Cambridge, MA: MIT Press.

Kahn, B. H. (Ed.). (1997). *Web-based instruction.* Englewood Cliffs, NJ: Educational Technology Publications.

Moore, M. G., and Kearsley, G. (1996). *Distance education: A systems view.* New York: Wadsworth Publishing Company.

Willis, B. (1993). *Distance education: A practical guide.* Englewood Cliffs, NJ: Educational Technology Publications.

Willis, B. (Ed.). (1994). *Distance education: Strategies and tools.* Englewood Cliffs, NJ: Educational Technology Publications.

SECTION VI

TRENDS
Our look into the crystal ball.

24

LOOKING AHEAD

Chapter Objectives:

1. *Project the historical developments of CBI to describe instructional forms which will be used in the future.*

2. *Project the developmental history of the computer to define what the instructional computer will be like in the future.*

3. *Predict new technologies which will be combined with CBI to change the patterns of instruction in the future.*

4. *Describe the CBI designer's tools of the future.*

Whither now?

Trying to predict the future of CBI would require three specialized crystal balls, one each to presage the futures of computer technology, cognitive science, and the culture of instructional design, respectively. In addition, it would require a wizard to predict the interplay of these technological and scientific currents. Though our wrong predictions will no doubt be hung around our necks, and despite the fact that no one will remember if, by accident, we guess the future correctly, we want to look over the hill, to the future of CBI. We do not want to look too far; we want to take a less ambitious peek at the near horizon to make some informed guesses about what will happen in the near future as the technology of computer-based instruction continues to mature. No holographic images in this chapter, no wristwatch computer terminals, but we hope to make some reasonable and realistic projections based on practical, economical, and theoretical considerations.

First, let's define what we're not going to predict. We will *not* worry about the mushrooming metrics of processor speed or storage capacity. The developer always looks wistfully to the future, saying, "...in a little while computers will have so much more memory, so why don't we..." Then there is the perennial issue of processor speeds, heard on almost every project. One of the authors began his career in a war with a customer about shoehorning an elementary school mathematics product into 16 kilobytes of RAM. Today this chapter is being written on a workstation with 32 megabytes of RAM—2,000 times as much. Speed, space, and their respective economies are working in our favor, and there is no reason to doubt they will continue to do so. So we will not concentrate on predictions based on the future computer's heroic size. There are other books that already do that.

We will try to define the CBI developer's world and the student's world, and the new personalities—mostly artificial—that might appear in them. Perhaps in this chapter it is also time for us to drop the term *computer-based instruction*, because it is likely that the boundaries which we see today between education and entertainment will probably blur. The day of *edutainment* is upon us, and the only question is, which will prevail: the *edu-* or the *-tainment*? We don't know if the CBI appellation will be the right term to describe the new type of product that emerges as our cultural technology, like our hardware and software technologies, continues to evolve.

We began our book depicting the struggle of CBI to establish itself as a central technology in our society. We compared the CBI question with other technologies which were themselves young once. As those technologies did once in their own early histories, CBI now faces the requirement to prove its economic practicality, its effectiveness, and its ability to fit into or change our daily routines. The computer has already passed this test. It is today a necessity, which we could prove to ourselves by trying to run our society and our economy without it.

In a few small areas of instruction, instructional computers have also proven themselves to be indispensable: in the training of pilots, in the training of astronauts, and in many areas where high-risk performances can lead to high-cost errors. But much of the CBI industry is still on trial—a novelty in search of its destiny. What will happen now? And how will it affect the future of the instructional computer? Here is a flurry of predictions.

Prediction #1: The computer will disappear: What we really predict is that computers will disappear from view. We believe that CBI is definitely a technology of the future. It will be more used, more popular, and more economical in the future. Moreover, it will come in more interesting forms (see below). But the computer itself and the monitor—both of which now sit within prominent view on the top of your desk—will disappear from sight, and in both stationary and portable learning locations what the learner will actually use will not look much like today's desktop computer. This disappearing act may take place through any of several scenarios:

Scenario 1: Vanishing into the desktop. The "desktop" computer may disappear by actually *becoming part of the desktop.* Envision a computer's parts spread across a desk top, lying flat on its surface. Now imagine those parts sinking into the top of the desk, still joined together as a functioning computer. The monitor, a 2-inch thick device resembling a picture frame, slides around the desk top, being positioned where it is needed. The keyboard, if one will be needed (and it will), is located beneath a sliding panel in the desk top or as a thin drawer on the front edge of it. A mouse or trackball may be supplied as a built-in feature of the desktop (possible), as a keyboard inset (very possible), or as a desktop plug-in (maybe). A microphone mounted in the monitor panel will facilitate communication with the computer, which will be able to recognize your voice. Remember, we are talking short-term projections here.

Scenario 2: The learning dock. The place where the computer is used may become a standard dock—a connecting point between a small personal computer appliance and a digital network. Many futurists see the growth of the network as a more prominent force in the future of computer-based instruction than growth in the power of the computer itself. Clearly there is a trend toward the network as a delivery channel for instruction and services of all kinds. So, a second sense in which the computer will disappear is in the reduction of the computer's prominence. Home computers will combine with TV in a way that is unpredictable at present, but the result will be that the home is connected with a network, presently called the Internet, especially its World Wide Web.

The computer itself in this strong network scenario may take the form of portable equipment capable of plugging into a hardware dock located almost anywhere. In a second version of this scenario, the computer may be supplied at the network terminus by the network provider just as the phone company today provides pay phones at the end of its phone lines (rent-a-puter?). Either way, the centrality of the computer is not the point; the point is that the computer connected to a network that has centralized instructional resources will be even more powerful.

Scenario 3: The anchored computer. This prediction foresees the day of the anchored computer, much as there are pay telephones everywhere today, only instead of providing a network connection for the user's computer to plug into, this scenario sees the computer as an anchored appliance, supplied at the end of the network. Memory cards carried by the student may be slipped into a slot on the anchored computer, initializing it with data and programs, checking the student's access permissions, and connecting the student to the appropriate sections of the net's resources.

Scenario 4: The system-contexted computer. In an earlier chapter we identified a scenario in which a student, learning to operate within a particular work context, might encounter the computer at first as the primary instructional device but over time see increasing amounts of real equipment from the workplace appearing as the computer becomes less and less prominent—vanishing ultimately from sight. This scenario is already evident in the training of airline pilots: flight simulators look like the working surfaces of airplanes—the cockpit. Numerous other work contexts will find this approach to training economically sound as well.

Prediction #2: The "lesson" as the primary unit of instruction will disappear: The nature of instruction will change. Most of our collective experience in school has put us in the habit of being instructed by *lessons* which teach us directly. There will be a purpose in the future for this type of instruction, but we predict that other forms of CBI will eventually predominate.

We believe first of all that things will begin to instruct themselves. This prediction is already starting to materialize. What we offer here is not so much a prediction as the beginning of a trend. The technology of object-orientation makes it easy to construct not only models and environments, but independent instructional features which communicate with these models and operate in parallel with them. Today when you use your data base or spreadsheet programs, you can run a second program which coaches you through basic procedures one step at a time. Not only does this form of user support reduce the level of need for unreadable user manuals, but it supplies the user with easy-to-use, rapid, and action-oriented assistance just when it is needed. Is this instruction? Of course it is, and the practice of the new learning takes place immediately.

We predict that this trend will widen and deepen. Not only will computer programs have their living support system, but non-computerized products will also be delivered to the user along with a computer object—a model of the product itself. As the owner runs the model, the product will be capable of describing itself, pointing out its key features, supplying a guided tour of itself, describing how it works, and making suggestions for its own operation, care, troubleshooting, and maintenance—whatever the owner wants. Your new house's first words to you might be, "Hi, glad to meet you. Let's take a look at me."

For these objects you may pay a price, but it will not be for computer program that makes it run: the *object player* will be free, and it will play many kinds of objects: your vacuum cleaner, your house, your dog, and your lawn. These objects will be more than just inventory lists and terminology machines. When you buy your lawn object, you will be buying a model of a lawn which you particularize to your own lawn by supplying it data on the soil, the weather in your vicinity, and the quality of the water. From there, you will be able to ask for recommendations and play "what if." (For instance, "What if I fertilize only three times this year?" "What if I water at night instead of in the morning?")

This *player/object* type of tool will be put to more than product support uses. It will also become the way to buy an encyclopedia in the future. Instead of buying a book containing words and pictures, you will purchase collections of objects. These will all *play* on the same object player. You will have more than an article on Napoleon: you will have a Napoleon object. And Napoleon will be purchasable in several degrees of completeness. You may buy the economy Napoleon for a song and ask him simple questions, see his military campaigns in low-detail, and learn somewhat about the world he lived in. Products somewhat like that are available now. But if you buy the gilt-edged Napoleon, you will have a rich object, capable of working in conjunction with your Early Europe object, and providing more rich explanations to your inquiries. Models within these encyclopedia objects will allow you to conduct self-directed studies: If you want to understand the atmospheric convection cells which girdle the earth, you will deal directly with a model of these cells which allows you to change key parameters, such as temperature at a particular spot, and observe the consequence.

The instructional objective will appear to be less prominent in these object products, but it will be there nonetheless, structuring the information the designer has decided to include with the object and the manipulations the student can perform on the object and its models. Models may come with their own set of suggested experiments and explorations. The instructional objective will be present, but objectives will be chosen moment-by-moment by the student rather than by set sequences of message provided by the designer.

Another form of instructional product which will become increasingly important will be the instructional problem. We are familiar with sophisticated products today which simulate complex systems—cities, economies, or the human body. Often these are marketed as games or tools for recreation, but the best of them are capable of instructing. What is missing from most of them is one or more specific problems for the user to solve. These problems, if chosen well, have instructional value. If sequenced properly, problems can be a more efficient form of instruction than didactics.

Prediction #3: Multimedia will remain important and improve, but it will become a less visible issue than it has been in the past: The pioneers of computer-based multimedia began in the early 1980s using videodiscs and specialized computer overlay boards to extend the display capabilities of the computer. A well-organized and much larger force later entered the CBI marketplace to popularize what we have come to know as *multimedia*, but it has taken only a few years for the original product introduction to be lost in a storm of innovation in computer display and display management tools.

Today's multimedia is a moving target, and its rate of development is breathtaking. Advances in 3-D and animated graphics pioneered on large, powerful computers during the 1980s now run on the average multimedia computer. Video segments stored on enormous memory drives now play routinely at speeds and resolutions that just a few years ago were headline news. Additional new developments waiting in the wings will be just as astounding when they make their entrance, and in the same half-life, the display techniques which are now so astounding will become merely the expected standard.

This is the reason that we say that multimedia will become a less visible issue. The quality of the computer display will continue to be important, but soon virtually everyone will be using that standard. There was a time when having a computer meant having either a multimedia or non-multimedia computer. This distinction divided the mainly-for-business-use computers from the training or marketing computers, which required more horse-power and more display sizzle. But today's businesses are moving to intranets—internal networks or webs which supply worker support, information, and training needs—which require multimedia-equipped computers to support the web software on which the intranet is built.

One of the discoveries of the next decade will be that multimedia itself is a display technology of great power but that it requires equally sophisticated techniques for product structuring, instructional featuring, and message construction in order to produce instructional resources of quality and effectiveness. The multimedia catalog products of today, which simply supply frame after frame of pictures or textual material, will be seen as little better than the picture book without additional design features to make them responsive to student inquiry, interaction needs, and goal-setting through adaptation to the student. It will not be just quality of display that raises a product above its peers, it will be quality of experience, and that experience will include being able to set knowledge goals, experiment, and obtain satisfactory explanations and understanding. The day of the multimedia computer will turn into the day of the instructional companion computer.

Prediction #4: Students will have an agent: When you use an instructional companion computer, you will not be alone. You will have not only a responsive companion in the learning process, but that companion will remember you from experience to experience. It will remember your style, your preferences, and your learning goals. It will help you reach those goals by suggesting experiences which lead toward them. It will also be able to influence those experiences as they occur, tailoring them to your methods of learning, and your prior knowledge.

Prediction #5: CBI development tools will be full-functioned, faster, and easier to use: Today's design tools for computer-based instruction, normally called authoring tools, are not really design tools; they are tools to simplify and speed *the creation of computer logic*. They allow a designer to express the logic of an instructional product, *but they do little to assist the designer to construct the design which the logic executes.*

In Chapter 22, we tried to describe the multiple levels at which a simulation product is designed and showed that computer logic design actually follows other, more important, levels of design. In Chapter 21, we tried to show how tutorial design begins with the design of an instructional strategy first, with computer logic following behind. According to this definition of the design process, only the final stage of product design—the computer logic building—is supported by authoring tools.

The CBI design tool of the future will help the designer create *instructional* designs first, before it supports the conversion of those designs into computer logic structures. This means that those tools will aid the designer in the construction of several types of design structure: the strategic structure, the problem structure, the environment structure, the model structure, and the dramatic structure. The design tools will have to support the designer not only in specifying these structures (strategies, problems, environments, and models) and linking them into larger organizational wholes, but also in converting them stage by stage into the producible elements (message elements, display elements, interfaces, and computer logic elements). This will not be as difficult to accomplish as it sounds, and some design tools have begun to move in this direction.

These tools will not consist of simple data entry ports like the tools of today. They will allow the data for the product to be produced as a natural by-product of the design process as it progresses stage by stage, until the point is reached where the data will have been generated which normally would be entered into the computer logic tool that today's authoring systems represent. This means that the design system will have created from the design the data that a designer is today forced to create off-line—or worse yet, at the keyboard. The design system will simple pour the design data directly over into the development tool, and the tool will produce the product automatically (well, mostly automatically!).

Prediction #6: Traditional delivery modes and organizations will be challenged: Not only will the instruction and the delivery and design systems for CBI change, but the educational and training contexts in which they are used will change as well. As products improve, they will be more capable of use by students anywhere and anytime. The use of computers in distance learning for CBI delivery will continue to increase at a breakneck pace, contributing to the (possible) decentralization of schooling. We give this as a tentative prediction, because many non-instructional factors will enter into decisions on school centralization and decentralization. There are voices in the educational community who hope that the school of tomorrow will be a smaller place, with more personal attention to give to the individual. Perhaps CBI technology will play an important role in this scenario.

The workplace and the home will become much more places of education and training. For those types of knowledge which permit it, training will tend to be given closer to the time of performance, and in many jobs, it will become impossible to tell the difference between job-aiding and training, because there will be no difference. For types of knowledge which do not permit learning by support, the instruction will still be possible at the workplace (after the phone is silenced), carried out over the network-based training system which will bring the needed resources to every desk in the company.

Finally, we predict that there will always be a need to educate and inform the mind in non-work-related ways. We believe that education is valuable in a free society as a means of keeping the society free. So as the computer proves its economic value, we expect that it will also prove its cultural value, as the most flexible and adaptable educational tool ever discovered, in truly educating people to think and to use their minds to their fullest potential.

Conclusion

There is much more to be said about designing computer-based instruction. This introduction has attempted to pull together basic principles from the major technologies which have collided to form the CBI field: instruction, instructional design, computers, and programming. To this book you must add your own continued study of a rapidly-evolving technology, which we are convinced will become one of the most important technologies of the twenty-first century.

Self-directed activities

- Make your own predictions about the future of computer-based instruction. Treat: (1) the future look and feel of instruction, (2) new instructional approaches which will emerge and become popular and economically appealing, (3) new tools for CBI design and development, and (4) new CBI delivery sites and tools for delivery.

Further reading

Gelertner, D. (1992). *Mirror worlds or: The day software puts the universe in a shoebox...how it will happen and what it will mean.* New York: Oxford University Press.

Gilder, G. (1994). *Life after television: The coming transformation of media and American life (rev. ed.).* New York: W. W. Norton & Company.

Havelock, R. G. with Zlotolow, S. (1995). *The change agent's guide (2nd ed).* Englewood Cliffs, NJ: Educational Technology Publications.

Maney, K. (1995). *Megamedia shakeout: The inside story of the leaders and the losers in the exploding communications industry.* New York: John Wiley & Sons.

Romiszowski, A. J. (1997). Instructional development for a networked society. In C. R. Dills and A. J. Romiszowski (Eds.), *Instructional development paradigms.* Englewood Cliffs, NJ: Educational Technology Publications.

Salisbury, D. F. (1996). *Five technologies for educational change.* Englewood Cliffs, NJ: Educational Technology Publications.

Russell, S., and Norvig, P. (1995). *Artificial intelligence: A modern approach.* Englewood Cliffs, NJ: Prentice-Hall.

Index

J

About the Authors

Dr. Andrew S. Gibbons designs instructional systems, technology-based instructional products, and tools and methods for instructional designers. His experience combines eighteen years of industry experience at WICAT Systems, Inc. and Courseware, Inc. (now Courseware/Andersen Consulting). He is currently an Associate Professor in the Instructional Technology graduate program at Utah State University. Dr. Gibbons has tried to combine academic and theoretic interests in instructional strategy and the design process with the search for tools that make possible high-volume production of innovative forms of computer-based instruction. His recent experience includes teaching, project management for large and small development projects, multimedia development, applied research, development of distance learning programs, innovative design projects, instructional theory, and consulting with government, businesses, and educational entities. Dr. Gibbons also currently serves as Director of the Center for the School of the Future at Utah State University, dedicated to the formation of teacher and parent networks for the support of continuous educational improvement. The Center promotes the implementation of classic diffusion principles and the diffusion of data-proven principles and best practices through a networked and mutually supporting professional-parent community.

Dr. Peter G. Fairweather has worked within the computer-based training and education industry for twenty-five years, and is the designer of nine authoring systems, including frame-based and object-oriented systems, systems for specialized functions (Mathematics), and for general use by CBI designers (WISE). Thousands of hours of computer-based instruction and simulation have been created using authoring tools Dr. Fairweather designed and constructed. Dr. Fairweather has also designed computer-managed instruction systems for use in integrated learning systems which have been installed nationwide. Before joining IBM Research, Dr. Fairweather was Vice-President, Instructional Systems Design, Jostens Learning Corporation. Prior to that, as Chief Scientist at WICAT Systems, he developed training simulation software in all content areas, consulting extensively on tools and methods with corporate, educational, and government heads. Dr. Fairweather has published extensively while in industry and while holding faculty positions at the University of Texas and Northwestern University. He currently works on projects related to distributed learning, intelligent tutoring, and assessment in K–12 and higher education as the Senior Manager of Education at the IBM T. J. Watson Research Center, Yorktown Heights, New York.